2 0 1 8

Year B-II

THE ALMANAC FOR PASTORAL LITURGY

SOURCEBOOK

FOR SUNDAYS, SEASONS, AND WEEKDAYS

Leisa Anslinger
Charles A. Bobertz
Donna M. Crilly
Joseph DeGrocco
Mary Dumm
Mary DuQuaine
Mary A. Ehle

Christopher J. Ferraro
J. Philip Horrigan
Timothy Johnston
Corinna Laughlin
Jason J. McFarland
Jill Maria Murdy

Stephen Palanca
Robert C. Rabe
Jakob Rinderknecht
Julie Pierce
Michael R. Prendergast
Trish Sullivan Vanni
D. Todd Williamson

LTP
LITURGY
TRAINING
PUBLICATIONS

Nihil Obstat
Very Reverend Daniel A. Smilanic, JCD
Vicar for Canonical Services
Archdiocese of Chicago
December 1, 2016

Imprimatur
Very Reverend Ronald A. Hicks
Vicar General
Archdiocese of Chicago
December 1, 2016

The *Nihil Obstat* and *Imprimatur* are declarations that the material is free from doctrinal or moral error, and thus is granted permission to publish in accordance with c. 827. No legal responsibility is assumed by the grant of this permission. No implication is contained herein that those who have granted the *Nihil Obstat* and *Imprimatur* agree with the content, opinions, or statements expressed.

LTP is grateful to the many authors and publishers who have given permission to include their work in this resource. LTP is especially grateful for contributing authors of past editions of *At Home with the Word; Foundations for Teaching and Preaching®; Children's Liturgy of the Word; Sourcebook for Sundays, Seasons, and Weekdays; Pastoral Liturgy®;* and *Catechumenate* for providing additional material. Every effort has been made to determine the ownership of all texts to make proper arrangements for their use. Any oversight that may have occurred, if brought to our attention, will gladly be corrected in future editions.

SOURCEBOOK FOR SUNDAYS, SEASONS, AND WEEKDAYS 2018: THE ALMANAC FOR PASTORAL LITURGY © 2017 Archdiocese of Chicago: Liturgy Training Publications, 3949 South Racine Avenue, Chicago, IL 60609; 1-800-933-1800, fax 1-800-933-7094, e-mail: orders@ltp.org. All rights reserved. Visit our website at www.LTP.org.

This book was edited by Danielle A. Noe, MDIV. Kris Fankhouser, Michael A. Dodd, and Christian Rocha were the production editors. Ana M. Stephenson was the cover designer, Anna Manhart provided cover art direction, and Jane Kremsreiter was the interior designer. Kari Nicholls was the production artist.

Cover art by Steve Musgrave © LTP.

Illustrations for Sundays and solemnities by Corey Wilkinson; seasonal icons by Kari Nicholls © LTP.

Printed in the United States of America.

ISBN 978-1-61671-341-6

SSS18

CONTENTS

INTRODUCTION

About *Sourcebook*

Sourcebook *for Sundays, Seasons, and Week-days 2018: The Almanac for Pastoral Liturgy* provides guidance regarding the various liturgical elements (music, environment, prayers, readings, and so on) so that communities can prepare liturgies rooted in the vision of the Second Vatican Council.

Sourcebook is organized to help you follow liturgical time in sequence. It begins with Advent, which is the start of the liturgical year, and it continues with Christmas Time. Next begins Ordinary Time, so named because the Sundays are designated by their ordinal (counted) numbers. *Sourcebook* tags the Sundays in Ordinary Time after Christmas Time and up until Lent as "Ordinary Time (during Winter)." This is not an official description or designation, but merely a chapter heading *Sourcebook* uses to differentiate between the two parts in Ordinary Time.

Next you will find Lent, followed by the Sacred Paschal Triduum, and then Easter Time. After the Solemnity of Pentecost, Ordinary Time resumes. *Sourcebook* refers to this longer stretch as "Ordinary Time (during Summer and Fall)." When Ordinary Time concludes, the next liturgical year begins, so this chapter takes us right up to the end of the liturgical year. A supplemental liturgical music preparation sheet and a checklist for those who serve during the Triduum are available online at www.ltp.org/t-resources.aspx. These sheets may be reproduced and distributed to your ministers for free.

Within each of the chapters of *Sourcebook*, you will find two sections: "The Liturgical Time" and "The Calendar." "The Liturgical Time" is organized into several parts:

- *The Meaning*: the theological meaning and history of the liturgical time or season

- *The Saints*: how the living witness of the saints can deepen and enrich liturgical time

- *The Liturgical Books*: what the *Lectionary for Mass, The Roman Missal*, and other ritual texts tell us about liturgical time

- *The Liturgical Environment*: ideas for the appearance of worship spaces

- *The Liturgical Music*: the musical expression of liturgical time and how to enhance it

- *Devotions and Sacramentals*: ideas to foster the parish's devotional life while emphasizing the primacy of the liturgy

- *Liturgical Ministers*: tips and formational notes for all liturgical ministers

- *Children's Liturgy of the Word*: how to prepare the Sunday children's Liturgy of the Word

- *Evangelization*: opportunities for evangelizing through the liturgy and the liturgical year
- *The Parish and the Home*: how to carry liturgical time from the parish to the domestic Church (at home)
- *Mass Texts*: original prayers for the Order of Mass (where options are permitted)

"The Calendar" is a straightforward almanac for each day of the liturgical year. You can look up any day of the year and find basic liturgical information as well as ideas for how to celebrate it. The primary purpose of *Sourcebook*, however, is to help you celebrate Sundays, solemnities, feasts, and all of liturgical time. For this reason, you will find most of the material in "The Calendar" devoted to Sundays, solemnities, and feasts, which include the following three sections:

- *Lectionary for Mass*: an explanation of how the Scriptures of the day relate to what is being celebrated
- *The Roman Missal*: insights into the prayers and suggestions about options; particular notes are provided for the third edition of the Missal
- *Other Ideas*: Additional ideas for parishes, families, or liturgies

Other days include additional sections:

- *"About This . . ."*: what the Church is celebrating on this day (solemnities, feasts, and memorials) and why
- *Today's Saint*: Biographies of the saints celebrated on that day

The Gospel according to Mark

THE primary evangelist for Year B is Mark. As with our other Gospel accounts, the earliest extant manuscripts of the Gospel according to Mark are anonymous and date from the fourth century after Christ. The earliest Christian legend that a Christian named Mark (see Colossians 4:10; Acts of the Apostles 12:12) wrote Mark's Gospel account comes to us from a second-century bishop of Hierapolis in Asia Minor, Papias, who tells us Mark was the interpreter of Peter. Scholars disagree on what Papias might have meant by "interpreter" and therefore disagree on how closely the Gospel stories in Mark are related to Peter's teaching. In addition, it is reasonable to conclude that Mark did have other written sources. He may well have had a written account of the Passion as well

as originally independent groups of stories, such as the five controversy stories that run from 2:1 to 3:6. Recent scholarship suggests it is not possible to determine how much Mark edited these earlier sources to fit his own purpose in writing his Gospel.

The original audience for Mark was probably living outside of the Holy Land in a place that was largely populated by non-Jews. We know this because Mark, in some places, appears to be confused about the geography of Palestine (see 5:1 and 7:31) and indicates that his audience would not be familiar with Jewish customs (7:4). He also at times translates Aramaic terms into Greek for his Greek-speaking audience (5:41; 15:34).

The date of the Gospel according to Mark depends largely on how one understands Jesus' prediction of the fall of the Jerusalem Temple to the Romans in AD 70. Those who believe this prediction was created by Mark and not actually spoken by Jesus understand this verse to refer to the actual destruction of the Temple in AD 70. Thus the Gospel must have been after that date yet early enough to have become a primary source for the other two synoptic Gospel accounts, Matthew and Luke, written some time in the two decades following Mark. Scholars who argue that it is not unlikely that Jesus himself would have made such a prediction about the fall of the Temple often date the Gospel according to Mark to around AD 60–70 and even more precisely to the probable time of Peter's death in Rome under Nero (c. AD 64).

It is best to understand Mark not as giving us information about the life of Jesus or as a source of Peter's teaching but rather as a Gospel created by an independent and fascinating theologian who crafted the story of Jesus to communicate deep theological insight about Christian life in Christ. How Mark does this is to take us deep into an understanding of the two primary sacraments of the earliest Christian Churches: the immersion in water known as Baptism and the sacred meal known as the Lord's Supper. This is the vantage point from which the remainder of this introduction will be presented.

The Gospel accounts of Matthew and Luke begin with separate stories about the birth of Jesus in Bethlehem and the early years of the Holy Family. Mark, on the other hand, begins with the baptism of Jesus who is, presumably, already a young adult. He immediately ties the story of the baptism to the story of the Cross at the end of the Gospel: Jesus is proclaimed Son of God in the first verse and at the foot of the Cross (1:1; 15:39); John the Baptist appears in the guise of the prophet Elijah who is called for by Jesus' detractors at the Cross (1:6; 15:36); the Baptism of the Spirit predicted at 1:8 happens at the Death of Jesus in 15:37; the heavens are torn open at the Baptism (1:10) and the Temple curtain is torn when Jesus dies (15:38). Moreover, Jesus himself within the Gospel according to Mark understands Baptism to be associated with his death (10:38–39). What this means is that Mark's account from its very first verse invites the reader to consider what it means to be baptized into the Death of Jesus.

In the earliest Christian Churches the practice of admitting uncircumcised Gentiles into the Lord's Supper to eat with the Jews was highly controversial. Paul in his letter to the Galatians describes vividly one encounter in Antioch when he confronted Peter and Barnabas for withdrawing from eating this meal with Gentiles (2:11–14). Mark appears to address this same issue in his Gospel account and presents an understanding of Baptism into the death of Christ as the primary means by which non-Jews (Gentiles) are brought into the Christian community with full participation at the Lord's Supper. Mark has Jesus state at 10:45 that his death is a "ransom for the many," which, in the context of the Gospel to this point, refers to the influx of Gentiles into the Christian community.

Gentiles who were baptized as Christians were isolated in ancient society. They could no longer participate in the myriad of pagan rituals that filled the life of the ancient cities (see 1 Corinthians 10:14–23) and, without circumcision, were not considered to be Jews by Jewish synagogues. This led to both the official and unofficial persecution described vividly in Mark 13:11–13. For Mark such suffering, entered into at Baptism, was participation in the Death of Christ. Yet just as Jesus' suffering and Death, begun at his baptism, led to his glorification, so also would suffering and death entered into at Baptism bring glorification to his disciples (8:35; 10:38–39).

It is, however, Mark's response to the issue of Gentiles and Jews eating the Lord's Supper together that binds the narrative of Mark into a timeless and powerful theological message of inclusivity. The first eight chapters of Mark depict Jesus himself as beginning the mission to the Gentiles, a mission that is both misunderstood and resisted by both his Jewish opponents and his earliest Jewish disciples. In chapter 2, for example,

Jesus heals a paralytic lowered through the roof into his house by "four men," an inclusive number in the ancient world (four winds, four corners of the earth), and commends their faith (2:5). In chapter 3 Jesus' Jewish family wants him to withdraw from the house (3:32) but Jesus responds by saying that his family is "whoever does the will of God" (3:31), undoubtedly a reference to the Gentiles who have gathered in the house with Jesus.

In Mark, Jesus also commissions the disciples for the Gentile mission. Peter and his brother Andrew are called by Jesus and told that they will become "fishers of men" (1:17). Later, upon the completion of the disciples' mission culminating in the first feeding narrative, the disciples discover they have, surprisingly, five loaves and two fish for the meal (6:38). The total (five + two) indicates the restoration of the Genesis creation in the Christian meal. Jesus commands the disciples to feed bread to the crowd of Jews and Gentiles and then Jesus himself gives the two fish to everyone gathered. Upon completion of the meal Mark tells us that "everyone ate and was satisfied" and that they took up twelve baskets (an allusion to the twelve tribes of Israel) of bread pieces (6:41–43). Immediately after this meal, when Jesus walks upon the water (an allusion to Baptism and Resurrection), the disciples are "surprised because they did not understand about the loaves" (6:52): they did not understand that on the basis of their baptismal death the Gentiles were to be part of the meal experiencing the Resurrection.

The first feeding narrative locates Jesus, his disciples, and the crowd somewhere in Jewish Galilee. The second feeding narrative (8:1–11) finds Jesus and the gathering outside of Jewish Galilee and in the Gentile area of the Decapolis (ten Greek cities, 7:31). The disciples' question at 8:4 ("how can one feed these people with loaves here in the Wilderness?") is a reference to the Gentiles who have gathered at the meal to eat with the Jewish disciples. Here, though, the venue has changed (we are on Gentile soil) and so have the numbers: the disciples come up with seven loaves (again creation restored) and some fish (the number seven is preserved). Again the disciples are commanded to feed the Gentile crowd and everyone eats (8:6–8). In the first feeding narrative Mark described five thousand males being fed (five is indicative of the five books of Moses) and twelve baskets of bread pieces being gathered (twelve is indicative of the twelve tribes of Israel). Here, however, Mark states that four thousand people were fed and seven baskets of bread pieces were gathered. Mark not only refers inclusively to the Gentiles but quite specifically to women as well.

Immediately following this, and in the course of another water and boat episode, the Jewish disciples fail to understand what has just happened. At 8:14 Mark tells us enigmatically that the disciples had forgotten to bring "loaves" but had one "loaf" with them on the boat. The ensuing conversation about being aware of the leaven of the Pharisees and of Herod leads Jesus to ask the disciples about the number of baskets of bread pieces they had taken up in the first and second feeding narrative (twelve and seven respectively): Jesus then asks his disciples what they do not understand about the one loaf they did have with them on the boat (8:21). Thus Mark has Jesus teach his Jewish disciples that the twelve (Jewish) and seven (Gentiles and women) baskets of bread pieces are all part of the one loaf of the Eucharist.

The next time in Mark that we encounter this one loaf is at the Last Supper immediately prior to the Passion and Death of Jesus (14:22–26). Here Jesus takes up the "one loaf," which the reader of Mark now knows constitutes Jews, Gentiles, men, and women and declares the one loaf to be his body. This is the body that will suffer and die only to be restored in the new creation that is the Resurrection of Christ. This is also all Christians, then and now, who have become part of the suffering and Death of Christ through Baptism and so joined with him in the new creation of Resurrection celebrated in the meal of the Resurrection.

Writing in a poor Greek style, Mark has created a brilliant theological narrative whose message is as relevant today as it was then: our Baptism unites all of us to Christ and joins us together at the Eucharistic meal to experience a new life and new creation united with God.

— Charles A. Bobertz, PHD

ADVENT

The Meaning

"**O** Come, O Come, Emmanuel!" Our sanctuaries and our homes ring with these ancient words of invitation and welcome as we embrace the season of Advent. Quieting ourselves, much as the coming of winter stills and quiets the natural world, we seek to prepare a place for Christ to come again and to be born anew—for his coming or "advent"—in our hearts and in our world. We remember his entry into human life as a vulnerable newborn, and remembering the Paschal Mystery, we also affirm when he will return in glory at the Parousia, the fulfillment of salvation history.

The coming of the Messiah was a source of hope and anticipation in the life of the people of Israel. Frequently subjugated and often enslaved, they looked to the coming of the savior of the Jewish people as a horizon of promise. In these weeks of Advent, we hear many stories of the covenant that God has entered into with his chosen people.

We also hear of the expansion of God's call to the entire human family through his Son, Jesus

Christ. We believe that the Messiah sent to save Israel is, in fact, the Savior of all people. All are called to come to God's holy mountain.

The invitation is not passive. We hear the voice of John the Baptist crying out from the wilderness, inviting all who would seek repentance to the waters of baptism. John does not sit silently, hoping that people will somehow find him, however much that might be to their benefit. His invitation to us is active. Similarly, Jesus reminds us to "be alert" (Mark 13:33) for the signs that redemption is at hand. The story of the Virgin Mary, who trusted and said yes to bearing God into human form, reminds us that when we hear God calling, our response should be trust and affirmation.

It is ironic that in our age, what should be a season of stillness, listening, and waiting becomes a season of frenetic busyness. In the bustle of "making" Christmas—decorating, buying gifts, preparing food, and entertaining—we can find ourselves exhausted and depleted. This can be true in our parishes as well as in our homes, where seasonal programs and special liturgies increase staff and volunteer workload. With the focus on the expectations of community members for certain types of Advent experiences, we can lose track of the richness of this season for evangelization and welcome.

Because we have other tasks demanding our attention, we may presume that if someone is new to town, they'll find the local Catholic Church in the phone book or on the Web. In our focus on our current community relationships, we may miss the challenge newcomers face as they try to make connections in this season, particularly if they are far away from friends and family. We have to actively remember that for the grieving, the lonely, the unemployed—for people struggling in any way—Christmas Time can be one of stress, not joy. They, too, need ways to meaningfully connect.

Advent is an ideal time to encourage community members to reach out and include people in the life of our parishes. This can be challenging for Catholics. While members may know of people who are rooted in the Catholic tradition, they may feel hesitant to invite them to join us at Mass, afraid that they'll be perceived as pushy or, even worse, holy rollers. We need to actively help people remember that we are inviting people to experience something wonderful and extraordinary when we bring them to the Eucharist: a relationship with a God so intimate that he chose to become one with the human family by taking on human form.

The Lectionary for Mass

THE traditional themes of waiting and expectation are never "out of season" during Advent. The Scripture readings for the Sundays of Advent offer us a rich fare of themes, attitudes, and imperatives.

The First Readings are from the great Hebrew prophet Isaiah and from 2 Samuel for the Fourth Sunday. These four readings frame a dialogue between the prophet and God. On the First Sunday this divine-human conversation opens with the prophet's lament, "Why do you let us wander, O Lord, from your ways?"

God's response on the Second Sunday is one of great concern assuring the people that they will be comforted and cared for as a shepherd cares for the flock. On the Third Sunday the prophet recalls that it was the Lord who anointed him to bring glad tidings to the poor, heal the broken hearted, and proclaim liberty to captives. The reasons for lamentation are past; there is cause for rejoicing. On the Fourth Sunday the conversation within the reading is between David and his Lord. We are drawn into this scene and reassured that indeed the Lord will take care of us and we too will inherit the greatness of God's own people.

The psalms portray the Lord as the one who looks kindly on his people, like a shepherd, a protector, and provider. The psalmist cries out to the Lord to "take care of this vine " (the people) that he has planted (Psalm 80:15). At the same time the psalmist expresses his trust that the Lord will be kind and faithful.

The Second Readings are like four parts of a single exhortation to the early Churches. Delivered by Paul and the author of 2 Peter (Second Sunday) they encourage the believers to live lives that are holy and blameless in anticipation of the Day of the Lord. There is an urgency about all this for the Day of the Lord will come "like a thief" (1 Thessalonians 5:2); the faithful must be watchful.

The Gospel accounts echo the exhortation of the epistles. Jesus tells his disciples to be watchful and alert. John the Baptist appears proclaiming the coming of the Messiah, and calling his listeners to repentance in preparation. On the Fourth Sunday the Gospel reveals the reason for all this anticipation: Mary will give birth to the Son of God.

The readings for Christmas Time celebrate the birth of the child Jesus, with all the details of that historic event as the Word becomes flesh and comes to dwell in the midst of humanity. The First Readings underline the hope of the first covenant people who look forward to a light for the nations. The psalms are hymns of joy exhorting the faithful to rejoice in the wondrous works of God.

The Second Readings have two principal themes: salvation comes from God and it is bestowed on all peoples.

The Gospel accounts proclaim the revelation of God in Jesus, Messiah, and Savior. The narratives of his birth, his baptism, and the visit of the Magi all celebrate the manifestation of divine intervention in the world. The response of the shepherds, the strange visitors from the east, and of the crowd at his baptism shapes our own response to this Good News: we are filled with joy!

The weekday readings for Advent present a rich tapestry for reflection. Most of the First Readings are from Isaiah and the majority of the Gospel texts are from Matthew. The Isaian passages speak of the future glory that the Lord will bestow on the people who will remain faithful to the covenant; even creation will be renewed and praise God. The Gospel accounts describe various teaching moments in Jesus ministry, explaining how the Kingdom of God is very different from the ways of thinking and acting of the listeners. The underlying theme is that God will bring about a new heaven and a new earth. Luke's account of the Gospel, which surrounds the Solemnity of the Nativity of the Lord, describes in careful and familiar detail the arrival of the One who will make all things new.

The Roman Missal

THE fervent expectation of the season is expressed throughout the proper prayers and chants of the Missal. At the start of the season our focus in on the Parousia as we "resolve to run forth to meet your Christ / with righteous deeds at his coming" (Collect, First Sunday of Advent). Journeying through the season we later recall more explicitly Christ's birth so that we "who are weighed down from of old / by slavery beneath the yoke of sin, / may be set free by the newness / of the long-awaited Nativity" (Collect, December 18).

Vestments for this season are violet, although on the Third Sunday of Advent rose-colored vestments may be worn. During Advent the Gloria is not to be sung or said except on particular solemnities and feasts. Another way we sustain the moderation of the season is to keep the music simple and to limit the use of musical instruments. Either Preface I or II of Advent should be used for the Eucharistic Prayer, according to the rubrics of the Missal. As such, we do not use Eucharistic Prayer IV because it cannot accommodate seasonal prefaces. The Missal offers other resources for the season, including a Solemn Blessing for Advent (for use on any Sunday in the season) and a sample formulary for the Universal Prayer in Appendix V. While the "O Antiphons" are part of the Liturgy of the Hours rather than the Missal, their theological depth might warrant them having some influence on the selection of music for Mass (although they do serve as the verses for the Gospel Acclamation from December 17–23). To be sure, the Entrance and Communion Antiphons of the Missal can also guide the range of music used during Advent.

Children's Liturgy of the Word

CHILDREN have a natural sense of anticipation and an innate capacity for excitement. For those who lead children's Liturgy of the Word, this is good news! It means you will not need to work so intensely to help the children appreciate the meaning of Advent. Many children will come to the celebration of the Word familiar with the season's symbols such as the Advent wreath and Jesse tree. You will want to have these as part of the environment in the space where you celebrate the Word with children. Place the Advent wreath in a central and fairly prominent location. You could have the appropriate number of candles lit as the children enter the space, or you could have a child assist an adult in lighting the candles as a first act after the children settle. Locate the Jesse tree in a space where the children can see and encounter it, but a place that allows the Word to remain the focus.

Children experience their surroundings through the senses. They particularly absorb meaning from what they see. Anytime the liturgical environment of your space changes, you will want to give the children time to acclimate to the newness either through a brief period of silence or with seasonal instrumental music as they settle in. When the children see violet cloths on the prayer table and underneath the children's Lectionary, they will want to know why. On Gaudete Sunday, the Third Sunday of Advent, the liturgical color is either violet or rose.

While time often is a premium for the celebration of the Word with children, you will also want to discuss the new environment with the children, perhaps as a part of the reflection, or briefly as the celebration opens. Make sure the children know that it is Advent. By questioning the children, lead them to know that Advent is a season of joyful anticipation for Jesus' coming. We prepare to remember that Jesus came in the past, to celebrate his presence with us now, and to affirm our belief that he will come again in glory. One of the ways we do this is to look at positive ways we can love one another and to change those ways we act that do not reflect Jesus' love. By engaging the children in the discussion of Advent in this manner, they will also come to see that aspect of repentance that is a part of the season's meaning. You might choose to change the words or music you use to express the meaning of Advent in accord with the Lectionary readings each week, but remember to have the children help you restate the meaning of the season each time you gather.

In terms of liturgical music, check with your music director or the leader of the music for the liturgy at which you will celebrate the Word with children. Inquire whether the assembly will sing a seasonal Advent psalm for the four Sundays and what Gospel Acclamation they will sing. If you are not a musician, ask about the "singability" of the chosen psalm or psalms and Gospel Acclamation for children. It is preferable for the children to sing the same and/or similar music as the main assembly. Doing so connects them with the entire worshipping community and assists them in their participation when they attend a liturgy in which the celebration of the Word with children does not take place. Give preference to having "live" music, keyboard or guitar accompaniment, and especially a cantor. Check with your music director about cantor availability. Perhaps high school youth might have the gift of leading the children in song. For more specific suggestions, see LTP's *Children's Liturgy of the Word: A Weekly Resource.*

The Saints

ADVENT is punctuated with celebrations of the saints, especially those of Our Lady. These commemorations have taken on added importance in different cultures as islands of light, warmth, and festivity in the dark and the cold of the end of the year. In many cultures, the optional Memorial of St. Nicholas on December 6 is an occasion for giving gifts to children, especially sweets. Similarly, the Memorial of St. Lucy on December 13 is an opportunity for a family celebration that centers on light and sweet rolls.

The December Marian observances are both tied closely to North America: Mary is the patroness of the United States under the title of the Immaculate Conception (December 8), and of the Americas under the title of the Virgin of Guadalupe (December 12). These observances appropriately fall in the first and second weeks of Advent as Mary is first to have waited and watched for the coming of the Lord. These two observances illuminate different aspects of our waiting. Each points us to the coming Christ and his mission to the world.

Mary's Immaculate Conception is not merely a preparation for the coming of her Son; it is also a vision of the fulfillment of his work. By special grace of God, she is preserved from sin from her very conception. Therefore she is already an image of the remade humanity that her Son brings about. This double meaning of the Immaculate Conception mirrors the double call to watchfulness in Advent. We prepare to welcome the infant in Bethlehem and look expectantly for his Second Coming and the remaking of the world.

Mary's appearance at Guadalupe calls us to a different kind of watchfulness. God is working for the salvation of all peoples and all cultures. The apparition to St. Juan Diego broadened the Church's vocabulary and vision. God's work is not limited to those whose ancestors have been Christians for millennia. Jesus is always the "cornerstone that ties the two together," as the O Antiphon for December 21 names him — no human division cannot be overcome by Christ.

The Liturgy of the Hours

LIKE Mass and the sacraments, the Liturgy of the Hours is our common, official prayer. Unlike other liturgies, we usually pray it as individuals. We may pray from books, tablets, or our phones. We pray in our homes and churches, in parking lots waiting for children's dismissal from school, and on subways as we go to work. While praying as individuals, we are united in this prayer and so as a community we find ourselves praying always, consecrating the world to God. Because the root of the Liturgy of the Hours is the Psalter, we are also tied with our ancestors in faith, praying hymns that may be three thousand years old.

In a parish's life, there are times when Mass may not be feasible or appropriate—gathering for meetings, holy days that are not obligatory, before leaving on parish trips, or even when Mass will be celebrated later in the day, such as on a retreat. This is the time for the Liturgy of the Hours. Many dioceses and parishes are experiencing the struggle of fewer priests. Occasions which used to be marked by Mass, such as the Girl Scout annual celebration or a school honors night, are now wondering what they should do. This is the time for the Liturgy of the Hours.

There is no need to "find something" to do in these circumstances. It is already here. There are many shorter versions available and when a musician is present to lead the psalms and canticles, only a small participation aide (if any) may be needed.

Since Advent is a new liturgical year, in what new ways can your parish use the Liturgy of the Hours? Note that the *General Instruction of the Liturgy of the Hours* asks us to apply the "principal of 'progressive solemnity'" (GILOH, 273). Don't be afraid to begin by using a shorter, adapted pattern for simple occasions. For example, begin with the introductory verse: "O God, come to my assistance . . . ." Then sing a common hymn followed by one, two, or three psalms. Begin with ones with which the assembly is familiar from Sunday Mass. Use the Scripture of the day and then the appropriate canticle. There are familiar settings in hymnals from many publishers. Intercessions, the Lord's Prayer, a concluding prayer, and blessing are familiar to all.

During Advent remember to light the wreath. If you are praying a common Evening Prayer, perhaps before a parish pastoral council meeting, lower the lights a bit and let the light of the candle and some silence settle our hearts and minds. If on Sunday you are using a seasonal psalm, pray it now. If singing is not an option, recite the texts. Remember this is not a time to rush—let the Spirit hover over you in prayer as you ask for God's presence in your discussions and deliberations.

In Advent, the Liturgy of the Hours honors the ancient tradition of the O Antiphons. These are taken from the antiphon to the Magnificat from December 17–23. Most of us know them as the verses from "O Come, O Come, Emmanuel." Consider using this hymn as a catechetical tool. This year we have a very short Advent, really only three full weeks. So be ready to move to the options for the O Antiphons on the Third Sunday of Advent.

The Rite of Christian Initiation of Adults

THE *Rite of Christian Initiation of Adults* as a rite of the Church unfolds in the course of the liturgical year. This process should not be rushed; both RCIA team members and those discerning initiation need time to attend to the movement of the Holy Spirit. In *Discerning Disciples: Listening for God's Voice in Christian Initiation*, Sister Donna Steffen, SC, says, "Discernment involves listening for and naming the various spirits that are operating" (6). Throughout the entire process, priests, deacons, catechists, and RCIA team members practice the art of discernment with each candidate seeking initiation. From the initial interview to the interview before the Rite of Election, those responsible for initiation take time to listen to candidates and accompany them as they listen to and respond to God's invitation. Article 43 of the rite says, "sufficient and necessary time . . . should be set aside to evaluate . . . the candidates' motives and dispositions" before the celebration of the Rite of Acceptance into the Order of Catechumens. Similarly, article 122 says, "there should be a deliberation prior to [the Rite of Election] to decide on the catechumens' suitableness."

The goal of this discernment is not to exclude individuals from the process, but to help people recognize God's grace and assist them in identifying how they are growing in the faith and how God is calling them to grow further. This may include naming areas of resistance, areas of joy and sorrow. An individual may need to learn to be vulnerable in the presence of God and how to listen with the "ear of the heart" (*Rule of St. Benedict*, prologue). In their listening, the priest, deacon, and/or catechist can help a candidate decide whether it is time to move from the Precatechumenate to the Catechumenate, from the Catechumenate to election, and so on. Those charged with formation need to develop a discerning heart and practice discernment in their own lives so that they can hone this skill. The team also needs to grow in awareness of their own biases so they do not cloud judgment. There are many resources available to help a team learn/practice the art of discernment. Prayer will be central in this process and in the formation of team and candidates alike. Take time study the book named above or learn more about Ignatian contemplation, the art of journaling, and get know spiritual directors in your parish or area who can assist with this process.

It is also important that the parish community understands its role in the process of Christian Initiation. The RCIA states, "The entire community must help the candidates and the catechumens throughout the process of initiation" (9). The community is not a silent onlooker, but actively participates in the rite through prayer, witness, as team members, ministers of hospitality, and so on. Most importantly, as the Body of Christ, they teach the candidates how to worship and live the Gospel. There should be many opportunities for the parish family to engage with the candidates. Personally knowing the candidates will allow members of the faithful to provide testimony when the time comes at the Rite of Acceptance and even at the Easter Vigil. In order to help the parish understand its role in the process, priests and deacons are encouraged to preach on the rites as they are celebrated and highlight the role of the assembly in the formation of these candidates. Parishes might consider publishing weekly articles in the bulletin to educate the assembly on the rite or even host a recruitment event to get more individuals involved in the process. There is a lot in the rite to explore so take a moment annually to reread and study the text.

The Sacraments of Initiation

Each candidate, their family, and the parish community go through a period of preparation prior to receiving the sacraments of initiation. Participating in the liturgy is an essential part of this process for everyone involved because it is the place of connection, to Christ, to the Church, and to our community of faith. When preparing for any of the sacraments of initiation, it is especially important for the candidates and their families to be in tune with the liturgical seasons of the Church because this is the cycle that will help to sustain their faith in the future.

When people are asked what keeps them coming to church they respond that it feels like family, that they feel connected to the community and each other, and it is a support system for everyday life as Christian disciples on the journey of faith. We celebrate that we are reborn into God's family through the waters of Baptism. Most often parents bring infants and young children to receive Baptism. This means that the congregation has a wonderful opportunity to show their support for the young family and welcome them into the family of faith. Since Advent is a time when we are very conscious of the pregnancy of Mary and the anticipated birth of Jesus, we are also reminded to attend to young families in the parish community.

Offering short programs like an Advent workshop for families after Masses or on Saturday morning the week or two prior to Advent is a quick and easy way to help young parents get to know each other and introduce them and the children to liturgical for the Advent. Offering simple Advent wreath crafts and decorating the tables with Advent colors of violet and rose will help families to establish and Advent traditions instead of jumping right into Christmas preparations.

The Rite of Penance

Advent begs us to do something quite contrary to our culture's expectations. We are asked to wait. The festive times of our Christmas celebrations have encroached upon all of December, making our homes and workplaces busy and stressful; often places of a hyperactivity.

However, there is joy in our Advent expectation. While we may begin to decorate, bake, and shop in anticipation of the celebration of the Incarnation, Advent insists we slow down and begs our vision to take a longer view, all the way to the Second Coming.

In this light, in reflection on the image of the Reign of God, how have we lived our out discipleship and how have we sinned? How do we participate in the social sins of our world? Advent asks us to remember the complexity of the web of sin. Our actions have ramifications beyond ourselves. This too is contrary to the wisdom of the world. This siren beckons us to rampant individualism. But the bond of humanity reaches across the world. How have we sinned again this truth? By our stinginess? Our greed? Our blinding need for self-righteousness that denies others' opinions, food, or freedom?

It is easy for parishes to give into the busyness of December and simply let our people avoid this sacrament altogether. However, this is contrary to the spirit of Mark, whom we read this year. His Gospel is filled with urgency, "Be watchful! Be alert!" (Mark 13:33).

Consider communal celebrations early in the season. If enough priests are not available for private confessions and absolution, there is still value in the gathering of the community for a non-sacramental service. At this time of the year, use readings and psalms that have a social justice dynamic. As you craft an examination of conscience, take a global view with a particular application. How may your parishioners be called to a deeper sense of the sinfulness of racism, sexism, or other forms of bigotry? Do we have a sense of caring for the earth? Have we reflected on the U.S. bishops' statements on immigration? Can we place ourselves in the shoes of our sisters and brothers displaced by war or terror?

Penances could then reflect a greater participation in healing these sins, such as contributing to coat drives, a commitment to recycling or perhaps a reduction in extraneous Christmas paraphernalia. If our communities have programs to learn about cultures other than our own, maybe it's time to discover how our neighbors see the world. Groups such as Pax Christi, Sojourners, Catholic Charities, or Catholic Relief Services are a wealth of information and suggestions.

For those unable to participate in the Penance services, think about publishing the examination of conscience and/or sample penances on the parish website, social media page, or in the church bulletin. While certainly not a substitute for the sacrament, it may be used as a preparation for a deeper sense of contrition.

The Order of Celebrating Matrimony

THE Sacrament of Matrimony is a beautiful expression of the working of the Spirit in the lives of disciples. "By the Sacrament of Matrimony Christian spouses signify and participate in the mystery of unity and fruitful love between Christ and the Church" (*The Order of Celebrating Matrimony*, 8). However, Marriage is also celebrated in the culture. Therefore, understandings and expectations can clash when we begin our meetings with prospective brides and grooms.

The introduction to *The Order of Celebrating Matrimony*, especially 1–11, describes the Church's understanding of this sacrament. If you have not read it in a while, perhaps this Advent is a good time to do so. If this is our view of Marriage, what understanding do your couples bring?

Marriage in American culture can be a byproduct of our consumerism. It's one more place where we can buy more, get more, show more. Television shows enourage not just one dress for the day, but even three. The media portrays outlandish reception halls, unrealistic ceremony sites, and what can only be described as over the top entertainment. Of course, all this comes with a large ticket price. The wedding day is a time for consumption and competition—be better than the last wedding you attended.

This is stark contrast to the Church. We want to talk about a Marriage, not just a wedding day. We want to discuss God acting in your lives for the rest of your life. As we begin a new liturgical year consider changes or adaptations to your process of preparation for the sacrament.

Start with the attitude. Do weddings bring joy to your parish's life or are they a burden? How we approach a couple sends a big message. If we can be sincerely happy for them, they will recognize it and fruitful dialog has a firm foundation.

Take some time rereading the introduction and ritual texts with the team that prepares for this sacrament. What insights can you glean? There are some wonderful resources as well that can help guide us.

With fresh eyes look at the materials what you provide for the engaged. Are they adequate and appropriate? Do they meet the couple where they are at or are they condescending and judgmental? If you discern that your process needs significant changes, don't move too fast. Take time, notes and consultation, maybe from the newly married, and prepare for the modifications you need to make. Don't make adjustments once preparation has begun. It is unfair to the couple; they are busy about many things. However, a good Marriage preparation is a wonderful gift from their Church community.

Encourage dialogue with the newly engaged. Consider reformulating the themes of the Introduction to the Marriage Rite in language that is useful for discussion. What expectation to they bring to the sacrament? What concerns? How do they see their Marriage as part of their spiritual journey? Where is the parish community in the Sacrament of Matrimony? What cultural expectations do they have that should be addressed early.

While Marriages can be celebrated in Advent, make sure the couple is of the same mind as the parish with regard to seasonal expectations. They may not be thinking about a blue-violet environment or an Advent wreath in their pictures. Also, December means Christmas to many. Make sure they are not thinking carols or trees until after December 25.

The Pastoral Care of the Sick

ONE of the traditional themes of the season of Advent is waiting. It could be said that there are three kinds or moments of waiting. There is the historical waiting of the Israelites that is proclaimed in the readings from the great Hebrew prophets during Advent. Their waiting was in anticipation of the coming of the Messiah. There is the liturgical waiting that Christians celebrate throughout Advent, marking the days of Advent as a journey to the celebration of the birth of Christ

in time and in our hearts. There is the spiritual waiting that shapes our whole life as we await the Second Coming of Christ in glory. This is the eschatological waiting we celebrate in Eucharist. In Eucharistic Prayer III we pray:

> Therefore, O Lord, as we celebrate the memorial
> of the saving Passion of your Son,
> his wondrous Resurrection
> and Ascension into heaven,
> and as we look forward to his second coming,
> we offer you in thanksgiving
> this holy and living sacrifice.

Those who celebrate the Sacrament of the Anointing of the Sick are often very conscious of what it means to wait. It may be that they are waiting for surgery, or for a report from some tests, or for relief from an illness, or for some assurance that they will regain a sense of wellness once again. It is during those times that they can benefit from the Sacrament of the Anointing, not only spiritually but emotionally. Indeed, many have said that the prayers and gestures of the rite have given them a sense that even their body and spirit are improved.

The rite for the *Pastoral Care of the Sick* offers many options for readings from Scripture. During Advent priests and pastoral care ministers could also choose readings from the Sundays and weekdays of Advent. Here are some suggestions:

◆ First Week of Advent: The psalm refrain for Sunday; the First Reading for Wednesday; the psalm for Friday; the psalm for Saturday

◆ Second Week of Advent: the Second Reading for Sunday; the psalms for Wednesday, Thursday, or Saturday

◆ Third Week of Advent: the First Reading for Sunday; the psalms for Sunday, Monday, or Tuesday

◆ Fourth Week of Advent: the psalm for December 19; the Gospel for December 21; the psalms for December 23 or December 24

The pastoral intent of the Sacrament of the Anointing of the Sick, with the Scripture readings, prayers, gestures, and presence of others is to take up the command of the Lord to the prophet Isaiah: "Comfort, give comfort to my people, / says your God" (40:1).

During Advent, a time of waiting in so many ways, the Sacrament of the Anointing of the Sick has a particular liturgical context that should not be overlooked. Those who are sick among us can be joined to the whole community of the faithful through the celebration of this sacrament. They can be remembered in the prayers of the assembly, thus making the whole people of God more aware that we all wait for the Second Coming of the Lord in glory.

The Order of Christian Funerals

THE Funeral Liturgy, while a time of sorrow, is also a time of praise and thanksgiving to our God for the life of our deceased sister or brother. It may be a time of pain, especially if the death is sudden or the person young. It may be a time of release if there has been long suffering or respite needed, the grieving having begun while our beloved has slipped slowly away. It may be a time of regret for words not spoken, or of healing and reconciliation. It may be a time of anger, loss, or seemingly inconsolable sorrow. It may be time for every affair under the heavens (see Ecclesiastes 3). It is assuredly a time of faith.

Clergy and lay ministers need to be aware of the graced and fragile time with which they walk with a family. They may be long time parishioners or new faces, but they are in a delicate spiritual space. Our ministry needs to reach out to them with assurances of Christ and fellowship in the Church. While funerals fall into the life of the parish usually without warning, they are powerful moments. How we work with the family can help heal or hurt for years to come.

Funerals in Advent can accentuate the sadness of death. The darkness of winter and the cold in the air remind us of the fleetingness of life and our own frailty. Nature has given us the environment for our worship. Don't be afraid to use it. Refer to the short days and the Advent wreath that counts time for us. The symbol of light in the darkness speaks volumes to the hurting.

Advent in some ways is the perpetual state of the Church. Use the symbols already present. We live in the in between time of Christ's Resurrection and his return. The white funeral pall in the midst of the purple of the Church expresses Resurrection in the midst of death. The large Paschal candle and the smaller, dwindling, Advent candles is another symbol of Christ's victory and the brevity of our lives. Use what surrounds the assembly. For our visiting family just a short explanation can give words to what their eyes see and their hearts already grasp.

One struggle is the choice of readings. Some parishes ask the family to make the selections. Others give them options on the readings other than the Gospel, reserving this to the priest celebrant. In this case, consider one of the Advent Gospel texts that lend themselves to speaking of the Second Coming.

Another concern may be choices in music. Since the secular culture largely ignores Advent and jumps to Christmas right after Thanksgiving, be wary of inviting the less churched families to randomly select music options. A consistent refrain of "No, we can't play that in church" sets a rather negative tone. Remember, we need to meet them where they are at, yet welcome them into our Church's liturgical life. Perhaps a list of songs that can be used in church should be provided. Most of our music has been recorded by the composer. Create a play list from which they can listen to selections while you plan with them. (Remember not to distribute music in violation of copyright.)

Don't forget to consider the Vigil Liturgy. How does your parish provide for this part of the *Order of Christian Funerals*? Do the priests and deacons lead the service? Are there trained lay leaders? In addition to presiding at prayer, who ministers as the reader? What about music? This is a wonderful time to show the love and concern a parish has for the family by surrounding them with support and witness beyond a single presider. Cantors who can lead simple, common hymnody and a psalm bring beauty to this liturgy. In addition, it allows the power of music to come forth from the grieving, giving them another place to profess and own their faith in Christ.

Many parishes work regularly with a few common funeral homes in their neighborhood. Discuss with them storing an Advent wreath to be placed by the casket. Then as you begin prayer, light the appropriate number of candles and allow for some silence. We all need a reminder of the importance of sacred space.

The Book of Blessings

THE obvious and most prominent blessing for use in this season is the Order of the Blessing of an Advent Wreath (*Book of Blessings* [BB], chapter 47), itself a sign of this light. The wreath is customarily made of a circle of evergreen branches with four candles — usually three violet candles and one rose-colored candle (for the Third Sunday of Advent), but four violet or four white candles are also acceptable. It should be of a size visible even from the back of the church, and should not obstruct the view of the ambo, altar, or presider's chair. Having such a wreath is not required, but is a long-standing traditional practice in a majority of parishes in the United States. The blessing should take place on the First Sunday of Advent or the evening before and can be celebrated within Mass (see BB, 1517–1520), in a celebration of the Word of God (see BB, 1521–1536), or during Evening Prayer after the Gospel canticle. While a priest, deacon, or a layperson may bless the wreath, if the rite is celebrated in the home it should be done by a parent or other member of the family. In this case the shorter rite (see BB, 1537–1540) is normally used. It is important to note that this blessing takes place only once. On subsequent Sundays of Advent, the appropriate number of candles are lit either before Mass or before the Collect without any accompanying ceremony or prayers.

The Order for the Blessing of a Christmas Tree (chapter 49) may take place in the last days of Advent, but because Christmas Day immediately follows the last Sunday of Advent this year, it would be better to to bless the tree on Christmas Eve (see the *Book of Blessing* commentary for Christmas).

The Liturgical Environment

THE color for Advent is violet, but it is a bluish-violet. The priest and deacon should wear vestments that are the same color. The altar cloth should be a simple white; however, altar scarves may be used as draping. Use the same blue-violet color as the vestments and other appointments. As always, the Liturgy of the Word and the Liturgy of the Eucharist should be the main focal point. You can add plants and flowers to the sanctuary during this season. Try to incorporate different vegetation that is indigenous to your local area at this time of the year. When preparing your liturgical environment this season, think of the often-quoted saying, "less is more." Keep the environment noble, dignified, beautiful, and simple.

Consider making your own Advent wreath, rather than purchasing a premade wreath. Cut branches from an evergreen tree (or purchase evergreen branches) and wire them together. Place the candlesticks in the boughs at varying heights. Add vegetation that is indigient to your part of the country—for example, in colder regions, you might add pinecones or holly or other berry branches. For a splash of color, add ribbons in shades of blue-violet that match the other fabrics in the liturgical space.

There are many options for placing the wreath. If you place it in the sanctuary, remember that it should not be directly in front of the altar. This may or may not be possible according to the space you have. If this is the case, find another suitable location.

Consider hanging banners that incorporate the symbols of Advent. As a team, read all of the weekly readings in addition to the Sunday readings in order to reflect upon the primary themes and symbols. During the enironment team meeting, talk about the different images that come to mind after having reflected on the Scriptures. talk about different ideas to use. You will need to select four symbols — one symbol for each week. Be sure to avoid Christmas symbols. For catechetical purpopes, include a short description about the symbol in the parish bulletin. Take photos of the banners and post on your parish social media page with a short description. Try starting an online faith-sharing discussion by inviting people to share their thoughts about the symbol and what it means to them. One year, my own parish created a Jesse Tree banner. Instead of using the shape a regular tree, we found one that was thinner and incoporated symbols such as the Star of David, the Chi-Rho, menorah, and other things that were a part of the life of Jesus! Refer to LTP's *Raise the Banners High! Making and Using Processional Banners*. This resource will help you create beautiful and expressive processional banners for use in the liturgy.

The Liturgical Music

THE images and references that pervade the liturgy in the Scriptures and orations during the first part of Advent (up through December 16) ought to also be the focus of the music. Hymns that focus on waiting, longing, light coming out of darkness, patience, and the justice and righteousness that will usher in the end times are appropriate. This is countercultural to the retail celebration of Christmas which began before Halloween and ends on December 26. Consider looking at *Within Our Hearts Be Born: The Michael Joncas Hymnary, Advent and Christmas* (OCP), a collection that offers hymn texts for the entire three-year Lectionary cycle for Advent and Christmas using some familiar traditional melodies as well as some newly created tunes.

While Advent is not a penitential season like Lent, it would be appropriate to sing the invocations of the Penitential Act using the third option in the Missal. Consider the setting based on "Warm the Time of Winter" by Lori True (GIA). If that hymn is used during the Entrance Procession, the melody will continue into the verses.

The Eucharistic Acclamations ought to be simple. If your assembly doesn't know the chant setting from the Missal, this is be a good time to introduce it.

Consider using one piece for the Communion Procession for all four Sundays of Advent to emphasize the unity of the season. "Jesus, Hope of the World" by Deanna Light and Paul Tate (WLP) is an excellent choice because of its Messianic references and easily memorized refrain. "Now in This Banquet" with its Advent refrain, "God of Our Journeys" by Marty Haugen (GIA), and "A Voice Cries Out" by Michael Joncas (OCP) are both good choices.

While many parishes offer a Christmas concert in December, it is more in keeping with the spirit of the season to offer Advent Lessons and Carols instead, particularly in the earlier part of the season modeled on the service that comes from King's College, Cambridge. This Lessons and Carols includes readings from Scripture and music (both hymns and choral anthems). If there are different musical ensembles in the parish, invite them all to participate. Each group could do one or two pieces on their own and then sing several combined pieces. The collection *Redeemer of the Nations, Come* by James Michael Thompson (WLP) offers a model for Lessons and Carols, which explores the treasury of the Church's Advent music and Scripture. The USCCB also offers a model on its website, www.usccb.org/prayer-and-worship /liturgical-year/advent/festival-of-lessons-and -carols.cfm. Keep the focus on Advent and let the story of the Annunciation be the focal point and culmination of the prayer service. "Mary's Story" by John Ferguson (GIA) tells the provocative story of the Virgin Mary's encounter with the angel Gabriel and the journey to visit her relative Elizabeth. It is arranged for reader, solo trumpet or flugelhorn, and organ and is intended that this piece be followed by Ferguson's "Magnificat." Save the Nativity story for late Advent and Christmas Time.

On December 17, the focus of Advent shifts from the Second Coming of Christ to his first coming in Bethlehem. The readings and orations set the stage for the Virgin Birth in Bethlehem. We hear a lot about Mary, Zechariah, Elizabeth, and the birth of John the Baptist. On the Fourth Sunday of Advent, since we again hear the story of the Annunciation, traditional Marian hymns like "Immaculate Mary" (LOURDES HYMN) or "Sing of Mary" (PLEADING SAVIOR) are appropriate, as are settings of the Magnificat. "We Sing with Holy Mary" by Alan Hommerding (WLP), set to the beloved THAXTED tune, could be done simply as a hymn tune or with Charles Thatcher's SATB choral arrangement with optional brass and string quartets.

It wouldn't seem like Advent without singing the traditional tune "O Come, O Come Emmanuel" (VENI EMMANUEL). Based on an ancient tune, this hymn mentions a different messianic title corresponding to the "O Antiphons" in each of its seven stanzas. Traditionally this hymn is used in the latter part of Advent although there are no hard and fast rules about this. Consider singing it as the recessional hymn on the Fourth Sunday of Advent. It could be done a capella or sung with a few handbells to keep everyone on pitch. Let the simplicity of the end of Advent leave the assembly longing for the grandeur and splendor of Christmas.

The Liturgical Ministers

PREPARE to provide spiritual formation for liturgical ministers during the year. Consider LTP's *Daily Prayer 2018,* which includes a Scripture reading, reflection, intercessions, and a closing prayer for each day of the liturgical year. *The Daily Mass Readings 2018: A Simple Reference Guide* includes the Lectionary numbers and citations for the readings. Providing these resources for liturgical ministers helps them to enter into the spirit of the liturgical year of the Church.

Advent is the perfect season to celebrate the Liturgy of the Hours with liturgical ministers and the entire community. Encourage liturgical ministers to use OCP's *Morning and Evening Prayer for the Commute* by Christopher Walker and Paule Freeburg or GIA's *My Morning Prayer* and *My Evening Prayer,* with music by various artists. These recordings of Morning and Evening Prayer can help to keep ministers linked to the Church's daily prayer.

If necessary Advent is the time to train new ministers that may be needed for the Christmas liturgies. Having enough ministers of hospitality on hand is important so that all who come to the threshold of the Church will be welcome. Consider including students who may have been away at college or former parishioners who may wish to serve in various liturgical ministries in the parish. Provide ministers of the liturgical environment a schedule indicating the times when the church and parish campus will be will be prepared for Advent which begins on December 3, 2017. Perhaps the church could be decorated following the Thanksgiving Day liturgy. Include a blessing for parents before childbirth (*Book of Blessings,* chapter 1, part VII) or a blessing of a mother before childbirth (*Book of Blessings,* chapter 1, part VIII) on the Fourth Sunday of Advent. Charge the parish liturgical commission to study the *Book of Blessings* and create a schedule for the upcoming liturgical year recommending days when blessings would be appropriate to include in the Sunday Liturgy or at other parish gatherings.

Other Prayers, Rituals, and Devotions

BEING one of the shortest of liturgical seasons, as well as running counter cultural to what is going on in the market place, makes the promotion of Advent traditions in the parish a challenge but well-prepared and executed rituals can set these days apart from the hustle and bustle of the season. What the Advent wreath does for the assembly on a weekly basis, the Jesse Tree does for the daily Mass-goers. The addition of symbols to bare branches for each day of the Advent season can be a time of scriptural catechesis in Old Testament personages. An excellent resource is published by Augsburg Fortress Press (www.augburgfortress. org) titled *The Jesse Tree: Stories and Symbols of Advent.* It not only supplies color symbols that can be cut out but daily prayers and Scripture citations. Producing an in-house brochure for Mass-goers can offer a prayer and scripture citation in conjunction for each symbol.

Advent offers children (and adults) an opportunity to learn more about the Advent saint, Nicholas, the precursor to Santa Claus. Usually falling around the Second Sunday of Advent, a visit from the bishop after a weekend Mass can include storytelling, distributing candy canes, gold coins, and holy cards. Visit www.stnicholascenter. org for products, crafts, and displays for use in a parish setting. One way to connect the prayer of the Church to prayer at home involves the setting up of the family crèche. Coordinate volunteers to fill small cellophane bags with straw, including a small card with the prayer for the "Blessing of a Christmas Manger or Nativity Scene," found in *Catholic Household Blessings & Prayers.* At the end of the Masses on one Advent weekend, the presider could bless the packets of straw and invite parishioners to take a bag home and add the blessed straw to their nativity scenes.

During his pontificate, St. John Paul II inaugurated "Bambinelli Sunday" on the Third Sunday of Advent. On this day, children are invited to bring the figure of the Infant Jesus from their crèche for a special blessing. Inspired by this ceremony, author Amy Welborn included the text of the annual papal blessing at the end of her children's book titled *Bambinelli Sunday: A Christmas Blessing,* published by Franciscan Media. Following the Prayer after Communion, children can be called forward at which time the presider can offer the blessing, ending with sprinkling the figures with holy water. As so many of our parishes are placed under the patronage of Our Lady, a novena in preparation for the Solemnity of the Immaculate Conception of the Blessed Virgin Mary can be a welcome addition to the parish's Advent calendar from November 30 to December 8. The Catholic News Agency (www.catholicnewsagency.com/resources/prayers/novenas/novena-to-the-immaculate-conception/) publishes a set of nine prayers for private or communal prayer, which includes a daily Scripture citation and reflection.

Evangelization

IN this season of anticipation and repentance, the Church's liturgies proclaim the advent of the gifts of light, warmth, home, love, and peace. John the Baptist and Mary, the Mother of God — the Mother of these gifts in the person of her Son, Jesus — show us the way to Christmas.

The questions for us in our parishes and homes are: How will we make straight the path for the Lord? How will we testify to the light? How will we say yes to God's coming in us? These are questions of evangelization. They lead us to reflect on the myriad of ways God calls us to prepare ourselves for Christmas, to support others in our parishes to do the same, and to reach out to our neighbors both near and far. Our task of evangelization in Advent is nothing less than communicating the beauty of this season that leads to the celebration of the birth of salvation in Jesus Christ.

Isaiah the prophet instructs us to do right, to give comfort to God's people, and to announce the coming of the Lord. The prophet's words are words of evangelization for both those old and new to the Christian faith. We look to the Second Readings, too, to guide us as we evangelize during this season. Our holiness and devotion, our prayer — indeed, our joy — brings us back to the Lord and shows others the path to him.

We watch. We remain alert. We live in hope, not fear. We put on patience. We slow our pace. We espouse humility as John the Baptist did. We assent to the Lord's will with Mary. Evangelization in this holy season rests on the orientation of our lives. Our Advent vocation presents itself once again as a re-focusing, a realignment of our lives on Jesus, the Savior and Redeemer of the world. We live out our orientation to the Savior in the ways we relate and interact with others in our homes, parishes, workplaces, and places of leisure.

You might choose to begin parish meetings that focus on Advent preparation with a brief discussion focused on how your parish or specific committee will embrace and model evangelization during this liturgical season.

The Parish and the Home

JUST hear the word "Advent" and many of us also hear in our memories the voices of children saying, "How long until Christmas?" This season is one of anticipation, preparation, waiting, longing for the coming of Christ at the end of time, and the celebration of the Incarnation in the season of Christmas.

In our homes and families, the way we mark Advent can help to balance what is often an especially hectic time of social gatherings, children's pageants, and shopping. Advent gives us reason to pause, reflect and hear the story of God's love afresh through the lens of our lives at home, in our workplace, cities, and world, as well as at our parish through the celebration of the Mass and sacraments.

Begin the season by talking as a family about how you will celebrate Advent this year. Consider special actions such as the following: participate in a gift or toy drive as a way of including those who are in need in your seasonal celebration, promise to pray together each day or evening, set aside one night each week for family time, mark a calendar with the special events that are scheduled for each person, note the Sundays of Advent in violet (rose on the Third Sunday), and make small slips of paper for family members to draw weekly with acts of kindness to perform as a way share the love of Christ with others.

One of the most common ways to celebrate Advent at home is with an Advent wreath, often a simple circle of greenery with four candles, three violet and one rose (or four violet or four white candles). Many parishes share a book with Advent prayers, or include a prayer for the blessing of the wreath in the Sunday bulletin. Including spontaneous prayer while lighting the candle(s) of the wreath each day encourages children to come to God in prayer, expressing what is in their hearts in unscripted fashion. Consider focusing your prayer on the week's corresponding virtue: Hope, Love, Joy, and Peace (you might use these as your banner symbols).

Several special solemnities and feasts hold particular appeal to children and include beloved traditions in many cultures: December 6, the Memorial of St. Nicholas, is often celebrated with small gifts being placed in the shoes of family members; December 8, the Solemnity of the Immaculate Conception, is a Holyday of Obligation and a wonderful opportunity to talk at home about Mary and her special role in the story of salvation; December 12 is the Feast of Our Lady of Guadalupe, often celebrated with prayer, music, and Mexican food.

While the focus of the time between Thanksgiving and Christmas is often on gift-giving and receiving, Advent urges us to focus on the love of God, which we anticipate in fullness at the end of time, and which we are called to bear to the world through our words and actions. Celebrating Advent well not only prepares us for Christmas Time. We will also give the greatest gift of all to our family — that of living and growing faith, shared within our family and beyond it.

Mass Texts

◆ TROPES FOR THE PENITENTIAL ACT, FORM C

December 3–December 16, 2017

You came to establish your eternal Kingdom of peace and justice: Lord, have mercy. R.

You stand at the gates of everlasting light and abolish the darkness of sin and death: Christ, have mercy. R.

You will come again at an unknown hour to judge both the living and the dead: Lord, have mercy. R.

December 17–24, 2018

In your coming among us, you reveal the eternal splendor of the Father: Lord, have mercy. R.

Born of the Virgin, you took our form to show us the way to salvation: Christ, have mercy. R.

You are Emmanuel, descended from David, King of the heavenly Jerusalem: Lord, have mercy. R.

◆ DISMISSAL FOR CHILDREN'S LITURGY OF THE WORD

December 3–December 16, 2017

My dear children, today, in God's Word, you will hear about Christ's promise to come back one day in "glory with salvation for your people." As we hear that same Word of God here, we will wait for you to come back so that together we may celebrate the Eucharist. Go in peace,

December 17–24, 2017

My dear children, today you will hear the Scriptures which speak about the things that happened when Jesus was born in Bethlehem. this happened because God loves us and we give him thanks. We will wait for you to come back to us here so that together we may give God thanks and praise in the Eucharist. Go in peace.

◆ DISMISSAL OF THE CATECHUMENS

December 3–16, 2017

My dear friends, this community now sends you forth to reflect more deeply upon the mystery of Jesus Christ who has been proclaimed to us in the Scriptures. He is the one who dwells among us and the one who will come in glory at the end of time. Know of our loving support of you and of our desire for you to gather with us around the altar of the lord so that together we may prepare for his final coming. Go in peace.

December 17–24, 2017

My dear friends, you who seek union with Christ's Church will now go forth to do what this season asks of each of us: wait and rejoice. As we await the celebration of Christ's birth and his coming in glory, we rejoice with you that he has called you to himself and chosen our community to nurture you in the faith.

December 2017
Month of the Divine Infancy

Optional Memorials in Advent

The Roman Missal commentaries below pertain to the seasonal weekdays or other obligatory observances. The following should be consulted for celebrating optional memorials during Advent:

On weekdays of Advent before December 17 . . . one of the following may be chosen: either the Mass of the weekday, or the Mass of the saint, or of one of the saints whose memorial is observed, or the Mass of any saint inscribed in the *Martyrology* for that day (GIRM, 355b).

On the weekdays of Advent from December 17 to December 24, . . . the Mass texts for the current liturgical day are used; but the Collect may be taken from a memorial which happens to be inscribed in the General Calendar for that day (GIRM, 355a).

3 (#2, LM)   violet
First Sunday of Advent

The Lectionary for Mass

◆ FIRST READING: Isaiah's prayer of lamentation is the cry of the people who believe that God has abandoned them in their distress. The tone of the lament appears to blame God who has allowed them to wander from the ways of God. But God's anger may be justified because the people have been sinful.

But the passage ends with a statement of hope: "O LORD, you are our father; / . . . / we are all the work of your hands."

◆ RESPONSORIAL PSALM 80: The theme of lamentation continues in the psalm. The psalmist cries out to God on behalf of the community. But the psalmist is confident that the Lord will respond and will once again look kindly on his people. The psalmist addresses God using images of shepherd and gardener, thus revealing a confidence that the Lord will surely tend to his flock, the vine he has planted.

◆ SECOND READING: At the beginning of his first letter to the Corinthians, Paul greets the people with a typical salutation of grace and peace. He gives thanks to God for the many gifts bestowed on them, reminding them that their good fortune is rooted in the grace of God. The end of the passage has an Advent tone; he reminds them that it is the Lord who will keep them faithful until "the end."

◆ GOSPEL: Mark's Gospel account sets the tone for our Advent spirituality: "Be watchful! Be alert!" A brief parable about the master and his servants underlines the urgency of Jesus' message. Just as the servants are to take care of the master's possessions until his return, so too are the Lord's disciples to take care of the gifts entrusted to them by God. Neither the servant nor the disciple knows when the master will return.

The Roman Missal

The Entrance Antiphon for the First Sunday of Advent, taken from Psalm 25:1–3, is a prayer for confidence. "To you, I lift up my soul, O my God . . . / let me not be put to shame . . . / let none who hope in you be put to shame." In the words of the old hymn, "'twas grace that taught my heart to fear, and grace my fears relieved."

The Collect for the first Mass of Advent echoes the Last Judgment parables of Matthew 25. The first part of the prayer recalls the wise virgins (see Matthew 25:1–13). We pray for the resolve to be among those who "run forth" with eagerness to meet Christ at his coming, carrying, not lamps, but "righteous deeds." The second part echoes the parable of the sheep and the goats (Matthew 25:31–46). We hope to be gathered with the sheep at his right hand, and "possess the heavenly Kingdom."

The Gloria is omitted, as it is for every Sunday of Advent. The Creed is said or sung.

The Prayer over the Offerings is also prayed on Mondays and Thursdays during the first three weeks of Advent. It expresses the divine exchange that takes place in the celebration of the Eucharist. We can only offer to God what God has already given to us; we pray that our devout celebration of the Eucharist "here below" will gain for us the eternal life of heaven.

The Creed is said or sung today. Preface I of Advent is the Preface prescribed for today (until December 16), and aptly so, as it lays out for us the two comings of Christ, namely, his first coming, when he assumed the lowliness of human flesh, and his Second Coming, the day that we watch for as we look forward to inheriting the "great promise," which is the foundation for our hopefulness. Our confidence in the future and our daring to hope are well founded, for they are grounded in Christ. Consider using Eucharistic Prayer III.

Other Ideas

There is no better time for people to experience the beauty of praying in their homes than Advent. Be sure to provide information on the history and use of the Advent wreath. This Sunday, the parish will bless the Advent wreath. It's an ideal moment to make prayers for blessing the home wreath available in print or online. Consider offering people the words of a simple Advent grace that they can use at meals, or the words to a familiar hymn like "O Come, O Come Emmanuel" to sing together as they light their family wreath. Be aware of respecting the copyright on all material that you share.

MON 4 (#175) violet
Advent Weekday

Optional Memorial of St. John Damascene, Priest, Doctor of the Church / white

The Lectionary for Mass

◆ FIRST READING: Isaiah announces a vision of peace for the people of God. They are invited to participate in this vision by approaching the mountain of the Lord, the place that symbolizes God's dwelling. There God will instruct them. In response they will turn their weapons into implements to till the earth as a peaceable people. The prophet's invitation is extended to us: "come, / let us walk in the light of the LORD."

◆ RESPONSORIAL PSALM 122: The first person pronoun indicates that this hymn is more a personal expression of joy and thanksgiving. It was a great honor to approach and enter the gates of the city, and then to enter the Temple. The psalmist rejoices in this blessing. The Temple of Jerusalem was also regarded as the dwelling place of God; it represented the heart of the relationship between God and the covenant faithful.

◆ GOSPEL: The healing of the centurion's servant is the second of three healing stories in this section of Matthew's account of the Gospel. In healing the Gentile's servant Jesus serves notice that he is not constrained by the social boundaries of his time; the compassion of the Father is available to all who believe. The remark of the centurion seems to be rather abrupt, but he recognizes that Jesus also has authority that allows him to do good. Jesus praises his act of faith.

The Roman Missal

The Entrance Antiphon for today's liturgy is based on Jeremiah 31:10 and Isaiah 35:4. The nations of the world hear the Word of God and watch for the Savior.

Today's Collect calls us to be alert and to be "watchful in prayer" as we "await the advent" of Christ.

The Prayer over the Offerings and the Prayer after Communion are the same as those used on the First Sunday of Advent.

The Communion Antiphon is based on Psalm 106 (105):4–5 and Isaiah 38:3. The Church waits for the Lord who will "visit us in peace."

Preface I of Advent is used until December 16. The Prayer after Communion (also prayed on Mondays and Thursdays during the first three weeks of Advent) contrasts earth with heaven.

Today's Saint

St. John of Damascus (or Damascene/c. 657–749) was a Syrian monk and priest, the "last of the Fathers of the Church." Islam had taken root in Syria, and John worked for the caliph for a time but left to enter the monastery of St. Sabbas near Jerusalem. He is best known for his defense of the veneration of images and his summary of the teachings of the Greek Fathers, *The Fountain of Wisdom*.

TUE 5 (#176) violet
Advent Weekday

The Lectionary for Mass

◆ FIRST READING: This reading from Isaiah is probably one of the most recognized of all Advent texts. Although the author envisions a new king for Israel that will do great things, the characteristics have been appropriated into the identity of the Messiah. Generations later, they are applied to Jesus. The stump of Jesse, the father of David, sets up the lineage of Jesus, who will bring about the vision of this oracle.

◆ RESPONSORIAL PSALM 72: The psalmist invokes the blessing of the Lord upon the king. The king was seen as God's appointment and hence he needed to govern in a manner similar to God's justice and providence. The psalmist prays that the king will do that. A particular characteristic of the king was his concern for those who could not care for themselves, the poor, the afflicted and the lowly. As with the First Reading, these attributes will be assigned to the future Messiah.

◆ GOSPEL: This reading occurs immediately after the seventy disciples have returned from their missionary activity to report to Jesus the wonderful things that have happened (see vv. 17–20). Jesus rejoices with them and offers a prayer of thanksgiving to the Father for this work of the Holy Spirit. Throughout his ministry Jesus affirms that it is the power of God that works through him; he is the vehicle of the Father's compassion.

The Roman Missal

The orations for today's liturgy remind the Church of God's great compassion and mercy. In the Collect, we ask God's "compassionate help" to meet the challenges of life, so that in all our trials we may be consoled by Christ's presence, and freed from "the corruption of former ways." Even as we are consoled by Christ's presence, we await his coming.

W E D 6 (#177) vioklet
Advent Weekday

Optional Memorial of St. Nicholas, Bishop / white

The Lectionary for Mass

◆ FIRST READING: This text is apocalyptic writing. It focuses on the future glory of God in which all God's people will share. "On that day" refers to end time. The celebration will be extravagant. A feast of "rich food and choice wines" will be provided; the shroud of oppression will be lifted. The pall of death will be no more. All this will take place on the mountain of the Lord, a symbol of the universal nature of God's reign.

◆ RESPONSORIAL PSALM 23 is surely the most beloved of the psalms; it is a hymn to the Lord as shepherd of his flock. The attributes of the shepherd portray a tender and loving image of the Lord. One of the shepherd's responsibilities is to make sure that the flock has sufficient food, although the pastures were sometimes rather sparse. But the Lord offers a plentiful table from verdant pastures; the blessings of the Lord go beyond human efforts.

◆ THE GOSPEL READING has two scenes that take place on a mountain. As noted in the First Reading, the mountain was a place of divine encounter, a place from which God's Word emanated and God's providence was found. Jesus sits down on the mountain, the posture for teaching. He heals those brought to him. But his "heart is moved with pity"; he wants to offer even more. There follows the account of the feeding of the multitude, an action that celebrates the remarkable compassion of God.

The Roman Missal

We know that only God's power can "prepare our hearts" for the coming of the Lord. In the Collect, we pray that we may be found worthy to come to the banquet of life, where we will receive "heavenly nourishment" from the Lord's own hands. In the Eucharist, we have the foretaste of that heavenly banquet.

Today's Saint

Little is known about this saint, the "wonder-worker," other than the fact that he lived sometime during the fourth century and was bishop of the city of Myra in Asia Minor. There is some evidence that he was imprisoned during the Diocletian persecutions and later condemned Arianism, a heresy that denied the Son was co-eternal with the Father. Many stories exist about St. Nicholas, but one most frequently passed down speaks of a poor man who could not feed or clothe his three daughters. Upon hearing of this man's dire situation, St. Nicholas tossed three bags of gold through his window one evening so the man could tend to his daughter's needs.

T H U 7 (#178) white
Memorial of St. Ambrose, Bishop, Doctor of the Church

The Lectionary for Mass

◆ FIRST READING: This reading is part lament and part an acknowledgment of the greatness of the Lord who protects his people from their enemies. The Lord is seen as having dominion in a city, a place of safety and peace. The people, who call themselves a nation, cry out to the Lord to "Open up the gates" so that they can enter. They seek refuge with the Lord, who will be their eternal Rock.

◆ RESPONSORIAL PSALM 118: The architectural image of the First Reading is present here. The Lord's enduring mercy provides a refuge for the people from their oppressors. The "gates of justice" could refer to the wisdom of the Lord or the faithfulness of the Lord that is available to those who acknowledge him as Savior. The last verse is a plea to the Lord for salvation and prosperity. It is a statement of faith in the Lord who "has given us light."

◆ GOSPEL: This reading comes at the end of a long teaching that started with the Beatitudes. Jesus states that simply knowing who he is is not enough to enter the Kingdom of Heaven. The mark of the disciple is hearing the Word of God and acting on it. He uses a comparison between the wise builder who constructed a house on rock, and the foolish one who built on sand. The first withstood the rigors of life; the latter did not. Both had a choice; the one who acts on the word is wise, indeed.

The Roman Missal

The prayers for today's memorial are found in the Proper of Saints for St. Ambrose. All the prayers are proper to the day. Consider using the Collect from the seasonal weekday to conclude the Universal Prayer.

Today's Saint

St. Ambrose (c. 340–397) was governor when he stopped the people's riot that erupted during the selection of a new bishop of Milan. The crowd cried, "Ambrose for bishop," and he was chosen, although he was just a catechumen. The Arian heresy—which denied the full divinity of Christ—divided the Church of his time. When Empress Justina demanded that Ambrose give his basilica to the Arians, he and his congregation locked themselves in and sang in what was the first recorded instance of antiphonal singing.

(#689) white

Solemnity of the Immaculate Conception of the Blessed Virgin Mary / Patronal Feastday of the United States of America

FRI 8

HOLYDAY OF OBLIGATION

About Today's Solemnity

Today is the Patronal Feastday of the United States of America and a Holyday of Obligation. Although our Gospel reading narrates the story of Jesus' conception, today's solemnity celebrates the Immaculate Conception of Mary, as she was conceived in her mother's womb. Prepared by God from the very first moment of her life to receive Jesus Christ, God's grace preserved Mary from sin from the womb to the end of her life, because of her role in the mystery of salvation as the Mother of God. Today's solemnity praises God for the hope and possibility that Mary embodies, as we turn to our Blessed Mother to learn from the first and most important relationship Jesus Christ experienced among us.

Mary's freedom from the sin of Adam and Eve is shown in today's Gospel. In Mary's response to the angel, she shows her willingness to place herself fully in God's hands, even when it promises to be difficult and requires great faith and trust.

The Lectionary for Mass

◆ FIRST READING: This familiar text from Genesis has been referred to under several titles: "The Fall, the sin of our First Parents" and "The Temptation in the Garden." It is a story of sin, understood as a refusal to follow a command from God. Its inclusion on this Marian highlights two aspects. In time it will be the offspring of the woman who will crush the presence of evil. And the designation of Eve as "the mother of all living" will be ascribed to Mary, the mother of all who live in Christ.

◆ CANTICLE: This is a hymn of praise for the marvelous deeds of the Lord. It will appear again for the Mass during the Day of Christmas. The exhortation of the psalmist to sing praises is rooted in the covenant. God has "remembered" his "kindness and faithfulness"; indeed, the goodness of God has extended to the very ends of the earth. Truly a new song is called for!

◆ SECOND READING: The opening lines of Ephesians are a form of a blessing for God. In this context a blessing directed toward God is also a form of thanksgiving for the blessings that God has bestowed on the faithful through Jesus Christ. The primary blessing is having been chosen by God "before the foundation of the world." Our adoption by God allows us to live lives that are "holy and without blemish."

◆ GOSPEL: Luke's account of the Annunciation bears some echoes to the First Reading. The woman Eve is chastised by God, but Mary is greeted with a pronouncement of grace and told she has "found favor with God." Her offspring will bring salvation to the people, not shame. The whole event gives witness to how God will bring about salvation. It is God who sends the messenger, it is God who names the child to be born, and it is God who will continue overcome all human boundaries, "for nothing will be impossible for God."

The Roman Missal

The texts for the Mass are found in the Proper of Saints.

That Mary was preserved from the stain of original sin from the moment of her conception is the theme echoed throughout the prayers for the Mass. Mary is always seen within the context of the Church, as the model disciple, and hence the second part of the Collect asks for her intercession that we too "may be cleansed and admitted to your presence."

Be careful of the phrase "prevenient grace" in the Prayer over the Offerings, it can be a bit of a tonguetwister! Priest celebrants will want to practice this prayer carefully.

The Preface is found right there along with the other texts for the day. As is common because it expresses the reasons we are giving thanks to God at this celebration, the Preface is a rich source for the meaning and theology of the solemnity we are celebrating, and it can be a splendid source for homiletic themes. Consider using Eucharistic Prayer II for Reconciliation.

It is a good idea to use the Solemn Blessing at the end of Mass suggested for today, which is the one titled "The Blessed Virgin Mary," number 15, the first choice under the "For Celebrations of the Saints" section.

In Advent, the Gloria is sung (preferred) or said only twice: the Immaculate Conception (today) and Our Lady of Guadalupe (December 12 in the dioceses of the United States of America). Choose a musical setting in the style of a fixed response by the assembly or a call and response of cantor and assembly. By having the liturgical musicians sing the intervening parts, this fosters singing the hymn and has the assembly learn its smaller part by doing it. A well-chosen setting may require little assembly rehearsal.

S A T 9 (#180) violet
Advent Weekday

Optional Memorial of St. Juan Diego Cuauhtlatoatzin / white

The Lectionary for Mass

◆ FIRST READING: The Lord speaks through Isaiah to those who are waiting for the day of the Lord which will be imminent or some time in the future. The people of Israel frequently turned to the Lord for relief from their current trials at the hands of their enemies. But they also looked forward to a time when they would enjoy the eternal glory of their God. In both cases they believed that the Lord would bless them in response to their cry. The examples in today's text of being nourished and having abundant crops are poetic metaphors for the graciousness of the Lord.

◆ RESPONSORIAL PSALM 147: The psalmist reminds his readers that waiting for the Lord is itself a blessing. To wait for someone is an act of faith; we believe that they will come to be with us. Our waiting for the Lord is a form of praise; we believe that God cares for us in our present situation. God is not far off.

◆ GOSPEL: The Gospel reading includes two important aspects of Jesus messianic ministry. The first is his compassion for the crowds. When he saw the crowds he saw more than a great number of people; he saw their innermost needs and brokenness. Matthew says "his heart was moved with pity," Jesus' compassion came from the heart, the source of true love. Only after he has ministered to the crowds does he commission the Twelve to go out to perform the same works of healing.

The Roman Missal

The orations focus on the Christ who will come and "free the human race from its ancient enslavement" (Collect). Use Advent Preface I.

Today's Saint

St. Juan Diego Cuauhtlatoatzin (1474–1548) was a native Mexican, a farmer, and a laborer. On December 9, 1531, on his way to attend Mass, he heard a woman call out from Tepeyac Hill. She was the Virgin Mary, and she asked Juan Diego to tell the bishop to build a chapel on the site. Juan Diego went to the bishop with the request, but the bishop scoffed at him. He returned with his cloak, or tilma, filled with roses, and when he unfurled it before the bishop, the woman's image was imprinted on the inside. The bishop believed, and the church was built. The image on Juan Diego's tilma is venerated as that of Our Lady of Guadalupe.

10 (#5) violet
Second Sunday of Advent

The Lectionary for Mass

◆ FIRST READING: The Word of God addressed to the people has a twofold message: God directs an unknown group of people to bring comfort to his people, and then directs the whole people to prepare "the way of the LORD!" The instruction to make a highway for God indicates that the Lord will come in glory. This *adventus* of the Lord is to be proclaimed to all peoples. The Lord will arrive in the image of a shepherd; he will feed his flock and gather the lambs "in his bosom."

◆ RESPONSORIAL PSALM 85: There is a sense from the words of the psalm, especially from the refrain, that the people are waiting for the Lord to reveal himself to them. They are confident that their Lord is "near indeed" and that the hoped for encounter will not be long. It will be a meeting of heaven and earth, of God and God's people, of truth and kindness, of justice, and peace. Even the land will prosper when the Lord returns.

◆ SECOND READING: The author of this reading makes an alarming prediction: the day of the Lord will come like a thief. In rhetorical fashion the author asks "what sort of persons ought you to be" in the meantime? He suggests that a life of holiness and devotion is needed as they await "a new heavens and a new earth." The theme of Advent is clearly underlined in this reading.

◆ TODAY'S GOSPEL and that for next Sunday present the preaching and mission of John the Baptist. It is clear that the expectation of the people is high as they stream out into the desert to hear John's message. John appears in the guise of the great prophets; is it possible that he really is announcing the advent of the Messiah? They do not want to miss it; they readily repent in anticipation. John's reference to the one who will come after him is further explained in next Sunday's Gospel.

The Roman Missal

A sense of urgency continues to be conveyed in the Collect as we pray that nothing may "hinder those / who set out in haste to meet your Son." However, any progress we make in our Advent journey of running to meet Christ is not due to our own merits, as noted in the Prayer over the Offerings. In fact, since we can do nothing on our own, we recognize our need for rescue through God's mercy.

The Gloria is not sung or said today. The Creed is said or sung today.

The Prayer after Communion asks that our participation in the Eucharistic offering will help us to be able to distinguish with wisdom the difference between the things of earth and the things of heaven—holding firm to the latter.

Preface I of Advent is assigned for today. Consider using Eucharistic Prayer I for Reconiliation and the Solemn Blessing for Advent at the end of Mass.

Other Ideas

Many dioceses undertake a second collection on the Second Sunday in December in support of the Retirement Fund for Religious. Sometimes this means a special speaker following the Prayer after Communion. Younger generations may not have the deep ties to the elderly sisters, brothers, and religious-order priests that impacted the lives of prior generations. Consider including a link to the funds website (www. retiredreligious.org) on your website and in the weekly bulletin. The fund is sponsored by the Conference of Major Superiors of Men, Council of Major Superiors of Women Religious, Leadership Conference of Women Religious, and United States Conference of Catholic Bishops. This is also the week that Filipino Catholics celebrate *Simbang Gabi* and Mexican and Central American Catholics celebrate *Las Posadas*.

M O N 11 (#181) violet
Advent Weekday

*Optional Memorial of
St. Damasus I, Pope / white*

The Lectionary for Mass

◆ First Reading: The prophets brought both good and bad news. The bad news was God's judgment; the good news God's salvation.

Today's oracle is very good news. The signs of God's salvation follow the unfolding of creation. First the world of nature will be regenerated. The signs are graphic and amazing. Then the people themselves will be restored to wholeness and prosperity. The signs of restoration become realities in Jesus' mission.

◆ Responsorial Psalm 85: The Israelites' relationship with God was an ongoing dialogue. They were partners in a covenantal friendship. The psalmist utters a prayer of hope that the Lord will respond to the needs of the people. They wait in hope for the peace and prosperity that they firmly believe God will bestow upon them. The divine-human conversation is imaged in the lines: "Truth shall spring out of the earth and justice shall look down from heaven." They will meet and embrace in peace.

◆ Gospel: Early in Jesus' ministry there are indications of the tension between Jesus and the religious leaders; it will eventually lead to his death. The healing of the paralyzed man is one such incident. When Jesus includes forgiveness of the man's sins, he oversteps the religious beliefs of the Temple authorities. After all, they say, only God can forgive sins. The people however were astonished and they praised God.

The Roman Missal

Are you prepared to hope? The Entrance Antiphon from Jeremiah 31 and Isaiah 35 reminds us God is near and we have no reason to be afraid. The Prayer over the Offerings and the Prayer after Communion are the same as those used for the First Sunday of Advent, but we read, hear, and pray them differently because of the context of today's readings. All the prayers allude to the mystery of God.

Today's Saint

As pope, St. Damasus I (†384) commissioned his secretary, St. Jerome,

to revise the Latin Bible in use at that time by translating the Old Testament from the Hebrew rather than the Greek version. The Vulgate remained the standard Latin translation until 1979. Damasus presided over the Council of Rome, at which the canon of scripture, or recognized books in the Bible, was set. He fought to counteract Apollinarianism, an over correction to Arianism that de-emphasized Christ's humanity. He is also known for the verses he composed to adorn the tombs of the martyrs in Rome.

T U E 12 (#690A or #707–712) white
Feast of Our Lady of Guadalupe

About Today's Feast

Today the Church throughout America (North, Central, and South) celebrates Our Lady of Guadalupe, Patroness of the Americas. Today is a feast in the United States of America, but in many Hispanic countries, such as Mexico, it is raised to a solemnity.

The story of the origins of the miraculous image of Our Lady of Guadalupe is well known. Juan Diego Cuauhtlatoatzin was a quiet, humble man, a poor peasant. When the Blessed Virgin Mary appeared to him and asked him to tell the local bishop to build a church in her honor, Juan Diego became a very reluctant messenger. The bishop would not believe him. So Mary filled Juan Diego's tilma, or cloak, with roses in December, and when he emptied out these beautiful flowers at the bishop's feet, there, imprinted on his tilma, was a wonderful image of the Virgin, dressed like a young Aztec woman.

The Lectionary for Mass

◆ First Reading, option 1: "Many nations shall join themselves to the Lord on that day" proclaims the prophet Zechariah. In presenting herself to St. Juan Diego, Our Lady of Guadalupe indeed reached many nations. Through the heart of a simple peasant, many were converted and came to know Our Lady and Jesus. This is a rich example of how the Lord chooses us to dwell among them.

◆ First Reading, option 2: This vibrant vision from Revelation is traditionally thought to reference the Blessed Virgin. Many of the images in this text are apparent in the story of the Mary's appearance to Juan Diego: the beautiful cape that "clothed [her] with the sun" and the "crown of twelve stars."

◆ Canticle: Our response today is not from a psalm, but from the Canticle of Judith. Judith was a great warrior and willing to do almost impossible tasks for the sake of her people. This hymn of praise was sung to her by King Uzziah, after she beheaded an enemy. While that may seem rather graphic, think of the many difficult moments in Mary's life, and it becomes fitting praise: "your deed of hope will never be forgotten / by those who tell of the might of God."

◆ Gospel: There are two options for today's Gospel. Luke 1:26–28 is the same Gospel that is proclaimed for the Immaculate Conception. Refer to that day on page 18 for information about this Gospel. The second option is from Luke 1: 39–47, detailing Mary's visit to Elizabeth. John the Baptist leaps for joy in Elizabeth's womb at the sound of Mary's greeting. This is almost like Juan Diego's reaction when Mary spoke to him. Would that we all leap for joy at encountering the Blessed Mother!

The Roman Missal

The orations for this Mass are found in the Proper of Saints. The Collect, Prayer over the Offerings, and Prayer after Communion are proper for today, so they replace the Advent texts.

The Gloria is sung or said today. The Creed is not said or sung.

You may use either Preface I or II of the Blessed Virgin Mary.

Given the references in Preface II to God's extension of "abundant mercy from age to age" and that God looks upon "the lowliness of [his] handmaid" this Preface might be a more appropriate selection for today's celebration. Consider using Eucharistic Prayer for Various Needs and Occasions I.

Each year parishes are uncovering the richness of celebrations of Our Lady of Guadalupe. Many music directors might find it to be a daunting task to prepare music for today's liturgy if they have little or no experience of the religious and cultural music connected to this feast.

W E D 13 (#183) red Memorial of St. Lucy, Virgin, Martyr

The Lectionary for Mass

◆ First Reading: The prophet places this passage in the mouth of the Lord. In the context of the covenant relationship God reminds the people to whom they are bound, and to whom they owe their loyalty. The prophetic oracle recalls the many feats that God has done for them and further that God never tires of acting on their behalf. God does not "grow weary."

◆ Responsorial Psalm 103: This psalm of blessing is also a hymn of thanksgiving. The psalmist addresses himself, calling on his soul to bless the Lord. The soul represents the whole being; body and spirit combine to give due praise to the Lord. The reason for blessing the Lord is threefold: he pardons, he heals, and he redeems. All these comprise the loving mercy of the Lord. Although the psalmist may be guilty of sin, the mercy of the Lord is even more abounding.

◆ Gospel: Jesus invitation to "come to me, all you who labor" is a gentle and reassuring gesture that brings us comfort and hope. The image of the yoke carries more than one meaning. Sometimes seen as a burden upon one's shoulders, it is also a form of harness that is used by two oxen. It helps to distribute the load that is being carried or pulled. Jesus says that his yoke, his teaching is not the yoke of the law. At the same time it suggests a partnership between us and the Lord in doing the work of the Father.

The Roman Missal

For today's obligatory memorial, the Collect is taken from the Proper of Saints for December 13. The Prayer over the Offerings and the Prayer after Communion are taken from either the Common of Martyrs: For a Virgin Martyr or from the Common of Virgins: For One Virgin. It would be a good idea to use the Collect of the seasonal weekday, Friday of the Second Week of Advent, as the concluding prayer to the Universal Prayer to maintain the connection to the liturgical time. Also, since there is no proper Preface assigned for today, Preface of Advent I may be used, and this would be another way of keeping a link with the season, although certainly the Preface of Holy Virgins and Religious or one of the Prefaces for Holy Martyrs are also appropriate choices. Consider using Eucharistic Prayer I.

Today's Saint

St. Lucy (c. † 304), even from a young age, had a burning desire to serve God and an infinite love for the poor. Living in Syracuse, a city in Sicily, she fell prey to the Diocletian persecutions, which eventually resulted in her martyrdom. She resisted a man, believed to be a Roman soldier, who tried to rape her. He, in turn, denounced her as a Christian and had her tortured and killed. Numerous legends revolve around her death, but one that has gained popularity is that she tore out her eyes in an act to resist her attacker. Her name in Latin, *Lucia*, comes from *lux, lucis*, meaning light; therefore, many northern countries honor her at this time of year when darkness is pervasive. Sweden celebrates the virginity and martyrdom of St. Lucy during a festival of light with a sacred procession of young girls clothed in white dresses with red sashes, and crowned with lit candles. She is the patron saint of those with eye troubles and those needing awareness.

THU 14 (#184) white
Memorial of St. John of the Cross, Priest, Doctor of the Church

The Lectionary for Mass

◆ FIRST READING: The Lord speaks through the prophet with a declaration of identity, beginning with "I am the LORD your God." There follows a litany of actions that the Lord will perform on behalf the people. These actions constitute a promise that God will act in the best interests of the people. In those situations that they could not alleviate on their own, God will act. In fact God will regenerate the whole of creation for their livelihood.

◆ RESPONSORIAL PSALM 145: The psalmist begins by addressing the people, calling on them to praise who God is and what God has done for them. Then he addresses the Lord directly. This address to God is a form of praise and thanksgiving for the works of the Lord. The singular attribute of the Lord is that no other king or reign is as great. The dominion of God is universal and eternal.

◆ GOSPEL: This passage follows Jesus' question to his disciples, "What did you go out in the wilderness to see?" He continues by extolling the role of John the Baptist as his precursor. Jesus is aware of the violence that greeted John. He

was imprisoned and yet his preaching of the Kingdom must continue for those who have ears to hear must hear. As John the Baptist encountered rejection so will Jesus, but that is part of his role as Messiah.

The Roman Missal

All three of the orations are from the Proper of Saints. They echo the mystical theology associated with St. John of the Cross. The Collect references his "outstanding dedication to perfect self-denial / and love of the Cross," asking that we might imitate those spiritual virtues. The Prayer over the Offerings requests that "we, who celebrate / the mysteries of the Lord's Passion, / may imitate what we now enact." The Prayer after Communion hails St. John as one through whom God has "wonderfully made known the mystery of the Cross" and prays that we may cling faithfully to Christ as we draw strength from participating in the offering of this Sacrifice. Consider using Eucharistic Prayer II.

Today's Saint

St. John of the Cross (1542–1591) grew up near Avila in poverty. His father died when he was young, and his widowed mother struggled to support the family. Shortly after his ordination in 1567, he met Teresa of Avila and was drawn into her reform of the Carmelites. The reform set Carmelite brother against brother, and John was even imprisoned but used the time to write the Spiritual Canticle. For this, and for his other great work, *Dark Night of the Soul*, he is considered one of the greatest poets to write in Spanish.

FRI 15 (#185) violet
Advent Weekday

The Lectionary for Mass

◆ FIRST READING: The foundation of the covenant was a pledge of faithfulness. This included God's

promise to protect and sustain them, and Israel's promise to remain faithful to God's commandments. Here the Lord reminds the people of their obligation. In response God will bestow blessings upon them. They will enjoy prosperity; their descendants will be many and their names will never be forgotten.

◆ RESPONSORIAL PSALM 1: This is one of the wisdom psalms. Its wisdom derives from observing the choices of human behavior. Those who are wise make good choices; they delight in the law of the Lord. Their counterparts take counsel from the wicked, they are among the sinners. The former are likened to trees that draw life from flowing water; they are fruitful. The latter have no roots; they are dried up like chaff and blown away in the wind with no purpose or usefulness.

◆ GOSPEL: The reading continues Jesus' description of John's mission and his own. "This generation" refers to those who would not and did not accept the testimony of John and who continued to reject his teachings. Jesus compares himself and John to those who play the flute for the children to dance. But "this generation" did not listen, they did not dance, they did not join in. Instead they condemned John for his ascetic life style, and Jesus the messianic bridegroom, for not fasting.

The Roman Missal

In the Advent propers, God has shown his salvation to the very ends of the earth! In the Collect, we pray that we may "be ever watchful" to the "coming of [God's] Only Begotten Son." See the Second Sunday of Advent for the Prayer over the Offerings and the Prayer after Communion.

^{S A T} **16** (#186) violet
Advent Weekday

The Lectionary for Mass

◆ FIRST READING: Elijah was regarded as fierce defender of the Lord. His holy zeal was renowned and he supposedly wrought more signs than the prophet Elisha. The author of Sirach, one of the wisdom books, portrays the passion of Elijah as coming from the Lord. He would reestablish the tribes of Jacob that had been decimated by wars and deportations. Generations later Jesus compares John the Baptist to Elijah, both of them displaying a great fire in their mission.

◆ RESPONSORIAL PSALM 80: The tone of the psalm is a lament. The people cry out to the Lord to reach out to them. They ask the Lord to help them "turn" to him; a reference to their need to repent of their ways. The Lord is addressed as shepherd, gardener, ruler and military leader (Lord of hosts). Each title has its own attributes, each one depicting how the Lord provided for the people.

◆ GOSPEL: The prophet Elijah, John the Baptist and Jesus are mentioned in relationship to each other. In response to the question of the disciples about the role of Elijah, Jesus tells them that the time of the prophet is past. They are now in the presence of a new reality. Even the role of John the Baptist is past. Jesus is the one who was foretold and he is in their midst. Nonetheless, he too will suffer and be rejected, as prophets before him, but the reader knows that that suffering will lead to glory.

The Roman Missal

Both the Entrance Antiphon and Responsorial use Psalm 80, and we see just how bold everything about this liturgy is today. To ask to see the face of God is a brave act of faith. Our readings speak of Elijah and flames, but that is exactly what our Collect promises as it speaks of the "splendor of your glory dawn in our hearts." We continue to pray with Advent Preface I.

The Prayer over the Offerings and the Prayer after Communion are repeated from Wednesday. There is a simplicity and straightforwardness in these messages that speak of the coming Christ. Practice different vocal inflections to explore their full meaning. Then you too may experience the fire of those chariots burning within your heart. How will you express your faith today?

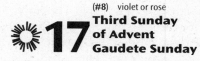

(#8) violet or rose
17 **Third Sunday of Advent Gaudete Sunday**

About Gaudete Sunday

The Third Sunday of Advent (like the Fourth Sunday of Lent) is a day of joy in the midst of our spiritual preparations for Christmas. It is traditionally called Gaudete Sunday, from the Latin of the Entrance Antiphon for today: *Gaudete in Domino semper,* "Rejoice in the Lord always; again I say, rejoice! The Lord is near" (Philippians 4:4 – 5). The antiphon captures the mood of the entire liturgy as we move into the second part of Advent: there is a sense of joyful expectation, an awareness that the fulfillment of God's great plan for us is near. That sense is strong in today's readings.

The Lectionary for Mass

◆ FIRST READING: It is not clear who the anointed one is that speaks this oracle. It may be a generic blessing of every prophet or of Isaiah himself. It is this passage that Jesus uses to initiate his public ministry after he reads it from the scroll in his hometown synagogue (Luke 4:16– 20). The mission of the anointed one is extended to those who are in special need of salvation, but the "year of favor" is clearly for everyone.

◆ CANTICLE: The text for the psalm is taken from Luke's account of the Gospel, the words we know as the Magnificat. It is a hymn of praise uttered by Mary during her visit with Elizabeth. The theme echoes that of the First Reading. The Lord is praised for "great things" that have been done for those who are lowly. But the Lord will bestow blessings on the whole people, just as he promised. The fulfillment of that promise will be realized in the coming of the Messiah.

◆ SECOND READING: Paul's exhortation to the Thessalonians is in light of the future coming of the Lord. This is apocalyptic writing; the coming of the Lord in glory is the reason for living in a particular way in the meantime. His instruction is terse: rejoice, pray, give thanks. In these ways they will make good use of their gifts and be ready and blameless when the Lord comes.

◆ GOSPEL: This passage from John is a more descriptive account of John's identity as the precursor of Jesus the Messiah. Although the focus of the question, "Who are you?" is on John, he makes it clear that he is not the one the Jewish people have been waiting for. John regards himself as a messenger, a herald of great news; his mission is to prepare the people for the coming of the Light that would transform their lives.

The Roman Missal

The Collect is a prayer for joy: we ask that we may reach the "joys of so great a salvation" and celebrate that salvation with "glad rejoicing" at Christmas Time. Even if the antiphon is not chanted, call attention to it or invite the congregation to recite it.

The Gloria is once again omitted. The Creed is said or sung.

Today's Prayer over the Offerings frequently reoccurs during Advent. In this prayer, we ask that the unceasing celebration of "the sacrifice of our worship," the celebration of the Eucharist, may accomplish God's saving work among us.

Even though the rubrics seem to indicate that the priest celebrant has a choice between Prefaces I and II of Advent, only Preface I can be used today. Preface II is not used until December 17. We are often impatient people. We are constantly given instant options: from the drive-through to the microwave. Yet the Prayer after Communion speaks of "divine sustenance." Word and Sacrament feeds us in a way no earthly fast food can. Wait for it. Consider using Eucharistic Prayer III.

Other Ideas

On Gaudete Sunday, we may light the rose candle of the Advent wreath. The name derives from the Introit (Entrance Antiphon) of Mass: Rejoice! At one point in the history of the season this Sunday was the midpoint of five weeks of fasting. On this day, as on Laetere Sunday in Lent, rose-colored vestments were allowed and flowers returned to the sanctuary. Consider singing the simple setting of the Entrance Antiphon as a round before Mass. A setting is available from Oregon Catholic Press (a recording of the setting is found here: www.ocp .org/compositions/8265). Set up a large billboard of blank construction paper on a portable partition at the entrance to the church. Ask

members to write, graffiti style, completion to the heading, "What gives me joy is . . ." Invite members to bring the infant Jesus from their home crèche to Mass for a blessing, like that done in St. Peter's square in Rome.

MON 18 (#194) violet
Advent Weekday

The Lectionary for Mass

◆ FIRST READING: In the verses preceding today's reading the leaders of the people are harshly criticized for not taking care of God's people. Today's text is the other part of that judgment; it is the promise of salvation by a future leader. This leader will spring from the household of David, a reference that in time is applied to Jesus. The reign of this future king will be one of wise judgment and security.

◆ RESPONSORIAL PSALM: In this royal psalm the psalmist prays for the reign of the king. He addresses God seeking a blessing on the leader of the covenant people. The prayer is for the king to not only share in the righteousness of God but to act as God would act. The critical test for the king is his compassion for the poor and the afflicted. His care of them must mimic the care of the Lord.

◆ GOSPEL: This is Matthew's account of "how the birth of Jesus Christ came about." Unlike Luke's account, which is a sort of first hand report of the angel's visit to Mary, Matthew's account is an explanation of what has already happened. Although he notes the marriage customs of the day, the passage is really about God's intervention in human history. The reference to Holy Spirit, both in Mary's pregnancy and in Joseph's dream indicates that it is God who directs the events that fulfill the prophetic tradition.

The Roman Missal

The orations used are those specifically assigned for December 18. Preface II of Advent is used again.

TUE 19 (#195) violet
Advent Weekday

The Lectionary for Mass

◆ FIRST READING: The mysterious pregnancy of Manoah's wife is one of several such incidents in the scriptures. Others include Abraham and Sara, Elizabeth and Zechariah, Mary and Joseph. The bearing of children was seen as a blessing from God since it was important that families have descendants to continue their name into future generations. The arrival of the "angel of the Lord," also called "a man of God" indicates that the Lord is intimately involved in the hope of the people and more than ready to care for them.

◆ RESPONSORIAL PSALM 71: The prayer of the psalmist is a typical prayer of lament. On one hand the psalmist cries out for assistance from the Lord in his present distress, and on the other he praises the Lord for past blessings. The image of the rock denotes the safety and trustworthiness. The Lord is the source of both.

◆ GOSPEL: There are similarities between the Gospel and the First Reading. In both readings, God's messenger, here named as Gabriel, announces an impending pregnancy for a woman who is elderly and barren. The wife of Manoah was not to drink wine or strong drink, but it is Elizabeth's child who will abstain form wine and strong drink. The angel appears to Manoah's wife and to Elizabeth's husband, Zechariah. In both scenarios the future of Israel is involved and the mission of the sons will be to further God's plan of salvation.

The Roman Missal

The prayers are those for December 19. The child born of Mary revealed God's glory to the world. In the Collect, we pray for right faith and due reverence as we prepare to celebrate the mystery of the Incarnation. In the Prayer over the Offerings, it is evident that we can offer so little, but we know that God's power is greater than our weakness. In the Eucharist, we receive a great gift from God, but the Eucharist is only a foretaste of the heavenly banquet. We ask God to "arouse in us . . . / the desire for those [gifts] yet to come" (Prayer after Communion).

W E D 20 (#196) violet
Advent Weekday

The Lectionary for Mass

◆ FIRST READING: The refusal of King Ahaz to ask for a sign from God is seen as a lack of trust and faith. The king's pretense at piety does not please Isaiah who announces that the Lord will nonetheless provide a sign. God will be faithful even if the king will not. The sign of the virgin birth is reinterpreted generations later in light of Jesus' birth. Both are seen as God's faithfulness to a promise of salvation.

◆ RESPONSORIAL PSALM 24: God is portrayed as creator in this hymn of praise. He is Savior and a divine dispenser of blessings on the pilgrims to the Temple. The mountaintop was regarded as a place of theophany, the seat of the Lord in glory. The tradition placed the Temple of Jerusalem on the highest mountain. It was there that the Lord received those who were worthy, both on the outside with "hands [that] are sinless" and on the inside with clean hearts.

◆ GOSPEL: Luke's familiar account of the Annunciation is rich with details and meaning. Joseph's lineage "of the house of David," the

presence of a heavenly messenger, Mary's virginity, the reference to Elizabeth's pregnancy, all point to the divine intervention that will change human affairs. The angelic announcement is countered by Mary's objection, but she is assured that the work of the Holy Spirit will prevail and the salvation of God will be fulfilled.

The Roman Missal

The prayers are those for December 20. The Collect extols Mary, who was filled with the Holy Spirit, and became "the dwelling-place of divinity" when the Word took flesh in her womb. We pray for the grace to imitate her by following her example of humble obedience to God's will. The Prayer over the Offerings reveals that Advent is about waiting in hope. Participating in the Eucharist, we have a pledge that one day we will possess fully the gifts for which faith teaches us to hope. In the Prayer after Communion, we ask for a share in the fruits of the Eucharist: "the joy of true peace."

T H U 21 (#197) violet
Advent Weekday

Optional Memorial of St. Peter Canisius, Priest, Doctor of the Church / violet

The Lectionary for Mass

◆ FIRST READING, OPTION 1: The Song of Songs refers to Christ as a lover, a gazelle, and a stag. In Christ, our winters are over, and we await him as a bride waits for her spouse.

◆ FIRST READING, OPTON 2: This hymn of the prophet is an exhortation for the people to praise the Lord. The reason for this joyful expression is twofold: the Lord has removed judgment against them and has turned away their enemies. It is not stated what the judgment had been for, but it is clear that the Lord has relented and this is cause for

great joy. Indeed, the Lord rejoices in the people and has come to dwell in their midst.

◆ RESPONSORIAL PSALM 32: This hymn of thanksgiving and praise has the nature of a liturgical prayer. The instruments of harp and lyre and the human instrument of voice are all called upon to sing a new song to the Lord. The reason for this exaltation is the steadfastness of the Lord and his choice of the people as his own inheritance. The imagery is covenantal; the work of the Lord is worthy of praise.

◆ GOSPEL: The account of Mary's visit to Elizabeth is a fitting prelude to the narrative of the nativity of Jesus. The exchange of greetings and obvious joy of these two pregnant women is touching. Elizabeth's greeting and the reaction of the child in her womb are indications that this is no ordinary event. Elizabeth's blessing on Mary and on the child is occasioned by Mary's faith. The joy expressed by Elizabeth is indicative of the great joy that the whole world will celebrate in a few days' time.

The Roman Missal

The Mass formularies are taken from those specific to December 21. The Advent Collect makes reference to the two comings of Christ: it acknowledges our rejoicing "at the coming of your Only Begotten Son in our flesh" and it asks that "when at last he comes in glory," we may "gain the reward of eternal life." The Prayer over the Offerings speaks of the transformation of the offerings that is to occur; as they are transformed "into the mystery of our salvation," the implication is that we who receive those gifts will also be transformed, for example, saved. The Prayer after Communion prays that our "participation in this divine mystery" will result in protection and abundant health in mind and body.

Today's Saint

St. Peter Canisius (1521–1597) was the first Dutchman to join the Jesuits. He is known as the second apostle of Germany for his work restoring Catholicism after the Reformation, writing a "German catechism," which defined basic Catholic beliefs in German. Peter felt that it was more effective to clarify the teachings of Catholicism rather than engage in polemics with the reformers. His last twenty years were spent in Switzerland, where he founded the Jesuit College that is the core of the University of Fribourg. He is credited with adding "Holy Mary, Mother of God, pray for us sinners" to the Hail Mary. This appeared for the first time in his Catechism of 1555.

FRI 22 (#198) violet
Advent Weekday

The Lectionary for Mass

◆ FIRST READING: A prior passage says of Hannah that God had "closed her womb" (see 1:6) in other words she was barren. She prayed for a child and in time she delivered a son, Samuel. Here she arrives at the Temple of Shiloh to give thanks to the Lord and to dedicate her son to the work of the Lord. Her husband Elkanah makes the requisite sacrificial offerings. Generations later a similar scene will unfold in the Temple of Jerusalem when Mary and Joseph present their child to the Lord.

◆ CANTICLE: This is Hannah's hymn of praise after she presented her son Samuel to the Lord in the Temple. The poetic words and structure of the hymn remind us of the hymn of Mary when visiting Elizabeth. This latter hymn is known as the "Magnificat." Hannah's heart "exults in the Lord" for the great things the Lord has done. The list of these actions speaks of a reversal of the fortunes of the people of Israel; God has truly brought blessings upon them.

◆ GOSPEL: Mary's hymn of praise is today's Gospel text. In the tradition of Hannah, Miriam, and Judith, Mary's exaltation of the Lord is filled with statements describing the marvelous works of God in the history of Israel. As God's plan of salvation has unfolded in the past it will now extend into future generations "from this day." Like the other women, Mary accepts her humble role in God's plan.

The Roman Missal

The Mass texts are those for December 22. We hear the prayers of thanksgiving proclaimed by Hannah and Mary in their songs of praise, and both our Lectionary readings and the Missal texts speak of God's compassion and rejoicing. There is much to unpack in the Prayer over the Offerings: "through the purifying action of your grace, / we may be cleansed by the very mysteries we serve." We are brought low in humble adoration, sometimes through suffering and pain—all so that God may raise us again, in a purer, sacred form. This is the sense of wonder and awe that we must bring with us to the liturgy, and that we pray about after we receive Communion. This is no small thing that the Lord is doing for us as we as we celebrate Eucharist and as we prepare for Christ's coming.

SAT 23 (#199) violet
Advent Weekday

Optional Memorial of St. John of Kanty, Priest / white

The Lectionary for Mass

◆ FIRST READING: Malachi means "messenger," and in this passage the Lord speaks through the prophet as messenger. The messenger's role is to make suitable preparations for the coming of the Lord. He is to "prepare the way" and to announce the coming, the "adventus" of the Lord. Generations later this task will fall to John the Baptist, the precursor of the Lord.

◆ RESPONSORIAL PSALM 25: The psalmist is anxious to know the ways of the Lord. The word "way" is repeated three times; the word "paths" is used twice. The psalmist could be asking about the ways of the Lord, or for the Lord to show him his own way. Both words appear to be a metaphor for how to live. If we know the ways of the Lord then we should live accordingly. But only the Lord can show us the right way.

◆ GOSPEL: We read of the birth of John the Baptist and the required Jewish initiation rites for a new born male child. The circumstances surrounding Elizabeth's pregnancy and the mysterious situation of Zechariah's inability to speak underline the extraordinary interest in this child. Even as Zechariah blesses God for his son the neighbors are filled with fear. Their fear could be understood as awe at this unusual event. John's mission as a messenger of God was already underway when he is only eight days old!

The Roman Missal

The Mass texts are those for December 23. The Collect acknowledges both the nearness of the celebration of the Nativity and the continued closeness of Christ who came in the flesh, asking that we may receive mercy "from your Word, / who chose to become flesh of the Virgin Mary / and establish among us his dwelling." In another acknowledgment of the closeness of the Nativity, the Prayer over the Offerings asks that the oblation offered bring about our reconciliation with God so that "we may celebrate with minds made pure / the Nativity of our Redeemer." Eschatology is emphasized and images from the parables of Jesus are used in the Prayer after Communion, as petition is made that "those you have nourished with these heavenly gifts" may be ready, "with lighted lamps, / to meet your dearly beloved Son at his coming."

Today's Saint

Also known as John Cantius († 1473), St. John of Kanty was a brilliant and multitalented Polish theologian and professor of Sacred Scripture at Kraków. In addition to his theological work, he was also a physicist and anticipated the work of Galileo and Newton. He was known for his spirit of poverty and humility and gave most of his professor's salary to the poor, keeping just enough to live simply. Miracles were attributed to him in his lifetime, and he became a very popular saint in Poland. Many churches founded in North America for Polish immigrants are named in his honor.

☀ 24 (#11) violet
Fourth Sunday of Advent

The Lectionary for Mass

◆ FIRST READING: This passage from 2 Samuel is a delightful conversation between David and the Lord. David has decided to build a fine house for the Lord, a place that would contain the presence of the Lord. The Lord will have nothing to do with this plan and tells David that he will continue to dwell in the midst of the people, wherever they are.

◆ RESPONSORIAL PSALM 89: The psalmist sings a hymn of praise to God for faithfulness to the promise given to David. The promise is in the form of a covenant, a bond between God and the people of God. This bond is based on fidelity and is intended to endure "through all generations." The ensuing relationship is not like a civil or political agreement; it has the nature of a relationship as familiar and intimate as that between a father and a son.

◆ SECOND READING: This passage concludes Paul's letter to the Romans. It is in the form of a doxology, a statement of praise for the revelation of God through the ages. Although the content of this revelation was not known in all ages, being "kept secret" from some, it is now fully revealed through Jesus Christ. This is the heart of the Christian Gospel and the reason for our celebration during this Advent-Christmas season.

◆ GOSPEL: Luke's account of the Annunciation brings us to the threshold of the celebration of the Nativity of the Word made flesh. Luke is careful to note that the event is part of the great plan of God; the house of David is represented by Joseph. The promise made to David is to be realized in a simple setting in Galilee, but its import will be to bring forth a kingdom that will have no end. Mary's response, first of fear and then of complete acceptance, helps us to identify with her as a model of a servant of the Lord.

The Roman Missal

Use the prayers for the Fourth Sunday of Advent rather than those for December 24.

The entrance antiphon is the *Rorate Coeli* or "Drop down dew from above, you heavens" (Isaiah 45:8). There are exquisite chant settings of this introit in English or Latin, as well as other beautiful choral arrangements. Just as the readings are shifting and leading us closer to the birth of Christ, so are our prayers. The theology presented in the Collect is a wonderful opportunity for liturgical preaching. It speaks of the angel proclaiming the Incarnation, but also connects the cradle to the Passion and the Cross. Similarly, the Prayer after Communion reminds us of "eternal redemption" and "salvation."

The Gloria is omitted. The Creed is sung or said. On this Sunday, Preface II of Advent is used. Consider using Eucharistic Prayer III.

Other Ideas

This year, the Fourth Sunday of Advent falls on Christmas Eve. As people enter in to the hubbub of gatherings with family and friends, consider educating them about the traditional Twelve Days of Christmas. While most people are familiar with the song, they may not realize that it originated as a catechetical tool to help people learn the important aspects of the Christian faith. Some families spread their present opening across the twelve days. Encourage people to give gifts of the heart (kindness or service) each of the twelve days between Christmas and Epiphany. In your parish bulletin or on your parish's website and social media page, provide a list of the special associations of each day (St. Stephen and Boxing Day, St. John the Apostle and "Wassail!" and so on) to help people mark this time.

CHRISTMAS TIME

The Meaning

THE ancient monastic *Rule of St. Benedict* includes many memorable lines, but perhaps no instruction points more powerfully to the meaning of the Christian life than, "Let all guests who arrive be received as Christ" (c. 53). On Christmas Day, we receive the Christ-child anew, God's gift of love and transformation taking flesh and dwelling in our midst. On that day, we often welcome dozens of people who are not normally in our sanctuaries each Sunday. What a wonderful moment to welcome the guest as Christ.

For many people, coming to a Christmas service or Mass is important, even if the rest of the year they are away from the Church. Our intent should be to create a wonderful experience for our parish community, but also for the many visitors who will come with friends, family, or by themselves to our sanctuaries.

Consider helping members of the Church extend active invitations to those with whom they'd like to pray. Facebook postings, particularly memes with pictures and text, can be shared from your parish page onto the pages of individuals. These images can also be e-mailed (a variety of memes about the Mass are found in LTP's resource *From Mass to Mission: Understanding the Mass and Its Significance for Our Christian Life, Leader's Guide*).

Consider extending invitations via e-mail to the entire parish membership list, letting people know Mass times or information about special activities. The data on Mass attendance in the United States makes it clear that only a small percentage of those on our parish rolls are in our pews each week. It's important to keep the information flowing to those who may be only loosely connected.

Make sure your parish website, social media page, and voicemail messages are current with Mass times and other information. If parking is an issue, consider having a site nearby where active members can park and be shuttled to the church, leaving more parking for newcomers and guests. During Christmas Time, encourage members to have open houses in their homes to which they can invite neighbors and other parishioners. Offer spiritual "conversation starters" or brochures about your community that they can give to those who attend. Or do a simple business card with relevant information that can be available at the back of the church and for individual use.

First and foremost, our liturgical services should emanate the joy, hope, and love of this beautiful season. People do not need to be reminded, directly or indirectly, that they are visitors. Even good humored ribbing about the pews being fuller than normal can be off-putting and make people feel that rather than cherished guests, they are interlopers. It's a good idea, in advance of Christmas Day, to remind people that their "spot" in the pews may need to be graciously shared.

Although you may have many beautiful hymns in your repertoire, encourage the music or choir director to include multiple familiar, traditional Christmas carols in the service. This can help people with the active participation we work for in all our Eucharistic liturgies. Be sure to have the wording of the current Missal responses easily accessible in the pews. While most active Catholics are more than aware that they should say, "And with your spirit," many people who have not regularly experienced the prayer over recent years will still need support to pray well, despite the fact that we have had the third edition of *The Roman Missal* for six years.

Be sure to think of ways that your parish can be engaged with the greater community in this season. The encounter is two way, not just about people coming into our church facilities. You might connect with your local food bank, provide workers for an organization feeding the hungry, or do outreach to senior centers and nursing homes. Consider a parish Christmas cookie baking party, and deliver the goodies to those who are homebound or alone.

The greatest welcome and evangelization we can offer, though, may simply be a loving smile and a warm greeting when we encounter new people. Scooting over and enthusiastically making room for someone can be as strong a message as anything we say.

Helping people realize that Christmas does not end on December 25 is important. Consider providing means by which members can honor Holy Family, Epiphany, and the Baptism of the Lord in their homes by providing special prayers or rituals, such as the blessing of the doors.

Christmas Time can be a remarkable moment to reawaken and reanimate our discipleship, and to discover new ways to welcome the guest as Christ.

The Lectionary for Mass

THE Gospel accounts proclaim the revelation of God in Jesus, Messiah, and Savior. The narratives of his birth, his baptism, and the visit of the Magi all celebrate the manifestation of divine intervention in the world. The response of the shepherds, the strange visitors from the East, and of the crowd at his baptism shapes our own response to this Good News: we are filled with joy!

The Lectionary texts speak of promise and fulfillment: the fulfillment of God's promises of old as they were recounted in the Old Testament. We see this especially in the Gospel according to Matthew. Matthew, writing for a community of Jews who had come to faith in Jesus of Nazareth, is quick to demonstrate how Jesus is indeed the fulfillment of God's promises by citing biblical texts to support this claim. We also hear in our readings, particularly those from the First Letter of Saint John, not only what is promised to us in light of the Christ event, but also what is commanded to us; we might even say *demanded* of us. It is the call to become ever more like Christ, to be increasingly receptive to God's grace so that we might be transformed through his power to become more and more like him. We are meant to become *like* him.

The Roman Missal

THE season begins with the Vigil of the Nativity of the Lord (or with Evening Prayer I if it is celebrated before the Vigil Mass) and ends with the Feast of the Baptism of the Lord. Besides Easter, "the Church has no more ancient custom than celebrating the memorial of the Nativity of the Lord and of his first manifestations" (UNLY, 32).

In this celebratory season the moderation of Advent falls away. Sing the Gloria, break out the instruments, make ample use of the organ or piano, adorn the liturgical space with joyous decorations, and (ministers) wear white or other festive vestments (gold and silver). There are three Prefaces for the Eucharistic Prayer in Christmas Time that can be used interchangeably. The Solemnity of Mary, the Holy Mother of God, has its own Preface and Solemn Blessing. The Baptism of the Lord has its own proper Preface. Just as in Advent we do not use Eucharistic Prayer IV because all Prefaces in the season are proper and Eucharistic Prayer IV has a fixed Preface. Other resources found in the Missal include a sample formulary for the Universal Prayer (appendix V), a Solemn Blessing for Christmas, which can be used where indicated by the rubrics of the Missal, and the Solemn Blessing for Epiphany. *The Nativity of Our Lord Jesus Christ* (from the *Roman Martyrology*) may be chanted or recited before the Christmas Mass during the Night, and the Announcement of Easter and the Moveable Feasts (in appendix I of the Missal) may be sung, after the proclamation of the Gospel, by a deacon or cantor from the ambo on Epiphany.

Children's Liturgy of the Word

CHILDREN love Christmas! As leaders of the celebration of the Word with children, you have the opportunity to help children experience Christmas as a season and not just the day or few hours of commercialism that secular society identifies it as. The Lectionary provides proper readings for the four Masses for the Nativity of the Lord (Christmas), so you will want to check with your director of liturgy or pastor to make sure you proclaim the same readings the main assembly will hear.

Strive to have the environment for the celebration of the Word with children mirror that of the main assembly. The liturgical color for the Sundays of Christmas Time, including the Feast of the Holy Family of Jesus, Mary, and Joseph; Solemnity of the Epiphany of the Lord; and the Feast of the Baptism of the Lord is white. Augment the environment in similar ways: perhaps a small Christmas tree and a few poinsettias. You might choose to have a few children and their parents help you set up the environment each time one liturgical season ends and another begins. Empowering their participation will help form them in the liturgical expression of their faith.

Discuss with your director of music the arrangements of the Responsorial Psalms for Christmas Time. Ask if the assembly will sing a seasonal psalm. Some children are auditory processors and will be able to pick up on the words when the cantor sings the refrain the first time. Other children are visual processors, so it might be helpful to have the words of the refrain either projected or simply printed in large letters on newsprint and posted where most children will easily see them. You will also want to find out whether or not the Gospel Acclamation ("Alleluia") will be repeated after the proclamation of the Gospel. Many parishes do this as a way of ritually focusing on the Gospel during the high liturgical seasons. Many parishes celebrate Baptisms on the Feast of the Baptism of the Lord. Find out whether your parish will have any Baptisms on that Sunday and what other Sundays they will. Consider the practice of bringing the children back to the main assembly to witness the Baptism, and perhaps gather around the font. If you choose to do so, the children would participate in the Prayer of the Faithful and the Renewal of Baptismal Promises with the main assembly rather than saying their own Creed and intercessions.

Finally, take a moment after the Mass concludes each Sunday during the Christmas season to wish children who participated in the celebration of the Word a "Merry Christmas." This is another small way to communicate the seasonal nature of Christmas to children.

The Saints

CHRISTMAS Time is a short season that is filled with commemorations of the saints, beginning with three feasts that celebrate the earliest witnesses to the Lord.

St. Stephen, celebrated on December 26 and often called "the protomartyr" or the first martyr, is the first of Jesus' disciples to be killed for preaching the Gospel (see Acts of the Apostles 6:8—8:1). On the other hand, St. John the Apostle (celebrated on December 27), is the only one of the Apostles to not die a martyr's death, according to tradition. His witness founded a community that produced several of our New Testament books. Sts. Stephen and John, then, mark out the beginning and the end of the Apostolic generation of first-hand witnesses to the Lord. Their very different deaths each witnesses to a life that overflowed with the love of the Crucified and Resurrected Lord. On December 28 we commemorate the innocents who unknowingly gave their lives in place of the Christ-child (see Matthew 2:16–18). Their silent witness stands against the tyrants of all ages who seek to hold on to power through violence.

After two feasts that turn our gaze back to the Holy Family (December 31) and Mary, the Holy Mother of God (January 1), we remember Sts. Basil and Gregory Nazianzen (January 2). These two theologians clarified how we speak about Jesus as God who became flesh, so to celebrate them in the season of the Incarnation is appropriate. We also celebrate the memory of three saints who witnessed to North America: Elizabeth Ann Seton (January 4), John Neumann (January 5), and André Bessette (January 6). Like Stephen and John, each of these saints was captivated by Jesus' call. They proclaimed his Gospel in the new world in different ways: one as a foundress in New York, one a bishop in Philadelphia, and one as a religious brother in Quebec. Each of these modern day disciples calls us to ask how the Gospel is to be lived in our own times and places, and to follow the Lord wherever he might lead us.

The Liturgy of the Hours

CHRISTMAS begins with Evening Prayer I on December 24. If you are new to praying the Hours, you will begin to have some insights into the structure of the Church's sense of time. Allow yourself to be wooed by it. There is a subtle shift in spirituality as we embrace this different rhythm.

The Church counts our high holy days beginning with sundown, evening. Many of us are only cognizant of this a few times of the year, such as Christmas Eve and the Easter Vigil. However, this pattern is always present. Each Sunday begins on Saturday Eve, for simplicity's sake usually reckoned as 4:00 PM. So the Saturday Mass is not for the sake of convenience, but in our Church world, we are already at the beginning of our Sunday celebration. This affects, therefore, all our patterns for prayers, readings, and feast day celebrations. In the Liturgy of the Hours, the prayer on the eve is considered "Evening Prayer I" while on the day it is "Evening Prayer II." Also, each new season begins again with "Week One." If you are not using a digital format for the Liturgy of the Hours, make sure you have adjusted your breviary (prayer book).

The time of Christmas is filled with feasts, especially at the beginning. Each celebration offers another vision of what the Incarnation means to us. Also note the subtle distinctions between each. For example, Thomas Becket on December 29 is an optional memorial while Holy Innocents on December 28 is a feast. This is where a paper format can be confusing. A digital breviary or calendar to finding the prayers may be helpful.

Notice that for the high feasts we are directed to use "Sunday Week One." As the beginning day of the Liturgy of the Hours it is our norm. What spiritual shift can we allow to occur in us when in prayer we are told to treat our day as a Sunday? There is a difference in allowing prayer to become for us a fundamental, guiding discipline, as opposed to something we do, a task to be accomplished and set aside.

The Octave of Christmas is the Solemnity of Mary, the Holy Mother of God, January 1. Since it falls on a Monday, the obligation will be abrogated. This is a great opportunity to offer a communal celebration of Morning Prayer. The psalms appointed are from Sunday Week One. As you consider an opening hymn, avoid the temptation to just sing any song about Mary. What is particular about this title, "Mother of God"? Historically, it was a source of great debate. Let's not be too casual.

Epiphany is assigned to the Sunday between January 2 and January 8, so this year it falls on January 7, 2018. Again, if you are using a non-digital resource be aware of this. Finally, Christmas Time will end on the Feast of the Baptism of the Lord, Monday, January 8.

Thematically Christmas moves from the Incarnation to the baptism of the Lord very quickly. It's as if Jesus grew up in a couple weeks. This is not the point. Be careful to avoid seeing Christmas as a birth of a baby rather than the Incarnation. How would this change affect your prayer and that of the parish community? How do you allow the themes of the feasts of the Christmas season to move your understanding of this great gift? More practically, how does it feel to continue praying Christmas each day while the culture has moved on weeks ago?

The Rite of Christian Initiation of Adults

THE Period of the Catechumenate is the time where the candidate becomes steeped in the Gospel. This encounter with the Gospel and the teachings of the Church forms candidates into disciples and trains them in the Christian life (see RCIA, 75). This period includes several minor rites that strengthen the candidate on the journey to Initiation. These can be easily overlooked if the RCIA team is unaware of them or rarely celebrated because the team is too content focused. When the Period of the Catechumenate is crammed into six or nine months, time is scarce. Any pause or redirection in a scheduled session becomes difficult. Celebrating the RCIA over the extended time that the rite envisions lets the catechumens relish this time and be immersed in the riches of our prayer and ritual.

The first rite belonging to this period is the Celebration of the Word of God. The ritual text outlines three options for this celebration. First are "celebrations held specially for the catechumens" (RCIA, 81). Consider a celebration of the word on a special retreat day for catechumens or at special gatherings in the parish (for example, parish feast days). The rite claims these special celebrations, "implant in their hearts the teachings they are receiving . . . [they] give them instruction and experience in the different aspects and ways of prayer . . . [they] explain to them the signs, celebrations, and seasons of the liturgy . . . [and finally they] prepare them gradually to enter the worship[ing] assembly" (RCIA, 82). Second, the rite reemphasizes that participation in the Liturgy of the Word on Sunday is crucial to Christian formation. Celebrating the word can also provide a perfect way to begin a weekly catechetical gathering. RCIA, 85–89, provides a generic outline to help the catechists or liturgy team plan this celebration. These rites can be lead by anyone.

The second series of rites belonging to this period are the Minor Exorcisms. RCIA, 90, says, "They draw the attention of the catechumens to the real nature of Christian life, the struggle between flesh and spirit, the importance of self-denial . . . and the unending need for God's help." The minor exorcism is normally celebrated during a Liturgy of the Word though RCIA, 92, says they can be prayed at crucial times for an individual candidate. As you discern the movement of the Spirit within the group, it will become clear when these need to be celebrated. Consider connecting these with the healing stories in the Gospels in Ordinary Time (for example, the Thirtieth Sunday in Ordinary Time). "A priest, a deacon, or a qualified catechist appointed by the bishop" can celebrate the minor exorcisms (RCIA, 91; see also RCIA, 12–16).

The Blessings of the Catechumens is the third minor rite during this period. "The blessings . . . are a sign of God's love and of the Church's tender care . . . they are bestowed on the catechumens so that . . . they may still receive from the Church courage, joy, and peace" on their journey (95). These are usually given at the end of celebration of the word, but you might find others ways to use them in your ministry. "A priest, a deacon, or a qualified catechist appointed by the bishop" can celebrate and may give the blessing (RCIA, 91; see also RCIA, 12–16).

The final option in this period is the Anointing of the Catechumens. Use this rite abundantly as it aids the catechumen to remain steadfast on the journey. "The anointing with oil symbolizes their need for God's help and strength" (RCIA, 99).

Using the Oil of Catechumens several times during the period is encouraged; the anointing is normally conferred after the homily in a celebration of the Word, at the Liturgy of the Hours, or even at Sunday Mass. Let this be a rich symbol of God's mercy and of the community's support and love. Review this section of the rite carefully so that you are familiar with all the options. Think creatively on how to incorporate them into the process.

The Sacraments of Initiation

THE Christmas season begins with the Nativity of the Lord at the Christmas Eve liturgy and each Sunday of the season we hear about the Holy Family and celebrate the experience of humanity awakening to the dawn of the Incarnation in the infant Jesus. We remember that Jesus is the reason we have people who come to the sacraments at all. Because Jesus, our Savior, was born we are baptized into his life, Death, and Resurrection. This is the core of our life of faith.

Christmas is a wonderful time for parish members to be especially welcoming and hospitable to family members who come to visit for the parish. It is a great evangelizing moment when you can reach out in love and support to a new family. Many parents wait a little longer to baptize their children and they may not yet have a parish home. When these young families have a good experience it opens up a lifetime of sharing faith.

By this time of year many parish children and teens will be in the midst of preparations for the Sacrament of First Eucharist and Confirmation. It is appropriate to add intercessory prayers of love and encouragement for all of the sacramental candidates.

The Rite of Penance

CHRISTMAS is more a time of celebration than reconciliation. However, we know that this season can bring with it both heart ache as well as healing. Christmas is when people are drawn home, physically and spiritually. How can your parish be open to visitors? Are we ready to receive back with open arms our sisters and brothers who may have wandered from the faith? Can we receive the returning in a spirit of reconciliation, not anger or mistaken triumphalism?

Are staff members available and ready to answer questions for the seekers? Be prepared, too, for some anger or misunderstanding. These emotions often mask deep pain. What materials are in your pamphlet racks? What posters on your bulletin board? Do they invite people home? Do they speak of returning, reconciling with God? Healing from pain?

What do we offer to the hurting or seeking at this time of the year? Perhaps the bulletin or website can list places where parishioner can find help: domestic violence shelters, therapists, addiction support groups, grief counselors. The schedule for Penance celebrations is also helpful.

While communal celebrations of Penance are rare during Christmas, do not neglect the importance of individual celebrations. Visitors often seek out a priest other than their own pastor. This allows for a freedom to address issues that perhaps are embarrassing for the person. When you inform local hotels of your Christmas Mass schedule, don't forget to include the Penance schedule and parish website address and Facebook page.

The Order of Celebrating Matrimony

WHAT a wonderful season for a wedding! The Church is decorated beautifully and spirits are high. This is a great time to include a carol or two in the liturgy. As our most familiar songs, Christmas music can inspire the assembly to participate. Encourage the couple to remember this when they assist in the music preparation.

When scheduling weddings during this season, remind the couple and parish support staff of the parameters of Christmas. December 25 is a Monday and the season will conclude with the Feast of the Baptism of the Lord on Monday, January 8. Therefore, the Christmas environment will still be in place for two weekends in January. This may be a blessing or a surprise.

When scheduling the date on the calendar it is wise to discuss your parish's seasonal environment.

A Nativity scene, especially a large one, may not be what the bride had in mind in January. Since flowers and other decorations are purchased quite a bit in advance, be sensitive to your couple and their needs.

Engagements commonly take place at Christmas. It is also a time when families, especially young adults come home for the holidays. These twenty-somethings are in a very flexible time of life. They are finishing school, finding their first job, moving into their first apartments, and getting engaged. Their new lives may be across the country. How do we welcome them home?

How do we do Marriage preparation when the couple is at a distance from us? Certainly they need to be encouraged to find a new parish in which to continue their journey of faith. However, because family and friends are in our neighborhood it is natural to want to celebrate the wedding with their parish of origin. Look at your website with the eyes of the newly engaged. Can they find information quickly? If you were just engaged, filled with excitement and enthusiasm, how would the site seem to you? A list of rules, or an invitation to celebration? Is it clear what the first steps are?

Evaluate your policy? Should a couple complete Marriage preparation in their new parish? How do we meet with them, especially as we prepare for the liturgy? Consider Facetime or Skype. These and other technological options can give us a better connection with the couple than by the phone. Do you have a parish wedding manual? Is it on the website? How about the readings or music options? Can you place a link to the music? Make sure that what they hear is similar to how it would sound for their wedding? There are many versions of Canon in D. Which sounds most like your music ministry?

How do we greet the less churched? Many of them may have come for Christmas Masses. Some are now looking for a spiritual home, yes others may be looking for a pretty place to get married. All are opportunities to invite, inspire and encourage the Gospel message.

The Pastoral Care of the Sick

THE many activities of parish life at Christmas Time are all wonderful celebrations that emphasize the nature of community and help to express the bonds of relationship within the parish and give it a feeling of joy and gratitude as the people of the Lord.

Many parishes engage in outreach projects like collecting gifts for a giving tree that are distributed to families in the larger community. The underlying motive is that no one is left out at Christmas.

Among those who often feel "left out" at Christmas are people who are home bound or hospitalized because of their health. There are also those for whom Christmas brings back memories of sadness related to a death of a loved one, either during this past year or in prior years.

The feelings of loss and loneliness can be overwhelming. The ministers of pastoral care need to be especially attentive to those who find themselves in such situations. The Sacrament of the Anointing of the Sick can bring great comfort to people whose health has not allowed them to join in the festivities of their parish family or to be with their own family members.

However, since other family members may be visiting from elsewhere during these days it would be a wonderful opportunity to bring them together for a celebration of the sacrament with the person who is ill. This happened in my own family a few years ago when my sister was very sick and we were able to gather for a celebration of anointing on December 23. She died the next day. The members of our family received great support from being able to gather in prayer with her.

The pastor and pastoral care visitors can take reminders of the parish to the sick person, for example the Christmas bulletin or a small plant to leave in the person's room. Some parishioners can be invited to pen notes or sign Christmas cards as a reminder that the person is still present in the thoughts and prayers of the parishioners.

Sometimes pastoral care visitors, including clergy, find it difficult to express the sense of joy that pervades this time of year when they are confronted with someone who is not feeling the same emotions. A possible conversation topic can be sharing stories and memories, both happy ones and those that are not as uplifting, about family traditions related to Christmas. This allows an opportunity for the sick person to feel included in the world around them, even as they are not as engaged as they once were.

There are several Scripture readings from this time that offer suitable reflections for the celebration of the sacrament. Suggestions include the psalm from the Feast of St. Stephen, martyr (December 26); the First Reading from the Feast of St. John the Evangelist (December 27); and the Second Reading (Year A) and the psalm (Year C) for the Feast of the Holy Family.

Since the Solemnity of Mary, the Holy Mother of God (New Year's Day), falls in this period of time, a communal celebration of Anointing of the Sick could be scheduled in the first few days of the new year. Those who are ill might see a spiritual connection between the comforting grace of the sacrament and their own desire to begin the year under the protection of Mary who brought such solace to her son in his suffering.

The Order of Christian Funerals

THIS season always seems too short. However, it is a very powerful time both in Church and in culture.

Be honest about the exhaustion clergy and lay ministers face at this time. It can make us cranky. Allow time for staff to celebrate with their families so they can be spiritual healthy to minister to the hurting.

Be also cognizant of the parish office schedule during the holidays. Make sure funeral homes can reach the church to make scheduling arrangements in a reasonable time frame. Families need to notify others and our openness to their struggles is one more act of care.

Christmas in the church is filled with images of Resurrection. Lights in many forms, evergreen, candles, white vestments. Let the environment inform your preaching. Many parishes also have time at the church for the body to lie in state prior to the liturgy. Where is this space in your church? What symbols and environment surround the body of loved ones? Are they put in a corner, or can simple, sacred space be created for use during this viewing time?

Some of the culture's Christmas values, such as family time, can be used to support our message of faith. For example, 1 Thessalonians 4 can be a common Scripture for Christmas funerals. In faith and power Paul writes to families who are also grieving. Again consider reserving some of the Sacred Scripture choices to the presider or preacher's discretion. This will allow for the funeral liturgy to be celebrated in the context of the season.

Some Christmas music is wonderful for funeral liturgies. Review the texts of your parish repertoire with this eye. For example, the last verse of "Hark, the Herald Angels Sing" masterfully ties together the Incarnation and Resurrection of Christ. "Hail the heav'n born Prince of Peace. Hail the Son of Righteousness. Life and light to all he brings, risen with healing in his wings. Lo, he lays his glory by. Born that we no more may die. Born to raise us from this earth. Born to give us second birth." There are many others as well.

The death of a loved one at Christmas can increase the pain. It almost seems contrary to the celebration. Be pastorally aware of this. The hurting is an open door to the healing message of the resurrection. However, make time for the family to tell their story. Discover their joys and sorrows in this place and time. Remember, each family is different and probably has an untold story too. Tread gently and lightly.

One example of helping the family heal at this sensitive time of the year is bestowing them with a symbol of the Church. Perhaps a white candle that is in the environment during the funeral maybe given to the family to be burned each Christmas when they gather. One of the prayers of the liturgy can be simply presented with the candle. For example, consider the opening prayer (option A) from the Vigil Liturgy.

The Book of Blessings

AT the very beginning of this season—on the Vigil of Christmas or sometime on Christmas Day—it is suitable to celebrate the Order for the Blessing of a Christmas Tree (see BB, chapter 49). As the *Book of Blessings* notes, this is a medieval European practice (see BB, 1570), but putting up and decorating an evergreen tree for Christmas

Time has become a nearly universal civil and religious custom in the United States. In its original Chrisitan context, the tree symbolized the tree of paradise lit with candles symbolizing the Light of Christ (see BB, 1570). The order of blessing can take place during a celebration of the Word of God (see BB, 1576–1591), or during Morning or Evening Prayer after the Gospel Canticle, where the intercessions, Lord's Prayer, and prayer of blessing take the place of the intercessions and concluding prayer of Morning or Evening Prayer (see BB, 1572). When celebrated in a church the minister of blessing should be a priest or deacon if present. The blessing can also take place at home, however, and in this circumstance a parent or other member of the family should lead the blessing, using the shorter rite (see BB, 1592–1596).

The Order for the Blessing of a Christmas Manger or Nativity Scene (see BB, chapter 48) normally takes place on the Vigil of Christmas, but can also be celebrated "at another more suitable time" (BB, 1542). St. Francis of Assisi is credited with making the first manger scene on Christmas Eve, 1223. Wall paintings of the manger scene go back to the fourth century, however (see BB, 1541). This blessing can be celebrated at church within Mass (see BB, 1562–1564), and at church or outside church—perhaps "during another service" such as a service of carols—during a celebration of the Word of God (BB, 1547–1561). It can also be celebrated at home, usually with the shorter rite (see BB, 1565–1569). While using the shorter rite is not forbidden in church, it seems the intent of the ritual book is that the home is the more suitable context.

Homes are traditionally blessed on the Solemnity of the Epiphany during Christmas Time, so celebrating the Order for the Blessing of Homes during the Christmas and Easter seasons (see BB, chapter 50) is most fitting. There is a longer and a shorter form, both of which take place within the home to be blessed. Take care to select the options in the rite most suitable to Christmas Time. A priest, deacon, or layperson may lead the blessing.

Family is a natural and recurring theme in Christmas Time. The Feast of the Holy Family is a perfect opportunity to celebrate the Order for the Blessing of a Family within Mass (BB, 62–67). Of course, this blessing can take place any time of the year, within Mass or outside Mass as a celebration of the Word of God. In places where an annual visit from the pastor to the homes of his parishioners is customary and feasible, note the Order for the Annual Blessing of Families in their Own Homes (see BB, 68–89).

The Liturgical Music

WHILE the secular world begins celebrating "the holiday season" well before Thanksgiving, the Church begins its celebration on the afternoon of December 24 and continues it until the Feast of the Baptism of the Lord. This creates a great challenge for liturgical musicians who have to fight the tides of the secular world and even the push from those who seem to want to celebrate the season earlier and earlier each year.

In many churches, Christmas Eve Masses are usually more crowded than Christmas Day. Be sure to spread the musical resources around so that all of the Masses are well staffed with musicians. Don't forget to include college students home for Christmas break who can be a valuable asset to the music ministry during this season.

In lieu of a concert preceding the Mass during the Night, consider hosting a service of Lessons and Carols. The musicians and the assembly will appreciate having a break in between some of the musical selections and more importantly, the spirituality that that Scripture readings bring to the music. The sermon from St. Leo the Great from the Office of Readings for Christmas offers a poignant reflection on the Incarnation. Lessons and Carols can end with the *Proclamation of the Birth of Christ* by the deacon or the cantor at the ambo just before the Entrance Procession.

As important as the celebration of Christmas is, it ranks second, just under the Sacred Paschal Triduum, in the Table of Liturgical Days (found at the end of UNLY). Christmas looks to Easter, points to the Paschal Mystery, and sets the stage for the Passion, Death and Resurrection of Christ. Martin Luther once said that the wood of the cross is the wood of the cradle. Several Christmas carols such as "Hark! The Herald Angels Sing" (MENDELSSHON), "What Child Is This" (GREENSLEEVES), and "We Three Kings" (KINGS OF ORIENT) explicitly reference Christ's Passion, Death, and Resurrection and should be used during the season. Some traditional carols tend to romanticize the scene in Bethlehem rather than depicting the poverty into which Jesus was born.

While people will want to hear some of these traditional carols, they can be balanced with contemporary settings that connect the Incarnation with the living out of the Christian Life. "Epiphany Carol" by Francis Patrick O'Brien (GIA), "What Child is This"/"Child of the Poor" by Scott Soper (OCP), and "Child of Mercy" by David Haas (GIA) are good examples. "Of the Father's Love Begotten" (DIVINUM MYSTERIUM) is an ancient hymn that emphasizes the Incarnation.

There are several Mass settings that utilize familiar Christmas melodies, including Jennifer Pascual's "*Resonet in Laudibus* Eucharistic Acclamations" (WLP), Howard Hughes' "Gloria for Christmastime (WLP), or "A Christmas Mass" by Paul Gibson (OCP). There will be likely be more visitors to Church during the weeks of the Christmas season than at any other time of year so selecting accessible and singable acclamations will help to foster a climate of hospitality and encourage participation.

Christmas carols should continue throughout the season up to and including the Baptism of the Lord. Since the season ends with a celebration Jesus' Baptism, which happened when he was an adult, hymns that celebrate the Incarnation while moving away from Bethlehem and images of the crèche would be more appropriate. Examples include "Joy to the World" (ANTIOCH) and "Songs of Thankfulness and Praise" (SALZBURG).

The Liturgical Environment

THE way you decide to incorporate the crèche, flowers, banners, wreaths, trees, greenery, and lighting into the environment is decided by many factors. Ideas to consider: What are some of the traditions used in your parish? How much room do you have to work with? Can you use real Christmas trees? Are there certain kinds of lights to use on your trees? Are you considering traffic flow and flower placement?

How to place these items is very important. Remember that the Liturgy of the Word and the Liturgy of the Eucharist should always be the focal points. Try to not put anything directly in front of the altar, but they can be off-centered.

The colors for Christmas are gold and white. You can use white pointsettias. If you use red flowers, still add white and gold colors on the pot covers and in the fabric you use for draping. It is very pleasing to the eye to have the flowers arranged at different heights. It is acceptable to have the top row of flowers almost even with the top of the altar (be sure not to put them on the altar or block the altar). To be safe I always make sure they are one to two inches shorter. If you have plant stands that are sturdy, but lack in eye appeal, you can drape those with fabric.

Trees are used to enhance the beauty of the season, not overtake it. Keep it simple. Setting them up to the right or left of the altar works well. If the trees are lined up, set the tallest tree the farthest away from the altar and the smaller ones closer. Use white lights on the tree, not colored lights. Cover the bottom of the trees with white or gold fabric so you don't see the tree stand or any of the electrical cords. Also use the "squint" eye test, to make sure the lights are evenly spaced on the trees.

It is a welcoming touch to put wreaths on the doors and around the church. Lighting these wreaths may prove to be problematic. Use battery-operated white lights so that you don't see the wires, or, instead of lights, add gold and white ribbon.

When setting up the crèche, make sure to use ground coverings that are as near to the likeness of a stable as possible. We use some green moss and hay. Don't be afraid to move the animal pieces close to where the infant will lie. Put hay in the manger, like they did for Jesus. Realism is the key. If you have a relatively large stable replica, put tree branches on the roof to soften the look of the wood.

The Liturgical Ministers

THIS year Christmas Eve falls on a Sunday. Consider putting up signup sheets for the various liturgical ministers needed for Christmas early in Advent. Whenever possible the sure to schedule ministers as family units and invite students returning from college to serve as well. Inquire with various groups in the parish to see if they are willing to help with the ministry of hospitality. Various parish ministers, especially musicians, sacristans, priests, and deacons, are often present for two or more liturgies on Christmas Eve or Christmas Day. Consider preparing a place where these ministers can have some down time and provide simple food and beverages for these co-workers in the vineyard. Make sure that all the ministers are thanked and recognized for their faithful service, especially ministers of music who will spend many hours rehearsing and preparing music for the Christmas liturgies.

Following the Epiphany liturgies (January 7, 2018), provide prayer texts and chalk for the domestic church to mark the doors of the home. Bring together the many liturgical, catechetical, and other ministers and volunteers in the parish, along with the parish staff, for an Epiphany party as a sign of gratitude for the work of all. Soon after the Advent, Christmas, and Epiphany celebrations have ended, bring together the parish liturgical commission along with parish musicians, presiding ministers, and members of the art and environment team to evaluation the season. What worked and didn't? Have the commission members write thank you notes to the various liturgical ministers. During the time of evaluation ask questions such as; what allowed you to capture the mystery of the Incarnation? In what ways did visitors feel welcome? Were enough traditional carols sung so that the assembly participated fully, consciously, and actively?

Other Prayers, Rites, and Devotions

Unfortunately in the secular world, the celebration of Christmas ends by the evening of December 25. How can parishes promote the celebration until the Feast of the Baptism of Lord (which is a Monday this year)? What does your parish do on New Year's Eve? Besides the vigil Mass for the Solemnity of Mary, the Holy Mother of God, how about offering prolonged exposition of the Blessed Sacrament and conclude with the celebration of Mass beginning at the stroke of twelve! Traditionally, the *Te Deum* is sung at this time. Many religious congregations may already be honoring the vigil in this way so why not open it up interested parishioners. Gather together after Mass for a champagne toast before all go their way.

One way to emphasize the continuation of the season is to host an evening of Epiphany Lessons and Carols or a concert of Christmas music bringing together all the musical talent of the parish for a grand finale! Many parishioners may welcome this opportunity to sit back and enjoy the sights and sounds of Christmas since all the busyness of the season has concluded.

What about promoting the blessing of the home? Volunteers can assemble small boxes stamped with the image of the Three Kings and include a small piece of chalk, grains of incense, and a small gold ball, cut from strands of gold chains that many people use in decorating during the season. These can be passed out as the assembly leaves Mass. Include the Blessing of the Home and Household on the Epiphany from *Catholic Household Blessings & Prayers* in the parish bulletin (you will need to acquire copyright permission from the USCCB). Be sure to include the directions for inscribing in chalk the lentil of the main door of the house with the characters 20+C+M+B+18. (The current year and the initials of the Three Kings: Casper, Melchior, and Balthazar). The initials also stand for *Christus mansionem benedicat* ("Christ bless our house"). When the parish school returns from Christmas vacation, a priest or deacon can go to each of the classrooms and inscribe the year on the door frame. In the past, the Ordo suggested an "increase of lights" on this day. Small battery powered votive candles could be placed around the parish crèche scene or window sills. (Real candles might not be a good option because of the usual abundance of straw and fire code laws in schools!)

Evangelization

Christmas Time affords us the opportunity to think about both how we evangelize through our liturgy and worship, and how our communal prayer leads us to proclaim the Good News as we go forth from the midst of the faith community. This year on the Feast of the Holy Family, we hear Simeon attest to the salvation that is come in the child Jesus; he is the light for revelation to the Gentiles. Anna gives thanks and speaks about the child to those waiting for the redemption of Jerusalem. They, along with Mary and Joseph, who faithfully brought their child to the Temple, are models of evangelization for us. They teach us the Good News of salvation is not just ours. The Good News belongs to peoples throughout the world. Our evangelization reaches to all who desire the way of Light. We, like the Magi, see the universal reach of the Christ star.

As we remember our Baptism on the Feast of the Baptism of the Lord, the transitional feast which ends Christmas Time and moves us into Ordinary Time, we accept once again the responsibility of our Baptism, to live in mission to others—even those we might not want to evangelize and welcome—the least, the lost, the homeless, the hurting, the refugees, those most vulnerable, those who are different from us in any way. May our evangelization reach to all of God's people, the Gentiles of today, as Christ himself extended the reach of the Good News in his own person.

The Parish and the Home

MAINTAINING Christmas as a season at home as well as within our parish is not as much about observing liturgical norms as it is about celebrating the love of God for us in Jesus Christ. Christmas is a season with much to teach us. As we take time to reflect upon the Incarnation, we gain insight into the divinity and humanity of Jesus. We may also glimpse the value of every human as one created in and called to live the image of this loving God in the world.

At home, leave decorations up throughout the season, including the Christmas tree for as long as possible. The season does not end until the Feast of the Baptism of the Lord, which is January 8 this year. Make the family table the place for prayer at dinnertime, and invite each family member to share a gift he or she has received each day, in recognition of the gift of the Christ-child. This practice will help each person recognize gifts received, large and small, in daily life, such as kindness shared, forgiveness received, or presence felt. Each Sunday, read a portion of the story of Jesus' birth, found at the beginning of the Gospel accounts of Matthew, Mark, and Luke, and the beginning of the Gospel according to John, which offers a theological reflection on the meaning of Christ's life. Share a favorite Christmas memory as a way of connecting this great love of God with the love shared within the family, and sing a favorite Christmas carol together.

On January 8, we celebrate the Feast of the Baptism of the Lord, the end of Christmas Time. As the decorations are packed away for another year, take time to look back on the blessings of the season that has just passed. Keep Christmas cards received and offer prayer for those who sent them as you unpack your decorations at the beginning of the next Christmas season!

Mass Texts

◆ TROPES FOR THE PENITENTIAL ACT, FORM C

You are the radiant splendor of the eternal God: Lord, have mercy.

You are the light to the nations and the glory of the whole human race: Christ, have mercy.

You are the Beloved Son of God and Savior of the world: Lord, have mercy.

◆ DISMISSAL FOR CHILDREN'S LITURGY OF THE WORD

My dear children, today you will hear the Scriptures that tell us who Jesus is and why he came to save us. We will wait for you here so that with this whole assembly, you may praise and thank God for sending us his Son. Go in peace.

◆ DISMISSAL OF THE CATECHUMENS

My dear friends, we now send you out to break open the mystery of Emmanuel, God-with-us, the Word of God which you heard proclaimed here today. it is Christ, whose light shines eternally, who will be your guide. Follow him with faith and go in peace.

December 2017
Month of the Divine Infancy

Optional Memorials during Christmas Time

The Missal commentaries below pertain to the seasonal weekdays or other obligatory observances. The following should be consulted for celebrating optional memorials during Christmas Time:

[ ]n days within the Octave of the Nativity of the Lord . . . the Mass texts for the current liturgical day are used; but the Collect may be taken from a Memorial which happens to be inscribed in the General Calendar for that day (GIRM, 355a).

[O]n weekdays of Christmas Time from January 2 . . . one of the following may be chosen: either the Mass of the weekday, or the Mass of the Saint or one of the Saints whose Memorial is observed, or the Mass of any Saint inscribed in the *Martyrology* for that day (GIRM, 355b).

(#13, #14, #15, #16)   white

M O N
25
Solemnity of the Nativity of the Lord (Christmas)

About Today's Solemnity

The events surrounding Jesus' birth are found only in Matthew's and Luke's accounts. In John's account, which was written later than the others, there is a totally different presentation of Jesus coming into the world, as "the Word became flesh" (John 1:14). The other Gospel accounts stress the humanity of Jesus while John's prologue stresses the divinity. The essence of the prologue that is important to proclaim is that God took on human flesh. God became incarnate in Jesus.

The Lectionary for Mass: Vigil Mass

◆ FIRST READING: Isaiah uses the first person pronoun making the reader understand that it is God who is speaking. Some catastrophe has befallen the nation and God will not rest until Jerusalem, which represents the whole people, is vindicated. God promises that they will be a new people; indeed, they will be espoused to God and become God's own delight. The marriage imagery underlines the covenant of love that God will establish.

◆ RESPONSORIAL PSALM 89: Like the passage from Isaiah it is God who speaks the words of the psalm. Once again the Lord refers to the covenant relationship between God and the people. The covenant was made with David and his posterity "for all generations." The fulfillment of that promise will unfold in the mystery of the Incarnation; God's Word will become flesh.

◆ SECOND READING: Paul's instruction in the synagogue of Antioch is a summary of his understanding of the historic breadth of God's plan of salvation. Paul mentions that there were two significant figures in the unfolding of God's plan: David and John the Baptist. The king and the desert preacher told their respective followers that God would raise up a Savior for Israel. Jesus the Messiah of the house of David and the one announced by John would be that Savior.

◆ GOSPEL: With his lengthy genealogy of Jesus, Matthew establishes Jesus' place in history and validates his lineage within the prophetic tradition, going back to Abraham. The shorter version omits these verses and recounts the details of Mary's pregnancy. The details about her and Joseph not being married, while interesting, are not really the point. The heavenly messenger, Joseph's dream, and the work of the Holy Spirit all speak of the mysterious action of God that is not hampered by human customs and boundaries.

The Roman Missal: Vigil Mass

The Gloria is sung or said; given the festivity of the occasion, the musical setting used should be a magnificent one indeed, as the text echoes the words of the heavenly host praising God's glory.

During the recitation or singing of the Creed, all are to kneel at the words "and by the Holy Spirit was incarnate," up to and including the words "and became man." Don't let the assembly be caught by surprise by this such that very few kneel or such that it winds up being awkward and haphazard. After leaving a silent pause after the homily, the priest may offer a spontaneous introduction to the Creed that explains how and when the kneeling is to take place, so that all might properly participate in this gesture that highlights the Incarnation.

The prayers for the Vigil Mass very much maintain the sense of vigiling as they speak of waiting and looking forward. There is a choice from among three for the Preface at this Vigil Mass—Preface I, II, or III of the Nativity of the Lord. These can be found immediately following the two Advent Prefaces. Note that if Eucharistic Prayer I, the Roman Canon, is used, there is a proper form of the *Communicantes* that is used.

The Lectionary for Mass: Mass during the Night

◆ FIRST READING: The oracle of the prophet Isaiah is a proclamation of salvation for all peoples. He uses the comparison of light and darkness to portray the great difference between the past and the future. The light will bring joy and prosperity to the whole land. What is more remarkable is that all this will come about through the agency of a child. The names given to this child-savior indicate his role and his God-given appointment. The Christian Gospel will ascribe all this to Jesus Christ.

◆ PSALM 96 is an exhortation to sing praise to the Lord for his salvation. This salvation is seen as one of the wondrous deeds of the past and it will be affirmed with the future coming of the Lord. The salvation of God is universal and cosmic; it will bring justice to all peoples. Heaven and earth are called to rejoice.

◆ SECOND READING: The pastoral epistle of Paul to Titus reiterates the universality of God's salvation noted in the First Reading. One of the graces of this gift of salvation is the strength to live worthy lives in anticipation of the return of "our great God and / Savior, Jesus Christ." The early Church could not know when that might be, but they could conduct themselves justly and devoutly in the meantime.

◆ GOSPEL: The narrative of Jesus' birth is probably one of the most familiar passages in Luke's account of the Gospel. When it comes to details for a story this is vintage Luke. Luke establishes the child's Davidic ancestry, thus placing him within God's plan of salvation. The humble details that surround his birth and his birthplace prefigure his future ministry to those who often lived on the edges of society. Yet the presence of the "heavenly host" clearly indicates the divine nature of this wondrous event.

The Roman Missal: Mass during the Night

The Christmas Proclamation should be done before Mass. The rubrics state that it should be sung or recited "*before the beginning* of Christmas Mass during the Night. It may not replace any part of the Mass" (emphasis added). Before the Mass begins—perhaps following a prelude or "carol service," sung by choir and congregation—a cantor could process to the ambo and chant the Proclamation, after which the opening notes of the Entrance Hymn or Introit would follow.

As with all Masses for this solemnity, the Gloria is sung or said. During the recitation or singing of the Creed, all are to kneel at the words "and by the Holy Spirit was incarnate," up to and including the words "and became man."

Preface III is a good choice; its mention of "the holy exchange" would echo the Prayer over the Offerings as explained above. Note that if Eucharistic Prayer I, the Roman Canon, is used, there is a proper form of the *Communicantes* that is used.

The Prayer after Communion gives voice to our joy at participating in the Nativity and asks that we "through an honorable way of life [may] become worthy of union with him."

Use the Solemn Blessing at the end of Mass, form #2, "The Nativity of the Lord."

The Lectionary for Mass: Mass at Dawn

◆ FIRST READING: This passage is a remarkable revelation about the state of the covenant people. First, the Savior is at hand, the time of waiting for salvation is over. Second, the arrival of the savior will bring about a change for them. They will no longer be "forsaken," as in their exile and felt abandoned by God. Now they will be "Frequented," God will be found dwelling among

them. The name Emmanuel, given to Jesus, will confirm this promise.

◆ RESPONSORIAL PSALM 97: The universal nature of the Lord's rule is the reason for the psalmist's call for rejoicing. The dominion of the Lord is heaven and earth, both are called to rejoice. The universal nature of the Lord's redemptive intervention is a common theme in the Christmas Scripture readings. This sets up the understanding that the Messiah is not just for the Israelites but for all the nations. This will cause tension throughout Jesus' ministry.

◆ SECOND READING: The focus of Paul's teaching is that salvation is a gift from God. It was not the "righteous deeds" of the believers that merited the "kindness and generous love" of God but it was because of God's mercy that they have a new life in the Spirit. This new life has been "poured out" upon them in Baptism, the "bath of rebirth." As the baptized they are to live lives worthy of this great gift.

◆ GOSPEL: The central figures in this Christmas narrative are the shepherds. At one time this Mass was called the Shepherd's Mass. The life of the shepherd was humble and poor; their social status was tolerated but far from being considered acceptable. That they should be visited by heavenly messengers is rather astonishing. They become bearers of great news. They offer us an example of openness and sincerity as we contemplate the mystery of the Incarnation.

The Roman Missal: Mass at Dawn

The Gloria is sung or said; given the festivity of the occasion, the musical setting used should be a magnificent one indeed, as the text echoes the words of the heavenly host praising God's glory.

During the recitation or singing of the Creed, all are to kneel at the words "and by the Holy Spirit was incarnate," up to and including the words "and became man."

Preface I of the Nativity, with its emphasis on light, shining glory, and the divine being made visible, is the most appropriate choice among the three possible Prefaces.

Note that if Eucharistic Prayer I, the Roman Canon, is used, there is a proper form of the *Communicantes* that is used.

Use the Solemn Blessing at the end of Mass, form #2, "The Nativity of the Lord."

The Lectionary for Mass: Mass during the Day

◆ First Reading: The tone of this reading is defined by the great news of salvation. Although salvation comes from the Lord, the messenger announces the "glad tidings." The role of the messenger is critical in bringing news, good or bad across the land. His arrival is either feared or welcomed. In this case his arrival is cause for rejoicing; his feet are celebrated for what they deliver! John the Baptist, the shepherds, and the angels were messengers of good news, and we are messengers of the Good News of Jesus Christ.

◆ Responsorial Psalm 98: This is an enthronement psalm. It celebrates God's victory over the entire cosmos. There is an indirect reference to the covenant. Unlike the people who forgot their responsibilities from time to time, God "has remembered his kindness and his faithfulness." The exhortation to praise the Lord requires instruments that are used for joyful celebrations.

◆ Second Reading: The Hebrew root of "word" denotes it as a verb, not as a noun. The Word of God is more action than object. When God speaks something happens. The author of Hebrews describes the Word of God as happening through the ages and now it has been fulfilled in Jesus, the Son

of God who "sustains all things by his mighty word."

◆ Gospel: The reading is presented in two forms: the shorter one is a theological statement; the longer one adds the narrative about John the Baptist. The Christology of the first part describes Jesus in the image of the Word of God, existing from the beginning. The word is the source of life, the light that overpowered the darkness. This image is central to the meaning of Christmas. The mention of John as a witness "to the light" places the arrival of Christ "the true light" in a historical context. The Word made flesh is thus established for all peoples and for all time.

The Roman Missal: Mass during the Day

The Gloria is sung or said. During the recitation or singing of the Creed, all are to kneel at the words "and by the Holy Spirit was incarnate," up to and including the words "and became man."

While any of the three Prefaces are appropriate, there may be a particular fittingness to using Preface III of the Nativity, insofar as it echoes the Collect with its mention of "the holy exchange." Note that if Eucharistic Prayer I, the Roman Canon, is used, there is a proper form of the *Communicantes* that is used.

Use the Solemn Blessing at the end of Mass, form #2, "The Nativity of the Lord."

Other Ideas

Be sure to sing plenty of Christmas carols this day. It is always fitting for the Communion song to include a familiar refrain ("Angels We Have Heard on High" or "The First Noel") so that the assembly can sing during the procession. Our society has been listening to Christmas music 24/7 for the last four weeks or so, our congregations have much of this music memorized. Also, con-

sider a festive sung response to the Universal Prayer.

TUE 26 (#696) red
Feast of St. Stephen, The First Martyr

The Lectionary for Mass

◆ First Reading: The joyous tone of Christmas is broken by the account of the martyrdom of Stephen. Although Stephen's death was sometime after the Crucifixion of Jesus it reminds us of the tension that developed between some authorities and the Christian conviction of the early Church. Stephen's posture, he "looked up intently to heaven," echoes that of Jesus on the Cross. Stephen's faith comes from being filled with the Holy Spirit.

◆ Responsorial Psalm 31: The psalmist cries out to the Lord to preserve him from his enemies and persecutors. The cry of the psalmist is also a statement of faith. He trusts that the Lord will be his "rock of refuge" and he will not perish. The words that Jesus uttered before his Death on the Cross were from this psalm: "Into your hands I commend my spirit."

◆ Gospel: Jesus' warning to the disciples of future persecution because of their confessing his name became true for Stephen. Jesus assurance that they would find the right words to speak when that time arrived may have given them little comfort, yet we recall that it was the words of Stephen that infuriated his persecutors. To speak the word of the Lord with conviction has always been a dangerous ministry, but Jesus reminds us that when that happens it is the Spirit of the Father that speaks through us. We are all instruments of the word of God.

The Roman Missal

The texts for this Mass are found in the Proper of Saints at December 26; all the orations are proper to the day. Since today is within the Octave of Christmas, the Gloria is sung or said at this Mass. One of the three Prefaces of the Nativity is used today. Be sure to use the proper form of the *Communicantes*, if Eucharistic Prayer I, the Roman Canon, is used.

Today's Saint

St. Stephen (c. † 34) is the protomartyr, the first martyr. Stephen was arrested and tried by the Sanhedrin for blasphemy. His fate was sealed when he had a vision during his trial and cried out, "I see the heavens opened and the Son of Man standing at the right hand of God" (Acts of the Apostles 7:56). He was taken out to be stoned to death by a mob, which included Saul of Tarsus. Stephen is shown in art with three stones and a martyr's palm, sometimes wearing a dalmatic, a deacon's vestment.

(#697)   white

W 27 Feast of St. John,
E   Apostle and
D   Evangelist

The Lectionary for Mass

◆ FIRST READING: Biblical scholars don't agree on the authorship of the Johannine epistles, but the prologue of 1 John is similar to the opening lines of John's account of the Gospel. The focus is on the "Word of life," very likely the person of Jesus Christ, and his importance in the Johannine community. The author notes that association with the Word is sensory: seeing, hearing, and touching. This association leads to public witness to what has been seen and heard. Believers are called to be witnesses of Christ.

◆ RESPONSORIAL PSALM 97: The psalmist makes bold statements concerning the glorious kingship of the Lord. The inference is that the Lord is enthroned in glory, surveying the heavens and the earth. Indeed the

whole cosmos glorifies the Lord: "the mountains melt like wax," "the heavens proclaim his justice," and "all peoples" see his glory.

◆ GOSPEL: There may be a hint of apostolic rivalry in this passage. John refers to himself as the one "whom Jesus loved"; none of the other evangelists give John that title. John records that he could run faster than Peter and reached the tomb first. Although he sees the burial cloths first, he deferred to Peter, who enters the tomb first. John also entered, but the closing line states that it was only John who "saw and believed." Apart from this slightly amusing exegesis, we owe John a great debt of gratitude for the Christology he has given the Church.

The Roman Missal

The texts for today's feast are found in the Proper of the Saints. The prayers from today's liturgy all include Johannine themes, including the Word of God brought to the Church from the Apostle John, which has "so marvelously [been] brought to our ears" (see the Collect); the "hidden wisdom of the eternal Word" revealed through John (see the Prayer over the Offerings), and the image of the "Word made flesh" in the Prayer after Communion. Preface I, II, or III of the Nativity of the Lord may be used and the Gloria is said or sung throughout the Octave of Christmas. You might consider using Eucharistic Prayer II.

Today's Saint

St. John (first century), Apostle and fourth Evangelist, is called the "beloved disciple" because of his close relationship with Jesus. Throughout his account of the Gospel, St. John, named as the son of Zebedee and brother of St. James the Greater, makes an appearance at significant moments in Jesus' life, specifically, at the Last Supper, the Garden of Gethsemane, the foot

of the Cross, and the upper room. These appearances point to the intimate relationship he had with our Lord. His account of the Gospel is quite different from the synoptic accounts (Matthew, Mark, and Luke) due to his high Christology (divine emphasis), which is proclaimed through symbolic language and poetic form. The eagle is the chosen symbol for John's account, ultimately representing the depth and height to which the human spirit must soar in order to grasp the meaning of John's text. Among his many important contributions to the Church, other scriptural writings are attributed to his name, including three epistles and the Book of Revelation.

T 28 (#698)   red
H   Feast of the Holy
U   Innocents, Martyrs

About Today's Feast

Herod the Great, fearing for his throne after the Magi told him about the birth of Jesus, ordered the execution of all male children in Bethlehem, hoping that Jesus would be among those killed (see Matthew 2:16–18).

Lectionary for Mass

◆ FIRST READING: The theme of light and darkness is used frequently in the Johannine writings to describe the difference between living in God and living in sin. The author of 1 John is aware that there are those in the community that do indeed live in sin. Even if they say that they do not, they still live in darkness. Those who confess their sin are forgiven through Jesus Christ, he is their advocate with the Father.

◆ RESPONSORIAL PSALM 12: The psalmist reminds his listeners that the hand of God has saved them in the past. Although his reference to the Exodus from Egyptian captivity is indirect, it appears that he is reminding the people that it was the intervention of the Lord that saved them from being overwhelmed by the waters. They were freed from "the snare" of captivity and are now free. Only the Lord could have done this for them.

◆ GOSPEL: Matthew's account of the massacre of the young boys in Bethlehem is the disturbing source of today's feast. There is a certain irony in the story. Joseph is told to flee to Egypt, the country where his ancestors had lived in captivity. The reader knows that the Holy Family returned safely from Egypt. Since the instruction came from a heavenly messenger the reader also understands that God is in charge and God's plan, spoken by the prophet, would be fulfilled.

The Roman Missal

The Mass formularies for today are found in the Proper of Saints for December 28; all the orations are proper to the day. Since today is a day within the Octave of Christmas, the Gloria is sung or said at this Mass. One of the three Prefaces of the Nativity is used today. Since we are within the Octave of the Nativity, be sure to use the proper form of the *Communicantes* if Eucharistic Prayer I, the Roman Canon, is used.

(#202)   white
FRI 29 Fifth Day within the Octave of the Nativity of the Lord

Optional Memorial of St. Thomas Becket, Bishop and Martyr / white

The Lectionary for Mass

◆ FIRST READING: Once again 1 John employs the image of light and darkness to instruct the community on right living. The measure of whether one is living in the light is in keeping the commandments of the Lord. To know the Lord is to live in the light and to walk in his ways. The author offers the example of loving one's brother as proof that they

live in the light. To hate one's brother or sister is to persist in darkness.

◆ RESPONSORIAL PSALM 96: The psalmist exhorts the people to sing songs of praise to the Lord. Singing the praises of the Lord is not only for their own benefit. It announces to everyone, "the nations," what God has done.

◆ GOSPEL: As devout Jewish parents Joseph and Mary follow the prescription of the law and take their child to present him to the Lord. The sacrificial offering is a gift of gratitude. The presence of Simeon is related to a revelation by the Holy Spirit; it is an echo of the work of the Holy Spirit in Mary's pregnancy. Simeon, who appears as a symbol of ancient wisdom, blesses the child in the form of a prophecy. The past and future of God's people have met in the child.

The Roman Missal

The prayers for the Octave Mass are found in the Proper of Time. Preface I, II, or III of the Nativity of the Lord may be used. Consider using Eucharistic Prayer III. The Gloria is said or sung throughout the Octave of Christmas.

Today's Saint

St. Thomas Becket (1118–1170) was born in London as the son of Norman parents. He received a good education at Merton Abbey, and later in Paris. When he left school, he became a secretary, a position of some prestige in a society with limited literacy. Eventually, he became assistant to Theobald, Archbishop of Canterbury. Recognizing his talent, Theobald sent him to the court of King Henry II, and eventually Thomas was named Lord Chancellor of England. In 1162, hoping to gain control over the Church, Henry had him installed as archbishop of Canterbury, but Thomas had a conversion, resigned as Chancellor, and thus

began a conflict between king and archbishop. When Thomas returned from exile in France and excommunicated Henry's followers, Henry said in a rage, "Will no one rid me of this meddlesome priest?" Four knights took this as a command and killed Thomas as he went to join the monks for vespers in the abbey church. The story is retold in T. S. Eliot's play *Murder in the Cathedral* and Jean Anouilh's play *Becket*.

(#203)   white
SAT 30 Sixth Day within the Octave of the Nativity of the Lord

The Lectionary for Mass

◆ FIRST READING: The writer equates the world and "the things of the world" as the source of evil ways. These pursuits are not from God, but with the word of God in them they will persevere.

◆ RESPONSORIAL PSALM 96: The charge in this psalm to praise the Lord is also given to all the nations because the whole of creation is the work of the Lord.

◆ GOSPEL: Luke introduces the prophetess Anna, a devout and elderly widow. She represents the people of Israel who have been "awaiting the redemption of Jerusalem." The city is synonymous with the nation. At the end of the rites of presentation the family returns home. Luke concludes his infancy narrative with the words, "The favor of God was upon him." The beloved son will soon emerge in his public ministry.

The Roman Missal

Today's Mass formularies are found in the Proper of Time section of the Missal, at December 30; all the orations are proper to the day. Since today is a day within the Octave of Christmas, the Gloria is sung or said at this Mass. One of the three Prefaces of the Nativity is used today. Since we are within the Octave of the Nativity, be sure to use the proper form of the Communicantes if Eucharistic Prayer I, the Roman Canon, is used.

(#17)   white

☀31 Feast of the Holy Family of Jesus, Mary, and Joseph

About Today's Feast

This liturgical feast has been on the Church calendar for about one hundred years, often on different dates. It is a "devotional" or "idea" feast that was inaugurated by Holy Family associations. Everything we know about the Holy Family, which is not much, comes from the Gospel accounts read over the three years. It celebrates the unity and love so evident in the family of Joseph, Mary, and Jesus.

The Lectionary for Mass

You may use the readings for Year B or Year A. What follows pertains to Year B.

◆ FIRST READING: The readings for this feast of the Holy Family take us back to Jesus' roots in the family of Israel. We hear of the first Jewish parents, Abraham and Sarah, who received their son (Isaac) as the child promised to them in their old age, the reward for their fidelity to God. From them, countless descendants as numerous as the stars have come forth.

◆ RESPONSORIAL PSALM 105: God remembers his covenant forever. So it was when he remembered his promise to Abraham (third and fourth stanzas) and Jacob, Abraham's grandson, with whom God renewed the covenant. The psalm is one of thanksgiving, not only in the house of Israel, but among the nations (Gentiles) as well.

◆ SECOND READING: The focus is on Abraham and Sarah, this time from the Letter to the Hebrews' account of their fidelity and trust in God. We also hear of Abraham's total obedience and complete trust in God even to the point of offering his son Isaac in sacrifice, the very one on whom the fulfilment of God's promises depended.

◆ GOSPEL: On the surface the Gospel describes the fidelity of the parents to the Jewish custom of presenting their first born male child to the Lord. As they do this in respect to the tradition, they encounter Simeon and Anna who represent that tradition and who acknowledge that a new tradition is unfolding in the child Jesus. Their waiting for the redemption of Jerusalem is over; the hope of the past has been fulfilled and the future is at hand.

The Roman Missal

The Collect holds in great esteem the Holy Family as a shining example to model our lives after. The Gloria is said or sung today. Since today's feast is on a Friday, the Creed is not said. The Prayer over the Offerings also looks to the Virgin Mary and St. Joseph to intercede for all families to live "firmly in [God's] grace and [his] peace." Preface I, II, or III of the Nativity of the Lord may be used. Consider using Preface II since it declares Christ restoring unity to all creation and calling humanity back to himself, a theme to be embraced by all families. Consider using Eucharistic Prayer III.

The Prayer after Communion calls on the Church "to imitate constantly the example of the Holy Family."

Other Ideas

Find a way this week to honor the holiness of all families through a parish gathering such as a potluck dinner. Or encourage people to set aside a "family night" this week to connect with each other, eat a meal, or play games.

January 2018
Month of the Holy Name

(#18)   white

M O N 1 Solemnity of Mary, the Holy Mother of God / The Octave Day of the Nativity of the Lord

NOT A HOLYDAY OF OBLIGATION

About Today's Solemnity

We are still in the midst of Christmas Time, and today the Church celebrates the Solemnity of Mary, the Holy Mother of God. One of the most outstanding characteristics of Mary is her willingness to know and do God's will. While we would like to follow her example, we wonder how she was so sure of it. Today's Gospel gives a clue. She reflected on events that happened and were happening. She meditated. In our busy lives today, we often overlook meditation as a prayer. Today is not a Holyday of Obligation.

The Lectionary for Mass

◆ FIRST READING: Scripture scholars suggest that this is one of the oldest pieces of poetry in the Bible. It is an ancient Jewish blessing bestowed by God through Moses. The threefold nature of the blessing invokes the graciousness of God upon the Israelites. If all that is promised comes to pass, the people will enjoy the peace and goodness that God desires for them.

◆ RESPONSORIAL PSALM 67: At first glance this psalm seems to be a petition for God's blessings. But when the psalm is read carefully or sung in a liturgical setting it takes on the form of a blessing. The first verse draws on the blessing of Aaron in the first reading. The subject of the blessings moves from "us" in the first verse to "the nations" in the second. Since the blessings of God are universal, all peoples will praise God.

◆ SECOND READING: In this short reading Paul states his understanding of God's plan of eternal salvation. The salvific action of God has existed from the beginning and is now revealed in and through Christ. The purpose of this event in time is to free everyone from slavery to the law as the source of salvation in order to be the sons (and daughters) of God and live in freedom. This freedom is not an unbridled human activity but a life under the free gift of grace.

◆ GOSPEL: This passage from Luke's account of the Gospel is similar to that for the Mass at Dawn on Christmas. In light of this Marian feast the focus is on Mary and Joseph as devout Jewish parents of Jesus. They follow the prescribed custom of circumcision which makes Jesus a child of the covenant. The name *Jesus*, which means "sav-

ior," is given to him in accordance with the instruction of the angel. Mary's contemplative posture gives us an example to follow in the face of the mystery of God's salvation.

The Roman Missal

The texts for this Mass are found in the Proper of Time section (the beginning of the Missal). The Gloria is sung or said, since it is the Octave of the Nativity and a solemnity. The Creed is said or sung.

The Preface assigned for today is Preface I of the Blessed Virgin Mary. For the last time this year, the proper form of the *Communicantes* for the Nativity of the Lord and its Octave is to be used if Eucharistic Prayer I, the Roman Canon, is chosen.

Interestingly, the formula of Solemn Blessing that is suggested at the end of Mass is the one for "The Beginning of the Year." Certainly the fact that this Mass is celebrated on New Year's Day (or New Year's Eve) makes this an appropriate choice, as the beginning of the new calendar year is an event that should be recognized, and one might argue it is therefore the preferred choice. Other possible Solemn Blessings, however, could be the one for "The Nativity of the Lord" (since it is the Octave of Christmas) and "The Blessed Virgin Mary" (since it is a Marian feast).

(#205)   white

Memorial of Sts. Basil the Great and Gregory Nazianzen, Bishops, Doctors of the Church

TUE 2

The Lectionary for Mass

◆ FIRST READING: At different times in 1 John, the author refers to those who have rejected Christ as dissidents, deceivers or false prophets. In this passage he calls them liars. The object of his comments may be those who were believers and have now denied their faith, or those who have lapsed in their faith. On the other hand there are those

who have been anointed. They are the ones who still hold to the teachings of Jesus the Christ; they will remain in Christ and in the Father.

◆ RESPONSORIAL PSALM 98: This is a call to joyful praise of the Lord. This psalm is used on the Sixth Sunday of Easter Time, Year B and also on Christmas Day. The psalmist praises the Lord for "wondrous deeds" in the past, deeds that have great affect on the present situation of the people. The kindness and faithfulness of the Lord, promised in the covenant, still exist. Praise of the Lord does not go out of date!

◆ TODAY'S GOSPEL passage is part of the evangelist's account of the identity and mission of John the Baptist. We learn about the Baptist through a series of questions and answers between John and two groups, Jews from Jerusalem and some Pharisees. Despite their respective efforts to connect him with the tradition of priests and prophets, John humbly replies that he is merely a messenger of one who will follow him.

The Roman Missal

The prayers for this Mass, all proper for the day, are found in the Proper of Saints at January 2. Since we are now outside the Octave, the Gloria is no longer sung or said on weekdays. The Collect asks that we may follow the example and teaching of bishops Sts. Basil and Gregory, putting it into practice in charity; the Prayer after Communion echoes that, asking that through our partaking of the Eucharist, "we may preserve in integrity the gift of faith / and walk in the path of salvation you trace for us." Consider Eucharistic Prayer II.

Today's Saints

Sts. Basil and Gregory became close friends as students in Athens. Together they fought against the

Arian heresy, which denied the full divinity of Christ. Their writings also aided the Church's understanding of the Holy Spirit and the Trinity. With Basil's brothers, Gregory of Nyssa and Peter of Sebaste, they are among the Capadocian Fathers. Gregory is known as "the Theologian" by the Eastern Churches. Basil is known as the father of Eastern monasticism and had a great influence on the development of liturgy, East and West.

W E D 3 (#206) white Christmas Weekday

Optional Memorial of the Most Holy Name of Jesus / white

The Lectionary for Mass

◆ FIRST READING: This text follows the one from yesteday and the author expands on what he means by being anointed. The anointed are those "begotten by him" who live a righteous life. This results from being the children of God and not the children of the world, because the world does not know God. This seems a bit odd since it is after all God's world. The use of the phrase "does not know" in this text means to not recognize or believe in God.

◆ RESPONSORIAL PSALM 98: The psalm selection for today repeats part of the psalm from yesterday and adds verses 5 and 6. These latter verses emphasize the psalmist exhortation to praise God by encouraging the use of musical instruments. In addition to joyful voices, festive instruments enhance the hymn of praise. Our own hymns of gladness also benefit from this combination of voices and instruments!

◆ GOSPEL: Today's reading follows the encounter of John the Baptist and those who wanted to know who he was. When he sees Jesus approaching John shifts the focus away from himself. He identifies Jesus as "the Lamb of God," an Isaian reference to the Suffering Servant. This image and title is often associated with Jesus, and Jesus uses it to refer to himself. The Baptist refers to the theophany of Jesus' baptism as proof that Jesus really is the Son of God.

The Roman Missal

Preface I, II, or III of the Nativity of the Lord may be used. If you are using the texts from the Proper of Time for Tuesday of the Weekday of Christmas, be sure to use the first Collect, "Before the Solemnity of the Epiphany," since two options are provided. Consider Eucharistic Prayer II.

Today's Optional Memorial

The name of Jesus is important. It means "God saves." His family does not choose the name of Jesus; rather, God gives it to him before his birth: "You are to name him Jesus," the angel tells Joseph in a dream, "because he will save his people from their sins" (Matthew 1:21). Jesus' name is both his identity and his mission. Jesus' name is powerful: "Whatever you ask in my name, I will do," he tells his disciples (John 14:13). In the letter to the Philippians, St. Paul sings a hymn to the power of Jesus' name: "God greatly exalted him and bestowed on him the name that is above every name, / that at the name of Jesus every knee should bend, of those in heaven and on earth and under the earth, / and every tongue confess that Jesus Christ is Lord, to the glory of God the Father" (Philippians 2:9–11).

T H U 4 (#207) white Memorial of St. Elizabeth Ann Seton, Religious

The Lectionary for Mass

◆ FIRST READING: The author continues his contrast of good and evil by indicating that there are "children of God" and "children of the Devil." The former have been begotten by God; they have the seed of God within them. The latter have no such lineage. However, the Son of God can and will destroy the works of the Devil. The example that the author gives to distinguish one from the other is whether they love their brother.

◆ RESPONSORIAL PSALM 98: The lectionary continues the use of Psalm 98. The first verse is repeated form Tuesday and Wednesday, calling on the people to "sing a new song" to the Lord. The idea of newness may not be in a new song that it is unfamiliar, but to sing what is already known with a newness of vigor and gladness. Even the sea, the rivers and the mountains are called to praise. The cosmic order can rejoice and even "clap their hands" in joy.

◆ GOSPEL: Jesus is identified by three titles in this reading: Lamb of God, Rabbi, which means "teacher" and Messiah. All three portray different aspects of Jesus' identity and mission. When two disciples ask where Jesus is staying they might be looking for his home or seeking to join those who already accompany him. The group gets larger as Andrew recruits his brother Simon Peter, and Jesus changes his name to Peter. As Peter's name is changed, so too will his life be changed.

◆ GOSPEL (SECOND OPTION): The second option presents Luke's genealogy of Jesus. Note the implicit reference to Jesus' conception through the Holy Spirit: "the son, as was thought, of Joseph" (Luke 3:23). Luke traces Jesus' ancestry all the way back to Adam, thus placing him in relationship with all humankind.

The Roman Missal

All of the prayers are proper for today and are found in the Proper of Saints at January 4. Although one of the two Prefaces of the Saints could be used, the preferred choice would be to use one of the Nativity Prefaces, in order to maintain the sense of Christmas Time.

Today's Saint

St. Elizabeth Ann Seton was born into an Episcopalian family and later in life joined the Catholic Church. She was married, a mother of five, and a founder of a religious order, the Sisters of Charity. At the invitation of the archbishop of Baltimore, Elizabeth founded a girls' school which gave rise to the parochial school system in the United States. She was canonized by Paul VI in 1975.

F R I **5** (#208) white
Memorial of St. John Neumann, Bishop

The Lectionary for Mass

◆ FIRST READING: The author of 1 John resorts to harsh words and a graphic example to emphasize his teaching. He recalls the murder of Able by his brother Cain as an example of the difference between those who are righteous and those who are evil. The righteous have love in their hearts, the evil have hatred. The love for brother and sister is a love like that of the Lord. This love must be more than just words; it must be put into action, "in deed and truth."

◆ RESPONSORIAL PSALM 100: The psalmist calls the people to five actions in their relation with the Lord: sing, serve, come before him, know, and enter his gates. In a way these are all part of the same activity; they are summoned to worship the Lord in all that they do. The summons is given to the "all the earth" for the goodness of the Lord is universal and his kindness endures forever.

◆ GOSPEL: The call to discipleship continues to spread as the first disciples invite others to follow Jesus. There seems to be a palpable excitement as John records these first days

of Jesus' public ministry. The gospel reader senses that these disciples, who will eventually be part of the Twelve are caught up in the mission this Rabbi, who is Jesus "son of Joseph, from Nazareth." The invitation of Philip to Nathanael, "come and see" is the invitation to all of us to seek the Lord in our life.

The Roman Missal

Preface I, II, or III of the Nativity of the Lord or the Epiphany may be used. The prayers for today's saint are found in the Proper of Saints.

Today's Saint

St. John Neumann (1811–1868) came to the United States from what is now called the Czech Republic with the dream of being a priest and missionary. Received with open arms by the bishop of New York, he was ordained and immediately asked to help build churches and schools for German immigrants and Native Americans. Needing spiritual support and companionship, he eventually entered a religious order, the Redemptorists, where he was made novice master and eventually vicar of all the Redemptorists in the United States. The larger Church recognized his holiness and affinity for leadership by appointing him bishop of Philadelphia, the largest diocese at the time. While bishop, he was an avid supporter of the work of religious orders, a proponent of Catholic education, and an advocate for the needs of immigrants.

S A T **6** (#209) white
Christmas Weekday

Optional Memorial of St. André Bessette, Religious / white

The Lectionary for Mass

◆ FIRST READING: The author of 1 John employs a Christology to instruct the faithful and to refute the dissidents. Jesus is the victor over the world because of his witness in water and in blood. In other

words, he was not only baptized for mission but also accepted death. There may have been some in the community who accepted baptism but rejected death as needed for Christian witness. The author states that one who is baptized in Christ must also be ready to die like Christ to achieve eternal life.

◆ RESPONSORIAL PSALM 147: The psalm underlines the relationship between God and God's people as a dialogue. God speaks and the people respond. It is always God provides the reason for praise; it is never the people's praise that causes God to act. The psalmist lists a number of deeds of God indicating that when God speaks abundant blessings flow upon the people.

◆ GOSPEL (first option): This brief text from Mark has two parts. In the first we read of John the Baptist's announcement of the arrival of Jesus as "one mightier than I." In the second we witness Jesus' baptism. John's stated unworthiness to "loosen the thongs of his sandals" is not meant to diminish his own role in preparing for the coming of the Messiah as much as it is intended to give due honor to Jesus. The baptism of Jesus marks the beginning of his public ministry.

The Roman Missal

The texts are found in the Proper of Time at the beginning of the Missal, after the Epiphany Mass during the Day, for Monday during the Weekdays of Christmas Time. Be sure you use the proper Collect—the correct one to use is the second one, for "Before the Solemnity of the Epiphany." For the Preface, you may use either the Preface of the Epiphany or one of the Prefaces of the Nativity. It might be advantageous to use the Preface of the Epiphany, in order to highlight these last days of Christmas Time. This option will be the same for each Christmas weekday between now and Saturday.

Today's Saint

St. André Bessette (1845–1937) was a brother of the Congregation of the Holy Cross in Montreal. A simple, holy man, André had a special gift of praying over the sick.

7 (#20) white
Solemnity of the Epiphany of the Lord

About Today's Solemnity

Today we celebrate that the child born in the darkness of night in a lowly manger is revealed as the manifestation (the meaning of *epiphany*) of God. Christ is revealed in many ways: as Lord, as King, as the one in whom God is present and acts. All of these manifestations are "lights" that shine on Christ, revealing a deeper understanding of who he is. All the readings for today reveal, in a way, a different manifestation of who Christ is for all who believe. Traditionally, three events in the life of Christ are remembered today as manifestations of God's presence and action through Christ: the visit of the Magi, the wedding feast of Cana, and the baptism of Jesus in the Jordan River. Lights have played an important role in today's solemnity. Parishes might follow this tradition by increasing the number of candles in church. They might be carried in the opening procession, or placed in the sanctuary, around the altar before Mass begins.

The Lectionary for Mass: Vigil and during the Day

◆ FIRST READING: Isaiah addresses Jerusalem, a symbol of the chosen people of Israel. He calls them to "rise up in splendor" because the light of Lord, the salvation of God has arrived. This great blessing brings a new mission for them. They will be a light for the nations; they will be the messengers of the wondrous deeds of the Lord. No longer will they be enslaved by other nations; in fact other nations will bring them riches from afar.

◆ RESPONSORIAL PSALM 72: The psalmist petitions God for blessings upon the king. The king not only acts on behalf of God but must have the justice and compassion of God. No small task for a monarch. One of the king's particular responsibilities is to treat the poor and the afflicted with special concern, just as the Lord would do.

◆ SECOND READING: The issue of the whether the Gentiles could inherit salvation without first becoming Jewish was a contentious one for the early Church. Paul, who came to be known as the Apostle to the Gentiles, makes it clear that God has always intended that the Gentiles receive the grace of salvation. Paul believes he has been appointed to reveal the truth that the salvation of God is open to all, because all are from God.

◆ GOSPEL: The importance of this story within the Christmas narrative lies in its theological meaning. Jesus' birth has significance far beyond the religious boundaries and expectations of his ancestors. The intervention of God in human history will have universal repercussions and people of every time and nation will be drawn to Son of God.

The Roman Missal: At the Vigil Mass

The Gloria is sung or said today. The Creed is said or sung. Light, splendor, brightness, shining, appearance—these are the themes that are conveyed in the three orations for this Mass. The Preface used is for the Epiphany of the Lord, which is found after the third Preface of the Nativity. There is no mention that the proper form of the *Communicantes* for the Epiphany of the Lord is to be used if the Roman Canon is prayed. This is because the Vigil Mass is a distinct Mass with its own set of texts and, as it were, its own focus. The proper form of the *Communicantes* for the Epiphany of the Lord only refers to "the most sacred day" whereas the form for the Nativity of the Lord, for example, has the option of using either "night" or "day." Thus, the insert should not be used at the Vigil Mass. Aside from that, there is a certain validity to using Eucharistic Prayer III at this Mass, which echoes Baruch in the line "from the rising of the sun to its setting." The same principle would apply for the Announcement of Easter and the Moveable Feasts (the "Epiphany Proclamation"—see below, At the Mass during the Day). Since no mention is made of it here but it is mentioned at the Mass during the Day, it is something that is envisioned to be done only on the day itself, not at the Vigil. Be sure to use the Solemn Blessing at the end of Mass, the one for the Epiphany of the Lord (#4).

The Roman Missal: At the Mass during the Day

The Gloria is sung or said today. The Creed is said or sung. The Preface assigned for today is the Preface of the Epiphany of the Lord, which can be found after the Preface III of the Nativity of the Lord. For the Final Blessing, be sure to use the Solemn Blessing for the Epiphany of the Lord (#4).

The Epiphany Proclamation

The Epiphany Proclamationg is optional. If done, it should be chanted from the ambo after the Gospel reading and before the homily. A deacon or cantor chants the Proclamation. No allowance seems to be made for the priest to do so. While *The Roman Missal* indicates that the Christmas and Easter Proclamations may be recited if no competent minister is available to sing them, and even includes the text without music, no such rubric is included for the Epiphany Proclamation, suggesting that if it is not chanted, it should be omitted.

Other Ideas

Have a parish Epiphany party, complete with a King Cake. Encourage children to dress as figures in the sacred story. Sing "We Three Kings" and remember the trust and courage of those who journeyed through danger to the crib of the Lord. Mark the doors of the parish with the traditional chalking of 20 + C + M +B + 18. Provide chalk and instructions to members. Encourage them to take holy water home and together bless the rooms of their homes.

This is also National Migration Week. In an age when millions are refugees and migrants due to war and other forces, we remember families throughout the world that face devastating hardship and displacement. Education on key issues via the parish bulletin, website, and social media page can help parishioners realize that the treatment of migrants and refugees is not only a political issue, but an issue of faith and justice as well.

MON 8 (#21) white
Feast of the Baptism of the Lord

About Today's Feast

The Feast of the Baptism of the Lord proclaims a theophany, a revelation or manifestation of the divine Sonship of Jesus by his anointing and appointment to his messianic office. It is the feast that proclaims the Baptism that elevates believers to the status of sons and daughters of God. The First Reading (and psalm) and/or the Second Reading from Year A may be used. The Lectionary commentary that follows below pertains to Year B.

The Lectionary for Mass

◆ FIRST READING: The oracle of Isaiah can be understood in two parts. The first is the invitation of the Lord to all peoples to be refreshed by the generosity of God. The offer of water and food are metaphors for the abundance of God's providence that is extended to everyone. The second outlines the way of life that is expected of the covenant people. They are to turn to the Lord whose Word will make them fruitful, just as the rain enriches the earth.

◆ CANTICLE: Today's canticle from Isaiah gives thanks to the Lord for he is the source of blessings. The symbol of water as a source of refreshment is like the gift of salvation that brings life to the people.

◆ SECOND READING: The author of 1 John presents a Trinitarian theology. Jesus comes from the Father ("is begotten") and the Spirit testifies that what God has accomplished in Christ is the truth. Jesus' mission on behalf of the Father began with his baptism, and ended in blood with his Death on the Cross. The heart of the Trinity is love, God's love of the son and the son's love of us. We participate in the life of the Trinity by loving both God and others.

◆ GOSPEL: The proclamation of John acts as a conclusion of the prophetic tradition. Jesus' arrival at the Jordan signals the beginning of a new tradition in the covenantal relationship between God and all God's people.

The Roman Missal

Two options for the Collect are offered in the Missal. The Prayer over the Offerings calls to our attention that the Holy Spirit is always the active transforming agent at work in the Church. The Preface is given right there along with the other Mass formularies for the day. The Prayer after Communion reminds us that, having been nourished with the sacred gifts, we must be God's children. The Gloria is sung today. Since today's feast of the Lord falls on a Monday, the Creed is omitted.

ORDINARY TIME DURING WINTER

The Liturgical Time

The Meaning

THE winter portion of Ordinary Time is but a few weeks. We may think that this time is ordinary in the sense of "run of the mill." However, the term *ordinary* derives from the word "ordinal," or numbered, as the Sundays in Ordinary time are numerically ordered. The time between the close of Christmas Time with the Baptism of the Lord and Ash Wednesday's introduction to Lent does not have to be fallow; it can be a time in which our faith can flourish and grow, "greening" in the spirit of this season's liturgical color. Perhaps one of the great opportunities of Ordinary Time — whether in winter or summer — is to make our discipleship visible not only through our words but also through our deeds. In this way, Ordinary Time becomes anything but ordinary.

The Lectionary for Mass

THE Lectionary helps us understand just how important it is for our liturgical assemblies by reminding us of our call to follow Jesus and guiding our reflection on who is the Messiah.

The First Readings in the Weekday Lectionary, Year II take us on a tour of the historical books of 1 and 2 Samuel and 1 Kings. The passages from these books introduce us to Saul, David, and Solomon, and their ups and downs leading the people of Israel. From faithfulness to infidelity and back again, their stories testify to God's mercy and constant care for his people. The Lord will forever triumph. There are days when the Lord's people will be divided, and out to get each other. There are days when the people forget their promise of covenant faithfulness and turn to worship idols. The story of the people of Israel—including the sins of the leaders—is also our story. Just as God continually calls them back, so God invites us to return to him. God's invitation for us to return to faithfulness in not an invitation reserved for Lent. Even in the first weeks of Ordinary Time, God invites for we need that invitation. The New Testament letter of James, from which the First Readings the two days prior to Ash Wednesday come, reminds us how God calls us to persevere in the face of temptations that stem from our distorted human desires. Yet when temptations get the best of us, God still invites us back through the mercy of Jesus Christ.

The Responsorial Psalms of the weekdays during this period of Ordinary Time reflect thanksgiving for God's faithfulness and mercy, as well as petitions for us to remain faithful to the divine statutes. They acclaim our Lord as the King of Glory. There is no other king like our God. Would that we could forever trust in God and mirror God's own faithfulness to us!

The Gospel readings take us from Mark 2 through Mark 8. As we make our way through thee texts, we hear over and over again narratives of Jesus teaching, exorcising demons, and healing the sick. We hear feeding miracles and the miracles of Jesus walking on water and the extraordinary event of Jesus calming the stormy sea. Many of these events greatly disturb the Pharisees and scribes, even those who might have thought themselves relatives of Jesus think he is not in his right mind.

Jesus and his disciples journey back and forth and from side to side of the Sea of Galilee multiple times. We journey with Jesus and his disciples (although we might forget on which side of the Sea of Galilee we are on!), as do the crowds who we hear are always there with them, and frequently arrive before them. The crowds are so desirous of Jesus and the power that emanates from him and his Word. While Mark portrays the Pharisees and scribes as troubled because Jesus teaches and heals on the Sabbath and his disciples do not follow human traditions, Mark also repeatedly references the hardness of the disciples' hearts. Often the disciples just do not understand Jesus and his teaching. Are we not the same some times? Let us take this period of Ordinary Time to see how our hearts can become less hard to the truth of the Gospel Jesus proclaims in his very person and mission. How can we remain faithful followers even knowing that there will be times when we are not accepted in our native place as happened to Jesus?

The Gospel reading for the Second Sunday in Ordinary Time is from John's Gospel account. Jesus, the Lamb of God, calls two of John the Baptist's disciples to follow him. Through this Gospel reading, we too, hear our own call again. The Gospel readings for the following three Sundays come from Mark. We hear Jesus' call to repent for the time of fulfillment is at hand. He teaches on a Sabbath and cures the sick. We know he is the Messiah, the Son of God. Yet once again we go on the journey with the Gospel writer, Mark, to delve deeper into his identity — even before Mark himself reveals it to his readers.

When we look at the First Readings for the Sundays during this period, we see they come from a variety of books of the Old Testament. 1 Samuel, Jonah, Job, and Deuteronomy are the books from which the First Readings are taken. The readings give us stories of call, questioning, and perseverance. They, like the weekday readings, remind us that God never leaves his people. For Christians, we believe God came to dwell among us in the Messiah, whose identity is gradually being revealed in the Gospel readings.

How to live in the interim before the Lord comes again is the subject of the Second Readings from 1 Corinthians in the Sunday Lectionary for this time. By his own example, Paul teaches us how to be single-minded in our proclamation of the Gospel. As he instructs the Corinthian community how to overcome some of their divisions, his teaching challenges us to find ways to live as cohesive come until the Lord comes again in glory. The source of our unity is Christ and the Gospel. The Responsorial Psalms of the Second through the Fourth Sundays in Ordinary Time are psalms of praise and thanksgiving. They too, like the weekday psalms for this period, ask God to instruct us in his ways. Psalm 95 calls us to harden not our hearts, but be open to the Lord.

During these brief weeks, the Lectionary also provides us with particular readings for the Feasts of the Conversion of St. Paul, Sts. Timothy and Titus, and the Presentation of the Lord. Perhaps as we come to the close of these weeks and arrive at Ash Wednesday, we might consider with Simeon how our eyes have seen God's salvation in Jesus Christ, and how his words and actions of healing, exorcising, and feeding have helped us to soften our hearts just a little more. How are we more mature disciples, open to the presence of the Lord in our lives at the end of this time? How have the Lectionary readings strengthened our faith so we are ready to begin the serious work of Lent?

The Roman Missal

WHILE we experience depths of reflection in Advent and Lent and heights of joy in Christmas Time and Easter Time, in Ordinary Time we get down to the business of living in Christ and being Church. Every Sunday is an Easter, a celebration of the Paschal Mystery. The weekly cycle constitutes Christians' most ancient cycle, in which we hear the Word, gather at table, and expect Christ's return in glory. We take time to contemplate the sacred mysteries, the life of Christ, and our life together. So, in the Fourth Sunday, we pray, "that we may honor you with all our mind, and love everyone in truth of heart" (Collect) and, in the Fifth Sunday, that "relying solely on the hope of heavenly grace, / [we] may be defended always by your protection" (Collect).

The Gloria and Creed are sung or said on all Sundays in Ordinary Time, but not on weekdays. On Sundays, we should use the prayers provided for that day in the Missal. Although it should be done with discretion, weekday feasts of special importance to a particular community (or of a higher rank in the General Roman Calendar) can be transferred to a Sunday in Ordinary Time, and

then we use the texts for that feast rather than those of the Sunday in Ordinary Time. On weekdays, though, we can use any of the thirty-three Masses in Ordinary Time, which brings out the unitive character of the season. We can use Eucharistic Prayer IV, which has its own proper preface, during Ordinary Time. When we use the other Eucharistic Prayers, however, there are eight Prefaces for Ordinary Time to choose from for Sundays. On weekdays we use one of the six Common Prefaces. As for the other seasons, there are sample formularies for the Universal Prayer in Appendix V.

Children's Liturgy of the Word

DEVOTE as much care to your preparation for children's Liturgy of the Word on the Sundays of Ordinary Time as you did during Advent and Christmas. Work closely with the liturgical musicians regarding weekly or seasonal psalmody and any change that will occur in the arrangement of the Gospel Acclamation. The cantor for the celebration of the Word with children should follow the same cantor principles and procedures as the cantor in the main assembly and use similar gestures to invite the children's participation.

Green is the color for Ordinary Time. Change any banners or cloths that you use to enhance the liturgical space where the children celebrate the Word to this color, and allow time for the children to notice and process the change on the Second Sunday in Ordinary Time. The Gospel on the Sixth Sunday in Ordinary Time is Luke's account of the Beatitudes. Decide whether or not you will have the Beatitudes visually posted somewhere in the liturgical space.

If your parish has small groups that meet weekly to discuss the readings for the coming Sunday, you might choose to participate in one of them. You might hear ideas you could use in the reflection with children. If you are unable to participate, consider contacting someone you know who does to see if they would be willing to share the essence of the discussion. Early to midweek, consider speaking with the priest or deacon who will be the homilist. Inquire about the core message they are mulling over for their homily. Perhaps you will want to choose to connect the children's reflection in some way to the homily the main assembly will hear.

Use or adapt the Prayer of the Faithful from LTP's weekly resource of *Children's Liturgy of the Word* and from the intercessions the main assembly will pray. Invite the children to contribute prayers before the final intercession for those who have died and now live in God's eternal Kingdom. Going forward, you might choose to discuss the possibility of a children's Liturgy of the Word team member serving as a member on your parish's liturgy committee or occasionally attending a meeting. This will enhance communication about seasonal details and changes.

The Saints

AFTER the business of Christmas Time, Ordinary Time in winter is a return to the quiet business of life. This is also mirrored in the calendar of saints, as there are fewer celebrations on the calendar. At the end of January, however, we once again have a group of saints' days. January 25 is the Feast of the Conversion of St. Paul. Christians of many confessions celebrate this octave of prayer in the eight days that run from January 18–25. It's an appropriate time, as Sts. Peter and Paul are both powerful symbols of the diversity of the early Church and its insistence on unity in Christ. St. Paul's mission to the Gentiles was controversial, and St. Peter was not always a supporter. During this week, Catholics and other Christians should pray for forgiveness, for wisdom, and for the unity that is the gift of Christ. The following day, January 26, the Church remembers two of Paul's associates, Sts. Timothy and Titus. Both men are described by Paul as eager coworkers who were motivated out of love for Christ and the Christian community. Traditionally, St. Timothy is regarded as the first bishop of Ephesus, and St. Titus the first bishop of Crete.

Two important women are celebrated at the beginning of February: St. Agatha on February 5, and St. Scholastica on February 10. St. Agatha was a virgin from Sicily who accepted martyrdom rather than break her vow to Christ. She is a widely beloved saint, and is invoked as help against fire, volcanic eruption, and earthquakes. She was the twin sister of St. Benedict and the Abbess of a community of nuns. In the *Life of St. Benedict,* written by St. Gregory the Great, Scholastica is the only figure who prevails over her brother. After their annual visit, she asks him to remain longer and he refuses (so that he does not violate his own *Rule*). Her prayer to God is answered, and Benedict is prevented from leaving by a rainstorm — Gregory's only explanation is that "she could do more because she loved more." Even the rigor of the rule is overcome by love.

The Liturgy of the Hours

WINTER Ordinary Time begins on Tuesday, January 9. Remember to begin again with week one of the Psalter.

January 15 is Martin Luther King Day. This is another opportunity to use the Liturgy of the Hours in your parish. Consider an Evening Prayer liturgy with the themes of justice and peace. If you need help with readings and psalms, begin with the Lectionary. Volume 4 has suggestions and these can be implemented into an evening prayer format. Some ideas for psalmody include Psalms 15, 113, 122, 131, and 146.

Because it is not Mass, this is also a great style of prayer to use for ecumenical services. Does your parish participate in the Week of Prayer for Christian Unity? If not, maybe this is the year to start. Are there projects or goals for your neighborhood? Can the local churches organize prayer around these events? Our tradition of Morning and Evening Prayer are well suited for this.

Ash Wednesday is February 14, Valentine's Day in the popular culture. Plan ahead for this natural conflict. Evening Prayer on the Sunday prior may be an option. Add a blessing for married couples or even have them renew their vows. The appendix of the ritual book for the Sacrament of Matrimony has options. If it is a family event, their children will experience an amazing witness to the sacrament. Since the presider for the Liturgy of the Hours may be a layperson, there is no need to add one more item to the pastor's schedule so close to Lent. Maybe a husband and wife can share the responsibilities. Make sure to discern carefully who has the gifts to lead prayer. Follow with a simple dinner and end with Night Prayer.

Music is always important. Again, with Lent looming just days away, be careful not to place burdensome expectations on your music minister. It's not necessary. While the psalms could be spoken, are there cantors in your parish who can lead common psalms acapella? Perhaps an instrumentalist can play appropriately and gently as the psalms are spoken. They can be said in an antiphonal format (side A one stanza, side B the next) or responsorial like at Mass or even communally.

The Rite of Christian Initiation of Adults

THE Period of the Precatechumenate or Inquiry is a special time in the RCIA process. Many parishes "celebrate" this period for only a few weeks in the fall. They advertise that the RCIA will begin on this or that date. This "school-year" model does not allow inquirers the opportunity to knock on our doors when the Spirit calls them or the time needed to explore their questions and discern whether they are called to enter the Catechumenate. Parishes need to evaluate their model of evangelization and ask how welcoming and hospitable they are to those who come seeking the Lord. The baptized are constantly called to give witness of their life in Christ in word and deed. It is the community's love and worship of Christ that draws people to inquire and ask about Jesus.

Liturgy committees and RCIA teams might consider developing an inquiry team. This team could include five to six families who rotate hosting an inquiry session once or twice a month (see RCIA, 38). This allows broad participation in the process without overburdening a few. Each month, the hosting family provides hospitality and shares their story (for example, how they came to know Christ, joys and sorrows, riches of the faith). This can allows candidates to begin naming God's grace in their own lives. Catechists must be equipped with the tools to tie these narratives together with the narrative of the Paschal Mystery. This is a time to explore the Gospel and to discern the movement of the Holy Spirit.

The Period of the Precatechumenate comes to end at the celebration of the Rite of Acceptance into the Order of Catechumens, which begins the Period of the Catechumenate. Parishes are encouraged to celebrate this rite several times during the year (see RCIA, 18, 44). This instruction presumes that a parish, as an initiating and evangelizing community, has an ongoing or year-round process where individuals can inquire about the faith at any time (precatechumenate); when it is discerned a group in the precatechumenate is ready to proceed to the next period, they are invited to celebrate the Rite of Acceptance. This should not be delayed if possible (see RCIA, 18.1).

This rite is the first time the candidates will publicly gather and "declare their intention to the Church and the Church in turn . . . accepts them as persons who intend to become its members" (41). The celebration of this rite is not automatic. For example, not everyone who inquires in April will be accepted in the summer or fall. Their inquiry period may last a bit longer. Each individual case requires discernment. Article 42 of the rite provides a few insights to help guide the process. Evidence of faith, initial conversion, repentance, and nurturing a life of prayer are some of the signs that help discern readiness.

The Rite of Acceptance is a rich celebration, and every attention needs to be given to its preparation and execution. It is also important the ritual does not overshadow the celebration of the Eucharist. The preparation team might especially consider the Second, Twenty-Fourth, and Twenty-Ninth Sundays in Ordinary Time. The Scripture readings on these days highlights the ritual action of taking up the cross and the journey of discipleship. Consider what ritual music the parish can learn to help highlight the action and draw the faithful into prayer. From the opening dialogue to the signing of the senses to the dismissal, carefully choreograph the movement from outside the worship space into the church so everyone is able to participate and witness this call to conversion.

Sacraments of Initiation

BAPTISM is the entryway into the Christian faith. With his baptism, Jesus showed us the way in the beginning of his ministry, he is our brother and we are all of God's children. It is appropriate to occasionally use our baptismal promises in place of the creed. Because members are often baptized as infants, it is helpful to invite the baptized to reflect upon their own initiation.

This may also help young parents to appreciate their own Baptism. We are baptized into a community of faith that has promised to support us spiritually and help us grow in the faith. It is essential that we walk the journey together.

The Eucharist is food for the journey of faith. We share food together with people we trust. Once again we celebrate gathering at the Lord's table in the community. It is an appropriate time of the year for children who are preparing for the sacrament individually to receive during a Sunday liturgy.

In Confirmation, "By [the] gift of the Holy Spirit the fiathful are more fully conformed to Christ and are strengthened with the power to bear witness to Christ for the buidling up of his Body in faith and charity" (*Order of Confirmation*, 2). The sponsors and the faith community gather to witness this commitment. We know that as disciples we are all companions on the journey. Candidates may attend a Confirmation retreat at any time of the year, it helps to engage the community in the preparation process when parishioners are invited to be prayer partners for the candidates.

The Rite of Penance

How shall Lent unfold this year? Mark's account of the Gospel is one of urgency directed toward the Cross. What does this mean in your parish, at this time? We can tend to both ignore or sentimentalize the cross. As you prepare to enter Lent, what type of Penance services will you offer? How many are needed? Do you/should you share liturgies with neighboring parishes? Don't let Ash Wednesday surprise you.

As you prepare, now is the time to involve others in the groundwork for the Lenten penance services, both sacramental and non-sacramental. Discern which type and when they will be celebrated. For example, will your school or faith formation classes have their own services? What would that look like? Perhaps it can be done by grade or a small cluster of grades. Since we're looking ahead there is time to invite the class or their leaders into a prayerful discussion about what are the sins and brokenness for them. Don't presume to know the world of sixth graders. Suggestions for the examination of conscience and readings may surface.

Remember to adapt the services to the ages involved, but don't rewrite the wisdom of the Church. It is important to root our younger disciples in the ritual tradition. It makes them feel like they belong (they do) and encourages participation since it has a familiar pattern. Also reflect on who will preside at the services. The wisdom from the *Directory for Masses with Children* can be applied here as well. Not everyone can speak to children skillfully. It is a gift. Even if the pastor is celebrating the sacrament, perhaps a catechist should offer a short reflection. Also, in non-sacramental services, remember liturgical gifts are not the same as catechetical gifts. Discern who has the appropriate ones for the ritual.

This same wisdom can be applied to other groups that gather in the parish. Now is the time to invite the women's group or their leaders to reflect on sinfulness and from what they hope to heal in Lent. The Knights of Columbus, youth group, and so on, should also add their wisdom. Consider too whether each group could have their own nonsacramental celebration during Lent in preparation for a parish sacramental celebration. Remember, we're attempting to not overburden our priests. Depending on your choices, others can help in this preparation.

The Order of Celebrating Matrimony

Our parishes have couples in various stages of Marriage preparation. Some are young adults. Some are older adults. Some are entering first marriages and some are beginning second ones. All are in need of the community's support and prayer.

There are many ways to invite the community to pray for the engaged. With their permission, include a picture on the parish website or social media page. On the week before the wedding, invite parishioners to pray for the couple or even attend the liturgy. You can even ask teens in the parish to be involved in not only prayer, but perhaps assisting at the weddings (which is a wonderful way to expose youth to the ritual aspects of Marriage rather than what they have already seen on TV or in movies). Young children can send them congratulation cards. What is needed? Be creative. Make sure that Marriage is seen within the context of the whole parish, not just as an outside event.

On the Sunday before Valentine's Day, February 11 in 2018, it is customary in many places to have a special blessing for couples celebrating significant anniversaries, such as 25, 50, and 60. See appendix III in the ritual book for appropriate prayers and the renewal of their commitment. If there will be a Mass for anniversaries on a day other than Sunday, see *The Roman Missal*, Masses for Various Needs and Occasions 11.

When do you bless engaged couples? An Order of Blessing is found in the ritual book, appendix II. This Order of Blessing is intended to be adapted (see OCM, 218). Notice too that this ritual may be led by a priest, deacon, or layperson (see OCM, 220). If Marriage preparation is a communal event involving many couples, perhaps the rite would be a way to end the day.

However, Marriage in our faith is more than just promises made between two people. It is joining of families. It is about a faith journey lived in the midst of our community. In this light, perhaps the blessing could be done a couple times a year. Parents with the appropriate gifts could take leadership roles in the prayer. In reflecting on the parish schedule, can you tie this prayer to another event? Perhaps a parish ice cream social, youth group, or even faith formation classes. Liturgy, while always about offering praise and thanks to God, has a catechetical dimension. This witness to our younger parishioners teaches them about the sacrament.

The Pastoral Care of the Sick

AFTER the "call" texts from John (Second Sunday) and Mark (Third Sunday), we read three successive healing stories from Mark on the Fourth, Fifth, and Sixth Sundays. In the first (Fourth Sunday), Jesus heals a man in the synagogue of an unclean spirit. In the second (Fifth Sunday), he heals Simon's mother-in-law, as well as many who were sick with various diseases. In the third story (Sixth Sunday), he heals the man with leprosy.

These Scripture texts provide the homilist with a breath of material for preaching about the remarkable intervention of God through the power

of the Spirit in human affairs, especially in the times when suffering and brokenness enter our lives. The encounters of Jesus with those he heals are moments of compassion and mercy.

The Sacrament of the Anointing of the Sick is the Church's ritual celebration of the mercy of God for our brothers and sisters who are ill. The prayers, readings, and gestures that comprise the rite speak so clearly of the tender care that the Father has for those who struggle with pain and weakness.

Since this sacrament, like all the sacraments, is more fully expressed when it is a communal celebration, the parish should consider arranging for such a celebration on one of these Sundays. Perhaps the obvious choice of the three Sundays is the Sixth Sunday in Ordinary Time (February 11), which is the World Day of Prayer for the Sick. It is also the optional Memorial of Our Lady of Lourdes, although the Sunday takes precedence over the observance. It was Pope John Paul II who added the designation to the memorial.

The Anointing of the Sick could take place during the Sunday liturgies using a shorter form of the rite. Such a celebration requires a good deal of preparation that includes announcements well ahead of time so people can make arrangements to be present. Extra ministers of hospitality will be needed for those who require assistance. Transportation from healthcare residences will need to be provided. Although a special liturgy could be scheduled apart from the regular Sunday Masses, there is a profound witness given to the whole parish when the sacrament is celebrated with the community. The pastoral notes for the rite speak of the witness that those who are sick give to others; a witness that reflects the redemptive grace that flows to all of us from Christ's own suffering.

Two other days during this season can be opportunities to highlight the place of this sacrament in the life of the parish. On the Feast of the Presentation of the Lord (Friday, February 2) it is customary to bless and distribute candles. (See *The Roman Missal* for the blessing). The Gospel passage from Luke tells the moving story of Jesus' parents meeting Simeon and Anna in the Temple. The Canticle of Simeon is a beautiful prayer for those who are experiencing great sickness, and could bring some comfort to those whose illness is terminal.

Pastoral care visitors could take one of the blessed candles to give to those they visit as a reminder that the whole parish continues to keep them in prayer. On Saturday, February 3, the Church celebrates the Memorial of St. Blaise. The custom of blessing throats on this day is kept in many parishes and could be part of a liturgy of anointing the sick. Pastoral care ministers may also bless the throats of those whom they visit on this day; the prayer of blessing is found in the *Book of Blessings* (see chapter 51).

The Order of Christian Funerals

THIS month between Christmas and Lent can be a busy and forgotten time. We are usually both looking backward in cleaning up Christmas and forward in readying ourselves for Lent. Funerals can seem like an interruption. Don't let them be so.

Take some time to evaluate your practices, especially how your parish attends to the Rite of Committal. A pastor's busy schedule, or two funerals on one day, may cause this part of the *Order of Christian Funerals* to be overlooked. While a much shorter part of the ritual, it gives closure to our prayer. Also, since it may occur in a chapel at the cemetery or at the grave side, the reality of death can be harsh and the Church's witness and care are important.

Reflection on the practical practices of your parish staff are also important. When a family or the funeral home calls, how are they greeted? What about inquiries from nonparishioners or family members, especially those who may have left the Church? They may not even know how to ask their questions. The support staff who answers the phone should be ready to help. What may seem like odd questions are usually a grieving person's struggle to ask for something difficult. It may be the first time they are preparing a funeral or they are embarrassed to call a church if they have not been with us for a while.

Ordinary Time is a great opportunity to go over with the support staff common questions or language that might be used by the less church going or non-Catholics. For example, when a family member inquiries about a "memorial Mass," what are they really asking? Is it a Mass with cremated remains present instead of a body? That is

still be a Funeral Liturgy. Perhaps they mean a second Funeral Liturgy, or another type of private celebration. It could also mean a Mass intention for a regularly scheduled liturgy. Whoever is answering the phone should be trained and ready with follow up questions asked in kindness. This is another opportunity for healing and gentleness, or it can be perceived as a time of judgment. Let's be ready and careful.

Adult faith formation around these issues may also help. It is helpful to explain all the parts of our beautiful Funeral Liturgy, as well as quell any concerns with regard to issues such as cremation. Invite a local funeral director and perhaps even a representative from the cemetery. This is not meant to be a sales opportunity for them, but it is a way for our parishioners to get a clearer view of what happens at the time of death. Since participants may be seniors or family members of ill parishioners, it also provides an opportunity to reassure them of the hope in our faith and of our care and concern for them.

The Book of Blessings

DURING this shorter period of Ordinary Time, the optional Memorial of St. Blaise takes place. It may seem odd that an observance remembering the fourth-century bishop of Sebaste in Armenia is popular in the United States and throughout much of the Christian world. But since the eighth century his cult has spread throughout the Church (see BB, 1625). St. Blaise's miraculous healing of a little boy with a fishbone stuck in his throat sparked the medieval imagination. Today, he is associated not only with healing diseases of the throat, but also healing and soundness of body in general. Using the Order for the Blessing of Throats on the Feast of St. Blaise (see BB, chapter 51) is customary in many parishes in the United States and makes sense, especially in those parts of the country where February 3 finds us in the depths of winter and cold/flu season. Indeed, "Part of the plan laid out by God's providence is that we should fight strenuously against all sickness and carefully seek the blessings of good health, so that we may fulfill our role in human society and in the Church" (*Pastoral Care of the Sick*, 3). This blessing can be especially evocative and memorable, as it uses two candlesticks blessed at the Feast of the

Presentation of the Lord, which takes place on the preceding day, February 2. Orders are provided for celebrating the blessing within Mass (see BB, 1630–1635), where the blessing of throats takes place after the homily and Universal Prayer, and within a celebration of the Word of God (see BB, 1636–1650). It can also be celebrated at Morning or Evening Prayer after the reading/responsory/homily and before the Gospel Canticle. For the sick or homebound, the blessing (probably the shorter rite; see BB, 1651–1655) can be given at home or at a healthcare or assisted living institution. Ideally, each individual present at the celebration is blessed, but when circumstances make this impractical the blessing may be said over the entire assembly at the same time.

The Liturgical Environment

ORDINARY Time during winter is very short; instead of thinking of it as the waiting period before Lent, perhaps it is a good time to re-group and think about what is happening in the life of Jesus. During this season, Jesus is leaving us signs to help us grow closer to him and to hold onto during his Passion.

In the readings we see that Jesus is inviting men to become his followers. They will later be known as his disciples. Since most of Jesus' disciples were fishermen, Jesus used their jobs to teach them how to become "Fishers of Men." In addition, Jesus was also performing many miracles, casting out demons, healing the sick.

So how do we incorporate these miracles, and make them visible to our congregations? How do we make an act become concrete, something we can see or touch? We might try by using different colors of green in our environment that mix well with the color blue. For example, the green shade of evergreen trees mixes well with many shades of blue. Water is also an underlying symbol these weeks. First of all, John the Baptist was the first person to know that Jesus was Lord, and he pointed out to two men that Jesus was "the Rabbi" they had been waiting for. John was also the person who baptized Jesus.

Since fish and nets are such a dominant visual aid in the readings, we could use pieces of fishing net as part of the environment. Drape blue fabric

and fishing net over a modest bench. To make it look realistic, try and find netting that is made from rope, like the Apostles would have used. Place pieces of stones on the floor to hold the fabric and netting in place. Seashells may be a little much, but play with them and see how it looks!

Use blue/green materials for banners and altar scarves. Something very beautiful for this time of year is a banner made to look like a mosaics by using different colors of blues and greens to resemble water and life.

Use the same fabric from the mosaics and add to the other aspects of the liturgical environment to create a cohesive look to the space.

The Liturgical Music

KEEP the music festive so that the transition to Lent will be noticeable. If you are going to use a new hymn at Easter, introduce it now and use it for a few weeks now so that it won't be new at Easter. Hymns focused on the Resurrection are appropriate any Sunday, not just during Easter Time.

If your parish is not accustomed to singing the proper Entrance or Communion Antiphons, Ordinary Time could be a good time to introduce the practice. *The General Instruction of the Roman Missal* lists four options for singing during the Entrance and Communion Processions. The first option is the antiphon from the Missal or the antiphon and psalm from the *Graduale Romanum*. The second is the antiphon and psalm from the *Graduale Simplex*. The third is a chant from another collection of approved psalms and antiphons. The fourth is another suitable liturgical chant. It is important to note that the frequent use of the word chant in the Missal does not mean the music during these specified times has to take the form of Gregorian chant, although it doesn't preclude it either since Gregorian chant has pride of place in the musical tradition of the liturgy.

The Missal's preference for the use of the appointed texts is a reminder of the universality of the Mass as people in every parish throughout the world use the same texts for worship, each in their own language of course. It also serves as a reminder of the pride of place of Scripture in the liturgy. After the Second Vatican Council, many parishes fell into the rut of what has been dubbed the "four hymn syndrome" meaning hymns were sung at the four transitional movements of the Mass: the Entrance Procession, the Preparation of the Gifts and the Altar, the Communion Procession, and the Recessional. Perhaps it is time to rethink that phenomenon and relook at what the Church envisions. A good approach to selecting the music for Mass is to include the best music of our two thousand plus year liturgical tradition with the best of the music that has been written in recent years.

Saint Meinrad Entrance and Communion Antiphons for the Church Year: Modal Settings of Roman Missal Texts in Modern Notation by Columba Kelly, OSB (OCP), a prayerful collection with several volumes, is a great resource for assemblies seeking to implement English chant into their repertoire. Two fine resources that draw upon the *Graduale Simplex* include the hymnal *By Flowing Waters* by Paul Ford (Liturgical Press) and the collection *Communion Chants for the Church Year* by Charles Thatcher (WLP). Other contemporary settings of the Missal antiphons and psalms have been published as well.

Liturgical Ministers

ONGOING training for liturgical ministers is essential for vibrant worship. Invite the homilists and preachers in your community to reflect on the texts of the liturgy, the various parts of the Mass and how the different liturgical ministries support the full, conscious, and active participation of the gathered Church. Consider having a day of reflection for liturgical ministers before the season of Lent begins. Invite the director of the (arch)diocesan office of worship or other liturgical experts in the local Church to provide ongoing formation liturgical ministers. Perhaps your parish could host a diocesan, vicariate, or deanery gathering. Include new and seasoned ministers in the training sessions. On the Sixth Sunday in Ordinary Time include a blessing for all who exercise pastoral service in the parish (see part VI of the *Book of Blessings*).

Other Prayers, Rites, and Devotions

DEPENDING when Easter falls, this span of Ordinary Time differs year to year and is actually replete with blessings, including the blessing of candles for the Feast of the Presentation of the Lord on February 2 or blessing throats on the following day in honor of St. Blaise on February 3. The Vatican keeps up their crèche in St. Peter's Square, as well as many Polish parishes, for the forty days following Christmas (this is a holdover from the pre–Vatican II liturgical calendar, wherein the Presentation of the Lord ended the Christmas season). Keeping those poinsettias looking fresh can be challenge.

Catholic Schools Week also occurs during this period, beginning the last Sunday of January. This might be a time to refresh children in their "Catholicity." Bring the students over for a tour of their own church, using this time to explain Catholic symbols, especially in architecture. If you're fortunate to worship in an older, more ornate building, one will not be without material to speak about. Take the older students on a field trip to neighboring churches. Many parishes are more than happy to host a group during a weekday.

This period of Ordinary Time also includes the Week of Prayer for Christian Unity at the end of January. This is an opportune time to teach children about other denominations and their places of worship.

Worldwide Marriage Encounter (www.WWME.org) promotes World Marriage Day on the Second Sunday of February (many times coinciding with St. Valentine's Day). This may be a time to honor married couples in the parish. After one of the weekend Masses, host a reception for all those couples celebrating an anniversary on the fives (5th, 10th, 20th, and so on; after five years, all parish couples have been honored). Either at the end of the Universal Prayer or at the end of the weekend Masses, invite all married couples to stand and offer a blessing taken from the *Book of Blessings*. Their witness of marital love is a wonderful sign of commitment to the assembly. And finally, don't let Mardi Gras get away without a one final hurrah! Many parishes invite parishioners to bring their blessed palm branches back to church weeks before Ash Wednesday to be burned.

This is also a good way of relieving people of dried palms and not knowing what to do with them in lieu of otherwise throwing them away. Gather the weekday assembly after Mass on Monday or Mardi Gras (Fat Tuesday) and burn them in a suitable container out front of church or in the parking lot. Encourage school children to bring their palms from home to be placed on the pile to be burned. A priest, deacon, principal, or teacher could lead everyone in a few short remarks before the palms are lit. Before all depart, sing one final rousing "Alleluia" as a way of bidding the acclamation farewell until the Easter Vigil.

News. They saw how much everyone wanted to see Jesus, to understand him, his power, his holiness, and his person.

Paul's teaching to the Corinthians to "glorify God in your body" (1 Corinthians 6:20) summarizes well our task of evangelization during this period of Ordinary Time. We do not know how much time remains before the Parousia, but we live confidently in the hope that if we proclaim the Gospel of Jesus Christ in our words and actions, we surely will share in it. We will know happiness beyond measure, as will those whom we evangelize and who, in turn, accept God's call to do the same.

Evangelization

WE hear the voice from the heavens in the Gospel according to Mark, "You are my beloved Son; with you I am well pleased" (Mark 1:11). Jesus' mission begins. Ours does, too, as we embrace anew our identity as God's beloved sons and daughters. Jesus is the Good News for us and for the world. During this portion of Ordinary Time, the opportunity presents itself once again for us to accept our call to follow Jesus and to live it out in new and deeper ways. We allow others to evangelize us, to help us deepen our faith. We reach out to those in our faith communities as we reevangelize each other. We turn to our neighborhoods, our cities, countries, and the world with the Good News of Christmas just celebrated. Christ is our midst as Savior and Lord. He leads us in the path to Jerusalem. His power, might, and compassion are the basis for us as to strongly and compassionately live as people of faith.

The Scriptures for brief weeks of Ordinary Time before Lent hold out to us models of faith and evangelization from the Old Testament such as Samuel, Jonah, Moses, and yes, even Job. The Gospel readings remind us that Jesus, the Lamb of God, is the One whom we invite others to behold. His Gospel of repentance and call to believe in the Gospel the message we proclaim. The power of exorcism and healing that emanates from him and the power of his Word is the power we offer to others through our kind words and healing touch.

As Jesus went from village to village, he invited his disciples to accompany him on his journey of evangelization. On the road, they learned what it means to live a life filled with the Good

The Parish and the Home

FOLLOWING the focus that Advent and Christmas Time provide, the brief season of Ordinary Time in winter can seem a let-down and may pass with little reflection without attentiveness to the grace of this season. In parishes, Ordinary Time may be a welcome period of relatively normal pace, as we settle into the rhythm of a new calendar year. Those who are responsible for the liturgy often take these weeks to review and evaluate the celebrations during Advent and Christmas, and anticipate the ones of Lent and Easter. In our families, it is easy to move from Christmas Time into Ordinary Time, which does not include regular participation in Sunday Mass, giving of time or attention to those in need, or making faith connections in our daily lives. Make this year one in which the ordinary becomes extraordinary by carrying the intentional faith focus of Christmas into the days and weeks of Ordinary Time in winter.

Place a green cloth on the family prayer or dinner table, along with green plants wherever possible. Give each family member a blank calendar for January and February. Mark Sunday Mass times, special family dates, and the various feasts and solemnities. Ask each member of the family to label each week with one special act of charity to which he or she commits for this season. Include a family sharing and check-in on Sundays, spending a little extra time together on this day. Explore a new form of prayer, devotion, or spiritual reading as a family in these weeks of Ordinary Time: *lectio divina* (sacred reading in which a few sentences of Scripture are used for reflection), the Rosary, reflection on the Sunday readings throughout the week, quiet prayer alone or together. Set aside an hour each week for this practice and invite family members to take turns leading your special time. Parishes may have a special faith formation gathering during this season to provide instruction and an experience of one of these prayer forms and to share resources for use at home.

Mass Texts

◆ Tropes for the Penitential Act, Form C

You are the Lamb of God who takes away the sins of the world: Lord, have mercy.

You are the light that illumines every darkness: Christ, have mercy.

You call each of us to follow you always: Lord, have mercy.

◆ Dismissal for Children's Liturgy of the Word

Beloved children of God, as you go forth to listen to the Sacred Scriptures you may be amazed at all the stories of what Jesus says and does. He asks his people to do many different things. When people do as he requests, great miracles can happen. Perhaps he is asking something special of you this day. Pray that God may open your ears to hear his Word in a new and special way. Go in peace.

◆ Dismissal of the Catechumens

My dear catechumens, as we send you forth to reflect on the Word of God, be mindful of the the many ways that he may be working in your lives, and in the lives of those around you. As the Scriptures unfold, you will see that God appears to ordinary people, in ordinary situations, and that he teaches us using examples found in nature and our daily lives. Incline the ear of your heart to God speaking to you this day. Go in peace.

January 2018
Month of the Holy Name

Weekdays during Ordinary Time

Except for the days of the First and Thirty-Fourth Weeks in Ordinary Time. *The Roman Missal* does not provide prayer texts for the weekdays in Ordinary Time. Instead, priest celebrants and those who prepare the liturgy may select from among the prayers provided for the Sundays in Ordinary Time.

Optional Memorials during Ordinary Time

On all Saturdays during Ordinary Time that do not have an obligatory memorial, a memorial to the Blessed Virgin Mary may be celebrated. The prayers may be selected from the Common of the Blessed Virgin Mary. Commentary below is only provided for Sundays, solemnities, feasts, and obligatory memorials.

The following should be consulted for celebrating optional memorials during Ordinary Time:

On weekdays in Ordinary Time, there may be chosen either the Mass of the weekday, or the Mass of an Optional Memorial which happens to occur on that day, or the Mass of any Saint inscribed in the Martyrology for that day, or a Mass for Various Needs, or a Votive Mass (#GIRM, 355c).

T U E 9 (#306 or #305) green
Weekday / First Week in Ordinary Time

The Lectionary for Mass

The following commentary pertains to Lectionary #306.

◆ First Reading: For an Israelite to be childless was considered a disgrace. Children were a blessing from the Lord. Hannah, one of the two wives of Elkanah, was barren. Peninnah, his other wife, had borne many children. Worse yet, Peninnah taunted Hannah because of it. We see Hannah in deep anguish and bitterness, quietly beseeching the Lord and making a promise to the Lord if he grants her prayer. Eli the priest at first misjudges her, but in the end blesses her. Note that Hannah's prayer and Eli's word of blessing moved her beyond her downcast state and the withdrawal and isolation described in yesterday's reading. Her trust was rewarded and she conceived a son.

◆ Canticle: Today's response is Hannah's prayer of thanksgiving when she offers her weaned son to the Lord in fulfillment of her vow (verse 11 of today's reading). Hear her prayer of thanksgiving within the context of her previous barrenness and rivalry with Peninnah.

◆ Gospel: The newly called disciples Andrew, Simon, James, and John follow Jesus as he begins his healing ministry. Notice that the cure of the man possessed with a demon occurs on a Sabbath and in a synagogue. Jesus' teaching contrasts with that of others whom the people have previously heard teach. Jesus teaches with authority. Neither the source of this authority nor the content of Jesus' teaching is specified. What we do know is the man with the unclean spirit attempted to cancel out Jesus' power by correctly identifying him as the Holy One of God. He thought his knowledge of Jesus' identity would show the spirit within him to be superior. The man's strategy did not work. Jesus drove the unclean spirit out, leaving the crowds amazed and wondering who Jesus is. We confess Jesus as God's Son, and his authority over life and death still amazes us!

The following commentary pertains to Lectionary #305.

◆ First Reading: Today, we meet Elkanah, the father of Samuel, and Hannah and Peninnah, Elkanah's two wives. Hannah, especially loved by Elkanah, was barren, a disgrace for an Israelite woman since children were seen as a blessing from the Lord. Peninnah had borne many children and so taunted Hannah for her barrenness. Hannah experienced deep anguish and grief, not only because of her barrenness, but because of Peninnah's reproaches.

◆ Responsorial Psalm 116 is a prayer that accompanied a sacrifice in the Temple. The psalmist, aware of all that God has done for him, publicly proclaims God's praise

◆ Gospel Jesus' ministry follows the conclusion of John the Baptist's. The Gospel Jesus proclaims is clear from the beginning of this short passage: the Kingdom of God is here—repent, and believe. In Mark, after Jesus' proclamation of the Gospel, he immediately calls the first disciples. As he passes by the Sea of Galilee, Jesus offers the invitation to come after him to two brothers, Simon and Andrew. They accept, leaving their boat and nets behind. Jesus also calls the sons of Zebedee who leave not only their boat and nets behind, but also their father. The proclamation of the Gospel and the call go hand in hand. Will you accept the call?

W E D 10 (#307) green
Weekday

The Lectionary for Mass

◆ First Reading: We hear the call of Samuel, the young son of Hannah, as he served in the Temple under the guidance of Eli the prophet. Note the comment of how in those days revelations of the Lord were uncommon, and also of how Samuel did not yet know the Lord. The verb know here connotes personal experience or relationship. Samuel was one quick to respond and be open to the instructions of his mentor. What a beautiful model Eli is for all the elderly in their relationships with children as one who teaches them to know the Lord. Because of Eli, Samuel is introduced to the Lord and learns to ask the Lord to speak to him.

◆ RESPONSORIAL PSALM 40: Samuel's response to the call he heard was, "Here I am." It is likewise the prayer of the psalmist: "Here I am, I come to do your will." The Lord speaks to the one who waits with openness.

◆ GOSPEL: Jesus' ministry of healing continues in today's Gospel reading. The ministry is personal as he heals Simon's mother-in-law who was sick with a fever. Having been healed by Jesus in the presence of his fledgling disciples, she serves them. The text informs us that, as evening came, the disciples led Jesus to others who were ill or possessed by demons. Indeed, the entire town came to the door of the house, evidence of how quickly Jesus' reputation was spreading. We also hear that Jesus performs many healings and exorcised many demons. Before dawn, still under the cover of partial darkness, Jesus left to recharge himself through prayer and quiet time away. But his disciples followed because people apparently inquired of them where Jesus was. Jesus heard the people's needs and went on to their towns to preach and heal.

THU 11 (#308) green Weekday

The Lectionary for Mass

◆ FIRST READING: The reading recounts the events of two battles in a Philistine attack on Israel, whose defeat is interpreted as God's punishment for sins. The last line of the reading speaks of the death of the two sons of Eli, Hophni and Phinehas. In 1 Samuel 2:12–36 (not included in the Lectionary) there is an important piece for understanding this story. Here we hear of Hophni and Phinehas's wickedness in taking for themselves some of the meat offered for sacrifice in a manner not in accord with tradition. In effect, they took the best for themselves first. Eli was aware of this but did nothing. The revelation given to the young Samuel (see 1 Samuel 3:11–18, also excluded from the Lectionary) predicts the punishment and Hophni and Eli's deaths. The Ark of the Covenant, a chest containing the tablets of the Law of Moses, was Israel's most sacred possession. It represented God's presence among them. Its loss was unbelievable tragedy.

◆ RESPONSORIAL PSALM 44 is a communal lament, prayed by Israel in the wake of defeat in battle (first stanza).

◆ GOSPEL: In today's Gospel, a leper kneels before Jesus desiring that Jesus cure him. The man does not demand Jesus heal him, but rather leaves the decision to cure him entirely up to Jesus by saying "If you wish. . . ." Jesus chooses to cure him and performs the healing with care and compassion. This healing is personal as are Jesus' others. As part of Mark's unfolding of Jesus' messianic identity, the Gospel account writer has Jesus instruct the healed man not to tell anyone what happened. He should simply show himself to the priest and be declared clean so he might be welcomed into the community again (see Leviticus 13—14). The man, however, did not follow Jesus' instructions. He made the matter public, and who wouldn't?

FRI 12 (#309) green Weekday

The Lectionary for Mass

◆ FIRST READING: The young servant of the Lord, Samuel, grew up to become a judge in Israel. In terms of biblical history, the judges were men and women who both arbitrated disputes and served as military leaders (see the Book of Judges for their stories). In his old age, Samuel appointed his two sons as judges, but they were not just judges. As a result, the people rejected them and asked Samuel to appoint a new leader. They did not want another judge, but a king, so that they could be like all the other nations. Samuel was distressed by their request, and in today's reading we hear the results of God and Samuel's discussion of the matter. God acquiesces even though he was not pleased with the request. The people, in fact, were replacing his sovereignty with those of a mere mortal.

◆ RESPONSORIAL PSALM 89 acclaims the everlasting covenant God made with David. David was Israel's second king and perhaps its greatest. In today's First Reading we hear of the very beginnings of the monarchy.

◆ GOSPEL: Today's Gospel text is not only about Jesus healing the paralytic because of his faith and that of his friends who lowered him through the roof, it also marks the beginning of the conflict between Jesus and his opponents: in this text, the scribes. The growth of the conflict will eventually lead to the plot to put Jesus to death. That Jesus told the paralytic his sins were forgiven leads the scribes to question his authority, since only God can forgive sins. It would have been much easier for Jesus to only forgive the man's sins, but he goes on to command him to rise and go home, an amazing miracle for many and disconcerting for others.

SAT 13 (#310) green
Weekday

Optional Memorials of St. Hilary, Bishop and Doctor of the Church / white; Blessed Virgin Mary / white

The Lectionary for Mass

◆ FIRST READING: We meet Saul who would become Israel's first king. In verses not included in today's reading, we hear of how Saul, failing to find the lost animals, sought out Samuel, a reputed prophet of the Lord, for help. Today's reading picks up in verse 17, with the Lord confirming his choice of Saul as the one to be anointed with oil and so designated as ruler of the people. Saul is also charged with delivering God's people from their enemies.

◆ RESPONSORIAL PSALM 21 is a prayer for Israel's king. It is the Lord's strength, not his own, that gladdens the heart of the king. The king, by virtue of his selection by the Lord and the anointing that signifies it, stands in special relationship with the Lord. The king is to be a blessing for all God's people.

◆ GOSPEL: Levi, whom the other lists of disciples name Matthew, was a tax collector sitting at his customs post, collecting not only the tariffs rightly owed, but probably monies above those. This money he could keep as profit. Surprisingly, Jesus calls him with the two simple words: "Follow me." Perhaps even more astonishingly, Levi follows and the next we know, Jesus is sharing a meal at table in Levi's house with many other tax collectors and sinners. Not unexpectedly, the smug Pharisees question Jesus about this, but he responds plainly: he calls sinners, not the righteous—or those who think they are already righteous.

Today's Saint

St. Hilary was the bishop of Poitiers, France, during the era of the Arian heresy, and he fought for the correct understanding and expression of the divinity of Christ. He was known as the "hammer against Arianism" and the "Athanasius of the West," after the bishop of Alexandria who fought the heresy in the East. The Christian world was so divided by Arianism that Hilary was exiled twice. His great contribution was the successful expression in Latin of the theology about Christ, or Christology, that had been developed in Greek.

☀ 14 (#65) green
Second Sunday in Ordinary Time

The Lectionary for Mass

◆ FIRST READING: Four times Samuel utters the phrase "Here I am." He desires to respond to whoever calls him, whether Eli or the Lord. Often we think that Samuel does not respond to the Lord's call until after Eli instructs him to say, "Speak, LORD, for your servant is listening." Yet the reading opens with the Lord calling to Samuel and Samuels first utterance of "Here I am." It seems as if Samuel knew from the beginning that the Lord was calling him, but perhaps what was necessary was his acceptance that he was indeed the Lord's servant.

◆ RESPONSORIAL PSALM 40: The first part of Psalm 40 conveys thanksgiving. The psalmist recounts the new song the Lord gave for nothing in exchange. For this, the author agrees to do the Lord's will. For all the Lord's wondrous deeds, we too, announce the Lord's justice to our liturgical assemblies and beyond.

◆ SECOND READING: Today's passage is from a section of the letter in which Paul deals with moral issues dividing the Corinthian community. His point is clear: avoid immorality. We are so united with Christ in our body that Paul instructs us that each person's body is the temple of the Holy Spirit. We are the Lord's individually and God will raise us—including our body— just as God raised Christ. The Christian community, the Church, is the Body of Christ, a connection Paul makes later in his letter.

◆ GOSPEL: The choice of two of John the Baptist's disciples to follow Jesus after John identified Jesus as the Lamb of God corresponds to Samuel's call in the First Reading. Jesus' invitation to the two disciples of John parallels the Lord's invitation to Samuel. As Samuel recognized it was the Lord calling, so the disciples recognize Jesus as the Messiah. Jesus, the Messiah, is the Lamb of God, a connection of titles early in the Gospel according to John, whose meaning the disciples will fully understand on the road to Jerusalem.

The Roman Missal

The Mass texts for today are found in the "Ordinary Time" section of the Proper of Time. The Gloria and the Creed are sung or said today.

The Collect acknowledges God as the one who governs "all things," and so asks him to "bestow [his] peace on our times." The Prayer over the Offerings reiterates how "whenever the memorial of this sacrifice is celebrated / the work of our redemption is accomplished." The Prayer after Communion highlights the unity of the faithful that is a constitutive element in the meaning of the Eucharist. It asks God to pour the Spirit of love on us so that those who have been nourished by the "one heavenly Bread" may become "one in mind and heart."

Any one of the eight Prefaces of the Sundays in Ordinary Time may be selected for today.

Other Ideas

The Week of Prayer for Christian Unity takes place from January 18 through January 25. This is a time when parishes and congregations worldwide come together and pray that Jesus' prayer, "I pray not only for them, but also for those who will believe in me through their word, so that they may all be one, as you, Father, are in me and I in you" (John 17:20–21) comes closer to fulfillment. Include a prayer for the reconciliation of the Churches in the Universal Prayer. Consider inviting a Protestant clergyperson to do a reflection after the Prayer after Communion. You can find resources for this day on the website of the Pontifical Council for Promoting Christian Unity.

MON 15 (#311) green
Weekday

The Lectionary for Mass

◆ FIRST READING: Samuel inquires of Saul as to why he disobeyed the Lord. Saul, however, misconstrues the sacrifice his men made as the fulfillment of the mission on which the Lord sent him. The Lord desires obedience rather than sacrifice. Acceptance is ours when we believe and live the Lord's command. At the end of the reading, Samuel informs Saul that because he rejected the Lord's command, the Lord rejected him as a ruler.

◆ RESPONSORIAL PSALM 50 follows upon the idea in the First Reading that the Lord extends saving power to those who live his commands. When we reject the dis-

cipline of the Lord's words, we sin. God shows salvation to those who live in praise and glory of the Lord.

◆ GOSPEL: The Pharisees' question about why Jesus' disciples do not fast follows upon the passage in which scribes who were also Pharisees witnessed Jesus and his disciples eating with tax collectors and sinners. Jesus responds to the Pharisees' question with the parable about the wedding guests not fasting while the bridegroom is in their midst. We learn in this Gospel reading that Jesus initiates a new time. The old time, in which external practices such as fasting determined one's relationship with the Lord, is no longer present. Love in Jesus Christ is the new wine that pours into new wineskins.

TUE 16 (#312) green
Weekday

The Lectionary for Mass

◆ FIRST READING: The Lord sends Samuel to Jesse of Bethlehem, for from Jesse's house will come the Lord's king. Samuel, a faithful servant, follows the Lord's command to go to Bethlehem. Once there, the Lord advises him to not judge by appearance or lofty stature as humans do for the Lord will look into the heart when he chooses a new king. Apparently, the Lord does not address his advice to Jesse, and so he goes through the ritual of presenting seven of his sons to Samuel thinking that the Lord has chosen one of them. We know unexpected the conclusion to this reading. David, the youngest—with a ruddy appearance—is God's choice. Anointed by Saul and filled with the spirit of the Lord, David undertakes his kingly mission.

◆ RESPONSORIAL PSALM 89: The refrain of the Responsorial Psalm affirms that God has found David as his servant-king. The first verse confirms the detail of David's

youth. The second describes his anointing as king and the Lord's strength, which is now always with David. The third verse presents the intimate father-son relationship that exists between the Lord and David. God is Father, Rock, and Savior for David and for us.

◆ GOSPEL: The Gospel reading, a continuous reading from Monday's Gospel text, finds the Pharisees once gain questioning the actions of Jesus' disciples who are picking heads of grain on the Sabbath. Jesus adept response, in which he uses David as an example of working on the Sabbath, connects today's Gospel reading with the First Reading. David's "work" consisted of eating the offering bread that only priests could lawfully consume, and then sharing that bread with his companions. As Christians, we see a Eucharistic reference here, and when we hear Jesus tell of the lordship of the Son of Man over the Sabbath. Our working of celebrating and living the Eucharist occurs every day of the week!

WED 17 (#313) white
Memorial of St. Anthony, Abbot

The Lectionary for Mass

◆ FIRST READING: David brought with him five stones and a sling. He was young and inexperienced. His opponent was Goliath the Philistine, a seasoned warrior armed with a sword, spear, and scimitar (a short sword with a curved blade). David's decision to engage Goliath in battle was probably not the wisest. Or was it? The wisdom of David's decision to take on Goliath rests in his experience of the Lord's care for him on previous occasions. His courage is the Lord's. The Lord will always triumph despite what the world sees as unfavorable odds.

◆ RESPONSORIAL PSALM 144: The Psalm connects directly to the First Reading in that it speaks of a king imploring God for assistance in battle. The psalm writer affirms strength comes from the Lord. In the third stanza (vv. 9–10), praise and thanksgiving become the psalm writer's song as the writer mentions David's victory by name. As we utter the Psalm refrain we express our confidence in the security the Lord our Rock provides us.

◆ GOSPEL: The Son of Man is Lord of the Sabbath. This we learned from yesterday's Gospel reading. Today's Gospel reading shows us just how consistent Jesus is. With the Pharisees closely watching him again, he heals a man with a withered hand. This is the last straw for the Pharisees as they immediately go forward to speak with the Herodians and begin to develop their plot to put Jesus to death. We know that even in death, the Pharisees do not triumph. Jesus does. He slays the Goliath of death. The victory over death belongs to the Lord of the Sabbath, the Lord of Life.

The Roman Missal

The Mass texts are proper for today and can be found in the Proper of Saints at January 17. The orations all echo the virtues of St. Anthony's life: his "wondrous way of life in the desert" and the need for self-denial in order to love God above all things (Collect), being free from "earthly attachments" so that "we may have our riches in you alone" (Prayer over the Offerings), and the saint's "glorious victories / over the powers of darkness" (Prayer after Communion). Although no particular Preface is indicated in the rubrics for today, certainly one should be chosen from among the two Prefaces of Saints or the Preface of Holy Virgins and Religious.

Today's Saint

Early in his life, St. Anthony of Egypt (251–356) discovered the importance of solitude in knowing oneself in relationship to God. Solitude provides the vehicle through which one battles demons and removes worldly distractions that distance the heart from the will of God. For nearly thirty years, St. Anthony journeyed in the desert, where he lived a life of solitary prayer and self-discipline — a life of utter dependence on God. After his time in the desert, he emerged as a man of balance, ready to share all he learned regarding the human thirst for God. Realizing that the spiritual life takes root within a community of believers, he founded a group of monks. While serving as abbot, a spiritual father, to the monks, St. Anthony mentored them in the ways of contemplative prayer and helped them overcome illusory thinking. His dynamic personality continued to attract individuals. As a result, he counseled a steady stream of pilgrims and laid the foundation for many monasteries.

THU **18** (#314) green
Weekday

The Lectionary for Mass

◆ FIRST READING: What starts out as jealousy on the part of King Saul because the women in their song of praise attribute only "thousands" slain to him, whereas they credit "ten thousands" slain to David, rapidly escalates to Saul wanting to kill David, the servant. The intervention of Saul's son, Jonathan, deescalates the situation such that it ends up in a peaceful resolution. David's good deeds Jonathon recounts to Saul convince the king that he should spare David's life. Even knowing Saul considered killing him, David holds no regrets and continues his life of service to the king.

◆ RESPONSORIAL PSALM 56: God empathizes with our troubles, even to the point of counting our wanderings and storing our tears. David trusted in this even as he was under attack by the Philistines and even as he continued to serve King Saul despite knowing that the king had considered putting him to death. We, too, trust in God even in the face of our real human fears. We believe God companions us each day and that God leads us to the land of living. Our God is the God of life, not death.

◆ GOSPEL: Jesus had cured many people and exorcised numerous demons. He now withdraws with his disciples near the sea. People from countless regions follow him — from Galilee and Judea — they come. From Jerusalem and Idumea, from Tyre and Sidon, even beyond the Jordan they travel to encounter him. His popularity was remarkable. His mission is expansive, for he seeks to bring life to all who would follow him. Yet the demons want to ward off his power by recognizing he is the Son of God. Neither the Pharisees nor the demons would succeed. Life in Jesus Christ will triumph. This we know and believe.

FRI **19** (#315) green
Weekday

The Lectionary for Mass

◆ FIRST READING: We move ahead six chapters in 1 Samuel for today's First Reading. The reading begins with Saul, accompanied by three thousand of his men, searching for and locating David in a desert cave. David's servants try to convince him of the glorious day this is that the Lord has brought the enemy directly to him. David initially agrees and cuts off an end of Saul's mantle. Regret, however, comes over David. He recognizes the Lord has anointed Saul and refuses to do him harm. Saul, for his part, honors David's generosity in doing him no harm. He attests that the Lord will surely anoint him king of Israel one day. For whom would go without harming the enemy who comes directly before him, but the one who is the Lord's?

◆ RESPONSORIAL PSALM 57 is known as a psalm of David, as is Psalm 56, from which yesterday's Responsorial Psalm came. David prays for God's mercy to be upon him. This is our prayer, too, as each time we pray the refrain we implore God for mercy twice. While in the desert cave, David took refuge from Saul. In the psalm, the reference to taking refuge under the shadow of God's wings reveals both the intimacy and power of divine refuge. The final stanza turns to praise of God for God's boundless mercy and faithfulness.

◆ GOSPEL: Jesus goes up the mountain where he calls the Twelve. These are the ones he chose by his divine authority. Jesus would accompany them and they would accompany Jesus, all the while learning to preach and to drive out demons. This would be the mission of the Twelve. They would carry forth the salvific mission of Jesus now and after his Death and Resurrection. Read the passage carefully and note how Jesus changes Simon's name to Peter, but also how the Evangelist Mark already early on in his Gospel account mentions that Judas Iscariot betrayed Jesus.

S A T **20** (#316)   green
Weekday

Optional Memorials of St. Fabian, Pope and Martyr / red; St. Sebastian, Martyr / red; Blessed Virgin Mary / white

The Lectionary for Mass

◆ FIRST READING: 2 Samuel narrates the history of David. Today's First Reading comes from the beginning of 2 Samuel. The reading begins with a statement of David's victory over the Amalekites. Then it notes that *on the third day* a man from Saul's camp came to David to report the deaths of Saul and his son, Jonathan. All were struck with grief. David's words of mourning express how important Jonathan had been to him. Recall that just two days ago on Thursday, January 18, 2018, the First Reading described how Jonathan intervened to deescalate the situation between David and Saul, and prevent Saul from killing David. David, now, will receive the divine anointing as king.

◆ RESPONSORIAL PSALM 80: The psalm is a lament of the people of Israel. They have tasted defeat and so, they pray in hope that the Lord will restore their fortunes. The people desire to see the Lord's face once again, to know the Lord's salvation, to experience solace from their relationship with their God who will no longer be angry with them.

◆ GOSPEL: The two brief verses that are today's Gospel serve as an introduction to the rest of Mark 3 from which we will read next Monday and Tuesday. We know this from the Gospel reading: Jesus and his disciples enter a house. They have arrived home, but the crowd is still with them. Presumably it is the size of the crowd that makes it impossible for them to eat. Because

---

of this Jesus' relatives accuse him of being "out of his mind" and want to apprehend him. As we will find out in the coming days, it is not really the size of the crowd and the inability to eat, which is the reason for Jesus' relatives thinking he is not altogether of sound mind.

Today's Saints

The Church celebrates the lives of two holy men today, Sts. Fabian († 250) and Sebastian († 288), both of whom were martyred for their faith. Very little is known about each of these martyrs, yet they continue to capture the hearts of Catholic Christians everywhere. St. Fabian was elected pope in 236, even though he was not a priest. During his pontificate, Emperor Decius came into power and began persecuting Christians who would not return to pagan worship.

St. Fabian was the first among many killed under this emperor's violent reign. While serving as a soldier, St. Sebastian was persecuted at the hands of Diocletian. According to legend, he was pierced with arrows so that he would die a slow and painful death, but this attempt on his life was unsuccessful due to his athletic stamina. He eventually became well enough to confront the emperor regarding the way Christians were being treated. This led to his execution.

☀ 21 (#68) green
Third Sunday in Ordinary Time

The Lectionary for Mass

◆ FIRST READING: Jonah's prophetic task was not easy. No wonder he refused it the first time God called. In today's reading, the Lord's word comes to Jonah for a second time, this time after the Lord rescued Jonah from the belly of the big fish by having the fish spew Jonah out onto the seashore. Jonah's calls the people of Nineveh to repentance based on his personal experience of God's mercy and opportunity to live a new life in God. God acknowledges the conversion of the Ninevites and God himself repented of the evil that he would have brought upon them.

◆ RESPONSORIAL PSALM 25 calls upon the Lord to teach us and instruct us in divine ways. The verses are the psalmist's prayer and ours that the Lord not only make those ways known to us, but that the Lord will guides us, have compassion on us when we stray. We acknowledge our sinfulness, our need for humility and the constancy of the Lord's presence by our side as our Teacher.

◆ SECOND READING: This brief passage is Paul's advice to the Corinthians about how to live in the interim before Christ comes again in glory. Paul believes that the Second Coming of Christ is imminent, so he conveys his instructions with a sense of urgency. Christians are to live in the knowledge of the Second Coming for this world is passing away. What lasts eternally is God's grace in the present and active in the Risen Christ, now alive in the hearts of those who believe. When Christians live in this knowledge, then their worldly actions will appear different than those who do not await the Lord.

◆ GOSPEL: Jesus proclamation to repent and believe in the Gospel parallels Jonah's call to the Ninevites to repent. What is unique is Jesus' proclamation is the preface to his announcement in which he states, "This is the time of fulfillment." Through our reading of the Gospel according to Mark, we, along with the disciples, will come to know that in Jesus' very person as the Son of Man who saves *is* fulfillment of all God's promises. Without fully knowing this, Simon and Andrew respond to Jesus' call to come after him and become fish for other followers. James and his brother John are the next to trust in the possibilities of what following Jesus could bring.

The Roman Missal

The Mass texts for this Sunday are found in the "Ordinary Time" section of the Proper of Time. The Gloria is sung or said today. The Creed is said or sung.

The Collect asks that God may direct our actions so that "in the name of your beloved Son / we may abound in good works." In the Prayer over the Offerings we are asking God to accept our offerings so that, in sanctifying them, "they may profit us for salvation." The Prayer after Communion asks that, as a result of receiving the grace of being brought to new life (for example, in the Eucharist), "we may always glory in your gift."

Any one of the eight Prefaces of the Sundays in Ordinary Time may be selected for today.

The deacon's or priest's use of the third option for the dismissal formula, "Go in peace, glorifying the Lord by your life," would make a nice connection with the Prayer after Communion.

Other Ideas

On January 22 each year, the Church dedicates a Day of Prayer for the Protection of Unborn Children. Remember this intention, as well, and make parish members aware of opportunities to serve women facing crisis pregnancies.

M O N 22 (#317) green
Weekday

Day of Prayer for the Legal Protection of Unborn Children / white/violet

About Today's Day of Prayer

On this day, the Church gives us prayers rooted in hope as the United States mourns the loss of millions of lives by abortion. In the Mass for Peace and Justice, we pray that all governments, especially our own, seek a truly just society, one in which the common good of all people, including the most vulnerable, is sought. In a very real way, we pray for the end of this genocide, the victims of which we remember with our violet vestments and mournful hymns. This Mass celebrates their brief lives, reminding us also of the beauty and sacredness of the lives around us, who have not yet been lost. We remember, we intercede, we hope — and the Church leads us in all three. We should remember that there may be members of our parish who are still in the process of reconciling with God and the Church because they have had an abortion. If able, provide counselors to support those who have participated in an abortion. Using this day to condemn rather than to show mercy causes unnecessary pain. We are called to show compassion and God's mercy as we restore all and renew all in Christ's love and life. You might also host a Rosary for life.

The Lectionary for Mass

◆ FIRST READING: David becomes the king of Israel. It was unanimous. All the tribes of Israel came to him and put forth their position on why he should be king: even when Saul was their king, David led the Israelites and brought them back. The Lord had said that David would shepherd the Lord's people and command them. Now it comes to pass. At thirty years of age, David makes an agreement with the Lord to be king and the people anoint him. David's reign is lengthy; its duration foreshadows the eternal reign of Christ in our hearts and lives.

◆ RESPONSORIAL PSALM 89 is also a community lament, as was yesterday's psalm. The people of Israel express grief over their defeats. They wonder how God, who had promised a kingly dynasty that would endure forever will make good on this promise. The stanzas for today's psalm come from the middle of Psalm 89 and recount David's anointing as king. His youth is not a deterrent to his reign for God's faithfulness and mercy will be with him. The psalm refrain affirms this truth.

◆ GOSPEL: The accusations of the scribes continue to increase in intensity. In today's Gospel, they level two charges against Jesus: he is possessed Beelzebul and he exorcises demons by the power of the prince of demons. Jesus does not shy away from their charges. Rather, he gathers the scribes around him and teaches them with a parable. In the parable, Jesus speaks of a divided kingdom and household. Divisions arise when people confuse the work of the Holy Spirit and the Evil One. Jesus' spirit was clean, not unclean, as the scribes asserted. They, not Jesus, blasphemed. They would

cause divisions in the kingdom and in households. Their spirits were unclean for the Holy Spirit, who fills Jesus and those who follow him, is the true Spirit.

The Roman Missal

According to GIRM, 373: "In all the Dioceses of the United States of America, January 22 . . . shall be observed as a particular day of prayer for the full restoration of the legal guarantee of the right to life and of penance for violations to the dignity of the human person committed through acts of abortion. The liturgical celebrations for this day may be the Mass 'For Giving Thanks to God for the Gift of Human Life' (no. 48/1 of the Masses and Prayers for Various Needs and Occasions), celebrated with white vestments, or the Mass 'For the Preservation of Peace and Justice' (no. 30 of the Masses and Prayers for Various Needs and Occasions), celebrated with violet vestments."

TUE 23 (#318) green
Weekday

Optional Memorials of St. Vincent, Deacon and Martyr / red; St. Marianne Cope, Virgin / white

The Lectionary for Mass

◆ FIRST READING: David brings the ark of the God to Jerusalem. A joyous occasion, indeed! Replete with ritual and sacrifice, David leads the people in dancing and singing. He blesses the people and serves them an abundant feast. Just as David and the people celebrated the presence of the Lord in their midst, we celebrate Christ present in the Word, the Eucharist, the assembly, and the priest who presides over our celebration.

◆ RESPONSORIAL PSALM 24: The people sang this psalm as the Ark of God was brought into the Temple. We are familiar with the psalm text from the song "The King of Glory."

While the psalm's refrain asks who the king of glory is, it also answers the question. The Lord is the king of glory who reigns over all the earth. We celebrate the Lord's presence in our midst as we joyfully acclaim him as we sing and pray the words of today's psalm.

◆ GOSPEL: Jesus is still in the house with his disciples and the crowd, presumably including the scribes who, in yesterday's Gospel reading accused him of being possessed by Beelzebub and driving out demons in the name of the prince of demons. Having taught in parable that a kingdom and house divided cannot stand, the discussion turns to address a personal topic. The crowd informs Jesus that his mother and brothers are outside asking for him. Jesus responds to the crowd with the well-known rhetorical question about the identity of his mother and brothers. He teaches that those seated around him are his mother and brothers because they do the will of God. Will we remain outside Jesus' home or come in?

Today's Saints

St. Vincent was from Saragossa in third-century Spain. He is also known as Vincent the deacon and served under St. Valerius, bishop of Saragossa. He was martyred in 304 during the persecution by the emperor Diocletian. Just before he was killed on a gridiron or grill, he was offered his freedom if he would throw a copy of the Scriptures on the fire that was prepared for him, but he refused. After witnessing Vincent's faith and heroism, his executioner converted to Christianity.

St. Marianne Cope (1838–1918) was born in West Germany, but a year after her birth the Cope family emigrated to the United States of America to seek work and educational opportunities. From a young age, she felt the call to enter religious life, which led to her decision to enter the Sisters of St. Francis in Syracuse, New York. She had a deep affection for the suffering and sick. Marianne was instrumental in the establishment of two of the first hospitals in the central New York area—hospitals that were open to all people regardless of ethnicity, religion, or race. While serving as superior general of her religious community, she accepted an invitation to care for the sick, especially those afflicted with leprosy, in Hawaii. Marianne joined the mission to Hawaii where she helped establish homes for leprosy patients and cared for St. Damien de Veuster of Moloka'i who contracted leprosy because of his ministry to the sick. Following the death of St. Damien, Marianne continued his compassionate ministry of care for leprosy patients. Marianne lived the Franciscan call to serve the "crucified," the most vulnerable, in society. The inclusion of her "feast day" as an optional memorial for the dioceses of the United States was approved by the Vatican in early 2013.

(#319)   white

W E D **24** Memorial of St. Francis de Sales, Bishop and Doctor of the Church

The Lectionary for Mass

◆ First Reading: The Lord communicates a prophecy to Nathan that he is to speak to David. The prophecy concerns the Lord's care for David in the present and the Lord's promise of an heir to David after he dies. Christians see the fulfillment of the promise of a Messiah in Jesus Christ. In the Messiah, David's house and kingdom lives on forever.

◆ Responsorial Psalm 89 echoes the covenant God made with David through which the Davidic dynasty will last forever. In this way, God shows his enduring love for his servant. Through the Messiah, Jesus Christ, God's love

comes to earth as human and embraces our humanity. God's love in Jesus Christ remains forever with us and all who believe. God is forever faithful. This we affirm as we pray today's psalm.

◆ Gospel: In today's Gospel reading we find Jesus no longer teaching from within a home, but in a boat on the Sea of Galilee. A large crowd still presents itself on the seashore. The parable of the sower and seed is fundamental to understanding Jesus' person and mission. We know this because at the end of the parable Jesus comments to those present with him and the Twelve that if they do not understand even this parable, how are they going to understand any of the parables he tells. Consider this parable and its interpretation in light of Jesus' teaching about a house divided and who are his mother and brothers from previous days' Gospel readings. Consider whether you will open yourselves to the rich soil of God's Word in Jesus Christ so that you bear fruit a hundredfold. Or will you choose the way of the seed sown on the path, the rocky ground, or the thorns?

The Roman Missal

The orations are proper for today and are found in the Proper of Saints at January 24. The prayers include mention of St. Francis de Sales by way of his gentleness, his meekness, his charity, and his being inflamed with the Holy Spirit. Although no particular Preface is indicated in the rubrics for today, the Preface of Holy Pastors would make sense, since St. Francis was a bishop.

Today's Saint

St. Francis de Sales (1567–1622), bishop of Geneva, contributed immensely to the development of spirituality through the publication of his book, *An Introduction to the Devout Life*. Living at a time when manuals on spirituality were writ-

ten primarily for clerics and members of religious orders, St. Francis' book provided a practical path to holiness for people from all states of life. He challenged the prevailing belief that only a select few could obtain sanctity. Along with his accomplishments in the area of an everyday, or lay, spirituality, he cofounded with St. Jane Frances de Chantal the Order of the Visitation of Holy Mary, a religious community of nuns that would move beyond traditional enclosure to a healthy blend of prayer and service to the poor. Together, Sts. Francis and Jane, with their close friends Sts. Vincent de Paul and Louise de Marillac, transformed the face of the Church in France. St. Francis has been named a Doctor of the Church.

(#519)   white

T H U **25** Feast of the Conversion of St. Paul the Apostle

About Today's Feast

Today's feast celebrates God's triumph, even in the most unlikely circumstances. Before Paul meets the Risen Lord on the Road to Damascus, he is Saul, dedicated to viciously persecuting the followers of Jesus Christ. Imagine yourself among those early Christians, and hearing that Saul, one of the most feared enemies of your community, has encountered the Lord and changed his life entirely to serve him from then on. Although certainly astonishing, the conversion of Paul is also deeply inspiring, for it tells us that God does not hold our mistakes against us, but rather calls us to turn our minds and hearts to follow his Son instead. The conversion of Paul is proof that no one is too far beyond the call of the Lord to follow, and that in Christ, change for the better is always possible.

The Lectionary for Mass

◆ First Reading Option 1: This is the second of three accounts of Paul's conversion found in the Acts of the Apostles. Paul's conversion is dramatic. A bright light blinds him, he falls to the ground, and the voice of Jesus speaks to him instructing him to get up and go to Damascus. There he will learn of his mission to preach the Gospel. Paul receives his sight back through the healing words of Ananias, a faithful observer of the Law. We learn of the deep continuity between the faith of our ancestors and faith in Jesus Christ. Our conversion to faith may not be as dramatic as Paul's, but through our Baptism and the washing away of our sins, God calls us, too, into mission for the sake of the world.

◆ FIRST READING, OPTION 2: The second option for today's First Reading is the first of three accounts of Paul's conversion recorded in Acts. There are details in this account not found in the account from Acts 22, the previous option for the First Reading. One detail of note is that Paul — at that time Saul — was unable to see for three days. The men who were traveling with him had to lead him by the hand to Damascus. Lives can change. Life can come from death. Like Paul who once persecuted followers of the Way, through our witness to the Gospel, people God can move people from unbelief to belief. Observe that Ananias's words in this account draw a connection not so much with the faith of the ancestors, but with the Holy Spirit who now resides in Paul. Through the Holy Spirit working in us, others come to recognize it is Christ who compels us to preach the Gospel.

◆ RESPONSORIAL PSALM 117: The refrain for today's Responsorial Psalm is the words of the Risen Christ's commission to the Eleven disciples. Jesus speaks these words to the disciples while they are at table. Despite their lack of belief when others told them they saw the Risen Christ, Jesus rebukes them, but still sends them into the world. The verses from Psalm 117 attest to God's steadfastness and faithfulness. Regardless of our hardness of heart, God works with us, forgiving us, sending us forth to proclaim the message of forgiveness and love to the world. For this, we sing "Alleluia, alleluia," the second option for today's Psalm refrain.

◆ GOSPEL: This Gospel reading comes from the longer ending of Mark and is the passage for today's Responsorial Psalm refrain. Jesus commissions the Eleven disciples before his Ascension to go into the world and proclaim the Gospel. The commission makes a clear distinction between the fate of those who believe and are baptized and those who do not believe. Those who believe will not only experience salvation, but they will also be able to exorcise demons, heal the sick, and speak new languages. All this believers will do in the name of the Risen Christ. The metaphorical language of believers picking up serpents and drinking deadly poison shows once again that Jesus is the Lord over sin and death. He is the life of the world.

The Roman Missal

Notice that the prayers have a very fervent nature to them, and this should be reflected throughout the liturgy. The Gloria is sung or said. Use Preface I of the Apostles. You may select from two options for the Solemn Blessing: Peter and Paul (#16) or the general one for Apostles (#17). The prayers clearly explain we are celebrating Paul's conversion and they ask us to follow his example and draw nearer to Our Lord. It is interesting to note that it speaks of stirring fire but that the fire is one of charity. One must use our fervor for the Lord in a kind fashion. The Spirit will fill us with wisdom and enlighten us on the path we must go. May we follow this wisdom, to be better witnesses in our prayer and in our lives.

(#321) white

FRI 26

Memorial of Sts. Timothy and Titus, Bishops

The Lectionary for Mass

◆ FIRST READING, OPTION 1: These verses come from the beginning of 2 Timothy, the second of three pastoral letters. Paul writes in a personal tone and expresses how much he longs to see Timothy again. The sincerity of Timothy's faith impresses Paul. He encourages Timothy to persevere in his proclamation of the Gospel. May we also continue to testify to the Lord and live the Gospel following Timothy's example of faith.

◆ FIRST READING, OPTION 2: The second option for the First Reading comes from the letter to Titus, the third of the three pastoral letters. These first four of these verses are Paul's lengthy greeting to his coworker, Titus. Paul affirms the faith they share in Christ Jesus, the Savior. Paul reminds Titus of the charge he has in Crete. As part of organizing the Church there, Titus needs to appoint presbyters in every town. The faith Paul and Titus share is our faith, too. We are heirs to the organization and tradition of the Church that stems from the early first century.

◆ RESPONSORIAL PSALM 96 is a hymn of praise inviting all nations to praise the Lord for his marvelous deeds. How appropriate this psalm is for the memorial of Sts. Timothy and Titus who diligently helped in spreading the Gospel. They proclaimed the Lord's marvelous deeds to the peoples they encountered. Through their organization of the early Church, they affirmed the kingship of the Lord and the equity with which the Lord rules. For this, we today continue to proclaim

God's marvelous deeds and sing new songs to the Lord!

◆ GOSPEL (#520): Take nothing. Go like lambs among wolves. Offer peace to the people in the homes you enter. Eat and drink what people offer as nourishment. Cure the sick. Proclaim the nearness of the Kingdom of God. This is the mission to which the Lord Jesus appoints seventy-two other disciples. The mission is not a solo mission, but one the disciples carry out in pairs just as we do not go it alone in living the Gospel mission today. We do so together, in the company of the angels and saints, and one another in our parish communities. Timothy and Titus proclaimed the Gospel and offered peace in communion with the believers in the early Church. They, too, were never solo disciples.

◆ GOSPEL (#321): Jesus appeals to his listeners' experience of nature to teach them the mystery of the growth of the Kingdom of God. Signs of the growth of a seed are visible, and while scientists today may be able to explain the process of growth, the force underlying it remains mysterious. Jesus' parables teach people with images and invite them to ponder their meaning. Can we hear with these same ears today?

The Roman Missal

The prayers are found in the Proper of Saints. Appropriately on this memorial, the Collect echoes the words of St. Paul's letter to Timothy (2:12). We pray that we may live "justly and devoutly in this present age" and so come to our "heavenly homeland." In the Prayer over the Offerings, we ask for "sincerity of heart," that we may be acceptable to God. We pray that the sacrament we receive may nourish us in the faith that was taught and "kept safe" by Sts. Timothy and Titus (Prayer after Communion). The Preface of Pastors is used.

Today's Saints

Sts. Timothy and Titus, first century bishops and martyrs, are celebrated together because of their joint association with St. Paul. Timothy is first mentioned in Acts of the Apostles 16:1–2, when Paul visits Lystra, in what is now Turkey. Timothy's mother was Jewish; Paul circumcised him so he would be accepted by the Jewish Christians. Timothy accompanied Paul on some of his journeys, and he is the one addressed in the letters to Timothy in the New Testament. Tradition says that Paul made him bishop of Ephesus in 65. He was martyred by stoning in the year 97 at the age of 80 for preaching against the worship of idols. St. Titus was also a disciple and companion of St. Paul. He was probably a Gentile, and Paul refused to have him circumcised because the Gospel freed Gentiles from the Law of Moses. Although he is not mentioned in the Acts of the Apostles, he is mentioned several times in Paul's letters and was probably commissioned to preach to the Gentiles. According to Paul, Titus was with Paul and Timothy at Ephesus and was sent to Macedonia to collect alms for the Christians in Jerusalem. He also spent time in Macedonia, Crete, and Dalmatia in modern-day Croatia. Tradition says that he was a bishop in Crete and died in the year 107.

SAT 27 (#322) green
Weekday

Optional Memorials of St. Angela Merici, Virgin / white; Blessed Virgin Mary / white

The Lectionary for Mass

◆ FIRST READING: We return to our reading from 2 Samuel after a two-day hiatus. In today's reading, we hear of David's anger with a rich man who took from a poor man in order to feed a guest. David, at Nathan's request to judge, deems the rich man deserves death. This was, however, a self-reflective parable. David had to take Uriah's wife as his wife. Together, they had a child. King David is quick to realize he sinned. His confession leads to Nathan's proclamation of the Lord's forgiveness, but as a consequence the child of David and Uriah dies.

◆ RESPONSORIAL PSALM 51 is a psalm of repentance and a lament. Today's verses come from the second half of the psalm known in Latin as *Misere mei, Deus*. When we pray this psalm, we align ourselves with David as he asks for a clean heart. We attempt to follow David's humble admission of his sinfulness as we ask God to create a clean heart in us.

◆ GOSPEL: We move ahead in Mark 4 from the parable of the sower and the seed to the narrative of Jesus calming the storm. For years, this beloved miracle story has helped to calm the anxieties and fears of many through the power of Jesus. Jesus is the author of life that comes through calm. Through the experience of the storm at sea, the disciples learn to trust in Jesus. Their fears and anxieties are real. Jesus never denies that. But in the midst of them, he calls his followers to mature in faith. This is our call, too. It is the call to "let go" and know that when rough waters come, we are never in the boat alone, but Jesus, the Son of God, is with us.

Today's Saint

Several miraculous occurrences, including restoration of sight and visions, surrounded the life of St. Angela Merici (1474–1540), a native of Desenzano in northern Italy. She was profoundly impacted by one vision in which she saw a great company of virgins and saints singing and playing instruments while descending from a staircase in the heavens. Based upon this vision, St. Angela founded a group of consecrated women known as the

Ursulines, dedicated to the education of young women, especially the poor. They were named after the fourth-century martyr and protector of women, St. Ursula, to whom St. Angela had a special devotion from an early age. Unlike the traditional customs practiced by those in religious orders, the members of this community did not wear habits, take vows, or live behind an enclosure. The women often resided with their own families, but met for instruction. St. Angela was gravely concerned that customary practices or rules not hinder the women from freely serving those in need.

☀ **28** (#71) green
Fourth Sunday in Ordinary Time

The Lectionary for Mass

◆ FIRST READING: Moses speaks about God raising up a prophet from the Israelites' kin. The people want this and God will fulfill their request. This gives the passage a messianic character. For Christians, the prophet God will raise up is Jesus. His words are the words everyone should heed. In a more general sense, we can interpret Moses' words at the conclusion of the passage to as instructions on how to discern true and false prophets. We are to listen to a prophet who speaks the Lord's words in the Lord's name, but not to one who speaks words other than those the Lord commanded. Responsorial Psalm 95:

Today's Responsorial Psalm is a common psalm for Ordinary Time. The opening two verses of this psalm invite us to worship the Lord, both joyfully and reverently, by singing in praise and kneeling in adoration. Our repetition of the refrain reminds us open our hearts when we hear God's voice rather than harden them as the Israelites did when they argued with God in Meribah and tested God at Massah.

◆ SECOND READING: Our reading is a continuous reading of Paul's First Letter to the Corinthians from the Third Sunday in Ordinary Time. Is Paul teaching a preference for the unmarried life in this brief passage? The anxieties of the unmarried man and woman, he says, relate to the things of the Lord, while the anxieties of the married man and woman relate to the world. Paul, however, begins his instruction with the same wish for both those unmarried and married: to be free from anxieties. The focus of everyone in the interim before Christ's Second Coming needs to be on Christ.

◆ GOSPEL: Today's Gospel continues our reading of Mark from where we left off on the Third Sunday in Ordinary Time. It marks the first appearance of Jesus teaching in a synagogue on a Sabbath. Mark does not tell us what Jesus taught; the Gospel writer only expresses the people's amazement at the authority with which Jesus taught. The event in the synagogue concludes with Jesus curing a man possessed by a demon even after the demon cries out in words wondering why Jesus' involves himself in the people's concerns and references him as the Holy One of God. Naming Jesus as such was the feeble, yet commonplace, attempt of the opposing power to triumph. The One who offers a new teaching of life, not death, triumphs.

The Roman Missal

The simple Collect echoes the words of Christ to the scribe who asked him which Commandment was most important: we are to "honor [God] with all our mind, / and love everyone in truth of heart." In the Prayer over the Offerings, we ask God to transform the "offerings of our service" and make them "the Sacrament of our redemption." In the Prayer after Communion, we pray that the "redeeming gifts" we receive may help the faith to spread. The sacrifice is offered not just for our own salvation, but for that of the whole world.

Other Ideas

This week, we celebrate the Feast of the Presentation of the Lord, when Mary and Joseph brought Jesus to the Temple. There, they meet Simeon and Anna, who recognize the unique destiny of the child. This is a good time for us to recognize and encourage the gifts of all the young people of the parish. We can also pray for many of them to embrace religious life and leadership, either as professed, ordained, or lay ministers in the Church. This is also the start of Catholic Schools' Week. Consider having guest speakers at a parish formation event or setting up tables with information about your local Catholic schools.

M
O **29** (#323) green
N **Weekday**

The Lectionary for Mass

◆ FIRST READING: An informant tells David that the Israelites have shifted their loyalty from him to Absalom. This causes David and his servants to flee Jerusalem. At the Mount of Olives, we find them weeping. The second half of the reading, which moves ahead to 2 Samuel 16, details David's encounter with Shimel, a man from Saul's clan, near Bahurim. Shimel curses David, yet David and his servants continue their journey leaving Shimel to his own negativity.

◆ RESPONSORIAL PSALM 3: This individual psalm speaks of the psalm writer's trust in the Lord. Just as David still faced adversaries in his reign as king, so too, we will encounter people who challenge us. Some we might even refer to as opponents or enemies. The text of the psalm reminds us that the Lord protects and sustains us even when people who challenge us surround us on all sides.

◆ GOSPEL: Jesus and his disciples arrive safely on the other side of the Sea of Galilee after encountering the storm. A man with an unclean spirit meets them as they disembark in the pagan territory of Gerasenes. The man's evil spirit announces that many demons exist in the area. The healing narrative takes a strange turn as the evil spirits then enter the swine in a large herd causing them to go down a steep bank and into the sea where they drowned. Jesus' power healed the man possessed by Legion and he was now in his right mind. Jesus' power of mercy and love triumphs again and again. This is Mark's narrative. This is our faith and the faith we cannot keep to ourselves. We must tell our family and friends—neighbors and strangers—as Jesus commanded the healed man to do.

TUE 30
(#324)   green
Weekday

The Lectionary for Mass

◆ FIRST READING: The First Reading tells us the death of Abasalom, King David's son. Deeply saddened by his son's death, we see David weeping and hear him crying out wishing he had died instead. The victory won that day had now turned into mourning as David's army joins him in grief.

◆ RESPONSORIAL PSALM 86: Today's Responsorial Psalm is also that of the Saturday after Ash Wednesday with a different refrain. Our refrain today asks the Lord to listen to our cries and answer them. In the verses of this lament psalm, we petition the Lord for mercy, to save our life, and to gladden our soul. We, like the psalm writer, devote ourselves to the Lord. We are the Lord's servants. We ask simply that the Lord hear our prayer.

◆ GOSPEL: Once again, we find Jesus crossing the Sea of Galilee. This time, he returns back to the other side to encounter Jairus, a synagogue official. Jairus pleads with him to cure his daughter who has been afflicted with a hemorrhage for twelve years. Interspersed in the narrative of the healing of Jairus's daughter is the cure of the woman who had suffered from a hemorrhage for twelve years. Her faith is so strong that she knows all she has to do is touch Jesus' cloak and he will heal her. Both the healing of Jairus's daughter and the woman with a hemorrhage reveal Jesus' power to us, a power of healing and love. Through these healings, the Gospel writer, Mark, leads us ever so close recognizing Jesus' identity as the Son of God, the Messiah, which Peter's confession will reveal to us in Mark 8:27–30.

WED 31
(#325)   white
Memorial of St. John Bosco, Priest

The Lectionary for Mass

◆ FIRST READING: The reading begins and ends with confessions of David. After asking for the Lord's forgiveness for numbering the people, David awakes to the words of the prophet Gad. In his message, he offers David three alternatives from which to choose. That one, the Lord will inflict on him and his people. David chooses pestilence and so the Lord delivers the plague. Many people died and the angel of the Lord readies a hand to destroy Jerusalem. But David confesses his sinfulness again. He is responsible, he says, not the people, and asks the Lord to punish him. David teaches all of us how to confess our sin and ask for forgiveness. Many times in our life we need to do this because in our humanity, we are neither perfect, nor God.

◆ RESPONSORIAL PSALM 32 is both a penitential psalm and a song of gratitude. The opening verse speaks of the blessedness of the person who has experienced the Lord's forgiveness. The psalm writer's own experience instructs us that once we set aside our ego enough to admit our sin, the beauty of God's mercy is ours. We will know God as our shelter. We will experience freedom like none other in the Lord.

◆ GOSPEL: Jesus has taught in parables, exorcised demons, and healed the sick. In today's Gospel reading, we find him back teaching in his native place still accompanied by his disciples. He is teaching in a synagogue on a Sabbath. Clearly, his teaching, like his exorcisms and healings, is powerful. Many who hear him question the source of his wisdom. They inquire if he is the carpenter who is the son of Mary and brother of James, Joses, Judas, and Simon. And they ask whether his sisters are present, too. Those who hear him take offense at his teaching. Their offense leads to Jesus speaking the oft-quoted saying about a prophet not being accepted in his native place. Lack of faith abounded there. Jesus—his person and mission—was refused, but not wholly, because he did cure a few sick people.

The Roman Missal

The Collect for St. John Bosco is proper. The remaining prayers may be taken from the Common of Pastors: For One Pastor or from the

Common of Holy Men and Women: For Educators.

Today's Saint

God gifted St. John Bosco (1815–1888) with the ability to read and interpret the signs of the times. Living during rapid industrialization and growing anticlericalism, he became very concerned about the emotional and spiritual livelihood of people, especially the plight of the young. St. John worked to provide positive and affirming environments, including orphanages and oratories, where the young could learn and recognize their infinite potential. In the spirit of his favorite hero, St. Francis de Sales, he founded the Salesians, a religious congregation devoted to works of charity, with an emphasis on empowering young people to become strong pillars of faith in a culture of instability. His work among young men living in the slums proved to be a worthy endeavor. Whether he was presiding at Mass or playing games with children or carrying the sick to hospitals, it was obvious he lived until his "last breath . . . day and night, morning and evening" for the neglected and abandoned (as quoted in *Butler's Lives of the Saints: January, New Full Edition*, p. 229).

February 2018
Month of the Passion of Our Lord

T H U **1** (#326) green
Weekday

The Lectionary for Mass

◆ FIRST READING: From now until Saturday, February 10, 2018, except tomorrow on the Feast of the Presentation, the First Reading will come from 1 Kings. In today's reading from this historical book, we hear David's instructions to his son, Solomon, as David's death draws near. David teaches Solomon

to follow the Lord's commands and the Lord will fulfill his promise to David that his lineage on the throne will continue. The reading concludes noting David's death, his long reign of forty years, and Solomon's succession.

◆ CANTICLE: Instead of a psalm, today's response is a canticle, and it comes from David's prayer of blessing to the Lord in another of the historical books, 1 Chronicles. Together with David and all those in the assembly centuries ago, exalt the Lord above all. We exclaim the Lord's sovereignty over all, and acknowledge the power and might in his hand from which all grandeur and strength come to us and to the world.

◆ GOSPEL: Jesus did not stop his mission with the rejection he experienced in his native place. Rather, in today's Gospel reading, we see him going around other villages in the area teaching. Not only does he teach, but he also calls the Twelve to go out two by two to continue his work of exorcising demons, healing the sick, and preaching repentance. The Twelve are to take nothing with them, save sandals and a second tunic. The power of Jesus is enough. They, like Jesus, did are to move onto another place when others reject them and their message. The Church today continues the work of the Twelve.

F R I **2** (#524) white
Feast of the Presentation of the Lord

About Today's Feast

The Feast of the Presentation of the Lord is rooted in everyday life. In faithful observance of the law of Moses, Mary and Joseph present Jesus in the Temple to consecrate him to the Lord. There they met the righteous Simeon and the prophetess Anna, for whom Temple worship was part of everyday life. God

rewarded their fidelity by allowing them to see the one who was Savior and to hold him in their arms. When the ceremony of presentation was completed, Mary, Joseph, and Jesus returned to their hometown. There, they created a home and a family life where Jesus grew up, becoming strong and wise, and the grace of God was upon him. The Feast of the Presentation of the Lord, on February 2, is also called Candlemas Day. According to Luke's account of the Gospel, Simeon recognized Jesus as the Messiah in the Temple and declared him "a light for revelation to the Gentiles, / and glory for your people Israel" (Luke 2:32). This sparked the tradition of blessing enough candles to last an entire year and to candle processions in churches and in the streets.

The Lectionary for Mass

◆ FIRST READING: This reading from the minor prophet Malachi contains the prophetic words that the Lord will send his messenger to prepare the way before him. The messenger will refine and purify such that the sacrifice of Judah and Jerusalem will satisfy the Lord. Later, Malachi 4:23 identifies the messenger as Elijah and in Matthew 11:10, Jesus quotes Malachi in reference to John the Baptist, who prepared the way for Jesus. The messenger paves the way for the coming Messiah, who we as Christians believe are Jesus Christ. He forever changes the world and us. He continues to refine us and purify us.

◆ RESPONSORIAL PSALM 24: In the context of today's Feast of the Presentation, the psalm reminds us that for Christians, the son Mary and Joseph presented in the Temple is the King of glory. We are to prepare ourselves to let him in this day and everyday.

◆ SECOND READING: Jesus fully shared in our humanity. For this reason, together with the fullness of his divinity, he was able to destroy death. He is the high priest who forgives sin through his once, for all sacrifice. We receive consolation from the fact that Jesus also shared in human suffering. Because of his suffering on the Cross, he is able to empathize with our suffering. He is our help and our salvation.

◆ GOSPEL: Simeon's song announcing that he has seen God's salvation in the child Jesus and the actions of the prophetess, Anna, giving thanks to God and testifying about the child to those who awaited Jerusalem's redemption form the heart of today's Gospel. How do we let Simeon's words and Anna's actions become ours today? When we find ways to follow the example of Simeon and Anna, even as our age advances, we embrace our call to proclamation and mission. Then, in the end, we, like Simeon, may say to God, "you may let your servant / go in peace." For peace, is seeing, knowing, and witnessing to the Messiah, the Son of God, Jesus Christ.

The Roman Missal

Everything is proper to today's feast, so all texts and rubrics are found at February 2 in the Proper of Saints.

The Blessing of Candles and the Procession

The Missal calls for this Mass to begin with the blessing of candles and a procession, in one form or another. Two possibilities are given in the Missal: "The Procession" and "The Solemn Entrance."

First Form: The Procession

All should gather in a place apart from the worship space where the procession will go to — for example, a smaller church, or perhaps a space in the parish hall, or perhaps even the gathering space of the church. The gathered faithful are to be already holding candles, so either the people bring candles with them or candles are handed to them as they gather. The priest, wearing white Mass vestments (although he may wear a cope at this point instead of a chasuble), and the ministers enter. There is no mention of a procession or of any singing, so the priest and the ministers just informally take their places. First, light everyone's candles and while this is done the antiphon suggested in the Missal (*Ecce Dominus noster* — "Behold, our Lord will come with power, to enlighten the eyes of his servants, alleluia" — or some other appropriate song is sung. If another song or chant is used, the words should speak of the imagery of light.

After the candles are lit and the singing is concluded, the priest begins with the Sign of the Cross and one of the usual forms of the Greeting for Mass. Then he gives an introductory address; he may use the exact words as provided in the Missal at #4 for the Feast of the Presentation of the Lord, or he may use similar words. The address as given in the Missal notes the passing of forty days since the celebration of the Nativity and recalls how "Today is the blessed day / when Jesus was presented in the Temple by Mary and Joseph." It goes on to speak of the meaning of this feast as Jesus "coming to meet his believing people" and how Simeon and Anna, enlightened by the Holy Spirit, recognized him. It ends with the exhortation that we should "proceed to the house of God to encounter Christ," particularly as we shall recognize him in the breaking of bread until he comes again. Whether the priest uses the exact words in the Missal or similar words, the point of the address is to encourage the faithful "to celebrate the rite of this feast day actively and consciously."

After the address, the priest extends his hands and blesses the candles using the exact words of one of the two prayers of blessing given at #5 in the Missal (Feast of the Presentation of the Lord). In the first prayer, which specifically recalls Simeon and which refers to "the Light for revelation to the Gentiles," the priest makes the gesture of blessing with the Sign of the Cross where indicated; there is no such gesture in the second prayer, which speaks more generally about light and God's glory.

Next the priest sprinkles the candles with holy water without saying anything. Then he puts incense into the thurible for the procession, receives his lighted candle from the deacon or another minister, and the procession begins with the words of invitation from the Missal, given by the deacon, or, if there is no deacon, by the priest himself.

With everyone carrying lighted candles, the procession, in the usual order (that is, thurifer, crossbearer, candlebearers, and so on), moves into the worship space while an appropriate antiphon or song is sung. This Missal offers two suggestions for antiphons: "A light for revelation to the Gentiles and the glory of your people Israel" or "For my eyes have seen your salvation, which you have prepared in the sign of all the peoples." The Latin text for the first option is provided in the Missal.

When the priest arrives at the altar in the church, he venerates it and incenses it, if incense is being used. He then goes to the chair where he changes from the cope into the chasuble, if he wore a cope for the procession. The Gloria is then sung, after which the priest prays the Collect and Mass continues as usual.

Second Form: The Solemn Entrance

When the procession as described above is not going to take place, then the assembly gathers in the church as they usually do, holding candles. The priest, along with the ministers and a representative group of the faithful, goes to a place in the church that is visible to the rest of the assembly. They can be at the doors of the church or even somewhere inside the church itself. Notice that it is presumed that more than just the priest and ministers will gather and move in procession; a certain number of the faithful are expected to participate in this. The priest wears white Mass vestments; no mention is made of using a cope in this form of the entrance.

The priest and the others arrive at the place for the blessing of candles, without any music or formal procession. Once they are in place, everyone's candles are lit, with an antiphon or song being sung, as described above (this may take a little bit of thinking-through ahead of time, so that it is not done haphazardly; ushers can be of assistance here). Once everyone's candles are lit, the priest begins in the same way as in the first form above, with the Sign of the Cross, Greeting, introductory address, and blessing of candles and sprinkling, followed by the procession, accompanied by singing; he uses the same texts as designated for the first form of procession. As in the first form, the priest incenses the altar when arriving there, if incense is being used, and then he goes to the chair, at which point the Gloria is sung and Mass continues in the usual manner.

At the Mass

The Collect makes a connection between Christ's being presented "on this day in the Temple / in the substance of our flesh" and the request that, by God's grace, "we may be presented to you with minds made pure."

The Prayer over the Offerings draws a parallel between the offering of the Son, offered as the Lamb without blemish for the life of the world, and the offering we make now with exultation, asking that our offering here and now be pleasing to God, as was the offering of the Son.

The Preface, found right along with the other texts for this Mass in the Proper of Saints, is a brief one, succinctly stating that the "co-eternal Son was presented on this day in the Temple / and revealed by the Spirit / as the glory of Israel and the Light of the nations." Because of this, "we, too, go forth, rejoicing to encounter your Salvation." This going forth to encounter salvation occurs on many levels: certainly in the journey of our life, but also as we continue forth with the offering of this sacrifice, where we will encounter Christ in the salvific power of the Paschal Mystery made present in the Church's anamnesis of the Eucharistic Prayer and in Christ's Real Presence in the Eucharist. This would be a good occasion to chant the introductory dialogue and Preface, in order to highlight the festivity of this liturgy.

Simeon is mentioned again, this time in the Prayer after Communion, as we pray that just as his expectation was fulfilled "that he would not see death / until he had been privileged to welcome the Christ," so too may we meet the Lord in the gift of eternal life.

SAT 3 (#328) green
Weekday

Optional Memorials of St. Blaise, Bishop and Martyr /red; St. Ansgar, Bishop / white; Blessed Virgin Mary / white

The Lectionary for Mass

◆ FIRST READING: In a dream while Solomon is at Gibeon, God simply says to the king, ask me for something and I will give it to you. How many of us would like to hear God say this directly to us! Solomon offers a deep-felt response that attests to the goodness God showed to his father, David, and acknowledges Solomon's own youth and inexperience on the throne. Solomon then asks for an understanding heart that will lead him to judge justly and

know right from wrong. God grants Solomon's wish and more because there has previously been no one quite like Solomon. Solomon will reign with riches and glory like no other before him. God does ask us directly like God asked Solomon. Is our response akin to Solomon's?

◆ RESPONSORIAL PSALM 119 is the longest psalm in the psalter at 176 verses. The six verses and psalm refrain come from early on in this acrostic psalm. In them, we pray along with the psalm writer, to follow the Lord's commands. We rejoice in the Lord's instructions and continually want to have wisdom to interpret and live them to the best of our ability. Our use of this psalm in today's liturgy could be seen as what we ask of God. Blessed be God for granting our request to follow keep his words.

◆ GOSPEL: Today, we proclaim the return of the Twelve after John the Baptist's death. The Apostles reported all they had done and taught to Jesus. They must have done so much that Jesus, following his own example, invites them to come away and rest. They had to go by boat to get away because of the throngs. But people so desired Jesus that they quickly traveled on foot to meet them when they disembarked. How intense their desire and longing of the people for Jesus was that the speed of their feet was faster than a boat under paddle power!

The Blessing of Throats

The optional Memorial of St. Blaise is the traditional day for the blessing of throats. Although the Missal is silent on it, the *Book of Blessings* states that throats may be blessed at Mass, following the Homily and the Universal Prayer. For pastoral reasons, it may take the place of the final blessing of the Mass. The formula of blessing is: "Through the intercession of St. Blaise, bishop and martyr, may God deliver you from every disease of the throat and from

every other illness: In the name of the Father, and of the Son, and of the Holy Spirit. Amen."

Today's Saints

Although St. Blaise († 316) and St. Ansgar (801–865) were separated by time, they both wanted to care for souls. While serving as bishop of Sebastea, in Armenia, St. Blaise was a visible witness of the Gospel, which eventually led to his martyrdom during the persecutions of Diocletian. His feast day is commemorated with a blessing of throats because legend says that he cured a young boy choking on a fish bone. St. Ansgar, born in France, was a monk with a missionary spirit. He longed to travel to distant lands to draw more and more souls to the saving message of Christ. His missionary endeavors were directed toward Scandinavian territory, thus earning him the title Patron of Denmark. He is credited with organizing missions to Denmark, Sweden, and Norway and building the first Christian Church in Sweden. Due to his excellent leadership and preaching skills, St. Ansgar was appointed archbishop of Hamburg.

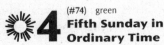

4 (#74) green
Fifth Sunday in Ordinary Time

The Lectionary for Mass

◆ First Reading: Job laments his sleepless nights and life of misery. He is hopeless, desperate to see happiness, but doubting whether he ever will. Many in our assemblies will resonate with Job's restlessness. Often people bemoan the misery that besets their lives. The world's misery frequently presents itself to us. As people of faith we might feel hopeless like Job, yet we still hope. We trust God's rest will overcome our insomnia and we hope in the beautiful dawn that follows and brings healing to misery.

◆ Responsorial Psalm 147 is a song of praise. In the verses of the Psalm for the Fifth Sunday in Ordinary Time, the psalmist praises God's gracious goodness for the Lord restored Jerusalem and brought her inhabitants back after the exile. The Lord heals broken hearts and binds wounds. The Lord knows each of us by name. Mighty and wise is the Lord who builds up the lowly and throws the wicked down to the earth. Our praise to the Lord we offer!

◆ Second Reading: The Gospel is everything to Paul. He preaches it not on his own accord, but out of an obligation that comes from God. In other words, God called Paul to serve as a minister of the Gospel. For his free proclamation of the Gospel, Paul's free reward is a life of grace in Christ. Paul's strategy for preaching the Gospel is to become all things to all people in the hopes of leading some to Christ. We might think his strategy is a recipe for burnout because no one can please everyone all the time, but pleasing people is not Paul's focus. The Apostle is single-minded about the Gospel and people's conversion to it.

◆ Gospel: Today's Gospel begins on the same Sabbath day as last Sunday's Gospel in which Jesus taught in the synagogue and healed the man possessed by an evil spirit. Inside the house of Simon and Andrew, Jesus heals Simon's mother-in-law not by uttering any words, but with the simple gesture of taking her hand and helping her up. This individual healing leads to a multitude of healings and exorcisms the same say after sunset as the entire town came to the doorstep of the house where Jesus was. Since it was the whole town that brought those ill or possessed, no wonder Jesus needed to renew him by going off to a deserted place to pray. This is exactly what he did the following day before dawn. Jesus' mission is clear: to preach, heal, and drive out demons with the divine authority given to him.

The Roman Missal

The Mass texts for today are found in the "Ordinary Time" section of the Proper of Time. The Gloria and the Creed are sung or said today.

The Collect asks that the Lord will keep us safe as we rely "solely on the help of heavenly grace." The Prayer over the Offerings prays for the transformation of the created realities we offer, that is, bread and wine, so that just as they are material sustenance for us, so too may they become "the Sacrament of eternal life." The Prayer after Communion highlights the unity of the faithful that is to be the result of their participation in the Eucharist. Being united in the one Body of Christ through "the one Bread and the one Chalice" (a presumption that the chalice is offered to the assembly at all Masses?) is the way that we "joyfully bear fruit / for the salvation of the world."

Any one of the eight Prefaces of the Sundays in Ordinary Time may be selected for today.

Other Ideas

On the first Sunday of February, Black History Month, the USCCB invites Catholics to pray for the African American Family. Reprint the prayer composed by Fr. Jim Goode, OFM (found here: www.usccb.org/issues-and-action/cultural-diversity/african-american

/resources/upload/2016-National -Day-of-Prayer-African-American -African-Family.pdf). Encourage community members to learn more about the particular generational burdens faced by African Americans in the United States that resulted from hundreds of years of slavery and the upheaval of reconstruction. Invite people to find ways to stand in meaningful solidarity with the African American community around issues of racial and economic justice. Help your community understand the rich, long history of African American Roman Catholicism by inviting in a speaker or showing Sister Thea Bowman's address to the USCCB (found here: www.usccb.org/issues -and-action/cultural-diversity /african-american/resources/) at a parish event. Include hymns that have been part of the life of this community at Mass (refer to the hymnal, *Lead Me, Guide Me, Second Edition*, published by GIA Publications).

M O N 5 (#329) red
Memorial of St. Agatha, Virgin and Martyr

The Lectionary for Mass

◆ FIRST READING: We move ahead five chapters in 1 Kings from this past Saturday in which we heard Solomon ask God for an understanding heart. Today's passage recounts the transfer of the Ark of the Covenant into the new temple building. The community of Israel is present for this solemn and festive occasion, although it is the priests who enter the holy of holies where the Ark will reside. The Lord's glory reveals itself in a cloud that fills the Temple. Solomon attests that the house they have built is one in which the Lord can live forever.

◆ RESPONSORIAL PSALM 132 is a hymn that was sung as the Israelites would carry the Ark of the Covenant into the Temple. Thus, it is a fitting Responsorial Psalm for today's First Reading in which the Lord is brought to his place of rest in the holy of holies. The psalm also prays that the Lord's priests may be clothed in justice and all they faithful joyfully shout for the Lord is with his people!

◆ GOSPEL: We advance about twenty verses in Mark 6 for today's Gospel. The Twelve have returned from their mission and gone away to rest with Jesus. Paradoxically, even while resting, they feed five thousand, get back in the boat and travel to Bethsaida. On the journey Jesus walks on water and the disciples think he is a ghost. The Gospel writer notes the disciples' had hardened hearts. This is the point at which today's Gospel passage begins. Crowds gathered once again as Jesus and his disciples came off the boat. On this occasion, the crowds recognized Jesus and went to bring people in the village to him in need of healing. Jesus might not have been welcome in his native place, but in the many villages and towns of Gennesaret, people flocked to him and he healed them. His was a ministry of healing. In his very person is healing for people then, and for us now.

The Roman Missal

The Mass text that is proper for today is the Collect, and it is found in the Proper of Saints at February 5. The prayer highlights St. Agatha's courage in martyrdom and her chastity. The Prayer over the Offerings and the Prayer after Communion will come either from the Common of Martyrs: For a Virgin Martyr, or from the Common of Virgins: For One Virgin. For the Preface, one of the two Prefaces of Holy Martyrs would be a good choice. Use Eucharistic Prayer I since she is included in the Canon.

Today's Saint

Agatha was born in Sicily, probably around the year 231, and is one of the women mentioned by name in Eucharistic Prayer I. According to legend, she was the daughter of a prominent family and was very beautiful. The Roman senator Quintianus wished to marry her, but when Agatha spurned him, he had her put in a brothel. In spite of this, Agatha held to her Christian faith. Quintianus then had her tortured by having her breasts cut off. She eventually died in prison in 253. St. Agatha is the patron of the city of her martyrdom, Catania, and is invoked against the fire, earthquakes, and eruptions of Mount Etna. In recent years, because her breasts were cut off as part of her torture, she is considered the patron saint of patients with breast cancer.

T U E 6 (#330) red
Memorial of St. Paul Miki and Companions, Martyrs

The Lectionary for Mass

◆ FIRST READING: Today we find King Solomon before the altar in front of the entire community of Israel where he leads them in pray. Solomon begins his prayer by praising God for his faithfulness to the covenant. The king wonders whether God indeed dwells on earth for neither the heavens—even the highest of heavens—can contain God. Nor can the Temple hold the Lord. Solomon then asks God to watch over the Temple and listen to the prayers he and the people of Israel will offer in it. We, too, desire God to listen to our prayers, for when we pray, whether in solitude or as part of a liturgical assembly, we always pray in communion with the whole Church.

◆ RESPONSORIAL PSALM 84: When have you so strongly desired to be in God's presence? Psalm 84 was originally sung by during the pilgrimage feasts by people longing to be in the presence of the Lord, in his courts. The pilgrim's desire to be with God was so deep that even their heart and flesh cried out for God. How comforting for the pilgrims and us to know that even the smallest of birds finds their home in God. Our home is also with God. God's dwelling place is indeed lovely!

◆ GOSPEL: The critical Pharisees and scribes make a return in today's Gospel. This time, they inquire of Jesus as to why his disciples do not follow the tradition of the elders and eat their meals with unclean hands. Jesus' response levels the charge against the Pharisees and scribes that they disregard God's commandment and cling to human tradition. Jesus calls the Pharisees and scribes to think seriously about the location of their heart. He bids us to do the same.

The Roman Missal

The Collect, which is proper for today, is found in the Proper of Saints at February 6. The prayer refers to God as "the strength of all the Saints," and asks that through the intercession of St. Paul Miki and companions, "we may hold with courage even until death / to the faith that we profess," just as they did. The Prayer over the Offerings and the Prayer after Communion are taken from the Common of Martyrs: For Several Martyrs. For the Preface, use one of the two Prefaces of Holy Martyrs.

Today's Saint

St. Paul Miki († 1597), a Jesuit priest, was one of the twenty-six martyrs of Japan. Feeling threatened by the growing influence of the Jesuits, the local governor had members of the Christian community arrested and thrown in jail. They were forced to walk 600 miles from Kyoto to Nagasaki as a deterrent to other Christians, but they sang the

Te Deum as they went. At Nagasaki they were crucified. When Christian missionaries returned to Japan in the nineteenth century, they found that a secret Christian community had survived by transmitting their beliefs and prayers from generation to generation.

W E D 7 (#331) green
Weekday

The Lectionary for Mass

◆ FIRST READING: The queen of Sheba needed to see Solomon's fame for herself so she made the journey to Jerusalem with her entourage. While there, she witnessed the extravagance surrounding him. She learned personally of his great wisdom by asking him questions, although the passage does not tell us the specific questions she asked. For Solomon's prosperity and wisdom, she blesses the Lord. Upon her departure, the queen herself gives Solomon with many gifts.

◆ RESPONSORIAL PSALM 37: Coming after the First Reading, the psalm reflects the example of justice and wisdom Solomon was to us and his people. The Lord will grant salvation to the just because they have put their trust in him. Once more, the questions return to us, how will the wisdom that comes from our mouth be like that of Solomon? How will we murmur the Lord's justice?

◆ GOSPEL: Jesus taught us to align our hearts with God's commandments and not cling to human tradition yesterday. Today's Gospel reading follows immediately from where yesterday's ended. The Teacher uses a short parable to teach the crowds that what defiles us comes from within us, not from outside us. The disciples, perhaps still with hardened hearts of Mark 6:56, do not understand. This is, however, a lesson that both the disciples had to understand and so do we. We must align our hearts with God's law.

T H U 8 (#332) green
Weekday

Optional Memorial of St. Jerome Emiliani / white; St. Josephine Bakhita, Virgin / white

The Lectionary for Mass

◆ FIRST READING: A change occurs in Solomon. The First Reading states that when the king was old, his heart was split between the Lord and strange gods, just as David's heart was divided. As a consequence of not keeping the covenant, the Lord would deprive Solomon of the kingdom. But the Lord, in his mercy, would not do this while Solomon was still alive, but would wait until after he died and not let his son inherit the kingdom.

◆ RESPONSORIAL PSALM 106 reflects how the people of Israel would call upon the Lord for mercy. For God's mercy, the people give thanks. But the psalm writer also describes how the people of Israel turned to idols, sacrificing even their sons and daughters to demons. The turn to idols aligns with the turn of Solomon's own heart recounted in the First Reading. Though we sin, we still pray to the Lord to remember us. Our hearts do trust in the Lord's mercy, even though at times our actions are not consistent with the covenant.

◆ GOSPEL: Jesus is now in the district of Tyre, perhaps for a bit of respite because today's Gospel reading tells us he entered a house and did not want anyone to know about it. But to no surprise, a woman comes to beg Jesus to heal her daughter possessed by an unclean spirit. The Greek Syrophoenician woman responds to Jesus' own statement with her own words that testify to the extension of Jesus' ministry beyond the Jewish people. Her words reveal her faith. Jesus sends informs her that the demon is gone from her daughter and sends her home. She, her daughter, and her home are at peace in the Lord.

Today's Saints

Jerome was born into a wealthy family, and before being led to study for the priesthood he was a soldier in Venice. As a priest, Jerome was greatly devoted to helping the poor and the disadvantaged. He founded hospitals, orphanages and an order of priests whose apostolate it was to care for the orphans.

Josephine was born in Sudan and at the age of nine was taken into slavery. Bought by an Italian diplomat, she was taken to Italy where she converted to Christianity at the age of 25. Three years later, after having been freed from slavery, she joined the Institute of the Canossian Daughters of Charity.

FRI 9 (#333) green
Weekday

The Lectionary for Mass

◆ FIRST READING: Our reading today narrates the meeting of Jeroboam and the prophet Ahijah the Shilonite on the road away from Jerusalem.

◆ RESPONSORIAL PSALM 81: Today's psalm reminds us that the Lord will always be our God. All the Lord asks of us is that we hear his voice and walk in his ways.

◆ GOSPEL: Jesus' ministry of healing continues as opens a deaf man's ears and restores his speech. *Ephphatha!* is Jesus' command. On the touch and word of Jesus, healing occurs. The Gospel writer, Mark, continues to have Jesus insist that people do not tell anyone what happened. But how unrealistic to have people keep such Good News to themselves! And they do not. Like stubborn children, the more a parent instructs them not to tell, the more they will tell.

SAT 10 (#334) white
Memorial of St. Scholastica, Virgin

The Lectionary for Mass

◆ FIRST READING: In today's reading, Jeroboam fears that the kingdom will return to David's house. He deals with his fear by instructing Rohoboam, king of Judah, to build temples on high places and consecrate priests who were not Levites. Joroboam continued his sinful ways, as did those in Israel who followed his lead and worshipped idols.

◆ RESPONSORIAL PSALM 106: We recently prayed Psalm 106, although with a different refrain and a few different verses, two days ago on Thursday, February 8, 2018. In today's refrain we affirm the Lord has been a refuge for his people in every age. The Lord has been, is, and ever shall take care of his children, even when the stray from him. This is the confidence we live in. This is why we, together with the psalm writer, we praise and thank God for always calling us back and extending his mercy to us.

◆ GOSPEL: As if teaching, exorcising, and healing were not enough on Jesus' part to reveal his identity to us, in today's Gospel he feeds the four thousand on seven loaves and a few fish. In his giving thanks, breaking bread, sharing of the bread with the crowd we know Jesus as the Messiah who feeds and nourishes us. He sustains us for the journey as disciples as he did the crowds who gathered around him. Feasting on his Body and Blood in the Eucharist, we are satisfied. And, as in today's Gospel, there is always more than enough to go around. Jesus will never leave anyone hungry. Our call as disciples is to follow the model he sets before us.

The Roman Missal

The Mass text that is proper for today is the Collect, found in the Proper of Saints at February 10. The Prayer over the Offerings and the Prayer after Communion are taken either from the Common of Virgins: For One Virgin, or from the Common of Holy Men and Women: For a Nun. For the Preface, choose either the Preface of Holy Virgins and Religious or one of the Prefaces of Saints.

Today's Saint

Information regarding the life of St. Scholastica is rather meager, but her legacy continues to live on. She was the twin sister of St. Benedict, the father of Western monasticism. From a young age (480–547) she expressed a deep desire to dedicate her life to God through the monastic vows: obedience, conversion of life (poverty and chastity), and stability. She founded and supervised a monastery of nuns near her brother's monastery at Monte Casino.

☀ 11 (#77) green
Sixth Sunday in Ordinary Time

The Lectionary for Mass

◆ FIRST READING: In the First Reading, we hear of the leper: "He shall dwell apart, making his abode outside the camp." It was a terrible fate for people to be cast out from the community. This story sets the scene for us to hear of Jesus' cure of the leper in the Gospel.

◆ RESPONSORIAL PSALM 32 is a hymn for those who know they have sinned and are overjoyed by God's forgiveness.

◆ SECOND READING: In today's reading, Paul tells the Corinthians what kind of example they should be. They should do everything for the glory of God, and avoid things that would cause offense.

◆ GOSPEL: Today's medical science has classified leprosy as a single skin condition, also known as Hansen's disease. In Jesus' time, though, *leprosy* was a term that referred to multiple skin disorders. The leper should not have been anywhere near Jesus nor close enough to speak with him. He broke the law. Yet Jesus did not shun the man. Instead, he listened when he approached him. Then Jesus broke the law by touching him. By breaking that law, Jesus showed his disciples and followers that God does not shun. We are not to shut anyone out from the community of the people of God.

The Roman Missal

The Gloria and the Creed are sung or said today. The Collect asks that our lives "may be so fashioned by your grace / as to become a dwelling pleasing to you." The Prayer over the Offerings reiterates that such transformation should be the heart of the oblation we make; as we make our offering in union at Mass with Christ's. In the Prayer after Communion we pray that, "having fed upon these heavenly delights" of the Eucharist, "we may always / long for that food by which we truly live."

Other Ideas

Ash Wednesday falls on February 14. Consider hosting a Mardis Gras party the day before with festive decorations. Eat pancakes and learn about why this day is called "Fat Tuesday."

MON 12 (#335) green
Weekday

The Lectionary for Mass

◆ FIRST READING: The final verses of the reading reveal how God's does not necessarily interpret earthly riches in the manner worldly people do. Humility, whether rich or poor, is what matters in the eyes of God.

◆ RESPONSORIAL PSALM 119: Today, we ask that the Lord be kind to us so we will live. We, like the psalmist writer have gone astray, but now we attempt to be faithful to God.

◆ GOSPEL: The Pharisees push Jesus for a sign from heaven as if his miracles and healings were not enough. Jesus' solemn response to them is terse. No sign will be given to people of this generation, he says. Then Jesus simply gets back in the boat and proceeds to the other shore, leaving the Pharisees to ponder not only response, but also why they thought it necessary to ask for a sign in the first place.

TUE 13 (#336) green
Weekday

The Lectionary for Mass

◆ FIRST READING: Today's First Reading from James picks up where yesterday's left off. In this passage James addressees the topic of temptation. He teaches that God is not the source of temptation, but rather our own distorted human desire is. From the lure of this desire, comes sin, and from sin, death. We are to persevere in the face of temptation, not allowing it to deceive us. God makes our perseverance possible, James teaches, because God desires to give us birth — to gift of us with life.

◆ RESPONSORIAL PSALM 94 is an individual lament. The words of the psalm clearly express the psalm writer's confidence that God's mercy will sustain him.

◆ GOSPEL: The disciples just cannot see the hardness of their own hearts. In today's Gospel reading, they forget to bring bread, although they do have one loaf. Jesus warns them against the leaven of the Pharisees and Herod, but the disciples think it is because they lack bread on this occasion. Jesus responds to them with five questions, trying to get at why they still do not understand. But they do not. May we open ourselves to the love and life that come through Jesus Christ, his Son, the Messiah.

LENT AND HOLY WEEK

The Liturgical Time

The Meaning

LENT is our season of prayer, fasting, and almsgiving, ancient practices dating back to the Israelites. Mentioned in a number of places in the Old Testament — particularly the Books of Job, Jeremiah, and Daniel — the sprinkling of ashes, wearing of sackcloth, and practices of fasting were the central gestures of sorrow and repentance for the chosen people.

The use of ashes for all the faithful at the start of Lent began in the tenth century. In many ways it is ironic that on the day we hear Jesus speak of praying, fasting, and almsgiving being done in secret, we participate in what may be the year's most public physical statement of our belief in him! As we are signed on the forehead with the Cross (a gesture that, with holy oil, is also part of Baptism, Confirmation, and Anointing) we are told to "Repent and believe in the Gospel." Alternatively, the formula "Remember that you are dust, and to dust you shall return" is used, which also points to the urgency of recognizing and reconciling our sinfulness. We are reminded that with our Baptism has come the responsibility to live our lives for the Lord.

While it is fine to wash the ashes off after Mass, many people keep them on their forehead throughout the day. Often, they are a discussion starter for people outside the Christian family or for those who have not been taught their meaning. Much in the way that our Muslim brothers and sisters have taught us the meaning of the Ramadan fast, Ash Wednesday provides an opening for us to share our faith and to highlight that our lives as followers of Jesus should be those of humble service to others.

Another visible practice that can be a good discussion starter about our faith is the abstinence healthy adults observe on Fridays. It's important to remember we don't do this to look or feel holy but to invite, through self-denial, inner purification by God. We also do this as an act of solidarity with those throughout the world who have less than we do. If we turn our abstinence into a treat (for example, having a lush, fish dinner in place of our ordinary fare) we almost defeat the purpose. Simple meals best reflect the purpose of this practice.

Likewise, the practices of fasting we undertake can be a witness. As children, many people learn to give up treats like sugary foods or television for Lent. As adults, we're encouraged to consider not only that from which we want to fast, but the deep hungers we hope Christ will fill as we create greater space within. Watching for ulterior motives ("I think I'll give up my morning mocha latte, and maybe by the end of Lent I will have dropped four pounds") is helpful. We can conserve the money saved in our fast for a work of kindness or charity. Or we can fast from behaviors. While restraining the angry retort, discontinuing gossip, or resisting mean judgments may not save us money, it might go further in bringing us closer to God.

As we evangelize in this season, we should stay open to inviting people to find out more about our faith. Recent research reveals that half of the adults who have been raised Catholic (52 percent) leave the Church at some point. But 43 percent of those who think of themselves as "cultural Catholics" can imagine that they might return to the Church at some point in their lives. Our invitation may be an important part of their process. Coming to Lenten fish dinners, the Stations of the Cross, special Bible studies, or other gatherings besides mass can be an easy way to experience returning to the Catholic community. Holy Week, with its vivid Palm Sunday start, can be another time to reexperience the richness of the Catholic expression of Christianity.

The Lectionary for Mass

THE forty-plus-day season of Lent is the time that we, as disciples, are invited to draw more closely to God. Across the world, Christians journey individually and as communities, following the pattern of Jesus' sojourn in the wilderness. Through practices of prayer, fasting, and almsgiving, we experience anew the ultimate expression of God's love as it is expressed in the Paschal Mystery of Christ's suffering, Death, and Resurrection. As we remember and reexperience the promises of God we are reminded not only of the limitlessness of God's power, but also the vastness of God's love and generosity.

This year, the Old Testament stories in the First Reading invite us into the rich history of the covenant. We hear of the destructive power of the flood and the salvific power of God. We journey with Moses and the Israelites out of slavery, through the desert and with them receive the Law, the Ten Commandments, on Mount Sinai. In the voices of the great prophets, we are called back to follow this law of the almighty more closely. Jonah reveals to us the power of surrendering to rather than defying God's will. Daniel, Micah, and Isaiah speak to us of turning from sin and returning to God completely. This is not a task to be put off to the future, but one to be embraced right now. The poetic Hosea offers us the loving invitation to return to right relationship with God with all our heart. And over and again, the psalmist reminds us that our God is not just a speaking, directing, law-giving God, but a God who listens.

In the words of the prophets, as well as in the psalm texts, we are repeatedly reminded that we are the descendants of Abraham. This lineage is a source of great gifts, but it also confers serious responsibilities. The covenant binds us, providing us with a framework for our lives. It does not arbitrarily restrict us in a negative way but guides our actions so that we live in a way that is pleasing to God and life-giving to all we encounter.

In the Gospel, we experience the challenges faced by Jesus in the last weeks of his ministry. Jeremiah will speak to us of how difficult it is to hear and respond to prophets, and Jesus echoes him as he observes that prophets are never loved in their own land. The local people are at times belligerent and ill disposed, resistant to listening to Jesus and receiving his call to repentance and radical love. The Jewish authorities escalate in their suspicion and hostility, and move beyond intellectual challenges to begin plotting a course to his Death.

None of this stops Jesus in his steady journey to Jerusalem and the Cross. We are left reflecting on how we respond to burdens, challenges, and deep struggles. Do we, like Jesus, use them to draw closer to God, or are we like the stubborn listeners to the prophets, who resist inviting God in more deeply as a source of healing and hope?

The purpose of the practices of Lent are many. Among them are spiritual growth and conversion of heart. At times, human life presents us with temptations. At other times, we rebel against our circumstances. In these holy days, Christ comes to us to further reveal the depth of God's love for us and deepen our response to it. No matter how far we have strayed, our loving God stands at the ready to respond to our repentance with love and forgiveness. With confidence and trust, we embrace our role as witness and follower once again in the journey to Calvary.

The Roman Missal

Lent, which runs from Ash Wednesday up to but not including the Mass of the Lord's Supper on Holy Thursday (see UNLY, 28), is a penitential season during which we prepare ourselves for the coming celebration of the Paschal Mystery during Holy Week, the Triduum, and Easter. The liturgical movement toward these great Sundays and solemnities hastens through the season. On the Fourth Sunday of Lent, for example, we pray in the Collect that "the Christian people may hasten toward the solemn celebrations to come." For the good of our sisters and brothers and for our own spiritual development, we take part in prayer, fasting, and almsgiving (see the Collect for the Third Sunday of Lent) to nurture humble, contrite, and merciful hearts.

The most profound expression of the penitential spirit of Lent transpires when we connect our spiritual preparation to the coming Baptism of our new brothers and sisters at the Easter Vigil, and, indeed, to our own renewal of baptismal promises on that day. Careful preparation must be exercised in parishes that have catechumens and elect participating in the RCIA process. The season concludes as we move into Holy Week and celebrate Palm Sunday with its three options for the Introductory Rite, and the Chrism Mass at which the bishop blesses the Oil of the Sick and Oil of Catechumens and consecrates the Sacred Chrism, and priests renew their Ordination promises.

Although Advent and Lent have different theological and spiritual themes, both require moderation in our liturgies and decoration of liturgical spaces. Music in general should be modest, and the use of instrumental music should be minimal. Ministers wear violet, but on the Fourth Sunday, they may wear rose and the sanctuary may be decorated with flowers. The Alleluia is not sung before the proclamation of the Gospel, and, as in Advent, we do not sing or recite the Gloria during Lent (except on feasts and solemnities). The First and Second Sunday of Lent each has its own proper Preface to the Eucharistic Prayer, which are always used. On the Third, Fourth, and Fifth Sundays of Lent in Year B, we use Preface I or II of Lent (when there is no Scrutiny). For weekdays, the Missal recommends Prefaces III or IV of Lent. The Eucharistic Prayers for Reconciliation are especially appropriate during Lent and they can be used with either their own Prefaces or with a Preface of Lent. As usual, Eucharistic Prayer IV should not be used when a proper Preface other than its own is required. There is no Solemn Blessing for Lent, but there are two sets of sample formularies for the Universal Prayer in Appendix V. Newly restored to this edition of the Missal are the Lenten Prayers over the People. One is provided for optional use for each day of Lent.

Children's Liturgy of the Word

The liturgical color changes from green, a color symbolizing hope, to violet, a color representing penance. During Lent, children's Liturgy of the Word leaders and assistants help children to realize the meaning of sin and repentance. They guide children to Easter Time, where they will renew their baptismal promises once again.

Those who participate in the celebration of the Word with children have many details to coordinate with liturgical and initiation ministries during these six weeks. You will need to be aware of any elect or candidates among the children so you might lead the children in prayerfully supporting them as they approach the Easter sacraments. Speak with your director of initiation about whether or not you have elect and therefore will celebrate the Scrutinies on the Third, Fourth, and Fifth Sundays of Lent. If your community will celebrate the Scrutinies during the same liturgy at which you also have children's Liturgy of the Word, you will need to make timing adjustments and most likely will have more time with the children. You will also need to find out from the director of liturgy or the priest celebrant whether Year A or Year B Lectionary readings will be proclaimed. Proclaim the same readings with the children as the main assembly will hear.

As always, discuss with the director of music the arrangements for the Responsorial Psalms and Gospel Acclamation. As part of the reflection on the First Sunday of Lent, you might ask the children about what they experience as different on this day and then discuss why the color and Gospel Acclamation change. If the response to the intercessions will be sung in the main assembly, consider singing the response with the children. You do not need to sing the same responses with the children all of the time, but some consistency helps unite the children with the main assembly. It also forms them so they are able to fully participate if they attend a liturgy at which the community does not offer the celebration of the Word with children.

Lastly, silence is always important in liturgy. In Lent, silence calms the spirit of children and aids their self-reflection. It leads them to recognize places where they have done wrong and need to repent. It teaches them that God loves them in the silence and depths of their hearts. Reflect on how you incorporate silence in the celebration of the Word. Consider lengthening the silence by ten to fifteen seconds at a few places so the pace of the celebration feels different to you and the children during Lent.

The Saints

DURING Lent, we the observances of saints continue, however, all memorials are considered optional instead of obligatory. The Feast of the Chair of St. Peter falls on February 22. This feast used to begin the Octave of Prayer for Christian Unity, before it was moved to February. On this day we give thanks for the unity that the popes are charged with guarding and fostering. We also remember the many saintly men who have given their lives as "Servant of the Servants of God."

St. Katharine Drexel, whose optional memorial falls on March 3, is perhaps the perfect saint to celebrate in the midst of our Lenten observance. Born to a very wealthy family, she dedicated her life to fasting, prayer, and almsgiving. She saw this as a response to God's free gift to us that is especially visible in the Eucharist. In the process, she founded her order, the Sisters of the Blessed Sacrament, along with Xavier University. Her love of neighbor and generosity of life is remembered across the United States, especially her work for the education of African American and Native American people.

Another ancient (optional) memorial falls shortly thereafter, that of Sts. Perpetua and Felicity on March 7. Perpetua was a nursing mother, and Felicity gave birth to a daughter in prison just before her martyrdom. The story of their martyrdom is one of the earliest accounts to be preserved, and their names are prominently remembered in the Litany of the Saints and in Eucharistic Prayer I.

On March 19, the Church remembers St. Joseph, husband to the Blessed Virgin and guardian of the Lord. Joseph is remembered as a gentle, thoughtful man who accepted the Lord's Word and took Mary into his own house. Because he is traditionally considered to have had Jesus present at his deathbed, he is traditionally asked to pray that Christians be given an equally holy death.

The days of Holy Week, of Triduum, and of the Easter Octave take precedence over other feast days. If your parish's or diocese's patronal feast falls on one of these days, it will be transferred to April 10, after the Easter Octave and the Feast of the Annunciation, which is itself transferred from March 25 to April 9 this year.

The Liturgy of the Hours

ASH Wednesday seems to always take us a bit by surprise. In many ways this is reflective of the grace of God. Be prepared for Lent. However, let's let God surprise us.

If you're not using a digital option, just follow the instructions in your breviary for which psalms are prayed on Ash Wednesday as well as the Thursday, Friday, and Saturday following. We begin "Week One" with the First Sunday of Lent. Also remember that the Alleluia is not sung or said.

Because of our traditional practices of prayer, fasting, and almsgiving, adding the Liturgy of the Hours to the parish schedule is a natural fit. Look at what events are being prepared for the season and begin and end with this prayer. For example, if you are having a parish mission, let Evening Prayer open each night. If there is a parish Friday fish fry, maybe schedule a service as the dinner time is ending. Saturday morning can be a good time for some, before they begin a busy day. Other parishes offer Evening Prayer on the Sundays of Lent and Easter, culminating in an ice cream social on Pentecost. This is a season people are generally open to adding prayer experiences to their lives. Seize the opportunity.

Since the Liturgy of the Hours is adaptable, adapt. If you are doing a Saturday morning, or an opportunity before school or work, be sensitive to people's time. Shorter may be better. If you are praying at a retreat, there may not be musical support. Then speak the psalms. Certainly if you are in the church, with a larger assembly and musicians, then allow for a fuller experience. The real point is to pray, and our style should support the best experience possible in any situation.

What about the shorter times of Daytime Prayer and Night Prayer? These can be easily prayed at lunch or before going to sleep. Many of us were trained as children to stop before climbing into bed and to say a prayer. As adults, these habits have fallen away, wrapped up in our own busyness or exhaustion. Maybe this Lent we can start again, and encourage our parishioners as well. Many don't even know these simple prayers exist. Make publications or websites available to them on your home page or church bulletin. Post a reminder on social media.

Morning Prayer each Friday includes the great penitential Psalm 51. This is often a seasonal psalm for Lent. The weekly repetition sears the words into our soul and we memorize the text without even trying. The psalmist speaks of the great themes and challenges of our Lenten journey. We must recognize mercy, name honestly our sin, turn to the Lord. We acknowledge that God never asked for empty sacrifices, but rather our hearts and our spirits attuned to the Lord. If you are praying communally on Friday and using this psalm on Sunday, consider preaching on it. Perhaps weave the sung version into your preaching and into the communal prayer experience as well.

Holy Week bridges us to the Sacred Triduum. Remembering the way the Church honors time, Lent will end prior to Evening Prayer on Holy Thursday.

Rites of Christian Initiation of Adults

IF we take our cue from the *Rite of Christian Initiation of Adults*, it becomes clear that the Lenten season is a time for the whole Church to slow down and examine herself in light of the Paschal Mystery. It is not really about giving up one's favorite food or TV program, but naming those areas in one's life that need healing, conversion, and renewal. The Christian community prays, fasts, and gives alms to deepen its communion with Christ as well as habituate itself to the life of a disciple. These practices aid us on the journey of repentance and healing. In this season, we find Christ calling us into the desert to wrestle with our sinfulness so that we might be renewed once again during the great feast of Easter.

The RCIA says this is a period of "intense spiritual preparation . . . and is intended to purify the minds and hearts of the elect" (RCIA, 139). Even though we focus our attention on the elect, this statement is true for the whole Church; the Lenten journey is one celebrated in community. We walk with each other and support one another as we grow in our "knowledge of Christ the Savior" (RCIA, 139). The whole parish community is on the journey of renewal and purification. Consider ways that the elect and the parish family can come together in prayer and reflection so that

Lent truly is an intense time in which our hearts and minds are renewed.

For catechumens, who have spent a full liturgical year in the Period of the Catechumenate (see *United States National Statutes for the Catechumenate*, 6) and have discerned their readiness for initiation, the beginning of Lent finds them gathered at the cathedral celebrating the second step in the process, the Rite of Election. In some dioceses, candidates for full reception also go to the cathedral to celebrate the optional Rite of the Call to Continuing Conversion. At the Rite of Election, the bishop announces what God has already done in the life of the catechumens and calls them to the Easter sacraments. The Rite of Election thus begins the third period in the RCIA process. This Period of Purification and Enlightenment is a time of retreat for the Church that coincides with Lent. This period is a time for the whole Church to cultivate its relationship to the living God.

The rite says that during this period, members of the elect should be preparing for the Easter sacraments. This preparation consists of prayer and "interior reflection [more] than . . . catechetical instruction" (RCIA, 139). Too often, those involved with RCIA use this period to continue formal catechetical instruction or finalize annulments instead of walking with the elect to learn the art of prayer as individual and as a member of the Body of Christ.

The primary ritual for the elect during this season is the celebration of the three Scrutinies. Each scrutiny is designed to "uncover, then heal all that is weak, defective, or sinful . . . [and] to bring out, then strengthen all that is upright, strong, and good" (RCIA, 141). Celebrated on the third, fourth, and fifth Sundays, these rites are so important that there is a special ritual Mass in the Missal with unique prayers. The Church also assigns the readings from Year A of the Lectionary because they help to highlight the process of conversion and enlightenment. As your community prepares for the scrutinies, consider inviting the parish together for prayer and reflection on what is sinful and in need of healing in the parish. This gathering will help you plan and shape the rite for each Sunday. Work closely with the musicians in the parish so that these rituals are celebrated with great care and reverence.

The Sacraments of Initiation

IT is often not customary for candidates to receive the sacraments during Lent, but it is possible, especially for the Sacrament of Confirmation because it is often scheduled based upon when the bishop is able to preside. It is a time of more intensive preparation with days of reflection and working on projects. The parish life is fully engaged in the Lenten season and it is an opportunity to invite candidates and their families to fully participate in the activities.

Parents and godparents are often interested in the role they will play in the Baptism of their child. They want to know what the expectations will be beyond the day of the Baptism. As members of the faith community we can support them by helping them to see that the sacrament is a sign of something bigger than the day it is experienced. The candidate is being baptized into something more, a new state of being and into a faith family. Whenever we have opportunities to convey this sensibility it is going to be transformative to the families.

Parishes usually offer the Sacrament of Reconciliation during the Lenten season. Inform parents that it is important to bring their children ages six and above to attend a Reconciliation service so that they are able to see their parents and other parishioners experience the sacrament prior to learning about it. This is a form of preparation for First Reconciliation. Confirmation candidates can also be encouraged to attend the Sacrament of Reconciliation as a part of their preparation of the reception of the sacrament since this is a regular part of adult Catholic faith.

The Rite of Penance

THE Church Fathers remind us that Lent has two characteristics: Baptism and Penance (see CSL, 109) Therefore, we prepare for and approach Penance in light of anticipating our renewal of Baptism at Easter. We are disciples on the road. How are we doing?

Is there a way that your community can weave together these ideas of discipleship and reconciliation? It's not a matter "beating ourselves up" for sin. It is about honestly acknowledging it, facing it, seeing the consequences of it for us and our world. Finally, it is about prayer, acknowledging God's grace and mercy, and repairing what we can. Said another way, contrition, confession, absolution, and penance.

Can we move our parishes into this idea of journey and away from seeing Lent as an endurance contest for God? Our Lenten disciplines naturally lead us to the sacrament. Can we nudge our parishioners to begin Lent by choosing actions (or inactions) that challenge them to a deeper relationship with God? Perhaps provide suggestions on the parish homepage or bulletin. For example, "Keeping the Sabbath holy" means worship, but also no work. Can we turn off our busyness to spend time with God and our family? This is very difficult in our culture. Can we confess that we are tied to our need for power, control or the affirmation that comes from work? Can we let go and experience our brokenness and God's mercy?

With an accent on Mark's journey to the cross, perhaps it's time to evaluate which Stations of the Cross are used in the parish. Is there a way of building a "progressive celebration" of reconciliation in the parish? For example, on one Friday invite parishioners to experience the stations which uses music, prayer, and Scripture. Be sure to utilize time for silence as well. In following week, perhaps at Evening Prayer, including preaching on the themes of the Stations, such as journey with the Lord through pain or solidarity with the disenfranchised. Then a celebration of the sacrament building on an examination of conscience rooted in your experience of the stations. This allows for a tie between the Lectionary, the season, and the sacrament.

Is your parish able to podcast some of these celebrations? While experience is better, a podcast may reach those seeking a renewed connection with the Church, but are not able or ready to join us yet. A simulcast of each of the celebrations would also be an option if you have the capabilities.

Another possibility is crafting at the beginning of Lent an examination of conscience to be shared throughout the season. While prayed in its fullness at communal celebrations of the sacrament, place parts of it in the bulletin or on the homepage weekly. If you have a Facebook page, this can be a great evangelization tool as well. Depending on which form of the Penitential Act you will be using, the reflections may also be utilized as invocations.

Be sure that your preparations allow for an appropriate amount of celebrations of the sacrament, communal and individual. Vary the days and time, or perhaps link them to other events, such as for parents during children's faith formation, or even during a fish fry. Making it convenient for our people is opening the door, inviting them to experience God's mercy.

The Order of Celebrating Matrimony

COUPLES do not often consult a church calendar when they are searching for dates for their wedding, especially if they are look at options over a year away. Lent, then, can come as a surprise and perhaps the proverbial fly in the ointment of their planning. This year Ash Wednesday is February 14, with Holy Week being the last week of March. While weddings are not expressly forbidden, the penitential nature of the season does not lend itself to this sacrament. Take care when discussing this with the couple. Some come to the church first to secure a date and are therefore more flexible. Others already have deposits made with the hall. While, their choices have ramifications, there are pastoral ways to approach the situation (see OCM, 32).

The Sacrament of Matrimony still take place in the context of our Church's life. The Lent environment, even at weddings, is red-violet and a bit stark. Some parishes have policies that do not schedule weddings this time, given the rest of parish activities in this season.

How can we best help our parishioners understand why Lent is not the most desirable time to celebrate this sacrament? Adult formation aimed at young adults may be helpful. Consider a "coffee house" setting, one that is comfortable and invites discussion. Talk about their ideas about a life partner. What do they hope for? What are their dreams? How about inviting couples who have solid Marriages of 10, 25, and 50-plus years. There is an incredible witness when encountering older couples, say in their 70s, who still have that spark in their eye when they look at their spouse. An older woman who can look at a twenty-two-year-old young lady and say, "Oh, I remember feeling like that." An older man who can admit, "I know those fears." Age has wisdom. Avoid parishioners who bring judgment, but encourage ones who can pass on the truths they've lived.

Then we can talk about Lent as a time for preparation for Easter, as engagement is a time of preparation for Marriage. Providing a connection to the parish that supports, listens to and sustains the faith of younger parishioners encourages them listen to the Church as well. They'll be more ready accept policies if they know we care and want to celebrate with them in the best possible way.

The Pastoral Care of the Sick

THE themes of reconciliation and healing are the spiritual touchstones for the season of Lent. Although the Sacrament of Reconciliation is the usual sacramental celebration during Lent, apart from Eucharist, the Anointing of the Sick can rightfully be included in the liturgical practices of the parish. In fact the Rite of Anointing includes an opportunity for the person who is sick to go to confession. There are many Scripture passages in the Lectionary readings for Lent that would be suitable selections for either a communal anointing liturgy or for the celebration with an individual.

Some parishes schedule an Anointing of the Sick during the Sunday liturgies on the Fourth Sunday of Lent. This is especially appropriate when the Gospel from Year A, the healing of the man born blind, is proclaimed.

But there are a couple of reasons why this might not be the best pastoral option. First, when the readings from Year A are proclaimed in Year B or C it is because the focus is on the elect who are in the final preparations for their initiation at the Easter Vigil. On this Sunday they will celebrate the Second Scrutiny. Adding a celebration of anointing of the sick tends to overload the liturgical celebration with extra rituals. Second, the Gospel passage is particularly long and, in parishes with a tight Mass schedule, the time needed for an Anointing can cause havoc with that schedule.

A better option is to schedule a communal Anointing of the Sick on the Monday of Holy Week. The Scripture readings for this weekday are especially suited for a celebration of the sacrament. An invitation should be extended to the

whole parish to participate in this liturgy. St. Paul reminds us that if one member of the Body of Christ, the Church, suffers, then all members suffer with them (see 1 Corinthians 12:26). When the Church gathers to pray for and support those who are ill it fulfills her identity as Christ's Body and exercises its ministry of compassion.

During Lent parishes often schedule special celebrations like the Stations of the Cross, Lenten missions, or other retreat like programs. It may be possible for those who are homebound to access these on the parish website and to have access to any printed material, like prayer booklets that pastoral visitors can bring to them.

The Sacrament of the Anointing of the Sick is more than a ritual event. It is part of a larger ministry within the Church that involves an ongoing effort to keep in touch with those brothers and sisters who are unable to join the faith community during their illness. In his letter to the early Christian community James encourages the faithful to pray over the person who is sick, stating that it is the prayer of faith that saves them.

Often those who are ill feel isolated from the parish community; every effort should be made to bridge that sense of separation that they experience.

A simple gesture is for the pastoral care visitors to take blessed ashes at the beginning of Lent to those they visit. The mark of ashes connects them to the Lenten journey of the whole Church. Also, by taking blessed palms to them they are reminded of their membership within the community of believers as they enter Holy Week. This also allows them to have a connection with the sufferings of Christ himself in a way that can be deeply moving and spiritually renewing.

The Order of Christian Funerals

As a penitential season, Lent and death have a natural bond. The images of the end of a long winter surround us. We are in the midst of disciplines and self-denial. Reflection on sorrow, suffering, and trials abound.

When we celebrate Christian funerals at this time it can be easy to stay with these ideas and metaphors. The deceased may have had a long illness or struggled for years with a chronic one.

However, for believers, we cannot stay in these comparisons. Yes, we need to acknowledge the pain and suffering. The cross is real, but death is not the end. Even in Lent, at a funeral we proclaim Resurrection. This is not to deny the pain the family may be in. We are not here to either ignore their grief and struggles or sugar coat them. As Church, we proclaim the whole story of our Lord's Passion, Death, and Resurrection.

Other images of Lent must also come to the fore. *Lent* means "spring." It is the time of a lengthening of days, even if it does not feel like it. Soon the buds will burst forth and birds will sing. These images are wonderful for funerals. The Christian theme of journey is also helpful.

The example of those preparing for Baptism may also be a helpful image. If you are using the Year A readings on the Third, Fourth, and Fifth Sundays, consider them as well for Funeral Masses. The dialogue between Jesus and the Woman at the Well speaks to growth of faith and the Lord's willingness to meet us where we are, loving us and accepting us. The Man Born Blind can be understood in the metaphors of light and darkness, but also Jesus' commitment to be with us, even if others have judged us as less worthy or outcast. This may speak volumes to those who have struggled with acceptance in their lives. The message of the raising of Lazarus is clear. Don't neglect the struggle of Mary and Martha's professions of faith. They can be read as declarations, surely. However, consider them too as faith in the midst of their loss, for Martha is a bit upset at Jesus in the story. The family at your funeral may feel the same way.

As you prepare for the Mass, consider the Preface which you will use this season. Preface II might be a good choice for the Lent. Also look to the alternate prayers in the ritual book. If you are using the Lazarus Gospel, perhaps use the alternate concluding prayer 2 (#408).

Do you change the Song of Farewell seasonally? See the alternate choices at OCF, 403. Few of these texts have musical settings. However, the musician can play instrumentally, having the cantor speak the responsory with interlude in between. Note that these may also be used during the Entrance Procession.

Do you use the option of the placing of Christian symbols? Many families purchase a cross for inside the casket during the viewing time. Especially during Lent, ask the funeral director to remove it before they close the casket. Then place it on the casket after the pall is placed. A simple declaration of the power of the cross may accompany your actions. Then present the cross to the family at the end of the liturgy, again accompanied by a simple statement expressing our faith and prayers for them in their loss and belief in the resurrection.

When giving options for music to the family, remember to remove songs with alleluias. In reflecting on your parish's repertoire, are there hymns that you will use on Lenten Sundays that may be used at the funerals. "Jerusalem, My Destiny" or "I Know That My Redeemer Lives" may be possibilities.

The Book of Blessings

LENT is the season during which we prepare ourselves for the coming celebration of the Paschal Mystery during Holy Week, the Triduum, and Easter. Among the Blessings Related to Feasts and Seasons, the *Book of Blessings* provides the Order for the Blessing of Saint Joseph's Table (see BB, chapter 53) for use on March 19, the Solemnity of St. Joseph. In some communities, it is the tradition to collect and bless food, especially bread and pastries, of which a large portion is given to the poor. Even in communities where this is not customary, particularly if there is a special devotion to St. Joseph, the practice could bring together the community for the sake of raising awareness about hunger and poverty in its local context. The normal form, which includes the Litany of Saint Joseph, takes place outside of Mass, and can be celebrated in a church or in some other suitable place. A shorter rite is also provided, which might be used at home, or even within Mass, even though the *Book of Blessings* does not explicitly state this as an option.

The Lenten season is a time of intense preparation of those to be initiated fully into the Church at Easter. Thus, both catechists and catechumens are in need of special support through prayer. For this purpose, the beginning of Lent is an appropriate time to use the Order for the Blessing of Those Appointed as Catechists (see BB, 491–508). This blessing can take place within Mass or within a celebration of the Word of God. Only a priest or deacon may use this blessing. A section titled Blessings of Catechumens is also included (see

BB, 519–521). This blessing prayer — actually a selection among nine options — is normally said at the end of a celebration of the Word, but it can also take place after a catechetical meeting, or even be said privately to bless individual catechumens. After the prayer, the minister lays hands on each catechumen one by one. A priest, deacon, or "qualified catechist appointed by the bishop" (BB, 520) may serve as the minister.

In places with a maritime culture, where fishing is a large part of the community's livelihood, or even where fishing is simply a popular pastime, the Order for the Blessing of Boats and Fishing Gear (see BB, chapter 22) would be appropriate for use during this time of year, or perhaps in Easter Time in places where the cold climate does not allow fishing to begin this early in the year. The concern here is primarily the safety of fishermen. We pray, then, for the soundness of boats, fleets, and gear, and for favorable weather. The blessing includes a litany invoking God to guide us in both calm and violent weather, to respect our natural resources, and to remember fishermen who have died or even lost their lives at sea. A shorter rite is also provided.

The Liturgical Environment

THE liturgical environment for Lent finds its inspiration in the liturgical life of the Church: in the Scripture narratives and images, in the Lenten devotions and practices, in the rites of the catechumenate, in the prayer texts of the Eucharist, and in the music.

For other seasons of the liturgical year, the environment and art ministry team often add items and arrangements to the liturgical space. During Lent the opposite might be the rule: by removing items so that the space reflects its own kind of fasting. Church documents generally say little about liturgical environment and this is also true for Lent. *The General Instruction of the Roman Missal* only notes that flowers should not be used to decorate the altar during Lnet (see GIRM, 305). Presumably, this means the whole sanctuary, as it is never advisable to place flowers on the altar itself. The exceptions are for Laetare Sunday and

for any feasts or solemnities that occur during Lent. Even on those days, the season should be obvious; therefore, use minimal decorations and these should be removed by the end of the day.

Other sources speak of a certain somber tone or spareness for the Lenten environment. This does not mean bare or boring. The careful selection of tetures and colors and the placement of vessels or containers and objects from nature can enhance the modd and spiritual focus of the season without being overstated or busy. Often a single item can be as effective as a collection or grouping of many things. Keep in mind that the scale of vessels and arrangements is important; all should be able to see them.

It is important to plan for the various celebrations that the parish holds during Lent, for example, Evening Prayer, Stations of the Cross, holy hour, a parish mission, communal celebration of the Rite of of Penance, and so on. Ministers of the liturgical environment need to keep these events in mind when preparing the arrangements for teh season. The primary principle for the liturgical environment applies during Lent as in all other seasons: the seasonal environment is to serve the ritual action and the spiritual message of Lent.

The Liturgical Music

THE *Ceremonial of Bishops* reminds us of the dual nature of Lent: "Through its twofold theme of repentance and baptism, the season of Lent disposes both the catechumens and the faithful to celebrate the paschal mystery" (CB, 249). Often the penitential aspect of Lent is given more attention than the baptismal aspect. Since Lent is not a forty-day reflection on Christ's Passion, not every hymn needs to mention it.

There is value in doing a common Entrance Hymn for the five Sundays of Lent to emphasize the unity of the season. Consider "Gather Us in Mercy Lord" by Gabe Huck and Tony Alonso (GIA), "This Is the Time of Fulfillment" by James Chepponis (GIA), or "Grant to Us, O Lord" by Lucien Deiss (WLP). Set to the familiar tune ST. FLAVIAN, "From Ashes to the Living Font" by Alan Hommerding (WLP) has a specific verse for each Sunday of Lent.

We Contemplate the Mystery, The Michael Joncas Hymnary: Lent and Triduum by Michael Joncas (OCP) offers hymn texts for the entire three-year Lectionary cycle for Lent and Triduum using some familiar traditional melodies as well as some newly created tunes.

To highlight the penitential nature of Lent, during the Pentitential Act the Kyrie could be chanted following the recited Confiteor and absolution by the priest. For a simple setting of the Kyrie, look at the tune from the chanted Litany of the Saints arranged by Richard Proulx (GIA). A more elaborate setting from *Cantus Missae* (GIA) could also be used.

Paschale solemnitatis and the *Ceremonial of Bishops* both recommend singing the Litany of the Saints during the Entrance Procession on the First Sunday of Lent as the Church ascends the holy mountain of Lent. This practice emphasizes the initiatory character of the season, particularly as catechumens are sent to the Rite of Election.

The extended use of silence in place of a hymn at the Preparation of the Gifts or at the end of Mass gives the signal that something unique is happening. *Paschale solemnitatis* states: "'In Lent the altar should not be decorated with flowers, and musical instruments may be played only to give necessary support to the singing.' This is in order that the penitential character of the season be preserved" (17).

The Eucharistic acclamations during Lent should be very simple and can even be done a cappella or with a simple flute or violin accompaniment. The chant setting in *The Roman Missal* is appropriate for Lent. Other simple chant-like settings include *Mass for Charity and Love* by Steven Warner (WLP) which utilizes the melody of "Where Charity and Love Prevail" by Paul Benoit (WLP) and Belmont Mass by Christopher Walker (OCP).

Many parishes pray the Stations of the Cross on Fridays during Lent. "At the Cross Her Station Keeping" (STABAT MATER) is the traditional tune associated with Stations but other alternatives include the refrains from "Now We Remain" by David Haas (GIA), "No Greater Love" by Michael Joncas (GIA), or "Jesus, Remember Me by Taizé" (GIA). Michael Ruzicki has a lovely setting for Stations published by Liturgy Training Publications, *A Light for My Path: Praying the Psalms on the Way of the Cross.*

Palm Sunday of the Passion of the Lord marks the beginning of Holy Week. "Hosanna to the Son of David" (HOSANNA, FILIO DAVID) is the appointed chant as the community gathers at the beginning of the liturgy and every parish should have it in its Holy Week repertoire. Once the procession is over and the Liturgy of the Word begins, the tone immediately changes as the focus shifts away from Christ's entrance in Jerusalem to his Passion and Death. The music from this point forward ought to reflect that shift. Choral anthems appropriate for this observance include contemporary arrangements like "The Silence and the Lamb" by Liam Lawton (GIA), "Pieta" by Tom Kendzia (OCP), "Wondrous Love" by James Clemens (WLP), or more traditional pieces like "Adoramus Te, Christe" by Theodore DuBois or "In Monte Oliveti" by Anton Bruckner. It would be appropriate to conclude the Mass with silence or with a simple Taizé chant such as "Jesus, Remember Me," "Adoramus Te Domine," or "Per Crucem."

The Liturgical Ministers

IN addition to the members of the assembly make sure all the liturgical minister in the parish are knowledgeable of the rites of iniation and model robust responses when the various rites of the catechumenal process are celebrated during this season of Purification and Enlightenment. Make sure rehearsals have been scheduled for all rites of initiation including the scrutinies, anointing, and celebrations of the Word of God so that all ministers and sponsors are well prepared and those involved clearly understand their role. Mull over the possibility of sending one or two readers from the parish out with the elect to break open the word following the dismissal. This will accomplish at least three things: give the regular RCIA catechists or team members a break, allow the elect to experience the breaking open of the Word with another disciple of Christ and third, potentially expand the pool of RCIA team members in your parish. Make sure schedules for liturgical ministers are given well in advance of the season. Consider gathering with the parish readers to break open the readings of the season and ask different readers to proclaim some of the texts for the season while giving each other feedback. Use a response such as: "I really like how you_____"; "I appreciate your understanding of the prophets words that helped to evoke_____"; or "you may want to consider_____ when proclaiming this text in the future." Make sure feedback is given in a nonjudgmental or non-threatening manner.

Have processional routes been mapped out for the various Lenten liturgies? Identify who will help facilitate the church on the move. Who will prepare the Triduum schedule for the website and what will the parish do to encourage greater participation in the liturgies of the three days? What time will the Easter Vigil be scheduled for? *Universal Norms for the Liturgical Year and the Calendar* tells us the vigil "should begin after nightfall" (UNLY, 21). Go to aa.usno.navy.mil/data/docs /RS_OneYear.php, from the United States Naval Observatory, to see what time the sun will set in your region on March 31. What are the conflicts that may arise such as spring break or sporting events, tournaments, and so on? Since our role as Church is to be countercultural contact the local school district or state athletic association and petition them to reschedule athletic events that conflict with the celebration of the Sared Paschal Triduum. You may not be able to make inroads this year, but provide them with the dates of the Triduum for the next several years out, coordinate this with the diocesan office of worship and the other liturgical Churches in you are such as Episcopalians, Lutherans, Methodists, and Presbyterians, and so on.If enough groups speak up perhaps things will change in the future.

Since the word *Lent* means "spring" consider inviting all the liturgical minister to the parish campus for a "Spring Cleaning Day." Begin with Morning Prayer and serve a light continental breakfast and then cluster groups of various ministers into working teams of six to eight. Assign them tasks such as cleaning pews, devotional spaces, and sacristies; have them file and organize music; conduct an inventory of vestments, linens, and banners (put aside anything that need to be laundered or repaired); polish any brass or silver candle sticks or hardware; make sure all lighting systems are in proper working order and replace fixtures if needed. You can add to this list to meet your own needs. Approximately forty-five minutes before folks finish with their tasks gather them in a large group and take them through a "mystagogical reflection" of sorts on this experience, using questions like; what did you learn about the behind the scenes work of liturgy in the parish? What did you learn about the other ministers your were linked with? What will you take from this day that will allow you to participate in the liturgy

in a fuller way? Serve lunch and end with Midday Prayer. Encourage each minister in the parish to invite a Catholic who no longer attends Mass to join them on the First Sunday of Lent. Welcome these brothers and sisters (without making them feel guilty for being away), host a coffee clutch following each Mass and have people voice the reason why they have been away. Be prepared to hear people's needs and meet them where they are at. Consider using some of the words of welcome that Pope Francis has been using in his preaching's and writings.

Make sure to examine your Paschal candle when it arrives to ensure it has no damage and when palm branches arrive make sure they are stored in a climate controlled environment until they are needed on Palm Sunday of the Lord's Passion. This is a good time review and prepare the annual budget for liturgy. Pray, fast, give alms, and celebrate as you "climb the holy mountain of Easter" (CB, 249).

Other Prayers, Rites, and Devotions

Catholics "do" Lent very well. Parish schedules abound in additional prayer times as well as offering various means of participating in almsgiving initiatives such as Catholic Relief Service's Operation Rice Bowl (www.crsricebowl.org). We seem more attune to this season than all the others. Utilizing the weeks of Ordinary Time might be a good opportunity for pastoral staffs and committees to evaluate the devotional practices of the parish and their resources. Only second to abstaining from meat on Fridays seems to be the weekly parish celebration of the Stations of the Cross. What resource does the parish use? The *Directory on Popular Piety and the Liturgy* tells us that whatever choice of texts are employed, "it is always preferable to choose texts resonant with the biblical narrative and written in a clear simple style" (DPPL, 135). The Church document on parish art and architecture *Built of Living Stones* even sees this devotional prayer as "a journey" or "a way" and cautions against the attempt to cluster stations together for expediency, because it eliminates the option of movement. Are those gathered invited to walk along with the leader from station to station?

As the *Via Crucis* (Way of the Cross) is to Christ, so the *Via Matris* (Way of His Mother) is to the Blessed Virgin Mary. This devotion was officially approved by Pope Pius VIII in 1815 but was being popularized by the religious order of Servites since 1668. Commonly known as the Seven Dolores (or Sorrows) of the Blessed Virgin Mary, these events are all scriptural in origin, unlike the traditional fourteen Stations of the Cross, which intersperse non-Biblical figures and moments such as Veronica and Christ meeting his Mother along the Way. The *Directory on Popular Piety and the Liturgy* refers to this devotion as "stages on the journey of faith and sorrow on which the Virgin Mary has preceded the Church, and in which the Church journeys until the end of time" (DPPL, 137). The *Via Matris* can be prayed anytime during the Lenten season, but has its roots of celebration on the Friday of the Fifth Week of Lent (the Friday before Good Friday) or on September 15, the Memorial of Our Lady of Sorrows. For prayer and hymn texts, visit www.catholictradition.org/Mary/7sorrows .htm. The site also includes beautiful artwork by the masters.

Evangelization

COVENANT faithfulness. We hold the security of this truth out to those we evangelize during Lent. God is always and eternally faithful. God never wavered in the covenant with Noah, Abraham, or Moses. God's people did. They, like we, were inconsistent, even sinful. Their following of the Ten Commandments was not always stellar. Often we falter, too. Evangelization in Lent is not about perfection. Rather, evangelization during these six weeks is about how we invite others into the covenant in which they are always God's people. Despite sin, despite infidelity, God always welcomes God's people back. The rainbow appears; the Resurrection is ours to participate in through our Baptism.

When we acknowledge our lack of faithfulness to the covenant and our need to for God's mercy and forgiveness, we evangelize. Most people in our neighborhoods and cities realize that even those of us who participate in an organized religion are not perfect. But when we acknowledge in humility our need for God, this causes others to take notice. For neither are perfect. God's promise of forgiveness and redemption is also available to them.

Often temptation will come upon us, but God's people, we live in confidence that transfiguration will also come. This is the hope our world desires. This is the hope of Jesus whom God draws others to through us and our parish communities this Lent.

Our catechumens and candidates turn to God for mercy in this final intense period of their preparation before they celebrate the sacraments of initiation. The three scrutinies are plentiful signs of God's strength, power, and compassion. They are signs that God's love and forgiveness in the Cross and Resurrection of Jesus triumphs over sin and death. God's new covenant in Christ lasts forever. Forever, we are God's people.

How will we lead others to know the God of the eternal covenant this Lent? How will we live the Law that God writes on our hearts? How will our lives produce the fruit of God's mercy so that others will want to become the seed that falls to the ground and dies with Jesus Christ? How will we invite those who are curious about what seems to them to be our inconsistent belief that life comes through death to walk the road to Jerusalem and enter the holy city? Through the Church's liturgy and our lives, may we accompany others to the joy of the Easter!

The Parish and the Home

PERHAPS more than any other liturgical season, Lent captures our hearts and minds, resulting in action that is driven by a desire to grow in Christian discipleship. Parishes often include opportunities for reflection, growth, reconciliation, and prayer in the Lenten observance. People anticipate Lent by determining their expression of prayer, fasting and giving for the season. With its sacrificial and spiritual nature, Lent appeals to us as a necessary and helpful time in which to re-orient our lives, calling us back to the self-giving way of life to which we are called.

Lenten violet and simplicity carry the liturgical season into our homes. Use the season as a time of spring cleaning, giving excess material possessions to those in need. Use a violet cloth at the family dinner or prayer table, and perhaps a few bare branches, a Bible open to the Sunday Gospel, and a single candle as a reminder that Christ's light shines through all darkness. Make a chart for each family member's Lenten promises, and support one another in keeping those resolutions. Make Sunday particularly special during this season by planning ways to spend part of the day together. Since Sunday is a "little Easter" even during Lent, begin the day with Mass, find ways to enjoy one another's company, and share time, attention, and care with those who are in need, lonely, or ill.

With its focus as a season of preparation for those anticipating the sacraments of initiation, Lent provides an opportunity to connect the entire community with those who will be initiated at the Easter Vigil. Parishes often list the elect and candidates in the bulletin. Keep the list and pray for them each day, along with their sponsors and catechists. Parishes may offer a special time for the community to learn more about the initiation process and the rites of the season. Talk within your family about the role of faith in your lives and what you learn from the witness of those who are preparing for initiation. Lenten celebrations of the Sacrament of Penance may also be a time to connect with children who participate in the sacrament for the first time, heightening our appreciation for Christ's mercy and forgiveness.

Since the weekdays of Lent retain the seasonal character, there are fewer solemnities and feasts to consider. Within the family, the Solemnity of St. Joseph on March 19 provides a distinct opportunity to reflect on the role of Joseph in the life of Jesus. Those of Italian descent hold this day in particular esteem. Customs on this day include special meatless meals and homemade bread, which may be shared within the parish, neighborhood, or extended family.

As the season builds toward the Sacred Paschal Triduum, holding fast to Lenten promises becomes challenging, particularly for children. Place a sign at the family table that shows the days remaining until Easter. Remind everyone of the reasons for the sacrifices. Children may take turns crossing the day off after sundown. With Palm Sunday of the Lord's Passion, Holy Week begins. Keep activities to a minimum in order to set the week apart from all others. Plan ahead to participate in the liturgies of Holy Thursday, Good Friday, and the Easter Vigil or Easter Sunday.

Mass Texts

◆ TROPES FOR THE PENITENTIAL ACT, FORM C

You are the Savior of the world, by whose Death and Resurrection we are redeemed: Lord, have mercy.

You are the suffering servant, by whose Death and Resurrection we are healed: Christ, have mercy.

You are the way, the truth, and the life, by whose Death and Resurrection we are given new life: Lord, have mercy.

◆ DISMISSAL FOR CHILDREN'S LITURGY OF THE WORD

My dear children, as you enter into this Lenten journey you are asked to put aside all that will sidetrack you. Put down your iPads, iPhones, iPods, and "I wants," and free yourself from all distraction, so that you may hear what God truly wants as you explore the Sacred Scriptures. The Word of God teaches us all and calls us ever closer to God throughout this holy season of Lent. May you always find wonder and joy in the gift God is offering you now. Go in peace.

◆ DISMISSAL FOR THE CATECHUEMNS AND THE ELECT

For those of you participating in the Rites of Christian Initiation, you have already experienced a long journey this year. You have nearly reached the fullness of your journey toward full communion in the Catholic, Christian tradition. Do not weary now or let the devil tempt you. Continue on your way. You are bound to have trials and wonderful "aha" moments of transformation and transfiguration. May you always find blessings now and in every day as you continue to turn toward God in your life. Trust in Jesus and the Cross to lead you home safely. Go in peace.

February 2018
Month of the Passion of Our Lord

Optional Memorials in Lent

The Missal commentaries below pertain to the seasonal weekdays or other obligatory observances. The following should be consulted when celebrating optional memorials during Lent:

If an obligatory memorial falls during Lent, it becomes optional. On the weekdays of Lent, except Ash Wednesday and during Holy Week, the Mass texts for the current liturgical day are used; but the Collect may be taken from a Memorial which happens to be inscribed in the General Calendar for that day, except on Ash Wednesday and during Holy Week (GIRM, 355a).

WED 14 (#214) violet
Ash Wednesday

About Ash Wednesday

In the early Church, when Lent was a time for the reconciliation of public penitents, the penitents would come to the church at the beginning of Lent, that is, on Ash Wednesday. They would wear a penitential garment, suggesting sackcloth, and be sprinkled with ashes. Then they would be ritually expelled from the assembly to do their penance for forty days, returning to the church on Holy Thursday, when they would be readmitted to the sacraments.

With time, the expulsion of penitents disappeared, but the ashes remained and became a call to penance of all the faithful. In the Scriptures, sackcloth and ashes are the signs of penance. The practice of using ashes from the palms of the previous year's Palm Sunday is a relatively new element of the liturgy, first appearing in the twelfth century. It adds another layer of meaning to this rich rite, reminding us of where we are headed—to the glory of Easter.

The Lectionary for Mass

◆ FIRST READING: The first step on the Lenten road is to change directions. We must turn back from the fascinating byways where we've wandered, the dead ends we've chosen, the roads to dark places. We must turn instead toward God from wherever we are right this minute. And not half-heartedly either. God wants our whole heart's attention because the heart houses the pilot who decides which way to take.

◆ RESPONSORIAL PSALM 51: Fully aware of sinfulness, the psalmist prays for God's help and for the clean heart, which alone can see God.

◆ SECOND READING: We can walk the Lenten road because Jesus came to get us in the deserts of sin where we've made our home. It's a demanding road, but we do not travel alone. And no, let's not even think about waiting till tomorrow morning or next Tuesday when we will have had more sleep, caught up with our to do list, or whatever other excuse delays us. The Lenten invitation is urgent. The time is now.

◆ GOSPEL: Danger awaits the Lenten traveler at the very first step. We can stop to look in the mirror, check out those ashes, compare penances with a friend, and decide we're looking pretty good. However, God has an uncomfortable habit of looking past appearances to learn what's in the heart, where no one else can see. And God's is the opinion that matters.

The Roman Missal

All the prayers and texts are proper for the day and can be found at Ash Wednesday in the Lent section of the Proper of Time toward the beginning of the Missal.

There is no Penitential Act today, since it is replaced by the distribution of ashes. There is no singing of the Gloria and the Alleluia is omitted until the Easter Vigil.

The rite for the blessing and distribution of ashes takes place after the homily. The priest celebrant, with any necessary ministers (for example, the bookbearer, and someone to hold the vessel with water, if needed), goes to the place where the vessel(s) with ashes is (are). His hands remain joined for the introduction (the rubric for which does *not* indicate "these or similar words"), and then he leaves a brief period for silent prayer. Then, with hands extended, he prays one of the two prayers of blessing. While both prayers include the gesture of making the Sign of the Cross over the ashes, the gesture has a somewhat different focus in each of the two prayers: in the first, the priest is asking the grace of God's blessing on those "who are marked with these ashes," and in the second, the blessing is invoked more specifically on the ashes themselves. Consequently, the gesture should match the action according to the words of the prayer. After the prayer, the priest sprinkles the ashes with water, but this is done in silence, without his saying anything.

Either one of two formulas is used to impose ashes: "Repent, and believe in the Gospel" or "Remember that you are dust, and to dust you shall return."

The rubric states simply that ashes are placed on the head of all those present who come up, as the formula is said. Customarily, this is done by the priest (or deacon or minister) dipping his (or her) thumb in the ashes, and then tracing the ashes on the person's forehead in the Sign of the Cross, although, technically, there is nothing that requires this. (Interestingly, we know, for example, that historically ashes have also been sprinkled on the top of people's heads.)

Singing is to take place during the imposition of ashes, and several possibilities are spelled out in the Missal. There are three suggested antiphons that can be used in connection with the verses of Psalm 51; a responsory is also suggested, or another appropriate song may be sung.

Be sure to provide the means for priests and other ministers to wash their hands after the distribution of ashes. Premoistened towelettes sometimes work better than plain water, although water and towels should also be available.

After the imposition of ashes (and the ministers' washing their hands), the Universal Prayer takes place; the Creed is not said. After the Universal Prayer, Mass continues as usual.

If the blessing and distribution of ashes takes place outside Mass, then all moves forward as described above, including all the readings and their chants as at Mass, but then, after the Universal Prayer, the priest simply blesses and dismisses the faithful, using the Prayer over the People given at the end of the Mass formularies. Interestingly, there is no specific mention in the rubrics that the Our Father is prayed when the blessing and distribution of ashes occurs outside Mass; they simply direct that the rite is concluded with the Universal Prayer, the blessing, and the dismissal of the faithful.

Use either Preface III or Preface IV of Lent. Both Prefaces are short and to the point, in keeping with the starkness of this day's liturgy.

For the dismissal, the priest is to use the Prayer over the People. There is no indication that this dismissal text is optional. The prayer is prayed with the priest's hands extended over the people. The prayer asks that God will pour out on us "a spirit of compunction" as a result of our doing penance, again pointing to the inward, spiritual conversion that should take place as a result of the outward actions.

Other Ideas

Consider preparing small containers of blessed ashes, so that ministers can take them, along with Holy Communion, to the homebound, to enable those who are unable to come to church to share in this special rite of new beginnings.

The Rice Bowl begins today and lasts throughout the Lenten season. Take advantage of the many resources provided by Catholic Relief Services (www.crs.org), including bulletin inserts, sample intercessions, and other suggestions for increasing our awareness of the needs of the world as we begin our Lenten fast.

The collection is for Aid to the Church in Central and Eastern Europe.

THU 15 (#220) violet
Thursday after Ash Wednesday

The Lectionary for Mass

◆ FIRST READING: How many Lents have you observed? One? Forty? Lent can lose its urgency with repetition, but the urgency is always there. Lenten choices — to do good or ill or nothing, to pray or watch TV, to carry someone else's groceries or just rush to our own car — are in fact a matter of life or death. They cause few ripples on life's surface, but they eventually determine where the journey ends, because Lent is a rehearsal for all of life, not just the span from here to Easter.

◆ RESPONSORIAL PSALM 1: Fidelity to God's law is the source of true happiness and flourishing life. The one who is faithful thrives, like a beautiful tree with deep roots and leafy branches in abundance.

◆ GOSPEL: Those Lenten sacrifices can look so inconsequential, so inconvenient, so artificial. Even as the day after Lent begins, we can start to rewrite our resolutions, trimming off a bit here, a bit there. "Be reasonable," whispers the voice

from the Eden's fruit tree. "Be good to yourself. Treat yourself." The question, though, is the one put by today's Gospel: what is real gain, what is real loss? The choice is ours.

The Roman Missal

The Collect is the perfect prayer for the beginning of Lent. We ask that God may be with us in all we do: inspiring our actions, helping them along, and bringing them to completion. In the Prayer over the Offerings, we ask God to give us his forgiveness, so that the offerings we make may give him honor. One of the four Prefaces of Lent is used today, and any one of the four is appropriate. In the Prayer after Communion, we ask that the "heavenly gifts" we have received may bring us both forgiveness and salvation. The Prayer over the People is a prayer that God, who made known the "ways of eternal life," will also guide his people along those ways.

FRI 16 (#221) violet
Friday after Ash Wednesday

The Lectionary for Mass

◆ FIRST READING: Fasting is one of the three great traditional works of Lent. However, the prophet reminds us that diet is not the determinant of holiness. Love is. Lifting the emotional yoke that chafes others' shoulders, refusing to reap a profit at others' expense, ceasing to hoard abundance from providence's warehouses when others need it, these are the real noes engraved on the key that opens the narrow gate onto the road to life.

◆ RESPONSORIAL PSALM 51 is the quintessential Lenten psalm. It is a prayer of repentance, a confession of sin, and a plea to God for a clean heart. The repentance God desires is conversion of heart.

◆ GOSPEL: Jesus' disciples had to fast from many cherished certainties, from the security of job and family, from all the hopes and plans they no doubt had, in order to be free to learn new ways of thinking, doing, and being from their Teacher. When ultimately they had to fast even from Jesus' daily companionship, they discovered they knew how to follow him even in dark hunger. And so will we.

The Roman Missal

The Collect is a prayer for the strength to complete the "bodily observances" we have undertaken this Lent. Our Lenten observance is a sacrifice that we offer to God. We pray that it will be acceptable to God, and strengthen "our powers of self-restraint" (Prayer over the Offerings). We do not fast from enjoyable things because they are inherently bad. We fast because it shows us the way to self-control. One of the four Prefaces of Lent is used today, and any one of the four is appropriate. In the Prayer after Communion, we pray for the fruits of the Eucharist, that we may be forgiven, and made ready for "the remedies of [God's] compassion." We are a people on a "pilgrim journey," and the disciplines we undertake during Lent are "age-old." In the Prayer over the People, we pray that, always giving God thanks, we may deserve to come into God's presence forever. Even though the Prayer over the People is optional on weekdays, it would be good to use it, to highlight the liturgical time.

S A T 17 (#222) violet
Saturday after Ash Wednesday

Optional Memorial of the Seven Holy Founders of the Servite Order / violet

The Lectionary for Mass

◆ FIRST READING: Saying no to selfishness is not enough. Love is not a negative. To take food we thought we needed and give it to someone hungrier, to abandon our own comfort to care for one afflicted with fear or loneliness or grief, to substitute a kind word for malicious gossip, or to worship when we would rather do something entertaining, all seem small enough, really. Yet the prophet's promises of reward suggest that none of them is as insignificant as we might imagine.

◆ RESPONSORIAL PSALM 86: is a prayer with just one plea: "Listen!" The psalmist asks God to listen over and over again: "Incline your ear . . . answer me. . . . Hearken. . . . Attend to the sound of my pleading" (86:1, 5, 6). Of ourselves, we are poor and helpless. We need God, God's help, and God's deliverance. We need to learn God's wisdom.

◆ GOSPEL: Isaiah begins to draw attention away from our behavior to God's, from our meager selfishness to God's extraordinary generosity. The Gospel points away from us to Jesus, who fasts from respectability in order to open a place for himself in the lives of sinners, there to make present in the flesh God's healing mercy.

The Roman Missal

We are weak, but we ask God to look with compassion on us, and protect us with the "right hand" of his majesty (Collect). In the Prayer over the Offerings, we ask God to receive the sacrifice we offer, which is a "sacrifice of conciliation and praise." The Eucharist we celebrate can cleanse us and make our minds "well pleasing" to God. The Eucharist we receive is a mystery and will always remain a mystery "in this present life," but it has power to help us toward eternity. One of the four Prefaces of Lent is used today, and any one of the four is appropriate. The Prayer after Communion prays for the protection of all "who have touched the sacred mysteries" in the celebration of the Eucharist. Even though the Prayer over the People is optional on weekdays, it would be good to use it, to highlight the liturgical time.

Today's Saints

The Founders of the Order of Servites were seven young men with one vision — to "be of one mind and one heart" (Rule of St. Augustine; the adopted Rule of the Servites, available from www.domcentral.org/trad/rule.htm), through common prayer, works of charity, and a special devotion to Mary, the Mother of God. Living in thirteenth-century Florence, the Founders of the Order of Servites (Friar Servants of Mary) were inspired to abandon their homes and businesses to seek a life of prayerful seclusion, eventually establishing themselves on Monte Scenario, called the "sounding mountain." These Friar Servants of Mary paid homage to Mary by living a humble and simple life. Their lifestyle drew young men from all over, which ultimately led to their establishment as a religious order. In the eighteenth century, a holy woman by the name of St. Juliana Falconieri was attracted to the lives of the seven holy founders and decided to consecrate her life to God, laying the foundation for the Servite Sisters.

☀ 18 (#23) violet
First Sunday of Lent

The Lectionary for Mass

◆ FIRST READING: The drama of the building of the ark, its loading, and the rising of the waters can overshadow what should be the most powerful moment in the story of Noah: The establishment of God's covenant with Noah and his descendants. This promise everlasting is the powerful covenant made with Abraham later in Genesis. The covenant is generated by God, who takes responsibility for its fulfilment, offering a sign of affirmation to humankind (the rainbow). Note the parallels between this account of God's promise and the process of creation in Genesis 1.

◆ RESPONSORIAL PSALM 25: The psalmist calls out to God for help and direction, affirming that they will be provided. Psalm 25 extols God's goodness and ability to lead his people in the way of truth. In many ways, these verses speak to the covenant, calling upon God to both remember his mercy and his promises.

◆ SECOND READING: The destructive power of water is now contrasted with the life-giving power of water in Peter's letter. In Christ Jesus, suffering is not meaningless but ennobled. The passage includes a creedal element, outlining the Paschal Mystery and its promise. The gift of Baptism is one of liberation for all, not salvation for a few as in the story of Noah.

◆ GOSPEL: In Mark, the beginning of Jesus' journey is his experience of forty days in the wilderness. His account is terser than that of Matthew and Luke, which also makes its message quite direct. Jesus has been tested, like the Israelites were tested by the forty years of wandering in the wilderness to the Promised Land and Noah was tested with forty days afloat in the flood waters. Under the protection of God's angels, he has triumphed, proving his readiness for his earthly mission. The number forty appears in dozens of places in the Bible, usually signifying a test that has been administered and passed. As we enter the forty

days of Lent, we can challenge ourselves to embrace the spiritual tests we are facing, transforming them— and ourselves —as we journey to Easter.

The Roman Missal

The Gloria is omitted today. The Creed is said or sung. The Preface to be used for this Mass is given on the pages right there along with the other texts for the Mass. The reason this Preface, "The Temptation of the Lord," is used today is obvious, since the Gospel reading for the First Sunday of Lent is always the account of the temptation of Jesus from one of the Gospel accounts. Consider chanting the introductory dialogue and the Preface today; if this is not the regular practice of your community, this can be a way of powerfully drawing attention to the solemnity of Lenten time (but be sure to prepare and rehearse your assembly as needed, especially if your people are not familiar with the responses!). The Prayer over the People is required, not optional, on the Sundays of Lent, and the text is given right after the Prayer after Communion.

The *Rite of Christian Initiation of Adults* includes an optional Rite of Sending of the Catechumens for Election. If your diocese celebrates the Rite of Election on the First Sunday of Lent, as suggested by the RCIA, then consider celebrating this Rite of Sending in your parish. Celebrating the rite is yet another way to catechize the entire parish about the meaning of RCIA and the journey the catechumens (soon to be elect) undertake. Also, the rite provides yet another opportunity for the catechumens to be supported in prayer by, and to receive the good wishes of, those who will soon be their brothers and sisters in Baptism. The rite takes place after the homily at Mass and is described in numbers 106–117 in the RCIA.

Other Ideas

Prior to this Sunday, make sure that the community has been provided with resources that will support a prayerful, holy Lent. This can include daily prayer resources or information about special Bible studies or other events (consider LTP's *Keeping the Seasons: Reproducibles for Lent, Triduum, and Easter 2018; The Way of Faith 2018: Keeping Lent, Triduum, and Easter Time; My Sacrifice and Yours* by Paul Turner; and *His Mercy Endures Forever* by Stephen S. Wilbricht, CSC). Educate people on the meaning of prayer, fasting, and alms giving, and invite people into a mature relationship with these practices. Consider programs like Catholic Relief Services Rice Bowl, a program designed to encourage prayer and fasting, learning, and giving. Communicate the times you will hold the Stations of the Cross (consider LTP's *A Light for My Path: Praying the Psalms on the Way of the Cross* by Michael Ruzicki) and let people know about regionally important events such as parish fish fries. On this weekend that leads up to Presidents' Day, find appropriate ways to remember this event honoring Washington and Lincoln. Do not place the American flag in the sanctuary or sing patriotic hymns at Mass (see the USCCB website on this policy: www.usccb.org/prayer-and-worship/sacred-art-and-music/architecture-and-environment/display-of-flags-in-catholic-churches.cfm), but consider including the words of the Gettysburg address or another speech in the parish bulletin or on your parish website or social media page.

MON 19 (#224) violet
Lenten Weekday

The Lectionary for Mass

◆ FIRST READING: The Ten Commandments offer us the roadmap to right relationship with God and right relationship with each other. These precepts are not quaint ideas, but powerful injunctions designed to lead us to our participation in the covenant that God has made with humankind. These religious and moral imperatives serve as the guide and touchstone for a life well lived. Without awareness of them, our spiritual health and growth are in question.

◆ RESPONSORIAL PSALM 19: The psalmist extols the life-giving power of God's Word. They are source of enlightenment and joy. While the exhortations of the Ten Commandments may seem restrictive, it is within their confines that humankind can flourish and grow. Christians believe that the ultimate source of God's Word is Jesus Christ, God's Word made flesh.

◆ GOSPEL: The sorting of the sheep and the goats is a powerful image in both Jesus' age and now. This seen of the final judgment depicts the Son of Man as a shepherd who will judge the nations as one might sort sheep and goats. The task of following the king are tied to showing compassion, mercy, and kindness to those who are the "least," including the stranger, the prisoner, and others who are deprived of earthly goods and therefore highly vulnerable. The practical instructions of this Gospel inform the Corporal Works of Mercy—feeding, providing shelter, clothing, visiting, and burying. The challenge in every age is to answer honestly, "Who is least among us," and upon identifying those persons, to take action both individually and collectively in their care.

The Roman Missal

Only by conversion and understanding of "heavenly teaching" can we benefit from the good works we offer to God this Lent (see the Collect). In the Prayer over the Offerings, we pray that the offering we make to God may change our lives, reconcile us to the Father, and bring us forgiveness. In the Prayer after Communion, we pray that the power of the sacrament we receive may bring us "help in mind and body" and "the fullness of heavenly healing." The Eucharist is food for body and soul. The Prayer over the People is a simple prayer that asks that God's people may receive the grace to see what needs to be done—and the strength to do it.

TUE 20 (#225) violet
Lenten Weekday

The Lectionary for Mass

◆ FIRST READING: Isaiah's typically evocative, poetic imagery reigns again in this exquisite passage on how God's Word flows and works. God's Word goes forth not only with power but with productivity. The rain and the snow bring water to the earth, ministering on God's behalf. It is through the creative speech of God that all things came into being, and it is through Him that all is nourished and sustained. Nothing that comes from God is wasted!

◆ RESPONSORIAL PSALM 34: God speaks, but also hears. When the just call out God, he hears their cries and are saved. To seek God is not just to find him, but to throw ourselves into his loving arms, presenting our needs to him as any child would do to a loving, listening parent. The wicked are not treated in the same way.

◆ GOSPEL: The disciples have seen Jesus center his life in prayer, and so they ask to be taught how to pray.

His beautiful answer—what we now call the Lord's Prayer—is grounded in lines from the psalms. Unfortunately, it can become so rote with recitation that we may find ourselves not attending to the meaning of its words. The great theologian of the early Church, Tertullian, believed that the prayer was "truly the summary of the whole gospel." While sometimes we may find it hard to pray, we cannot say in honesty that we don't know how to pray. Dietrich Bonhoeffer, the Lutheran theologian, minister, and martyr in the hands of the Nazi regime, observed, "The Lord's Prayer is not merely the pattern prayer, it is the way Christian must pray. If they pray this prayer, God will certainly hear them. The Lord's Prayer is the quintessence of prayer. A disciple's prayer is founded on and circumscribed by it" (*The Cost of Discipleship*, p. 165).

The Roman Missal

We do not undertake "bodily discipline" in Lent for its own sake, like athletes or dieters. Rather, through this observance, we grow in "yearning" for God (Collect). In the Eucharist, we bring "temporal sustenance," bread and wine, and in his goodness God transforms them into food for eternal life (Prayer over the Offerings).

Controlling our desires can help us to correct our priorities—to "love the things of heaven" (Prayer after Communion). Any one of the four Prefaces of Lent can be used today. Even though the Prayer over the People is optional on weekdays, it would be good to use it, to highlight the liturgical time. In this prayer, we pray that God may be with us in all the trials of life—our consolation in grief, our perseverance in times of trial, our protection in danger.

WED 21 (#226) violet
Lenten Weekday

Optional Memorial of St. Peter Damian, Bishop and Doctor of the Church / violet

The Lectionary for Mass

◆ FIRST READING: Jonah, himself forgiven and restored in God's favor, is called a second time by God. He sets out to complete the task of calling the "great city of Nineveh" to repentance. (The superlative "great" is used multiple times throughout the book of Jonah, emphasizing both the extremity of the task and the greatness of God's action.) The Ninevites respond with repentance; their hearts turn, the essential act to which all who observe Lent are called.

◆ RESPONSORIAL PSALM 51: The psalmist, like the king of Nineveh, trusts that when one turns to God in humility, God will show mercy. The verses of Psalm 51 are a perfect prayer of repentance, inviting God's healing presence and care. While burnt offerings were an important part of observance, the psalmist recognizes that they pale compared to a true change of heart.

◆ GOSPEL: This story from Luke reminds us, as do many others, of how deeply steeped was Jesus in the teachings of the prophets. The people of his day, and in so many ways ours, look for signs to support belief. "Where is the evidence?" we ask. The people of Nineveh were saved not by seeing a wonder, but by trusting the prophet—a prophet who experienced a resurrection of sorts when, rather than being consumed by the great fish, he was spit up alive on the shoreline. The queen referenced is the Queen of Sheba, who visited Solomon and opened up great trade routes of their age. Jesus challenges the listeners: One greater than Solomon and greater than Jonah is among them, and yet they cannot hear. The

Resurrection of Christ is foreshadowed, a sign that will be the ultimate sign of God's power and love.

The Roman Missal

We pray that the Lord may "look kindly" on us, so that our bodily self-restraint may lead to renewal in mind (Collect). For our sake God makes our gifts into the Sacrament of Christ's Body and Blood. We pray that this same sacrament may be for us "an eternal remedy," food for everlasting life. Any one of the four Prefaces of Lent can be used today. Even though the Prayer over the People is optional on weekdays, it would be good to use it, to highlight the liturgical time. In the Prayer after Communion, we pray that the sacrament we have received may bring us "unending life."

Today's Saint

St. Peter Damian (1007–1072), born to a large Italian family, entered a Camaldolese Benedictine monastery comprising hermit monks who followed an austere life of fasting and prayer. Dedicating himself to the study of Scripture and the Fathers of the Church, he gained a reputation among the hermits as being both a gifted scholar and spiritual guru. Although he lived in a monastery, removed from the world, St. Peter was a powerful voice of reform in the Church. He spoke out against clerical abuses, challenged bishops to recommit themselves to their vocation, and announced the need for a reformed papacy. Recognized for his ability to lead, he was made abbot of his monastery and later installed as bishop of Ostia. As bishop, he never lost sight of his calling to be a monk. He was so influential in the Church that Pope Leo XII declared him a Doctor of the Church.

THU 22 (#535) white
Feast of the Chair of St. Peter the Apostle

About Today's Feast

The chair of a bishop, called the *cathedra*, is the symbol of his foundational ministry to be a teacher of faith to his Church community. What then can we learn from Peter, the rock of our Church? His extraordinary confession of faith in this passage teaches us courage to confess truth, even if it may sound far-fetched by everyday standards. Peter listened to the Spirit of God in his heart and proclaimed Jesus as Christ, Son of the living God. When Jesus asks "Who do you say that I am?", each of us is presented with the same question. What is the Spirit of God prompting us to proclaim? Today's feast, attested to as early as the mid-fourth century, has its roots in the *Parentalia*, or commemoration of dead relatives and friends celebrated between February 13 and 22. At this commemoration, a chair, or *cathedra*, was left empty for particular deceased persons. Since the actual date of Peter's death was unknown, it came to be remembered on February 22, eventually becoming a celebration of his taking over the pastoral responsibility of the Church of Rome.

The Lectionary for Mass

◆ FIRST READING: The Church, from her founding at Pentecost, exists to bear the Good News of Jesus Christ to the world. Here, Peter speaks a clear message to the presbyters, an office now called "priest," about how their leadership should be exercised. They are to follow the example of Jesus, overseeing those in their care as a Shepherd. This is not only a role of tending and directing, but of humble service and personal example.

◆ RESPONSORIAL PSALM 23 is resonant for listeners, as it is very likely the best-known and best-loved of all the psalms. The shepherd gives the king all that he needs: rest, refreshment, comfort, courage, and protection. Overflowing with gratitude, the psalmist remembers that just as he has been blessed with the presence of God's constant care in the past, he will receive it today and in the future. This message of trust and hope informs how Christians relate to Christ Jesus and those who lead in his name.

◆ GOSPEL: The humanity and foibles of Peter make him one of the most accessible, understandable figures in all of the New Testament. Here we see Peter at his finest. Jesus knows that the region is buzzing with talk, but more important is how those who follow him see him. Here, Peter's ready response is completely on target. Jesus, seeing his stalwart personality, renames him Petrus, a name derived from the Greek word for "rock." All of us know people who are the "rock" we count on when life is uncertain or stormy. Our Church leaders can be such a rock, providing counsel, care, and radiating the love of God when we are most in need.

The Roman Missal

Everything is proper to today's feast—all texts are found at February 22 in the Proper of Saints. All of the orations include mention of St. Peter, as might be expected, focusing on his teaching and on our need to hold fast with integrity to the faith that has been both confessed and taught by Peter. In fact, this idea of the Church's faith being built upon the faith of Peter is expressed in the liturgy even before the orations: in the Entrance Antiphon, taken from Luke's account of the Gospel, we hear, "The Lord says to Simon Peter: / I have prayed for you that your faith may not fail, / and, once you have turned back, strengthen your brothers." The Gloria is sung or said today. There is no Creed.

The Collect presents an image of the surety and strong foundation that we can have when we rely on the faith confessed by Peter, as particularly evidenced by the role that Jesus gave to Peter after the Apostle's confession of faith in the Lord: we ask that "no tempests may disturb us" because we have been set "fast / on the rock of the Apostle Peter's confession of faith." Again acknowledging that it is only through Peter's teaching that the Church can hold the faith in all its integrity, the Prayer over the Offerings also recognizes St. Peter as the shepherd of the Church.

The Preface assigned for today is Preface I of the Apostles, which expresses how through the blessed Apostles God continues to watch over the Church to protect his flock always. The Prayer after Communion speaks of the Eucharistic celebration as "this redeeming exchange," asking that our nourishment "by communion in the Body and Blood of Christ . . . may be for us a Sacrament of unity and peace." Thus, the prayer brings to the fore the importance of unity that is at the heart of both the Petrine ministry, even down to our day in the role of the pope, and the celebration of the Eucharist. It is suggested in the Missal to use a Solemn Blessing at the end of Mass, the formula of blessing titled "The Apostles." It would be a good idea to use this today.

FRI 23 (#228) violet
Lenten Weekday

Optional Memorial of St. Polycarp, Bishop and Martyr / violet

The Lectionary for Mass

◆ FIRST READING: Ezekiel contrasts the past and the present, highlighting that the old self can be overcome, and the new self, in turn, is received by God with joy. What matters most is not what has been accomplished, but the conversion

of heart that God desires. The radical forgiveness of God may not be "fair," but it certainly is life-giving and powerful, calling us to rigor in living virtuous lives and embodying God's ways. Repentance is followed by forgiveness, always.

◆ RESPONSORIAL PSALM 130: The psalmist cries out to God in the face of calamity. Despite the dire circumstances, he trust in God's promise and fidelity, willing to wait on the Lord. Every human person has faced moments when afflictions seem too great to bear, and yet trusting in God's promise, they find the faith to endure.

◆ GOSPEL: Jesus does not dismiss the law of the prophets; rather, he elevates the core of what it offers to an entirely new level. It is not enough to not kill; even anger unleashed on others must be addressed and reconciled. This exquisite pattern of reconciliation — facing an issue, addressing it, and coming healed and whole to the prayer of the community — remains to this day a powerful model for the Christian life. The Scribes and Pharisees were trained to obey the law, but there is something more than the formality of particular proscriptions or restraints. The law imposed by Jesus upon his followers will not be simply about the letter of the law but its spirit.

The Roman Missal

Any one of the four Prefaces of Lent can be used today. Consideration might also be given, in light of the Gospel's call for us to be reconciled with one another (especially before bringing our gifts to the altar), to using Eucharistic Prayer for Reconciliation II, as it describes in its Preface how it is through the power of the Spirit "that enemies may speak to each other again, / adversaries join hands, / and peoples seek to meet together" and how the

Spirit "takes away everything that estranges us from one another."

Today's Saint

St. Polycarp, an esteemed Christian leader, lived during the first half of the second century and was a friend to many who personally knew Jesus. He converted to the Christian faith under the influence of St. John the Evangelist. St. Polycarp later became bishop of Smyrna, in Turkey, around the year 96. He fought many of the gnostic heresies that were beginning to overtake the early Church. When there was a controversy over the celebration of Easter, the Churches in Asia Minor sent Polycarp as their representative to discuss the issue with Pope Anicetus. The Romans tried to burn Polycarp at the stake (when he was in his late 80s) but, when he survived that, they finally stabbed him to death with a dagger.

SAT 24 (#229) violet
Lenten Weekday

The Lectionary for Mass

◆ FIRST READING: Moses completes the deliverance of God's law to the people by exhorting them to give themselves, heart and soul, to observance. The covenant with God moves in both directions: from God to his people, and from the people to Him. This agreement binds them to him, and they are called to "walk in his ways." If they do this, they will be blessed.

◆ RESPONSORIAL PSALM 119: We are reminded that following God's law is not a burden to be shouldered but a gift to be embraced. God calls us to diligence: We don't follow the law here and there, willy nilly, but make it the centerpiece of our lives. Once the law is known to us, it is incumbent upon us to make God's ways our ways, to "walk" with him and to "seek" him always.

◆ GOSPEL: Jesus continues to illuminate how following him calls people to live the fullness of the implications of the law. Anyone can love the one who loves them in return; how much more difficult it is to love the person who is a persecutor. The ultimate demonstration of the exhortation to love ones enemies is offered at the end of the Gospel, where Jesus prays for forgiveness of those who are crucifying him. We may shrink from the idea that we should be perfect as God is perfect, but made in God's image and likeness, and baptized into Christ's life, Death, and Resurrection, we strive for nothing less.

The Roman Missal

In the Collect we pray that we may seek "always the one thing necessary," so that while we undertake works of love, we may worship the Lord. The Eucharist is the reward of saints, and food for sinners. We pray that these "blessed mysteries" may restore us and make us worthy to receive them (Prayer over the Offerings). We have been refreshed by a "divine mystery," "imbued with heavenly teaching." We ask that God may accompany us on our way with his consolations (Prayer after Communion). We long for God's blessing. We ask that his benediction may strengthen us to follow his will, and rejoice in his gifts (Prayer over the People). Any one of the four Prefaces of Lent can be used today.

☀ 25 (#26) violet
Second Sunday of Lent

The Lectionary for Mass

◆ FIRST READING: The story of the near sacrifice of Isaac is one of the most gripping and disturbing of the many stories related to the covenant in the Book of Genesis. It is worth noting what God does not ask, in the end, of Abraham, rather than focusing on his initial request. Ours is not a capricious God putting humanity to terrifying tests, although the test does reveal the extraordinary willingness of Abraham to listen to God. Scholars suggest that this startling story points to the fact that Abraham's God is one that does not demand human sacrifice for appeasement, as do the gods of the many neighboring cults of the time.

◆ RESPONSORIAL PSALM 116: The psalmist voices his willingness to believe even in the face of terrifying affliction. In response to his release from agony, he offers God prayer and thanksgiving, echoing the response of Abraham who offers a sacrifice of a ram in thanksgiving to God. Like Abraham, like the psalmist, we are called to surrender ourselves to God in the manner of a servant. God in turn cherishes each one of us.

◆ SECOND READING: To close his observations on what it means to live life in God's Spirit, Paul speaks to what having God with us looks like. One with Christ, we can count on God's presence and fidelity. While there may be those who try to condemn, they cannot succeed, because Christ is our intercessor.

◆ GOSPEL: Peter, James, and John accompany Jesus up the mountain, where they experience him transfigured. They see his glory revealed in the company of the great prophets and representatives of the law of Israel, Moses and Elijah. In his terror, Peter resorts to the practical: Perhaps they should contain the moment by erecting dwellings for the three. God names Jesus as his "beloved Son," echoing the proclamation made in the first chapter of Mark at the Baptism of the Lord in the Jordan. Jesus exhorts his companions to keep the experience a secret, a theme that weaves throughout the Gospel according to Mark when Jesus' identity comes into question.

The Roman Missal

"Of you my heart has spoken: Seek his face" (Psalm 27:8/Entrance Antiphon). The second option for the Entrance Antiphon is from Psalm 25 (24). The Collect shows us the way to see God. God has commanded us to listen to the Word of his Son. We pray that, fed by his divine Word, our sight may be "made pure" so that we too may "behold your glory." It clearly connects with the Gospel reading of the Transfiguration. The imagery in the prayer all but puts us in the Transfiguration scene. The Gloria is omitted today. The Creed is sung or said.

In the Prayer over the Offerings, we ask that our sacrifice may cleanse and sanctify us for the celebration of Easter. The Preface to be used for this Mass is given on the pages right there along with the other texts for this Mass. Titled "The Transfiguration of the Lord," the Preface clearly recalls and gives the meaning of the Transfiguration: "to show, even by the testimony of the law and the prophets, / that the Passion leads to the glory of the

Resurrection." Consider chanting the introductory dialogue and the Preface today; if this is not the regular practice of your community, this can be a way of powerfully drawing attention to the solemnity of Lenten time (but be sure to prepare and rehearse your assembly as needed, especially if your people are not familiar with the responses!). The Prayer after Communion is a simple prayer of thanksgiving for the grace of being "partakers . . . of the things of heaven" while still on earth. The Eucharist is our everyday Transfiguration!

The Prayer over the People also echoes the Gospel account of the Transfiguration, with its prayer that we may be faithful to the Gospel of the Son of God, and one day attain "that glory whose beauty he showed in his own Body." The Prayer over the People is required, not optional, on the Sundays of Lent, and the text is given right after the Prayer after Communion.

The RCIA offers the option of celebrating the Penitential Rite for the baptized candidates. It is designed to be celebrated on the Second Sunday of Lent, but it may be celebrated on a Lenten weekday or at another suitable time. If the Penitential Rite is celebrated on the Second Sunday of Lent, the Mass and the readings are from that day; if it is celebrated on another day, appropriate readings from the Lectionary are used, and the Collect provided in the rite is prayed. This rite follows a pattern similar to the Scrutinies; instead of focusing on preparation for Baptism, however, the texts and prayers look to preparation for Reconciliation. The candidates will receive the Sacrament of Reconciliation before they are confirmed, share in the Eucharist and, if appropriate, are received into the full Communion of the Catholic Church.

There is no ritual Mass for the Penitential Rite as there are for the Scrutinies. There is no com-

bined rite for the Scrutinies and the Penitential Rite. The prayers and other texts of the Scrutinies are specific to the elect; they include prebaptismal exorcisms, which are not appropriate to the baptized (see RCIA, 445–472).

Other Ideas

This Sunday we hear the Transfiguration account from Mark. As we reflect on the powerful story of Peter, James, and John experiencing Jesus as he truly is—the glorified Son of God—we can present resources to help individuals see in new or transformative ways. This is a good time to highlight supports for addiction recovery, Marriage enrichment, domestic violence intervention, and more. Also, the candidates for full communion in the Church will come forward with their sponsors to participate in the Penitential Rite (see above). Be sure to include prayer for them in the Universal Prayer, and use the bulletin to help the community better understand the various rites pertaining to the initiation of adults, particularly the Church's recognition of Baptism received in other Christian denominations.

MON 26 (#230) violet
Lenten Weekday

The Lectionary for Mass

◆ FIRST READING: Daniel's prayer is a heartfelt confession of the shortfall of the people of Israel in living up to their side of the covenant. They have not followed the commandments and have turned a deaf ear to the prophets. Daniel is frank and condemnatory of the people, who must turn in shame from God. Still, he grasps with hope the promise of forgiveness that God has made to those who will turn away from sin and return to him.

◆ RESPONSORIAL PSALM 79: There would be little hope for

humankind if God judged us only on our sinfulness and not on our contrite willingness to return to his ways. This lament recognizes that the people have brought suffering upon themselves, but it also confirms that God has the power to relieve their agony.

◆ GOSPEL: The followers of Jesus are not called to righteous condemnation of each other but a full-bodied posture of mercy. Nothing less than mirroring the extraordinary mercy of God is expected. In the time of Jesus, great weight was given to judging others — who was following the law, how well, and meting out consequences. To be in relationship with one another is to be poised to extend loving forgiveness. This calls the question of who we are poised to evaluate, to judge, and to even condemn in our own time.

The Roman Missal

In the Collect, God teaches us to undertake physical penances for the good of our souls. We ask for the strength to "abstain from all sins," and to carry out God's loving commands. In the Prayer over the Offerings, we pray that all whom God allows to participate in these sacred mysteries may be "set free from worldly attractions." In the Prayer after Communion, we pray that the Communion we receive may cleanse us of our faults, and "make us heirs to the joy of heaven." In the Prayer over the People, we pray that with God's grace, we may be faithful in prayer to God, and truly love one another.

T U E 27 (#231) violet Lenten Weekday

The Lectionary for Mass

◆ FIRST READING: In full prophetic voice, Isaiah calls out to his listeners to turn away from sin and return to the Lord. As he speaks to

Judah about Jerusalem, he evokes the names of two great, recognizable cities that paid consequences for their sinfulness: Sodom and Gomorrah. The situation is dire, and Isaiah calls the people out — set things right! There is still time to turn the blood-red stain of sin into the purity of white snow.

◆ RESPONSORIAL PSALM 50: This psalm records a ceremony in which God, mediated through the priest, speaks to his people. While other Gods are sated with sacrifices, the God of Israel requires the sacrifice of old ways and old behaviors. The greatest sacrifice offered to God is the praise of God's people who have lived the principles of the covenant, not paid lip service to them.

◆ GOSPEL: The popular idiom "walk the walk," usually contrasted with "talk the talk," may very well derive from these words of Jesus. The scribes and the Pharisees are adept at telling people how to follow the law, but do not live the law to its fullest in their own lives. It is insufficient to be conspicuously pious if the showy display is not backed up with a life lived in the light of the law. The closing exhortation of the greatest being the servant is most fully embodied in Jesus Christ himself, who "took the form of a slave," in the words of Paul. Here we are called to rigorously investigate our own grandiosity, and to turn to each other in humble service in the manner of Christ.

The Roman Missal

Since we will surely fall without God's help, in the Collect, we pray that the Lord may assist us always, protecting us from harm and pointing us toward salvation. Through this sacred mystery God can work his "sanctification" in us, cleansing us of sin and leading us to heaven (Prayer over the Offerings). One of the four Prefaces of Lent is used today. In the Prayer after

Communion, we ask that the heavenly "refreshment" we receive at the Lord's table may increase our devotion, and help us with God's reconciling love. In the Prayer over the People, we ask God to hear the "cries" of our prayer and lead us from "weariness" to rejoicing.

W E D 28 (#232) violet Lenten Weekday

The Lectionary for Mass

◆ FIRST READING: Jesus himself notes that prophets are never loved in their own land! This is true for Jeremiah, who after challenging the community to return to God, is treated with contempt. His adversaries plot to destroy him. Note that the plotters think that they can destroy God's prophet and yet still maintain a relationship with God. Their tactic will be defamation — destroying Jeremiah by twisting his words against him. Jeremiah exhorts God to hear them, and to be alongside him in his trial.

◆ RESPONSORIAL PSALM 31: This psalm of lament points to the destructive power of hateful speech. Like Jeremiah, the psalmist faces plots and the threat of death. In affirmation of God's salvific power, the psalmist affirms that God will rescue him from the grasp of persecutors.

◆ GOSPEL: As he travels to Jerusalem and the fulfillment of his destiny, Jesus tells the Twelve what to expect. This is the third time in Mark's account of the Gospel that Jesus predicts his Passion. We are not offered the reaction of the Apostles. Instead, the focus shifts to the mother of James and John, and her concern about their status. Those who will sit alongside him are those who are able to embrace his understanding of greatness. To be a servant, a slave, of others is the pattern of the Christian life, and God will look favorably on those who embody this in their own discipleship. In a culture focused on achievement and status, this teaching invites us to consider a new order for human relationships.

The Roman Missal

In the Collect, we ask God to keep his "family," the Church, "schooled always in good works," to surround us with his protection, and to lead us to heaven. Lent is this school for our souls. The Eucharist is a "holy exchange" (Prayer over the Offerings). We offer to God the sacrifice his Son offered for us, and in return, God gives us forgiveness. The Communion we have received is our "pledge of immortality." We pray that it may "work for our eternal salvation" (Prayer after Communion). The Prayer over the People asks God for everything we need to live the Christian life: grace and protection, health, love, and devotion.

March 2018
Month of St. Joseph

THU 1 (#233) violet
Lenten Weekday

The Lectionary for Mass

◆ FIRST READING: Jeremiah uses contrast to present two types of human character. The person who places his trust in humanity, with all its faults and failings, is doomed. The person who trusts in God thrives, even in time of drought. The poetic image of the tree, stretching its roots down and remaining anchored in the face of adversity, is a vivid picture of what is possible for any person who sinks their spiritual roots deep in God.

◆ RESPONSORIAL PSALM 1: The image of the tree planted near fresh water appears in numerous places in the Old Testament—Job, Numbers, Ecclesiastes, Ezekiel, and, as heard

today, Jeremiah. In a region characterized by barrenness and desert, the precious gift of constant water is a vivid image for the nourishment of God's life-giving presence.

◆ GOSPEL: The story of the rich man and the poor man Lazarus completes a series of teachings by Jesus on money. The issue here is not that the rich man had money, but that he was blind to the suffering of another—a person who was literally right at his front door. Where he might have stewarded the financial gifts he was given in service to others, instead his focus was only on his own pleasure and well-being. It is too late for the rich man to learn his lesson; Jesus says it is even too late for the rich man's brothers, who should have attended to the exhortations of the prophet to care for the poor, the widow, and the orphan. The ironic twist at the end is that there will be those among Jesus' listeners who will not believe in the Resurrection—even coming back from the dead will not change their hearts.

The Roman Missal

Today's Collect brings to mind how the purification we undergo during Lent can restore us to innocence, as it asks that being caught up in the fire of the Holy Spirit, "we may be found steadfast in faith / and effective in works." The Prayer over the Offerings again highlights the necessary connection between our exterior behaviors of Lenten disciplines and our interior dispositions and conversion: those disciplines are supposed to both be a sign of and bring about the inward, spiritual realities. The Prayer after Communion prays that the sacrifice we have just celebrated may truly be active and strong within us.

FRI 2 (#234) violet
Lenten Weekday

The Lectionary for Mass

◆ FIRST READING: The acute sibling rivalry among the sons of Israel comes to a bad end as the brothers plot to kill the favorite, Joseph. Reuben and Judah both modify the vile plot: Reuben would try to save him by having him placed in the cistern (perhaps to be rescued later), and Judah connives to sell him to the Ishmaelites. Reuben returns just after this incident, and tears his garments in despair.

◆ RESPONSORIAL PSALM 105: The story of Joseph, which in the Book of Genesis reads like an exciting short novel, is remembered here. The devastation of the famine is mitigated by God's agent, Joseph, whose interpretation of dreams allows Egypt to store food for the time of trial—and save the family of Israel. These are but a few of "the marvels the Lord has done" worth remembering.

◆ GOSPEL: The parable of the vineyard, offered to the chief priests and elders, is an indictment of the ways in which the people have rejected God and his prophets. It evokes events to come, pointing to the reality that the leaders of the people will be the first to reject and kill the messiah. The parable also evokes the destruction of the Temple by the Roman Army in the year AD 70. Notice that while Jesus incenses the leaders, the people are able to hear his powerful message and embrace him as a prophet.

The Roman Missal

The Collect asks that our penance may purify us, and lead us "to attain the holy things to come." In the Prayer over the Offerings, we ask for God's "merciful grace" to prepare us to celebrate these mysteries, and to lead us to "a devout way of life." Prefaces I–IV are the choices once again today. While any one is appropriate, perhaps Eucharistic Prayer for Reconciliation I, with its own Preface, would be a good choice for today, insofar as that Preface tells how God is rich in mercy, offering constant pardon, how he never turned away despite how humanity broke the covenant again and again, and how now is a time for turning back. In the Eucharist, we receive a "pledge of eternal salvation" (Prayer after Communion). We pray that we may "set our course" toward the redemption God has promised. In the Prayer over the People, we ask for "health of mind and body," so that we may use these precious gifts for "good deeds."

SAT 3 (#235) violet
Lenten Weekday

Optional Memorial of St. Katharine Drexel, Virgin / violet

The Lectionary for Mass

◆ First Reading: These verses comprise the upbeat conclusion to the book of Micah. The prophet exhorts God to bring back an age of abundance. His image is of God as Shepherd and his words evoke images of the forgiveness, and compassion of God. This prayer, and other passages, should support Christians in not reducing the God of Abraham to a punishing God, but to encounter him as the God of Jesus Christ, a God of fidelity and love.

◆ Responsorial Psalm 103: The magnificent verses of Psalm 103 remind us of all the positive characteristics of God. His kindness and mercy inspire us to bless God with all our being. The vastness of God's forgiveness and the scope of our redemption are vividly envisioned here.

◆ Gospel: The story of the prodigal son evokes a range of reactions in people. Who do they relate to? Is it the righteous son who has not lost anything and yet feels slighted that

the brother who transgressed is so fully forgiven? The contrite, desperate wastrel who comes crawling back, hoping for even the tiniest shred of kindness? The effusive, forgiving even profligate father, who flaunts social convention to embrace his beloved child? In keeping with today's themes of God's vast love and forgiveness, the father embodies what all of us would hope for when we return to God in humble repentance: An open-armed, over-the-top reception filled with forgiveness and love.

The Roman Missal

Prefaces I–IV are the choices once again today. While any one is appropriate, perhaps Eucharistic Prayer for Reconciliation I, with its own Preface, would be a good choice for today, insofar as that Preface tells how God is rich in mercy, offering constant pardon, how he never turned away despite how humanity broke the covenant again and again, and how now is a time for turning back.

Today's Saints

St. Katharine Drexel (1858–1955), a wealthy and worldly heiress from Philadelphia, did not spend her fortune on houses or jewelry, but on the establishment of institutions and missions dedicated to the marginalized. Due to her financial means, she had the privilege of traveling to various parts of the country where she became keenly aware of the oppression of Native Americans and African Americans. She dedicated her entire life, including the founding of a religious community known as the Sisters of the Blessed Sacrament, to the empowerment of these groups through education (that is, launching the first Catholic college for African Americans, and starting 145 Catholic missions and twelve schools for Native Americans). Regarding the purpose of the

Sisters of the Blessed Sacrament, St. Katharine said, "Ours is the spirit of Eucharist—the total gift of self" (as quoted on the website of the Archdiocese of Philadelphia, www.archdiocesephl.org/rigali/cardhom/drexel04.htm).

4 (#29 or #28) violet
Third Sunday of Lent

The Lectionary for Mass, Year B

◆ First Reading: The first weeks of Lent focused us on our relationship with the law as people of the covenant and followers of Jesus. Here, we experience the power of God's voice in the giving of the law. To follow these precepts is to remain in right relationship with God and with each other. The language of the law is "you" and "me," an intimate address that reflects the direct connection between God, the nation, and each and every individual.

◆ Responsorial Psalm 19: Following God's law is not a burden; rather, it is the source of "everlasting life." His precepts are perfect, a source of rejoicing and enlightenment. How often we relate to moral guidance, laws, or commandments as restriction or burden, when in fact they create a life-giving framework in which humankind can live. The preciousness of God's guidance is vividly depicted in the final verse.

◆ SECOND READING: It is challenging for us to try to imagine how utterly outside the cultural conceptions of the day was the image of Christ who died on a Cross and rose again. In our age, we too want "signs" or evidence to prove things; we also use intellect to shape answers and guide our thinking. To claim Christ as the Risen Lord is to leap, with the fleet feet of faith, into the mystery of an incarnate God who has entered into human experience for our redemption.

◆ GOSPEL: John's vivid depiction of the cleansing of the Temple offers us insight into Jesus' outrage at the abuses in the Temple precinct. The money changers and those selling unblemished animals for sacrifice were gouging the traveler and the poor, who had no recourse but to purchase what they needed from extortionists. In doing this, Jesus stands within the tradition of the prophets, who come to Israel to call her back to sanctity. The Talmud calls for the very sanctity that Jesus seeks. His bold disruption of commerce, and the revenue it provided to the less-than-scrupulous is experienced as very threatening, as is his comment that he can raise the Temple up in three days. This comment—about his body but perceived as a threat to the holy building—is very likely the moment that set in motion the desire of the Temple authorities to turn him in to Rome.

The Lectionary for Mass, Year A

◆ FIRST READING: The passage from Exodus is rich with images and layers of meaning. The reader might well be surprised at the grumbling of the people against Moses; after all, God had delivered them from Egypt. It appears that they are really dissatisfied with God and ask, "Is the Lord in our midst or not?" The response of God to Moses' plea is an unconditional gesture of concern for the people. Out of a lifeless rock, in the middle of a desert God provides living water. This happened at Massah (which means "testing") and Meribah (which means "dissatisfaction"), but the greater meaning of this place is found in the intervention of God on behalf of a people thirsting for life.

◆ RESPONSORIAL PSALM 95: This liturgical hymn praises the God of the covenant. The psalmist issues a fivefold invitation to praise, "Come let us sing . . . let us acclaim . . . let us come . . . let us bow down . . . let us kneel." The image of God echoes the First Reading; God is the "Rock of our salvation." Here one imagines a great rock, one that speaks of strength and security, something one could depend on to be in place forever. Such is the role of the Lord in the life of the people. The psalmist ends with an exhortation that recalls the First Reading: "Harden not your hearts as at Meribah."

◆ SECOND READING: Paul's theology of justification occurs a number of times in his letters. One aspect of his teaching is that this justification is not merited by believers; it is pure grace and comes from God through Jesus Christ. In fact, we were sinners and still God has chosen to save us. This grace is the love of God that is "poured into our hearts." This baptismal imagery reflects Paul's' understanding that it is through baptism that we enter into the life, Death, and Resurrection of Christ.

◆ GOSPEL: This is the first of the three great stories of John that take us toward the end of Lent. The baptismal imagery is obvious and the conversation between Jesus and the Samaritan woman is layered with meanings. Jesus stops at the well of Jacob because he is thirsty, but it is the woman who is refreshed. Through the course of the conversation Jesus identifies himself with one of the "I am" statements that will occur in the Gospel accounts for the next two Sundays. He becomes the source of a new life for the woman and she becomes an evangelist, bearing the news that she has found the Messiah.

The Roman Missal

There are two options for today's Entrance Antiphon. The second, taken from Ezekiel 36:23–26, is especially appropriate when the scrutiny of the elect is celebrated: "I will pour clean water upon you." We are burdened by sin, but God has given us a remedy in the Lenten disciplines of prayer, fasting, and almsgiving. The Gloria is omitted today. The Creed is sung or said.

We pray in the Collect that we, who are weighed down by a heavy conscience, may be lifted up by God's forgiving mercy. With the sacrifice we make, we ask God for forgiveness and reconciliation. We who ask these blessings must "take care to forgive our neighbor," as Jesus taught (Prayer over the Offerings).

When the Gospel about the Samaritan woman is read, the proper Preface for the Third Sunday of Lent is used. It is found in the Proper of Time. It reflects beautifully on the encounter at the well. Jesus asks the Samaritan woman for water, and gives living water. Jesus is on fire for her faith, and he gives "the fire of divine love." Consider chanting the introductory dialogue and the Preface today; if this is not the regular practice of your community, this can be a way of powerfully drawing attention to the solemnity of Lenten time (but be sure to prepare and rehearse your assembly as needed, especially if your people are not familiar with the responses!).

The Prayer after Communion expresses the mystery of Holy Communion: "we receive the pledge" of what is "hidden in heaven," and are fed on earth with "Bread that comes from on high."

We pray that we may come to the "true completion" of this mystery which is already at work in us.

The Prayer over the People echoes the golden rule: we ask this one grace, to abide in love of God and neighbor, and thus to fulfill the whole of God's commandments. The Prayer over the People is required, not optional, on the Sundays of Lent, and the text is given right after the Prayer after Communion.

If your parish is celebrating the First Scrutiny with the elect, then, according to a rubric in the Missal, the proper prayers should be used; these Mass formularies are found in the "Ritual Masses" section of the Missal, under segment I — For the Conferral of the Sacraments of Initiation; #2 — For the Celebration of the Scrutinies; A — For the First Scrutiny. For the actual ritual of the scrutiny itself, consult RCIA, 150–156. The scrutiny takes place after the homily.

Other Ideas

Over the next three weeks, special rites called the Scrutinies will be prayed over the elect who are making their final preparations to be fully imitated at the Easter Vigil. This is a time for strengthening and repentance. The community can stand in solidarity with the catechumens by participating in "24 Hours for the Lord," an initiative of Pope Francis that happens on the Fourth Friday of Lent. Consider offering this celebration in your parish, beginning with penitential prayer service and the Sacrament of Reconciliation (catechumens and elect of course do not participate in this rite), and followed by a vigil with Eucharistic adoration (see LTP's resource, *Guide for Celebrating® Worship of the Eucharist Outside Mass* by John Thomas Lane, sss). This initiative is designed to create a global moment of prayer for the Catholic community and is part of the new

evangelization. In the words of Pope Francis, "Let us not underestimate the power of so many voices united in prayer!" (found here: www.novaevangelizatio.va/content/nvev/en/news/24h-2015.html). Please note that the optional readings for the Third Week of Lent may be used on any day this coming week (see Lectionary #236).

M O N **5** (#237) violet
Lenten Weekday

The Lectionary for Mass

Please note that the optional readings for the Third Week of Lent may be used on any day this week (#236).

◆ FIRST READING: The great prophet Elisha is the successor of Elijah. The story of the cleansing of Namaan has an almost theatrical quality, the cast including his wife, the young girl, the two kings, the loyal servants and of course the willing but judgmental Namaan. He longs for healing, but he finds the simplicity of what is offered an affront. In the midst of the displays of power, we see the strong, straight forward faith of the people of Israel, particularly the young girl who speaks with the boldness and confidence that sometimes comes from young people. In his cure, Namaan finds evidence for believing in Israel's God.

◆ RESPONSORIAL PSALM 42: Nothing is more fundamental to staying alive than having access to water. Without it, we perish. This psalm is written from the perspective of someone who is living apart from Israel, and the tender longing and hope with which it speaks touch our hearts. At the time, to be distant from Jerusalem meant being distant from God, who dwelled there in his holy Temple. The psalmist remains confident that he will once again come to God's altar.

◆ GOSPEL: Here we see the depth of Jesus' knowledge about the prophets and their messages as he recounts two great events in the lives of Elijah and Elisha. These prophets, and others, were resisted or ignored. Jesus, too, experiences a rebuff from many of the people to whom he speaks. His comment that "no prophet is accepted in his own native place" is prescient; after challenging the people in the synagogue, the chase him off from his home town in a rage. Like the listeners in the synagogue, we do well to meditate on which messages we are willing to hear and which we are not, and who we can listen to and who we resist — including Jesus.

The Roman Missal

The Collect for today notes how the Church needs God's compassionate cleansing and protection, because without it, the Church cannot stand secure; the prayer reminds us that unlike any human society or association, the existence of the Church is rooted in God, and without that divine union, she does not exist. The Prayer over the Offerings refers implicitly to the holy exchange that takes place in the Liturgy of the Eucharist: we offer our gifts of bread and wine as tokens of our service, indeed, of our very selves, and we pray that they will be transformed into the "sacrament of salvation." The Prayer after Communion asks that our sharing in the sacrament will result in purification and unity. Any one of the four Prefaces of Lent can be used today. While any one is appropriate, you might also consider using Eucharistic Prayer for Reconciliation II with its own Preface. The themes of universality and of salvation being extended to those thought to be outsiders as presented in the readings would be continued in phrases such as the Church's being "an instrument of your peace among all people" and bringing together "those of every race and tongue" to "the unending banquet of unity" that are found in the second part of the Prayer. Even though the Prayer over the People is optional on weekdays, it would be good to use it to highlight the liturgical time.

TUE 6 (#238) violet
Lenten Weekday

The Lectionary for Mass

◆ First Reading: The touching and humble prayer of Azariah (also called Abednego) from the midst of the fire of the furnace. He and his two companions have been condemned for their unwillingness to worship Nebuchadnezzar's golden statue. He extols God's mercy and affirms their faith, even though the furnace is being stoked. An angel comes, dispelling the heat of the furnace in response to his prayer.

◆ Responsorial Psalm 25 cries out to the Lord for mercy. The psalmist knows that he is a sinner, but he also trusts that God can set him aright. With a contrite heart, he affirms that the God of Israel is a God of compassion and justice, one who leads the humble. A lament, he trusts that God will hear his plea.

◆ Gospel: The human mind, aware of crimes that are incomprehensible, wants to apply reason to the question of forgiveness. Is there a limit? Peter probably thought he was being bold in suggesting the "seven times" of this Gospel. Jesus instructs otherwise. For the Christian, forgiveness is a constant, something that is, for all intents and purposes, unlimited. The illustration of the merciless servant and the harsh response of the master drives home Jesus' point. Notice that the master forgives the servant; the latter's opportunism and mean spiritedness is in contrast to the king's generosity.

The Roman Missal

We pray in the Collect for God's continued grace, that we may dedicate ourselves to his "holy service," and receive his help in our need. We pray in the Prayer over the Offerings that the sacrifice we offer may cleanse us of sin, and be pleasing to God. In the Prayer after Communion, we ask for "pardon and protection" through our sharing in the Eucharist. In the Prayer over the People, we ask God to drive sin away from us, so that we may remain safely under his protection.

WED 7 (#239) violet
Lenten Weekday

Optional Memorial of Sts. Perpetua and Felicity, Martyrs / violet

The Lectionary for Mass

◆ First Reading: Moses speaks to the people, calling on them to remember what has been given to them. He is calling them to observance of the law, and to hold it in its integrity — a "whole law" that has been given to them. The people have firsthand experience of what it means to keep the law, and the destruction that comes when they forget it — as was the cast.

◆ Responsorial Psalm 147: The psalm offers praise to the creative, protective God who brings forth the riches of the earth. The God of Israel has shown them favor, and the fact that they are his chosen ones is extoled. All of Jerusalem is called upon to give him praise in thanks for the gifts and the mercies that God has extended to them.

◆ Gospel: Jesus emphasizes by stating the fact twice, that he is not among the Jews to abolish but to fulfill the law and the prophets. In him, a deep and true meaning of the law is being revealed for the people. The phrase "these commandments" may also be referencing the teaching of Jesus, not just the Decalogue and other laws. The disciples are exhort-

ed to obey and teach, as Jesus has modelled. This passage is the opening of the Sermon on the Mount, which will unfold for listeners the expansive way in which Jesus holds the law.

The Roman Missal

Lent is a school in which we learn "holy restraint" (Collect). We pray that we may learn from our Lenten observance, and from God's Word, to be devoted to the Lord and united in prayer. The Prayer over the Offerings is a prayer for the protection of all those who "celebrate your mysteries." In the Prayer after Communion, we pray that our sharing in the heavenly banquet may make us holy and cleanse us from "all errors," so that we may see the fulfillment of God's promises in heaven. In the Prayer over the People, we ask for "a resolve that is pleasing" to God, for we know that those who are conformed to God's Word will experience his favor.

Today's Saints

In the year 203, Sts. Perpetua and Felicity were martyred in the amphitheater at Carthage. Their crime was professing faith in Jesus Christ. Perpetua was a wealthy noblewoman, the mother of a young son; Felicity was a humble slave girl, who gave birth to a daughter just a few days before she died. These women, so different in their circumstances, were united in their death. The names of these heroic women are included in Eucharistic Prayer I, alongside the names of Apostles and martyrs. They lived today's Gospel, praying for their persecutors.

THU 8 (#240) violet
Lenten Weekday

Optional Memorial of St. John of God, Religious / violet

The Lectionary for Mass

◆ First Reading: The thing that prevents the people from walking in the ways of the Lord is hardness of heart. What should be a fleshy, soft, living thing can become calcified. This image appears in multiple places in the Old Testament as well as in the Gospels and Epistles. The heart represented the entire person—thoughts, feelings, and all activity. To have a hard heart is to become impenetrable.

◆ RESPONSORIAL PSALM 95: The beauty of Psalm 95 is its invitation, over the ages, to God with a soft, open heart. The psalm is an invitation to worship, a call to the Temple where God can be encountered. The image of the shepherd and the flock is offered, and the reference to Moses reminds the people—and us—that we can turn from God at the very moments we need God most.

◆ GOSPEL: Here, the astonishing gift of freedom offered to the man who was possessed by a demon is met with the darkest possible interpretation. This is not work done in the power of God, but in the forces of darkness. Others demand another sign. In this story we see illustrated the theme of hardness of heart. Jesus uses logic to address them—if the power was from Beelzebub, then would the evil one drive out his own demon? More important still is his observation that they stand at a crossroad: Accept that the Kingdom of God has come to them or be scattered.

The Roman Missal

At the midpoint of Lent, there is somewhat of a sense of urgency in today's Collect, which takes note of the journey we are on toward the celebration of Easter. Referring to that upcoming feast as "the worthy celebration of the Paschal Mystery," the prayer asks that as that feast draws closer, "we may press forward all the more eagerly" toward it. Thus, we are again reminded of the ultimate purpose of our Lenten journey, which is

to share in the risen life of Christ celebrated at Easter. The Prayer over the Offerings is a prayer for cleansing. We must be cleansed "from every taint of wickedness," and freed from "false joys," if we are to bring our gifts to God and receive "the rewards" of his truth. In the Prayer after Communion, we pray that the sacrament which renews us may bring us salvation. We will know this salvation "in mystery" through the sacraments, but it must also be expressed "in the manner of our life." God is the source of everything, "all that we are." We ask his grace, that we may "seek what is right" and "do the good we desire" (Prayer over the People).

Today's Saint

St. John of God was a Portuguese friar who became a leading religious figure. After a period in the army in Spain, he began to distribute religious books, using the new Gutenberg printing press. At one point, John had an intense religious experience that resulted in temporary insanity. He was thrown into a mental institution, and while there, he realized how badly the sick and the poor were treated. Once he recovered, he spent the rest of his life caring for them. In Granada he gathered a circle of disciples around him who felt the same call and founded what is now known as the Brothers Hospitallers of St. John of God.

F R I 9 (#241) violet
Lenten Weekday

Optional Memorial of St. Frances of Rome, Religious / violet

The Lectionary for Mass

◆ FIRST READING: Return to God is the essence of Lent. Here, Hosea reminds the people, and us, that God awaits us, eager to heal and love. All we need do is bring hearts of repentance. The magnificent images drawn from nature of God coming to Israel like the

dewfall and the response of abundant growth and multiple fragrances is a vivid image to embrace. To experience conversion is to surge with life and beauty.

◆ RESPONSORIAL PSALM 81 was most likely a psalm of worship, perhaps used at one of Israel's harvest festivals. These verses recount the action of God in liberating the people from the slavery of Egypt. The words of the first commandment are embedded in the verses. We also hear God's longing for the return of the relationship of love and sustenance that he offers.

◆ GOSPEL: While the scribes are often suspicious and hostile in the Gospels, here we have a sincere, interested scribe who seeks to understand Jesus. Upon hearing his response, his honest, affirmative answer demonstrates both his own knowledge and that of Jesus. The Shema ("*Hear, O Israel! / The Lord our God is Lord alone!*") is a centerpiece in Jewish spirituality to this day. The two commands offered by Jesus are those offered to Moses (Deuteronomy 6:2 and Leviticus 19:18). Mark's audience is Jewish, and they, too, would have known the centrality of Jesus' answer in the Judaism of his day. Notice that after this honest, kind interaction, no one dares to challenge him further.

The Roman Missal

In the Collect, we ask God to pour his grace into our hearts, for it is only by his grace that we can observe "heavenly teaching," and be "drawn away from unruly desires." It specifies what we want God's grace to do for us: we ask that "we may be constantly drawn away from unruly desires" and more closely obey the "heavenly teaching," which has been given to us as a gift. In the Prayer over the Offerings, we ask God to "look with favor" upon the sacrifice we offer, that these gifts may be pleasing to him and bring salvation to us. In the Prayer after Communion we pray that as a result of sharing in the sacrament, God's strength will be at work in us completely, "pervading our minds and bodies" and bringing us "the fullness of redemption." God has given us gifts, but not for ourselves alone. We need to spread these gifts, "far and wide" (Prayer over the People).

Today's Saint

St. Frances of Rome was born in Rome to wealthy parents. Although she wanted to enter a monastery, her parents married her off to Lorenzo Ponziano, commander of the papal troops in Rome. It was a happy marriage that lasted forty years. Her husband was often away at war, and Frances spent her time praying, visiting the poor, and caring for the sick. Eventually, her example inspired other wealthy women to do the same. Frances founded a lay congregation of Benedictine Oblates now known as Oblates of St. Frances of Rome.

S A T 10 (#242) violet
Lenten Weekday

The Lectionary for Mass

◆ FIRST READING: The frustration of God is heard in the voice of Hosea. As do all the prophets, Hosea calls upon the people to return to God, but he bemoans the recalcitrance of the people. The theme of the third day appears here, the day upon which the wondrous act of God will occur. This is the pattern that will appear in the resurrection, and which we remember each time we recite the Creed.

◆ RESPONSORIAL PSALM 51 may be the most vivid and expressive of the penitential psalms. The psalmist calls out to God for forgiveness, remembering that sacrifices are not the heart of the matter — a transformed heart is what is desired. Authentic sacrifice is offered when one is rightly related to God, and when Jerusalem is rebuilt — both literally and figuratively — they will please God.

◆ GOSPEL: Jesus is consistently opposed to righteousness in all its forms in the Gospels. The contrast of the pious yet filled-with-himself Pharisee and the pariah of the community, the tax collector, is stark. Embedded in this story is the tension between faith and works, a bone of contention in the Christian community since the Reformation. The repentant tax collector would have shocked the listeners. Jesus is turning social order on its head, and at the same time underlining the magnitude of the embrace of his Father, who, as Hosea and the Psalmist notes, desires love, not just rote observances.

The Roman Missal

The Collect connects our observance of Lent with what they are oriented toward, namely, celebrating with joy the Paschal Mystery at Easter; that is the focus our hearts should be set on. The Prayer over the Offerings prays simply that it is by God's grace that we can approach the celebration of the mysteries, and so we ask that our minds may be made pure. The prayer includes an interesting phrase about the mysteries, as it asks that we may offer God "fitting homage . . . in reverently handing them on." The phrase can remind us of how our celebrations of the Eucharist are not isolated actions, but instead should be seen as actualizations that perpetuate the one offering made by Christ, that offering made present in our space and time through the Spirit. The Prayer after Communion asks for heavenly assistance so that we might seek God with all our hearts and be granted what we request. Perhaps too we can hear the phrases "minds made pure" and "fitting homage" in light of the virtue of humility that is emphasized in the Gospel. While any one of the four Prefaces of Lent can be used today, perhaps Preface III with its reference to God's will that we "humble our sinful pride" would echo the Gospel reading. Even though the Prayer over the People is optional on weekdays, it would again be good to use it.

11 (#32 or #31) violet or rose
Fourth Sunday of Lent

The Lectionary for Mass, Year B

◆ FIRST READING: After the reign of King Josiah, a number of kings have led the people poorly, subjugating the people to the Egyptians. Although Jeremiah has witnessed to Nebuchadnezzar's place as the servant of the Lord meting out deserved punishment against Judah, the unfaithful Zedekiah revolts against Babylon. Nebuchadnezzar destroys both Judah and Jerusalem and the Babylonian captivity begins. After 70 years, Cyrus, the good king of Persia, calls for the rebuilding of the Temple and allows the Jews to return to Jerusalem for this critical task.

◆ RESPONSORIAL PSALM 137: To lose Jerusalem and the Temple was to lose access to God. The people grieve in their captivity, and their captors demand entertainment from them — their laments should be replaced with songs of joy and gladness. But the songs of Zion are songs of worship, and they would be desecrated if sung outside of the worship of the Temple.

◆ SECOND READING: The Epistle reminds us that we are saved by the pure and unfettered gift that is the grace of God. We are reminded that it is God who gives, and we who receive by this beautiful passage, and that even if we are "dead in our transgressions," as were the people of Judah in their exile, God awaits us with salvific, healing grace.

◆ GOSPEL: Jesus has been conversing with the Jewish leader and teacher Nicodemus, who is both open and curious about Jesus, coming to him in the night and affirming that clearly Jesus must be from God, or he would not be able to perform such signs. Nicodemus wants to understand what it means to be reborn. Jesus begins his answer with a reference to the miracle performed by Moses in the book of numbers, where a bronze serpent on a stick is raised and the people are saved (a confusing passage for Bible scholars given the prohibitions of the second commandment). Jesus, too, will be raised on wood—the Cross—but his death is one death for the salvation of all, for all time. Verse 16 may be one of the most widely known verses of scripture in the United States due to its appearance in popular culture.

The Lectionary for Mass, Year A

◆ FIRST READING: The selection and anointing of David as the king of the Israelites initiates a new era in the history of the people of God. It is clear from the account that God is the one who makes the decision, a choice that is not based on the normal criteria. Once again, the ways of the Lord are not the ways of human beings. Despite his humble beginnings the spirit of the Lord

will guide David and he will establish a great nation. The house of David will be renowned; in a future generation another shepherd will spring from the Root of Jesse, of the family of David.

◆ RESPONSORIAL PSALM 23: The "Good Shepherd" psalm is surely one of the most beloved passages of the Bible. The psalmist uses the very familiar image and role of a shepherd to identify the Lord and to describe the intimate relationship that the Lord has with his people, the sheep of his flock. Like the shepherd, the Lord is protector, provider, and nurturer. The tender care that the Lord provides the whole flock and even a single one of them becomes the mark of Jesus' own ministry generations later.

◆ SECOND READING: The contrast of darkness and light is one of several such contrasts that occur in the Lenten Scriptures. Others include temptation and transformation; thirst and overflowing water; fasting and feasting; blindness and sight; death and new life. Paul reminds the Ephesians that they once lived in darkness, a spiritual state before their faith in Jesus Christ, but now they live in the light. The Easter imagery here is obvious and it serves to prepare both the elect and the baptized to hurry toward the celebration of Christ, the Light of the world.

◆ GOSPEL: The contrast of darkness and light underscores both the healing of the blind man and the teaching of Jesus about who is spiritually blind and who can truly see. The encounter between Jesus and the man born blind confronts the religious thinking of the crowds and the religious leaders. It becomes a vehicle for Jesus to expose them to the intervention of God in human affairs and to see if their faith is ready to accept him. When the man regains his sight, he professes his belief in the "Son of Man." Like the

Samaritan woman, he becomes the bearer of Good News, if only the others can see it.

The Roman Missal

Traditionally, this Fourth Sunday of Lent marks a joyful relief amidst the seriousness and somberness of the many weeks of preparation for Easter. Hence, today is called Laetare Sunday, a name that comes from the Entrance Antiphon for this Mass: "Rejoice, Jerusalem, and all who love her. / Be joyful, all who were in mourning; / exult and be satisfied at her consoling breast" (Isaiah 66:10–11). Even in Lent, a time of fasting and repentance, we rejoice, because we know that God is love, and our loving God will provide for all our needs. Rose-colored vestments may be worn, and the altar may be decorated with flowers. However, the Gloria is still omitted today. The Creed is still sung or said.

In the Collect, we ask for "prompt devotion and eager faith" as we hasten toward the "solemn celebrations" to come — the Paschal Triduum of the Lord. "With joy" on this Laetare Sunday, we bring our offerings to God, and ask that they may be received "for the salvation of all the world" (Prayer over the Offerings). The Preface that is given on the pages right there along with the other texts for this Mass, "The Man Born Blind," is to be used today. Do not use Preface I or II of Lent; that is meant for other years when that Gospel is not read. Using the motif of humanity's being led out of darkness into "the radiance of the faith," the Preface relates how being "born in slavery to ancient sin" (that is, original sin) is to be in darkness, and how we are led out of that darkness "through the waters of regeneration." The theme of the Sacrament of Baptism as enlightenment could not be clearer here, a reference so appropriate as the Church approaches the Easter Vigil when the elect will be baptized and the faithful will renew their baptismal promises. Consider chanting the introductory dialogue and the Preface today; if this is not the regular practice of your community, this can be a way of powerfully drawing attention to the solemnity of Lenten time. Be sure to prepare and rehearse your assembly as needed, especially if your people are not familiar with the responses! The Prayer over the People is required, not optional, on the Sundays of Lent, and the text is given right after the Prayer after Communion.

If your parish is celebrating the Second Scrutiny with the elect, then, according to a rubric in the Missal, the proper prayers should be used; these Mass formularies are found in the "Ritual Masses" section of the Missal, under segment I — For the Conferral of the Sacraments of Initiation; #2 — For the Celebration of the Scrutinies; B — For the Second Scrutiny. For the actual ritual of the scrutiny itself, consult RCIA, 164–170. The scrutiny takes place after the homily.

Other Ideas

Today is Laetare Sunday. In medieval times, this was a day to visit the cathedral, or "mother church" of the diocese. Perhaps a parish-sponsored trip to your local cathedral, with an informational tour, can be offered. To celebrate Laetare Sunday in their homes, invite parishioners to place roses on their table or plant a rosebush. Today the collection for Catholic Relief Services takes place which funds relief worldwide, including help to migrants and refugees. Please note that the optional readings for the Fourth Week of Lent may be used on any day this coming week (see Lectionary #243).

MON 12 (#244) violet
Lenten Weekday

The Lectionary for Mass

Please note that the optional readings for the Fourth Week of Lent may be used on any of the remaining days of this week (#243).

◆ FIRST READING: Isaiah presents a vision of what the new Jerusalem will look like. It will be a place of joy and happiness, not a place of conflict, sorrow and weeping. The people will thrive and live, having lives of great length and abundance, although death will still exist. This is a picture of the fullest imaginable experience of life and blessing.

◆ RESPONSORIAL PSALM 30: God is praised for his rescuing powers in this vivid, narrative psalm. The enemy will not prevail; sickness and death will not prevail. Although night may be experienced, with its darkness and mourning, the dawn will come again and with it comes rejoicing and dancing. This psalm moves through stages. It starts in a space of peace, and then turns to the agony of trouble. Next the psalmist surrenders his pain to God in prayer, and God in turn lifts him up, returning him to a place of thanksgiving.

◆ GOSPEL: Jesus is back at the location at which his ministry first began: Cana. Again, the challenge is what will be the bedrock upon which belief rests. Is it signs and wonders? Or is it faith in God's promise and the messiah? The nobleman asks for what he needs, and is willing to take God's gift on Jesus' terms, not his own. His faith must be deeper than it first appears, for it first appears to be more of a demand of proof given Jesus' initial response. The reward for the little bit of faith he expresses is tremendous. This Gospel is a healing reminder to us all that we do not need vast faith or exemplary faith for

God to work in our lives: we simply need some faith, which may not only be powerful for us, but for those that surround us, as in the household of the royal official.

The Roman Missal

Only God can see the big picture. We pray that God will guide the Church according to his "eternal design," and come to our aid in "this present age." God is present, now and for ever (Collect). By the sacrifice we offer, we pray that we may leave behind "earthly ways" and grow in "heavenly life" (Prayer over the Offerings). In the Prayer after Communion we ask God to renew us, sanctify us, and lead us to eternal life. Any one of the four Prefaces of Lent is equally appropriate today. The Prayer over the People continues the theme of renewal present in all today's prayers. We ask God to renew his people "within and without," so that they may not be hindered by the pleasures of the flesh, but persevere in their "spiritual intent" — hope for the life to come.

TUE 13 (#245) violet
Lenten Weekday

The Lectionary for Mass

◆ FIRST READING: Ezekiel's exquisite vision of the water flowing out of the Temple is so beautiful as to be almost sublime. The rains fall from heaven, but they rise up from the earth to nourish all that the water touches. Here, water is a source of healing, sustenance, and abundant life. From a place where there once was destruction and barrenness, the fullness of the divine life springs forth.

◆ RESPONSORIAL PSALM 46: God is hope and deliverance in time of trouble, always extending his saving hand. The image of the stream rising within the city of God contrasts the destructive power of the raging storm in the first verses. Our storms may be literal or figurative; the power of nature, or the raging interior distresses that are too often part of human life. In every case, the psalmist reminds us, we need to trust that God is in our midst.

◆ GOSPEL: Jesus comes to the pool at Bethesda, where all around people are suffering. Their misery is extraordinary; every form of human need is present. All are hoping that the waters will be a source of healing. The man with whom Jesus speaks is particularly heartbreaking. He has been ill for thirty-eight years, and although he has made it to the pool, he is unable to reach it. Moved to pity, Jesus asks this most miserable person if he wants to be healed. This seems a strange question given the setting and the desperation of the man, but rather than challenge Jesus, he simply speaks of his need for help. Both the man and Jesus are subject to the ire of those around, Jesus for healing on the Sabbath and the man for carrying his mat: both actions of work. Unlike the Gospel according to Mark, where Jesus invites those around him to keep his power secret, here Jesus identifies himself and invites the man to witness to what has happened to him.

The Roman Missal

We pray that the ancient Lenten practices we observe — "the venerable exercises of holy devotion" — may "shape" our hearts, so that we may come "worthily" to the celebration of the Paschal Mystery (Collect). We give to God what God has given to us, and we pray for awareness of the Creator's loving care for us, and for the spiritual "healing / that brings us immortality." God cares for us, body and soul (Prayer over the Offerings). We ask God to purify and renew our minds with the sacrament we share, both now and in the future. Any one of the four Prefaces of Lent is equally appropriate today.

Although the Prayer over the People continues to be optional on weekdays, its consistent use would mark the daily liturgies of Lent in a significant way. The simple text asks for the grace of perseverance, that God's people may receive the good things God's love and "kindness" wills for them.

WED 14 (#246) violet
Lenten Weekday

The Lectionary for Mass

◆ FIRST READING: The "time of favor," also called the "acceptable" time and the "day of salvation," signifies the start of a new dispensation. God's servant will come and carry God's message of hope and restoration. Some commentators see the servant as the messiah; others as Isaiah speaking of himself. The closing lines, which evoke the steadfast, unending love of a mother, are a vivid reminded that God, who is neither male or female, can be spoken of in feminine as well as male metaphors.

◆ RESPONSORIAL PSALM 145: Nine of the psalms in the Psalter, among them Psalm 145, use the literary form of acrostic as an organizing factor. The letters of the Hebrew alphabet, in order, start each line. This feature may indicate that the psalms were written before they became part of oral tradition. Psalm 145 extols the goodness of God and his majesty; we might even say what makes God great is his goodness.

◆ GOSPEL: The intimate, empowering connection between Jesus and his Father is illuminated in this discourse. The Father is operative in history: he gives life and raises the dead. Through his power, the Son is also operative in human history. Those that encounter his life-giving word and embrace it will have eternal life. Jesus has been fighting the Jewish leaders about God's power

and how it operates in him. The two resurrections — one to eternal life, another to condemnation — make a strong closing point to those gathered. In some ways, this discourse unpacks for us the theology behind the hearing of the man with the mat at Bethesda. Just as God works on the Sabbath, Jesus — one with his Father — works on the Sabbath.

The Roman Missal

In the Collect, we call on God, who rewards the just and forgives the repentant. We pray that we who acknowledge our sinfulness may receive God's pardon. The Prayer over the Offerings is a prayer for renewal. We ask God to wipe away the old, and increase the "grace of salvation" and new life within us. One of the four Prefaces of Lent is used today. While any one of the four is appropriate, perhaps, in light of the Collect's focus on repentance, either Preface III, with its direct reference to self-denial and humbling our sinful pride, or Preface IV, with its mention of how bodily fasting restrains our faults, would be good options. The Prayer after Communion echoes St. Paul: "A person should examine himself, and so eat the bread and drink the cup. For anyone who eats and drinks without discerning the body, eats and drinks judgment on himself" (1 Corinthians 11:28–29). We pray that the sacrament which God gives us as a "heavenly remedy" may not bring us judgment. We ask God's protection so that we may do "what is good in this world," and so reach God, our "highest good" (Prayer over the People).

THU 15 (#247) violet
Lenten Weekday

The Lectionary for Mass

◆ FIRST READING: The Israelites, freed from bondage, are straying. The golden calf is not a new God, but an idol that they have created.

Some scholars suggest that a group, under Aaron's leadership, broke away. They had found insufficient the image of the Ark of the Covenant offered by Moses, and replaced it with a more powerful symbol for God, that of a bull. Moses pleads on their behalf, and God relents.

◆ RESPONSORIAL PSALM 106: The psalmist evokes the episode of the creation of the golden calf during the Exodus. In this psalm, eight incidents of the people's rebellion are recounted. Moses, the mediator, comes to the aid of the people, reminding God of the promise of the covenant. Their restlessness has caused them to disobey, acting without God's direction. This willfulness can impede us, too, from listening for and seeking to do God's will.

◆ GOSPEL: Within the tradition of the people, testimony to God's actions and witness to his ways have played a central role. John has offered clear testimony, but he was not believed. Even the Father himself has offered testimony, but the people would not hear him. Jesus has performed compelling works, and if all that is not enough, Moses has spoken and has not been believed. This is a strong indictment of his listeners, who are preoccupied with their own thinking and position and unable to listen to the power of God.

The Roman Missal

The Collect for today sets a tone of humility and it reminds us of the purpose of our Lenten penance: it should correct us and school us in doing good works. The prayer also asks for perseverance so that we might "come safely to the paschal festivities." Again there is the undertone in this prayer of calling on the Lord for help as we continue through the long haul of Lent. The Prayer after Communion

again points to the purification that comes to us through the sacrament, as it asks that we be granted "freedom from all blame." The sense of how participation in the Eucharist brings new life and heals us from our burdens is highlighted as the prayer asks "that those bound by a guilty conscience / may glory in the fullness of heavenly remedy." The Prayer over the Offerings asks for cleansing and protection through the offering we make in sacrifice. Although any one of the four Prefaces of Lent is equally appropriate today, perhaps Preface I of Lent would work particularly well to echo the orations, with that Preface's mention of "minds made pure," being reborn, and being led to "the fullness of grace." Although the Prayer over the People continues to be optional on weekdays, its consistent use would mark the daily liturgies of Lent in a significant way.

FRI 16 (#248) violet
Lenten Weekday

The Lectionary for Mass

◆ FIRST READING: For a long time, the Book of Wisdom was attributed to King Solomon. It is recognized by the Catholic Church as deuterocanonical, part of a secondary canon of the Bible, but it is not recognized by Protestant communities. In this passage the wicked are described. They revile and condemn others, condemning the just man to death. This chapter is seen as prophesying the Passion of Jesus Christ.

◆ RESPONSORIAL PSALM 34: Is there any human person who lives a full life who manages to avoid being broken hearted? Most likely not. The psalmist offers assurance that God will stay true to the just person.

◆ GOSPEL: The timing of this story takes place during Sukkoth,

the harvest festival in which thanksgiving is given for the abundance of the land. It is also the time that the Jewish people recalled and honored two of the miracles of the Exodus: the appearance of the pillar of fire to lead the Israelites and the gift of water in their time of trial. Jesus has been threatened, but he nevertheless goes to Jerusalem, although in secret. Rumors start buzzing; Jesus abandons his cover and challenges them to recognize who he is. The question of timing arises. Shortly after this passage, Jesus will offer the people the image of himself as living water, the fulfillment of God's promise to the Israelites and to all who are born into the covenant.

The Roman Missal

The Collect for the Lenten Weekday reminds us that the penances we undertake during Lent are gifts that have been given to us from God as "helps for us in our weakness." As a result, those helps have healing effects on us, effects that we should receive with joy and reflect in the way we live daily "a holy way of life." The Prayer over the Offerings asks for cleansing so that we might approach the source of this sacrifice with purity; thus, the prayer reminds us that our worship can never be mere outward ritual, but must always draw us more deeply into the mystery being celebrated. The Prayer after Communion for the weekday uses the contrast between old and new to ask that we leave former ways behind and "be renewed in holiness of mind." The prayer reminds us that reception of the sacrament is never a passive reception but must represent the offering of self and the openness to transformation of a life that is continually being renewed in Christ.

SAT 17 (#249) violet
Lenten Weekday

Optional Memorial of St. Patrick, Bishop / violet

The Lectionary for Mass

◆ FIRST READING: In his lifetime, Jeremiah was sent by the reformer King Josiah to preach to those in the northern kingdom and in Judah. This passage recounts the distrust and animosity with which that mission was met. The idea of those who should be trustworthy acting in conspiracy is a true affront. The would-be murderers were most likely priests, a parallel to the animosity shown to Jesus by the Jewish authorities.

◆ RESPONSORIAL PSALM 7: The just man can take refuge in the Lord, who will be his safeguard and salvation. To be accused is devastating, but to be an innocent accused is even more horrifying. God, who sees all things, will allow the psalmist to prevail because the charges are false, if terribly threatening.

◆ GOSPEL: The people are torn between recognizing who Jesus is— a prophet, the Christ—and their expectations. The differences of opinion are causing division, even a call for his arrest. The Temple guards take the problem to the Pharisees. There, the open minded and level headed Nicodemus weighs in: He doesn't take a side, but points to the importance of following the prescripts of the law. The hubbub dies down. The story calls into question the ways in which our own expectations can thwart God. Do we have limiting ideas of what God's presence looks like or who God's grace can flow through?

The Roman Missal

The Lenten Collect once again reminds us that without God we can do nothing: "without your grace / we cannot find favor in your sight." The Prayer over the Offerings points out that even in bringing our oblations we are not yet perfected, and we may in some way be defiant of God's will; nonetheless, in our offering to God, we pray that he will assist us in conforming our will to his own. This prayer, then, reminds us of the willingness to have our will transformed. This must be an inherent part of participating in the offering of the sacrifice. The Prayer after Communion for the Lenten Weekday again asks for purification so that we may be pleasing to God.

Today's Saint

Many legends have developed around St. Patrick (390–460), from driving snakes out of Ireland, to using the shamrock to explain the Trinity; however, his popularity stems beyond these stories, to his missionary zeal and astonishing ability to inspire faith. He was sold into slavery at a young age and eventually freed, and so he wanted people enslaved by doubt and skepticism to know the liberation found in Jesus Christ. Although he had little education, he was appointed bishop of Ireland. His many accomplishments include the conversion of Ireland, ordination of clergy, consecration of virgins, and organization of missions to evangelize Europe. St. Patrick's life has a universal appeal; therefore, his feast day is celebrated by the Roman Catholic Church, the Church of England, the Episcopal Church in America, and the Evangelical Lutheran Church in America. He also makes an appearance on the Russian Orthodox calendar. Today is a solemnity and Holyday of Obligation in Ireland. Parades, corned beef and cabbage, and service projects usually mark this special day of our favorite Irish saint. Remember to celebrate this saint and to think of the outreach associated with him. Consider serving at a local food pantry as part of your Lenten concern for the poor.

☀ 18 (#35 or #34) violet
Fifth Sunday of Lent

The Lectionary for Mass, Year B

◆ FIRST READING: After calling the people back to the Lord, Jeremiah shifts his tone and offers a message of hope. In contrast to the rooting up and tearing down of the first chapter, he now speaks of building. God is not only offering a renewed covenant, but a new covenant written on the hearts. The passage is stylistically like Hosea, using many of the same words.

◆ RESPONSORIAL PSALM 51: This great hymn of repentance reminds us that a return to God is possible. Crying out for forgiveness, and affirming the great compassion of God, the psalmist asks God to create within him a "clean heart," a true transformation of his entire person. God is both faithful and gracious, willing to restore to wholeness those who ask for help.

◆ SECOND READING: To obey is one thing; to obey to the point of death is obedience of an almost unfathomable magnitude. In this chapter, the writer compares Christ to the high priest Melchizedek. The passage contrasts the total humanity of Christ with his divinity, through which eternal salvation is achieved for all humankind.

◆ GOSPEL: Jesus has entered Jerusalem in jubilant glory, welcomed as a king. Now he must convey to his companions the destiny he walks. Now the time has come, and it is to death that he must travel. The path to true eternal life is going to involve giving up earthly life. The agricultural metaphor of the seed that dies in order to produce fruit; harvest cannot be achieved without it. Notice that the conversion of the Greeks is mentioned at the outset. This message comes not only to the Jews, but to all people. A powerful voice underscores the truth of what Jesus is saying, but not all can hear it correctly.

The Lectionary for Mass, Year A

◆ FIRST READING: Ezekiel announces to the people of the covenant God's fourfold promise to them: the graves of the dead will be opened, those who have died will be brought to life, the people in exile will be brought back to their land, and the spirit of God will be given to them. The promise of restoration prefigures the promise of Christ for all those who believe in him and sets up the Gospel story of the raising of Lazarus from the dead. The promise of the Lord God is affirmed in signs and in words. "I have promised and I will do it, says the Lord."

◆ RESPONSORIAL PSALM 130: The prayer of the psalmist is a supplication. The psalm was at one time known as the *Miserere*, which also included words from Psalm 51. Both psalms are a plea for the Lord's mercy. The psalmist calls on the Lord to be attentive to his plea believing that only the Lord is able to give him strength to withstand "the depths" in which he finds himself. The psalmist doesn't give any indication what this might be, or why he is in this state. The focus of his pleading is on the kindness of the Lord; no one else can raise him up.

◆ SECOND READING: In Paul's theology of the body, the word "flesh" could mean two things: the physical body or that part of human nature that is prone to sinfulness, as in the ways of the flesh. The opposite of this is the way of the spirit, the way of goodness and right judgment. In today's reading he denounces the way of the flesh, though he doesn't give examples as he does in other cases. It is Spirit of Christ that overcomes the flesh and brings a new way of life to those who believe in him.

◆ GOSPEL: The story of the raising of Lazarus draws us into the human grief of a family and of Jesus himself. The story has more than one purpose and several layers of meaning. It is first a prelude to the Death and Resurrection experience of Jesus himself. Second it includes another of John's "I am" statements, the declaration by Jesus of his identity, "I am the resurrection and the life." A third aspect of the story is Jesus' affirmation that those who believe in him will also rise to new life; death will not sever the bonds of relationship between Jesus and those he loves. Jesus brought comfort to Mary and Martha; his message brings comfort to us.

The Roman Missal

The Fifth Sunday of Lent can be seen as a turning point in the Lenten journey as we enter the final days of this season with less than two weeks left before we begin the Sacred Paschal Triduum. The Missal includes a rubric pointing to a practice that can serve as a visual reminder to the assembly that we have reached this point in Lent: the practice of covering crosses and images in the church may be observed beginning with this Sunday. Images and statues are covered until the beginning of the Easter Vigil; crosses, however, are uncovered sooner, remaining covered only until the end of the Celebration of the Lord's Passion on Good Friday. Consider doing this in your church so that the faithful continue to be engaged in the somberness and tone of Lent through the visible environment of the worship space. Also, as with the previous two Sundays, there are two sets of Mass formularies from which to choose today. Use either the Mass for the Fifth Sunday of Lent if you are not celebrating the Third Scrutiny or the Mass for the Third Scrutiny if you are celebrating that ritual. The Gloria continues to be omitted today. The Creed is sung or said.

The Preface that is given on the pages right there along with the other texts for this Mass, titled simply "Lazarus," is the Preface that is to be used today if the Year A readings are done for RCIA, and the Gospel account of Jesus raising Lazarus is the text assigned for the day. Consider chanting the introductory dialogue and the Preface today. If this is not the regular practice of your community, this can be a way of powerfully drawing attention to the solemnity of Lent (but be sure to prepare and rehearse your assembly as needed, especially if your people are not familiar with the responses!). The Prayer over the People is required, not optional, on the Sundays of Lent, and the text is given right after the Prayer after Communion.

If your parish is celebrating the Third Scrutiny with the elect, then, according to a rubric in the Missal, the proper prayers should be used; these Mass formularies are found in the section "Ritual Masses," under segment I — For the Conferral of the Sacraments of Initiation; #2 — For the Celebration of the Scrutinies; C — For the Third Scrutiny. For the actual ritual of the scrutiny itself, consult RCIA, 164–170. The scrutiny takes place after the homily.

Other Ideas

The Solemnity of St. Joseph, earthly father of Jesus, is celebrated this week on March 19. In the Italian community, observation includes the creation of a special shrine to St. Joseph. The use of a three-tiered table represents the Holy Trinity, and includes a statue of the saint surrounded by greenery. A solemnity with special meatless foods, such as minestrone, seafood, and fava beans, is shared. Afterward, children reenact the Holy Family going to three homes. Turned away from all but the last, this ritual is called "Tupa, Tupa," or "knock, knock," and is strikingly similar to *Las Posadas*. The day ends with everyone receiving prayer cards, St. Joseph medals, and a lucky blessed fava bean. Offer community members the Litany to St. Joseph today, and add the prayer to St. Joseph to the end of the praying of the Rosary.

(#543) white

MON 19 Solemnity of St. Joseph, Spouse of the Blessed Virgin Mary

About Today's Solemnity

Joseph was the foster father of Jesus, the man entrusted with his care and upbringing. We know that Joseph was a "righteous man" who protected Mary from disgrace after she was found to be pregnant with Jesus (Matthew 1:19). Like the earlier Joseph in Genesis, he received instruction and reassurance from God through dreams. The Gospel gives little information about him, save that he was an artisan who lived in Nazareth, was a descendant of David, and went to Bethlehem for a census, causing Jesus to be born there in fulfillment of the prophecies.

When warned in a dream that Jesus was in danger because of the evil intentions of King Herod, Joseph took Jesus and Mary to live in exile in Egypt until he learned that Herod had died (see Matthew 2:12–15). As a result, Jesus was spared the fate of the Holy Innocents.

After the account of Jesus' being lost and found in the Temple during a pilgrimage, Joseph is not mentioned again. We can infer that he had died before Jesus began his ministry; he was certainly not alive at the time of the Crucifixion, because he would have been the one to claim Jesus' body, not Joseph of Arimathea. Catholic tradition describes him as dying in the arms of Jesus and Mary, and so he is invoked as the patron of a happy death.

Because he was a man who worked with his hands, he is the patron of workers and especially carpenters. Devotion to St. Joseph developed rather late, and was popularized by St. Bernardine of Siena during the fifteenth century.

The Lectionary for Mass

◆ FIRST READING: The Lord does not speak directly to King David, but communicates through his prophet, Nathan. David has wanted to build a house for the Lord, but the plan is reversed: The Lord himself will build the house, and it will come through David's son. Here, the house is not a dwelling but a dynasty. Some consider this passage a form of personal covenant between God and his servant David, who he has chosen to rule over the people.

◆ RESPONSORIAL PSALM 89: This psalm of community lament includes verses that reference the place of King David as God's appointed leader. The king has been established, and God has promised that his line will rule forever.

But the Davidic king has been defeated; the voices of the people the hardships and trials faced by the community, calling on God to remember and keep his promises to David.

◆ SECOND READING: The image of fatherhood, so appropriate for this solemnity, is developed further in the Epistle. The covenant exists and it is something dependable, but it is only fulfilled in mutuality. Without the faith of the believing people, it cannot be fulfilled. Yes, the law is to be recognized and followed, but it is through a lived, expressed faith that the covenant comes into its fullness. Abraham, the great father of all, has been tested and it is his trust in God that matters most.

◆ GOSPEL, OPTION 1: We could have no better Lenten model than Joseph, who is asked to leave behind the carefully constructed world of laws that has hitherto defined and circumscribed his righteousness so that he is free to travel forward into an unknown future governed not by written laws but by God's astonishing mercy.

◆ GOSPEL, OPTION 2: This unique story in Luke offers us a sense of Jesus' relationship with both his earthly and heavenly Father. We can imagine the terror struck into the heart of Joseph when it is discovered that the mischievous adolescent has not packed up and traveled with the community's caravan. Eventually he is discovered, peaceful and inquisitive, learning from the rabbis in the Temple. Although still young, Jesus would have already been receiving religious instruction in his home, including the Hallel psalms, the Mishnah (interpretations of the law) and prayers like the Shema. We can understand the tug on both sides: the protectiveness of mother and father, and the longing of the Son of God to deepen and expand his understanding.

The Roman Missal

The Entrance Antiphon, based on Luke 12:42, speaks of Joseph as the "faithful and prudent steward, / whom the Lord set over his household." The Collect presents Joseph as a model for the Church. Just as Joseph watched over Christ in his infancy, so the Church must "watch over / the unfolding of the mysteries of human salvation." Since today is a solemnity, the Gloria and the Creed are said or sung today. We pray that we may imitate the "loving care" of St. Joseph's service of the infant Christ (Prayer over the Offerings). The Preface is subtitled "The mission of Saint Joseph," and, like the Entrance Antiphon, speaks of Joseph as the steward of God's household, watching "like a father" over the Son of God. The Prayer after Communion is a prayer for the protection of the Church on this Solemnity of St. Joseph.

TUE 20 (#252) violet
Lenten Weekday

The Lectionary for Mass

Please note that the optional readings for the Fifth Week of Lent may be used on any of the remaining days of this week (#250).

◆ FIRST READING: Here we hear the passage about the plague of serpents sent upon the complaining, ungrateful Israelites referenced in last week's Gospel on the Fourth Sunday of Lent. The Israelites seem to have a selective amnesia, forgetting over and over again the trials and travails of life under Pharoah. Their recall seems only to be of the food and water they received as slaves. The punishment is harsh; serpents are sent to bite them (*saraph* also translates as "serpent"). They quickly plead with God, for the situation with deadly venom is far worse than the lack of food and water.

◆ RESPONSORIAL PSALM 102: While many of the psalms of lament are communal, Psalm 102 is individual. The psalmist's personal distress causes him to groan and cry out for assistance, recounting the extremity in which he finds himself. He beseeches God to hear his prayer and act on his behalf, asserting that

by doing so God will be remembered for generations to come.

◆ GOSPEL: This passage finds Jesus using the phrase "I AM" three of the forty-five times it appears in John's Gospel. The use of this phrase is often emphatic, implying his divinity. The "I AM" is related to the meaning of the Hebrew name of God (YHWH), a four-letter construction that means "I am." The name of God, revealed to Moses, was never to be spoken but only written, thus the transliteration YHWH with its common translation "Lord." This reference anchors Jesus in the story of Moses and also begins answering the question in the minds of those around him: Is this the Messiah?

The Roman Missal

The Collect today includes an important petition, namely, that we may persevere in obeying God's will. Again, the prayer seems to recognize our need for encouragement and strength to maintain the long discipline of Lent. There is an interesting result of that perseverance that is mentioned: so that "the people dedicated to your service / may grow in both merit and number." Perhaps this phrase could remind us of the importance of giving good example to those preparing for initiation; our witness as we persevere through Lent can have a direct effect on their coming into the faith.

The Prayer over the Offerings recognizes the reconciliation that is brought about between God and humanity as a result of our participation in the sacrifice; through it, we can ask God, who is full of compassion, to pardon our offenses. The Preface assigned for today is Preface I of the Passion of the Lord, as it will be every day this week. Use this Preface even if you are using one of the two Eucharistic Prayers for Reconciliation (it is not required to use the Preface that goes

with the Eucharistic Prayers for Reconciliation). The Prayer after Communion notes how a constitutive dimension of being human is to seek what is divine. Although the Prayer over the People continues to be optional on weekdays, its continued use would mark this late Lenten Weekday in a significant way.

WED 21 (#253) violet
Lenten Weekday

The Lectionary for Mass

◆ FIRST READING: Faithful Shadrach, Meshach, and Abednego refuse to worship the idol that King Nebuchadnezzar has erected. They will go to their deaths rather than worship a god other than the God of Israel. The king is so enraged he has the furnace stoked even hotter. The faithful three are tossed into the furnace. Rather than burning alive, the three are seen walking around the furnace in the company of a fourth figure. Seeing the angel and the fact that they are unharmed causes the king to bless their God. Canticle: Today, a selection from the psalter is replaced by the moving words of the prayer of Azariah (Abednego). Rather than focusing on their plight, Azariah sings praise to God, blessing God in his Temple upon his throne. In some ways, we join our voices with those of Shadrach and Meshach affirming Azariah's words.

◆ GOSPEL: The question of worshipping the one true God is developed further today in the Gospel according to John. Jesus invites those listening to follow him, but they reject his Messianic claims by clinging to their ancestry. They are the descendants of Abraham. But Jesus offers them truth; the truth that will offer them the ultimate freedom. Again, they cling to Abraham, but Jesus calls them out. If they were truly living under the law, they would not be threatening him with death. He is the divine liberator, if only they could see clearly.

The Roman Missal

God himself awakens devotion in us. We ask him to enlighten those who have been "sanctified by penance" this Lent, and to hear us when we cry out to him (Collect). We ask God to "receive back" the sacrifice he has given us, that it may be "for our healing" (Prayer over the Offerings). The Preface assigned for today is Preface I of the Passion of the Lord, as it will be every day this week. Use this Preface even if you are using one of the two Eucharistic Prayers for Reconciliation (it is not required to use the Preface that goes with the Eucharistic Prayers for Reconciliation). The sacrament we receive is "heavenly medicine," purging evil and strengthening us with God's protection (Prayer after Communion). God has given us our hope in his compassion. In the Prayer over the People, we ask him to let us feel his mercy as well.

THU 22 (#254) violet
Lenten Weekday

The Lectionary for Mass

◆ FIRST READING: Shakespeare noted in the play *Romeo and Juliet*, "What's in a name?" For God, everything. Today we hear of the renaming of Abram, who will now be known as Abraham, a word that signifies a multitude. It is through Abraham that Jews and Christians (through Isaac) and Muslims (through Ishmael) find their patrimony. The abundance of the covenant is described in this passage.

◆ RESPONSORIAL PSALM 105: The verses of psalm 105 offered today affirm the vast, eternal covenant God entered into with Abraham. This promise of relationship is enduring. The psalm echoes the conversation between Abraham and God in Genesis. Although

Ishmael, the child of Hagar and Abraham, will have many descendants, it is through Isaac, the son of Abraham and Sarah, that the promise of the covenant is fulfilled.

◆ GOSPEL: The discourse in chapter eight of the Gospel according to John contrasts those in the community that believe that Jesus is the Messiah and those who do not. Here the conversation takes a threatening turn. Those gathered know that the Messiah will be a descendent of Abraham. Jesus has just accused the naysayers that they do not behave like children of Abraham. They turn antagonistic, but Jesus does not respond directly to their questions. Rather, he affirms his relationship with God and God's activity in and through him. This passage must be treated sensitively. Translations that reference "the Jews" have been used to foster anti-Semitism.

The Roman Missal

In the Collect, we ask for the grace of perseverance "in holy living," so that we may be "full heirs" of God's promises. We offer the holy sacrifice not only for our own conversion, but for "the salvation of all the world" (Prayer over the Offerings). As with the other days this week, the Preface assigned for today is Preface I of the Passion of the Lord, and it should be used even if you are using one of the Eucharistic Prayers for Reconciliation (it is not required to use the Preface that goes with the Eucharistic Prayer for Reconciliation). Through the sacrament of which we partake here and now, we pray to be "partakers of life eternal" (Prayer after Communion). In the Prayer over the People, we ask that we may reject those things that displease God, and instead be filled "with delight" in God's commandments.

FRI 23 (#255) violet
Lenten Weekday

Optional Memorial of St. Turibius of Mogrovejo, Bishop / violet

The Lectionary for Mass

◆ FIRST READING: This discourse recounts the trials that Jeremiah is experiencing as he is attempting to do God's will. While initially he rails against God, his thoughts turn to the power of the almighty: who will be with him and vanquish the persecutors? He recognizes that while circumstances may test faith, ultimately God is worthy of trust.

◆ RESPONSORIAL PSALM 18: The images of psalm 18 — rock, fortress, refuge, and deliverer — evoke thoughts of many classic hymn texts. God is the staunch protection against enemies of all sorts, and reminiscent of Jeremiah, the psalmist knows that God will hear his cries and respond. In contemporary culture, the approach to prayer may be tame; today we are reminded to cry out to God, who will hear.

◆ GOSPEL: The story of the clash between Jesus and those Jews who do not believe continues. They are so irate that they are ready to stone him. They accuse him of claiming to be God. Jesus points out that he is not blaspheming, and encourages them to examine his works. The mystical theological observation "the Father is in me and I am in the Father" is Jesus' response. The Gospel according to John was written after the Christian community was established. In this period, the relationship between the Jewish followers of Jesus and greater Jewish society has become hostile.

The Roman Missal

There are two options for the Collect today. The first prayer is a prayer for pardon, asking that we will be set free from "the bonds of the sins / we have committed in our weakness." The second option notes how in this liturgical time the Church imitates the Blessed Virgin Mary "in contemplating the Passion of Christ," and therefore the prayer goes on to ask that through her intercession "we may cling more firmly each day / to your Only Begotten Son / and come at last to the fullness of his grace." Thus, in a certain sense, this second prayer puts us at the foot of the Cross along with Mary, clinging to Jesus even throughout his Passion and Death, and prepares us well to enter into the celebration of Holy Week. The Preface assigned for today is Preface I of the Passion of the Lord; remember to use it even if you are using one of the Eucharistic Prayers for Reconciliation (it is not required to use the Preface that goes with the Eucharistic Prayer for Reconciliation). Continue to use the Prayer over the People as well.

Today's Saint

St. Turibius of Mogrovejo (1538–1606) was born into the Spanish nobility and dedicated his life to bringing Christianity to the native peoples of Peru as the missionary archbishop of Lima. He traveled the whole of his enormous diocese, usually on foot, evangelizing and baptizing as he went. Among those he baptized and confirmed were St. Rose of Lima and St. Martin de Porres. St. Turibius also founded the first seminary in the Western hemisphere and built roads, schools, chapels, hospitals, and convents. He is remembered for his defense of the native peoples against the injustices of the Spanish government.

S A T **24** (#256)   violet
Lenten Weekday

The Lectionary for Mass

◆ First Reading: Ezekiel speaks not only of the release of the captives in Babylon, but of the recreation of Israel through the gathering of all the people scattered about the region. God's vision is that all shall be one, led by David the king. Yet again the covenant is confirmed; a covenant of peace for all for all time. The image of the Shepherd King is, of course, an image for Jesus familiar to Christians, who see this passage as foreshadowing the reign of the Messiah.

◆ Canticle: Chapter 31 of the Book of Jeremiah focuses on the new covenant that God will establish with Israel, and bears striking similarity to passages in Hosea. The verses offered here focus on the joy that is unleashed when God fulfills his promise. The exiles stream to God's holy mountain, where sadness is transformed into glorious celebration.

◆ Gospel: This passage occurs immediately following the story of the raising of Lazarus. While some have believed, others are alarmed and suspicious, and go to the leaders to report Jesus' activity. The Sanhedrin, the court, is summoned. It is valuable to remember the terror Rome had struck into the Jewish community, which was living in a hostile occupation. The only way to contain the movement gathering around Jesus, in the minds of the Jewish authorities, is to eliminate him. Jesus remains out of sight, but the Passover feast will draw him to Jerusalem and his destiny.

The Roman Missal

The Collect prays for those who have already been called to eternal life. There is much emphasis on forgiveness of sins, as if the prayers themselves are cajoling us one last time to seek the Sacrament of Reconciliation before Holy Week starts, or to implore Christ in his mercy, to take on whatever is lacking in our penance. As we share in both the suffering of the Lord, and the table of the Lord, may we truly become "sharers of his divine nature" as the Prayer after Communion suggests.

(Gospel with palms, #37; #38)
red

25 **Palm Sunday of the Passion of the Lord**

Editorial Note

The Solemnity of the Annunciation of the Lord is usually celebrated on March 25. This year, the solemnity is transferred to the next available date on the calendar, which is the Monday after the Second Sunday of Easter. Please refer to page 180.

About Palm Sunday

Branches of palm, olive, or sometimes even budding willow are ancient symbols of victory and hope, as well as of new life. The procession celebrating Jesus' entry into Jerusalem overflowed with praise and excitement, as onlookers waved these triumphant branches and proclaimed their blessings. Yet in a few days, they will cry, "Crucify him!" The crowd's change of heart illustrates the problem of holding God to our expectations. The crowd expected a liberating leader, the Messiah, to free them from Roman oppression. Jesus instead takes up his Cross and invites us to do the same. Through his Death and Resurrection he is indeed a liberator, but from death and sin, not from Rome. But unable to see past their need, the crowd's disappointment turns into anger and a death order. As we enter Holy Week, Palm Sunday teaches us to let God be God, and to trust in God's wisdom not only to meet but shatter and exceed our expectations.

The Lectionary for Mass

◆ THE GOSPEL AT THE PROCESSION: Jesus entered Jerusalem in triumph and left in ignominy. He entered carried by a donkey colt, hailed by the crowds with branches and hosannas. He left walking, even stumbling under the weight of the Cross, to the place of execution outside the city walls, jeered there by the bystanders. Lent is a season of paradox, a season of contradictions, a season of successes and failures, culminating in the great paradox of the Cross, where all apparent failure yields to the ultimate triumph of life over death.

◆ FIRST READING: As we enter Holy Week, the readings focus on the reason for Jesus' suffering and Death. This selection from one of the four Suffering Servant songs summarizes well Jesus' ministry, why he was rejected, how he responded, and what ultimately led to his suffering and Death. Through it all, Jesus trusted in God, knowing he would never be disgraced for attuning himself to God's ways.

◆ RESPONSORIAL PSALM 22 is a lament psalm, the typical pattern of which recounts the experience of bad things happening to a good person. The suffering is narrated, usually in vivid detail, with the psalm concluding on a note of trust, confidence, and assurance that with God, suffering and death are not the last word.

◆ SECOND READING: This well-known text from Paul's letter to the Philippians speaks of Jesus' *kenosis*, or emptying of his God-self in order to become fully human. In becoming human, Jesus chooses not to grasp onto divinity but rather empties himself, "taking the form of a slave" (7). He humbly and fully accepts all the limitations that being human entails, while being totally "obedient" (8),

that is, attuned and oriented, to God's ways. Such a lifestyle brought about opposition, rejection, and ultimately death at the hands of those unwilling to tolerate such a challenging message. Throughout, Jesus trusted in and turned to God for strength and courage.

◆ GOSPEL: Mark's Passion narrative highlights Jesus' willingness to empty himself out for others. He does not resist his fate. Rather, he accepts it as the inevitable result of aligning himself with a God who invites all to empty themselves for the sake of others. Such a mission is not easily accepted by most individuals, which is exactly why Jesus became fully human. Both fully human and fully divine, Jesus shows us that not only is it possible to live out that mission, but that is what God has always desired of us.

The Roman Missal

A careful reading of the Missal by all those involved in the preparation of today's liturgy will help ensure a smooth flow to the ritual. All the texts are found in the "Holy Week" section of the Missal that follows Saturday of the Fifth Week of Lent in the Proper of Time.

All Masses today take place with the Commemoration of the Lord's Entrance into Jerusalem, "to accomplish his Paschal Mystery," in the words of the Missal; that Commemoration takes place using one of three forms: the Procession, the Solemn Entrance, or the Simple Entrance. The Missal indicates that the Procession (the first form) or the Solemn Entrance (the second form) takes place before the principal Mass and that the Solemn Entrance, but not the Procession, may be re usually celebrated with a large gathering of people (note, therefore, that the Missal envisions the first form, the Procession, taking place only once, whereas the Solemn Entrance may be used at as many Masses as is deemed pas-

torally advantageous in light of the gathering of the people).

First Form: The Procession

This form of the commemoration takes place with all gathering at a place other than inside the church to which the procession will go — either a smaller church, or perhaps a parish center room, or perhaps even outside. The faithful already hold palm branches.

The priest and the deacon wear red vestments; the priest may wear a chasuble, or he may wear a cope and then change into a chasuble when the procession is over. At the appointed time, the priest, deacon, and other ministers go to the place where everyone is gathered. The Missal does not indicate that this is any kind of a formal procession per se, so it can be an informal gathering of the clergy and ministers as they arrive at the place of beginning. The Missal does state, however, that "meanwhile" (while the ministers are assembling, or perhaps even while all are gathering, not just the ministers, to create a prayerful environment as all arrive) an antiphon or an appropriate song is sung; the antiphon suggested is from chapter 21 of Matthew's account of the Gospel: "Hosanna to the Son of David; blessed is he who comes in the name of the Lord, the King of Israel. Hosanna in the highest."

After this singing and when all have arrived, the priest begins with the Sign of the Cross and the usual liturgical greeting for Mass, followed by an introductory address. For this introduction, he may use the words given in the Missal (#5, at Palm Sunday of the Passion of the Lord); if he uses his own words, it is important that he convey the invitation for the faithful to participate actively and consciously in the celebration this day.

After the address, the priest says one of the two prayers of blessing. Only the first option includes the gesture of making the Sign of the Cross by the priest; the second one does not. The first prayer specifically asks God to bless the branches, and then goes on to ask that we "who follow Christ the King in exultation, may reach the eternal Jerusalem through him." The second option focuses more on the people "who today hold high these branches to hail Christ in his triumph," asking for their faith to be increased and their prayers to be held, so that they "may bear fruit for you by good works accomplished in him." Whichever prayer is used, however, the branches are next sprinkled after the prayer, in silence.

Then the deacon, or the priest if there is no deacon, proclaims the Gospel account of the Lord's entrance according to the proper cycle of Lectionary readings in the liturgical year; the Missal states this is done "in the usual way," meaning that there should be the greeting "The Lord be with you" and the announcement "A reading from the holy Gospel according to . . ." as is always done. Incense may also be used here. The third edition of *The Roman Missal* has the texts for this first Gospel reading right there in the Missal, which makes things much easier.

The Missal notes that after the Gospel, a brief homily may be given. The key word concerning this homily would seem to be "brief," if one were to be given at all—it's optional. Then an invitation is given by either a priest, deacon, or lay minister, using the words in the Missal or similar ones, to invite the people to begin the procession.

The procession is led by the thurifer, if incense is used, followed by a crossbearer. The Missal specifically points out that the cross that is carried should be "decorated with palm branches according to local custom." The cross is carried between two ministers with

lighted candles. Behind this follow the deacon with the *Book of the Gospels*, the priest, the ministers, and then the faithful (note that the priest celebrant is not at the end of the procession, but rather walks before the people). Singing takes place during this procession, with various options suggested in the Missal; other appropriate songs may of course be chosen.

Keep in mind in your preparations that it will be important to choose music that will be able to be sung easily by the choir and the people as they move along in procession. Think through the route that will be used and how the movement will affect people's ability to sing. Think of ways to maintain the singing. *Sing to the Lord: Music in Divine Worship* (STL, 93–94) points out that while recorded music should not normally be used in liturgy, the use of recorded music to accompany communal singing during a procession outside is an exception. Therefore, if necessary, look into resources for having prerecorded music broadcast. For example, your choir could record the singing ahead of time, and then that recording could be broadcast outside via a bell tower or some other external speaker system, and that music would support and enhance the assembly's singing while they are processing to the church.

The Missal notes that a second song or a responsory is sung as the procession enters the church; thus, the music should change.

Then, as the procession enters the church, the priest goes to the altar, venerates it, and, if appropriate, incenses it. The people, meanwhile, continue to process into the church. He then goes to his chair, changes from cope to chasuble if necessary, and, when all are in the church, the singing ends. The priest goes right into the Collect of the Mass, and then Mass continues in the usual

way; the other Introductory Rites are omitted.

Second Form: The Solemn Entrance

This form of the entrance is used at Mass when the first form, the procession, is taking place or has taken place at another Mass, or when a procession outside the church cannot otherwise take place for some reason.

In this case, the priest, ministers, and, if possible, a small group of the faithful gather somewhere other than the sanctuary, but preferably at a place where the people can see the rite. All are already holding branches in their hands.

An antiphon or another song is sung while the priest approaches the place where the rite is to begin, and then the Sign of the Cross, liturgical greeting, introduction, blessing and sprinkling, and proclamation of the Gospel all occur as described above. After the Gospel, the priest, ministers, and small group of the faithful process solemnly through the church to the sanctuary while an appropriate song is sung. Then, arriving at the altar, the priest venerates it and then goes to the chair, where, omitting the Introductory Rites, he says the Collect of the Mass after the singing ends. Mass then continues in the usual way. The Missal makes no provision for the priest to wear a cope in this form of entrance; he wears the chasuble.

Third Form: The Simple Entrance

Essentially, this form of entrance is the same as any other Sunday: the priest proceeds to the altar while the Entrance Antiphon with its psalm or some other suitable song is sung; he arrives at the altar, venerates it, and then goes to his chair; and then he begins Mass with the Sign of the Cross, greets the people as usual, and Mass continues. In this form, the usual Introductory Rites would occur.

At the Mass

There are special instructions for the proclamation of the Lord's Passion: it is to be read without candles and without incense, and there is to be no greeting before the proclamation and no signing of the book. It is customary in many places to have several people participate in the reading of the Passion, not just the priest and deacon. However, the part of Christ should, if possible, be read by the priest. Only a deacon asks for the blessing of the priest before reading the Passion, as he does before reading the Gospel. Your community may wish to consider chanting the Gospel; this is a wonderful way of highlighting the solemnity of the day.

The Missal goes on to note that there should be a homily after the narrative of the Passion, but interestingly the adjective "brief" is used again.

The Creed and the Universal Prayer take place as usual.

The Preface assigned for today, "The Passion of the Lord," is given right there in the Missal along with the other texts for this Mass. The Preface is a very succinct proclamation of how Christ, though innocent, "suffered willingly for sinners" in order to save the guilty.

Other Ideas

The palms used in the liturgy are blessed today. Many communities enact a Palm Sunday procession outside the church if the weather is temperate. Some invite the children of the community to play instruments in a joyful opening procession within the sanctuary to a traditional hymn like "Ride on, Jesus, Ride!" Help the community to respond joyfully in this moment by waving their palms, an ancient tradition mentioned in the Torah (Leviticus 23:40) and the Book of Maccabees (2 Maccabees 10:6–8). Many people take their palms home to hang over their crucifix.

Some cultures weave the palms into crosses or into elaborate figures. Encourage community members to resist weaving during Mass, which can be a distraction to those around them. The dried palms will provide the ashes for Ash Wednesday, transforming the moment of triumph into the beginning of our annual Penitence. It is also customary to dine on figs on Palm Sunday, a tradition tied to Jesus cursing the fig tree shortly after entering Jerusalem (see Mark 11:12–14). When preparing for Palm Sunday, be conscious of the many environmental issues surrounding the harvesting of palm fronds, especially the Chamaedorea or Bella Palm. Although the majority of palms are used for palm oil, the harvest of this plant is linked to the depletion of the rain forests in Mexico, Central America, Indonesia, and other areas. The workers are often exploited, underpaid, and discriminated against; they live in impoverished and unhealthy conditions. The wildlife is at risk — habitats are destroyed, animals are killed, and endangered species become more at risk. Know your supplier. Ask questions. Be responsible and good stewards of natural resources. Look for fair-trade, sustainable, wild-life, and eco-friendly distributers. Catholic Relief Services (www.crs.org/) has partnered with the Lutheran World Relief (lwr.org/) and the Presbyterian Church U.S.A. (www.pcusa.org/) to sell eco-friendly palms. Inform parishioners (via parish bulletin, social media) about your efforts to go green and protect God's creation.

This week, make sure people are aware of all the times for the celebration of Triduum and Easter Sunday.

M O N **26** (#257) violet
Monday of Holy Week

The Lectionary for Mass

◆ FIRST READING: On Passion Sunday, we hear the full horror of Jesus' tortured suffering and death unfold. However, the Holy Week readings, culminating in the reading of the Passion according to St. John on Friday, take us deeper into the mystery. We are asked to recognize that God's plan forges meaning and hope out of the darkness. The Sufferer is no victim of circumstance but an active partner in the victory of justice, which will emerge from the tomb on Easter Sunday.

◆ RESPONSORIAL PSALM 27: With the Lord as light and salvation, the psalmist confidently and courageously faces his adversaries. There is no cause for fear.

◆ GOSPEL: Mary of Bethany recognizes what Judas does not. With prophetic insight, she anoints the Messiah, whose title means "anointed one," for the climax of his mission. Judas can see no deeper than common sense, blinded in this case by desire for personal gain. Jesus' gathered enemies can see no farther than a religious and political threat. Jesus credits Mary's insight as the true one: he is the one sent to achieve the work of redemption through his very death and burial.

The Roman Missal

The fact that we are now in Holy Week is marked by the assignment of a new Preface — Preface II of the Passion of the Lord is assigned for today. The Preface makes specific mention that "the days of his saving Passion and glorious Resurrection are approaching." In view of this, it might be better to use this Preface and not replace it with the proper Preface if one of the Eucharistic Prayers for Reconciliation is used (it is not required to use the Preface that goes with the Eucharistic Prayers for Reconciliation). In fact, it might be advantageous to highlight a certain starkness of these days of Holy Week through using an economy of words; along those lines, perhaps Eucharistic Prayer II would be a good choice for these last three days before the Sacred Paschal Triduum. Its direct statement of "At the time he was betrayed and entered willingly into his Passion" makes it perhaps especially appropriate for these three days.

TUE 27 (#258) violet
Tuesday of Holy Week

The Lectionary for Mass

◆ FIRST READING: This second Song of the Suffering Servant continues to name the Servant as the new Israel, in and through whom light will dawn on a darkened world as the salvation accomplished through the Passion spreads "to the ends of the earth."

◆ RESPONSORIAL PSALM 71: The psalmist in distress cries out for God's deliverance. God is—and has been even before the psalmist's birth—rock, refuge, stronghold, and teacher. The experience of salvation leads to grateful proclamation of the Lord's deliverance.

◆ GOSPEL: What Isaiah foretold of the Suffering Servant, what Mary of Bethany proclaimed by her anointing, Judas Iscariot, Simon Peter, and indeed all the disciples except John, Mary the mother of Jesus, and the other faithful women will betray, deny, or flee in the days to come. The hard reality of the Gospel, which John describes as the ultimate conflict of darkness and light, is too much for them to bear, as it can be for all of us. However, after the Resurrection, Jesus does not betray or deny or flee them but welcomes them back.

The Roman Missal

Today's Collect prays that we may receive pardon through our celebration of "the mysteries of the Lord's Passion." The Prayer over the Offerings asks that we may be given a share in the fullness of the sacred gifts in which we have been made partakers. The Prayer after Communion makes a connection between the earthly liturgy and the heavenly liturgy as it asks that having been nourished by the saving gifts in this present age, we may be made "partakers of life eternal." Preface II of the Passion of the Lord, first used yesterday, is again assigned for today.

WED 28 (#259) violet
Wednesday of Holy Week

The Lectionary for Mass

◆ FIRST READING: The Word made flesh lives the word of salvation he proclaims to all who will hear. His fidelity is obedience to the work God has given him. His love is made visible in his own decision to the turn the other cheek when he is beaten, tortured and humiliated for the salvation even of his enemies. Those who accuse him of wrong will fade before the dawning of the true Light.

◆ RESPONSORIAL PSALM 69 is a psalm of lament, vividly describing the sufferings endured by one of the chosen people—all for the sake of God. The last stanza attests the psalmist's confidence that God will deliver him.

◆ GOSPEL: Judas is finally unable to bear the burden of his own betrayal. Lest Jesus' statement of "woe" satisfy too quickly our easy desire for defeat and revenge upon the villain of the story, let us recall his plea for forgiveness on the cross. His statement of woe may be read as dire warning of the ill to befall the betrayer, or it may be read as an expression of his defeated and grieving love for the disciple who turned away and then died of his own despair. Love, not vengeance, is the Gospel for which Jesus died.

The Roman Missal

Preface II of the Passion of the Lord, used on the previous two days, is once more assigned for today, and the connection throughout these last three days of Lent can be maintained if, having used Eucharistic Prayer II on Monday and Tuesday, it is used again today.

SACRED PASCHAL TRIDUUM

The Liturgical Time

The Meaning

Having prepared ourselves during Lent and Holy Week, we move to the greatest celebration of the Christian liturgical year: The Sacred Paschal Triduum. The Triduum begins with the Holy Thursday Evening Mass of the Lord's Supper and continues through Evening Prayer on Easter Sunday (see UNLY, 19). During this time, we are in a sense outside of time. Through the rites of the Triduum, we transition from Lent to Easter Time, from red vestments to white, from death to resurrection, and from human frailty to the fervent hope of eternal salvation in Christ, who "is our salvation, life and resurrection, / through whom we are saved and delivered" (Entrance Antiphon for Holy Thursday Mass of the Lord's Supper).

The liturgy of the Sacred Paschal Triduum is, in most settings, the most beautiful communal prayer of the year. Still, many parishes have many members who have never experienced these three days.

Many people mistakenly relate to Christmas as the central Christian holiday. The summit of the liturgical year is, in fact, the Sacred Paschal Triduum. The Triduum is a symbol and sensory rich event. Fire, water, and incense take us beyond our intellect into the ancient and beautiful roots of our faith. Use the bulletin throughout Lent to catechize people about the Triduum in small bites, and regularly encourage people to set aside the time to share in the Mass of the Lord's Supper, Good Friday of the Lord's Passion, and the Mass of the Resurrection of the Lord at the Easter Vigil. Experiences like the Washing of the Feet, the empty tabernacle, the Adoration of the Cross, gathering around the new fire, listening to the stories of God's covenant, and the return of joyful "Alleluias!" are powerful, even visceral, experiences. Pope Francis has grown awareness of the Triduum through his visible performance of the washing of the feet in new and unexpected places like nursing homes and prisons. As parishes, we can build on the great interest in the Holy Father by tying his teaching and witness to that of our own parish homes.

Consider creating a flyer or other promotional piece that not only provides information about the timing of the various Masses, but also a brief description of each moment in the three days of prayer. Invite people to come to any of the times the community has gathered. Consider having members share, briefly following the Prayer after Communion in Lent, about the meaning of this liturgy in their lives. People who have been initiated at the Vigil in recent years might be particularly good candidates for this role.

If your community is aging, reach out to see if elders who have been regular participants are in need of transportation help. As people age, they may be reticent to drive in the evening, even though the Triduum is important to them.

Consider having a special hospitality desk or table for all three days at which visitors or those who have been away for a while can find out more about the community from enthusiastic representatives. Develop an information packet that they can take with them if they are interested, or provide an opportunity for e-mail information sign ups.

The Triduum is an ideal moment to turn all of the parish's liturgical ministers into evangelists. Consider a special training before or during Lent in which extraordinary ministers of Holy Communion, servers, readers, cantors, and hospitality ministers can be trained in the basics of providing a warm and meaningful welcome to people. An act of simply having everyone who is not serving but in the pews actively greeting those around them can make a difference.

The Lectionary for Mass

WE hear a lot of Scripture during the Paschal Triduum. Counting Easter Sunday, there are eighteen Scripture readings and ten psalms. All of them are important. The readings, especially the nine readings of the Vigil, build in a remarkable way, leading us through the story of salvation history from the very dawn of time straight to the Resurrection of Jesus Christ. During the Triduum, let the Liturgy of the Word speak to the parish in its fullness.

The readings for the Triduum carry us into the very heart of the Old and New Testaments. There are great narratives—the sacrifice of Isaac, the crossing of the Red Sea, the Passion according to John, the Resurrection narrative according to Matthew. There are rich prophetic readings from Isaiah, Baruch, and Ezekiel. There is wonderful poetry, like the song of the suffering servant from Isaiah, and the song of the Israelites after the crossing of the Red Sea. And there are key readings from the letters of St. Paul, readings that teach us about Eucharist and proclaim with utter confidence the truth we celebrate at Easter: that Christ is risen, and that we will rise with him through our Baptism.

In scheduling and training readers for the Paschal Triduum, this great variety of readings should be considered. If possible, have a different person do each reading during the Triduum. Work with the readers on the special demands of the reading they are assigned. A prophetic reading should not be read in exactly the same way as a narrative, and a poem demands different pacing, a different style of proclamation, than does an intricate passage from St. Paul. The reading or chanting of the Passion according to John has challenges of its own. It is not a Passion play, and yet it certainly is dramatic. Careful preparation on the part of the readers (and cantors) can help the assembly to hear the rich and wonderful variety in the readings to which we are treated during these three days.

The Roman Missal

WHILE there is not room here to even begin laying out the details for celebrating the Triduum, some over-arching recommendations might be helpful. The introduction to the Triduum in the Missal instructs us to sing well and to prepare carefully. Indeed, it is crucial that everyone involved in preparing the liturgies of the Triduum and serving in a ministerial capacity (ordained and lay) should engage in a careful reading of the (lengthy and detailed) rubrics and instructions in the Missal and then prepare the parts pertaining to them with care. This pertains especially to those responsible for preparing the rites of initiation, which culminate at the Easter Vigil. It is also true that during these solemn days it is even more important than usual to sing the parts of the liturgies that are meant to be sung, and to make fuller use of the chants provided in the Missal. Sing the Gloria when it returns on Holy Thursday. Sing the Solemn Intercessions on Good Friday. Sing the *Exsultet* and intone the threefold Alleluia at the Vigil. If it is not practical for the chants to be sung well, however, it is probably best not to sing them unless the rubrics absolutely require it. For this reason, the Missal also suggests that communities without sufficient resources to perform the rites "with dignity" should join in the celebrations at the cathedral or large parish church. Celebrating the days at an Abbey church would be another solution.

Children's Liturgy of the Word

ENCOURAGE family participation in the holiest three days of the liturgical year. The symbols, rituals, and Scripture readings of these days proclaim our faith and lead us to renew our baptismal promises at the Easter Vigil. The rituals of the presentation of the oils and foot washing on Holy Thursday, the Adoration of the Cross on Good Friday, and the procession with the Light of Christ, the celebration of the sacraments of initiation with the elect, and the sprinkling with holy water at the great Vigil of Easter offer opportunities for young and old and those in between to experience their faith in deep and profound ways.

Children embrace ritual and symbols. Explicitly invite families to participate in the liturgy of these three days.

The Saints

THE days of Holy Week, of Triduum, and of the Easter Octave, take precedence over other feast days. If your parish's or diocese's patronal feast falls on one of these days, it will be transferred to April 10, after the Easter Octave, and the Solemnity of the Annunciation itself will be transferred from March 25 to April 9 this year.

The Liturgy of the Hours

THE Sacred Triduum is all about prayer. These three days are our holiest and demand us to be attentive to all that God has done and the great crescendo in the history of salvation. We need to do only the work necessary, and for parish ministers, this is a lot. However, we should prepare well, clear our schedules as best we can, and attend to our fundamental stance: prayer and praise of our God.

All our liturgical life is tied together. Symbols, spoken words, sung acclamations weave in and out of our prayer lives. Nowhere is this connection more striking than in how the community prays the Triduum. It's more than rules about when to say what. There is an integral integration between the liturgies that teaches us and fills us. Internalize the directions. Allow the power of the prayer precedence.

The Triduum begins with the Mass of the Lord's Supper on Holy Thursday evening. Evening Prayer is said only by those who do not attend this liturgy. Note, it is the evening Mass that has priority. Many parishes pray Night Prayer at the Altar of Repose. It may be used as a way of signaling that for security reasons it is time to go so the building can be locked. It is also simply a way of praying communally. Respecting that this is a solemn, rather quiet time, less is more, so speaking the psalm is appropriate. If there is a strong vocalist, or a simple instrument like guitar or flute, use it to gently offer support. This is not a time for power or overwhelming brashness.

The Church recommends that the community gather for Good Friday Morning Prayer or the Office of Readings. The Altar of Repose is an appropriate space. The tone is the same. Again, we encounter Psalm 51. If our Sunday setting for Lent is appropriate to today, perhaps we can sing. However, the somberness of Good Friday prevails. Note that Evening Prayer is said only by those who do not participate in the Liturgy of Good Friday.

Holy Saturday is a time of preparation and waiting. Again the Church recommends Morning Prayer or the Office of Readings. Today we should try to avoid as much work as possible and live in the anticipation of Easter. Night Prayer is not said by those who participate in the Great Vigil.

Can your parish celebrate the end of Triduum with Evening Prayer on Easter Sunday? Depending on the culture of your parish, perhaps add a bit of festivity. An ice cream social or some other way of celebrating is in order.

The Rite of Christian Initiation of Adults

THE Sacred Triduum is at the heart of the liturgical year and central in the RCIA process. The ritual text provides texts for the "Preparation Rites on Holy Saturday" (see RCIA, 185–205), the "Celebration of Initiation" (see RCIA, 206–243), and texts for the celebration of the combined rites (see RCIA, 562–594). As the liturgy team prepares for these high holy days, they might consider including a brief dismissal of the elect and catechumens on Holy Thursday and Good Friday. On Holy Thursday, the dismissal is celebrated after the Washing of the Feet; on Good Friday, after the Adoration of the Cross. Since dismissals have been celebrated weekly, the group is well equipped to break open the Word without a catechist present. This allows the RCIA team to be present for the entire liturgy. There are many resources on the market that can help the group in their discussion. Careful preparations by the RCIA team will help this go smoothly and can be very effective.

Holy Saturday, the day we commemorate Jesus' descent into hell, provides an opportunity for the parish community to gather in prayer as the elect make their final preparations for the Easter sacraments. The rite provides some general guidelines and options, but there is some freedom in how this time might be structured. Since all the baptized have entered into the time of the paschal fast, the rite urges the elect to do the same. The RCIA says, "The elect are to be advised that on Holy Saturday they should refrain from their usual activities, spend their time in prayer and reflection, and, as far as they can, observe a fast" (185.1). These directives give weight to the importance of this preparation. Since the RCIA should include the whole parish, the liturgy committee and RCIA team might consider hosting a morning of reflection and prayer for the whole parish, with a focus on the elect. Celebrate Morning Prayer or a Liturgy of the Word with the recitation of the Creed (see RCIA, 185.2). The Lord's Prayer can be presented too if it was deferred after the Third Scrutiny (see RCIA, 185.2). Make sure you have trained ministers (for example, readers, hospitality) to assist with this gathering. The prayer can be followed by a mini-retreat time. This is a time to gather the whole parish for prayer in preparation for the Easter Vigil. Carefully read the rite so you are familiar with the options and be creative with the ways you engage the community in contemplating the Paschal Mystery. Holy Saturday can be a real graced time.

As the sun sets and darkness consumes the earth, the Church prepares herself for the greatest of all vigils. The elect who have been preparing for months or maybe even years, finally gather to celebrate the third step in the process, which is Initiation. This liturgy has many details so it is important that all the ministers involved are carefully prepared and familiar with the rite. It is also important that the team has coached the elect to make their responses with fervor so the community hears them and can support them. The US *National Statutes for the Catechumenate* has a strong preference that this night be reserved for those celebrating initiation (see NSC, 26, 32–33). If, for pastoral reasons, the parish discerns that it is necessary to celebrate Full Reception and the Completion of Initiation on the same night, a combined rite is provided (see RCIA, 562–594). Use the symbols of water, oil, processions, and so on abundantly. The NSC encourages Baptism by immersion since it "is the fuller and more expressive sign of the sacrament" (17). Remember that children of catechetical age (that is, even years and older) are to receive all three sacraments of

Initiation (canon 852.1). Finally, the newly baptized are called neophytes and begin a period of mystagogy.

The Sacraments of Initiation

ENCOURAGE families who are preparing for the sacraments this year to participate in the Triduum liturgies. These liturgies are some of the most meaningful and inspiring worship services of the whole year and are highly encouraged for candidates who are preparing for sacraments of initiation because the Paschal Mystery comes alive each year during these worship services.

The Easter Vigil on Saturday night is a wonderful time to invite sponsors and godparents to attend the liturgy because it is very inspiring. Oftentimes parents of young children avoid the lengthy liturgy because of tired children and bedtimes. However, if they are able to get a babysitter and attend the vigil they will have a deeper sense of the beauty of the Christian life that they bring their child to in the sacrament of Baptism.

Since First Eucharist is about preparing to receive the Body and Blood in Holy Communion, it is especially helpful for children to attend the Holy Thursday liturgy of the Lord's Supper. Consider inviting children who are preparing to receive to take part in the footwashing.

Confirmation candidates can also be invited to take part in the footwashing, either as having their own feet washed or by assisting the priest with making sure the water and towels are replenished during the rite. They may also serve as greeters, readers, cantors (if they are trained), and choir members. This helps to make them more visible to the community and helps them to feel an essential part of the liturgical life of the parish.

The Rite of Penance

WHILE the Missal notes that the Sacrament of Penance may be celebrated on Good Friday, consider carefully the reasons for doing so. How do we encourage our parishioners to live and embody the great movement from the Mass of

the Lord's Supper, through the Liturgy of Good Friday to the Great Vigil and Easter Sunday? If we have embraced a journey motif, let's continue it. The Lectionary will guide our steps. The broad definition of mercy demonstrated by Pope Francis encourages us to live freely in the grace of God. Our sacramental celebrations during Lent give us courage and new eyes and ears to meet our Lord this Triduum.

The Order of Celebrating Matrimony

THE Sacred Triduum is our holiest season. Now we celebrate our most important truths: the Passion, Death, and Resurrection of our Lord Jesus Christ. Everything bows before the triduum. These days are like no other. The Sacrament of Matrimony, therefore, is forbidden on Good Friday and Holy Saturday (see OCM, 32). While it is possible to celebrate the sacrament without a Mass on Holy Thursday morning, this would be in extreme pastoral circumstances. Our hearts and minds are turned to the Lord alone during these sacred days.

The Pastoral Care of the Sick

ALTHOUGH there are some restrictions on the celebration of ritual Masses during the Sacred Triduum, for example weddings and funerals, the Anointing of the Sick can be celebrated for a person who is ill at any time. Normally a communal Anointing of the Sick would not be scheduled during the Sacred Triduum. Holy Communion may be taken to those who are sick at any time during the Sacred Triduum. The exception is on Holy Saturday when Communion can only be given if the person is dying. In that case the rite for Viaticum is celebrated (see chapter 5, Celebration of Viaticum, *Pastoral Care of the Sick: Rites of Anointing and Viaticum*).

At some point during Holy Week the oils to be used for sacramental rites in the parish are blessed by the bishop during the Chrism Mass that is celebrated at the cathedral church of the diocese. Traditionally this liturgy is celebrated on Holy Thursday, although some dioceses schedule it on another day. Many parishes choose to "receive" the blessed oils in a brief rite just prior to the celebration of the Liturgy of the Lord's Supper on Holy Thursday evening.

In this ritual each of the blessed oils is presented, a prayer of thanksgiving is said and the vessels of oil are placed in the ambry. Often the oils are presented before the congregation by one or more liturgical ministers involved with the sacramental celebrations that include one or more of the blessed oils. Ministers of pastoral care would present the Oil of the Sick. Again, this brief ritual serves to connect the entire parish with the many individuals whose sacramental journey is not always as visible within the congregation. It also reminds the parish of its own ministry toward those who are sick. The Rite for the Reception of the Holy Oils is found in this *Sourcebook* on page 160.

It is most fitting that Communion be taken to those who are unable to join the assembly for the liturgies of the Sacred Triduum. Perhaps the ideal time to do this is after the Liturgy of the Lord's Supper on Holy Thursday. Sending forth the pastoral ministers after this liturgy makes a strong statement on how the Body of Christ, the Church extends beyond the gathered assembly and embraces those whose absence is yet present in the prayer of the community.

However, this might pose a practical concern in that the liturgy, which is normally scheduled in the evening, may not be concluded until quite late. This might not be the best time to be visiting the homes or healthcare residences of those who are sick. The other option would be after the Communion Rite on Good Friday.

The Order of Christian Funerals

NOTE that Funeral Masses are not celebrated on Thursday of Holy Week or during the Paschal Triduum. This may present pastoral challenges, so be prepared to assist the grieving in understanding our reasons for this practice. The power of faith in the Lord's Passion, Death, and Resurrection which we celebrate with great devo-

tion at this time may or may not be understood or accepted. This is real and grief is real. However, our witness to placing God first is important. Pastoral care is important. Be ready with compassion for the intense feelings that may occur. Make sure the support staff is ready too. Perhaps a reminder call to the local funeral homes of our discipline may help. While funerals in the context of the Liturgy of the Word may be permitted on Holy Thursday, effort should be made to avoid this option.

Be ready too for the Vigil Liturgy services on Easter Sunday in preparation for a Monday funeral. The time of these may need to be adjusted from your standard.

The Book of Blessings

DURING this short season, we are in a sense outside of time. Our minds and spirits are full with contemplation, reflection, prayer, and commemoration, with processing, singing, seeing, venerating (and so on!). The days are full with rites already. As such, the Triduum is not a usual time for using the *Book of Blessings*, but it quickly returns to use during Easter Time. However, before we come to Easter Sunday—the "Sunday of Sundays," the *Book of Blessings* offers an opportunity to reflect on one particular aspect of our Lenten preparation: fasting. While fasting throughout the Triduum is no longer required, except on Good Friday, some of the faithful still take on this fast. Indeed, it could be especially fruitful for those elect who will be fully initiated into the Church at Easter. In addition, many of the faithful still fast from meat every Friday during Lent. In the Order for the Blessing of Food for the First Meal of Easter (*Book of Blessings*, 1701–1723) we recall our Lenten fast and celebrate the return to our normal, heartier diet. We can also remember those for whom even the meals of our Lenten fasting would be a feast.

This blessing is best suited to the time immediately before or after the Easter Vigil, or even Easter Sunday morning. Food for the first meal after the fast is brought together, either at the church or in another place appropriate for a gathering of the faithful. As with most of the other blessings, this one can be led by a priest, deacon, or layperson. The normal, longer form would work best before the Easter Vigil or at the church on Easter morning. The shorter rite is appropriate for after the Easter Vigil, when the long liturgy and late hour might make the longer form impractical. Either form can be celebrated at home.

The Liturgical Environment

THE Paschal season is the season of Christian initiatio. As such, the environment for Holy Week and the Triduum should be carefully prepared with the sacramental experience of the elect and those called to continuing conversion in mind.

Of course, the font is central. So also is the place at which Confirmation will be celebrated, and the altar. Just as the "Three Days" make up one great liturgy, the celebration of these sacraments forms on initiatory process. The environment in which it takes palce can make this unity clear, or it can obscure it and treat the three sacraments as separate and unrelated pieces.

When considering how each of these places might be prepared, we should, then, think of them as forming one path of initiation. In many churches, the font is found in the rear of the nave, at the entrance to the assembly. Ritually, this underlines that Baptism is entrance to Christ's Body, the path through being one with his Body. It marks out the beginning of a path through Confirmation to the altar, which the newly baptized will approach for Eucharist with the rest of the assembly for the first time. There, they will be one with Christ's Body, reciving what they are, and becoming what they receive.

The place of Baptism should be as lush as possible, made verdant with plants and be well lit. The explanatory symbols can also be made more visible: consider using a candle with some substance and an alb for the white garment. Give those being baptized some time to change and welcome them back to the assembly clothed as one of God's people. The RCIA stipulates that an appropriate song may be sung between the celebration of Baptism and Confirmation. this can allow enough time for both a change of clothes and the procession to the sanctuary. Practicality shouldn't be overlooked either. Especially when baptizing by immersion or infusion, people will need a dry set of clothes

and a place to change. Also, many church floors can be slipper when wet; the careful placement of a mat or towel can prevent slips or falls.

Confirmation does not require much by way of environment, except for attention to space. There should be enough room for those being confirmed, their sponsors, and the minister of the sacrament. Of course, chrism is necesary, as well as means for the celebrant to clean his hands after the celebration of the sacrament.

Of course, the place of the Eucharist will recieve special attention in any feast day environment. It might mirror the garden imagery of the Baptismal font or be lighted with more candles than usual. It is appropriate to bring out the best vessels that the church has for this liturgy, just as one would bring out special dishes for family occasions. But there is no need to overdecorate the altar. The new life of plants and the inescapable draw of light can be enough. The best liturgical environments draw our eye and involve us in the action without drawing attention away from the actions that take place in their midst.

The Liturgical Music

THE music during the Sacred Paschal Triduum should be carefully chosen to reflect the fact that these are the holiest and most sacred days in the liturgical calendar. There are ancient rituals enacted on these days that we don't see at other times of the year. The music that accompanies these once a year rituals ought to be very familiar to the assembly and sung year after year, like wearing shoes that are comfortable and well broken in. There are ancient melodies and/or texts that are provided in the Missal that should be given pride of place during the Triduum:

Holy Thursday: Mass of the Lord's Supper

- ◆ Entrance Antiphon ("We Should Glory in the Cross")
- ◆ Seven Antiphons for the Washing of the Feet
- ◆ Chant for the Preparation of the Gifts ("Ubi Caritas")
- ◆ Transfer of the Most Blessed Sacrament ("Pange Lingua")

Good Friday—The Celebration of the Passion of the Lord

◆ The Solemn Intercessions

◆ The Showing of the Holy Cross

◆ The Adoration of the Holy Cross ("The Reproaches" and "Faithful Cross the Saints Rely On")

◆ Communion (Psalm 22)

Easter Sunday of the Resurrection of the Lord: The Easter Vigil in the Holy Night

◆ T e Lighting of the Paschal Candle

◆ The Procession

◆ The Easter Proclamation (*Exsultet*)

◆ Glory to God in the Highest

◆ Alleluia

◆ Litany of the Saints

◆ Blessing of Baptismal Water

◆ Sprinkling with Blessed Water ("Vidi Aquam"/ "I Saw Water Flowing")

◆ Communion Antiphon ("Christ Our Passover" and Psalm 18)

◆ Solemn Dismissal

◆ Easter Sunday of the Resurrection of the Lord: At Mass During the Day

◆ Communion Antiphon ("Christ Our Passover" and Psalm 18)

◆ Solemn Dismissal

There is an ancient principle that suggests that during the Church's most solemn days, the most ancient rituals are preserved. The Church's liturgy is not a museum piece meant to be looked at for its historic value. Rather, it is a living and growing reality that preserves its very best tradition for its holiest days as it also seeks to embrace the best of what is new and modern. If new music is used for the Triduum, it should, if possible, be introduced months in advance so that the assembly becomes familiar with it. The collection, *I Shall Live* by Tony Alonso (WLP), brings fresh life to the texts of the ritual music in *The Roman Missal* with some new and some traditional melodies, such as *Pange Lingua Gloriosi*, woven into the music. Check out LTP's resource *Guide for Celebrating © Holy Week and the Triduum*, a valuable tool for music

ministers and others involved in the preparations for the Sacred Paschal Triduum.

Everyone in the parish music ministry should be invited to participate in the liturgies of the Triduum. Space and other temporal limitations may not allow everyone to sing together at every liturgy, however a creative approach will give everyone who is able the opportunity to participate in one or more liturgies. During the Church's holiest days, a unified and inclusive music ministry will assist in helping the parish pray well.

The Liturgical Ministers

AT the heart of the liturgical year the number of rehearsals and tasks can be intimidating. Pastoral musicians and other ministers who run a marathon through the "Three Days" are often frazzled, so provide opportunities for them to contemplate the mysteries during these sacred days and provide them with bottled water and light snacks so they can remain adequately hydrated and fed as they exercise their ministry. Create a check list for each day of the Triduum, especially for sacristans, musicians, presiding ministers and RCIA team members. Make sure all readers have practiced with the microphone at the ambo or other places where the Scriptures will be read, especially those who are proclaiming the Passion. Put someone in charge of the lighting, especially for the Easter Vigil and charge someone to coordinate the various processions that occur during the Triduum. Make sure a team of people have a clear understanding of the larger picture so nothing is left to only one person. Make sure the deacon or cantor who will chant the *Exsultet* is well rehearsed early in the season of Lent and not just a few days before the celebration of the Paschal Triduum.

Other Prayers, Rites, and Devotions

DURING these solemn days, the principal liturgies of the three days take precedence. Many pietistic practices made popular by waves of immigrants who came to the United States at the turn of the century still have significant meaning to second and third generation Catholics. But with proper catechesis, many devotional aspects of the Triduum are still valuable today. Parish organizations often schedule or promote pilgrimages to neighboring churches, often times numbering seven, after the Holy Thursday evening Mass, to spend some quiet time at prayer before the Blessed Sacrament. Keep in mind, this time should not be seen as "touring local churches" but maintaining a sense of prayer even at the times of traveling from parish to parish, whether it be praying the Stations of the Cross, reciting a decade of the Rosary, or reading sections of the Passion narrative.

Good Friday offers many opportunities for devotional prayer throughout the day and night. The majority of parishes already offer the Stations of the Cross. This could be an opportunity to expand the service to include brief musical refrains interspersed, for example after a scene is described, the choir could sing a brief refrain from the Taizé collection or a verse from a Lenten hymn. The traditional presentation of "The Seven Last Words of Christ" could be scheduled. The composition by Théodore Dubois, included in the *St. Gregory Hymnal* (GIA), was a parish staple for years. In between each of the sung statements, a brief homily is given, reflecting on the given scriptural quote. The *"Tre Ore"* or the "Three Hours" invites people to solemn prayer from Noon until 3:00 PM. The Jesuit priest, Fr. Alphonsus Messia (died 1732), is said to have devised this devotion in Lima, Peru. It was introduced to Rome around 1788 and spread around the world. In 1815, Pope Pius VII decreed a plenary indulgence to those who practiced this devotion on Good Friday. This time includes the presentation of the Seven Last Words, Stations of the Cross, and traditionally ended with the proclamation of St. John's Passion. As the Passion is already part of the principle service of Good Friday, its best to leave the reading to the main liturgy.

It is customary, especially in the Polish communities, to bless Easter foods on Holy Saturday. The placement of this tradition is a holdover from the pre-Conciliar days when the Easter Vigil was anticipated and therefore, the Lenten fast was over and the newly blessed holy water was available. Many parishes celebrate this blessing either in the morning or afternoon of Holy Saturday, but the proper place is either at the end or after the Easter Vigil. The *Book of Blessings* does make reference

to both "before" and "after" the celebration of the Easter Vigil. Pastoral sensitivity should prevail. If the ritual is held before the Vigil, the service could be celebrated in a gathering space, activity center, or gym, or even outside (weather permitting), and incense used instead of holy water. During Holy Week, parishioners could be invited to bring items for their first Easter meal to the Easter Vigil, placed on a table before the start of the Mass for a blessing at the conclusion. This change of custom may take some time, especially in parishes with a long history of daytime blessings.

Evangelization

THE word *Triduum* is unfamiliar to many. Even lifelong Catholics pause when they hear this Latin word uttered. The first challenge of evangelization during this sacred time is how we let people know the meaning of these three days and why they are so significant to us. How do we welcome "outsiders" into what seem to be "insider" language and rituals?

On Holy Thursday, we process with oils. We wash feet. We remember and make present the first celebration of the sacrifice of the Eucharist. On Good Friday, we proclaim the Passion of the Lord and affirm that the obedient, suffering servant is the new high priest. We process with a cross and adore it affirming, too, that this Cross is the tree of life on which our Savior hung and through which eternal life came. At the Easter Vigil, we tell story upon story of our history of our faith. We announce the Resurrection of our Savior through music, the liturgical environment, and proclamation of the Easter Gospel. We welcome new members through the sacraments of initiation. All these rituals might seem strange to newcomers, or at least unfamiliar. We will want to consider in our parishes how we celebrate these rituals so those who might be coming for the first time will feel welcome to enter into them.

A question of evangelization focuses on how we build energy and excitement in our parish communities as the Sacred Triduum draws near. While the length of these liturgies is a practical concern, especially for those with young families and the elderly among us, we need to find ways to not let this discussions dominant our liturgy committees. These are the days we show forth to others our very identity as Christians. Ponder ways the liturgy will occur outside of the physical structure of the Church so that passersbys might take notice and perhaps inquire about what is taking place, or even join a procession. Perhaps they might be reminded that Easter is close upon us, and consider participating in liturgy on the Sunday of the year when we celebrate with delight the Lord's Resurrection.

Consider how you will invite the people of your communities to react with joy and embrace the visitors who enter into their midst to celebrate Easter. Frustration and gloomy faces because of crowded parking lots and pews do not evangelize, but hospitality and pleasure at the many people who want to sing "Jesus Christ is Risen Today" with us, most certainly do! Our call to evangelize during these three sacred days is a call to infuse every aspect of the life of our parish and home with the reverence of these days and make Easter joy palpable in all we do.

The Parish and the Home

THE way in which we celebrate the Sacred Paschal Triduum communicates much to all who participate, and even to those who do not. The more emphasis we place on the three days as time set apart, the greater the likelihood that the parish and its people will grow as a community who puts first things first, center life and action on Jesus Christ, learn from his sacrifice and self-giving love, and live as members of Christ's Body in the world.

Within the family, some preparation will go a long way to make Triduum days to anticipate and honor rather than ones that have little bearing on life and faith. Even young children can and should participate in the liturgies, learning the special nature of them simply by hearing, seeing, and sensing the difference in tone and character. Older children may be invited to retell the story of Jesus' washing the disciples' feet, Last Supper, agony in the garden, betrayal, trial, scourging, Crucifixion, and Resurrection. Create a family "Gospel" book to tell the Good News of Christ's life, Passion, Death, and Resurrection, with places for each family member to write a prayer, reflec-

tion or example of how he or she has served others, suffered persecution or betrayal, the death of a loved one, and new life following a time of darkness.

Ask each family member to take responsibility for learning about one of the Triduum liturgies and helping the family to prepare. Share that even though on the calendar, it appears to be four days, when we count from sundown to sundown, the days actually number three. Parishes might include a walk-through of the Triduum in Lenten or Holy Week offerings, enhancing the full participation of all who gather. Invite last year's elect to offer brief witness in bulletin or newsletter articles, sharing the impact of initiation and of the liturgies in their lives. Ask someone to share a brief testimony to the power of the Triduum at the end of the Palm Sunday of the Lord's Passion Mass, urging everyone to participate in this year's Triduum liturgies. Since each liturgy includes special elements, exploring these will help each person to understand, enter into, and reflect upon them as the three days progress. Add an element to the family prayer or dinner table for each of the days: bread and wine for Holy Thursday, a cross or crucifix for Good Friday, a basin of water for Holy Saturday, and a lily and/or Alleluia banner for Easter Sunday.

Some parishes invite parishioners to participate in Holy Saturday Morning Prayer with the elect. A blessing of the food for the Easter feast may also be part of the parish's tradition on Holy Saturday. Those who prepare the liturgical environment and liturgical ministry may gather prior to each of the liturgies for prayer and may linger following the celebrations for quiet social time together. These special moments within the Triduum provide additional connections between prayer and life, marking people, time, and action as sacred.

Mass Texts

◆ TROPES FOR THE PENITENTIAL ACT, FORM C (HOLY THURSDAY)

You are the unblemished Lamb, given for our salvation: Lord, have mercy.

You are our Passover, leadng us from slavery into new life: Christ, have mercy.

You are the servant of God, who calls us to follow your example of self-less love: Lord, have mercy.

◆ TROPES FOR THE PENITENTIAL ACT, FORM C (EASTER SUNDAY)

Your Resurrection bestows upon us every spiritual blessing from the heavens: Lord, have mercy.

You have made us adopted sons and daughters of the Father: Christ, have mercy.

You have redeemed us by your Death and Resurrection: Lord, have mercy.

◆ DISMISSAL FOR CHILDREN'S LITURGY OF THE WORD (EASTER SUNDAY)

My dear children, today you will hear about the Resurrection of Christ from the dead. God the Father raised Christ just as we pray he will one day raise us to new life. We will wait for you hear so that together we may give him thaks and praise in the Eucharist. Go now in peace.

◆ DISMISSAL OF THE CATECHUMENS AND THE ELECT (HOLY THURSDAY)

My dear friends, tonight in the Gospel, you heard of the selfless service to your brothers and sisters which is the Christian charity you will inherit when at last you are one with us around the table of the Lord. Go now in peace to reflect mor deeply on the word you have heard.

◆ DISMISSAL OF THE CATECHUMENS (EASTER)

The Church is renewed in the living waters of Baptism, as Easter joy resounds in our hearts and upon our lips. As you grow to know Christ more and more each day and follow in his footsteps, you will long for these waters and the newness of life they contain. We, your brothers and sisters, join with you in prayer, as you share with each other the Word of God. We patiently wait for the day when you too will share fully in the Paschal feast of the Lord. Go in peace.

March 2018
Month of St. Joseph

(#39)   white

**Thursday of
Holy Week
(Holy Thursday)
Evening Mass of
the Lord's Supper**

THU **29**

About the Evening Mass of the Lord's Supper

This evening Lent ends and the Church enters the Sacred Paschal Triduum, gathering to pray, building toward the prolonged vigiling of Saturday night. This evening's celebration, the Mass of the Lord's Supper, is the threshold liturgy of the Triduum. It commemorates the institution of Eucharist and the priesthood, as well as Jesus' command of love and service. It should be the only parish Mass today, even if varied language groups make up the parish community. Another Mass is celebrated only with permission of the bishop, and it should not dissuade people from attending the principal Mass. Aside from the possibility of the Chrism Mass, no other Masses are celebrated today.

Preparing this liturgy and the others of the Triduum can be enormously stressful if not reviewed well in advance. Avoid scheduling rehearsals during Holy Week; conduct them instead during the last few weeks of Lent. While there should be one overall coordinator for the Triduum liturgies, it helps greatly to have people responsible for each ministry and willing to rehearse each group. Rehearsals calm anxiety and ministers will be able to identify the processional routes, the stations for the washing of the feet, musical cues for movement, the location of readings and petitions, as well as the placement of needed liturgical items.

It is interesting to note that the Missal gives a series of instructions for the whole Sacred Paschal Triduum; these are listed before the rubrics for Thursday of the Lord's Supper. Liturgy committees would do well to take note of these important instructions and reflect on how they can best be implemented in their parish celebrations.

First, the centrality of these days as the preeminent days for celebrating the Paschal Mystery is noted, since on these three days the Church solemnly celebrates "the greatest mysteries of our redemption, keeping by means of special celebrations the memorial of her Lord, crucified, buried, and risen" (rubric for Triduum, 1).

The Paschal fast is also mentioned. The fast is to be kept everywhere on the Friday of the Lord's Passion, but the Missal goes on to recommend that it be prolonged through Holy Saturday. Catechesis about this Paschal fast might be useful for parishioners, because its meaning differs from that of the Lenten fast. While the Lenten fast is centered on penance, conversion, and renewal, the Paschal fast is more focused on preparation and anticipation (in a sense, almost being too excited to eat!); it is a way of preparing to come, "with spirit uplifted, to the joys of the Lord's Resurrection" (rubric for Triduum, 1). The Paschal fast helps us to enter into *kairos*, the "time outside of time" that characterizes the continual anamnesis of the Three Days, which, in some sense, are actually one.

A second rubric cautions that a sufficient number of lay ministers is required in order to fittingly celebrate the Sacred Paschal Triduum. Thus, what is true all year long must be especially in evidence during the Church's most sacred days, namely, that liturgical celebrations are diversified actions celebrated by the entire Body, and that a variety of ministers is needed, in proper number, so that the fullness of the Church's liturgical ministries may be in evidence. While "good enough is never good enough" is a maxim that should always apply to the Church's liturgical celebrations, the necessity of allowing the rites to be celebrated in all their fullness, which includes an adequate number of lay ministers, is heightened during these days.

In actuality, the point about lay ministers simply underscores the importance of the full, conscious, and active participation of the faithful during the celebrations, and this is the point that is highlighted next. The Missal points out that "the singing of the people, the ministers, and the Priest Celebrant has a special importance in the celebrations of these days, for when texts are sung, they have their proper impact" (rubric for Triduum, 2). Thus, the Missal is calling on communities to sing the rites during these days, and indeed these are the days to sing as many of the texts as possible—maybe even all of them! Furthermore, the full participation of the faithful is so important that the Missal makes a special reminder to pastors to catechize their people about the meaning and order of the celebrations. If we take this seriously, then we understand that catechesis about the Sacred Paschal Triduum through bulletin articles, preaching, workshop sessions, and adult education courses is as important a part of liturgical preparation as are the flow charts, gathering of props, and sprucing up of the environment and the vestments.

A third notation specifies that the liturgies of the Sacred Paschal Triduum "are to be carried out in cathedral and parochial churches and only in those chosen churches in which they can be performed with dignity, that is, with a good attendance of the faithful, an appropriate number of ministers, and the means to sing at least some of the parts" (rubric for Triduum, 3). For some, this might be a challenge to a radically new understanding of the rites. The liturgies of these days are not formalities or simple prayer experiences that can be performed perfunctorily just for the sake of giving people a nice experience; they are liturgies that are supposed to be powerful expressions of the very heart of what we believe and who we are. Thus, it is essential that these liturgies be celebrated with the dignity and fullness of expression that their nature demands. Small communities and other groupings of the faithful — small communities of religious, nursing homes or other institutions, schools, and even mission parishes — may need to ask some very difficult questions about their ability to celebrate these liturgies properly, and perhaps consider joining with larger communities.

The Lectionary for Mass

◆ First Reading: The profound story of the final acts of God that produce Israel's freedom from captivity in Egypt are now recounted. Moses has demanded their release, and Pharaoh's obstinacy has resulted in nine horrifying plagues. Water has become blood; frogs, lice, flies, and locusts have been sent; disasters of hail, fire, and darkness have been unleashed, and the people have been afflicted with boils. Now God sends the devastating death of the firstborn. Israel will be spared by following the directions offered here. An unblemished male lamb will be

sacrificed, and the doorposts marked with its blood. The flesh of the lamb will be consumed by people who stand ready to leave — "loins girt," sandals on, and a walking staff held in the ready for departure. This done, God will "pass over" the homes of the chosen people. God instructs the people through Moses to memorialize this moment every year. To this day, observant Jews recount and remember this powerful moment of deliverance in the Seder, the festive meal of Passover, by telling this story in the liturgy contained in the Passover.

◆ Responsorial Psalm 116 offers thanksgiving to God, who has delivered his people. The God of the covenant has done great things. Having escaped trials and suffering, the response is to extol the greatness of God in thanksgiving. To "call upon the name of the Lord" is to pray in gratitude. The lives of those who love God are precious, including those who have died. The "cup of salvation" mentioned in the first stanza is a reference to an offering made to God upon deliverance from death; the "blessing cup" in the antiphon evokes the third ritual cup of wine in the Passover celebration. This night of Holy Thursday, the cup that is shared is the blessing cup that contains the Blood of Christ — a cup that has represents our salvation. The antiphon is drawn not from the psalm but from the reading from 1 Corinthians that is about to be proclaimed.

◆ The Second Reading is from Paul's letter to the growing community in Corinth, an important city of commerce in Greece. It is believed that Paul stayed in Corinth longer than he stayed in any other city, and his letters reflect an intimacy and familiarity with the life and concerns of people to whom he writes. Here, in the midst of a narrative addressing issues in the litur-

gical assemblies in Corinth, Paul offers us the earliest description of how the Eucharist was instituted. In the account, he first establishes himself as an authoritative recipient of the Lord's instructions. Paul did not know Jesus in life, and his conversion en route to Damascus as described in the Acts of the Apostles does not mention the Eucharist. Rather, the authority that has passed on the Lord's direction is most likely the early Christian community, the Church, which speaks with authority. The description here, which ties past, present, and future together, recounts our Eucharistic practice to this day. It is fitting that on the day we celebrate the Last Supper, we are reminded of this core belief.

◆ Gospel: The exquisite, poetic narrative from the Gospel according to John describes the actions of Jesus Christ at the Passover meal we now call the Last Supper. John's telling focuses on washing the feet of the disciples rather than the institution of the Eucharist. While foot washing was a common task in the time of Jesus, it was also a menial task. Listeners in the life of the early Church would have found this account almost shocking; for the one who is Lord to take on a task relegated to slaves. Here, an everyday task become a ritual that totally upends social convention. From the first letter to Timothy, which mentions washing the "feet of the holy ones," we know that this practice became a part of Christian hospitality. This practice demonstrated the reality that while Christians might have to accommodate the dominant social conventions of their day, within their own communities, a new world order was established that was consistent with the reign of God. In this passage, we experience, yet again, the enthusiasm and grandiosity of Peter, who at first resists the Lord, and then offers his entire body for cleansing. The foot washing of the Holy Thursday liturgy is more than a quaint custom; it is a direct access to an embodied experience of what Jesus Christ asks of all his followers: self-forgetting, humble service, and radical hospitality. To use the categories of cultural anthropologist Victor Turner, this ritual — then and now — is a transformation of roles and status with a horizon from the present to the future, unlike a ceremony, where the horizon is past-to-present and where status is confirmed and often elevated.

The Roman Missal

Before the Mass texts are given, the Missal lists special instructions that pertain to the celebration of the Evening Mass of the Lord's Supper, some of which are worth highlighting here. First to be noted is that the Mass is celebrated in the evening, "with the full participation of the whole local community and with all the Priests and ministers exercising their office" (*The Roman Missal*, Thursday of the Lord's Supper, 1). Thus, once again the importance of the community gathering as the one body with a variety of roles and ministries in evidence is affirmed; in fact, it is ancient tradition that all Masses without the participation of the people are forbidden on this day (see PS, 47). Another rubric mentions that flowers are permitted as decorations, but there should be moderation; we are not yet at Easter. This moderation applies to the place where the Blessed Sacrament will be reserved after Mass; *Paschale solemnitatis* specifies that this space must be conducive to prayer and meditation, and therefore demands sobriety, and abuses are to be suppressed (see PS, 49). Nor is the place of reservation to be made to resemble a tomb, because the chapel of repose is not representing the Lord's burial; rather, it is for the custody of the Eucharistic bread that will be dis-

tributed in Communion on the next day (see PS, 55).

There is no mention in the Missal about the reception of the Holy Oils. However, it has become an accepted practice in the Dioceses of the United States to present the oils to the community who in turn receives these oils to be used throughout the year. This rite is included in *Sourcebook* on page 170.

The Entrance Antiphon, taken from chapter 6, verse 14, of Paul's letter to the Galatians, sums up the mystery we are celebrating throughout the days of the Sacred Paschal Triduum. It's a mystery that can only be understood by living in its truth: "We should glory in the Cross of our Lord Jesus Christ." How is it possible to find glory in the midst of suffering and death? It's possible because through Christ's suffering and Death "we are saved and delivered." That's the mystery that is the heart of the Christian faith, the mystery that is celebrated in every liturgy, and the mystery that is the raison d'être of the Christian life — it is the Paschal Mystery that through Christ, with him, and in him, death becomes life and self-emptying leads to fullness.

The Gloria returns this evening, and it should be sung with joy and fullness; the Missal mentions that bells are rung. Outdoor bells could be rung in the carillon; bells inside the church may be rung by choir members, or altar servers and other ministers, perhaps even by members of the assembly. After this joyous ringing out of the glory of God, the bells are to remain silent until the Gloria of the Easter Vigil. To further highlight the seriousness and uniqueness of the days of the Triduum, a rubric notes that "during this same period [between the Gloria of the evening Mass on Holy Thursday and the Gloria at the Easter Vigil], the organ and other musical instruments may be used only so as to support the singing."

The Collect for this Mass draws our attention to this night's Eucharist being linked to the Last Supper, which is referred to in the Second Reading, with the meaning of the supper being clear: it is the meal Jesus "entrusted to the Church" as "the banquet of his love," "a sacrifice new for all eternity." The effects of participating in that sacrificial banquet are also made clear: we are to draw "from so great a mystery the fullness of charity and of life."

This evening is one of the rare occasions when the Missal specifies for the homilist the themes he is to touch on. The priest's homily is to shed light on "the principal mysteries that are commemorated in this Mass, namely, the institution of the Holy Eucharist and of the priestly Order, and the commandment of the Lord concerning charity." As will be noted several times below, the connection between participation in the Eucharist and living a life of love cannot be overlooked, and that connection should be at the core of the meaning of this Mass. The institution of the ministerial priesthood is commemorated because of the close connection between priesthood and the Eucharist; it is the priest who acts in the person of Christ the Head (*in persona Christi capitis*) within the liturgical assembly and without whom the Eucharist cannot be celebrated. Notice, however, that there is nothing in the ritual for this evening about priests renewing their promises; the place for that is at the Chrism Mass and it has no place in this liturgy. It is something that is meant to be led by the bishop; there are no texts for it at the evening Mass, and it should not be added.

Sacrificial charity and sacrificial living are ritualized in the washing of feet, which, as the Missal notes, follows the homily. Although technically optional, the ritual has such power that one might rightly question why a community would not celebrate it. The unique power of this startling gesture should be allowed to stand on its own and should not be obscured by gimmicks or adaptations. Yes, it is uncomfortable, especially (and ironically) not for the one doing the foot washing, but for the one having his or her feet washed (it's not unusual for people to be shy and reticent about doing this); yes, it is countercultural; yes, it can be awkward. However, all three can also be said about Christian humility and sacrificial love. Resist the temptation to weaken the gesture by changing it to a washing of hands. Nor is there any foundation in the Missal for anyone other than the priest celebrant to wash feet; he functions as the sacramental image of Christ the Head at all other parts of the Eucharist, so why should there be the need to mute this representation during this rite, which is part of the Eucharist? True, all are called to wash one another's feet, that is, serve one another, but the same call to service (and unity) is true of every Eucharist, and the priest exercising his liturgical function alone at other times does not negate or lessen the assembly's participation in the mystery; the same is true here. Therefore, also to be avoided is diminishing the power of the gesture by having others, whether they be clergy or laity, join the priest celebrant in washing feet.

As you prepare for the Sacred Paschal Triduum, parishes should be aware that a decree issued on January 6, 2016, changed the rubrics of *The Roman Missal* to allow for washing the feet of women and girls during the liturgy on Holy Thursday. At the direction of Pope Francis, the Congregation for Divine Worship and the Discipline of the Sacraments has decreed that rubric 11 on Holy Thursday read: "Those chosen from among the People of God are accompanied by the ministers. . . ." (In the

Ceremonial of Bishops, the wording will change in nos. 299b and 301.) The "Decree concerning the Rite of the 'Washing of Feet'" can be found at www.vatican.va. Pope Francis notes, "After careful consideration I have decided to make a change to *The Roman Missal*. I therefore decree that the section according to which those persons chosen for the Washing of the feet must be men or boys, so that from now on the Pastors of the Church may choose the participants in the rite from among all the members of the People of God. I also recommend that an adequate explanation of the rite itself be provided to those who are chosen." This means parishes may choose men, women, the young and the old, the healthy and the sick, clerics, consecrated persons, and laypeople.

Also, no specific number is mentioned, and therefore it need not be limited to twelve. While twelve is a customary number, any number can be used, and the people chosen should adequately reflect the makeup of the community. People of all ages, including young children, may be asked to have their feet washed; people of different races and language groups may be included; at least one of the elect preparing for initiation at this year's Easter Vigil may be included.

Next, the only location mentioned is "a suitable place." Therefore, there is no need for this rite to take place exclusively in the sanctuary; in fact, there are several reasons that would argue against that practice. Certainly, the visibility of the rite would be an important factor. Having multiple stations throughout the church would allow for a maximum number of people to be up close to the action as it is taking place. (This is also one way of reinforcing what is true for all liturgy — that the liturgical action takes place in the entire worship space, not just in the sanctuary.)

Additionally, there can be something very touching — part of the meaning of humble service — to have the priest celebrant move throughout the assembly, going to those before whom he will kneel, rather than having them come to him. However, the suitability of various locations must be carefully considered: how will chairs be placed and then removed in such a way that this action does not draw undue attention to itself? Will the priest be able to kneel easily enough, and will the necessary ministers have access to assist him? What about numbers of pitchers, basins, and towels — how will they be made available, taken away, and who will see to this? None of these details are insurmountable; they need only be thought through in advance so that specific needs can be prepared for and the action can be carried out smoothly, with a minimum of distraction.

Also of interest is the statement that the priest removes his chasuble if necessary; given the action to be performed, one would think it is necessary, for ease of movement. However, there is no mention of the priest tying a towel around his waist, which is nonetheless a custom that many priest celebrants do; the Gospel for the Mass mentions that Jesus did so before he washed the disciples' feet. The rubric goes on to mention that the priest goes to each person and, assisted by ministers, pours water over each one's feet and then dries them. The plural "feet" is used, which would seem to indicate that both feet of each person are to be washed, not just one. (Many priest celebrants have the custom of kissing the feet of the people as well, after washing them.)

While the rite should not be unduly prolonged, neither should it be hurried; the fact that several examples of antiphons are given in the Missal indicate this. The meaning of the rite is revealed in the antiphons:

it is all about Jesus' example of love, humble service, and sharing in Jesus' life by following him.

After the washing of feet, the priest washes and dries his hands, puts the chasuble back on, and the Mass continues with the Universal Prayer as usual. The Creed is not said. After the Universal Prayer, Mass continues with the preparation of the altar and the presentation of the gifts.

Rarely does one find in the Missal a specific rubric about the procession with the gifts, but there is one given here: it is mentioned that gifts for the poor may be presented along with the bread and wine, with those gifts being carried in procession by the faithful. This harkens back to the ancient practice of the Church, where everyone brought something for the offering, and some of the offerings would be set aside for the poor. Such a procession would be a stark reminder of the practical charity that must be a consequence of our participation in the Eucharist — we cannot truly share bread at the Eucharistic table unless we are also sharing bread with the hungry outside the Eucharist. Perhaps these offerings on Holy Thursday can be an impetus for catechizing the faithful at other times about the offering of self that is the heart of our participation in the Eucharistic sacrifice. Certainly the sight of everyone processing forward to bring their gifts to the altar, with the gifts of bread and wine that will be transformed through the power of the Spirit being carried last, would be a powerful sign of the participation of all the faithful. The Missal's suggestion of the antiphon to be chanted, *Ubi caritas*, "Where true charity is dwelling, God is present there," highlights the unity of meaning between the foot washing, which was just completed, and the bringing forward of the offerings for the celebration of the Eucharist.

The Prayer over the Offerings offers a succinct summary of the very essence of liturgical theology: "whenever the memorial of this sacrifice is celebrated / the work of our redemption is accomplished" (one suspects that the homilist could well include this theme in his preaching). To the degree that we are aware of and appreciate what is taking place in our midst here and now (the work of our redemption), that is the degree to which we can be said to be participating worthily in the mysteries.

The Preface assigned for this Mass is Preface I of the Most Holy Eucharist, and the text, with musical notation, is given along with the other texts for this Mass; one could argue that this is revealing the Church's preference for the priest celebrant to chant the Preface. The text itself zeroes in on the core of Eucharistic theology. As it recalls Christ offering himself "as the saving Victim," it also notes how the Eucharist was instituted as the pattern of his sacrifice, and therefore the offering of the Eucharist is the memorial of his offering and sacrifice. Participation in the Eucharist means to join one's own offering with the self-offering of Christ that is made present through anamnesis. This is further emphasized as the Preface goes on to note, "As we eat his flesh that was sacrificed for us, we are made strong, and, as we drink his Blood that was poured out for us, we are washed clean."

The complete text for Eucharistic Prayer I, the Roman Canon, is given along with the other texts for this Mass. This allows for an easy use of the special inserts for the *Communicantes* ("In communion with those"), the *Hanc igitur* ("therefore, Lord, we pray"), and the *Qui pridie* ("On the day before he was to suffer"), which are used at this Mass. However, while it might be argued that, given these special inserts, there is a certain preference

for using the Roman Canon, it is not required (as indicated by the rubric at number 17, "When the Roman Canon is used . . ."), and so Eucharistic Prayer III could also be used. (Prayer II because of its brevity would not be appropriate, and Eucharistic Prayer IV is disqualified because of its proper Preface.)

There is a special rubric concerning Holy Communion: after distribution, a ciborium with hosts for Communion tomorrow is left on the altar. The Prayer after Communion makes an eschatological reference as it asks that "just as we are renewed by the Supper of your Son in this present age, so we may enjoy his banquet for all eternity." This is the last prayer that will be proclaimed at this liturgy; the transfer of the Blessed Sacrament follows immediately.

The transfer of the Blessed Sacrament is rather simple and direct. After the Prayer after Communion, the priest, after putting incense in the thurible, goes to the Blessed Sacrament and incenses it three times. He puts on a white humeral veil, rises, takes the ciborium, and uses the ends of the humeral veil to cover it.

A procession is then formed, led by a minister with a cross, flanked by ministers with lighted candles; although the people are not mentioned, if the place of repose is in another location, the assembly will join the procession, following these ministers. Other ministers with lighted candles may follow the assembly, preceding the minister carrying the smoking thurible, who is directly in front of the priest carrying the Blessed Sacrament. During the procession, a suitable Eucharistic chant is sung; the Missal suggests *Pange, lingua*, excluding the last two verses (the *Tantum ergo*), and it might be argued there is a certain fondness for using this chant.

Upon reaching the place of repose, the priest places the ciborium in the tabernacle, but leaves the door open. Placing incense in the thurible, he incenses the Blessed Sacrament while kneeling and while the *Tantum ergo* or another Eucharistic chant is sung. After this, the tabernacle door is closed.

Next comes a period of adoration in silence (note that the door is to be closed before the period of adoration). After a period of silence, the priest and ministers rise, genuflect, and then depart, but with no formal procession—this is simply a functional leaving of the ministers, not a ritual departure. Adoration by the faithful before the Blessed Sacrament continues, but the Missal notes that midnight is a demarcation point for adoration: "after midnight the adoration should take place without solemnity" (rubric, 43). However, there is no requirement to continue adoration past midnight, but only "for a suitable length of time during the night." Thus, there is nothing to prevent a parish closing the period of adoration at midnight.

Notice that there is no formal or specific dismissal to this liturgy; thus, emphasizing that the liturgies of the Sacred Paschal Triduum are, in some sense, one continuous liturgy. After the liturgy, at an appropriate time, the altar is stripped and crosses are removed from the church, if they can be; if not, they should be veiled (number 57 of *Paschale solemnitatis* notes that the veil should be red or purple, unless they have already been veiled on the Saturday before the Fifth Sunday of Lent). This stripping is done without any ritual or solemnity.

The Missal makes a final note that if for some reason the Passion of the Lord is not celebrated in the same church on the next day, then Mass ends in the usual way, and the Blessed Sacrament is reserved in the tabernacle as usual, without any procession or adoration.

A good resource which discusses the procession with the Blessed Sacrament is *Guide for Celebrating Worship of the Eucharist Outside Mass* by John Thomas Lane, sss (LTP).

The Reception of the Holy Oils

The holy oils are blessed and consecrated at the Chrism Mass, celebrated by the bishop with the priests of diocese in the cathedral on the morning of Holy Thursday, or on a more convenient day before Easter. Following the Chrism Mass, the pastor or his delegate then brings the fresh oils back to the parish in time for the celebration of the Triduum.

The Chrism Mass wonderfully highlights the importance and meaning of the holy oils. However, most of the faithful never participate in this liturgy, and may not even be aware that the oils are renewed each year in preparation for Easter. Thus, the Church provides an optional rite for the Reception of the Holy Oils in the parish community: "The reception of the Holy Oils may take place in individual parishes either before the celebration of the Evening Mass of the Lord's supper or at another time that seems more appropriate" (*Roman Missal*, Thursday of Holy Week, 15).

The rubric in the Missal does not provide much guidance about how this reception is actually to take place. For that, we need to go to the supplemental materials prepared for the dioceses of the United States, available at www.usccb.org/prayer-and-worship/liturgical-year/triduum/reception-of-holy-oils.cfm, and printed in this *Sourcebook* on page 160. This short rite engages the whole assembly, with acclamations for the people, texts that express the purpose of each of the oils, and individual parishioners designated as presenters. (It would be especially powerful if these rep-

resentatives joined the pastor at the diocesan Chrism Mass.)

Note that with the third edition of *The Roman Missal*, the time for the reception has changed. The oils are no longer received as part of the gifts procession; instead, they are presented before Mass begins. This timing can be challenging. If the ambry is located near the entrance of the church, it could work well to receive the oils near the doors just before the entrance procession of the Holy Thursday Mass. As he receives each of the oils, the priest could place it directly in the ambry. The rubrics suggest that the oils can also be placed on a table in the sanctuary, but this could be awkward before Mass begins, since the priest would then have to make his way to the doors of the church for the entrance procession. If your church's "geography" does not make for a graceful reception of the oils, you might consider doing this optional rite at a different time, for example before or after a weekday Mass shortly following the Chrism Mass.

If your community gathers for Night Prayer, invite them (with readers and musicians) earlier for additional Eucharistic adoration. Prepare a time of interwoven Scripture and song using some excerpts from the Gospel according to John, chapters 13–17 (see *Paschale solemnitatis*, 56).

(#40)   red

FRI 30 Friday of the Passion of the Lord (Good Friday)

About Good Friday

On this day, the parish community gathers to prayerfully recall the Death of Jesus "in the hope of their resurrection" (Prayer over the People, Good Friday). Because his Resurrection is inseparable from his Death, the Lord's Passion is truly celebrated. We remember last night's words from St. Paul: "We should glory in the Cross of our Lord Jesus Christ, / in whom is our salvation, life and resurrection, / through whom we are saved and delivered."

A rubric in the Missal describes how the environment in the church expresses the somber mood of the day: the altar should be completely bare, without cross, candles, or cloths. The liturgy is to begin at three o'clock in the afternoon or later; a time before then is not envisioned. It is a liturgy consisting of three parts: the Liturgy of the Word, the Adoration of the Cross, and Holy Communion.

The liturgy may be repeated later with the permission of the diocesan bishop, and this is important. For people who work and/or who would otherwise be unable to attend the afternoon liturgy but who are looking to attend a service to mark the day, it would be preferable for them to be able to experience the liturgy of the Church. Certainly devotional celebrations such as Stations of the Cross can be scheduled on this day, but as much as possible we should be encouraging people to pray the official liturgies of the Church. Finally, there is a specific rubric mentioning that this liturgy "by its very nature" may not be celebrated in the absence of a priest; therefore, a deacon may not preside.

The Lectionary for Mass

◆ FIRST READING: Isaiah, the great prophet, speaks to his age and ours in the First Reading as he describes the experiences of the servant of the Lord. This famed passage is one of four "servant songs" in this book of Israel's prophetic literature. Many Christian and most Jewish scholars assert that at the time of its writing, the "servant" of whom Isaiah speaks is the nation of Israel. Christian have a long history of reading the narrative as a prediction of the Passion of Jesus. It is referenced in the narratives of all four Gospel writers. Isaiah, whose name means "salvation of the Lord," addresses the people as Assyria is rising as a cruel and destructive power. This remarkable passage can be divided into three parts. The opening lines speak of God's servant's appearance. Listeners are warned that how things appear is not necessarily how they are; while the servant's appearance is battered beyond recognition, he suffering will be transformed into glory. Next we hear about the purpose of the servant's suffering. His suffering is like that of Job, misunderstood by onlookers. In fact, his suffering is not the result of his own actions; rather, he has taken on the sins of the people, the onlookers who scoff. The servant's death atones for them all—through his actions, he has restored their right relationship with God. Finally, we hear of the triumph of the servant as God's exalted one. God's work has been done in and through him. His trust and surrender are rewarded profusely; his endurance and faith are vindicated by God.

◆ RESPONSORIAL PSALM 31 is a lament and also a statement of trust. The psalmist calls out to God for rescue in the face of total degradation. The vivid descriptions ("an object of reproach," "a laughing-stock," "a dread to my friends," "like the unremembered dead," and "a dish that is broken") all describe the devastation of being an outcast. This is a picture of human suffering in the most vivid terms. Still, the psalmist asserts a depth of trust in God that transcends the horrific circumstances. He affirms his faith in God, in rescue, and in blessing. On Good Friday, this psalm recalls for us the context of the words "into your hands I commend my spirit," uttered in faith by Jesus as he dies on the Cross.

◆ SECOND READING: Jesus Christ the High Priest has been given by God. No longer are ongoing sin offerings needed; unlike the human high priest of the Temple, Christ has offered himself up, once and for all people. Christ, God entering into human flesh and experience, understands all the joys and trials of human life. His followers can come to him "confidently," knowing that he sees our lives for everything that they are, and that we will receive grace and mercy. Like us in every way except for sin, Christ is now the path to salvation for those who listen to him and follow him. Jesus has become one with human struggle, and has seem human sin in its most extreme in the actions of those who have crucified him unjustly. His response is sympathy, and our response is boldness— to take ourselves to him fully, in love and obedience.

◆ GOSPEL: John's depiction of the Passion has a number of qualities that make it unique. It begins in the garden with the arrest of Jesus.

Under cover of darkness, Judas leads the soldiers and guards of the Temple to seize Jesus. Jesus, completely in control of the situation, steps forward. From the very start of the Gospel, Jesus has been aware of his divine destiny; he is the Word made flesh that came to dwell with humankind. His words to his captors are "I AM," a divine revelation that causes them to recoil from him. The protective posture he takes toward the disciples around him remind us that he is the Good Shepherd, an image used by Jesus earlier in the Gospel. He is brought to the Jewish authorities: first to Annas, who then sends him to the high priest, Caiaphas, for questioning. Jesus is composed throughout; he is at peace despite the fact that the charge against him—blasphemy—carries the death penalty.

Placed between the descriptions of his interrogation are two of the three episodes in which Peter denies that he knows Jesus. This story appears in all the Gospel accounts; here, we see the effusive, grandiose personality displayed in the foot washing reduce to fear and equivocation. Fear and frailty have overcome his commitment to witnessing, the heart of discipleship.

Jesus is then escorted to Pilate, the Roman governor of Judea. The responses of Jesus to Pilate's questioning (a dialogue unique to this Gospel) make clear the crime of which he is accused: claims to kingship (albeit not an earthly one), a political offense against the empire. However, Pilate is aware that Jesus has not led a rebellion, and falls back on his privilege of releasing a convicted criminal at Passover. The crowd choses Barabbas; boldly threatening Pilate himself—if he does not do as they demand, Pilate is "no friend of Caesar." Jesus is scourged, crowned with thorns, and taken away to be crucified.

Throughout it all, Jesus is dignified. In this Gospel account, Jesus, the Lamb of God, moves through persecution to a fate that he accepts. Embracing the Cross, he accomplishes God's plan for salvation.

Many images are juxtaposed in this Gospel: darkness versus light, belief versus unbelief; earthly kingdom versus heavenly kingdom. Probably the greatest of all is the contrast between life and death, the triumph of goodness over evil.

The Roman Missal

Just as last night's liturgy had no formal ending, so today's has no formal beginning—one liturgy flows into the next in the unity of these days. Wearing red Mass vestments, the priest and deacon simply go to the altar in silence and, after reverencing it, prostrate themselves; all others in the assembly kneel. Then, after a period of silence, the priest rises and goes to the chair. He should take care to make sure that the period of silence is noticeable. It has been said that true silence begins only when the shuffling, rustling, and other noises end, and so the priest should allow for a prolonged period of true silence on this particular day.

At the chair, the priest prays the prayer. This prayer is not a Collect, and the invitation "Let us pray" is omitted, further showing both the stark nature of this liturgy and the way this liturgy flows from the previous one. The priest has a choice from among two prayers. The first option asks God to remember his mercies and to protect his servants, because they are the ones for whom Christ shed his blood and established the Paschal Mystery. The overt use of the phrase "Paschal Mystery" is striking, and it reminds us of the total mystery we are celebrating through the Sacred Paschal Triduum. The second option asks that just as we have borne "the image of the man of earth," that is, Adam, so too, "by the sanctification of grace," may we "bear the image of the Man of heaven." Bearing the image of Christ is possible because by his Passion he "abolished the death inherited from ancient sin."

The Liturgy of the Word takes place, with the Lord's Passion read in the same way as it was read on Palm Sunday of the Lord's Passion. After the reading of the Passion, a brief homily is preached; the rubric goes on to mention that at the end of the homily "the faithful may be invited to spend a short time in prayer" (rubric 10). Certainly this day above all others calls for noticeable periods of silence.

The Solemn Intercessions follow. A deacon or lay minister sings or says the invitation while standing at the ambo. Then all pray in silence for a while, followed by the priest saying or singing the prayer with his hands extended. A rubric mentions that it is traditional for all to kneel for silent prayer after each invitation to prayer, as the deacon may add, "Let us kneel" and "Let us stand." While technically optional, one could argue a certain preference for following this tradition on this day: it highlights the solemnity of the intercessions, and the unusual gesture serves to further mark off the rites of the Sacred Paschal Triduum as rites that occur only once a year to mark our central and holiest days. A key element, however, would be to make sure the people are left to kneel silently for a long enough period of time, lest the kneeling and standing become simply a distracting (and perhaps unintentionally comical) series of down-and-up, down-and-up movements.

There are ten intercessions provided by the Missal: for the Holy Church, for the pope, for all orders and degrees of the faithful, for catechumens, for the unity of Christians, for the Jewish people, for those who do not believe in Christ, for those who do not believe in God, for those in public office, and for those in tribulation. The titles reveal the universality of these prayers as the Church expresses her concern and intercedes for the whole world. It is significant that on one of her most solemn days, the Church spends so much time pleading for the well-being of the entire world.

Following the Solemn Intercessions, which conclude the Liturgy of the Word, comes the second part of the liturgy, the Adoration of the Holy Cross. The Holy Cross is first shown, and then it is adored; there are two forms for the showing, and there are two ways that the adoration may take place.

In the first form of the showing, the deacon, accompanied by one or more ministers, goes to the sacristy and then returns in procession, accompanied by two ministers carrying lighted candles, carrying the Cross, which is covered with a violet veil, through the church to the middle of the sanctuary. There the priest receives the Cross and, after uncovering a little of its upper part, elevates it while singing the "Behold the wood of the Cross . . ." After responding, "Come, let us adore," the people kneel and adore the Cross in silence for a brief period while the priest stands and holds the Cross up. Then the priest uncovers the right arm of the Cross, again raising it, and then singing "Behold the wood of the Cross . . ." and the rest taking place as the first time. Lastly, he uncovers the Cross completely and the same sequence of events occurs. In the second form of showing, the priest or the deacon, accompanied by one or more ministers, goes to the door of the church and takes up the unveiled Cross as the ministers take up lighted candles. Then, in procession, they move through the church to the sanctuary, stopping in three locations — just inside the entrance to the church, in the middle of the church, and in front of

the entrance to the sanctuary — at which times the priest or deacon elevates the Cross, sings "Behold the wood of the Cross . . ." with all responding "Come, let us adore." A rubric states that also in this second form the people are to kneel and adore the Cross in silence for a brief moment, as in the first form.

For the Adoration of the Cross, one option is to have the priest or deacon, after carrying in the Cross, hand over the Cross to ministers to hold at the entrance to the sanctuary, or at some other suitable place, with candles placed to the right and left of the Cross. At that location, the priest celebrant, possibly with chasuble and shoes removed, approaches the Cross, followed by the clergy, lay ministers, and the faithful, all coming in procession. The sign of reverence to the Cross can be varied: a simple genuflection, a kiss, or some other meaningful gesture. Consider inviting everyone to remove their shoes before approaching the Cross; there is nothing that forbids this, and the strangeness of this gesture not only reinforces the uniqueness of the days of the Triduum, but also makes a statement about the holiness of the ground we walk in adoring the instrument of our salvation.

It is clearly stated that only one Cross should be used for adoration, so parishes should avoid using multiple crosses. When the assembly is so large that approaching individually is not feasible, a second option is given for the adoration. (It should be noted, however, that several people can approach the Cross and venerate it at the same time, to accommodate a larger number of participants. There is no need to rush this part of the liturgy, and the music that is suggested would seem to indicate that more than just a brief time should be accorded to the adoration.) In this second option, the priest, "after some of the clergy and faithful have adored"

(the Missal does not specify who these "some" are), takes the Cross and invites the people in a few words (of his own choosing — no text is given) to adore the Holy Cross, after which he holds the Cross high for a brief time while the faithful adore it in silence. The Missal suggests and gives the texts for an antiphon, the Reproaches, and/or the hymn *Crux fidelis* to be sung during the adoration; other suitable songs may be used as well, and a rubric mentions the *Stabat Mater* as another possibility, in addition to some other "suitable chant in memory of the compassion of the Blessed Virgin Mary."

When adoration is finished, the Cross is carried to its place at the altar, where it stands with lighted candles, which are placed either around the altar, on it, or near the Cross. The third part of the liturgy, Holy Communion, now begins with the altar being prepared with a cloth, a corporal, and the Missal being placed on it. While this is being done, the deacon, or, in his absence, the priest, wearing a humeral veil, brings the Blessed Sacrament from the place of repose to the altar while the assembly stands in silence. The Missal specifically notes that the deacon or priest uses "a shorter route," indicating that this is not in any way to be an elaborate procession; it is simply more of a functional bringing of the Blessed Sacrament to the altar for Holy Communion, although appropriate marks of honor for the Real Presence are nonetheless used — the humeral veil, and two ministers with lighted candles accompanying the Blessed Sacrament. As the Blessed Sacrament is placed on the altar, candlesticks are placed on or around the altar.

If the deacon brought the Blessed Sacrament to the altar, the priest goes to the altar once the ciborium is uncovered, and he genuflects upon arriving there. He then introduces the Lord's Prayer, which is prayed with its embolism and doxology, followed by a private prayer of the priest, his genuflection, and then the "Behold the Lamb of God . . ." with the response, "Lord, I am not worthy . . ." Communion is then distributed, during which Psalm 22 or another appropriate song may be sung.

When the distribution of Holy Communion is completed, the Blessed Sacrament is taken by the deacon or another minister to a place prepared outside the church. Of note here is that there seems to be a preference for the priest not to do this; if a deacon is not present, then perhaps another minister would be a more appropriate choice. No mention is made of candles accompanying the Blessed Sacrament, so this too is a simple action of returning the sacrament to its place of repose, and is in no way a procession or movement with a great deal of solemnity; this is in keeping with the tone of the day. If required, the Blessed Sacrament may be placed in the tabernacle, although it would appear the preference is to use a place outside the church.

The liturgy ends as starkly as it began. After the Blessed Sacrament has been removed, the priest prays the Prayer after Communion. Then follows a simple dismissal: the deacon or priest invites the people to bow down for the blessing, the priest extends his hands over the people, and he prays the prayer. Then they simply depart after genuflecting to the Cross. There is no procession by the ministers or the faithful; it is a simple dispersing.

After the liturgy, the altar is stripped, but the Cross remains with two or four candlesticks; people should be encouraged to pray before the Cross.

(#41)   white

Easter Sunday of the Resurrection of the Lord: The Easter Vigil in the Holy Night

SAT **31**

About Holy Saturday Morning

Christ was in the tomb; he lay in darkness in the womb of the whole world. Holy Saturday commemorates that day and has a character all its own. It is a quiet day of meditation, reflection, and anticipation, especially for the elect preparing for Baptism. Although there is much to do, don't let it just be a day for decorating the church. During the day, invite people to pray Morning Prayer and vigil in front of the crucifix in the barren church.

There is no Mass during the day, and Holy Communion may be given before the Vigil only as viaticum. Reconciliation and Anointing of the Sick may be celebrated today. Ministers to the sick should make every effort to visit the sick during Good Friday and Holy Saturday, sharing with them some of the readings and bringing the prayers of the community. During the day today we continue the Paschal fast. The elect should be fasting in preparation for their Baptism, and the faithful may join them in solidarity of spirit. This recommendation dates back to about the year 100, where it appeared in the *Didache*. Linked to the past, we continue this discipline in a prayerful spirit. The climax of the Sacred Paschal Triduum,

the Easter Vigil, begins after darkness has fallen, officially forty-five minutes after dark. You can find the exact time for the setting of the sun in your area by consulting the Navy website (aa.usno.navy.mil/data/docs/RS_OneYear.php). The Easter Vigil launches us into Easter Time, and it should not be confused with Holy Saturday itself. The color for the morning is violet.

About the Vigil

Shattering the darkness, the great Paschal candle is lit with the Easter fire, five wax nails of incense are embedded, and it becomes the symbol of the crucified Christ. The Paschal Mystery, already celebrated in various ways since the Evening Mass of the Lord's Supper, is clearly and joyfully announced from the very beginning of the Vigil liturgy. It is in the light of the Paschal candle that the liturgy continues to unfold. The Easter Vigil is the most beautiful of all liturgies. Ranking highest among the celebrations of the liturgical year, it should rank highest in the spiritual life of the parish community, not a small task in places where Christmas is considered the high point. Encourage all parishioners to take part by offering good, solid catechesis and invitations in advance. If the community has been involved in the journey of the catechumens, they will want to be present and surround them for this celebration.

The four parts of the Easter Vigil move us through a gradual unfolding of the Paschal Mystery of Christ. The great fire immediately dispels the gathering gloom. The Liturgy of the Word reveals the path of God's plan throughout salvation history. The Liturgy of Baptism draws the elect through the baptismal waters into the promise of eternal life and renews the baptismal belief of the faithful. The Liturgy of the Eucharist brings the celebration to the climax of the banquet of the Lamb, as we experience the presence of the Risen Christ in our midst.

The Missal gives several introductory and explanatory rubrics for the celebration of the Easter Vigil. Some comments about them are noted here.

This night's Vigil is explicitly described as "the greatest and most noble of all solemnities." The importance and grandeur of this evening's celebration cannot be emphasized too strongly, and parishes must resist any temptation to abbreviate the rites or to enact them in a perfunctory way. Feeble excuses such as "it's too long for the people" are in fact insulting to the people of God—their spiritual wherewithal when the rites are done in all their fullness is quite hearty; let's not shortchange the people of God on "this most sacred night."

The Vigil is to take place "during the night," so that it begins after nightfall and ends before daybreak on the Sunday. This is an absolutely crucial and nonnegotiable point, as strongly stated by PS, 78: "This rule is to be taken according to its strictest sense. Reprehensible are those abuses and practices that have crept into many places in violation of this ruling whereby the Easter Vigil is celebrated at the time of day that it is customary to celebrate anticipated Sunday Masses." The starting time, then, is to be after nightfall: thus, depending on the date of Easter and in what part of the country you live, the time will vary.

The Easter Vigil is made up of four parts: the Solemn Beginning of the Vigil or *Lucernarium*, the Liturgy of the Word, the Baptismal Liturgy, and the Liturgy of the Eucharist.

First Part: The Solemn Beginning of the Vigil or *Lucernarium*

The Vigil begins with the church in darkness. The Missal states that "a blazing fire is prepared in a suitable place outside the church," and that the people gather around the fire. The intent is clear that this is to be a bonfire, more than just a few small flames flickering from a table-top hibachi. As a later rubric describes, the blessing of fire may be adapted if difficulties arise constructing a bonfire. In such cases, the people may gather in the church as usual, and at the door of the church the rites of blessing the fire and preparing the candle take place.

The liturgy begins with the Sign of the Cross and the priest offering a greeting to the people "in the usual way," presumably using one of the liturgical greetings for Mass; unlike the Good Friday liturgy, the Easter Vigil is a Mass. The priest then instructs the people about the meaning of this night, "in which our Lord Jesus Christ / passed over from death to life," and that we keep this memorial in "the sure hope / of sharing his triumph over death / and living with him in God." The instruction may be given using the exact words in the Missal or similar words of the priest's own choosing.

The priest then blesses the fire, after which the candle is prepared. The rubric simply states that one of the ministers brings the Paschal candle to the priest; while therefore any minister may do this, perhaps it is fitting, if a deacon is carrying the candle into the church, for him to be the one to do this, in a sense taking custody of the candle. The lines of the cross, the alpha and omega, and the numerals of the current year are cut into the candle; this preparation of the candle is not optional. Thus the rite presumes that a real candle that is actually prepared in this way is used; *Paschale solemnitatis* clearly states that it "must be made of wax, never be artificial, be renewed each year, be only one in number, and be of sufficiently large size so that it may evoke the truth that Christ is the light of the world" (PS, 82).

Plastic tubes that hold oil canisters and have permanent symbols, where only the last numeral changes from year to year, should be avoided at all costs!

After the cutting of the cross and other signs have been made on the candle, five grains of incense may be inserted in the form of a cross, with the accompanying words. This part is optional.

Next the priest lights the Paschal candle from the new fire with the accompanying words sung or said. A little careful preparation and rehearsal will ensure that all goes smoothly at the beginning of the Vigil; it can become rather awkward managing the various items needed and matching the gestures to the words, and making sure all the necessary things are handy, so think this through ahead of time.

Once the candle has been lit, the procession forms. Ministers take burning coals from the fire and place them in the thurible, and the priest puts incense into the thurible in the usual way. A deacon, if present (otherwise, any other suitable minister), carries the candle. The order of procession is: first the thurifer with the smoking thurible, then the deacon or other minister with the candle, followed by the priest with other ministers, and finally the people, all carrying unlit candles. Note that the priest precedes the people, and that candles are not yet lit.

The same three stations as used for carrying in the cross on Good Friday are used again: the door of the church, the middle of the church, and in front of the altar. At each station the candle is lifted high and "The Light of Christ" is sung, with the people's response. Only the priest's candle is lit after the first "Light of Christ" and its response; then, after the second, the people's candles are lit; after the third, the Paschal candle is placed in its stand that is located next to the ambo or in the middle of the sanctuary.

The Missal is clear that it is at this time that the lights are turned on in the church, although the altar candles are not yet lit. Although there has arisen the custom of not turning the church lights on until later, usually during the Gloria, it is clear that the rubrics do not call for this. The powerful symbol of the light of the Paschal candle is being emphasized in that once it is brought into church, its brightness completely illumines everything.

With the Paschal candle in its stand, the priest goes to his chair, and after handing his candle to a minister so his hands are free, he puts incense in the thurible and blesses the incense as at Mass. The deacon asks for and receives the blessing from the priest in preparation for singing the Easter Proclamation (Exsultet). The blessing is the same one given before the Gospel at Mass, except that the words "paschal praise" are used instead of the word "Gospel." After receiving the blessing, the deacon incenses the book and the candle, and then proclaims the Easter Proclamation at the ambo or at some other lectern; the assembly remains standing and holds lighted candles. The choice as to whether to use the ambo or some other lectern can be made based on the arrangement of your church. Presumably, if the ambo were some significant distance from the Paschal candle, it might be advantageous to use a lectern that is right next to the candle.

It is possible for someone other than the deacon to sing the Exsultet, with the Missal specifically mentioning the priest celebrant or a concelebrating priest, although a lay cantor is another possibility. One presumes the decision will be made according to which person will be able to proclaim such an important piece best. Note the omission of certain lines in the case of a layperson singing the Proclamation. Immediately after the Proclamation, all extinguish their candles.

Second Part:
The Liturgy of the Word

This Vigil is referred to as "the mother of all Vigils," and so nine readings are provided, seven from the Old Testament and two from the New, an Epistle and a Gospel reading. Considering the importance of this liturgy, all nine readings should be considered, "so that the character of the Vigil, which demands an extended period of time, may be preserved." Liturgy committees and preparers, and indeed all parishioners, should understand that the solemn Easter Vigil is not just another Mass, nor is it even just "a long Mass"; it is a Vigil, and a Vigil takes time. It is part of the experience of "time outside of time," the sacred time of the Triduum that was begun on Holy Thursday night and is reaching its climax this night. Any attempts to truncate or abbreviate the experience should be avoided. The Missal is clear that using all nine readings is the norm and is preferred. Nonetheless, the Missal does admit of the possibility of reducing the number of readings "where more serious pastoral circumstances demand it." One might take special note of the deliberate use of the word "serious," which is weightier than just preference, impatience or, as noted above, a misguided sense that the people cannot handle it. In the case of a shortened Liturgy of the Word, at least three readings should be read from the Old Testament, both from the Law and the Prophets, and the accompanying Responsorial Psalms should be used; additionally, the reading of chapter 14 of Exodus and its canticle is always to be used—it cannot be omitted.

The priest gives an instruction, using the words of the Missal or his own words, to invite the people to listen to the Word of God "with quiet hearts" and reminding them to meditate on how God has saved his people throughout history and especially by sending his Son as Redeemer.

The Missal gives prayers to follow each of the Scripture readings; in some cases, the priest has a choice between two prayers.

After the last Old Testament reading, followed by its Responsorial Psalm and prayer, the altar candles are lit and the priest intones the Gloria. Since the Missal gives the notation for the priest to sing, there would seem to be indicated a preference that the priest do this. After he intones the Gloria, the assembly then takes up the hymn. Bells are rung during the hymn, but no further specification of this is given; it simply says "according to local custom," so this can be left open to the creativity of the parish—perhaps the choir rings bells, or servers, or even members of the assembly who have brought their own, or any combination or all of these! When the Gloria is concluded, the priest prays the Collect.

After the Collect, the Epistle is proclaimed. After the Epistle, all rise and the priest solemnly intones the triple Alleluia, with the Missal specifically noting that he raises the tone by a step each time, and all repeat after him. However, if the priest is not capable of singing this properly, it is possible for a cantor to do so. Incense is placed in the thurible as usual, and the deacon receives the blessing as usual. Only incense is carried in procession with the Book of the Gospels; the Missal explicitly states that candles are not used. Finally, there is a rubric stating that the homily is not to be omitted. The importance of preaching on this holiest of nights is underscored by this rubric.

The Lectionary for Mass

◆ FIRST READING: The Vigil of Easter begins in darkness liturgically and in the darkness of the wonder of the creation account of Genesis. A formless wasteland awaits the creative hand of God. All is primordial chaos waiting to be called into order. Note that this darkness is not part of what God creates; symbolizing terror and evil, its source is left in mystery.

It is worthy to note the narrative voice used in the creation account. Creation is a creative and dynamic process but also a participative one. God's actions are not done alone; rather, he invites all that he has created to join in the process of bringing forth new creations: "let the water teem" and "let the earth bring forth."

At every juncture, God observes what has been accomplished, and declares each day's effort "good." Most good in the eyes of God is the creation of humankind—made in God's image, created male and female. This sixth day of the creation receives the most in-depth description, and humankind is called to stand in dominion over all of God's handiwork. This great trust is not about enslaving the earth or using it in destructive ways.

◆ RESPONSORIAL PSALM 104: The psalmist praises what God has produced in creation. The first seven strophes of the psalm are in harmony with the seven days of creation recounted in the Book of Genesis. After the psalmist blesses God, speaking of God's as clothed in a garment of light, he offers descriptors of the wonders that surround him: the mountains, the waters, the birds, the grasses that feed cattle, and more. Witnessing the indescribable wonders of the natural world, the psalmist cannot refrain from again extolling gods "manifold" works and joining in a cry of praise and blessing with all of creation.

◆ RESPONSORIAL PSALM 33: As an alternative to Psalm 104, a different song of creation may follow the First Reading: Psalm 33. It, too, praises God for the wonders of nature. This psalm envisions that the waters of the ocean are contained as in a flask, confined as though in cellars in the deep. Notably, Psalm 33 includes morality among God's creations.

God's word is "upright," all God's works are "trustworthy," God loves "justice and right," and the earth is full of God's "kindness." Here is echoed the belief from the First Reading that what God made is "good." We praise God not just for the things that are, but for the goodness of things that are. Christians interpret one of the verses of this psalm as a prophecy for our belief in the Holy Trinity: "By the word of the Lord the heavens were made; / by the breath of his mouth all their host." In one verse we find references to the Lord, the Word, and the breath, images of the Triune God, preexisting all that is.

◆ SECOND READING: To contemporary ears, God's demand for the sacrifice of Isaac by Abraham is nothing short of horrifying. How could God, who has given this child to Sarah and Abraham late in their lives, demand Isaac's life? This passage is read in both Christian and Jewish liturgies (the Easter Vigil and Rosh Hashanah, respectively). We do not know from the account whether Isaac was a young boy or a youth; we do know he is old enough to carry wood.

Significant is the word test in the first line. Abraham has already, in effect, sacrificed his son Ishmael by driving him and his mother off into the wilderness in response to Sarah's anger.

Now God asks for the ultimate sacrifice—the death of Abraham's remaining son. One interpretation of this passage is that the test at hand is to see whether Abraham will do anything for God as his faithful servant. In fact, he binds his son and places him on the altar of sacrifice. His surrender to God is complete, and thus Isaac is spared and a ram offered in his stead.

Another interpretation is that the point of the story is that God does not, in fact, demand this sacrifice. Through the action of the angel, God stays the hand of Abraham at the critical moment to demonstrate that while God demands faith, he does not demand human sacrifice as was practiced in some other religions of the day. God's covenant with Abraham is reiterated. His descendants will be as numerous as the stars in the sky.

This story is referenced in the letter to the Hebrews. Many of the early fathers of the Church (Augustine, Tertullian, Origen, Ambrose, and others) saw in Isaac a scriptural type of Christ. The wood on Isaac's shoulders was seen as parallel to the wood that would burden the shoulders of Jesus Christ as he walked the path to Golgotha. Like Abraham and Isaac, God the Father and Jesus were seen as walking to the ultimate sacrifice, together.

◆ RESPONSORIAL PSALM 16: This psalm speaks to the trust the psalmist places in his God. No other gods will be worshipped; only the Lord, who will be set "ever before" him. The whole body is swept up in this experience. The heart is glad and the body confident.

◆ THIRD READING: The story of God's fidelity to the covenant with the chosen people now moves to an episode in the Exodus. Freed from bondage, they are on the march away from their former captors, but the Egyptian army is in pursuit. The people, in terror of being overcome by Pharaoh's soldiers, panic and accuse Moses. God responds by calling them forward, producing the miracle of the parting of the Red Sea (the text reads *yam suf*, the "sea of reeds"). Dry land appears, and the Israelites move ahead. God is manifested in this story both in the angel that is leading the people and in the column of cloud and the pillar of fire that go before them, pointing the way. Upon achieving safety, the waters close in and destroying the pursuing army. While contemporary scholars debate the precise nature of this historical event, it is perhaps more valuable to focus on the act of faith in this story. The Israelites, despite their fear, place themselves in God's hands.

◆ **CANTICLE:** Having been saved from attack, the people—filled with gratitude and joy—sing to God in this passage commonly referred to as the Song at the Sea. Not surprisingly, given the 430 years of captivity, the structure of this song reflects the Egyptian poetry of the time. The themes, however, are reminiscent of those found in the Wisdom literature, particularly the Book of Deuteronomy. This poem is believed to be one of the Bible's oldest compositions, and very likely was an independent work at some point. God's love is steadfast, as demonstrated in this salvific miracle.

◆ **FOURTH READING:** The prophet begins his exhortation by evoking a passage in Hosea wherein God casts off his bride, Zion. In fact, the wife is not abandoned. Like a loving spouse, God embraces Israel. This simile—being "like a wife forsaken and grieved in spirit" whose husband has a change of heart—underscores the irrevocable contract of God's covenant with his chosen people, Israel. God has promised from the time of Noah not to destroy the earth, and the constancy of his love is underlined. The beautiful words spoken to Israel, "my love shall never leave you nor my covenant of peace be

shaken" underpin the Church's teaching found in the Vatican II document *Nostra aetate* (NA): "God holds the Jews most dear for the sake of their Fathers; He does not repent of the gifts he makes or of the calls he issues" (see NA, 4).

◆ **RESPONSORIAL PSALM 30** offers a song of thanksgiving for being delivered from death. The voice is either that of an individual who has been cured of illness. Restored to health, the psalmist bears witness to the mercy of God. The name of God, "LORD," appears six times in the verses used at the Easter Vigil. The speaker is not content to praise God alone; all are invited to join in the hymn. The "faithful," or *hasidim*, are the keepers of hesed, the mutual covenant of love with God. The pains of life, such as weeping or anger, are momentary. The psalmist cries out in closing, asking for God's pity and help in the fight against complacency. The psalm ends as it opens, with praise and gratitude.

◆ **FIFTH READING:** In this passage, Isaiah speaks of the generosity and abundance of God. All are invited to come to the water, to the feast. The banquet that God spreads is rich and filling, a meal that gives life. In many ways, the account echoes the description of the Wisdom Woman in the Book of Wisdom, who stands at the crossroads beckoning all to come to her feast. In the context of the Easter Vigil, the themes of welcome to the water and to a table of plenty set the stage perfectly for the Sacrament of Baptism that will be received by the RCIA catechumens, and the Eucharist that will be spread for them, the candidates and all. God's ways are beyond comprehension to humans, and yet his self-gift is done through the natural world and in a manner that can be understood by every person.

◆ **CANTICLE:** The words of Isaiah are now presented antiphonally, an

appropriate response to the passage that was just proclaimed. In the face of the abundance of God's gifts, the answer is to burst forth joyfully in song with words of thanks and praise. The third verse features the phrase, "the holy one of Israel," a term used in a number of places in Isaiah. This name for God stands out among the prophets, and echoes the experience the prophet had in his vision, where the seraphim sing to God, "Holy, Holy, Holy!"

◆ **SIXTH READING:** This reading is drawn from the Book of Baruch, part of the apocrypha. While these books are not accepted by Jews or Protestants, Catholics recognized them as part of the biblical canon at the Council of Trent and they are also included in the Bible by the Greek and Russian Orthodox Churches. Baruch, believed to be Jeremiah's secretary, has stayed behind in Babylon with a community of the people of Israel after Cyrus has released them from captivity. This beautiful passage extols Wisdom. To know Wisdom is to know God, thus the powerful invitation to embrace her and to embrace God's law, the Torah.

◆ **RESPONSORIAL PSALM 19:** This beautiful prayer extols the life-giving Word of God. God's law is perfect, refreshing. It is just and fair, a source of rejoicing and enlightenment. Fear of the Lord, awe and wonder before him, is the natural response to the goodness and generosity of God. Knowing God's law and receiving it is the greatest possible gift. In this psalm, we see the Torah—the words of life in the law—as both preeminent and also central, more precious than any other part of God's creation.

◆ **SEVENTH READING:** Although the people have been scattered due to their wickedness, God is about to restore Israel. Ezekiel explains to the people that the glorious period that is about to unfold has been done for her not because of worthiness, but because of God's own character—he acts in a manner consistent with the greatness and glory of his holy name. Israel is to be restored not by virtue of her merit, but because of God's power and holiness. God will gather, purify and cleanse, and restore the people, who will receive a "new heart." The images of this passage uplift and reassure, particularly the strong assertion of the closing verse: "You shall be my people, and I shall be your God."

◆ Responsorial Psalm 42: This psalm is used when Baptisms are celebrated. Swept up in the grief that comes with separation from God, the psalmist cries out, wondering when he will go to God and see him once again. This lament is of a person who is not able to join in the Temple worship in Jerusalem. Confident, he asks God to take him to the holy mountain, God's dwelling place. To return to the altar of God is to be swept up in joy and gratitude. The themes of thirst and running streams echo the Sacrament of Baptism which is to be conferred at the Easter Vigil.

◆ Canticle: This canticle from Isaiah may be used if Baptisms are not celebrated.

◆ Responsorial Psalm 51: This psalm may be used if Baptisms are not celebrated. This penitential psalm is one of the great laments in the entire Book of Psalms. Calling out to God, the psalmist asks for a clean heart—akin to the clean heart God promises in the reading from Ezekiel. The psalmist ask for restorative action by God; in turn, he will become someone who helps others to know God's ways and return to God. The greatest offering is not a burned offering, but the transformation of the self into someone who is both humble and contrite.

◆ Epistle: Having heard of God's greatness, and Israel's return to God with all of her heart, we now hear Paul's beautiful description of who Christ is and what he has done for his followers. Baptism has truly united Christ's followers with him, not only in his life but in his full destiny. To be baptized it to have died and risen with Christ, and to share in his glory forever. To be baptized is to be set free from sin and to share in the entirety of Christ's promise. Having let go of the "old self," Christians are now empowered to live their lives for God.

◆ Responsorial Psalm/ Gospel Acclamation: This hymn of victory would have been sung by the people upon entering the precincts of the Temple. Its glorious words reintroduce the Christian community to the cry of "Alleluia!" which they have not spoken since before the commencement of Lent. Through the victory that has been achieved, the people know that they, truly, are God's chosen ones. Likewise, the Christian community, knowing what has been achieved once and for all people in Christ, raise their voices to extol the fulfillment of God's promise.

◆ Gospel: All four accounts of the Gospel message reach a climax to sound this chorus. Christ is risen! Mark opens his report of the Resurrection with a rather pedestrian statement: the women had gone shopping. The stores would have been closed for the Sabbath, but on the next day, the women bought the spices they needed to anoint Jesus. This detail reveals that they had no clue what awaited them at the tomb. To report the rising of Jesus, Mark carefully notes the rising of the sun. To help interpret the newness of the Resurrection, he says that it is the first day of the week.

The ordinariness of the story returns. The women see a large stone and wonder who will roll it

back for them. Then the women are amazed to see a young man clothed in white. They hear the most important news that has ever been spoken: "[Jesus] has been raised; he is not here." They see the empty tomb. They receive the commission to report this Good News. The young man instructs them to tell the disciples—and Peter. Apparently, Peter was going to need a special message because of his misbehavior and his doubts, but also because of his leadership among those who would hear the word. Each of us needs that from time to time. We always rely on the message of those who have received a deeper insight into their faith.

Third Part:
Baptismal Liturgy

The Baptismal Liturgy begins after the homily. The rites take place at the baptismal font, so the priest goes there with the ministers, unless there is to be a procession to the font (see below). If, however, the font is in a location where it cannot be easily seen by the faithful, then a vessel with water is placed in the sanctuary. Notice the importance given to the participation of the entire assembly—it is crucial that they be able to see what is going on. This is in keeping with the main thrust of the renewal of the liturgy.

Next the elect are called forward and presented by their godparents or, in the case of small children, are carried by their parents and godparents. It is admittedly odd that the Missal refers to them as catechumens when, in fact, the terminology used in the *Rite of Christian Initiation of Adults* refers to them as the elect. The Missal does not give any specific texts for this calling forward and presentation.

If there is to be a procession to the baptistery or to the font, it begins now, and the order of procession is clearly noted: a minister with the Paschal candle leads the procession, followed by those to be baptized and their godparents, then other ministers, the deacon, and lastly the priest. (Thus, if there is to be a procession to the font, the priest and the ministers do not immediately go there.) The Litany of the Saints, given in the Missal, is sung during the procession. Names of some saints may be added, especially the saint for whom the parish is named, and other patron saints, for example, of those to be baptized. Also, if there are candidates to be baptized, the priest adds a prayer at the end of the litany.

If there is no procession to the font, the priest addresses the assembly using the words given in the Missal, or words similar to them. The Missal provides a text not only for the case when Baptisms are to take place, but also for the case if no one is to be baptized, yet the font is still to be blessed.

There is a third possibility: that no one is to be baptized, and that no font is to be blessed. In that instance, there is no Litany of the Saints, and the Blessing of Water takes place at once.

After all have arrived at the font and the Litany ends, the priest blesses the baptismal water, with has hands extended during the prayer. The Missal gives the text of the prayer first with musical notation and then without, indicating a certain preference for singing the prayer. The prayer includes the gesture of lowering the Paschal candle into the water either once or three times and then holding the candle in the water for the remainder of the prayer, with an acclamation sung (or said) by the assembly as the candle is lifted out of the water. If no one is to be baptized and if the font is not to be blessed, there is a completely different introduction and blessing prayer for the priest to use.

When Baptisms are to take place, they take place immediately after the blessing of the baptismal water

and the acclamation of the people. The Missal first directs the priest to the appropriate ritual (that is, either the *Rite of Christian Initiation of Adults* or *Rite of Baptism for Children*) for the prescribed questions and answers concerning the renunciation of sin. There is also a mention that if the anointing of adults with the oil of catechumens has not already taken place at some point before this (that is, as part of any earlier preparatory rites), then it is to occur now. This, however, conflicts with the *Rite of Christian Initiation of Adults*, 33.7, which states that in the United States, "the anointing with the oil of catechumens is reserved for use in the period of the catechumenate and in the period of purification and enlightenment and is not to be included in the preparation rites on Holy Saturday or in the celebration of initiation at the Easter Vigil or at another time." As of this writing, this point would seem to be in need of clarification.

Next the priest questions the adults, and the parents and godparents of children, about the faith, again as indicated in the respective rites. Interestingly, the Missal admits of an option that, should the number of those to be baptized be very large, the priest may, immediately after the response of those to be baptized and the parents and godparents of children, also ask for and receive the renewal of baptismal promises of the entire assembly. Presumably, this option is offered as a way of not unduly prolonging the ritual when the numbers are large.

After the professions of faith, the priest baptizes the elect and the children (here the Missal does refer to the adults as the elect!). While no mention is made of the manner of Baptism, it would be good to reflect on what the *Rite of Christian Initiation of Adults* and *Rite of Baptism for Children* ritual books say

about the suitability of and preference for immersion.

After the Baptisms, the infants (that is, children under the age of discretion) are anointed with chrism (this is the anointing on the crown of the head, as described in the *Rite of Baptism for Children*). Next white garments are given to all the newly baptized, adults and children, followed by the lighting of the baptismal candles from the Paschal candle. The Missal states that the Rite of Ephphetha is omitted for the infants.

The explanatory rites completed, there is a procession back to the sanctuary (unless, of course, these rites have occurred in the sanctuary) in the same order as before, and with the newly baptized carrying their lighted candles. The Missal suggests singing the baptismal canticle *Vidi aquam* during this procession, or some other appropriate song.

Finally, the Missal notes that once the procession has returned to the sanctuary, the adults are to immediately receive the Sacrament of Confirmation according to the proper ritual book. (Priests who baptize an adult or a child over the age of discretion have, by law, the faculty to confirm and should do so.)

After the Rites of Baptism and of Confirmation are complete, or after the blessing of water if there have been no Baptisms, the renewal of baptismal promises for the assembly takes place. All in the assembly hold lighted candles (although it does not make sense for the newly baptized to participate in this, since they have just done so; it can be powerful for them to watch the "veteran" Catholics renew what they themselves just did for the first time). The introduction to the questions, which may be said by the priest using the exact words in the Missal or other similar words, makes reference both to the Paschal Mystery (the very meaning of what we are doing) and the fact that this celebration comes as the fruition of the Lenten observance; the reference to Lent serves to reinforce a sense of the "Ninety Days," so to speak, of Lent-Easter. Two forms of questions for the renunciation of sin are given, and then there are the traditional questions for the profession of faith, followed by a conclusion by the priest. The priest then sprinkles the assembly with the blessed water while an appropriate baptismal song is sung, perhaps the *Vidi aquam.*

A rubric indicates that during the sprinkling the newly baptized are led to their place among the faithful. In practice, the adults may need some time to put themselves together, especially if Baptism was done by immersion. Drying off, changing clothes, and getting ready to rejoin the assembly can take place in another location while the assembly renews their baptismal promises and are sprinkled, with the neophytes rejoining the assembly during or immediately after.

After the sprinkling, the priest returns to the chair and the Universal Prayer is prayed in the usual way; the Creed is omitted. The Missal makes specific mention that the newly baptized participate in the Universal Prayer for the first time; it's a significant moment for them as they exercise this important function of the priestly people of God—that of interceding for the needs of others and of the whole world—and its importance should not be lost on them or on the entire assembly.

Fourth Part: The Liturgy of the Eucharist

After the Universal Prayer, the Mass continues as usual with the beginning of the Liturgy of the Eucharist. The Missal makes specific mention of the desirability of having the bread and wine brought forward by the newly baptized adults and/or by the parents or godparents of newly baptized children. Thus

is their participation in the offering of the sacrifice for the very first time duly highlighted. Needless to say, high priority should also be given to bringing forward and consecrating all the bread that will be needed for Holy Communion; it is fitting, given the newness of life that is central to this celebration, that any consecrated bread remaining from Good Friday has perhaps been consumed, or at least, is not used for this Paschal celebration.

The Prayer over the Offerings makes yet another explicit reference to the "paschal mysteries," asking that the Lord accept our prayers along with these sacrificial offerings, so that we might be brought "to the healing of eternity" through those mysteries.

Preface I of Easter is the Preface prescribed for this Mass, and the phrase "on this night" is used. The Preface succinctly announces the Paschal Mystery: "by dying he has destroyed our death, and by rising, restored our life."

There are special inserts that are to be used in the Eucharistic Prayer; be careful, as these can be tricky because the inserts are found in the ritual Masses section toward the back of the Missal, under "I. For the Conferral of the Sacraments of Initiation; 3. For the Conferral of Baptism." Eucharistic Prayer IV would be excluded from use this night, because of its proper Preface, but Prayers I or III would be good choices (II might not be appropriate to the solemnity of the occasion, due to its brevity, although there is nothing to absolutely forbid it). Eucharistic Prayer I, the Roman Canon, has these three special inserts and proper forms: at the *Memento Domine* ("Remember, Lord, your servants"), found in the ritual Masses section; a proper form of the Communicantes, used from the Mass of the Easter Vigil until the Second Sunday of Easter, and found right within the text of

the Prayer; and a proper form of the *Hanc igitur* ("Therefore, Lord, we pray") with two variations: one variation is found right within the text of the prayer itself, used from the Mass of the Easter Vigil until the Second Sunday of Easter, and a second variation is found in the Ritual Masses section, with this second variation perhaps being a better choice for use this night if Baptisms have occurred. The inserts for Eucharistic Prayers II and III are found in the ritual Masses section and are inserted in the places as indicated in the rubrics (there is only one insert for each prayer).

The Missal reminds the priest that before the "Behold the Lamb of God . . ." he may briefly address the newly baptized "about receiving their first Communion and about the excellence of this great mystery, which is the climax of initiation and the center of the whole Christian life." Those words in and of themselves can be the basis for the priest's remarks, and one would think it most beneficial to take advantage of this opportunity to offer extemporaneous remarks to highlight this important moment in the lives of the newly initiated and of the entire community.

The appropriateness of the newly baptized along with their godparents, their Catholic parents, spouses, and the catechists, indeed, the entire assembly, all receiving Communion under both kinds is highlighted, and it is hoped that this is a common practice of the parish.

The Communion Antiphon, taken from chapter 5 of 1 Corinthians, refers to Christ as "our Passover" and enjoins us, since he has been sacrificed, to "keep the feast with the unleavened bread of purity and truth." The Prayer after Communion asks God to pour out on us "the Spirit of your love" so that the nourishment of the Eucharist might make us "one in mind and heart." Once again, unity is emphasized as the goal of receiving Holy Communion.

The text for a Solemn Blessing is given and should be used. A rubric indicates that this Solemn Blessing may be replaced by the final blessing formula from the *Rite of Baptism of Adults or of Children*; interestingly, while such a formula is given in the rite for children, there is no such formula in the rite for adults. Use of the formula from the rite for children would make sense if only children were baptized this night; otherwise, stick with the text given in the Missal. Lastly, the dismissal is chanted, by the deacon or by the priest, with the double Alleluia. This solemn dismissal is used throughout the Octave of Easter—that is, also on Easter Sunday, on the weekdays of Easter Week (within the Octave of Easter), and on the Second Sunday of Easter. It is not used, however, on the other weekdays or Sundays of Easter Time, being used again only at Pentecost.

April 2018
Month of the Holy Eucharist

(#42, or Gospel #41, or at an afternoon or evening Mass, Gospel #46)   white

 1

Easter Sunday of the Resurrection of the Lord
SOLEMNITY

About Easter Sunday

The celebration of the Resurrection of Jesus Christ continues into Easter Sunday morning. Easter Sunday marks the end of the Triduum and is the first day of the Easter Octave. The celebration of the Triduum concludes after Vespers and the great fifty days begin. Forty days of fast yield to fifty days of feast. On Easter Sunday, many of those who were present the night before return, especially the neophytes. In addition, there may be many people attending who have not been to church in a while. Have plenty of hospitality ministers to greet and seat them. Have enough seats and enough worship aids so all can participate. Insert words of welcome and a description of the parish into the worship aid or bulletin. Perhaps you will make them feel so welcome that they will return to church because of you.

It is not surprising that in many parishes some of those baptized at the Easter Vigil, those still "wet behind the ears," wake up on Easter Sunday morning and go to Mass.

Their excitement cannot be contained. If this is the case, invite the neophytes to wear the white garment donned at the Easter Vigil to Easter Sunday Mass. Some parishes celebrate the receptions into full communion and/or the completion of sacramental initiation at a Mass or Masses on Easter Sunday morning. Others schedule these events on Sundays during Easter Time. This laudable practice helps distinguish the baptized from the unbaptized at the Easter Vigil. Without the additional ceremonies, the Vigil is celebrated much more smoothly, and Easter Time, the great fifty days, then takes on the characteristic of being an extended time of initiation. Be sure to include the names of the neophytes in the Universal Prayer (Prayer of the Faithful) at the Sunday Masses on Easter Sunday and throughout Easter Time. If the parish celebrates Easter Evening Prayer, consider inviting the neophytes to that celebration.

The Lectionary for Mass

◆ FIRST READING: On Easter Sunday morning, the First Reading takes us to the home of Cornelius, a devout man who was also a Roman centurion. He has had a vision in which he has been instructed to send for Peter, who also has had a vision that calls into question the Jewish food purity rules about which animals are clean versus unclean. In this passage, we hear Peter recount the story of the life, Death, and Resurrection of Jesus Christ. While all he has accomplished has been witnessed to by the prophets, the redemption of the Risen Christ has been accomplished for all people, including the gentiles. Anyone who believes and bears witness to him will be forgiven.

◆ RESPONSORIAL PSALM 118: More verses of the song of victory, Psalm 118, are heard this morning. God's mercy is not a one-time reality; it endures across the ages.

God will protect those who believe, who are rescued through his power. The final verses (22–23), in which the rejected stone is mentioned, are recited by Jesus in reference to himself in the Gospel accounts of Matthew, Mark, and Luke. They also appear in Acts, Ephesians, and 1 Peter. Jesus has not fit the blueprint expected for the rebuilding of God's house.

◆ SECOND READING: Both of these selections for the Second Reading exhort the followers of Jesus Christ to set aside the old self and old life in favor of the new life they have been given in Christ. In the letter to the community in Corinth, Paul utilizes the metaphor of leaven. The image of yeast, a small bit of which can raise a great deal of flour, is one of the predominant images for the role of the laity in the constitutions of Vatican II. Laypeople are called, through their faith and holiness, to "work for the sanctification of the world from within as a leaven" (*Lumen gentium*, 31).

◆ SEQUENCE: The Easter sequence is sung today before the Gospel. Carefully select an arrangement that can be easily played so that the sequence leads into the Gospel Acclamation. The cantor should sing the sequence at the ambo. After finishing the text (which may also be congregational) the cantor moves to the cantor stand while instrumental music continues to be played. Once at the cantor stand, the music segues into the Gospel Acclamation. Two themes stand out in the Easter sequence, *Victimae paschali laudes*. The first is God's victory in Christ who redeems and reconciles humanity with God. The second is that of witness as it calls on Mary to proclaim the Resurrection by recounting her experience of the empty tomb. The song ends with the hopeful, joy-filled cry, "Have mercy, victor King, ever reigning!" The Easter sequence may be sung each

day of the Octave. It is required on Easter Sunday.

◆ GOSPEL: On Easter, we proclaim not the presence of the Risen Christ, but the empty tomb. Mary of Magdala, Peter, and the "other disciple whom Jesus loved" are the key characters, as is the empty tomb. Mary can only surmise that the body has been stolen as she rushes to Peter. Peter and the beloved disciple run to the tomb. The beloved disciple gets there first, but waits for Peter to arrive before entering. Both Mary and the beloved disciple seem to acknowledge Peter's priority status among the disciples. Peter arrives and enters the tomb followed by the beloved disciple. Both see the burial cloths but no body. The beloved disciple sees and believes. Peter does not yet appear to believe for "they did not yet understand the Scripture that he had to rise from the dead."

Like the disciples, we acknowledge that Resurrection belief is a mystery. Scripture continues to sustain us in that belief. The living witness of those who believe, however, concretized in lives of care, concern, and reconciliation, is the clearest proof that the Lord is risen and active among us. Let us always continue to intensify our witness to the Resurrection by continuing the Risen Lord's ministry.

The Roman Missal

The Gloria is used today, and of course, today is a day for great flourish and solemnity in the selection of musical settings.

The Penitential Act is prayed unless replaced by the rite of sprinkling. However, it is probably best to replace the Creed with the renewal of baptismal promises. The text for it is not given again at the Mass during the Day; the priest will need to refer to the text used at the Easter Vigil. If this is done, the sprinkling that follows does not replace the

Penitential Act. The Penitential Act should take place as usual.

The Collect uses the important phrase "on this day." Our participation in the liturgy on this day is our participation in the salvation won for us and made present for us; therefore, it is on this day that God, through his only begotten Son, has "conquered death / and unlocked for us the path to eternity." Therefore, we pray that "we who keep the solemnity of the Lord's Resurrection" may rise to new life through the renewal brought by the Holy Spirit.

In the Prayer over the Offerings, we express that we are offering the sacrifice by which the Church "is wondrously reborn and nourished" filled with "paschal gladness." Preface I of Easter is again, as at the Vigil, the Preface assigned for today. Because of this, use of Eucharistic Prayer IV is again precluded, and perhaps Eucharistic Prayers I or III would be better choices than Eucharistic Prayer II, given the festivity of the day. The only inserts or special forms to worry about are the "In communion with those" and the "Therefore, Lord, we pray" as indicated within the text of Eucharistic Prayer I; there are no other special inserts.

The three-part Solemn Blessing from the Easter Vigil may be used again at this Mass, and the dismissal with the double Alleluia is used, preferably sung.

Other Ideas for the Triduum

The three-day liturgy of the Triduum is the most beautiful but in many ways the most logistically complex of the entire year. Be sure to hold a training run through for all of your readers so that they are well prepared. Likewise, those who are distributing ashes, managing foot washing vessels and towels, or carrying incense on Good Friday should be given the gift of practice in advance. Expand your horizons to tap more than the "usual suspects" for these roles. Consider teens, young families, and elders. This is an ideal time to invite new participants into liturgical ministry. But bear in mind that even the best planned and practiced liturgy may have bumps. Have back up batteries, and a plan if the new fire is thwarted by weather. Emphasize in the bulletin and on the website and social media page that this is one, great liturgy but invite parishioners to join any part if they cannot be present for the entire experience.

Easter is a time when we welcome many visitors. We also may see many members that are not regularly with us on Sunday. In advance, strategize on how to handle larger numbers in the pews.

This is a good time to choose hymns that are established and familiar to most people. Be sure to have a supply of worship aids that will help people pray the prayers of *The Roman Missal*. The Paschal candle, symbolizing the light of Christ is a centerpiece throughout Easter Time. Consider offer-

ing the meaning of the symbols and dates placed on the cross to community members, or the historical significance of the use of lilies at this time of year. Eggs, a sign of spring and fertility, also feature in Easter. Inform people of the hope in Resurrection represented in the egg. The legend of Mary Magdalene and the red egg is also fascinating, and may be the origin of Easter eggs (see www.catholiccompany.com /getfed/mary-magdalene-first-easter -egg/).

RECEPTION OF THE HOLY OILS

Introduction

1. It is appropriate that the Oil of the Sick, the Oil of Catechumens, and the holy Chrism, which are blessed by the Bishop during the Chrism Mass, be presented to and received by the local parish community.

2. The reception of the holy oils may take place **before** the Mass of the Lord's Supper on Holy Thursday or on another day after the celebration of the Chrism Mass.

3. The oils should be reserved in a suitable repository in the sanctuary or near the baptismal font.

4. The oils, in suitable vessels, are carried in procession by members of the assembly.

5. The oils are received by the Priest and are then placed on a suitably prepared table in the sanctuary or in the repository where they will be reserved.

6. As each of the oils is presented, the following or other words may be used to explain the significance of the particular oil.

7. The people's response may be sung.

Reception of the Holy Oils

Presenter of the Oil of the Sick:

> **The oil of the sick.**

Priest:

> **May the sick who are anointed with this oil**
> **experience the compassion of Christ and his saving love,**
> **in body and soul.**

The people may respond:

> **Blessed be God for ever.**

Presenter of the Oil of Catechumens:

> **The oil of catechumens.**

Priest:

> **Through anointing with this oil, may our catechumens**
> **who are preparing to receive the saving waters of Baptism**
> **be strengthened by Christ to resist the power of Satan**
> **and reject evil in all its forms.**

The people may respond:

> **Blessed be God for ever.**

Presenter of the Holy Chrism:

> **The holy Chrism.**

Priest:

> **Through anointing with this perfumed Chrism**
> **may children and adults, who are baptized and confirmed,**
> **and Priests, who are ordained,**
> **experience the gracious gift of the Holy Spirit.**

The people may respond:

> **Blessed be God for ever.**

EASTER TIME

The Liturgical Time

The Meaning

THE Solemnity of Easter and its season can be incredibly sweet, literally and figuratively. Lilies grace the sanctuary, jelly beans and other candies have been given and received, and symbols like the egg and the bunny remind us of fertility and new birth. In many regions of the world, the land is greening and spring has either commenced or is around the corner.

Easter can be a good time to provide an active "come home" program for people who have stepped away from the Church. Unlike Christmas, with its frenetic preparation and busyness, Easter can feel more open and less harried. The parish community has experienced, hopefully, the journey of catechumens and candidates into full membership in the Church. If they have attended the Easter Vigil, they have experienced an important moment in the process of Christian initiation. Witnessing adult Baptism, Confirmation, and first Eucharist adds a deeper valence to the importance of this journey not only for the individuals who have participated, but for the Church as a whole. Consider using a parish program like Inviting Catholics Home or Catholics Come Home, or your individual diocesan program. It is important to be sensitive in this undertaking and to consider a structured process that is designed to cover many issues with care and consideration.

People step away from the Church for many reasons. Some seem small, but they are significant in the life of that person, such as a rude parish secretary who made getting married in the Church a chore rather than a moment of joyful inclusion. Others have been seriously wounded by the representatives of the Church, such as victims of sexual abuse and those who love them. The depth of their pain may make returning feel almost impossible. The most important people in this process are parish members who must be empowered in a variety of ways. First and foremost, they need simple training on how to invite people in a way that is comfortable for them and respectful of those with whom they are speaking. Being told "we are having an event for the fallen away" is anything but attractive, and while it may seem obvious to avoid phrases like that, people still need help in developing a new vocabulary.

Use social and print media to share the message as well. Facebook posts and Twitter tweets can be brief and engaging, inviting people to come to a "coming home" information session. Billboards, which may seem passé in this electronic age, can also be effective.

Welcome back experiences can also be framed as an "updating" for people. It is remarkable how many people operate under misapprehensions about what the Catholic Church teaches due to outdated catechesis or misguided representations from film or television.

One of the groups that may also be in need of a welcoming, evangelizing message are the households on the parish rolls who do not attend Mass regularly. Sadly, many of these folks have children in religious education but do not find time to participate in the Sunday Eucharist. As with those who have taken a longer break from being with us, we need to handle these households sensitively. All sorts of things intrude on Sundays. Perhaps the adults in the household don't see eye to eye about attending Mass. Or maybe someone is working multiple jobs and Sunday is literally their only day of rest. Staying open and supportive is best.

We do well when we bring the same love and enthusiasm to those that are set apart from the community as did Jesus. His interest in and welcome to Zacchaeus, Levi (later Matthew), the Syrophoenecian mother, the Samaritan woman at the well, and other marginalized people in the Gospel accounts can be our example.

The Lectionary for Mass

"**W**HY are you standing there looking at the sky?" (Acts of the Apostles 1:11).The two men dressed in white garments pose this question to Apostles in the First Reading from the Acts of the Apostles on the Solemnity of the Ascension of the Lord. The question of the men dressed in white is a question for all who prepare the liturgies, reflect on the Lectionary readings, and embrace the truth of Easter Time that Christ is alive, not dead, and is present among us through the Holy Spirit. The readings of Easter Time remind us that God raised Christ from the dead, he has ascended to the heavenly throne and sits at the Father's right hand, and he will return again in glory. Ours is the task in the interim before Christ returns to witness, to testify, to proclaim the Gospel, to live the Good News of healing and hope as the disciples and Apostles, and all those who belonged to the early Church did.

The First Readings for both the weekdays and Sundays of Easter Time come from the Acts of the Apostles. We follow the development of the early Christian communities as leaders such as Peter, John, Stephen, Philip, Paul, Barnabas, Timothy, and Silas preach the Gospel of new life in Christ despite persecution, imprisonment, and trials before the Sanhedrin. We hear of unexpected conversions not only of Paul, who previously had persecuted Christians, but also of Paul's jailer, and Crispus and his household. Gamaliel, a Pharisee in the Sanhedrin, surprises us with the manner in which he stands up to the ruling council, telling its members that if the witness of Peter and the other Apostles indeed comes from God, the Pharisees and Sadducees will not succeed in destroying it.

The readings from Acts chronicle the ministry of the Apostles and followers of the Way as it extends from the Jews to Gentiles. We learn how the early community of believers held everything in common and how it was of one heart and mind in the Risen Lord. Even the question of which, if any, of the Jewish laws new Gentiles believers would have to abide by to become members of the Christian community did not fracture the fledgling Church. So united was the witness of early believers to the Resurrection, through their leaders and representatives they worked together to come to a decision on the question of how to incorporate Gentiles into their Churches.

Praise and thanksgiving mark the tone for the majority of Responsorial Psalms during Easter Time. We sing of the Lord's goodness (Psalm 89) and affirm the Christ risen from the dead as the stone rejected by the builders who is now the cornerstone (Psalm 118:22). The psalms themselves paint the picture of the Lord's reign extending to the ends of the earth—he reigns both in heaven and on earth. We pray to the Lord to keep us safe (Psalm 16), knowing that we, like the Apostles will suffer for our faith. Ours is the longing to dwell in the Lord's house (Psalm 27) and for the Lord's mercy (Psalm 33), for we desire a home with the Father whose Son he raised from the dead. For his Resurrection and the gift of new and eternal life, we praise the Lord in our assemblies, the assemblies of his people (Psalm 22).

The message of love—of God and of one another—in the Second Reading, from the First Letter of St. John, seems simple enough this Easter Time. Yet is it really? The passages from the first of the three Johannine epistles challenge us to love in word and in deed, to not only say we follow God's command, but to also believe in his Son, and to live out our belief in our actions. While often brief, the Second Readings from 1 John will leave us and our liturgical assemblies with much to ponder about how we will go forward in love to live as God's children in the world.

It's almost as if we do not want the Octave of Easter to end, as day after day the Lectionary provides us with a Gospel reading that recounts a post-Resurrection appearance of the Risen Christ. We can imagine ourselves in the place of those who encounter the Risen Christ near the empty tomb, on the road to Emmaus, at the shore of the Sea of Tiberias, and behind the locked doors. The Gospel passages the Lectionary provides call us to trust in the peace of the Risen Lord. Truly he comes to offer the disciples and us the gift of his peace and mercy. We only need believe once again this Easter Time as we hear Jesus' offer of peace multiple times, including on Divine Mercy Sunday, the Second Sunday of Easter.

After the Easter Octave, the weekday Gospel readings come almost solely from John's account of the Good News. As we move forward in his Gospel account, we wonder with Nicodemus about what it means to be "born from above," we hear of God's great love for the world, and for his Son. If we believe in Jesus, we will have eternal life—the gift of Easter. By the fourth and fifth weeks of Easter Time, we hear of the marvels of Jesus: he feeds thousands on a pittance of five loaves and two fish and walks on water. In the Gospel passages, Jesus self-identifies through "I Am" statements as the Bread of Life, the Gate, and the Way, the Truth, and the Life. On Good Shepherd Sunday, the Fourth Sunday of Easter, Jesus' words announce he is the Good Shepherd. On the Fifth Sunday of Easter, he states he is the True Vine and the Father, the Vine Grower. There is really nothing more for which his disciples or us could ask.

Yet during the final weeks of Easter Time we, along with Jesus' disciples, learn we must let go. The Lectionary gives us beautiful passages from Jesus' prayer for his disciples in the Gospel according to John. Jesus prays to his heavenly Father for his disciples, his friends. He knows their road will be arduous, because they remain in the world. He wants the Father to keep them safe and make them holy. In many of the Gospel readings, we hear Jesus explain to his disciples that the Father will send the Advocate, the Holy Spirit, to be with them, to continue to teach them and guide them. Most of the time, the disciples do not fully understand what Jesus tells them, but Jesus consoles as he reminds them the Advocate will companion them in the truth.

On the Solemnity of the Ascension, Jesus commissions his disciples. "Go into the whole world and proclaim the gospel to every creature" (Mark 16:15). By virtue of our Baptism, this is our commission as well as that of the first disciples. The Gospel for the Vigil of Pentecost proclaims the flowing of living waters, while the Gospel for Pentecost during the day speaks of the coming of the Spirit of Truth, the Advocate.

The Spirit will be with us as we live as followers of the Risen Christ in the time before he comes again in glory. When we sing the refrain of Psalm 104 at the Pentecost Vigil and on Pentecost Sunday, we pray, "Lord, send out your spirit, and renew the face of the earth." The Lord's is the Spirit who will lead us to believe, to follow the command of love so that the world might see the fruits of the Spirit in action—the fruits of "love, joy, peace, patience, kindness, generosity, faithfulness gentleness, self-control" (Galatians 5:23). The Second Reading at the Pentecost Vigil reminds us of these fruits.

The Lectionary readings for Easter Time shows us that we are Christ's friends as his disciples were. Sts. Stanislaus, Mark, Athanasius, Philip, James, and Mathias are saintly friends who offer encouragement as we delve deeper into the mystery and reality of our Easter faith. We are Easter friends to one another and to the world. Our friendship with the Risen Lord and one another we enact as we embrace our mission — as we testify and witness — as we extend the Gospel to the ends of the earth, and as we affirm the gift of eternal life that is ours in Jesus. We know Christ reigns with the Father in heaven, but we do not want to remain looking at the sky for too long. Our work now is to spread the Gospel, to proclaim the saving power and glory of God, to go forth in mission. Eternal life is God's promise to us through his Risen Son, the Son who nourishes us with the Bread of Life each time we celebrate Mass. Go forth in the peace of Christ, Easter friends. Your joy will be complete!

The Roman Missal

Every Sunday is a celebration of Easter, and the entire cycle of the liturgical year is one celebration of the Paschal Mystery. Still, we can call Easter Sunday the "Sunday of Sundays." As the Missal reminds us, the entire season of Easter, from Easter Sunday, through the Ascension of the Lord, to Pentecost Sunday is "one 'great Sunday'" (UNLY, 22). This Great Sunday proclaims joy for our life in Christ, victory over sin and death, and a resounding Alleluia! As we pray in the Collect for the Third Sunday of Easter, "May your people exult for ever, O God . . . / so that, rejoicing now in the restored glory of our adoption, / we may look forward in confident hope / to the rejoicing of the day of resurrection."

This is the season when we pull out all the stops (literally and figuratively): music is joyous and the adornment of our liturgical spaces can be appropriately extravagant. Vesture is white, and in the United States it can also be gold or silver. There are five Prefaces for Easter. Preface I of Easter is used on Easter Sunday (as at the Easter Vigil), and through the Octave of Easter, including the Second Sunday of Easter (Divine Mercy Sunday). From the Monday after the Second Sunday of Easter up to the Ascension of the Lord, any of the Easter Prefaces may be used. On Ascension there are two Prefaces to choose from. After Ascension through Pentecost any of the Easter and Ascension Prefaces may be used, and, of course, for Pentecost, we use its proper Preface, "The Mystery of Pentecost." Whenever we use the Roman Canon (Eucharistic Prayer I), it is important to use the proper forms of the *communicantes* and *hanc igitur*, where this is indicated in the Missal. Take care to use the appropriate prayers on the days surrounding the Ascension, which vary according to whether it is celebrated on Thursday or the following Sunday. The rubrics in the Missal are complicated but clear in this regard. The twofold Alleluia is sung from Easter Sunday through the Second Sunday of Easter, and then again at Pentecost. Similarly, the Easter sequence (*Victimae Paschali Laudes*) should be proclaimed on Easter Sunday and may also be proclaimed each day of the Octave, including the Second Sunday of Easter. On Pentecost Sunday, its squence (*Veni, Sancte Spiritus*) must be proclaimed. These texts should be sung if at all possible, which will require a lot of practice. To conclude Easter Time as joyously as possible, it is a good idea to use the new extended form of the vigil for Pentecost.

Children's Liturgy of the Word

Easter Time resounds with the joy of the Resurrection! For seven weeks leading up to the Solemnity of Pentecost we proclaim the Risen Christ and hear stories of the beginning of the Church. The Lectionary readings include many visual images that will resonate with children. If you have older children who participate in the Liturgy of the Word or serve as assistants and are strong readers, consider asking them to proclaim one of the readings other than the Gospel. Make sure to give them the reading well ahead of time so they can practice and learn how to pronounce any challenging words, names, or places.

Many parishes offer children's Liturgy of the Word on Easter Sunday. If this has not been your practice, discuss the possibility with your team and pastoral staff. If you choose to celebrate the Word with children on Easter Sunday prepare yourself and the liturgical space for a larger number of children than usual. When the priest celebrant invites the children forward ask him to welcome those children who are visiting on Easter.

New children might be reticent to participate, so welcome their parents to come with them.

The liturgical color for the Easter Sunday and the following six Sundays is white (gold and silver may also be used). On the Solemnity of Pentecost the color changes to red. The principles for decorating the environment for the liturgical space for the celebration of the Word with children follow those for the main assembly space. An Easter lily or two is a must in the space for as long as possible throughout Easter Time!

The Lectionary provides separate sets of readings for the Pentecost Vigil on Saturday and for the Masses during the Day on Pentecost. Check with your director of liturgy or pastor regarding the readings that will be proclaimed. If you provide the Liturgy of the Word with children on the eve of Pentecost, use the vigil readings if those are the readings the main assembly will hear. Also, discuss an arrangement of the Pentecost sequence that would be suitable for children. Easter Sunday also includes a Sequence before the Gospel Acclamation. Make a similar decision with regard to this sequence as for Pentecost.

In terms of the Lectionary readings, you will also want to coordinate with the director of liturgy or pastor on the Solemnity of the Ascension of the Lord. Find out whether your diocese celebrates this solemnity on a Thursday as a Holyday of Obligation or transfers its celebration to the Seventh Sunday of Easter. This is important so that the children hear the appropriate readings proclaimed and the readings that are consistent with the main assembly.

Let the Easter Alleluias resound throughout the season. Often parishes will have a trumpet player or other instrumentalist who could augment the Easter joy by contributing his or her musical talents. High school youth frequently have the capability to play the refrain for the Gospel Acclamation in tune and with the correct rhythm and intonation. Check with your music director to see if an instrumentalist might be available and willing to play the Gospel Acclamation with the children especially on Easter Sunday and Pentecost, but perhaps throughout Easter Time. Give them the music well ahead of time to practice. See if the music director is willing to work with him or her. Decide whether you will repeat the Gospel Acclamation after the proclamation of the Gospel in accord with the practice of the main assembly. Ask the children about the meaning of "Alleluia" and why we sing "Alleluia" again during

Easter Time. As with Christmas Time, wish the children a "Happy Easter" on each of the Sundays of Easter Time.

The Saints

EASTER Time is a fifty-day prolongation of the Easter festival. It consists of a couple of parts, and understanding those parts helps to understand how our celebration of this central mystery of Christianity relates to our memory of the remarkable women and men of Christian history. The center of the liturgical year is the Sacred Paschal Triduum, the three-day long liturgy that extends from the Holy Thursday Evening Mass of the Lord's Supper through Good Friday to the Easter celebration that runs from Holy Saturday evening into Easter Sunday. The second part is the "octave" or eight-day extension of Easter that runs through Second Sunday of Easter (April 8). Each of the days of the Triduum and the Octave take precedence over everything else on the calendar. After the Octave is over, the calendar returns mostly to normal, except that the Sundays of Easter, as reflections of the principle feast, also take precedence over other celebrations (that is, ritual Masses cannot be celebrated on Easter Sunday). What this means practically is that celebrations of the saints that would normally fall on the days taken over by Holy Week, the Triduum, or the Easter Octave are not celebrated. If those days are solemnities, like the Annunciation this year, they are transferred to the first available day, that is, the Monday of the Second Week of Easter (April 9). Because the feasts of the patron saint of a parish or diocese are solemnities for those places, (for example, St. Isidore of Seville parish; his feast is usually April 4) and is then transferred to the first available day.

Every season colors how we remember the saints whose feast days fall within it. During Easter Time, it might be particularly good to thank God for the witness to the Resurrection that saints have provided. This is of many different kinds: St. Mark (April 25) wrote a Gospel account, while St. Anselm (April 21) and St. Catherine (April 29) taught the Church how to believe in the Risen Christ. St. Damien Joseph (May 10), showed us the power of the Resurrection in his work in a leper colony in Hawaii, as Pope St. John I (May

18) did through his martyrdom. The Church sees the Risen Christ working in his Body, especially through the saints who give their lives in many different ways, but for the one Lord.

The Liturgy of the Hours

WHAT better time to offer praise and thanks? Since Easter is April 1 this year, in some of our colder climates the weather may or may not cooperate with our internal joy. This too is blessing. Resurrection is real, no matter the externals. Whether the day is warm or a late snow storm arrives, it is still Easter. The unexpected is part of the message of the season. Certainly the women were anticipating to anoint a body, not find an empty tomb.

Our prayer is like that too, filled with the unanticipated presence of God. While the words for Liturgy of the Hours are right in front of us, on our tablet or in a book, the Spirit has more in mind. There is a certain reluctance on some people's part to use a "prayer book." It seems old fashioned and obsolete. However, nothing is farther from the truth. By giving ourselves the gift of not planning, not being in control, we give God a rightful place. We let God take charge and speak to us from texts prayed over the years all over the world. As Easter is celebrated again and again, year in and year out, so too does the Lord breathe new life into us each year. It is time for something ever ancient and ever new. Eternal truth is eternal, yet takes on new form in every age.

So we open our hearts and minds in Easter joy! The Alleluia is back! Even if we pray independently at home, sing, or at least put on some Easter music that enlivens your heart. Remember, it's a joyful noise that we are told to make and to the play before the Lord.

As in the Christmas season, during the Octave, the psalms are taken from Sunday Week I. Each day of this first week is Easter Sunday all over again. Note that the Solemnity of the Annunciation will be on April 9. If you are using a nondigital breviary, go to the prayers for March 25.

There are a number of opportunities during Easter Time to celebrate the Liturgy of the Hours in common, even if in an abbreviate form. How do you end the catechetical season? Gather the children, catechists, and parents if possible in Church. Make sure the Paschal candle is lit. Hopefully, a music minister is available. There are a number of settings of the Psalter with which the children should be familiar.

The same applies as we make ready those celebrating Eucharist for the first time or perhaps our Confirmation candidates. Whenever we bring groups of children and adolescents together in prayer, it is right for them to take on liturgical roles, especially so in the Liturgy of the Hours. Try to make sure they understand they are serving God and others. This is not the time for one more photo op or a reward for some who have earned the right. It is their right and responsibility by their Baptism. Yet we need to honor that not all of us have been given the same gifts. A younger person is capable of proclaiming the Word to their peers, but they should be able to be understood. Perhaps a group can provide ideas for a short preaching. Remember, a priest or deacon is not required to lead this prayer. Even if the pastor is available, the director of the program or a catechist can function as a presider. What would it say to your community if the pastor sat with the community and another person led this prayer?

The Rite of Christian Initiation of Adults

THE beginning of Easter Time is also the beginning of the fourth period of the Rite of Christian Initiation of Adults. Regarding this Period of Mystagogy, the rite says, "This is a time for the community and the neophytes together to grow in deepening their grasp of the Paschal Mystery and in making it part of their lives through meditation on the Gospel, sharing in the eucharist, and doing works of charity" (RCIA, 244). Notice that this is a period for all for all the baptized and the goal is to deepen everyone's knowledge of the life, Death, and Resurrection of Christ. This is the period of ongoing conversion— of falling in love with Christ over and over and over. It is this love, this union, which moves each of us to act within the world.

The process of mystagogy is not attending a weekly "class," or signing up for a particular ministry in the parish or even attending one or two socials. Mystagogy is a lifelong process, in which the baptized are invited to break open their experiences of participating in the sacraments. Reflecting on the experience of receiving the sacraments (the smell of chrism, gasping for air coming out of the font, the taste of the Eucharistic bread and cup) opens our hearts and minds to God's grace in our lives. It deepens our knowledge of God and draws us deeper into the heart of Christ.

People often ask how one does mystagogy. The work of mystagogy is the work of engaging one's own spiritual life through reflection on the Gospel, celebrating eucharist, and doing works of charity. "Its main setting is the so-called Masses for neophytes . . . the Sunday Masses of the Easter season" (RCIA, 247). The Sunday Mass is so important in nurturing the life of the neophyte and the whole Body of Christ that the rite even says, "Special places in the congregation are to be reserved for the neophytes and their godparents" (RCIA, 248). This directive demonstrates that mystagogy unfolds in the midst of the assembly where the Word is proclaimed and the Eucharist shared. The encounter with the Risen Christ at Mass rouses our hearts so that upon leaving the worship space and being filled with compassion, we reach out to the poor and marginalized, those suffering or in need of reconciliation. In turn, our encounter with "Christ of the Streets" leads us back to worship to encounter once again God's gift of love.

The US *National Statutes for the Catechumenate* state that postbaptismal catechesis "should extend until the anniversary of Christian initiation, with at least monthly assemblies" (NSC, 24). One way to sustain these monthly assemblies is to engage the entire parish in mystagogy. Since mystagogy is not a class, consider developing a parish team that creates opportunities for prayer and fellowship (for example, *lectio divina*, Liturgy of the Word, Taizé) each month, paired with a parish potluck. Specifically, during Easter Time, the parish can celebrate Paschal or Baptismal Vespers. This Evening Prayer includes processions, a sprinkling rite, and an opportunity to reflect on the sacraments received at the Vigil. There are a few resources available. This could be an opportunity for the whole parish to deepen their knowledge of the Paschal Mystery and continue to unpack their experience of partaking in the sacraments and sacramental life of the Church. Finally, the bishop, if he is unable to celebrate the sacraments of initiation with the new members should gather

them for Mass and a social so he can get to know the flock. The cathedral may even consider celebrating Paschal Vespers where the bishop preaches a mystagogical homily with the neophytes, godparents, and the whole Church gathered.

The Sacraments of Initiation

ONE of the central motifs of Easter Time is the new life of Baptism. Through Baptism, we come to share in the life of the Risen Christ. Baptisms often take place during Easter Time, and the Rite of Blessing and Sprinkling of Water frequently replaces the Penitential Act at the beginning of Mass.

Parishioners renew their baptismal commitments in the Rite of Sprinkling. The Gospel readings unpack the meaning of the Easter event and help the assembly to celebrate and remember that what God the Father did in his Son Jesus is being done in our lives today. The period from Easter Sunday to Pentecost is the ideal time to celebrate the Sacraments of Initiation in the midst of the assembly.

Work with the liturgy and music directors to emphasize the Rite of Sprinkling and the renewal of baptismal promises at the Masses where Baptism, first Eucharist, and Confirmation are celebrated. Parishes have varied practices for the celebration of first Holy Communion. Some celebrate in a large group and others celebrate individually with families or throughout Easter Time with smaller family groups. If at all possible do not celebrate first Holy Communion at a Mass separate from the Sunday assembly. A "first" Eucharist is the first time a person shares fully at the table, and this should happen on Sunday, the Day of the Lord, when the community gathers for the central act of worship. To separate them from the assembly does not make good liturgical sense.

Prepare the celebration(s) with the liturgy and music directors. If you have a large number of children celebrating, you may want to look at the relevant directives in the *Directory for Masses with Children*. This directory is available in the first volume of *The Liturgy Documents* from Liturgy Training Publications. Since initiation is a call to mission, develop a specific final blessing and dismissal that explicitly includes the first communicants.

Since most Confirmations are presided over by the bishop, it is not always possible to celebrate during Easter Time, but it is appropriate if possible to arrange it.

During the week before Pentecost or the week before Confirmation, plan an afternoon or evening of reflection with the Confirmation candidates and their sponsors on the theme of being anointed for service as an element of initiation into the Christian community.

The Rite of Penance

THE Great Fifty Days turns our minds and hearts to the new life of the resurrection. While Lent is our high penitential season, mercy is part of the daily life of Christians.

The Second Sunday of Easter is also the Sunday of Divine Mercy. How shall you celebrate? Depending on the number of priests in your parish, consider a dialogue with neighboring parishes. The burden in the joy of doing Triduum well can be exhausting for both clergy and lay ministers. Sharing the work of Penance celebrations for the Divine Mercy Novena may be the answer.

How does your parish celebrate Easter? For many this is a time for First Communions. What does the immediate preparation look like? Is there a time for a celebration of Penance with the children? Avoid putting it too close to Eucharist. Neither sacrament should get overlooked. The *Rite of Penance* has suggestions for use with young people. Maybe slightly older children can help design an appropriate examination of conscience.

They have insights into language that speaks to younger children as well as possible occasions for sin. If the sacrament is to reach children well, teens and even middle school age children have many ideas that can guide adults. Another helpful resource is your parish's faith formation textbooks and website. They also offer examples of services with children.

What about the parents? As first teachers of their children, have we given them opportunities to model this sacrament? Inviting families to celebrate together is one option. If you're having whole families individually confess sin and receive absolution, make sure you consider the amount of time appropriate and the resources you have. One priest and a large number of family members may make it too long for children.

Another option is to have a unique communal celebration designed keeping these parents in mind. Again, invite others who "have been there" to guide the selection of appropriate music, readings, and give ideas for the examination of conscience. Make sure the examination of conscience and preaching are geared to the real life of parents in your community. Be careful to keep the power of this season balanced with the need of mercy and forgiveness. We have moved on from Lent. Our liturgies should feel like it.

Easter is also often a time for Confirmation. At what age is this celebrated in your diocese. For children or teens, be aware if they have yet celebrated Penance for the first time. If not, how should they be prepared? A good understanding of sin, sinfulness, and social sin—as well as the power of mercy is needed in our culture. Penance as a sacrament allowing us to live in the freedom of God's children is a powerful witness for Easter. This is especially true as we make ready our confirmation candidates. Reflect on how Penance interfaces with your program of preparation for Confirmation.

Do you have adults, those already baptized and sharing in Eucharist, who are now preparing for Confirmation during this Easter Time? Have they yet celebrated Penance or done so recently? This may also be a great opportunity to reach out to neighboring parishes and share a communal celebration. Always keep in mind those who are gathering and the season. Penitential liturgies need to reflect what we are celebrating on Sunday.

The Order of Celebrating Matrimony

EASTER Time is usually a very busy time sacramentally. With our very early Lent, Pentecost is May 20. Many weddings, therefore, will probably take place during the Ordinary Time.

Is there a pattern established in your parish for when sacraments of initiation are celebrated during Easter Time? For example, are the first celebrations of Eucharist scheduled for the third week of Easter? Or are infant Baptisms normally on the Second or Sixth Sunday of Easter? In any case, make sure that all the sacramental moments in the life of the parish are on the calendar. Be aware of the time commitments and recovery needs of not only the priests and deacons, but also the music ministers, pastoral ministers, faith formation directors, maintenance staff, and hospitality coordinators.

It is in this context that we celebrate weddings. We expect to be busy during Easter, but there is no need to overschedule. The couple rightly expects the music minister to be fresh and exuberant and the presider to have a wonderful homily ready. Ministers, ordained and lay, are human and Easter can be an exhausting time. Look at the whole picture and appropriately place weddings on the calendar.

Does your parish have wedding coordinators? This is a wonderful ministry. It can help take a burden off the staff as well as demonstrate the love and support of the parish for the couple. This is a great way for whole families to get involved. Parents can coordinate the rehearsal and help direct the bride and groom, while younger children may be altar servers. However, if you do have volunteers coordinate the rehearsal and work with couples, be sure that they are trained and well-versed with the Catholic rituals surrounding Marriage.

Take some time to reflect on how your parish organizes the rehearsal. What is the expectation? Why do we have one? Practically, the most difficult part may be the Entrance Procession. Once that is completed, nervousness wanes a bit and the liturgy begins to flow smoothly. Of course the vows (consent) themselves can be a bit nerve wracking for the couple. In the meeting at which the final liturgical decisions are made, it can be helpful to provide the couple with a completed "order of service" as well as a short list of expectations for the rehearsal.

When all the participants have arrived for the wedding rehearsal, a simple prayer will help all to direct their hearts, minds and energy to the real reason they have gathered: the work and call of God in the lives of the couple. It may be in the context of this prayer that some of the cultural requests of the bride and groom that are not appropriate for the wedding liturgy can be honored. The pouring of sand, lighting of extra candles or painting a common picture, while not fitting for Mass, can be included in the prayer this evening.

Make sure an appropriate time is spent both in prayer and in practicing for the liturgy. Do not neglect the readers and Communion ministers who will also need some time to feel comfortable in their roles. Even if they minister in their own parish, placement, the presider's instructions, microphone usage, and so on, should be discussed.

The Pastoral Care of the Sick

THE rites of the *Pastoral Care of the Sick* are firmly rooted in the theology of the Paschal Mystery. As the Church continues to celebrate the life, Death, and Resurrection of Christ during Easter Time she does so with thanksgiving for the redemptive grace of Christ's sacrifice and for the outpouring of a new life of freedom and mercy through his Resurrection.

In the Gospel readings for Easter Time, we encounter the remarkable words and gestures of Jesus as he assures us of the love of the Father. His greeting of peace to the disciples (Second and Third Sundays) is passed on to us in the words and gestures of the Eucharistic liturgy. No matter what our situation in life we yearn for the peace that only the Lord can give.

On the Fourth and Fifth Sundays we hear two of the "I am" statements from John's Gospel account. The image of Jesus as the Good Shepherd (Fourth Sunday) brings great comfort us whenever we encounter brokenness in our lives. On the Fifth Sunday we are reminded that Jesus is the vine and we are the branches. He is the source of our life and the strength that we need to bear fruit as disciples. The message for us on the Sixth Sunday is simply this, "As the Father loves me, so I also love you."

Celebrating the Sacrament of the Anointing of the Sick during Easter Time affirms the ministry of the Church as the ministry of Christ at work in the world. The pastoral notes for the *Pastoral Care of Sick* state that this ministry is the common responsibility of all Christians. Parishes are encouraged to explore various ways of reaching out to those who are sick.

Pastoral care ministers take up their ministry on behalf of the whole parish, but others could be encouraged to join this ministry or to offer a "ministry of accompaniment" from time to time. This might include accompanying the priest or pastoral visitor to residences and hospitals where there are a number of sick persons. In addition to the few moments that elapse for the actual rite, whether for Communion or an Anointing by a priest, some time could be spent simply visiting with the person who is sick. Sharing stories about the life of the parish, reading Scripture passages, or passages from their favorite book, assisting them to take a walk, if they are able, are some ways to accompany them, as a good shepherd might for those who need a gentle touch in life.

During this time of the year many parishes focus on recruitment of new members for their ministry teams and offer opportunities for ongoing formation of those who are already active in their respective ministries. Such efforts find an obvious link with the readings from the Acts of the Apostles, the source of the First Reading for the Sundays of Easter Time. Many of these passages speak of how the early Christian communities developed ways to take care of their brothers and sisters, thus offering the Church today a worthy example of ministry. The early communities were especially concerned for those who were often left aside, widows and orphans, the poor and the sick.

Today the Church has many ministries and agencies that can respond to the needs of many people. We are all called to continue our efforts to bring the healing and merciful love of the Lord to all those who are members of the Body of Christ.

The Order of Christian Funerals

Funeral liturgies in Easter are ritually powerful moments. The symbols of Christ's triumph over sin and death are everywhere. The white of the vestments and pall are echoed throughout the church. Preaching during this season has many clear options: renewal, spring time, the conquering of darkness by the light of Christ. Baptism and the newly blessed water are front and center.

How do you celebrate the Introductory Rites? Is the family already seated, or are they able to witness the "sprinkling with holy water"? Consider having at least the immediate family present around the font, especially if it takes place at the entrance to the church. Then they can accompany the casket with the pall bearers in the procession.

It is important for them to see this action and hear the ritual words. There is no need for any further explanation here.

How much water do you use? While pouring a huge amount may be impractical, it should be clear that water is falling on the casket. Does your aspergillum need to be cleaned or replaced? The brush style usually displaces more water. If the funeral takes places with cremated remains, this sprinkling is also to take place (see OCF, 433). Note that there is no pall in this case.

The ritual envisions that the Paschal candle is in proximity to the casket. Where is it in your sanctuary? During Easter the immensity of the light of Christ both guiding the deceased and overpowering death is a wonderful visual for the assembly. This too may be part of the homily.

While we are surrounded by symbols of the Resurrection and Easter joy, we must yet be careful. The family of the deceased could be in great pain. This does not mean we change the environment, but rather we are even more sensitive to the assembly gathered. Help them to recognize the truth of the message, even if emotionally they are far from joy. As the hymnist writes, "No storm can shake my inmost calm." We can put the family in touch with this calm, even if they are as yet in great sorrow. This is the truth of the message too: faith is more than emotion. It is our rock and fortress.

Remember to use the prayers for the Easter Season, C in *The Roman Missal*. Consider also Preface I, which speaks strongly of resurrection.

If you are reserving the choice of the Gospel to the preacher, look to the Sunday Gospel accounts of Easter Time or the stories of the Resurrection. We can never hear these too many times. Often families are so caught up in remembering their beloved dead, that they may lose sight of the praise and thanks to God of the liturgy. The stories of Resurrection, so clearly tied to the story of salvation, can help move them out of their insulated musings and forward to healing in the truths of faith.

Easter music is also a wonderful choice for funerals. There are many powerful hymns of this season. If the family is choosing some of the music, then have a seasonal entrance or dismissal. "The Strife Is O'er," "Jesus Christ Is Risen Today" or "Sing With All The Saints in Glory" are some examples. The psalm as well could be the seasonal one used in the parish, such as an arrangement of Psalm 118.

The Book of Blessings

As at Christmas Time, homes are traditionally blessed during Easter Time, so celebrating the Order for the Blessing of Homes during the Christmas and Easter Time (see BB, chapter 50) is most fitting. There is a longer and a shorter form, both of which take place within the home to be blessed. Take care to select the options in the rite most suitable to Easter Time. A priest, deacon, or layperson may lead the blessing.

Mother's Day, since it always falls on a Sunday in Easter Time (second Sunday of May), has long been commemorated in many churches in the United States, often with a blessing and a flower for each mother present. The Order for the Blessing of Mothers on Mother's Day (see BB, chapter 55) is not a full rite of blessing, but rather a set of three adaptable intercessions to be added to the others of the day, along with a Prayer over the People, which on this day can replace the Solemn Blessing of Easter Time. Because the blessing takes place during Mass, the Prayer over the People (blessing prayer) would naturally be said by a priest or deacon.

Depending on the local climate and common local professions, the Order for the Blessing of Fields and Flocks (see BB, chapter 26) might fit well within Easter Time and the spring season. The fertility of fields and pastures, as well as the successful birth of newborn livestock are concerns weighing heavily on the minds of farmers during this time of the year. Unlike most other blessings, the introduction to this one says, "the minister [priest, deacon, or layperson] should adapt the celebration to the circumstances of the place and the people involved" (BB, 969). In a rural context, when planting season falls during Easter Time, the Order for the Blessing of Seeds at Planting Time (BB, chapter 27) provides an opportunity to pray for protection from floods, hail, and heavy wind, as well as for healthy seeds, abundant blossoms, sprouting plants, and fruitful vines—all in hopes of an abundant harvest at the end of the season. This blessing can also be adapted to local context and circumstances. It provides both a longer and shorter rite.

Finally, where there is a special devotion to St. Joseph the Worker, or where May Day is celebrated, it might be appropriate to use the Order for the Blessing of Tools or other Equipment for Work (see BB, chapter 24) on May 1. In addition to the normal form, a shorter rite is provided for use whenever just a single tool or piece of equipment will be blessed (see BB, 939–941).

The Liturgical Environment

Lucky for us (and thanks to the Great Vigil) the liturgical environment has everything it already needs for Easter Time—flowers, banners, beautiful music, and, best of all, the church smells great from the Easter lilies! The church was brought back to "life" at the Vigil—now the life continues.

There is not a lot to change in the environment between the Vigil and Easter morning. Remember to fill the holy water fonts (stoups) at the church entrances before the first Mass begins. Make arrangements with the head usher to have a plan for seating the overflow parishioners. If you use extra chairs, have them ready to set up, or if you have another room or parish hall that is equipped with online screening, then it is our responsibility to make sure the environment is appropriate for "Mass." Include in this environment the same kind of flowers, bulbs, and greenery that are used in the main sanctuary.

The main responsibility of the environment team during the seven weeks of Easter is to water the flowers, prune deceased and wilting flowers, and keep the sanctuary (and other areas) free of dead leaves. A helpful (and practical) way to keep the lillies alive longer is to pick off the yellow stamen. Make sure not to overwater the flowers. It is advisable to check the flowers twice during the first two or three weeks. Some of the flowers will last a long time and some flowers will only last a week. Be prepared to swap out flowers with greenery or pretty pieces of fabric. White or gold is appropriate as well as soft pastels. When the flowers are no longer visually appealing, a nice idea is to put them out in the narthex for the parishioners to take home after Mass, or if the church needs some flowers around the outside of the building, plant them in the flowerbeds. Easter lilies come back the next year but unfortunately not by the next Easter. For Pentencost, add reds, oranges, and golds to the existing Easter environment.

The Liturgical Music

THROUGHOUT Easter Time we continuously proclaim the Resurrection of Christ and his victory over sin and death. An abundance of sung Alleluias should permeate the Liturgy throughout the season. St. Augustine once wrote: "We are an Easter people and Alleluia is our song." The music during Easter need not always mention or focus on the empty tomb, particularly later in the season when the Gospel accounts move from Christ's post-Resurrection appearances to the Apostles to the Johannine images of the Good Shepherd, the Vine and the Branches, the unity of the Church and the coming of the Spirit. Easter is also about what it means to live the Christian life as we imitate his command to love one another.

The weekdays of the Octave of Easter are ranked very high on the Table of Liturgical Days and should be celebrated as Solemnities of our Lord. Consider adding music to the daily Mass on these days to heighten the sense of solemnity. Even if an organist and cantor can't be scheduled, someone could lead the singing of a few Easter hymns, the Gospel Acclamation, and Eucharistic Acclamations. The solemn dismissal, with its double Alleluia, is sung at the end of Mass and the Liturgy of the Hours throughout the entire Octave of Easter, and again on Pentecost.

The Missal offers the option of replacing the customary Penitential Act with the blessing and sprinkling of water on Sundays, especially in Easter Time. Five antiphons are suggested, although any hymn baptismal in nature could be substituted, particularly one with an abundance of alleluias. "Out of Darkness" by Christopher Walker (OCP), with its Easter verses, appropriately emphasizes the priesthood of the baptized and could be used for the sprinkling rite.

The Eucharistic Acclamations throughout Easter Time ought to be the parish's finest setting, perhaps even one that is only used during this season. The fasting and simplicity of the forty days should give way to the feasting and exuberance of the fifty days.

The month of May has traditionally been associated with the Blessed Virgin Mary. Marian hymns that focus on the resurrection are especially appropriate during the Easter Season. Examples include "Be Joyful, Mary" (REGINA CAELI), the plain chant *Regina Caeli*, "Sing We of the Blessed Mother" (OMNI DIE DIC MARIAE), and "Song of Mary" by Dan Schutte (OCP). Consider the lovely a cappella choral setting of *Regina Caeli* in the collection Four Pieces for Marian Feasts by Lisa Stafford (WLP). "Immaculate Mary" is better suited for Advent or the Solemnity of the Immaculate Conception, and "Hail, Holy Queen" is more appropriate for the Queenship of Mary or the Assumption of the Blessed Virgin Mary.

First Communions typically take place during Easter Time. Even if the celebrations are held on Saturdays, be sure to use music that the assembly sings on Sundays with appropriate texts that echo the faith we profess while avoiding cute, childlike music. If the children will be processing into the Church during the Entrance Procession, consider a hymn with a refrain, perhaps even a setting of Psalm 34: "Taste and See." Music that is familiar is best since family members will likely be watching the children rather than looking at a booklet or hymnal. For the Communion Procession consider "The Supper of the Lord" by Laurence Rosania (OCP), "Come to the Banquet" by James Chepponis (GIA), and "Draw Near" by Steven Janco (WLP). Invite members of your adult or youth choirs to sing for First Communions to support the assembly singing and to sing an anthem at the Preparation of the Gifts.

With so much energy and preparation put into Lent and the Triduum, keeping the enthusiasm going for the entire season of Easter can be a great challenge. Consider offering an Easter concert or Easter Lessons and Carols. Bring the life giving message of Christ's resurrection to those in nursing homes or hospitals. *Universal Norms for the Liturgical Year and the Calendar* reminds us that "The fifty days from Easter Sunday to Pentecost are celebrated in joyful exultation as one feast day, or better as one "great Sunday" (UNLY, 22).

The Liturgical Ministers

BE sure to review the May calendar, since it is often one of the busiest months of the year in people's lives, especially with the celebrations of *Cinco de Mayo*, end of the school year, graduations and Mother's Day. You'll want to have a sub-list on hand during this busy time. Schedule college students returning home for summer as liturgical ministers. Soon after the Lent/Triduum celebrations have ended, bring together the parish liturgical commission along with liturgical ministers, parish musicians, presiding ministers, and members of the liturgical environment team to evaluation the season—what worked and didn't? Invite members of the assembly to participate as well and come together first in small groups. Ask questions such as: what allowed you to go deeper into the Paschal Mystery? What symbols or rituals spoke to you or stirred up your faith and explain why? What did you hear or feel as you heard the texts of the Missal or Lectionary proclaimed? Consider writing thank you notes to the varies ministers in the parish. Celebrate with simple food and beverages and give thanks for the good work you do on behalf of the holy people of God.

Other Prayers, Rites, and Devotions

Now that the forty days of fasting have ended, the fifty days of feasting begins! The Blessing of the Family Table on Easter Sunday can easily be promoted in the parish by offering parishioners the opportunity of taking some of the newly blessed Easter water home, by either providing small holy water bottles to be filled from the font (or prefilled) as people are leaving the Easter Vigil.

The *Directory on Popular Piety and the Liturgy* states: "It is also an opportunity to invite the faithful to live according to the Gospel, and to exhort parents and children to preserve and promote the mystery of being 'a domestic church'" (DPPL, 152). What the Stations of the Cross or the *Via Crucis* does for Lent, the Stations of the Resurrection or the *Via Lucis* does for Easter Time. This pious exercise has developed over the recent years in many regions. In the same fashion of the Stations of the Cross, the faithful meditate on the various appearances of Jesus from his Resurrection to Ascension, concluding with the Pentecost event. Although there is no official list or ritual, several publishers have compiled their own service. Some suggested resources include *Via Lucis: The Way of Life* (2013, Novalis Publications), *Stations of the Resurrection: The Way of Life* (2007, Liguori Publications), and *Journey into Joy: Stations of the Resurrection* (2001, Paulist Press).

The devotion to the Divine Mercy has gained worldwide attention with the canonization of St. Faustina Kowalska as well as the feast day being entered into the universal calendar by St. Pope John Paul II in 2000. Even though the recitation of the "chaplet" is sometimes prayed daily by devotees, this devotional prayer must be placed in proper perspective in regard to its celebration on the Second Sunday of Easter. The celebration of the Octave of Easter takes precedence. The communal recitation (or even chanting) is best suited for its traditional time at 3:00 PM. This afternoon prayertime may be accompanied by the Exposition and Benediction of the Blessed Sacrament or the recitation of the Glorious Mysteries. Parish leadership might do well to properly promote this devotion during the later weeks of Lent or even in the Palm Sunday or Easter Sunday parish bulletins.

How does your parish keep and promote the Pentecost Novena (the original novena by the way!)? On May 4, 1897, Pope Leo XIII proclaimed "We decree and command that throughout the whole Catholic Church, this year and every subsequent year, a novena shall take place before Whit-Sunday (Pentecost) in all parish churches." St. Pope John Paul II reiterated Pope Leo XIII's command for a worldwide Pentecost novena. The *Directory on Popular Piety and the Liturgy* suggests: "Where possible, the Pentecost novena should consist of the solemn celebration of vespers" (DPPL, 155). If your parish has never celebrated the Liturgy of the Hours this may be an excellent time to introduce parishioners to this ancient liturgical prayer. Pre-printed daily orders of worship can be downloaded (by subscribing) to www.ebreviary.com.

The month of May is devotionally known as the month of the Blessed Virgin Mary. A little known ritual, the Order of Crowning of the Image of the Blessed Virgin Mary published by the United States Conference of Catholic Bishops, (www.usccb.org), provides texts for three services: within Mass, within Evening Prayer, and within the Word of God. Parishes that have a strong tradition of May Crownings will benefit from examining this ritual.

Evangelization

WE love to celebrate Easter! We do so for seven weeks. Yet how does the world know the meaning of "why" we love to celebrate Easter for so long? Easter Time provides us with the opportunity to show forth the reason for our faith. Without Easter, there is no Resurrection, no Christianity. But with Easter comes a new way of being now and in the future. In Easter Time, we are sent out over and over again in mission. Our mission is a gentle offering of the peace Jesus extends to his disciples. Multiple time in Gospel readings this season, we hear Jesus say, "Peace be with you." Easter evangelization means we repeat these words to the people in our parishes, our homes, and our world.

Over and over again, we also hear we are witnesses to Jesus' Death and Resurrection. We must testify to this. Our love of God and one another is our testimony. Often, however, we fall short in this love—on our parish committees, in our competition to be the best liturgical minister, the best cantor, the favored son or daughter, in our unwillingness to compromise and need to have our way, and in our hesitation to bring our faith into our daily lives. That is why Easter Time provides us with an opportunity to reevangelize—ourselves and other believers—to renew our baptismal faith. The call to repentance and conversion we hear is our call to renewal and our message to the world. The call has not ended with Lent just as the work of faith does not end with Easter; Easter is only the beginning.

Let us go into the world to proclaim the Gospel, to drive out demons, to speak the language of faith, and to heal the sick. Jesus sends us to do nothing less. The Spirit accompanies us and we accompany each other, holding all things in common as a community of faith. This is Easter evangelization. And, when new disciples come to us as Saul came to the disciples, even though we might be afraid, let us listen to their stories and see how they have spoken for the Lord. Let us through our liturgies and worship, welcome new inquirers and disciples into our midst this Easter Time, for the Father calls us all children of God.

Each Sunday of Easter Time may we exit through the church doors in mission taking the message of Easter with us to the streets, our workplaces, and our places of recreation. Let us, children, youth, and adults alike witness to Resurrection in our families, to our friends, and yes, to those we encounter but do not know.

The Parish and the Home

AT the parish, Easter Time is often filled with the celebrations of the Reception of Baptized Christians into the Full Communion of the Catholic Church (when not celebrated at the Easter Vigil), first Communion, and Confirmation. As often as possible, these celebrations take place within the context of the Sunday liturgy, which helps all who are present to deepen their appreciation of the call of Baptism to ongoing conversion in Christ. This, combined with the sprinkling rite within the liturgies of Easter Time, and the readings from the Acts of the Apostles and Gospel narratives insures that Sunday will maintain its Easter focus throughout the season.

At home, carry a few elements through the entire season at the family prayer space: an Easter lily, Bible opened to the story of the Resurrection, and a family member's baptismal candle. On Easter Sunday, create an Alleluia banner that will hang or be placed near the family table. Ask each member to draw a symbol of the season or to write a word or phrase that captures the meaning of Easter for her or him. Invite each person to share something learned or realized through the observance of Lent, and how this will influence their living in the future.

Many parishes list the readings for the coming Sunday in the bulletin. Using these as a guide, take time each week to read the story of the early community of believers found in the Acts of the Apostles. Reflect on this story in light of your experience as individuals and within the parish community, and plan activities that will encourage growth in discipleship and mission. This could be a perfect time for the parish to celebrate what is and to talk together about the hopes and dreams of parishioners for the future of the parish. As individuals and within the community, be attentive to the needs of people in your local town or neighborhood. Invite neighboring Christian congregations to join together for evening prayer, a shared meal, and an act of service on behalf of the poor in the area. Encourage teens to join with Confirmation candidates to share their experience of faith. Offer opportunities for people to inquire about the faith or to gather in seasonal small faith groups.

May 20 is Pentecost Sunday, which is often a time in which parishes invite members to renew or offer their gifts in ministry. People are sometimes invited to wear red, the color of the Holy Spirit, and the newly initiated may be invited to offer a brief witness at the conclusion of Mass or to be present for a parish-wide social.

In the final weeks of Easter Time, encourage people of all ages to make a renewed commitment to live as Easter people, as disciples of Jesus Christ whose faith shapes all aspects of their lives, and who live as witnesses to the life that Christ offers.

Mass Texts

◆ TROPES FOR THE PENITENTIAL ACT, FORM C

Lord Jesus, your Resurrection bestows upon us every spiritual blessing of the heavens: Lord, have mercy.

Lord Jesus, you have made us adopted sons and daughters of the Father: Christ, have mercy.

Lord Jesus, you have redeemed us in your Blood and forgiven us your sons: Lord, have mercy.

◆ DISMISSAL FOR CHILDREN'S LITURGY OF THE WORD

My dear children, the readings that you will hear to day tell us of Christ's Resurrection from the dead. God has promised to give us new life also–a life that will never end. Listen carefully to these readings of Easter joy, so that you will be able to come back here and with us give God thnanks and praise in Jesus Christ. Go in peace.

◆ DISMISSAL OF THE CATECHUMENS

My dear friends, today have heard with us the great mystery of Christ's Resurrection as proclaimed in the Scriptures. Go now to reflect upon this mystery sot hat you might see how Christ is the fulfillment of every promise God has made to us through the prophets. Know that we long for the day when you will share with us at this banquet table of the Lamb, who lives now and for ever. Go in peace.

April 2018
Month of the Holy Eucharist

Optional Memorials in Easter Time

The Missal commentaries below pertain to the seasonal weekdays or other obligatory observances. The following should be consulted when celebrating optional memorials during Easter Time:

> [O]ne of the following may be chosen: either the Mass of the weekday, or the Mass of the Saint or of one of the Saints whose Memorial is observed, or the Mass of any Saint inscribed in the Martyrology for that day (GIRM, 355b).

(#261) white

M 2 Monday within the
O   Octave of Easter
N   SOLEMNITY

The Lectionary for Mass

The **Easter Sequence**, *Victimae paschali laudes,* is a song of praise to the Paschal victim that also reflects the Gospel account of Mary's encounter with the Risen Lord. It may be sung throughout the Octave of Easter. It should precede the Gospel and be sung from the ambo. Consider the arrangement, accompaniment, and pacing—the sequence can transition nicely into the Alleluia, giving time for the cantor to move from the ambo to the cantor stand.

◆ FIRST READING: On Easter Monday, we read from Acts of Peter's proclamation to everyone staying in Jerusalem. Peter's proclamation is the basis of our faith. He testifies to Jesus' person and mission, and his Death and Resurrection. Even David, he tells, foreshadowed the Resurrection of Christ. Then and now, we all witness to the Resurrection.

◆ RESPONSORIAL PSALM 16: In the words of the psalm writer, we ask God to keep us safe. The Lord is our hope; he gives direction to our lives. Day by day, the Lord companions us in our journey. When we open ourselves to the Lord's guidance, truly we will know the ending joy that comes from being in his presence. Ultimately, the psalm writer instructs us that the path the Lord shows us with lead to our eternal happiness at God's right hand.

◆ GOSPEL: Mary Magdalene and the other Mary ran to tell the disciples about the empty tomb. The Gospel from Matthew informs us that it was Jesus who met the women on their run, not that the women met him. The Risen Lord offers the women and us an invitation to encounter him. Should we choose to accept his invitation, he will quell our fears, as he did those of the two Marys, and we can continue uninhibited in our proclamation of the Resurrection. We proclaim the truth, while others, like the guard, will chose to proclaim untruths about Jesus' Resurrection such as the disciples stole the body, solely for the sake of their selfish gain.

The Roman Missal

Our long journey through the desert has brought us "into a land flowing with milk and honey" (Easter Entrance Antiphon)!

We praise God who adds "new offspring" to the Church through Baptism, and we pray that all remain faithful to their Baptism throughout their lives (Collect) and "attain unending happiness" (Prayer over the Offerings). We pray for the abounding grace of the "paschal Sacrament" (Prayer after Communion) we receive on this Easter day.

The Gloria is sung or said today, as it is every day within the Octave of Easter.

Preface I of Easter is assigned for today, and, as specified at the text for the Preface, the phrase "on this day" is used. If Eucharistic Prayer I, the Roman Canon, is used, the special inserts are used.

The solemn dismissal with the double Alleluia is sung or said today, as it is throughout the Octave of Easter.

(#262) white

T 3 Tuesday within the
U   Octave of Easter
E   SOLEMNITY

The Lectionary for Mass

◆ FIRST READING: We continue today to hear from Peter's proclamation on the day of Pentecost. The crucified Jesus is Lord, Peter tells the Jewish people. Peter then announces the call to repent and be baptized. Through Baptism, God forgives sins and we receive the gift of the Holy Spirit. Three thousand accepted Peter's words and were baptized. To this day, people continue to accept, repent, and be baptized.

◆ RESPONSORIAL PSALM 33: The Lord delivers us from death. The psalm writer acknowledges this, and through the Risen Christ, we profess this as our faith. We know the wondrous truth of the psalm refrain that the Lord's goodness fills the earth. The Lord's justice and kindness overcome all death and famine for the Lord brings life and nourishment.

◆ GOSPEL: Jesus wept at the death of Lazarus, the brother of Mary and Martha. Mary Magdalene weeps first outside the empty tomb, and then peering into it. The two angels first ask her why she is crying. Then, when Mary Magdalene turns around, Jesus asks her the same question. Yet it is not until Jesus exclaims her name that she recognizes him. Jesus advises her to let him go so he might ascend to the Father. Mary Magdalene went on to tell the disciples she had seen the Lord. She let go and proclaimed the Resurrection. Will we?

The Roman Missal

God gives us "paschal remedies" that we may have "perfect freedom" and rejoice both on earth and in heaven in Christ's Resurrection (Collect). We pray that God may protect us (Prayer over the Offerings) and prepare us for eternal life (Prayer after Communion). The Gloria is once again sung or said today.

Preface I of Easter is again assigned for today, and, as specified at the text for the Preface, the phrase "on this day" is used. If Eucharistic Prayer I is prayed, remember to use the special inserts.

The solemn dismissal with the double Alleluia is sung or said today, as it is throughout the Octave of Easter.

(#263)   white

WED 4 Wednesday within the Octave of Easter
SOLEMNITY

The Lectionary for Mass

◆ FIRST READING: Peter heals a man crippled from birth who was outside the Temple gate. The man desired money, but Peter and John have none to give. Instead, Peter offers the healing power of Jesus Christ. Peter takes the man by the right hand and raises him up, a connection not to be lost during the Octave of Easter. The man leaps, stands, walks, and jumps, all to the glory of God. People are amazed! They have seen the glory of Easter in the healed man, but do they recognize it and believe in the Risen Christ?

◆ RESPONSORIAL PSALM 105: The Responsorial Psalm invites us to rejoice and thank God for his wondrous deeds. Like the man who was crippled, we praise God for the new life he gives us. We rejoice that God forever is faithful to his covenant. We join our praise today with all the descendants of Abraham who rejoice in the Lord.

◆ GOSPEL: The disciples never wanted to believe that Christ had to suffer and die. But on the road to Emmaus, the Risen Christ again

instructs them in this truth. He interprets Scripture for them. But it was not until he was with the disciples at table, and blessed, broke, and shared bread with them, that they knew who he was. The disciples' journey back to Jerusalem where in community with the Eleven and others, they, too, share their experience of the Risen Lord.

The Roman Missal

Each year the Church is gladdened by the celebration of Christ's Resurrection; we pray that we may experience the joys that Easter promises (Collect). We ask for "salvation of mind and body" (Prayer over the Offerings), that we may be cleansed of our former way of life and transformed into "a new creation" (Prayer after Communion). The Gloria is once again sung or said today.

Preface I of Easter is again used today, as is the phrase "on this day." If Eucharistic Prayer I is used, the special inserts are also again used.

The solemn dismissal with the double Alleluia is sung or said today, as it is throughout the Octave of Easter.

(#264)   white

THU 5 Thursday within the Octave of Easter
SOLEMNITY

The Lectionary for Mass

◆ FIRST READING: Peter preaches to the people in Solomon's Portico and tells them it was not the power of Peter and John that healed the crippled man in yesterday's reading, but the power of the Risen Christ working through them. God glorified the One who was put to death and raised up his servant. Repent and be converted, Peter instructs the crowd, for Jesus Christ is the one God raised from among prophets for us to be like him and to bless you forever.

◆ RESPONSORIAL PSALM 8: We marvel at our place in God's scheme

of creation through today's psalm. Particularly in Easter Time, it is good that we sing, "O Lord, our God, how wonderful your name in all the earth!" This text echoes the narratives in Genesis, reminding us of the stewardship of creation to which we are called, as people who have been "crowned . . . with glory and honor," of whom God is mindful, which is made clear through the Passion, Death, and Resurrection of Jesus Christ.

◆ GOSPEL: Today's Gospel reading follows directly from yesterday's reading. The two disciples returned to Jerusalem and as they recount how they recognized Jesus in the breaking of the bread, Jesus comes into their midst and offers peace. Fear and anxiety overtakes the disciples, and they think Jesus is a ghost. As he often does, Jesus extends an invitation to them to trust, to believe, to have faith. In his own words, Jesus explains that he is the Christ, the fulfillment of the Law of Moses, the psalms, and the prophets. We, as the disciples, are witnesses to this.

The Roman Missal

We continue to pray for the neophytes and for all the baptized, that we may be one in faith and in "the homage of their deeds," the praise they offer to God by the good work they do (Collect). We offer the sacrifice of the Mass for the newly baptized and for ourselves (Prayer over the Offerings). We pray that the "holy exchange" of the Eucharist may bring us present help and "eternal gladness" (Prayer after Communion).

The Gloria is sung or said today, as it is every day within the Octave of Easter.

Once again Preface I of Easter is the Preface to be used for today, and the phrase "on this day" is used. If the Roman Canon is used, be sure to use the special inserts.

The solemn dismissal with the double Alleluia is sung or said today, as it is throughout the Octave of Easter.

(#265) white

FRI 6 Friday within the Octave of Easter
SOLEMNITY

The Lectionary for Mass

◆ FIRST READING: In today's First Reading, the priests, the captain of the Temple guard, and the Sadducees get involved. Their frustration with Peter and John proclaiming Jesus to the people and teaching them about the Resurrection of the dead leads them to arrest the two. The next day, members of the high-priestly class inquire of them as to the power or name that has led them to heal and preach? Undeterred and filled with the Holy Spirit, Peter witnesses to Jesus Christ, the crucified and Risen One. Salvation, he acclaims, comes only through Jesus Christ!

◆ RESPONSORIAL PSALM 118: We also sing Psalm 118 on Easter Sunday, although with a few different verses and with verses 24 as the refrain. Psalm 118 is also common psalm for Easter Time. As Christians, we acclaim Jesus Christ as the cornerstone each time we repeat the refrain of today's Responsorial Psalm. We believe that in him, God's mercy endures forever. Would that we witness like Peter in the First Reading so others might know salvation through him.

◆ GOSPEL: The post-Resurrection appearance of Jesus occurs in today's Gospel at the Sea of Tiberias. Simon Peter leads a group of people in an unsuccessful nighttime fishing excursion. At dawn, Jesus stands on the shore, and true to the disciples' history, they do not recognize him. Since Jesus is about providing food for people, he instructs them to at the net over the right side of the boat. After catching so many fish, the disciples struggle to pull in their net. The disciple whom Jesus loved first recognized him, then upon his word, so did Peter. At breakfast the other disciples do not even need to ask the Lord who he is. They know.

The Roman Missal

The Paschal Mystery is God's covenant with us, to reconcile us to himself. We pray that we may profess our faith in this great mystery, and express our faith in the way we live our lives (Collect). We pray that our offering may draw our minds from earth to heaven (Prayer over the Offerings). We ask God to redeem all he has saved through Christ's Passion, that they may rejoice in his Resurrection (Prayer after Communion).

The Gloria is sung or said today.

As with all the days this week, Preface I of Easter is assigned for today, and, as specified at the text for the Preface, the phrase "on this day" is used. If Eucharistic Prayer I, the Roman Canon, is used, the special inserts are used.

The solemn dismissal with the double Alleluia is sung or said today, as it is throughout the Octave of Easter.

(#266) white

SAT 7 Saturday within the Octave of Easter
SOLEMNITY

The Lectionary for Mass

◆ FIRST READING: The man who Peter and John cured is still with them. The crowds are still praising God for what happened. But the leaders are troubled with the confidence of Peter and John. The authorities order the two to leave the Sanhedrin so they might confer about what to do. Ironically, the authorities think Peter and John to be uneducated and ordinary men, and yet they, who are supposedly more astute, decide on a stern warning for Peter and John not to speak in Jesus' name. Do they think this will work? Of course not! Peter and John boldly state that it is impossible for them not to speak about Jesus—the crucified and Risen One!

◆ RESPONSORIAL PSALM 118: Once again, our Responsorial Psalm comes from Psalm 118. We, like Peter and John, cannot but help proclaim the Lord and give thanks to him. Death has not won the victory. The power of the Lord to bring life has! For this, we give thanks in the words of the psalm writer.

◆ GOSPEL: On Saturday of the Octave of Easter, we hear the last of the post-Resurrection appearances of Jesus. Today's Gospel from Mark tells of three appearances of the Risen Christ knit together into one unit. Jesus appears on the first day of the week to Mary Magdalene, two of Jesus' companions, and the Eleven at table. There is no question about Jesus' identity on the part of Mary Magdalene and the first two companions, but the Eleven do not believe their testimony. After rebuking the disciples for their disbelief and hardness of heart, Jesus sends them into the world as proclaimers of the Gospel. Let us go with them.

The Roman Missal

In many of our parishes, we saw the newly baptized in white garments as they emerged from the waters of new life. In the Collect, we pray that those who have been reborn in Baptism may be clothed "with blessed immortality." The prayers echo the "delight" and "joy" of Easter Time (Prayer over the Offerings), as we pray that all who are renewed by the sacraments may share in the resurrection of the body (Prayer after Communion).

The Gloria is sung or said today. Preface I of Easter is to be used today, although today is the last weekday for which it will be exclusively assigned. The phrase "on this day" is again used, as are the special inserts for Eucharistic Prayer I if that prayer is selected.

The solemn dismissal with the double Alleluia is sung or said today, as it is throughout the Octave of Easter.

(#44)　white

8 Second Sunday of Easter (or Sunday of Divine Mercy) / Octave Day of Easter

About this Sunday

The Sunday of Divine Mercy is a day established by Pope John Paul II as "a perennial invitation to the Christian world to face with confidence in divine benevolence the difficulties and trials that humankind will experience in the years to come" (Congregation for Divine Worship and the Discipline of the Sacraments, May 23, 2000). In a way similar to Passion Sunday (Palm Sunday) or the Fourth Sunday of Easter (Good Shepherd Sunday), the Second Sunday of Easter bears the additional title of Sunday of Divine Mercy.

This is not a new solemnity or feast, nor does it celebrate a new or separate mystery of redemption, but rather, it leads into the continuing celebration of God's mercy during Easter Time. As the Octave Day of Easter, the Lectionary readings and prayer texts highlight the mystery of divine compassion that underlies the Church's Easter faith.

The Lectionary for Mass

◆ FIRST READING: This summary of the early community of believers at Jerusalem depicts an ideal community, one we can strive to emulate. Would that we, like they, see our unity in the one heart and mind of Jesus Christ and hold everything in common, for everything ultimately belongs to the Lord! The community took care of everyone's needs as it centered its work on witnessing to the Resurrection and living out the message of new life in the Risen Christ.

◆ RESPONSORIAL PSALM 118: As we sing this song of thanksgiving today, may its words help us give voice to our Easter joy for there is nothing, not even death, which will put an end to the Lord's mercy. For Christians, Jesus is the cornerstone who was rejected and sentenced to death on a tree, but who now lives forever. Truly this is the Lord's day!

◆ SECOND READING: Throughout the Sundays of Easter Time, the Second Readings come from the First Letter of John. Today, we hear words from the final chapter of this letter. These words instruct us that love of God's children is intimately connected to love of God and obeying God's commandments. Faith conquers all that is evil in the world. God's children have confidence in this truth for we believe Jesus Christ conquered death. And, when our memory lapses in regard to this truth, we only need listen to the testimony of the Spirit.

◆ GOSPEL: Peace is Jesus' gift to the disciples when he appears to them in locked room. "Receive the Holy Spirit," he says. You have the power to forgive sins. Even on the basis of the disciples' testimony, Thomas did not believe they had seen the Lord. Would we have is the question this Gospel passage leads us to ponder today. Perhaps knowing Thomas's doubt, Jesus appears again a week later offering the same gift of peace, and not judging Thomas at all, invites him to see for himself that Jesus is indeed his Lord and God.

The Roman Missal

As the eighth day of the Octave of Easter, this Sunday completes the Easter Octave, and the Missal texts continue to strongly emphasize the meaning and effects of sacramental initiation. Historically, this day was given the name *Dominica in albis*—the last day for the neophytes to wear their white baptismal garments.

Keep in mind, given the baptismal character of all of Easter Time, that the Rite for the Blessing and Sprinkling of Water is a good option to take advantage of. The rite may be used as a memorial of Baptism in place of the Penitential Act at the beginning of Mass on Sundays, and parishes and liturgy preparation groups would do well to do this on all the Sundays (and any other major celebrations) during Easter Time. The rite is found in Appendix II at the back of the Missal. The priest and ministers enter as usual, and the priest greets the people as usual. Then, standing at the chair (or perhaps going to the baptismal font), with a vessel containing water to be blessed nearby, he calls the people to prayer and then blesses the water; be sure to use the third option, the prayer during Easter Time. Salt may be blessed and added to the water if that is the custom of the people.

After this, the priest sprinkles himself, the ministers, and the people, ideally moving throughout the church. One of the chants suggested in the Missal or some other appropriate song is sung during the sprinkling. After the sprinkling, the singing ends, and the priest returns to his chair and prays the closing to the rite. After this prayer, the Gloria is sung.

The splendid Collect is a prayer for the grace to recognize the Christ in whom we have been baptized, whose Spirit gives new life, and whose blood redeems us. The Prayer over the Offerings includes a special optional insert for the newly baptized The Gloria and the Creed are sung or said today.

Preface I of Easter is assigned for today, although today will be the last Sunday for which it will be the only one to be used; the phrase "on this day" is again the proper phrase to be used among the possible choices. Consider chanting the introductory dialogue and the Preface today, and every Sunday during Easter Time; if this is not the regular practice of your community, this can be a way of powerfully drawing attention to the festivity of the liturgical time, and in particular if this was the practice during Lent, this can be a way of highlighting the continuity of the liturgical times (but be sure to prepare and rehearse your assembly as needed, especially if your people are not familiar with the responses!). If Eucharistic Prayer I is selected, the proper forms of the "In communion with those" and the "Therefore, Lord, we pray" are still used, as it is the Octave of Easter.

The simple Prayer after Communion asks that the "paschal Sacrament" may have an ongoing effect on our hearts and minds.

If a Solemn Blessing is to be used, it is the Solemn Blessing for Easter Time, found at number 6 in the "Blessings at the End of Mass and Prayers over the People" section of the Missal immediately following the Order of Mass. Notice how the third section of the blessing continues the baptismal theme of Easter by its specific reference to that sacrament.

Finally, for the last time until Pentecost, the solemn double Alleluia dismissal is used.

Other Ideas

Just as we should encourage people to realize that Christmas Time is more than December 25, now we remind people that Easter Time lasts a full fifty days, beginning with the Octave of Easter which commences Easter Sunday. Octaves are rooted in the practices of ancient Israel, where a feast would be honored for seven consecutive days. The Church celebrates two octaves (Christmas and Easter). Each of the days of the Octave of Easter is a solemnity, the highest of liturgical feasts. At Mass each day, the Gloria should be sung or recited, and the double Alleluia sung at dismissal. If people cannot attend each daily Mass, encourage them to pray the readings of each day using a print or online resource. Family members can greet each other with the greeting of the Eastern churches used at the cracking of boiled eggs: "Christ is risen!" with the response, "He is risen indeed!"

(#545) white

MON 9 Solemnity of the Annunciation of the Lord

About Today's Solemnity

Today's solemnity is usually celebrated on March 25; however, this year, the date falls within Holy Week. However, the Annunciation is so important to our lives of faith it is transferred to the first available date on the calendar, which is today, the Monday after Holy Week. On this solemnity, we remember when the angel brought to Mary the amazing news that she would be the mother of God's Son. On this day, as in Christmas Time, we contemplate the wonder of the Incarnation: in Jesus, God took on our flesh, becoming like us in all things but sin.

The Annunciation is a Solemnity of the Lord, but it is also a day to give thanks to and for Mary. The Gospel account of the Annunciation in Luke reveals a great wonder: God sought the free consent of a young girl to carry out his plan for us. God asked for help! No wonder so many artists throughout the ages have chosen to depict this moment of decision that changed the world for ever.

The Lectionary for Mass

◆ FIRST READING: Ahaz is stubborn and refuses to ask for a sign from the Lord, thinking it will tempt him. The prophet Isaiah seems frustrated. His words to the house of David communicate the message that the Lord will provide a sign even without being asked. The sign will be a virgin who will give birth to a son and who will be named "Emmanuel." God is indeed with us!

◆ RESPONSORIAL PSALM 40 is a psalm attributed to David. We come to do the Lord's will as David did. On this solemnity, we acknowledge the epitome of the One who does God's will is Jesus Christ, Emmanuel, God with us. He announced God's justice. He is the model of sacrifice we are to follow. His, the kindness, we are to live out.

◆ SECOND READING: No longer are holocausts and sin offerings necessary. Jesus Christ offered himself once for all. He is the living sacrifice. He is the One who came to do the Father's will. Notice how our passage references Psalm 40 in its use of the terms holocausts and sin-offerings and how the passage, too, speaks of the Son of God as coming to do God's will. A direct connection between the Second Reading and the Responsorial Psalm is infrequent.

◆ GOSPEL: The Gospel is the beloved narrative of the Annunciation. Mary's fiat echoes the theme of doing God's will found in the Responsorial Psalm and the Second Reading. May we let her willingness to do what God asks of her resonate with us on this Solemnity of the Annunciation. May we, too, say let the Lord's will be done. For who would have thought that a virgin could conceive a son and that her son, God's Son, would rise from the dead!

The Roman Missal

All the Mass texts for this solemnity are proper for the day and can be found in the Proper of Saints at March 25. The Gloria is sung or said.

The theology underlying the words of the Collect reflects the understanding that as a result of the Incarnation, humanity is given a share in divinity. Not unlike the prayer the priest prays at the mixing of a little water into the wine ("By the mystery of this water and wine / may we come to share in the divinity of Christ / who humbled himself to share in our humanity"), this Collect asks, insofar as God willed that his Word should take on human flesh, that we "may merit to become partakers even in his divine nature."

The Creed is said today in observance of the solemnity. Today is one of two times (the other being at the Masses on the Nativity) when all genuflect, instead of bow, at the words "and by the Holy Spirit was incarnate of the Virgin Mary and became man." Be sure your assembly is prepared for this; the priest can give a brief explanation of this in his introduction to the Creed.

The Prayer over the Offerings highlights that it is the Church that is making this offering (notice what this means in terms of liturgical theology—the entire assembly makes the offering, not just the priest), and, in so doing, she (the Church) is recognizing that her life began with the Incarnation of the Son. In God's acceptance of this offering, we pray that the Church "may rejoice to celebrate his mysteries on this Solemnity."

The Preface assigned for today is given right there along with the other Mass texts for the Solemnity of the Annunciation of the Lord in the Proper of Saints. Titled "The Mystery of the Incarnation," it relates Mary's hearing "with faith" about the Christ who was to be born "by the overshadowing power of the Holy Spirit." The text goes on to relate how, by bearing the child in her "immaculate womb" the promises made to the children of Israel were fulfilled and the hope of the world was realized.

The Prayer after Communion expresses our confession in Jesus as "true God and true man" as among the "mysteries of the true faith," and asks that we may attain eternal joy "through the saving power of his Resurrection."

No Solemn Blessing or Prayer over the People is designated for the end of Mass, but if you desired to use one, certainly Solemn Blessing #15, "The Blessed Virgin Mary," would be appropriate for today.

TUE 10 (#268) white
Easter Weekday

The Lectionary for Mass

◆ FIRST READING: Unity of heart and mind. This is the hallmark of the early Christian community of believers. No one was in need. All shared everything in common. The Levite, Joseph, called Barnabas by the Apostles, even sold his property and gave the money to the Apostles. So great was the desire to build up the community and witness to the Resurrection of Jesus Christ.

◆ RESPONSORIAL PSALM 93: Easter affirms Christ's kingship. The refrain for today's Responsorial Psalm provides us the opportunity to acclaim the Lord's reign as King. For Christians, Christ is King in his life, Death, and Resurrection. The Apostles witnessed to this, the Church throughout the centuries has professed it, and we continue to testify to this in the world of the twenty-first century.

◆ GOSPEL: Having completed the Octave of Easter, we move on from the narratives of the post-Resurrection appearances to reading through the Gospel according to John. We begin in chapter 3 with a passage in which Nicodemus is the central character. Jesus instructs Nicodemus that he must be born from above, but this Pharisee and ruler of Israel does not understand Jesus' words. In his solemn teaching to Nicodemus, Jesus explains that the descending Son of Man has gone to heaven by relating God's lifting Jesus up to Moses lifting up the serpent. Through the Son of Man who descends and ascends, everyone who believes will experience life forever with God.

The Roman Missal

On the weekdays of Easter Time, the Prayer over the Gifts and the Prayer after Communion are repeated week by week. Commentaries are included for these prayers on the Easter Sundays when they occur. Each day has its own unique Collect. The Collect for today reminds us that we, too, are called to that apostolic task, "to proclaim the power of the risen Lord."

WED 11 (#269) red
Memorial of St. Stanislaus, Bishop and Martyr

The Lectionary for Mass

◆ FIRST READING: The message of Easter life that comes through the Risen Christ cannot be confined. Even when the high priest and the Sadducees jail the Apostles, their imprisonment does not least long. An angel of the Lord comes during the night and frees them. The next morning, the high priest and the Sadducees find the Apostles back in the Temple area teaching.

◆ RESPONSORIAL PSALM 34: The Responsorial Psalm expresses gratitude to the Lord for hearing the cry of the poor. No matter our fears—or perhaps the fear the Apostles had when the high priest imprisoned them—the Lord will deliver us from our anxieties that we might continue to taste and see his goodness. The reference to the angel of the Lord in the final stanza (v. 8) provides a connection to the First Reading.

◆ GOSPEL: Life comes through death. As Jesus continues to teach Nicodemus, we learn of God's tremendous love for the world, and the gift of eternal life available to those who believe. God's invitation to choose light over darkness is an invitation to live in the truth of his only-begotten Son, Jesus Christ. Many Pharisees refused the light. We do not yet know how Nicodemus will respond. But how will we respond this Easter season?

The Roman Missal

The proper Collect is found at April 11 in the Proper of Saints.

Today's Saint

Noted for his compassionate concern for the poor and for his wise counsel, St. Stanislaus (1030–1079) was appointed bishop of Krakow. His consecration as bishop was met with great joy on the part of the people. While serving as bishop he spoke out against King Boleslaus, an unjust and cruel man who incited fear in the people of Poland. St. Stanislaus, outraged by the oppressive behavior of the monarch, declared that an unjust king has no place in the Church. In response, the king defamed his reputation, eventually ordering guards to kill him, but they refused. The king took matters into his own hands by stabbing him with a sword. St. Stanislaus, the martyr, is the patron saint of Poland and the city of Krakow.

T H U **12** **(#270)** white
Easter Weekday

The Lectionary for Mass

◆ FIRST READING: The court officers bring the Apostles before the Sanhedrin once again where the high priest inquires of them about the strict orders he had given them not to teach in the name of Jesus. The high priest cannot even say Jesus' name, as he refers to it as "that name." Peter and the Apostles are resilient. They respond to the high priest by simply stating the kerygma. The Apostles will not cease to preach Jesus' name. They, too, could face death like Jesus because the high priest and Sadducees are so afraid of the truth they preach.

◆ RESPONSORIAL PSALM 34: The refrain for today's Responsorial Psalm is the same as yesterday's. The opening verse is the same, while the other verses differ. Today's verses describe the Lord's confrontation with those who oppose him. The Lord will hear the cries of the just and the broken hearted. Those who seek to ruin his name, along with those who oppose the teaching of Peter and the Apostles in the First Reading, the Lord will destroy for his name means life, not death. The goodness of God's life we can taste and see!

◆ GOSPEL: Jesus concluded his words to Nicodemus, and in today's Gospel we hear the final testimony of John the Baptist. John's words are part of his response to those who inquired of his disciples about ceremonial washings and why everyone is coming to Jesus for baptism. John testifies to the greatness of Jesus who is above all. Jesus, the Son of God, speaks God's words and does not place a quota on the gift of the Spirit. Believe in the Son, John says, and you will have eternal life.

The Roman Missal

Having just celebrated the Sunday of Divine Mercy, we are reminded of God's love and mercy: "may by his likeness to ourselves / bring us reconciliation" (Collect) and may we "be conformed to the mysteries of [his] mighty love" (Prayer over the Offerings).

Any of the Prefaces for Easter may be used.

F R I **13** **(#271)** white
Easter Weekday

Optional Memorial of St. Martin I, Pope and Martyr / red

The Lectionary for Mass

◆ FIRST READING: Gamaliel advises the Sanhedrin to have nothing to do with Peter and the other Apostles, and to let them go. Gamaliel warns that they might come from God and if so, the members of the Sanhedrin would then be fighting against God. They would not win. Before the Apostles are sent out, they receive a flogging. Yet they continue their work of preaching and teaching in the name of Jesus Christ. Their perseverance is a model for us who proclaim Christ's name during the Easter season and after.

◆ RESPONSORIAL PSALM 27: Today's Responsorial Psalm is also the psalm for Friday of the First Week of Advent, although the refrains differ. The psalm writer proclaims the Lord is his light, his stronghold, and refuge. These words become ours today. And, in light of the First Reading, we can see how the Apostles were steadfast in their proclamation of the Gospel. The Lord provided them refuge from their fears and from those who would do them harm. They sought to dwell in the Lord's house forever as we do.

◆ GOSPEL: Five barley loaves and two fish. That was all it took for Jesus to feed the five thousand. On the basis of this miraculous sign, the people professed Jesus as the Prophet, "the one who is to come into the world." Yet after their profession, Jesus quickly withdraws for he sensed that the wanted to make him their king, a worldly king. But the Gospel writer John will make sure his audience knows that Jesus is the King who reigns from the cross, and the cross is the cross of life.

The Roman Missal

In the Collect, we ask God for hearts disposed to prayer and praise. Any of the Easter Prefaces may be used.

Today's Saint

Martin I was a Roman of noble birth, and had a reputation for intelligence, learning, and charity. He fought against the Monothelite heresy, which claimed that Jesus had two natures—human and divine—but only one will. At that time, the government was deeply involved in theological controversies. If the Church was torn by doctrinal conflicts, the emperors felt it threatened public order. They sought peace at all costs, even sacrificing orthodoxy. Martin was tried by Emperor Constans II in Constantinople, and was imprisoned and exiled. He died from mistreatment at the hands of fellow Christians in 655.

SAT 14 (#272) white
Easter Weekday

The Lectionary for Mass

◆ FIRST READING: Today's First Reading recounts the selection of the seven from among the community of disciples to care for the widows who were being neglected in the daily distribution. The Apostles prayed and laid hands on the seven chose. Through the ministry of these seven and the other disciples and Apostles, the word of God continued to spread and priestly leaders rose up in obedience to the faith. The early church was growing.

◆ RESPONSORIAL PSALM 33: Those of us who place our trust in the Lord, also pray for God's mercy. Like the psalm writer, we know the Lord will deliver us from death. No matter what we hunger for, the Lord will feed us is in times of famine. For this, we sing and give praise to the Lord whose word is living and active throughout the earth.

◆ GOSPEL: If we would see Jesus walking on water, would we believe it really is he? The disciples were afraid in his presence as he approached their boat at sea. Their response was a natural human response in the face of the unknown. At Jesus' word, they immediately wanted to welcome him into their boat. But he need not come aboard, for the boat just then arrived at the shore of Capernaum. In the Gospel according to John, the disciples are beginning to recognize that Jesus is his Word. He is the Word made flesh.

The Roman Missal

There are two options for today's Collect. In the first, we beg God to "set aside . . . / the bond of sentence" written by our sins and cancel it through the Resurrection of Christ. In the second, we see "the gates of mercy" flung wide through the Paschal Mystery, and we pray that we may "never stray from the paths of life."

15 (#47) white
Third Sunday of Easter

The Lectionary for Mass

◆ FIRST READING: Peter addresses the Israelites after he has cured a man who was crippled from birth. His words are accusatory, letting the people know they rejected the Holy and Righteous One and put him to death. Peter's words are also affirmative. In them, Peter testifies that the God of their fathers is the same God who raised Jesus, the Holy and Righteous One. Jesus' suffering fulfilled the message of the prophets; his Resurrection is God's ultimate act of fidelity, fulfilling his promise of life to his people. Paul calls the Israelites to repentance and conversion. Our call to change does not stop with Lent. It continues in the Easter Season!

◆ RESPONSORIAL PSALM 4 seems a rather somber hymn for the Easter Season. The psalm's subdued nature reflects the psalm writer's confidence in God's gentle strength and power. In the refrain, we ask the Lord to shine his face upon us. We want to see God and to live in his image and likeness as he created us. We celebrate with the psalm writer the wonders God has done for us — and, as Christians, especially the wonder of his Son's Resurrection!

◆ SECOND READING: From the final chapter of John, from which last Sunday's Gospel was taken, we move back to an earlier part of the letter. Are we in Lent? You might ask this question as you read the three short verses of today's Second Reading. Sin is the obvious topic of the passage. We hope to remain faithful in love to God's commandments. We hope not to sin, but the author of the letter is realistic. God's children will sin. Yet all is not lost. Jesus Christ with advocate for us with the Father. Jesus Christ died as expiation for our sins and the sins of the whole world. For this, we are grateful.

◆ GOSPEL: Jesus offers peace once again to the disciples, as we heard him offer last Sunday. The disciples do not believe it is he. Jesus recognizes that they are troubled, and invites them to see his hands and feet for themselves. Easter joy fills the disciples. Jesus eats with them and breaks open the Scriptures for them. Their growth in faith continues. Ours must, too, in Easter Time as we strengthen ourselves for lifelong witness to the Risen One.

The Roman Missal

It would be a good idea to again use the Rite for the Blessing and Sprinkling of Water. The rite is found in Appendix II at the back of the Missal and it replaces the Penitential Act. The Gloria and the Creed are sung or said today.

The Collect is full of joy—the joy of "the restored glory of our adoption" in Christ, the joy of "the day of resurrection," the joy of a new "youthfulness of spirit."

The Prayer over the Offerings continues the joyful tone of the texts by describing the Church as "exultant" as we offer these gifts, again asking that the offerings will "bear fruit in perpetual happiness."

Any one of the five Easter Prefaces may be selected for today; if Preface I is chosen, remember that the correct wording is "in this time." Consider chanting the introductory dialogue and the Preface today, and every Sunday during Easter Time, in order to highlight the ongoing festivity of the season.

In the Prayer after Communion, we ask that all who share in the "eternal mysteries" may one day know the resurrection of the body.

You might consider using the solemn blessing for Easter Time, found at number 6 in the "Blessings at the End of Mass and Prayers over the People" section of the Missal immediately following the Order of Mass. Remember that a regular formula for dismissal is used, not the solemn double Alleluia.

Other Ideas

Baptisms often take place at Sunday Mass as well as at other gatherings of couples and their children. Too often, people see this as an addition that makes the Mass "too long." Catechesis via the bulletin, website, and social media page can help people remember that Baptism is not a sacrament celebrated in isolation, but one that also includes the commitment of the community to help the infant, child, or adult continue to grow in faith. Invite family members to take out Baptismal candles and photos of family Baptisms to support remembering the joy they experienced at this sacrament. This year, the Third Sunday of Easter falls during tax week in the United States (tax day is usually April 15; however, since this is not a business day in 2018, it is moved to April 17). Consider offering information on stewardship. Have members considered contributing, or even tithing, a portion of the money they receive in their income tax refund?

MON 16 (#273) white
Easter Weekday

The Lectionary for Mass

◆ FIRST READING: The next three days we hear about Stephen's ministry and martyrdom. Today's passage begins by informing us that Stephen worked many great wonders and signs and that many people also could not understand the grace and wisdom with which he taught. The elders and scribes brought Stephen, like Peter and the Apostles, before the Sanhedrin. There, those in the Sanhedrin heard testimony that accused Stephen of blasphemy.

◆ RESPONSORIAL PSALM 119 occurs as a Responsorial Psalm frequently throughout the liturgical year. Today's refrain comes from the very first verse of the longest psalm in the Psalter. The words of the refrain affirm the blessedness of those, like Stephen, who follow the Lord's Law despite others speaking out against them. The verses chosen for this day reflect the beauty of the Lord's statutes as most of the one hundred seventy-six verses of this psalm do.

◆ GOSPEL: It is the day after the disciples saw Jesus walking on water. Today's Gospel is much about the observant crowd keeping track of who's in what boat and where they are going. The disciples go in one boat unaccompanied by Jesus. Other boats came from Tiberias (recall this is near where Jesus had blessed the bread and fed them). The crowds did not find Jesus or his disciples yet, so they got into the boats again and went to Capernaum. They find Jesus there and he tells them that they are looking for him because he filled them with bread. He instructs them on the food of eternal life and upon their inquiry of what to do to gain this food, simply says, believe in the one God the Father sent. Every time we receive the Eucharist, we profess our belief in Jesus, the One who gives us the gift of eternal life in his very Body and Blood.

The Roman Missal

We must leave behind the "old self with all its ways" and "live as Christ did." Our sharing in "the healing paschal remedies" is transformative, making us more like Christ (Collect).

Any one of the five Easter Prefaces may be used today; the readings don't seem to necessarily suggest any one more appropriate than another, although perhaps Preface I, focusing in general on the Paschal Mystery, with its mention that "dying he has destroyed our death, / and by rising, restored our life," would resonate well with the orations.

TUE 17 (#274) white
Easter Weekday

The Lectionary for Mass

◆ FIRST READING: Perhaps Stephen had a suspicion that if he continued to boldly preach the glory of God present in Jesus Christ the crucified and risen Savior he would face persecution, even death, at the hands of the people, elders, and scribes. Today's First Reading begins with Stephen rebuking the people and leaders for their stubborn opposition to the Holy Spirit present in the people who foretold the coming of the Righteous One and in the Righteous One himself. The people's anger took over and they stoned Stephen. Yet as he was dying Stephen gave his spirit over to the Lord whom he served and prayed for the forgiveness of those, even Saul, whose sin led to his death.

◆ RESPONSORIAL PSALM 31: The Responsorial Psalm comes from the same psalm as we sing as Good Friday. The psalm is a lament, but even as such, the psalm writer still expresses confidence in the Lord. In the words of the psalm writer, we pray that the Lord refuge and grant us safety. We trust in the Lord to let his face shine on us. With Stephen, and in the words of Jesus on the Cross in Luke's account of the Gospel, we commend our spirit into the Lord's hands.

◆ GOSPEL: Following upon yesterday's Gospel in which Jesus taught the crowd to believe in the One who gives the food of eternal life, today's Gospel reading finds the same crowd asking Jesus for a sign that would help them believe. It is the crowd who references the manna their ancestors received in the desert. Jesus' solemn response reminds them it was not Moses who provided the food in the desert, but the Father in heaven. The Father's bread gives life forever to the world, Jesus says. Then, in an "I am" statement, Jesus identifies himself as the Bread of Life.

The Roman Missal

Today's Collect continues Easter Time's overall emphasis on sacramental initiation with reference to "those reborn of water and the Holy Spirit," as it asks for "an increase of the grace you have bestowed"; this increase is available through the Eucharist, which is the culmination of and renews the life of grace begun at Baptism.

The Prayer over the Offerings, recently used this past Sunday, expresses the joy of the Church, a joy that originates in the new life given at Easter and finds fulfillment in the happiness of the Kingdom of God. The Prayer after Communion, also repeated from Sunday, asks that those who have been renewed by eternal mysteries—pointing to how every celebration of the Eucharist is our present participation in the Paschal Mystery—may "attain in their flesh / the incorruptible glory of the resurrection," thus, like the Prayer over the Offerings, reminding us of the eschatological fulfillment that awaits us.

Any one of the five Easter Prefaces may be used today. Perhaps, in light of the First Reading from Acts, which portrays Stephen's death as paralleling Jesus', we could find in Preface V of Easter, with its mention of Christ our Passover being sacrificed, its reference to the oblation of Christ's Body, and its mention of Christ "commending himself to you for our salvation," an echo of both Jesus and Stephen handing themselves over in death. that this exchange—this liturgical celebration —"may bring your help in this present life / and ensure for us eternal gladness."

W E D 18 (#275) white
Easter Weekday

The Lectionary for Mass

◆ FIRST READING: Life was not easy for the early followers of Jesus in the Church of Jerusalem. They faced persecution for their belief in Jesus. We know from yesterday's reading that the people killed Stephen for his proclamation of the faith. Today's reading recounts Stephen's burial by devout believers, but also Saul's ongoing attempt to destroy the Church. The reading concludes on a positive note, describing how Philip went to Samaria proclaimed Christ, exorcised demons, and healed the sick. In Jesus Christ, death and destruction never have the final word. Life and joy do.

◆ RESPONSORIAL PSALM 66: The Responsorial Psalm reflects the joy that the people of Samaria experienced when Philip preached Christ to them and continued the mission of Jesus to exorcise demons and heal the sick. This psalm of praise assists us as we continue to express our Easter joy and praise of God for the tremendous deeds he has done in Jesus. Resurrection joy is our song as Christians as we pray the words of today's psalm.

◆ GOSPEL: We continue to proclaim Jesus' words from the Bread of Life discourse in the Gospel according to John over the next few days. In today's Gospel, Jesus expands on his identity as the Bread of Life. He communicates to the crowds how he came down from heaven to do the will of the Father. All that has come to him, he says, he will not lose for the Father deeply desires that all who see the Son, believe in him, so that eternal life and the Resurrection on the last day may be theirs.

The Roman Missal

Today's Collect emphasizes God's initiative in saving us, as it points to "those you have endowed with the grace of faith," and it again reminds us to look beyond our present participation in the Paschal Mystery toward our full participation as it asks that God give us "an eternal share in the Resurrection of your Only Begotten Son." The Prayer over the Offerings speaks of the ongoing power of the Paschal Mystery in our life, asking that "the renewal constantly at work within us /

may be the cause of our unending joy." We should always remember that the effects of the Lord's Resurrection are ongoing in our lives, especially through the liturgy (in the words of the prayer, "these paschal mysteries").

In the Prayer after Communion we once again hear the felicitous phrase "holy exchange" as we pray that this exchange—this liturgical celebration—"may bring your help in this present life / and ensure for us eternal gladness."

Any one of the five Easter Prefaces may be selected for today; perhaps Preface II, with its theme of new life in Christ, would resonate well with what was said above concerning the orations.

THU 19 (#276) white
Easter Weekday

The Lectionary for Mass

◆ FIRST READING: On the road from Jerusalem to Gaza, Philip joins up with an Ethiopian eunuch who was reading from the Isaiah (see 53:7) about the prophet being led to the slaughter. The eunuch's question to Philip is not an indifferent one. Rather, the eunuch begs for an answer as to whom the prophet Isaiah refers. Without hesitation, Philip proclaims Jesus to him. The evidence the passage gives of the eunuch's conversion is his Baptism by Philip. It is the eunuch who sees the water along the route. Philip baptizes him and joy of Christ is his—the same joy that is ours.

◆ RESPONSORIAL PSALM 66: The refrain of today's Responsorial Psalm is the same as yesterday's. The entire earth cries out to God with joy! The opening verses speak of the life God has given the souls of his people (see vv. 8–9). In the other three verses, the psalm takes a personal turn, and the writer declares gratitude and blessing for

how God rescued him. Perhaps the words of this psalm are words the eunuch would have sung after his Baptism. They are our words of praise and gratitude today.

◆ GOSPEL: We continue to read today from the Bread of Life discourse. The passage today follows after a few verses that recount how the Jews were murmuring about Jesus because he claimed he is the Bread of Life. As today's reading begins, Jesus tells them to stop mumbling and complaining among themselves. He proceeds to teach them and the crowds of his relationship to the Father. Just as Jesus is the living bread from heaven come down to earth, so the Father will draw all who believe back to him. All this the Father does through Son for the sake of the world.

The Roman Missal

The Collect points to our ongoing celebration of the fifty days of Easter Time, and the mystery we focus on, as it asks that we experience God's "compassion more readily / during these days when, by your gift, / we have known it more fully." The mention of having been "freed from the darkness of error" can, of course, call to mind the illumination that occurred at Baptism, another theme that runs throughout Easter Time.

The Prayer over the Offerings expresses how this "wonderful exchange" makes us partakers of the very life of God (that is, in the liturgy the very work of our redemption is accomplished). Being made sharers in the life of God, however, the prayer reminds us that we must "make it ours by a worthy way of life."

The Prayer after Communion returns to the old way of life/new way of life motif, asking that we be led to the new way.

Among the Easter Prefaces to be used today, perhaps either II, with its reference to "children of light" or IV, with its statement that "the old

order [is] destroyed, / a universe cast down is renewed, / and integrity of life is restored to us in Christ" would continue the themes found in the orations.

FRI 20 (#277) white
Easter Weekday

The Lectionary for Mass

◆ FIRST READING: The text for today's First Reading was also proclaimed on the Feast of the Conversion of St. Paul. The passage from Acts is first of three narratives of Saul's conversion. Saul's conversion teaches us that with Jesus, change happens. Even dramatic change such as going from persecuting followers of the Way to preaching the Gospel is possible. Like Saul, we never know how or when Jesus will come to us, and more often than not, we will need the assistance of another disciple such as Ananias to assist us in our new way of life.

◆ RESPONSORIAL PSALM 117: The brief two verses Responsorial Psalm takes as its refrain the Risen Christ's commission of the Eleven in the longer ending of Mark's account of the Gospel. The simplicity of the verses draws us to praise God for God's faithfulness and kindness for God never tires of responding to us in this manner even if we weary in our own faithfulness.

◆ GOSPEL: True food and true drink is the topic of today's passage from the Bread of Life discourse. Christ's own Body and Blood is the true food and true drink. His is the Body and Blood come down from heaven to nourish believers. His is the food and drink of eternal life. Some of the Jews do not understand this and argue with one another about it. They want to know how Jesus can give his own flesh for them to eat. Will his explanation be enough for them to believe? How will our reading of today's Gospel lead us to a deeper appreciation of the true food and true drink of the Eucharist?

The Roman Missal

The grace of Easter is not a moment in time, but a lifetime! We have already come to know "the grace of the Lord's Resurrection," yet we continue to pray that "through the love of the Spirit" we may "rise to newness of life" (Collect).

The various references to living in newness of life, and the Gospel's reference to having life because of our feeding on the Bread of Life might make Easter Prefaces I or II likely candidates for use today.

SAT 21 (#278) white
Easter Weekday

Optional Memorial of St. Anselm, Bishop and Doctor of the Church / white

The Lectionary for Mass

◆ FIRST READING: Today's First Reading begins with a summary of how the Church was growing through Judea, Galilee, and Samaria. Then the passage recounts two healings by Peter. First, Peter heals Aeneas, a man who had been bedridden for eight years. Second, at the request of two men whom the disciples had sent, Peter goes from Lydda to Joppa and heals Tabitha, a disciple. As a result of the work of Peter and the other disciples, many of the people of Lydda, Sharon, and Joppa came to believe. Our work for the Lord during the Easter season and beyond also leads people to believe.

◆ RESPONSORIAL PSALM 116: In the refrain, the psalm writer poses the question that perhaps Aeneas and Tabitha could also have asked after the Lord healed them through Peter. The Lord has done so much good for me, how is it possible for me to return his kindness? We use some of the verses of this psalm on Holy Thursday. We pray with the

psalm writer in thanksgiving for the salvation brought through the Lord that we will offer thanksgiving fitting to him.

◆ GOSPEL: Students balk when teachers present challenging material to them. The disciples who heard Jesus say he is the Bread of Life and that they must believe in him whom the Father sent to have eternal life, found this difficult to accept. They murmur just like others who might not have been disciples murmured in yesterday's Gospel reading. Yet Jesus is a realist. He knows that some will chose to believe and other not to believe. Finding Jesus' teaching just too problematic, we hear that many of the disciples went back to their old way of living. The Twelve remain, although Jesus already knows the one who will betray him. May we let the joy of Easter Time buoy us so we might continue to believe in the Bread of Life.

The Roman Missal

Baptism is central to Easter Time and a theology of this sacrament is evident in today's prayers: "You have been buried with Christ in Baptism, / through which you also rose" (Entrance Antiphon); "in the font of Baptism / [God has] made new" (Collect); may we "attain the gifts that are eternal" (Offerings); and "keep safe . . . / those whom you have saved by your kindness" (Communion).

Today's Saint

St. Anselm was born around the year 1033 in Aosta, then part of the Kingdom of Burgundy, today part of Piedmont in the Italian Alps. Hearing of the reputation of his countryman, Lanfranc, who was prior of the Benedictine abbey of Bec in Normandy, Anselm entered the monastery there at the age of twenty-seven. When Lanfranc was named abbot of Caen, Anselm succeeded him as prior of Bec, and fif-

teen years later in 1079, he became abbot. In 1070, Anselm's mentor Lanfranc was made archbishop of Canterbury in England, and when he died in 1109, William II of England seized the lands and revenues of the archdiocese and left the office of archbishop empty (at this time, bishops were appointed by kings). Finally in 1093, public pressure forced William to appoint Anselm archbishop of Canterbury. Anselm's term as archbishop was not easy. He was forced into exile twice because of his support of the Gregorian Reform, which tried to do away with lay investiture, the power of secular authority to appoint bishops. Anselm is a Doctor of the Church and is called the Father of Scholasticism for his works of theology.

(#50) white
Fourth Sunday of Easter
22 Good Shepherd Sunday

About Good Shepherd Sunday

The Fourth Sunday of Easter is traditionally referred to as Good Shepherd Sunday. Hearing the Shepherd's voice, followers recognize and know it is their God. Safe in the knowledge that they cannot be taken from the hand of the Shepherd, those who hear his voice follow as faithful believers willing to go where God calls and sends them. When all the clamor of false voices and seductive distractions threaten to overwhelm, we have only to listen carefully to be led to do the work of the Father.

The Lectionary for Mass

◆ FIRST READING: Peter's good deed of healing a man who was crippled from birth is under examination by the Sanhedrin. Would that our testimony to the person and power of Jesus Christ be as forthright as his! Peter's testimony includes a citation of Psalm 118:22. In quoting this verse, Peter identifies Jesus as the cornerstone through whom salvation comes. No one else saves humanity!

◆ RESPONSORIAL PSALM 118: Our Responsorial Psalm comes from Psalm 118, the same psalm from which our response on the Second Sunday of Easter came. The refrain is the verse Peter's cites in the First Reading from Acts. The verses of the Responsorial Psalm assist us in expressing our thanks and gratitude for all God has done in Jesus Christ as he now lives forever as the cornerstone!

◆ SECOND READING: How much love the Father has for us! We are God's children — not later, but now! Our future, God is yet to reveal. But we have confidence that because of the gift of God's Son, who became like us in all ways but sin, we too, will be like God when we see him as his truly is. We will live forever with the Risen Christ who is one with the Father.

◆ GOSPEL: Jesus knows those who follow him. He would do anything, including laying down his life for his sheep. We know he did suffer and lay down his life. We also know he rose to be the one shepherd of the one flock. Jesus' leadership contrasts starkly with that of a hired man who shepherds sheep he does not know and love. Today we allow the Gospel to remind us of how blessed we are to have Jesus as our Good Shepherd and to have his un-

dying love for us to guide is in our faith and Easter witness.

The Roman Missal

On this Good Shepherd Sunday, the Missal texts are full of images of shepherds.

Continue to use the Rite for the Blessing and Sprinkling of Water, as discussed for the Second Sunday of Easter, or, if you haven't been using it, consider beginning to do so. This rite, found in Appendix II of the Missal, replaces the Penitential Act.

The Gloria is sung today. The Creed is said.

In the Collect, we pray that "the humble flock" may follow "the brave Shepherd" (Christ) to where he has gone — to the very "joys of heaven."

The Prayer over the Offerings is one of "delight," "renewal," and "joy."

While any one of the five Easter Prefaces may be selected for today, certainly Preface III with its reference to Christ as "the Lamb, once slain, who lives for ever," would be appropriate. Continue or begin chanting the introductory dialogue and the Preface today, in order to highlight the ongoing festivity of Easter Time.

The Prayer after Communion, addressed to God, the "kind Shepherd," asks that the whole flock redeemed by Christ's Blood may come to "eternal pastures."

You might consider using the solemn blessing for Easter Time, found at number 6 in the "Blessings at the End of Mass and Prayers over the People" section of the Missal. Remember that a regular formula for dismissal is used, not the solemn double Alleluia.

Other Ideas

This week, on the Feast of St. Mark, was traditionally celebrated as the Major Rogation. *Rogation*, which derives from the Latin word *rogare*, meaning "to ask." Although

not required by the Second Vatican Council, on the days of Rogation we seek God's mercy and ask for his blessings, particularly on gardens, farms, and other agricultural endeavors. This is a day, also, to pray for healing in the wake of the disasters that often befall the natural world such as droughts, floods, hurricanes and blizzards. In this time of growing awareness of the critical need for care of creation, it is also a time to raise awareness about conservation and ecological action. Today is also Earth Day which can be a day of prayer and action for the parish both on its own property and throughout the town or city. Consider making plans with another Christian congregation or a community from another faith tradition to honor our common call for protecting God's creation. This Sunday is also known as Good Shepherd Sunday and the World Day of Prayer for Vocations.

MON 23 (#279) white
Easter Weekday

Optional Memorials of St. George, Martyr / red; St. Adalbert, Bishop and Martyr / red

The Lectionary for Mass

◆ FIRST READING: The episode in today's First Reading takes place after Peter had been in Cornelius's house and baptized many of its members. Cornelius and his family were Gentiles and this appalled the Jewish Christians of Jerusalem. Peter takes time to explain why he entered Cornelius's house and baptized Gentiles and all throughout his explanation references the working of the Spirit within him and the others. In all humility, Peter himself as a person who will not hinder God's work. Peter's explanation was convincing as the Jewish Christians ceased objecting. God's mission does extend to Jews and Gentiles alike — indeed, to all people!

◆ RESPONSORIAL PSALM 42: The psalm writer who was writing outside of Israel and away from Jerusalem profoundly longs for God's presence. Like a deer longs for running water, the psalm writer's soul desires God. Thanksgiving is the appropriate response when we encounter the Lord in our lives. This is the psalm writer's response. Surely, this was the response of Cornelius and his household.

◆ GOSPEL: From the Bread of Life discourse we skip ahead to chapter 10 in John's account of the Gospel. Jesus' solemn teaching in which he identifies himself as the gate for the sheep occurs immediately after his healing of the man born blind. The Pharisees thought they could see, but their sin remains. It was the blind man who acknowledged Jesus. When we recognize Jesus, we, too, are no longer blind. We are a part of the flock whom Jesus leads to salvation.

The Roman Missal

It is by God's gift that we celebrate the Paschal Mystery here on earth; we pray that we may "rejoice in the full measure of . . . grace / for ages unending" (Collect). Time intersects with eternity.

Any one of the five Prefaces of Easter may be used today.

Today's Saints

St. George (c. † 303) was a soldier from Syria who was in the guard of emperor Diocletian. Although historians believe that he did, in fact, exist, the details of his life have been obscured by the many legends that grew up around him. The Golden Legend, a thirteenth century collection of saints' stories, relates the account of George slaying a dragon. He is honored by Catholics, Anglicans, Lutherans, the Orthodox, and even adherents of Islam. St. George is shown in art as a soldier on a white horse slaying a dragon, while carrying a white shield with a red cross. This red cross on a white background is known as St. George's Cross and is on the flags of several countries, including England and Georgia.

St. Adalbert (c. 959–997) came from a wealthy Czech family. He became bishop of Prague before the age of thirty, but resigned because paganism persisted among the Christians there. Adalbert went to Rome and became a Benedictine monk, but in 993, after only four years, the pope sent him back to Prague to resume his role as bishop. He founded the first monastery in the Czech region, but during an uprising, all of his brothers were murdered, and Adalbert had to flee Prague. Adalbert then went to evangelize in Hungary and Poland, where he was welcomed by the rulers. He then went to Prussia where, following the custom of Christian missionaries, he chopped down the sacred oak trees to show the people that the trees were not supernatural. For this he was executed in April, 997. He is honored by both the Catholic and Orthodox Churches and is a patron saint of Bohemia, Poland, and Prussia.

TUE 24 (#280) white
Easter Weekday

Optional Memorial of St. Fidelis of Sigmaringen, Priest and Martyr / red

The Lectionary for Mass

◆ FIRST READING: The message of the Gospel went out to the Greek as well. Paul and Barnabas met up in Antioch where they taught a large number of people. There they met with the Church, and, while the passage does not tell us how the decision was made, it does report that going forward from the conversations in Antioch, the disciples were called Christians.

◆ RESPONSORIAL PSALM 87 is a song of Zion. The Jewish people in diaspora who journeyed to Jerusalem, could take comfort in the Psalm's words for they, too, are among the peoples the Lord loves. As Christians, our roots are in the Jewish faith. Jesus was a Jew. The earliest of believers also were. This psalm connects with the First Reading from Acts because we are now hearing the extension of the early Christian community to Jew and Greek alike. For this all nations praise the Lord!

◆ GOSPEL: Some of the Jews directly ask Jesus to tell them straightforwardly if he is the Christ. Jesus responds directly by saying he told them, but they did not believe. Those who do not believe are not his sheep. Those who believe are in the Father's hands forever. The Gospel concludes with Jesus' statement of the unity between the Father and him, a union in which we believe the fullness of divinity accords itself to both the Father and the Son.

The Roman Missal

Any one of the five Prefaces of Easter may be used today.

Today's Saint

St. Fidelis was a German Capuchin. His baptismal name was Mark, but when he joined the order, he took the name Fidelis, which means "faithful." Fidelis was known for his charity and prayer, and when he became superior of a Capuchin friary, many in the local area returned to Catholicism as a result of his influence. At the behest of the Habsburgs, who ruled parts of Europe at the time, Fidelis went to the north of France to reconvert the people there. Although he was protected by Austrian soldiers, he was captured by Calvinists, who murdered him when he refused to renounce his faith.

WED 25 (#555) red
Feast of St. Mark, Evangelist

The Lectionary for Mass

◆ FIRST READING: Mark, perhaps a disciple of Peter and Peter's colleague in the Church of Rome, sends his greetings. Mark's well wishes follow verses that provide instructions to the Christian community. The instructions advise community members to put on humility and to be sober and vigilant for the Devil roars like a lion near them. The grace of God will continue to strengthen all those whom God calls in Christ Jesus.

◆ RESPONSORIAL PSALM 89 is a communal lament over the defeat of the Davidic king. Despite the fact that the psalm is a lament, the psalm writer still praises the Lord, not just now but forever. Trust that the Lord will remain faithful to his promise that the Davidic dynasty will endure, the psalm writer proclaims the Lord's wonders. We join today in this praise of God together with St. Mark the Evangelist, whose account of the Gospel reveals the Good News of Jesus Christ, the Messiah, the Suffering Son of God who was raised to new life.

◆ GOSPEL: Today's Gospel is the commissioning of the Eleven from what we know as the longer ending of Mark. The passage also includes an account of Jesus' Ascension after the commission the Eleven to continue his work of preaching, exorcising, and healing. After Jesus takes his seat at the Father's right hand, the Eleven fulfill their commission, not alone, but together with the Lord who labored with them.

The Roman Missal

The prayers for the feast are found in the Proper of Saints. The Gloria is said or sung today. Preface II of Apostles is used. In the Collect we pray that we may learn from the Gospel according to Mark to "follow faithfully in the footsteps of Christ." The Prayer over the Offerings is a prayer for the Church, that she may "always persevere / in the preaching of the Gospel." We pray that the Communion we have received may make us strong in the faith that St. Mark proclaimed (Prayer after Communion).

Today's Saint

According to tradition, Matthew and John were Apostles. Mark was not, although he could have been an eyewitness to the events he describes in his Gospel account. He is thought to have been a friend and disciple of Peter, and we know from New Testament references that he ran into some difficulties with Paul. We know that his account of the Gospel of Jesus Christ was written in Rome between the years 60 and 70, following the martyrdom of Peter and Paul. Mark's symbol is a winged lion, an allusion to the desert wilderness with which his Gospel account begins. Mark is the patron saint of Venice, and his relics are venerated in the great cathedral of San Marco.

THU 26 (#282) white
Easter Weekday

The Lectionary for Mass

◆ FIRST READING: We find Paul and his companions in a synagogue in Antioch today, although without John who went back to Jerusalem. They listen to the Law and the prophets, and then, upon the invitation of the synagogue officials to speak, Paul arises and begins a lengthy exhortation on the Davidic ancestry of Jesus, the Savior. Today's First Reading concludes with Paul remarking John the Baptist's ministry heralding the coming of the One whose sandals he is not worthy to unfasten.

◆ RESPONSORIAL PSALM 89 has the same refrain and opening two verses as yesterday's. The other verses come from about halfway through the lament. These verses attest to David's anointing as God's servant-king, and how God will remain faithful through David. As Christians, we believe God's faithfulness will last forever in Jesus Christ, the resurrected One and Savior, whose lineage we trace back through David and his ancestors.

◆ GOSPEL: We move ahead three chapters in John from where Tuesday's reading concluded with Jesus' statement of the oneness between the Father and him. Since that statement in the Gospel according to John, Jesus has raised Lazarus, the Sanhedrin has held a session which resulted in a plan to kill Jesus, Mary anointed him at Bethany, and he entered Jerusalem. Jesus speaks in today's Gospel after he has washed his disciples' feet. His words teach us about servanthood and about receiving both his Father and him. He knows his betrayer is a disciple who has eaten of the food he gave.

The Roman Missal

Any one of the five Easter Prefaces may be selected.

FRI 27 (#283) white
Easter Weekday

The Lectionary for Mass

◆ FIRST READING: Paul's speech in the synagogue that he began in yesterday's reading continues today. His words about Jesus' ancestry in yesterday's First Reading lead to his proclamation today about Jesus' death, Resurrection, and post-Resurrection appearances. Paul says many now are witnesses to the Good News of Jesus Christ, the fulfillment of God's promise. We join our witness today with those who have gone before us in the faith.

◆ RESPONSORIAL PSALM 2: Psalm 2 is a royal psalm in which the psalm writer speaks about how God anoints the king with divine power to rule in his name. As Christians, we interpret the king in this psalm as the Lord's anointed, the Messiah, Jesus Christ, whom God sent to as a fulfillment of his promise. Jesus is God's Son, his beloved. He is the King who will reign forever, the King to whom we witness.

◆ GOSPEL: After announcing Judas's betrayal, giving the New Commandment of love to his disciples, and predicting Peter's denial, we move head to today's Gospel reading in which we hear Jesus identify himself as the Way, the Truth, and the Life. His departure is near, but for those who follow him, he will make ready of place where they can reside together with him and his Father. Often we ask, like Thomas, how we will know the way to where Jesus is. The witness of the Church in the liturgy together with the witness of our companions in faith help to remind us that it is indeed Jesus himself who is the Way.

The Roman Missal

In the Collect, we pray that all who have been redeemed by the blood of Christ may have life and protection from God, "author of our freedom and of our salvation."

Any one of the five Easter Prefaces may be used today, although perhaps using Preface I, II, or IV, with their explicit mention of the life we share in Christ, would provide an echo of the Gospel reading.

S A T **28** (#284) white
Easter Weekday

Optional Memorials of St. Peter Chanel, Priest and Martyr / red; St. Louis Grignion de Montfort, Priest / white

The Lectionary for Mass

◆ FIRST READING: From Paul's speech in the synagogue, we turn today to his address to the Gentiles. Paul quotes from the prophet Isaiah to support his mission to the Gentiles. Salvation is not solely for one corner of the earth, but extends to the ends of the earth. Who would not be delighted, as the Gentiles were, with the Good News Paul offers? Some of the Jews provoked important women and men who worshipped in the community to organize the persecution of Paul and Barnabas. Filled with joy, not sadness, they shook the dust from their feet and moved on. Our joy remains, too, even in rejection, for the Holy Spirit fills us as we proclaim the Good News, just as the Spirit filled Paul and Barnabas.

◆ RESPONSORIAL PSALM 98: A psalm of the Christmas season is our Responsorial Psalm today. The refrain from Psalm 98:3cd announces God's salvation reaches to the ends of the earth. Joy permeates the verses of the psalm, which affirm the wondrous deeds of the Lord. The connection between Easter and Christmas is real and obvious. God's only-begotten Son whom he sent is the Risen One, the Savior of the world. Our response to God's gift is our joyful song. Our song is our witness to the world.

◆ GOSPEL: As we continue to read in the Last Supper discourse of Jesus, we hear Philip ask Jesus to show the disciples the Father. Jesus' response reveals that Philip and the other disciples do not yet understand his words about the oneness of he and the Father. The Father dwells in Jesus and works through

---

him, Jesus says. Thus, those of us who believe in Jesus will continue to do his work — and even greater ones. When we dwell in Jesus, we also dwell with the Father.

The Roman Missal

In the Collect, we pray that what we do today — "our present observance" of the Paschal Mystery of Christ — may benefit us for eternity.

Today's Saints

St. Peter Chanel (1803–1841) was a French missionary to Oceania. Although he encountered many difficulties and made few converts, Peter was able to say, the day before he died for his faith, that "it does not matter if I die. Christ's religion is so deeply rooted on this island that it cannot be destroyed by my death" (Office of Readings, p. 1792). He was right. Within two years, the entire island was Catholic, and the faith remains strong there to this day.

St. Louis Grignion de Montfort (1673–1716) was a priest, the founder of two religious communities (the Daughters of Wisdom and the Company of Mary), and a great apostle of devotion to the Blessed Virgin Mary. His book, True Devotion to Mary, is widely read to this day.

☀ **29** (#53) white
Fifth Sunday of Easter

The Lectionary for Mass

◆ FIRST READING: Saul (Paul) comes to Jerusalem and wants to join the community of disciples. Since he had a history of persecuting followers of the Way, the disciples feared him. Barnabas, however, sponsored him to the Apostles. He brought Saul before the Apostles so they could hear of his conversion. The passage recounts no debate about Paul joining the community of disciples. All we read is that he went about proclaiming the Lord with the Apostles. New disciples, faithful followers are always welcome in the community of believers. We nurture each other, as the community cared for Paul as the Hellenists tried to kill him. Together in the Lord, we build up the Church.

◆ RESPONSORIAL PSALM 22 is a common psalm for Holy Week, and is the psalm for Palm Sunday. Today, we use different verses from Psalm 22 to praise the Lord in the midst of the assembly of his people. As followers of the Lord, our praise is always united with that of the Church. We proclaim the Lord from generation to generation in communion with all who have gone before us and those yet to come.

◆ SECOND READING: Believe in God's Son, Jesus Christ. Keep his commandments. Love one another. Love by your actions. When we do these things, we can have confidence that we will remain in Jesus Christ. We will know his Spirit alive in us! We will be Easter people for the world and for one another.

◆ GOSPEL: Jesus' call for us to glorify the Father by bearing fruit and becoming disciples is clear. The way we do this is by remaining united with Jesus, the true vine and the Father who is the vine grower. Stay the course is essentially Jesus' message. He will always remain in us. Ours is the call to remain in him and bear luscious fruit for the world. Ours is the consolation that we do not have to do anything on our own. In fact, we cannot do anything without the true vine. His is the support and encouragement we live our Easter faith.

The Roman Missal

Even though we are at the Fifth Sunday of Easter, the season is still reverberating with the joy and enthusiasm of the sacramental initiation that occurred at the Easter Vigil: the Collect makes explicit reference to "those you [God] were pleased to make new in Holy Baptism." The prayer goes on to ask that those newly baptized will "bear much fruit / and come to the joys of life eternal." The meaning of Baptism continues to be center stage in the liturgical theology of Easter Time. We ask God to "constantly accomplish the Paschal Mystery within us," so that all the baptized may bear fruit and come to eternal life is not something that happened: it is something that is happening. It is a "wonderful exchange" indeed that has made us "partakers of the one supreme Godhead"! And yet, that is what we are through our sharing in the Eucharist (Prayer over the Offerings).

Every day is Passover, in the sense that every day we are called "to pass from former ways to newness of life" (Prayer after Communion).

Continue to use the Rite for the Blessing and Sprinkling of Water, as discussed for the Second Sunday of Easter, or, if you haven't been doing it, there's no reason why it cannot be used this week. This rite, found in Appendix II of the Missal, replaces the Penitential Act.

The Gloria is sung or said today, as is the Creed.

Any of the five Easter Prefaces may be selected for today. Continue to chant the introductory dialogue and Preface in order to highlight the ongoing festivity of Easter Time, especially if it is not your practice to do so during Ordinary Time.

Consider using the Solemn Blessing for Easter Time, found at number 6 in the "Blessings at the End of Mass and Prayers over the People" section of the Missal. Remember that a regular formula for dismissal is used, not the solemn double Alleluia.

Other Ideas

The readings today are powerful reminders that Christ is the vine and we are the branches. Growth occurs when we remain in him and bear fruit. As his disciples, we are called not to just any sort of love, but the self-sacrificing, critically aware love that Jesus showed those who journeyed with him in life. For many people, when thinking of spreading God's love, the image of missions to other countries may come to mind. In the United States and its territories, there are many dioceses that cannot support basic pastoral needs. This week, the annual Catholic Home Missions appeal will take place. This grant-making agency of the USCCB provides resources that empower missionary activities, including critical help and pastoral services to mission parishes. It also provides financial support for training seminarians, lay ministers, and special ministers who serve ethnic groups in the eighty-seven Latin and Eastern Catholic dioceses.

MON 30 (#285) white
Easter Weekday

Optional Memorial of St. Pius V, pope / white

The Lectionary for Mass

◆ FIRST READING: In Iconium, the Jews and Gentiles and their leaders attempt to stone Paul and Barnabas. The two astute and resilient men flee to Lystra and Derbe, where Paul heals a crippled man. The crowds who witnessed the healing do no understand and choose to acclaim Paul and Barnabas gods. The two would have none of it and persist in their preaching of the living God come down from heaven.

◆ RESPONSORIAL PSALM 115: The refrain for the Responsorial Psalm supports the focus of the First Reading that we give glory to God's name, not to any human beings. We owe all to God for God's loving mercy. We honor God because he has made the heavens and earth. As Christians, we believe God's glory is manifest wholly and completely in Jesus Christ.

◆ GOSPEL: Jesus instructs the disciples in the way of love. Those who love him, he says, the Father loves. Love of Jesus and adhering to his word go together. Consistency matters in this regard. A disciple cannot love Jesus and not follow his commands, and vice versa. Jesus promises the disciples that the Father will send the Advocate, the Holy Spirit to continue to teach them and offer reminders of Jesus' own instruction.

The Roman Missal

In the Collect, we pray for God's abiding presence, that his "right hand" might perpetually help us and defend us "from all wickedness."

The Prayer over the Offerings, makes it clear that what we offer is a participation in the sacrifice of the Eucharist.

The Prayer after Communion asks that the fruits of the Eucharist we just celebrated will "increase in us" and be poured "into our hearts."

Any of the five Easter Prefaces may be used.

Today's Saint

St. Pius V (1504–1572) was a Dominican theologian, elected pope in 1566. His primary task as pope was to implement the reforms of the Council of Trent, which had concluded three years before. During his pontificate, seminaries were reformed, a new Missal was published, and the Catechism and Breviary were also revised. Pius retained his white Dominican habit when he became pope; since that time all the popes have worn white.

May 2018
Month of Our Lady

T U E 1 (#286) white
Easter Weekday

Optional Memorial of St. Joseph the Worker (559) white

The Lectionary for Mass

◆ FIRST READING: Paul and Barnabas had their ups and downs as they sought to grow the early Church. Today's First Reading tells us how some Jews for Antioch and Iconium converted the crowds and stoned Paul. They thought Paul had succumbed to death, but yet when the other disciples came around him, he got up and was able to continue his mission with Barnabas. The two first went to Derbe and then back to Lystra, Iconium, and Antioch where they appointed presbyters and helped the communities to organize the Church. Through it all, Paul and Barnabas are clear in their exhortation to the fledgling disciples new to the faith: hardships are a reality, but persevere will lead you to the Kingdom of God.

◆ RESPONSORIAL PSALM 145 reminds us that it is together, not alone, that we make the wonders of God's Kingdom known. Like the early followers of Jesus, we support in each other today as we persevere in faith and proclaim God's mighty works done in Jesus Christ. His Kingdom lasts forever, his reign lives on for all generations.

◆ GOSPEL: Having told the disciples that the Father will send the Advocate, Jesus now offers them the gift of his peace. He is honest with the disciples as he communicates the reality that he is going away, but will also return. Though this is difficult news for the disciples, he invites them to rejoice with him that he is going to the Father. As we listen carefully to Jesus' words, we also hear his confidence

that the world truly has no power over him for he loves the Father and does the Father's will. Jesus calls us to follow his example of love and obedience.

The Roman Missal

We ask for "constancy in faith and hope," so that we may never doubt the promises of our faith (Collect).

Any one of the five Easter Prefaces may be used today.

Today's Saint

Today you may celebrate the optional Memorial of St. Joseph the Worker, a relatively new addition to the calendar. It was introduced by Pope Pius XII in 1955, as an alternative to secular May Day celebrations of the worker, which originated in Communist countries and which did more to promote Communist propaganda than to promote the worker. Pope Pius XII urged workers to look to St. Joseph, the carpenter, and to see the dignity inherent in human labor, which could become a source of holiness.

W E D 2 (#287) white
Memorial of St. Athanasius, Bishop and Doctor of the Church

The Lectionary for Mass

◆ FIRST READING: Should Gentile believers have to follow the Mosaic law in order to be welcomed into the early Church? In Antioch, Paul and Barnabas hear dissenting opinions on this matter. Rather, the causing a division in the early Church, the community decides to send them and some of the others to Jerusalem to meet with the Apostles and presbyters. The Council of Jerusalem ensues.

◆ RESPONSORIAL PSALM 122 was sung by pilgrims as they journeyed to Jerusalem. How appropriate that this psalm accompanies our First Reading in which Paul and Barnabas and other disciples journey to Jerusalem to meet together to resolve dissension in the early Church. Joy fills this Psalm. The pilgrims rejoice to go to Jerusalem to praise the Lord. There, they will come into the Lord's house.

◆ GOSPEL: Now that Jesus has told his disciples that he must leave and go to the Father, he exhorts his disciples to remain in him as he remains in them. Using a parable-like technique, Jesus speaks of himself as the true vine and the Father as the vine grower. When you bear fruit, he instructs his disciples, you glorify the Father. Jesus warns, however, that the reverse is also true. If they do not remain in him, they will be thrown out because they cannot bear fruit. Will we choose to remain in Jesus or not and support in bearing fruit as his disciples?

The Roman Missal

The prayers for the memorial are drawn from the Proper of Saints. They recall that Athanasius championed Christ's divinity in a time when the Church was divided by heresies. We "profess, as he did, an unblemished faith" (Prayer over the Offerings) in "the true divinity of" Christ (Prayer after Communion).

Today's Saint

St. Athanasius was a fourth-century deacon and bishop who lived in Alexandria, Egypt. He is best known for his lifelong struggle against Arianism, or the heretical belief that God created a son who was neither coeternal nor coequal with the Father. He attended the Council of Nicaea with his bishop, Alexander, and his theological work Three Discourses against the Arians provided the foundation for arguments against this heresy. He was exiled more than five times because of his views, spending more than seventeen years of his episco-

pate outside his diocese. Because of his contributions to the faith, he is a doctor of both the Western and Eastern Churches.

THU 3 (#561) red
Feast of Sts. Philip and James, Apostles

The Lectionary for Mass

◆ FIRST READING: Our First Reading comes from the beginning of the next to last chapter in 1 Corinthians. Paul opens this chapter by reminding the Corinthian community of the Gospel he preached to them. Paul reiterates the kerygma he proclaimed: Christ died for our sins, was buried and was raised on the third day. He appeared many times after his Resurrection. This is the faith the Corinthians share and which is the source of their unity. This is the faith into which we were baptized. This is our Easter faith!

◆ RESPONSORIAL PSALM 19: The first half of Psalm 19, from which today's Responsorial Psalm comes, declares the glory of God. The message of God's glory goes throughout the earth. God's beauty touches everything. God's Word and commands lived out by his faithful servants leave testify to his goodness.

◆ GOSPEL: This Gospel, less the opening verse was proclaimed last Saturday, April 28, 2018. See the commentary on that day for more background. The opening verse of today's Gospel, in which Jesus identifies himself as the Way, the Truth, and the Life, concluded the Gospel reading on Friday, April 27, 2018. Read in the context of the feast of the Apostles, Sts. Philip and James, we hear Philip's statement to Jesus to show us the Father, as our statement, too. We know Philip came to know Jesus, though, he might not have initially understood all Jesus said. May the example of the Apostles Philip and James lead us to deepen our belief in Jesus, the

Way, the Truth, and the Life. When we need guidance in following Jesus, may we ask him—for as he teaches at the end of the Gospel—anything we ask in his name, he will do. Today, we ask in communion with Sts. Philip and James.

The Roman Missal

The texts for this Mass are proper and are located in the Proper of Saints section of the Missal, at May 3. The Gloria is sung or said today, since it is a feast.

The Collect notes how we are gladdened by this feast day each year, asking the prayers of the two Apostles that we might be granted a share in Jesus' Passion and Resurrection, and so see God in eternity.

The Prayer over the Offerings, a short and direct prayer, simply asks the Lord to receive the offerings we bring on this feast day and, in so doing, to "bestow on us religion pure and undefiled."

The Prayer after Communion gives a nod to the Communion of Saints as it observes how together with the Apostles, Philip and James, we contemplate God in his Son and thus "may be worthy to possess eternal life."

The Preface, proper for today, is one of the two Prefaces of the Apostles. Also, in place of the usual final blessing at the end of Mass, the Solemn Blessing for "The Apostles" may be used.

Today's Saints

Two of the chosen Twelve, Sts. Philip and James (first century), grace the liturgical calendar today. Although few details are known about St. Philip, Scripture portrays him as one who leads others to Christ. St. Philip introduces his friend Nathaniel to Jesus, and points to Jesus as the source of nourishment in the feeding of the five thousand. He also highlights Jesus as the path to the Father in the

Last Supper account. St. James "the Lesser"—not to be confused with St. James "the Greater" (he is honored on July 25)—was gifted with a special appearance of the Risen Christ (see 1 Corinthians 15:7). Throughout history it was believed that he authored the letter of James, but recent biblical scholarship considers this to be unlikely. Both Sts. Philip and James died as martyrs, shedding their blood for the sake of the Gospel. They are most likely celebrated together because the Basilica of the Twelve Apostles in Rome is dedicated to them.

F R I 4 (#289) white
Easter Weekday

The Lectionary for Mass

◆ FIRST READING: The Apostles and presbyters at Jerusalem in concert with the whole Church decide to send Judas and Silas as representatives back to Antioch along with Paul and Barnabas to deliver a letter to the community there. Whether or not the letter is the result of the Council at Jerusalem or not, scholars still debate. The letter is straightforward: Gentiles merely need to a few dietary laws and not engage in unlawful marriage. Rejoicing followed the delivery of this communiqué. The Gospel of new life is for everyone!

◆ RESPONSORIAL PSALM 57: You can hear the words of thanksgiving of the psalm refrain on the lips of the Christian community at Antioch once they received the letter placing very limited requirements on Gentiles in order for them to participate fully in the Christian community. For God's mercy and faithfulness, the psalm writer gives thanks. Attributed to David, this psalm could be related to when David flees into a cave to avoid harm by Saul.

◆ GOSPEL: Love is Jesus' commandment, but not just any kind of love. The love with which Jesus instructs the disciples is love modeled on his own love for them. Service and sacrifice define Jesus' love. Would the disciples lay down their lives for him as he will do for them? This love is the love of true friends. The three words "love one another" capture Jesus' command to us and for all will believe in him in future generations.

The Roman Missal

Any one of the five Prefaces of Easter might be used equally well today.

S A T 5 (#290) white
Easter Weekday

The Lectionary for Mass

◆ FIRST READING: Paul and Barnabas separated over a dispute about whether or not to travel with John (who was also known as Mark). In today's First Reading, we find Paul with a new partner in the work of the Gospel, a disciple named Timothy. Paul receives a vision to travel to Macedonia. The vision leads them to seek passage there, for they believe God's call is for them to proclaim the Good News of the Gospel of Jesus Christ to the people in Macedonia.

◆ RESPONSORIAL PSALM 100: Today's Responsorial Psalm, like many during the Easter Season, resounds with joy. Psalm 100 is processional psalm often used as people entered the Temple courts. In liturgy, we come before God with our gifts of joyful praise. We trust that the Lord is God and we belong to him. Delight seems the appropriate response for God's faithful friendship.

◆ GOSPEL: Jesus commands us to love one another as he loves us. He lays down his own life for us on the cross and asks of his followers the willingness to do the same. Yet the hardships that will come upon disciples are part of the difficult news

Jesus conveys to his disciples in today's Gospel reading. The world might hate the disciples just as it hated Jesus. Yet if the world would know the Father, the situation could be different.

The Roman Missal

Through Baptism, God gives us "heavenly life" and makes us "capable of immortality." We pray that we may "attain the fullness of glory" (Collect).

Of the five Easter Prefaces that can be used today, it is Preface IV of Easter, with its mention of "the old order destroyed," that perhaps provides an echo of the Gospel reading of the day, in which Jesus talks to his disciples about being hated by the world.

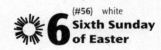

6 (#56) white
Sixth Sunday of Easter

The Lectionary for Mass

◆ FIRST READING: Cornelius and the members of his household meet Peter in today's First Reading. Peter speaks to them of God's impartiality and acceptance of all who believe. God's Word alive in Jesus Christ extends to all—Jew and Gentile alike. Those who hear the Word are welcomed into the community of faith. They, too receive the gift of the Holy Spirit. At the end of the reading, Peter questions whether anyone can withhold the baptismal waters from Cornelius and his household. They were baptized in the name of Jesus Christ for God's grace knows no bounds. That is why it is grace.

◆ RESPONSORIAL PSALM 98 acclaims the Lord for making his salvation known. The revelation of God's saving power we affirm in when we give voice to the Psalm refrain. As Easter people, for us there is nothing like God's saving power in Christ Jesus, nor will there ever be. This power extends to the ends of the earth. Through our witness, we invite others into the gift of God's salvation.

◆ SECOND READING: Love and God are intimately connected. Love comes from God. Love became flesh in Jesus Christ who suffered, died, and rose. From the love of God's Son came life—life for us through him. This, the author of 1 John defines as love. It is what God does for us. It is the expiation of our sins through his Son. When we love God and one another, we link ourselves directly to God. We know God.

◆ GOSPEL: Today's Gospel passage follows immediately in John's account from where the Gospel on the Fifth Sunday of Easter ended. Love is the theme connecting all of today's readings. The Father loves the Son. The Father's Son loves his disciples to the point he considers his disciples friends. His commandment is love; love one another. In love, we as his disciples bring forth fruit into the world.

The Roman Missal

Continue to use the Rite for the Blessing and Sprinkling of Water, as discussed for the Second Sunday of Easter. If you haven't been doing it, there's no reason not to use it this week. This rite, found in Appendix II of the Missal, replaces the Penitential Act.

The Gloria is sung or said today, as is the Creed.

We pray that we may not only celebrate Easter, but live it, so that "what we relive in remembrance / we may always hold to in what we do" (Collect).

In the Prayer over the Offerings, we pray that our prayers may rise up with our offerings, so that we may be transformed as they are, "conformed to the mysteries of your mighty love."

Any one of the five Easter Prefaces may be used equally appropriately today. Continue to chant the introductory dialogue and Preface in order to highlight the ongoing festivity of the season, especially if it is not your practice to do so during Ordinary Time.

In the Prayer after Communion, we ask for an increase in the fruits of the Eucharist, which is the "paschal Sacrament."

Consider using the Solemn Blessing for Easter Time, found at number 6 in the "Blessings at the End of Mass and Prayers over the People" section of the Missal. Remember that a regular formula for dismissal is used, and not the solemn double Alleluia.

Other Ideas

The entire month of May is dedicated to the Virgin Mary, who is celebrated as Queen of Heaven. Many communities hold a crowing of the statue of the Blessed Mother with a simple wreath of roses or a modest crown. Invite parish members to bring flowers to place before her statue as well. Households can place a statue of the blessed mother in a prominent place, and create a small altar with flowers and candles. Include hymns to the Blessed Mother in the liturgy where they fit at mass. Set aside a moment each day for praying the Rosary, perhaps after or before daily Mass, to honor this month. Consider study groups about Mary and Marian piety. The website of the International Marian Research Institute at eh University of Dayton (www.udayton.edu /imri/) is an excellent source of material about the Blessed Mother.

During Easter Time, parishes celebrate group and individual first Communions with children. If it is not your parish's practice, consider having first communicants receive for the first time at Sunday Mass (see LTP's *Guide for Celebrating® First Commuion*). Help members consider what types of gifts will be lasting and meaningful for first communicants, such as Bibles, Rosaries, saint statues, and prayer books. Thursday is the Solemnity of the Ascension, a Holyday of Obligation (in some dioceses, Ascension is transferred to what would have been the Seventh Sunday of Easter).

M O N 7 (#291) white Easter Weekday

The Lectionary for Mass

◆ FIRST READING: Imagine the scene. Paul had found a place of prayer outside the city gate of Philippi along the river. A beautiful spot he had found, not only for prayer, but to engage in holy conversation. The conversation he had was with a woman named Lydia. Lydia listened to Paul's message of Good News and she, along with her household, became believers and were baptized. She invites Paul and his companions into her home, a sign of her hospitality in the Lord.

◆ RESPONSORIAL PSALM 149: Read in the context of today's First Reading, the refrain expresses how happy the Lord is in his people. How happy the Lord must have been when Lydia her household believed and were baptized! Surely, her household sang God's praises as the psalm invites us to do on this Monday of the Sixth Week of Easter!

◆ GOSPEL: The coming of the Advocate does not take away the disciples responsibility to testify to Jesus. Though Jesus states it as a reality that the journey for the disciples will get difficult, he also exhorts them to remain committed to their mission. Even when the disciples' hour comes, and they might face death, Jesus wants them to remember what he has told them: they know and believe in Jesus and the Father. The two are one, and their care and love for the disciples will endure forever.

The Roman Missal

We ask for "the fruit produced by the paschal observances," that Easter may have an effect in our lives (Collect).

TUE 8 (#292) white
Easter Weekday

The Lectionary for Mass

◆ FIRST READING: After the Baptism of Lydia and her household, Paul exorcises an evil spirit from a slave girl working as an oracle. Her owner's were upset with Paul's miraculous deed because they profited from the girl and the spirit of the Python serpent within her. Thus, they chose to drag Paul and Silas into the public square where the crowd attacks them. Today's First Reading picks up at this point. The magistrates imprisoned the two, but while Paul and Silas prayed and sang to God, a severe earthquake occurred and the doors of the jail opened. Paul and Silas were freed by the power of God and free in the Lord. The freedom they experienced is the freedom they offer to others through the Gospel they preach. The jailor and his household recognized this as they believed in the Lord Jesus and were baptized. Unlikely converts, perhaps, but God's salvation knows no bounds.

◆ RESPONSORIAL PSALM 138: The psalm writer thanks God for coming to his aid in a time of distress. The words of the psalm profess salvation in God and gratitude for the strength the Lord gives. In light of the First Reading, Paul and Silas surely could pray these words for the Lord came to their aid and freed them from prison. God's help in Jesus Christ has also come to the jailor and his household. For God's saving grace they and we give thanks!

◆ GOSPEL: Letting a loved one go is difficult. Jesus sees the grief in his disciples after he informed them that he must leave and return to the Father. In today's Gospel, Jesus explains to the disciples that it is indeed better that he go so the Advocate might come. Jesus also conveys a word of warning to the disciples about the world. The Advocate, he advises them, will judge harshly against those who do not believe and have condemned the Father who reigns over heaven and earth.

The Roman Missal

The Collect is a simple prayer for a share in the Resurrection of Christ. The Prayer over the Offerings asks that "we might always find delight in these paschal mysteries" which will "ensure for us eternal gladness" (Prayer after Communion).

WED 9 (#293) white
Easter Weekday

The Lectionary for Mass

◆ FIRST READING: Today we find Paul in Athens. His speech at the Areopagus addresses the Athenians in a way they will understand. Paul affirms their religiosity, but then moves from that to proclaim the one God who created the world and is Lord of heaven and earth. This God forgives times of ignorance and infidelity. Without using the name Jesus Christ, Paul proclaims, this God has selected a man who he raised from the dead. Paul's talk of the Resurrection of the dead intrigued some of the Athenians, while others mocked him, and other became believers. We are among the believers and those who continue to want to hear more about the Resurrection of the dead. Paul's message is the Easter message!

◆ RESPONSORIAL PSALM 148 summons all creatures in heaven and earth to praise the Lord. Male and female, kings and princes, children, youth, and those mature in age, praise God! Is not the picture of diverse people that the psalm writer calls to praise the Lord, an image of our assemblies that gather for worship today? Notice the phrase in the Sanctus that echoes the psalm refrain ("Heaven and earth are full of your glory").

◆ GOSPEL: Jesus continues to speak with his disciples. He informs the disciples that even though he has more to tell them, he will not say more because he recognizes they cannot handle what he might say. Jesus reminds the disciples that he will not abandon them. The Spirit, Jesus says, will lead them to the truth. The disciples will share in what belongs to Jesus and the Father.

The Roman Missal

If tomorrow is celebrated as the Ascension, this Mass is celebrated in the morning. The evening Masses should be for the Vigil of the Ascension (see page 203).

◆ FOR THE MORNING MASS: The Collect today reminds us how every celebration of the Eucharist unites us with the Communion of Saints: we participate in the fruits of Jesus' Resurrection now, through our liturgical celebration of the mysteries, while the saints already share in the fullness of the Resurrection in the Kingdom. In the Prayer over the Offerings we again hear of "the wonderful exchange effected in this sacrifice," which should become the pattern for every aspect of our life; growing in that conformity to the life of Christ is the goal of liturgical celebration. The Prayer after Communion presents the effects of our participating in the "heavenly mysteries" as passing "from former ways to newness of life."

(#58)   white

T
H
U
10

Solemnity of the Ascension of the Lord

HOLYDAY OF OBLIGATION

About Today's Solemnity

The distinct celebration of the Ascension of the Lord was unknown in the first three and a half centuries. The chronology of dating the Ascension to forty days after Easter exists only in the Acts of the Apostles. In the Gospel according to Luke, the Ascension appears to have taken place much earlier, even on Easter Day. The original ending to Mark's account of the Gospel did not include the Ascension at all, and it can only be inferred from Matthew's conclusion. When fourth-century Egeria mentions a celebration forty days after Easter in Bethlehem, it may have been for the Holy Innocents. But by the fifth century the observance seems to be universally accepted.

In the dioceses where today is celebrated as the Ascension, it is a Holyday of Obligation.

The Lectionary for Mass

◆ FIRST READING: The opening of the Acts of the Apostles is today's First Reading. The introduction to this book connects it to Luke's first volume, his narrative of the Gospel, noting that his Gospel account described what Jesus taught and did, his post-Resurrection appearances, up to his Ascension. Now Jesus tells his disciples they will receive the Holy Spirit and they are to go forth as Jesus' witnesses to the far reaches of the earth. Jesus ascends to the Father, but the Apostles are left staring at the sky until two men in white garments inform them of more Good News: Jesus will return in glory!

◆ RESPONSORIAL PSALM 47: Today's refrain directly connects to Jesus' Ascension into heaven where he now reigns with the Father. What a joyful occasion this is indeed! Let clapping, shouts of joy, and songs of praise tell the world that the Lord reigns forever.

◆ SECOND READING: The One who ascended into heaven is also the One who descended to earth. One with us in all things but sin, Christ is the One who came down to earth and returned to the Father. Jesus Christ, the Son of God, is the one who gives us the gifts to preserve the unity of the one Church, the Body of Christ. The seven unity statements that open the reading reminds us of how strong the bond of faith is among those who believe. We are united in the one Lord who now has return to his Father.

◆ GOSPEL: The Great Commission is today's Gospel reading. With the mere command "Go," Jesus sends his disciples into the world to proclaim the Gospel. Their commission is ours today by virtue of our Baptism. The Lord worked wondrous signs through them as they spread his Word. On this Solemnity, may we look around and see the amazing signs the Lord continues to work through those who witness to him throughout the world in the twenty-first century!

The Roman Missal

Two sets of Mass formularies are given for the solemnity, one for the Vigil Mass and one for the Mass during the Day. A rubric before the texts for the Vigil Mass explains that where the Solemnity of the Ascension is not observed as a Holyday of Obligation, it is observed on the Seventh Sunday of Easter.

◆ AT THE VIGIL MASS: Remember that the Creed is said today as is the Gloria.

The Preface assigned for this Mass is either Preface I or Preface II of the Ascension. Preface I makes explicit that the purpose of Christ's Ascension was "not to distance himself from our lowly state," but rather so that we "might be confident of following where he, our Head and Founder, has gone before." Preface II states the same thing in a slightly different way, noting that the purpose of the Ascension was so that "he might make us sharers in his divinity." As with the Sundays of Easter Time, it would be a good idea to chant the introductory dialogue and Preface today.

If the Roman Canon is used as the Eucharistic Prayer for this celebration, remember that there is a proper form of the *Communicantes* ("In communion with those . . ."); it is found within the prayer itself, on the page that lists the several different forms of the *Communicantes*.

There is a special Solemn Blessing specifically for the Ascension of the Lord that can be used for the final blessing at the end of Mass, and it would be good to make use of it. We're not at Pentecost yet, however, so the solemn double Alleluia dismissal is not yet used. Stick with one of the usual dismissal formulas.

◆ AT THE MASS DURING THE DAY: There is no reason not to use the Rite for the Blessing and Sprinkling of Water, especially if it has been used on the Sundays throughout Easter Time. Baptism into the Paschal Mystery means immersion in the fullness of the mystery, which includes Christ's ascended glory. The rite is found in Appendix II of the Missal and replaces the Penitential Act. The Gloria is sung today. The Creed is said.

The priest celebrant has a choice from among two Collects for today. The first option sets a tone of gladness and joy as it notes that "the Ascension of Christ your Son / is our exaltation" because we, his Body, are "called to follow in hope" where he, our Head, has gone. The reality that liturgy is at its core a celebration of our participation in the mysteries of Christ cannot be stated emphatically enough, and this prayer is yet another example of how this truth is basic to the meaning of liturgical celebration. The second prayer asks that, since we "believe that your Only Begotten Son, our Redeemer, / ascended this day to the heavens," we may be granted to even now dwell in spirit "in heavenly realms." Notice too the important assertion of "this day," an important reference to the salvific reality being made present in our own time and space. The Creed is said today.

See the comments about the Vigil Mass for some thoughts about the two options for the Preface, which are the same for the Mass during the Day, and for the proper insert if Eucharistic Prayer I is used.

As with the Vigil Mass, it would be good to use the special Solemn Blessing specifically for the Ascension of the Lord as the final blessing at the end of Mass. Since we're not at Pentecost yet, one of the usual dismissal formulas, not the solemn double Alleluia dismissal, is used.

THU 10 (#294) white
Easter Weekday

In some dioceses, today is celebrated as an Easter Weekday. The commentaries that follow are for this day. You may also celebrate the optional Memorial of St. Damien de Veuster, Priest / white

The Lectionary for Mass

◆ FIRST READING: From Athens, Paul journeys to Corinth where he meets Aquila who share Paul's tent making trade. The passage tells us the Paul stayed with Aquila, and on the Sabbath days, he held forums in the synagogue with both Jews and Greeks. We do not know from this passage if Aquila became a believer, but what we do know if some Jews opposed Paul's preaching that Jesus was the Christ. Paul decides to move forward by taking his message to the Gentiles. Ironically, the reading ends by noting the Crispus, a synagogue official, and his household became believers and were baptized.

◆ RESPONSORIAL PSALM 98: In light of today's First Reading, the victory of the Lord the Psalm speaks about reflects the victory of new life in Jesus Christ for those who believe. Salvation touches every part of the earth. Jews and Gentiles alike can rejoice in God's saving power extended to them by Jesus, who as Paul proclaims, is the Christ.

◆ GOSPEL: Again Jesus reminds the disciples that shortly they will not see him. Yet all is not lost, as he also lets them know that after a brief time, they will see him again. The disciples question Jesus' words. They want to know more about what the "little time" means. Jesus can tell exactly what the disciples are discussing, and so he responds by solemnly teaching them that their sorrow with turn to joy. Would that the world know this joy so that its initial joy while the disciples grieve would last.

The Roman Missal

If the Ascension is celebrated in your diocese on Sunday, then today's prayers are from Thursday after the Sixth Sunday of Easter in the Proper of Seasons.

Today's Saint

After years of missionary work in the Hawaiian Islands, Damien (1840–1889), a young priest from Belgium, sought to align himself even more with the "crucified" in society. He requested to be stationed on the island of Moloka'i. Outraged by the deplorable conditions on the island, he sought to restore dignity to the lepers and diseased who were sent there to die. Outraged by the deplorable conditions of the island, he sought to restore a sense of dignity. Within a short period of time, the sick were living in clean houses instead of caves, and upon death they were given a proper burial rather than being dumped into mass graves. Even though leprosy was highly contagious, he chose to remain in close contact with the people. Damien eventually contracted the disease and died from it.

FRI 11 (#295) white
Easter Weekday

The Lectionary for Mass

◆ FIRST READING: After receiving a vision that God will protect him in Corinth, Paul settles there. His preaching insights some Jews to rise up against him, but Gallio, the proconsul of Achaia, will have nothing to do with resolving doctrinal disputes. His authority only extends to Roman law. Those who had risen up against Paul seize Sosthenes, a synagogue official, and beat him. Despite the conflicts and persecution, Paul remains in Corinth for a long time, and then bids farewell to continue his mission in Syria.

◆ RESPONSORIAL PSALM 47 proclaims God's kingship with certainty. God governs the earth and its inhabitants. The inheritance of the earth's peoples is God's glory. Verse 6 in the third stanza Christians interpret as a reference to Christ's Ascension. Christ ascends to the Father and now sits at his right hand on the throne. To the risen and ascended Easter King, we sing praise!

◆ GOSPEL: The Gospel reading today begins with a repetition of the verse with which yesterday's Gospel ended. Jesus uses the event of woman giving birth to a child to explain to the disciples the shift they will experience in their emotions from sorrow to joy as Jesus departs and then returns. When a woman gives birth to a child, the anguish of labor gives way to the joy of seeing and holding the child she has brought into the world. The disciples' sadness will shift to pure delight when they see their Lord again.

The Roman Missal

The Missal acknowledges that in some regions the Solemnity of the Ascension, observed on the Seventh Sunday of Easter, has not yet been celebrated, and so it provides a choice for the Collect.

The first Collect is the one to be used if the Ascension was celebrated the day before. It acknowledges that God restores us to eternal life through Christ's Resurrection, and so it asks that we be raised up "to the author of our salvation, / who is seated at your right hand." The prayer then goes on to confess how our Savior will come again in majesty, therefore asking that. "those you have given new birth in Baptism / may be clothed with blessed immortality." Notice how the prayer skillfully weaves together various themes we have been hearing throughout Easter Time, incorporating them with the most recent aspect of a focus on Christ's Ascension into glory.

The second Collect is the correct choice for those places where the Solemnity of the Ascension is celebrated on the upcoming Sunday. This prayer more generally asks that what God has promised may be accomplished so that "all your adopted children" (we can hear the language of Baptism here) may attain what has been foretold — eternal life and happiness. The Prayer over the Offerings, in a somewhat similar theme as the

second Collect, begs both that the blessings that have been given by God may not be lost, and that we may "attain the gifts that are eternal." The Prayer after Communion echoes this petition. The choices for the Preface today include any one of the five Prefaces of Easter or the two Prefaces of the Ascension. For communities that celebrated the Ascension yesterday, it would be most beneficial to highlight the unique nature of these days as time Pentecost by using one of the Ascension Prefaces. For other communities, one of the Easter Prefaces should be used.

SAT 12 (#296) white
Easter Weekday

Optional Memorials of Sts. Nereus and Achilleus, Martyrs / red; St. Pancras, Martyr / red

The Lectionary for Mass

◆ FIRST READING: Paul traveled from Cenchreae to Ephesus, and from Ephesus to Caesarea, and then on to Antioch. Today's First Reading finds him departing Antioch for Galatian country and Phrygia. The rest of the reading focuses on the work of Apollos, a Jew whose homeland was Alexandria. Apollos proclaimed God's Word in the synagogue at Ephesus, but as the reading mentions, Priscilla and Aquila advised him on how to be more precise. From Ephesus, Apollos went on mission to Achaia, where he, like Paul, taught that Jesus is the Christ.

◆ RESPONSORIAL PSALM 47: The refrain attesting to God's kingship over all the earth draws our attention to the ongoing spread of the Gospel that we hear in the First Reading. The last three verses from Psalm 47 for today differ from the verses in yesterday's psalm. Note particularly verse 10, in which we, as Christians, recognize the God of

Jesus Christ is the God of Abraham enthroned above.

◆ GOSPEL: Like yesterday, today's Gospel reading begins with a repetition of the concluding verse from the previous day's Gospel. Jesus' words to the disciples are simple, yet profound. Ask anything of the Father in Jesus' name, he tells them, and you will receive it. The Father will honor the disciples' request for he loves them deeply, just as they love his only-begotten Son, Jesus. Soon Jesus will tell his disciples and us more clearly about the Father.

The Roman Missal

Notice that there are two options for the Collect today, to be used depending on when the Solemnity of the Ascension of the Lord is observed. When he ascended into heaven, Christ promised his Holy Spirit to the Apostles. We ask for a share in those same "spiritual gifts" (Collect).

Today's Saint

The information we have regarding the lives of St. Nereus and St. Achilleus comes from an ancient inscription written in their honor by Pope Damasus I. While serving as second-century praetorian soldiers, they had a conversion experience resulting in the choice to relinquish their weapons for the Gospel of peace. Because they refused to succumb to idol worship, they were beheaded during the reign of Trajan (98 –117).

St. Pancras († 304), a Roman martyr, was a casualty of the Diocletian persecutions. After moving to Rome he converted to Christianity, thus making him a target of the anti- Christian ideology of the reigning emperor. He was beheaded at the age of fourteen; his death gave rise to a strong cult of followers. Stemming from St. Pancras' popularity among the faithful, a monastery in Rome and a church in Canterbury were dedicated to him.

☀ **13** (#60) white
**Seventh Sunday
of Easter**

*In some dioceses, the Solemnity of
the Ascension of the Lord is transferred to the Seventh Sunday of
Easter. If this is the case in your
diocese, please use the readings
and prayer texts from the Ascension. Please see page 198 in this
Sourcebook for commentary.*

The Lectionary for Mass

◆ First Reading: Proclaimed in
the context of the Seventh Sunday
of Easter, we focus on how the ministry of the Apostles continues in
the early Church. A new leader is
chosen through discernment and in
communion with other Apostles and
believers. The Eleven, now Twelve
again, will continue their proclamation of the Risen Christ and the new
life he offers.

◆ Responsorial Psalm 103:
The Lord's throne is in heaven the
refrain tells us. Following upon the
First Reading for the Seventh
Sunday of Easter, the psalm invites
us to bless the Lord with our entire
being as those who are Apostles do.
The Lord rules over all, yet ours is
the task now to show others the way
to him.

◆ Second Reading: Now, nearing the final days of Easter Time,
we hear these words again. The
message is simple, yet profound.
The words this Sunday as the past
few Sunday are words of love. God

is love. We know this because he
sent his Son as the Savior of the
world. We go forth and carry on his
work as he returns to the Father.
Ours is the call to teach others how
to live in God's love. We do this
within a communion of faithful
people who can constantly reminds
us of God's love and our ongoing
invitation from him to live in it.

◆ Gospel: Joy is Jesus' wish for
his dear ones, his disciples. He
knows he took care of them while
he was with them on earth, but he
must return to the Father. So now
he prays that the Father watch over
them while they are still in the
world. He does not want his followers removed from the world, for
then they have no impact on the
world. Bind them to the truth and
make them holy are Jesus' desires
for the disciples and us.

The Roman Missal

If you are in a region that observes
the Solemnity of the Ascension
today, refer to the comments on
page 198 for the celebration of
Mass today. What follows is for the
Seventh Sunday of Easter.

Continue to use the Rite for the
Blessing and Sprinkling of Water,
as has been done, it is hoped, on all
the Sundays of Easter Time. If this
has not been the case, it can nonetheless still be used today if desired.
Remember that this rite, found in
Appendix II of the Missal, replaces the Penitential Act. The Gloria
and the Creed are sung or said.

We believe that Christ has risen
and ascended to his Father; in the
Collect, we pray that we may experience his abiding presence in
our midst.

We pray that the "acts of devot-
edness" we bring to God in the celebration of the Eucharist may help us
to "pass over to the glory of heav-
en" (Prayer over the Offerings).

The Ascension is a fact, and a
promise of future glory, because
we believe that "what has already

come to pass in Christ," the Head of
the Church, "will be accomplished
in the body of the whole Church"
(Prayer after Communion).
Although the choice of the Preface
may be taken from among the
five Easter Prefaces or the two
Ascension Prefaces, it would seem
to be pastorally advantageous to
use one of the two Prefaces of the
Ascension. Continue to chant the
introductory dialogue and Preface.

Use the solemn blessing for
Easter Time, found at number 6 in
the "Blessings at the End of Mass
and Prayers over the People" section
of the Missal, and one of the regular formulas for dismissal is used.

Other Ideas

Because Easter Time does not end,
continue to keep the Paschal candle lit and placed by the ambo until
after Evening Prayer on Pentecost.

Today is Mother's Day. In the
Universal Prayer, include prayers
for mothers facing challenges, including those who are pregnant,
facing infertility, mourning, endangered, and more. If you set aside
a moment after the Prayer after
Communion for a blessing, consider expanding the approach beyond those "who are mothers."
Many women feel sadness and loss
on this day because they have not
had a child for which they longed.
Consider inviting all women "who
have shown someone a mother's
love" to stand and be recognized
with a prayer or the presentation of
a flower. Invite community members to honor their godmothers as
well as their mothers.

M
O **14** (#564) red
N **Feast of St. Matthias,
Apostle**

The Lectionary for Mass

◆ First Reading: In the reading, Peter summarizes Judas'
betrayal and the necessity, according to the Scriptures, of another
taking his place to witness to Jesus'

Resurrection. A group of about one hundred and twenty brothers and sisters in the faith surfaced the names of two men Joseph and Matthias, as candidates to fill Judas' position. After offering a prayer of discernment, those gathered cast lots. Thus, Matthias became the new chosen Apostle.

◆ RESPONSORIAL PSALM 113: The psalm writer calls upon the assembly to offer praise befitting of God for no other God is like him who sits upon the throne on high. The refrain speaks of the seat the Lord gives to a new leader among the existing leaders of the Lord's people. In light of today's First Reading, we can visualize Matthias taking his seat among the existing Eleven Apostles to praise and glorify the Lord. Ours is the call to follow the example of praise and glory of our leaders in faith who shepherd us to the Lord. Ours is the call to praise so that by our example, others also might come to believe.

◆ GOSPEL: The Gospel focuses our attention on how Matthias fulfilled Jesus' command to the disciples to love another. His as a ministry that would contrast with Judas Iscariot's betrayal and failure to love Jesus in the end.

The Roman Missal

The prayers for the feast are found in the Proper of Saints. The Gloria is said or sung today. One of the Prefaces of the Apostles is used. The Collect alludes to the fact that St. Matthias was chosen by lot to take the place of Judas among the Twelve. We pray that, through his intercession, we may "be numbered among the elect."

Today's Saint

St. Matthias was chosen by the Holy Spirit to replace Judas as a member of the Twelve. Today we commemorate this Apostle, whom the Scriptures tell us had been in the company of the Lord from the time he was baptized by John until the time he was taken up to heaven.

TUE 15 (#298) white
Easter Weekday

Optional Memorial of St. Isidore / white

Lectionary for Mass

◆ FIRST READING: Paul announces his return to Jerusalem. Unsure of the fate that awaits him there, he is certain about one thing: that he will continue in the ministry of witness to the Gospel of the Lord Jesus. He informs the presbyters of the Church of Ephesus that he will not be responsible for what happens to them because he fulfilled his mission of proclaiming God's plan to them.

◆ RESPONSORIAL PSALM 68 praises God for his help in the past as he led the Israelites out of Egypt and accompanied them as the settled in the land of Canaan. Together with the psalm writer in the verse 20–21, we bless the Lord who is our salvation and in whom we have confidence is with us now and will be forever, even through the passage of death.

◆ GOSPEL: Jesus' prayer from John 17 from which we read the rest of this week, is the climax of his teaching in John 16. The prayer begins with Jesus' acknowledgment that his hour has come. He prays that the Father will glorify him and for his disciples to receive the gift of eternal life. The world is not among the concerns in Jesus' prayer, but only the ones the Father has given him. These he holds dear. These are the ones who have believed and through their own ministry have already glorified him. Jesus knows when he leaves them, they will remain in the world and will need the Father's love.

The Roman Missal

Although the choice of the Preface may be taken from among the five Easter Prefaces or the two Ascension Prefaces, strongly consider using one of the two Prefaces of the Ascension as a way of highlighting the unique liturgical time in which we find ourselves, in between Ascension and Pentecost in days that pray for the coming of the Spirit.

Today's Saint

Today we honor Isidore the Farmer, rather than the Doctor of the Church, Isidore of Seville. Isidore the Farmer was born in Madrid to poor parents who sent him to work for a landowner. He was very devout and married a like-minded woman, Maria, who also became a saint. Isidore attended daily Mass and was often late arriving at the fields, but he managed to get his work done nonetheless. He shared the little he had with the poor. He is the patron of farmers; it is fitting to remember him in the northern hemisphere's agricultural season.

WED 16 (#299) white
Easter Weekday

The Lectionary for Mass

◆ FIRST READING: Paul finishes his address to the presbyters of the Church of Ephesus at Miletus in today's First Reading before he bids farewell to return to Jerusalem. He exhorts the presbyters to care for each other and their flock. He is honest with the leaders of the Church letting them know that they will face persecution. Yet Paul instructs them to be resilient, faithful in the missions to proclaim Gospel as he was. A concluding prayer together concludes their time together, as did the genuine hospitality of the leaders escorting Paul to the ship that awaited him.

◆ RESPONSORIAL PSALM 68: Surely, Israel sings praises to God!

In today's Responsorial Psalm, which comes from the same Psalm as yesterday's, the psalm writer even encourages the defeated enemies of Israel to confess God's power. The God of Israel desires to be their God, too, for Israel's God is truly the God of all the kingdoms of the earth.

◆ GOSPEL: Hold them in your name. Keep them safe from the Evil One. Make them holy in the truth. Jesus asks all this of the Father for his disciples. It is obvious how much Jesus cares for his followers. Theirs is a deep, close friendship. They have seen each other through much in their mission and ministry. In his prayer, Jesus asks for his love and support that stem from the Father's own love to strengthen the disciples for what lies ahead.

The Roman Missal

The choices for the Preface today include any one of the five Prefaces of Easter or the two Prefaces of the Ascension. It would seem most beneficial to highlight the unique nature of these days as time in between the Ascension and Pentecost by using one of the Ascension Prefaces.

THU 17 (#300) white
Easter Weekday

The Lectionary for Mass

◆ FIRST READING: Paul was wary of the fate that awaited him. We move ahead a few chapters in Acts from yesterday's First Reading and find Paul before the Sanhedrin. Pharisees and Sadducees were both members of the ruling council. Paul identifies himself as a Pharisee who was on trial for hoping in the Resurrection of the dead. The Pharisees, of course, could find nothing wrong with Paul, while the Sadducees dismissed his hope in the resurrection because they themselves did not share this confidence. Paul's life was at risk that troops brought him back to the compound.

He witnessed in Jerusalem, now the Lord tells him, he must do the same in Rome. We, too, witness to the Resurrection wherever the Lord sends us in our lives.

◆ RESPONSORIAL PSALM 16: Today's Responsorial Psalm was also used on Monday of the Octave of Easter, April 2, 2018. Surely, Paul prayed similar words to that of the refrain in which we ask God to keep us safe. We, like Paul, also express our hope in God in the second half of the refrain. God will guides us in the path of our life, and though we might face danger, we still will taste joy in God's presence. Our heart and body, spirit and soul, our whole being exudes confidence that the Lord always remains with us.

◆ GOSPEL: Jesus expands his prayer in today's passage to include those who will believe on the basis of the disciples' witness. He asks the Father to include these new believers in his circle of love. The love of the Father and the Son is not exclusive to them, but is an open embrace drawing in the disciples and all who will believe in the name of Jesus Christ, the Word made flesh.

The Roman Missal

The choices for the Preface today include any one of the five Prefaces of Easter or the two Prefaces of the Ascension. It would seem most beneficial to highlight the unique nature of these days as time in between the Ascension and Pentecost by using one of the Ascension Prefaces.

FRI 18 (#301) white
Easter Weekday

Optional Memorial of St. John 1, Pope and Martyr / red

The Lectionary for Mass

◆ FIRST READING: Paul asserted Jesus was alive, when the authorities claimed he was dead. In today's First Reading we find Paul before

King Agrippa and his sister, Bernice. The two were notorious for the lack of kindness to the Jerusalem community. No one can find reason to charge Paul with any crime. The only issue they have with him relates to his proclamation of the Risen Christ. Paul will have a chance to defend himself in front of the k†ing in the following chapter of Acts, and then, still a prisoner, he will set sail for Rome with others held in captivity.

◆ RESPONSORIAL PSALM 103: We acclaim the Lord enthroned in heaven in the refrain. Along with the psalm writer we bless God with our entire being. We rejoice in the Lord's kindness and trust that he forgives our sins. We praise the Risen Christ who ascends to the Father and now sits at his right hand. Jesus is the Risen Christ to whom Paul ceaselessly witnesses.

◆ GOSPEL: From the conclusion of Jesus' prayer in yesterday's Gospel we journey ahead four chapters in John. The Risen Christ has revealed himself to the disciples and shared breakfast with them. Our scene begins with Jesus inquiring of Simon Peter about his love for Jesus in comparison to the other disciples. Three times Jesus asks and Simon Peter is nothing less than consistent in his responses—always professing his love and stating the Lord should know Simon loves him. Jesus leaves Simon Peter with two simple words: "Follow me." He will have to follow, feeding and tending Jesus' sheep, even to the point of his own death.

The Roman Missal

Through Christ's Resurrection and the Spirit's light, "the gates of eternity" stand open before us. We pray that our sharing in God's great gifts may deepen our devotion and strengthen our faith. The choices for the Preface today include any one of the five Prefaces of Easter or the two Prefaces of the Ascension.

Today's Saint

St. John I († 526) was a native of Tuscany and was elected pope when quite elderly. Despite his protests, he was sent by the Arian King Theodoric to Constantinople, where he was to convince Emperor Justin to moderate his decree against the Arians. Theodoric threatened reprisals against Orthodox Christians in the West if he failed. When John returned, Theodoric had him arrested on suspicion of conspiring with the emperor. He died in prison of ill treatment.

S A T 19 (#302) white
Easter Weekday

The Lectionary for Mass

◆ FIRST READING: We move ahead a few chapters in Acts for today's final weekday First Reading of the Easter Season. Paul is now in Rome, but still imprisoned. He requests to speak to the leaders of the Jews for he believes in his witness to Jesus—the One who suffered, died and rose—he carries the "hope of Israel." The end of this passage is the end of the Acts of the Apostle. Two years Paul remained in prison, though in his own private dwelling, where he remained steadfast in his proclamation of God's Kingdom and taught about Jesus Christ. Would that our faith be as strong as Paul's and our witness as consistent!

◆ RESPONSORIAL PSALM 11: Once again, our psalm writer reflects on the Lord's throne in heaven. From his throne in heaven, the Lord watches over humankind. The Lord distinguishes between the just and the wicked such that the just will gaze on the Lord's own face as the refrain tells us. Certainly Paul was among the just; his fidelity to the Gospel something we ought to emulate.

◆ GOSPEL: We complete our weekday journey in the Gospel according to John today with the conclusion of the evangelist's narrative. Jesus responds to Peter's question about the beloved disciple who is following him. Peter is overly concerned about the disciple whom Jesus loves that he needs to remind Peter of the two words he previously spoke to him: follow me. The Gospel reading concludes with the summary statement about the beloved disciple's testimony and writing down of it. Most telling as the Easter Season comes to an end is that so much more could have been said about what Jesus did! Would that our faithful and continuous testimony help take the place of all the books that could have been written to contain his marvelous signs!

The Roman Missal

Notice how the Missal's designation of "At the Morning Mass" clearly distinguishes this Mass from the Vigil of Pentecost, which will be celebrated later the same day, in the evening.

The Collect, perhaps somewhat curiously, does not specifically mention the Holy Spirit (except in the Doxology, of course), but it does convey a sense of completion or coming to a close with its phrase about "we who have celebrated the Paschal festivities"—throughout these fifty days. The prayer goes on to ask that we may "hold fast to them in the way that we live our lives," thus affirming the goal of all liturgical celebration—that what we celebrate in ritual (dying and rising; offering ourselves in union with Christ) may be lived out in daily life.

The Prayer over the Offerings does explicitly mention, in a way that connotes a sense of anticipation and excitement, that the Holy Spirit is indeed "coming near," as it asks that the event "prepare our minds for the divine Sacrament, since the Spirit himself is the remission of all sins."

The notion of our being prepared fits well with this point in the liturgy at the Prayer over the Offerings as part of the Preparation of the Gifts; the mention of the remission of sins reminds us of one of the fruits of participation in the Eucharist, namely, forgiveness.

The Prayer after Communion uses the old/new motif that we have heard so often throughout Easter Time, as it begs that "as we have been brought from things of the past to new mysteries [both in this Eucharistic celebration and throughout the whole fifty days of Easter Time, which are coming to a close today], so, with former ways left behind, we may be made new in holiness of mind [the concrete transformation to be brought about through our participation in the mysteries]."

The choices for the Preface today include any one of the five Prefaces of Easter or the two Prefaces of the Ascension.

20 (#62/#63) red
Solemnity of Pentecost

About Today's Solemnity

The Greek word for Pentecost (*pentēkostē*) means "fiftieth," and in early Christianity it referred to the entire fifty days of Easter. The roots of Pentecost can be found in the Jewish festival of Weeks (Shavuot), the fifty-day celebration following Passover (Exodus 23:16). It was a harvest festival in which the first fruits of the harvest were offered to God in gratitude. It eventually became associated with the giving of the Torah on Mount Sinai. Early Christians reinterpreted the Jewish festival as a commemoration of the coming of the Holy Spirit, since Acts records that the Holy Spirit came to the disciples when the festival of Pentecost was fulfilled (see Acts 2:1–11). The celebration of Pentecost may begin on Saturday afternoon or evening with the Vigil. By the end of the fourth century in the West, Pentecost became a time for the initiation of those not baptized at Easter. Thus, a night vigil was added like the Easter Vigil for this purpose. With this early history in mind, this is a most appropriate time to initiate those who were not ready at the Easter Vigil, or (not and) to celebrate the Reception of Baptized Christians into the Full Communion of the Catholic Church (see RCIA, 473).

The Lectionary for Mass: Vigil

◆ READING, OPTION 1: This ancient story of Babel is thought by many scholars to be an etiology which explains the many languages found throughout the world. It is also a story of humanity's relationship with God: the people build the city with the tower to "make a name for ourselves," implying that they do so separate and apart from God. As such, it is a continuation of the story of the garden. The Lord responds not by destroying the city or tower but by scattering them throughout the earth.

◆ READING, OPTION 2: In this encounter between Moses, the Israelites, and God, the people assent to listen to God's voice and heed it, establishing a covenant between God and the people of Israel. God is presented as both near (the people will be his special possession) and powerful (the theophany on the mountain). Moses is designated as the leader who goes up to the mountain on behalf of the people.

◆ READING, OPTION 3: The vision of dry bones being brought to life by God in Ezekiel presents the hope of new life and restored relationship with God following the long exile of the people. It is a statement of the power of the promise of God to take what seems lost and to make it new: the Lord's spirit will be placed within the people, they will be settled into their land, and will therefore know the Lord.

◆ READING, OPTION 4: In this vision from the prophet Joel, the Lord pours his spirit upon all, equally. Young and old, male and female, even upon servants and handmaids, the spirit is given to all who call upon the name of the Lord, and they will see visions and dream dreams. God will work great wonders and signs on the day of the Lord. Those who call upon God's name comprise a remnant of faithful ones, survivors whom the Lord shall call.

◆ RESPONSORIAL PSALM 104: This psalm of praise declares the majesty and glory of God as a response to any or all of the designated readings, linking these stories of God's love and the spirit of God with the Second Reading and Gospel that follow. Through our proclamation of this song, we ask God to renew the outpouring of the Spirit upon us, and upon the earth. All of creation is a sign of God's greatness; the spirit of the Lord brings life and renewal.

◆ SECOND READING: In his letter to the Romans, Paul depicts the present and the future of our life in Christ. We have received the Holy Spirit and yet wait for the redemption of our bodies in the initiation into eternal life. Hope for something already seen is not true hope; we wait with endurance for the ful-

fillment of the promise of union with God through the Spirit. Yet in our present, incomplete life in Christ, the Spirit is with us in our weakness, strengthening and interceding for us.

◆ GOSPEL: This passage is set on the last day of the feast of Tabernacles, a weeklong harvest celebration that included remembrance of the Exodus water miracle. Water was taken daily from the pool of Siloam to the Temple and poured over the altar with prayers for winter rain. In this context, Jesus says that we are to come to him, through whom living water will come. He says this in reference to the Spirit who has not yet descended upon the disciples.

◆ RESPONSORIAL PSALMS and Collects at the Extended Vigil:

◆ Genesis 11:1–9: Sing Psalm 33:10–15. Use the prayer for Wednesday of the Seventh Week of Easter.

◆ Exodus 19:3–8a, 16–20b: Sing the canticle of Daniel 3:52–56. Use the prayer for Tuesday of the Seventh Week of Easter.

◆ Ezekiel 37:1–14: Sing Psalm 107:2–9. Use the prayer for Friday of the Seventh Week of Easter.

◆ Joel 3:1–5. Sing Psalm 104, as on Pentecost Sunday. Use the prayer for Monday of the Seventh Week of Easter. Following this prayer, sing the Gloria. Then pray the Collect Prayer of the Vigil of Pentecost. The reading from Romans follows and Mass proceeds as usual.

The Roman Missal: Vigil

◆ EXTENDED VIGIL: The Missal gives rubrics and texts to be used for the extended celebration of a Pentecost Vigil, and it is hoped that every parish will take advantage of such a celebration for its parishioners. Instructions are even given if a parish wishes to celebrate First Vespers (Evening Prayer I) in common. This might be something for communities to consider as a way of highlighting the Liturgy of the Hours as something that is meant to be prayed by every baptized Christian, not just the clergy.

If Evening Prayer I is not to be celebrated communally and Mass is to begin in the usual way, then all is done as usual for the beginning of Mass, including the Kyrie (Lord have mercy), after which the priest prays the Collect of the Mass. This would be an ideal occasion to use the Rite for the Blessing and Sprinkling of Water, found in Appendix II at the back of the Missal, especially if your parish has been doing this on all of the Sundays of Easter Time. Even if you have not been making use of this rite, today is a perfect occasion to do so as it brings together the themes of Paschal Mystery, Easter Time, Baptism, and the Holy Spirit, and its use allows the enactment of the ritual to convey the sense of fullness and completion so appropriate for this solemnity. Remember that this rite takes the place of the Penitential Act. It's important to note, however, that in this extended Vigil, the Collect would be prayed by the priest immediately after the concluding prayer, "May almighty God cleanse us of our sins . . . ," not the Gloria, which comes later (see below).

After the Collect, an address is given to the people, using the exact words in the Missal or words similar to them. The address asks the people to follow the example of Mary, the Apostles, and the disciples who persevered in prayer and who awaited the Spirit as promised by the Lord. We follow that example by listening "with quiet hearts to the Word of God," meditating "on how many great deeds God in times past did for his people" and praying "that the Holy Spirit, whom the Father sent as the first fruits for those who believe, may bring to perfection his work in the world."

After this follows an extended Liturgy of the Word modeled on the Liturgy of the Word at the Easter Vigil. The Missal refers us to the readings proposed as options in the Lectionary, with a Responsorial Psalm and a prayer corresponding to the reading following each one. (It is possible to have a period of sacred silence in place of any of the Responsorial Psalms.) The Missal then goes on to give the texts for prayers that correspond to each of the readings and their subsequent psalms. It is then after the Fourth Reading that the Gloria is sung.

When the Gloria is completed, the priest then prays the Collect in the usual way; this time, the Collect used is the text found as the first one given as the Collect for the Simple Form of the Vigil Mass, the "Almighty, ever-living God, who willed the Paschal Mystery. . ." After this, the reader proclaims the Epistle, Romans 8:22–27, and everything continues in the usual way. The texts for the remainder of the Extended Form of the Vigil Mass are taken from the Simple Form of the Vigil Mass, which follows in the Missal. Commentary on those texts is provided below.

◆ SIMPLE VIGIL: If the Extended Form of the Vigil is not being celebrated, then all occurs as usual at Mass; however, there are still proper texts that must be used for the Vigil Mass, distinct from the Mass during the Day.

As with the extended form of the Vigil Mass, the simple form would be an ideal occasion to use the Rite for the Blessing and Sprinkling of Water, found in Appendix II at the back of the Missal, especially if your parish has been doing this on all of the Sundays of Easter Time. Even if you have not been making use of this rite, consider doing so now. Remember that this rite takes the place of the Penitential Act. The Gloria immediately follows the prayer the priest prays as the con-

clusion to the Rite for Blessing and Sprinkling of Water.

In the simple form of the Vigil, either one of the two Collects given in the Missal may be used. The second prayer was discussed above, under the extended form. The Preface assigned for today is the Preface of Pentecost, the text for which (both with and without musical notation) is given along with the texts for the Mass during the Day, two pages further along (this might be a little confusing; the priest celebrant should be sure to check this ahead of time). Given the festivity of the day, it would be a good idea to sing the introductory dialogue and the Preface, especially if this has been the custom on Sundays throughout Easter Time. Note that if Eucharistic Prayer I, the Roman Canon, is used, there is a proper form of the *Communicantes* ("In communion with those . . ."), which mentions the traditional image of the Holy Spirit as tongues of fire.

A formula for Solemn Blessing is suggested, the formula titled "The Holy Spirit" (number 8 under "Blessings at the End of Mass and Prayers over the People"), and it would be good to use this formula. Since it is Pentecost, the solemn dismissal with the double Alleluia returns for use one last time before Easter Time next year.

The Lectionary for Mass: Mass during the Day

◆ FIRST READING: Luke's account of Pentecost is filled with symbolism, and yet it is concise in its description of the centerpiece of the action. More than the Spirit's actual arrival, Luke describes its effect on the people. Luke tells us that Jesus' followers were waiting and hoping for something they were probably incapable of anticipating; they had no idea what God would bring about in and through them. But their very anticipation opened the way for the Spirit to enflame them with the desire and ability to preach the Gospel.

◆ RESPONSORIAL PSALM 104 celebrates God's greatness manifested in the works of creation. The selection we pray today homes in on the fact that all that exists has God as author and sustainer.

◆ SECOND READING: The reading begins with Paul's assertion that "No one can say 'Jesus is Lord,' except by the Holy Spirit" (1 Corinthians 12:3). While that sounds like an almost magical formula to prove one's faith, Paul's intention here is something else entirely. He is dealing with a community competing about who is the greatest, most gifted, most spiritual, and so on. Paul's simple proclamation summarizes the more than forty verses that follow: all Christians have received the gift of the Spirit and are called to spread the Spirit's gifts.

◆ SEQUENCE: This Sunday, the Church sings one of the four sequences, or ancient, poetic songs that precede the Gospel Acclamation on solemn occasions. In the Pentecost sequence, *Veni, Sancte Spiritus*, the Church prays for the Holy Spirit to come. In beautiful, poetic titles, the sequence calls on the Father of the Poor, the Comforter, Divine Light, Sweet Rest, and

Healer, asserting that in the absence of the Holy Spirit, we have nothing. When the Holy Spirit is present, we have the Lord's salvation.

◆ GOSPEL: Jesus clarifies the essence of the disciples mission (and ours). Where Matthew describes apostleship as teaching and baptizing, John summarizes the whole mission as forgiveness. The disciples have received Jesus' peace and his Spirit, and now they and those who come after are charged with making the peace of forgiveness present in the world until the end of time.

The Roman Missal: Mass during the Day

As with either the extended form or the simple form of the Vigil Mass, the Mass during the Day provides an ideal occasion to use the Rite for the Blessing and Sprinkling of Water, found in Appendix II at the back of the Missal, especially if your parish has been doing this on all of the Sundays of Easter Time, and strong consideration should be given to this. Remember that this rite takes the place of the Penitential Act. The Gloria immediately follows the prayer said by the priest at the end of the rite.

The text for the Preface, both with and without musical notation, is proper for today and is given right there at the place in the Missal along with the other texts for the Mass during the Day. See above for com-

mentary on the Preface, as well as for notes concerning the proper insert if Eucharistic Prayer I is used.

The formula titled "The Holy Spirit" (number 8 under "Blessings at the End of Mass and Prayers over the People") is suggested for use as the final blessing, and it would be good to do so. Remember that since it is Pentecost, the solemn dismissal with the double Alleluia is used today, one last time before Easter Time next year.

Other Ideas

Among the traditional symbols for this day is the dove, the image of the Holy Spirit descending upon Jesus at his baptism by John in the Jordan. This is a good weekend to highlight the gifts of the Spirit conferred in Baptism and Confirmation for the community. Wind and fire also symbolize Pentecost. The liturgical color of this day is red, representing the Holy Spirit, and parishioners (especially liturgical ministers) can be encouraged to wear red clothes to Mass. Some parishes have members who speak languages other than English proclaim the Universal Prayer in these languages. This represents the gift of tongues given on Pentecost to the followers of Jesus (be sure to provide a worship aid with the translation of the prayer texts). Others provide birthday cake as part of after-Mass hospitality.

ORDINARY TIME DURING SUMMER AND FALL

The Meaning

AFTER our full participation in the forty days of Lent, the Triduum, and the fifty days of Easter, we now return to counting or numbering the weeks, not the days, of the liturgical year. Ordinary Time, which will take us through the summer and fall, comprises the thirty or so weeks that are not marked by major feasts. The longest stretch of Ordinary Time begins after Evening Prayer on the Solemnity of Pentecost and continues up to the start of the new liturgical year on the First Sunday of Advent. The seasons of the Church reflect the rhythms of our lives, with peak moments and times of quiet growth. The liturgical color of Ordinary Time, green, reminds us that this is still a season of growth in our discipleship, a time to continue maturing into the followers of Jesus Christ we are meant to be.

The Lectionary for Mass

THE journey through the Lectionary during Ordinary Time in Summer begins with the two "idea" solemnities of the Most Holy Trinity and the Body and Blood of Christ, when the First Readings come from the Deuteronomy and Exodus, Old Testament books of the Pentateuch, and the Second Readings comes from Romans and Hebrews. We proclaim Jesus' Great Commission of the disciples in the Gospel according to Matthew and Mark's account of the Passover in which Jesus instructs his disciples to take and eat his Body, and drink of his blood. These two solemnities set the course for the rest of Ordinary Time by giving us our mission to baptize and teach others to observe Jesus' commandments and also letting us know that Jesus is food for our journey of faith. Disciples, new and old, will never want for food and drink.

The First Readings for the weekdays of this period of Ordinary Time come from both the Old and New Testaments. We hear readings from 1 and 2 Peter, Jude, and 2 Timothy before moving on to the historical books of 1 and 2 Kings to recall the stories of Elijah, Elisha, and Naboth. God's people struggle with faithfulness, yet God's mercy and covenant faithfulness remain. In this, we rejoice! The month of July brings us First Readings with prophetic warnings from Amos, Hosea, Isaiah, Micah, and Jeremiah. Micah tells us the Lord requires justice and Hosea reminds us that God espouses his people as his beloved forever. Jeremiah, Nahum, Habakkuk, and Ezekiel bring the Lord's Word to us in August. Priests and princes rejected and scorned Jeremiah was rejected and scorned, but the prophet still delivered news of a new covenant in the Lord. Ezekiel faced a rebellious house. Sometimes we are no less rebellious today and in need of hearing the prophet's message about how the Lord shepherds his people justly in contrasts to the evil leaders of the day. We find hope knowing dry bones come to life in the Lord! As August comes to a close, the First Readings again come from the New Testament. Paul's second letter to the Thessalonians and his first letter to the Corinthians

encourage us to stand firm in the wisdom of our faith though to the world it is folly.

The weekdays of Ordinary Time in summer begin with Gospel readings from Mark. Once the middle of June comes, we proclaim Gospel readings from Matthew until the beginning of September. When we move into Ordinary Time in Fall, Luke becomes our source for the weekday Gospel readings. Each evangelist trains us in the fundamentals of discipleship. Jesus' power and authority, his identity as Son of Man and Son of God is the basis of discipleship. He invites us to follow him, to live the commandments, to be salt and light for a world in need, to heal and dispel demons. We are his mothers and brothers when we hear and act on the Word of God. Woe to us should we not champion God's Word.

Parables teach us about the Kingdom of Heaven and whom God invites to its great feast. Parables, as clearly as parables do, instruct us that the last will be first in the Kingdom. Servanthood is discipleship and humility the primary of all characteristics of the disciple's life.

Weekday First Readings from 1 Corinthians, Proverbs, Ecclesiastes, Job, Galatians, Ephesians, Philippians, Titus, Philemon, and 2 and 3 John remind us of the expansion of the Wisdom of the Gospel mission to all peoples as schools and parish programs ramp up in the fall, and the pace of life quickens with the changing seasons.

Proclaiming and living Wisdom is never an easy task. Job's story clearly illustrates this point. Disciples of Jesus, however, do not proclaim Wisdom by themselves. Paul teaches us that we are many members of one Body. From Ephesians we learn, Christ is the Head of the Body, the Church. Three John speaks of us as co-workers in the truth. We support each other in keeping the commandments and preaching sound doctrine.

The First Readings on the Sundays of Ordinary Time during Summer and Fall come from a similar variety of books as the weekday readings. Genesis, Exodus, Deuteronomy, and Numbers represent the Pentateuch and 1 and 2 Kings, the historical books. The prophets Isaiah, Ezekiel, Amos, and Jeremiah prompt not only call us back to faithfulness, but present us with the wondrous works of the Lord of justice who opens the eyes of the blind and makes the mute speak.

From the Tenth Sunday in Ordinary Time through the Sixteenth Sunday, the Gospel readings come from Mark. For five Sundays from the Seventeenth Sunday through the Twenty-First

Sunday, we proclaim selections from the Bread of Life discourse in John. We hear not only is Christ the Bread of Life, but he is the Living Bread. We who eat this Bread will have eternal life. Going forward, we return to the Gospel according to Mark only to learn that sharing in the Bread of Life does not make the disciples' road any easier. Take up our cross and follow the One who predicts his own Passion, Death, and Resurrection. Inherit the Kingdom of God loving God and others, and by selling all your possessions. Witness to the Truth of Jesus whom Pilate seems to think is King of the Jews. Live as a disciple for God's Kingdom that is already, but not yet, only to be fully realized in heaven, not in this world.

The final weekdays of the liturgical year the Book of Revelation is the source of the weekday First Readings, while on the final two Sundays the First Readings comes apocalyptic work of Daniel. Jesus fulfills Daniel's vision of "one like a son of man" coming.

The Second Readings on the Sundays in Ordinary Time in Summer and Fall come from 2 Corinthians, Ephesians, James, and Hebrews, and culminate in the proclamation Jesus as the Alpha and Omega in a passage from Revelation proclaimed on the solemnity of Christ the King. Jesus' high priesthood expounded on in Hebrews is the "once for all" priesthood of the King. There is no need for any other sacrifice. He is the source of the Church's unity spoken of in Ephesians. We are doers of his Word according to James.

Will we inherit eternal life? Will we feast in God's Kingdom? The Lectionary readings for Ordinary Time in Summer and Fall open many avenues for reflection on our journeys of faith and those of our parishes. Even when the readings turn toward judgment and remind us to be vigilant for the Lord's coming at the close of the liturgical year, we continue to sing our praise to the Lord in the psalms and acclaim him as our inheritance and our King. We are blessed for the Lord has chosen us to be his own (Psalm 33:12b). The chosen will feast. Eternal life will be theirs. This God promises.

The Roman Missal

WE continue our journey through Ordinary Time between Pentecost Sunday and the First Sunday of Advent. Again, this is a time to focus on the fundamentals of our faith and to grow in understanding of the Paschal Mystery through Word and Sacrament. Vestments in this season are green: the color of new life and nature symbolizes our hope of eternal life and our new life in Christ. We keep Sunday as the primordial Christian gathering. The Collect of the Thirty-Third Sunday brings the theology of the season together well when it prays, "Grant us . . . / the constant gladness of being devoted to you, / for it is full and lasting happiness / to serve . . . / the author of all that is good." At the end of the season, we celebrate the Solemnities of the Lord. These celebrations focus our attention on the multivalent manifestations of Christ: Trinity, Eucharist, Sacred Heart, and King of the Universe.

In addition to those details provided earlier for Ordinary Time during Winter, there are several other details to keep in mind during this season. The Missal provides several Solemn Blessings (6) and Prayers over the People (26), for example, which can replace the simple blessing at the end of Mass. Their use would be most appropriate on Sundays. Throughout Ordinary Time, the Missal systematically provides two options for the Communion Antiphon: the first from the psalms and the second (almost always) from the Gospel accounts. While either is always permitted, it is best to choose the one most in harmony with the Gospel of the day. Each Solemnity of the Lord in Ordinary Time has its own proper Preface. The first Sunday after Pentecost is the Solemnity of the Most Holy Trinity, while on the second Sunday after Pentecost we celebrate the Solemnity of the Most Holy Body and Blood of Christ (Corpus Christi). The optional sequence for this Solemnity (*Lauda Sion*) should be sung after the Second Reading if possible. On the Friday after Corpus Christi, the Church celebrates the Solemnity of the Most Sacred Heart of Jesus. The final Sunday of the liturgical year, after a long and fruitful journey through the Paschal Mystery is the Solemnity of the Our Lord Jesus Christ, King of the Universe. This celebration points to the culmination of our hope—that time at the end of time and outside of time when all the universe is restored and "the whole creation, set free from slavery, / may . . . ceaselessly proclaim your praise" (Collect).

Children's Liturgy of the Word

THE return of Ordinary Time begins with the two "idea" solemnities, the Most Holy Trinity and the Most Holy Body and Blood of Christ. The liturgical color for both solemnities is white. The lengthy season of counted Sundays concludes in November with the Solemnity of Our Lord Jesus Christ, King of the Universe, for which the liturgical color is also white. Otherwise, the liturgical color is green. Consider making a transition in the environment after Labor Day by adding accents such as fall leaves to the prayer table. As always, anything in the environment should be real and from nature, not plastic.

Whether your parish takes a hiatus from celebrating the Liturgy of the Word with children in the summer or not, Ordinary Time in summer provides an opportunity to evaluate how the celebrations of the Word with children have gone over the past months. Gather your team together to discuss what has worked well and what needs improvement. Begin or end with a potluck or picnic. Decide how you will recognize the ministry and service of those involved on the team. Depending on the number of volunteers you have, being involved in children's Liturgy of the Word can be a huge commitment, especially for those who serve as the prayer leader and lead the reflection, and for those involved in leading the music ministry. Consider how you will recognize and thank the volunteers.

The Lectionary readings in Ordinary Time provide a chance for us to reflect on how God calls us to live out our baptismal call to ministry and service. This is true both for adults and children. As such, Ordinary Time is a good time to recruit new members to the ministry of the Word with children. Try to gear up for the fall before the rush of Ordinary Time in Fall occurs after Labor Day in September. Train new leaders and assistants as early as possible or even integrate them in during the summer months by having them observe a few celebrations of the Word before you set them off on their own.

Prepare appropriate psalmody with the music director and familiarize yourself with the Gospel Acclamation the main assembly will use. If it is an appropriate arrangement for the children, see check on the availability of a cantor. Many parishes switch the Gospel Acclamation early in September to mark a transition to a new segment of Ordinary Time, although the splitting of Ordinary Time into the periods of Summer and Fall is not an official distinction. Check to see if your parish changes the Gospel Acclamation. A shift in environment will signify Christ the King and the conclusion of the liturgical year. To aid in acclaiming Christ the King with the children, see if an instrumentalist like a trumpet player might be available to play the Gospel Acclamation or intersperse the refrain from "To Jesus Christ Our Sovereign King" in the reflection on the readings. For more detailed suggestions, see LTP's *Children's Liturgy of the Word: A Weekly Resource*. Go through this lengthy period of Ordinary Time with an eye to how the Liturgy of the Word forms children to live as Jesus' disciples in age-appropriate ways. Allow the Word to speak to the children in a prayerful, not structured catechetical, manner. Theirs is the Kingdom of God.

The Liturgy of the Hours

FOLLOWING Pentecost, we are back in Ordinary Time. Notice that this is a return, so we do not begin again with week one. Monday, May 21, is in the Seventh Week in Ordinary Time, which is Monday of the third week of the breviary.

Ordinary Time is counted time, a way of numbering of our days. This is the foundation of the Liturgy of the Hours. We return to settle in for a while. Our high feasts are over. We are in a new place in our journey because of our disciplines and our celebrations of the year.

This is a great time to evaluate our prayer practices. Do we find it difficult to pray Morning and night? Is there a way to better organize or structure our activities that prayer time is not neglected? Perhaps this summer we can pray outside, at home or at a park. Is it time to add an app to our phone, giving us freedom to pray while we wait for a baseball game to start or practice to be over? On a trip, hand the phone or tablet to your family while you drive. Let them lead and you can respond. It's a great way to encourage children to lead this prayer.

If you have more time in the summer and fall, consider the Office of Readings. These may be prayed any time and offer us great insights from the Church Fathers as well as longer texts from sacred Scripture. Most Catholics do not have the opportunity to mine such a wealth of wisdom. The Office places it right in front of us. Even if you are not in the position to pray the Office daily, once or twice a week is a good start. Take it slow. There's no rush and some of the texts are very thought provoking. You will most likely discover new ideas. Journaling with this prayer may assist you in processing the wisdom of our ancestors.

If you have a printed breviary (rather than a digital resource), look to the back of the book. There is much to explore. The Commons are there and even if you are not regularly praying the Office, you may discover homilies and teachings to feed your prayer. The Office for the Dead is available when a loved one or neighbor has died.

Some publications also have additional prayers and poetry. In the parish, if you are responsible for preparing common celebrations of the Liturgy of the Hours or other prayer experiences, this section is of great value. Since the busyness of parish life has waned a bit prepare your resources for next year. Consider creating a journal or folder for each season or event and make notes for yourself with ideas, prayers, songs and references. Now is a great time for research and creativity.

Praying the Liturgy of the Hours is a wonderful catechetical opportunity. The repetitive nature of the prayer teaches us about the Christian faith. If you work with children or adults, perhaps plan on praying with a seasonal psalm or using one of the alternate texts. A meeting with the parish music minister can be of great value. There are many settings of the palms and canticles, some of which you may not be aware. Start in your own backyard before doing a lot of research. There is probably something wonderful at hand.

The Rite of Christian Initiation of Adults

THE Period of the Catechumenate, the second period in the process, commences at the celebration of the Rite of Acceptance into the Order of Catechumens. The rite says that "the duration of the catechumenate will depend on the grace of God . . . [it] should be long enough–several years if necessary–for the conversion and faith of the catechumens to become strong" (RCIA, 76). This paragraph might surprise some, along

with the requirement, found in article 6 of the US *National Statutes for the Catechumenate*, that a convert must spend a full year as a Catechumen and an Elect before being initiated. There is, however, much wisdom in the intentional and gradual process of incorporation into the community (see RCIA, 4).

Conversion takes time. The RCIA team should not rush this process as if the candidate is checking off boxes on a race to Easter, but truly accompany them and discern with them. Those involved with RCIA ministry must reconcile the fact that some will move through the process more quickly than others will. They do not enter the catechumenate as a "class," but as pilgrims on a journey of conversion. Like the precatechumenate, the catechumenate should also be accepted as members of the Order of Catechumens when they are ready. This will mean that the catechumenate is a year-round ministry. Such an approach requires a team who can support this process and focus on this period. Moreover, if the process is more than six or nine months, there will be no worry about a candidate "missing" any catechesis and formation. Recognizing that the spiritual journey takes time, the rite invites catechumens to enter into the liturgical year, and through it to encounter the Risen Christ.

The catechumenate is the time for formal catechesis. When the catechumens gather, begin with prayer or reflection, allow time to mingle and meet others from the parish (see RCIA, 80), and spend time discussing a particular topic. "A suitable catechesis is . . . planned to be gradual and complete in its coverage, accommodated to the liturgical year, and solidly supported by celebrations of the word" (RCIA, 75.1; see also RCIA, 78). The art of catechesis is "nothing other than the process of transmitting the Gospel, as the Christian community has received it, understands it, celebrates it, lives it and communicates it" (*General Directory for Catechesis*, 105). The time spent in this period must draw the catechumens deeper into the heart of Christ and help them grow in knowledge of the Paschal Mystery.

Within the catechumenate, the minor rites (such as anointing) can be celebrated to help mark the process of conversion and to strengthen and purify the candidate (see RCIA, 75.3, 79). More information on these is found in the Christmas section of this resource.

A final note on the US *National Statutes for the Catechumenate*, which was approved by the

United States Conference of Catholic Bishops in 1986. As particular law for the United States, these statutes provide elaboration and clarification on how the RCIA should be implemented. If you are not familiar with them, please take time to study them with your team. They provide insight on how to minister to the Catholics who are baptized but uncatechized, as well as directives applying to those being received into full communion. Being familiar with the bishops' guidance in this document will help us to better implement the RCIA.

The Sacraments of Initiation

WHILE the Baptismal preparation programs are usually offered at the parish on a continual basis throughout the year, the programs for Eucharist and Confirmation usually start at the beginning of the school year.

Supporting families with infants before and after Baptism needs to be a key ministry of the Church. This is a special time in the development of the family's faith patterns. So, finding ways to connect with young parents as they raise their young children will help them to see the parish faith community as an integral part of their life.

There are more parents who delay Baptism for one reason or another, so each parish will need to be flexible in order to meet the needs of families with different situations who are ready to bring their children to the sacrament. This may include Baptism for young children as well as a RCIA process for children between the ages of seven and eighteen (see LTP's *Guide for Celebrating® Christian Initiation with Children*).

Children who attend Mass with their families grow up with a natural desire to participate in the Eucharist. The whole family greatly anticipates the day when their child is ready to join them at the table of our Lord Jesus. When the preparation program begins in the fall it is important to emphasize to the parents that weekly attendance at Mass is one of the most important things they can do together as a family to help their child prepare for the sacrament. Children need to be at the age of reason in order to receive Communion, this is usually at seven years old. Children ages seven and above are capable of having a close personal relationship with Jesus. They are also able to make

the connection that Christ is the Bread of Life, he wants us to remember him in the sacrament of the Eucharist and to receive the gift of his Body and Blood, new life and food for the journey of faith.

The preparation for the Sacrament of Confirmation really begins at Baptism, continues through the reception of Eucharist and is fulfilled when the young person desires to confirm their belief in the Catholic faith and receive the gifts of the Holy Spirit through the ritual anointing of the Sacrament. The formal program of preparation in the parish usually lasts one to two years depending upon the norms of each diocese. Oftentimes the period of preparation begins or is at least continued each fall. Once again, weekly attendance at Mass is an essential component of the program. It may also be helpful to invite the candidates for Confirmation to write Mass journals, reflecting upon the readings, the homily, and their experience at church in order to have a deeper awareness of how to connect to the liturgy as a young adult in the Catholic Church.

The Rite of Penance

OUR long period of Ordinary Time provides ample opportunity for creativity or lethargy. Which will we choose? Let's not neglect this sacrament. Take time to consider your own parish location, time table and charisms.

This is a time of weddings for many parishes. How do we spiritually prepare the couple? Do we ever prepare the attendants? Is the rehearsal just for practicing a procession? This may be an opportunity to encourage the wedding party to celebrate Reconciliation. Go beyond merely reminding them. Perhaps have a communal celebration with all those celebrating Marriage during these months. Open it to the couples, their families and friends. Maybe neighboring parishes can work together. Make sure to design the service for the engaged.

What else happens in your parish, or what could, that provides an opportunity for formation and education in this sacrament? For example, do you have a Vacation Bible School? What are the themes this year? If mercy or forgiveness are present, don't lose sight of the opportunity to include a mention of this sacrament. Many VBS programs are written for Protestant churches, even if they say "Catholic" on the marketing brochure. Also, VBS is a great time to evangelize. Seize the chance to correct misunderstandings. Be careful to evangelize (proclaim the Good News) not proselytize.

Is your parish in a vacation spot? Great! Can you get your parish schedule and/or website in hotel lobbies or in the guide book in each room? Travelers often look for this information. Let's make it easy for them. Include not just the Mass times, but times for Penance and directions.

This is also a good time to make sure our neighboring nursing homes and assisted living facilities have your correct schedules and contact information. If the situation is right, maybe it would be beneficial to have a communal celebration at the facility or arrange to bring the guests to the church.

Even if you are not in a destination spot, Summer usually brings visitors. Make sure the times for Masses and penitential celebrations are readily available. Check the church doors for signage, the website and even outgoing answering machine message.

The Order of Celebrating Matrimony

ORDINARY Time provides the most common time for celebrations of the Sacrament Of Matrimony. As parish ministers too spend some time in relaxation and rejuvenation, it may be helpful to gather the staff and those volunteers responsible for preparation and liturgical preparation for weddings. It's time to share ideas, wisdom gleaned, and perhaps make adjustments to our practices. Consider a simple follow up evaluation of each wedding. For example, ask the couple how the community could better support them during their engagement? Which of the pieces of the preparation were the most and least helpful? Then review the answers with open hearts and be ready to make some changes. Using an online service such as survey monkey may produce more responses than a paper evaluation form.

It is also often helpful to review the ritual text and parish policies. Is everyone clear on which rite is used when and why. The norms are found in the ritual OCM, 33–36. How do we approach Marriage between a Catholic and another

Christian, or a Catholic and a person who is not baptized? Pastors are reminded that they are the "ministers of Christ's gospel for all" and therefore should also offer care to the non-Catholics who are part of the marriage celebration (OCM, 37) What might this look like? While we respect our differences, especially with regard to the reception of Eucharist, how can we model our lived faith to those gathered? This is not a time for triumphalism. Can we gently and directly explain the liturgy in a manner that invites participation and information. Think liturgical catechesis. Go beyond just the practical to allow the family and dear friends, as well as the couple themselves, insights into the blessings and beauty of the Catholic tradition.

Reflect on the alternate texts for the Marriage liturgy. Chapter IV of the ritual includes many beautiful options. Part I are options for readings. Oftentimes couples are simply given a resource and asked to select a reading. Once you know them a bit, discuss the reading options and why you feel a particular choice would be important at their wedding. Consider reserving the Gospel to the priest or deacon who will preach.

As you reconsider the alternate texts that follow the readings, perhaps note in the margins of your personal copy when certain prayers might be used. For example, some of the Collects speak of the blessing of children. This would not be appropriate for an older couple.

The Church also provides alternate prayers for the blessing of rings. Is there one that speaks to your experience of a particular couple? There are also different choices for the Nuptial Blessing. As with all the prayers, we can often defer to what is common or expedient. While the sentiments expressed may be similar, the poetry by which each are prayed feels different to our ears. Pray the texts aloud with your team and discuss. What did each hear? To which are you drawn and why?

One rarely exercised option for the celebration of Marriage is during a regular Sunday Mass. Of all the possibilities, this speaks most clearly to the place of Marriage in parish life. For couples who were raised at your church, who may have been baptized there, Confirmed and join in Eucharist weekly, this is their family. Many have watched this bride or groom grow in faith and knowledge. They want to witness the Marriage. They too are happy and excited for the couple. No one expects to be invited to the reception; that is a private party. However, the sacrament is public and deserves the joy and participation of the community.

In this case, the prayers for the Mass of Sunday are used. The celebration of the sacrament takes place at the usual time after the homily. The Universal Prayer should include an intercession for the couple and the Nuptial Blessing is also included at the appropriate time. During Ordinary Time, the Church allows for an adaptation within the Liturgy of the Word. One of the readings may be chosen from the selections provided for the sacrament of Marriage (see OCM, 34).

Choosing this option moves Marriage into its rightful place as an integral part of parish life, not a private and external gala. It also provides a catechetical moment, especially for teens and young adults who otherwise may rarely participate in a wedding.

The Pastoral Care of the Sick

DURING these weeks of the liturgical calendar the Sacrament of the Anointing of the Sick can be considered within the context of Ordinary Time and against the backdrop of the Scriptures, especially the Gospel passages from Mark and John.

When we think of the liturgical life of the Church, there is nothing really "ordinary" about how the community of faith celebrates the unfolding of the Paschal Mystery in its midst. The Church continues to explore the grace and the demands of the mission of the Risen Lord. In every time and place men and women are formed and reformed as faithful disciples.

On the first few Sundays of this period the Gospels are from Mark's account. The texts describe Jesus' expectations of the household of faith. There follows five Sundays with texts from chapter six of John's account of the Gospel, the so-called bread of life discourse. The final Sundays of Ordinary Time return to readings from Mark's Gospel account in which Jesus teaches the disciples, and us, that a firm commitment is needed to be part of his mission and to be members of the household of faith. This commitment is focused on inclusion and compassion for everyone.

The experiences of suffering, illness, and death have no time or season in the scope of human affairs. The encounters of Jesus with those who sought his words of comfort and healing touch often occurred in the most ordinary circumstances in people's lives.

The Sacrament of the Anointing of the Sick is intended to bring that same ministry to people today. There are many options for the prayers and readings provided in the liturgy of Anointing and for the pastoral visitation of the sick. These various choices are based on the particular situation of the person who is ill. For example, in the Rite of Anointing there are specific prayers for someone in extreme illness, in advanced age, before surgery, for a child or a young person (see chapter 4, 125). Another issue that should be noted here is that Part II of the rite for *Pastoral Care of the Sick* is the Pastoral Care of the Dying. Many of the rites within this area of pastoral care can be led by a lay pastoral minister; for example, the Celebration of Viaticum, Commendation of the Dying, and Prayers for the Dead. Again, there are many options for the prayers and readings that can be chosen to best suit the particular circumstance. In these situations it is likely that members of the person's immediate family are present. The pastoral minister should be attentive to their emotional and spiritual needs as well. The ritual words and gestures are intended to bring comfort and strength to the dying person as well as those who accompany them at this difficult time. The solicitude of the whole Church is expressed through the rite and is made visible through the presence of those who have taken up this ministry of compassion.

If the parish has not scheduled an opportunities for the pastoral care ministers to gather for some form of renewal in their ministry (as noted above for Easter Time) this is an ideal time to do that. A number of topics could be addressed in such a session, for example, the history of the Rite of Anointing, the theology of suffering, and the ministry of the Church as the ministry of Christ. The prayers and Scripture readings found in the various rites offer rich spiritual nourishment for such gatherings. Those who take up this ministry need to nourish their own spiritual well being on a regular basis.

The Order of Christian Funerals

SUMMER finds us in a sea of beauty and presumably a slower pace in parish life. Now is a good time to evaluate and plan.

One suggestion is to make a list of the ideas in that have served the community well in the past year. Are there hymns, prayers, and readings that you'd like you preserve for next year's funerals? What ideas did not work, or what happened for which you wish you were better prepared. Now is the time to take stock and be ready.

Start with the ritual book itself. If you have an older copy, make notes to draw attention to options of which you were unaware. Have you ever used the prayers for married couples or parents? There are also prayers for less common situations, such as a deceased non-Christian married to a Catholic (OCF, part V, 36) See the alternatives for the Song of Farewell. (OCF, 403) If certain words strike you as particularly appropriate, perhaps the music minister knows a musical setting of it.

In prayer, reread the "General Introduction" to the ritual again. It is a beautiful reflection on our common prayer. Are there elements that refresh you? Challenge you? Are there old practices that need renewal or new ones that could be considered?

Are you prepared in case of the death of a child? This is an exceedingly difficult time for all. Does the parish have an appropriate pall? If this tragedy occurs, pastoral sensitivity suggests that you've made preparations. The ritual has the prayers for both a child who has been baptized and one who has not.

In reflecting on the number of funerals your parish celebrates, is it time to train lay ministers to lead the Vigil Liturgy? Is it time for a renewal of ministers? Are there readersand cantors willing to lead prayer at funeral homes? The witness of the community is an important element in the time of grief. When a cantor leads a simple setting of a psalm or common hymnody to begin or end prayer, we place on the lips of the grieving words of hope, faith and healing. If possible, this is a wonderful ministry.

As you evaluate the Funeral Mass, do not neglect the Vigil Liturgy and Rite of Committal. Note the placement of the remembrances by family members is during the vigil after the Concluding Rite (see OCF, 80). Are there times to use the Office of the Dead instead of the vigil service? What about the prayers provided for Gathering in the Presence of the Body or Transfer of the Body? Is it time to make changes to how your parish celebrates these rites?

Moving into autumn, we return to images of death and the brevity of life. How does your parish honor the dead in November? All Souls' Day holds a special place in many cultures. Instead of mass on this day, consider using the Office of the Dead. The gentle singing of psalms provides the assembly a different way to praise God and reflect on the loss of their loved ones.

The Book of Blessings

OUR journey through Ordinary Time resumes after Pentecost Sunday and continues until the First Sunday of Advent, roughly mid-May through early December. The many Sundays of this season offer insight, examples, and guidance on our journey to the end of the year and to the start of a new one, where we delve into the liturgical cycle again and hope to do so even more deeply this time around. Perhaps the Order for Visiting a Cemetery on All Souls' Day (see BB, chapter 57) is the most important among the blessings we might use during this season. Broadening our commemoration of those who have died also broadens our consideration of the hope we have because of our faith in Christ. The order of blessing can take place immediately after Mass if the cemetery is close by and a procession is feasible. In this case, the usual blessing and dismissal of the Mass are omitted, and a suitable song or psalm is chosen for the procession to the cemetery. It can also take place at another time. In this case, the procession is usually omitted and a psalm or song is sung after all have gathered at the cemetery. A priest, deacon, lay minister, or simply a family member may lead this blessing, which may also be used on Memorial Day, on any anniversary of death or burial, or when a gravestone or cemetery monument is erected.

On the Third Sunday of June, and especially if the blessing of mothers took place on Mother's Day, we can use the Order for the Blessing of Fathers on Father's Day (see BB, chapter 56). Like the blessing for mothers, this blessing is not a full rite, but a set of intercessions to be added to those of the day and a Prayer over the People.

In the spirit of blessing mothers and fathers, the Orders for the Blessing of Elderly People Confined to Their Homes (see BB, 344–375) might be appropriate on or around Grandparent's Day (September 9). Several forms of the rite are provided. Of course, not all grandparents are infirm or confined to their homes! Because the introduction to this blessing states it may be adapted "to the circumstances of the place and the people involved," however, with some creativity it could be modified to suit grandparents in general. In a similar spirit, the Orders for the Blessing of Children (see BB, 135–173) or the Order for the Blessing of Sons and Daughters (see BB, 174–194) might be used on or around Children's Day (second Sunday of June).

Two events that are often preoccupying at this time of year are the annual vacation and the beginning of the school year. Early in the summer, soon after the school year ends, using the Order for the Blessing of Travelers (see BB, chapter 9) or even the Order for the Blessing of Various Means of Transportation (see BB, chapter 21) could be useful by helping mark and bless this important time in the lives of many individuals, couples, and families. As the end of summer approaches and the new school year looms, communities could use the Order for the Blessing of Students and Teachers (see BB, chapter 5). The Order for the Blessing of Tools or Other Equipment for Work (see BB, chapter 24) might be suitable for Labor Day, the first Monday of September, especially if it was not used on May 1.

As the cold of winter approaches, the fragility of life becomes more apparent and the danger to livestock is real. In some places there is a custom of blessing animals on October 4. The Order for the Blessing of Animals (see BB, chapter 25) can be used for this purpose on or around this date.

The most prominent holiday of this season in the United States is Thanksgiving Day, the last Thursday of November. To bless this special time, when families come together to feast and give thanks, the *Book of Blessings* provides the Order for the Blessing of Food for Thanksgiving Day (see BB, chapter 58). The faithful should bring food items to be used at their holiday meals for the blessing.

By this time of the year, harvests have been gathered. The most appropriate time depends on the local climate and crops, but the Order for a

Blessing on the Occasion of Thanksgiving for the Harvest (see BB, chapter 28) is another blessing suitable to this season. In this blessing, we give thanks for our food, those who labored in planting, tending, and harvesting it, and the abundance of the earth — or even the fragility of this abundance in places suffering from drought, disease, or pestilence. Celebrating this blessing can also be a time to remember those millions in the world who go hungry every day. Rural communities are the most obvious contexts for this blessing, but it might be used even in urban communities as a way of recalling the food cycle that is so often obscured in city life.

The Liturgical Environment

As Easter Time draws to a close, the Solemnities of the Most Holy Trinity and the Most Holy Body and Blood of Christ march by. The great rush of the typical parish spring slows. People begin to look forward to the winding down of parish pgoramming, to the end of school, and to slipping back into the easy progression of Ordinary Time.

This time can provide an opportunity to reflect on how the liturgical environment has worked during the previous year, and to remember those things that people wanted to improve on for next year. Bigger changes require more lead time, especially if they will require engaging the services of liturgical artists, whether these are parish members or outside professionals.

As you consider each season, you might consider the following questions:

1. How did the environment support the parish's worship? What worked well?

2. Were there areas in which it might have distracted from the liturgy itself?

3. Were the chief liturical actions framed and supported by the environment?

4. Where should the balance lie between repitition (people knowing what to expect) and novelty (keeping the environment fresh and interesting)?

5. How are finances and time budgeted for the environment?

6. Are major seasonal pieces (such as the Advent wreath or the Cross for Good Friday) suitably well made and in good repair?

7. Are the furnishings and vestments in good repair? Is there a long-term plan for maintaining and refreshing these items?

8. What about the space itself? Does it fit the gathered assembly? Is it in good repair? Are people able to see and hear? Does it encourage them to participate?

Answering these questions together should provide your group with a common sensibility of what needs might present themselves going forward. Some of these will be easily dealt with at the next season (for example, "we need to move the palms so that they don't block the view of the altar"). Others will have budget implications and may need involvement from members of the community. Starting the conversation now can let everyone prepare for future needs together, hopefully with a shared vision of what needs to occur.

The Saints

DURING the long stretch of Ordinary Time that extends from Pentecost to Advent, the observances of the saints serve as punctuation. They briefly change the colors in our churches and reminding us of the purpose of the Gospel we preach: lives lived fully in God's love. There are many feast days during this time, but three categories of feasts dominate the calendar.

The first of these include the biblical story of the Visitation (May 31), and a number of feasts that have grown up to celebrate Mary's life as mirror of her Son. Her Assumption (August 15) mirrors his Ascension (May 10/13). Her Nativity (September 8), recalls his Incarnation, as does the Nativity of his cousin, John the Baptist (June 24). John and Mary are unusual among the saints in that they the calendar commemorates both their birth and the end of their earthly lives. John's martyrdom is celebrated on August 29. Mary is also celebrated as Queen of Heaven (August 22), Lady of Sorrows (September 15), and Our Lady of Mount Carmel (July 16).

There are also quite a few feasts of Apostles that fall during this season. St. Barnibas is remembered June 11, Sts. Peter and Paul on June 29, and St. Thomas on July 3. St. James the Greater is commemorated on July 25, St. Bartholomew on August 24, and St. Andrew on November 30. These feasts of the Apostles would usually be joined by that of St. Mary Magdalene on July 22, but that feast falls on a Sunday this year and is not celebrated except in places under her patronage.

Perhaps the largest group of remaining saints on the calendar during this season consists of the founders of religious orders. These men and women received a special calling to gather others around a shared vision of the Gospel. Some of these names are immediately recognizable: St. Benedict (July 11); St. Ignatius Loyola (July 31), St. Francis (October 4), and St. Clare (August 11); St. Dominic (August 8), St. Vincent de Paul (September 27), and St. Frances Xavier Cabrini (November 13). Some less well-known names include: St. Philip Neri (founder of the Oratorians, May 26), St. Norbert (Founder of the Order of Premontre, June 6), and St. Camillus (Founder of the Camillians, July 18). All of these remarkable men and women continue to enrich the Church through their spiritual children, and we do well to thank God for them.

The Liturgical Music

MANY choirs take a break from rehearsals during the summer. Some stop singing for liturgies as well, at least for a few weeks. It can be helpful for choir members to take a break and to participate as a part of the worshipping assembly for some time. A break could give members the opportunity to recruit new choir members as well. Small business cards with an invitation to the first rehearsal of the season could be given to choir members to hand out to those they hear singing around them at Mass.

The summer is a great time to form an intergenerational unison or two-part choir. This is a great opportunity to involve college students who are home for the summer or the high school students and adults who are just too busy during the school year to make a weekly commitment. Instead of rehearsing on a weeknight, the choir could rehearse for a half hour before Mass. Even if choir takes a break for the summer, there should always be someone leading the music at Mass.

Both prayer and community building are such important parts of ministry. In September, when the ministerial year picks up again, consider starting off with a retreat or Evening of Prayer for the music ministry. Include some time for prayer and, of course some social time at the end. If there are multiple ensembles in the parish, bring them all together.

The Liturgical Ministers

Communicate early with ministers who may be away for all or part of the summer and make sure enough ministers are scheduled for each liturgy. Give those ministers who need a break time off and provide training for new ministers. If you hold a procession on the Solemnity of the Body and Blood of Christ (Corpus Christi), make sure you create a map for the route the procession will take and ensure someone can monitor traffic along the way (depending on your route a parade permit may be required from your city or local municipality). During the summer hold an ice cream, lemonade, or iced tea social for ministers, volunteers, and parishioners. Consider holding a ministry fair in the fall and announce the event for several weeks in advance. Send letters, provide notices and announcements in the bulletin on the parish website and at announcement time during Mass. Remember, however, that the best way to find new ministers is with a personal invitation. Have parishioners who are currently serving in various ministries share their story and if you have a sign-up for new ministers be sure to follow up with them in a timely manner. Provide resources for various ministers along with an outline for each ministry including responsibilities and the time commitment required. Recognize people's gifts, talents and time commitment and thank them for their service.

Other Prayers, Rites, and Devotions

This long stretch of Ordinary Time is replete with saints' feast days and observances. The end of September honors the archangels Michael, Gabriel, and Raphael. St. Michael is the patron saint of police officers which offers a wonderful

opportunity to honor the parish's local police force. Depending on the precinct's schedules, either invite officers to a weekend Mass for a blessing followed by a reception or on the patronal feast day of September 29, invite the parish school to gather to show appreciation by offering a blessing of the officers. Many times, officers may perform a group roll call for the assembly. St. Michael holy cards or medals can be given to those assembled. Any show of appreciation to these men and women who put their lives in danger daily for our safety and protection will be welcomed.

October has traditionally been set aside as the month of the Holy Rosary. A weekly communal celebration of the recitation of the Rosary may include the proclamation of Scripture associated with the particular mysteries. The parish school can be encouraged to gather weekly for the praying of the Rosary. Barton Cotton (www.bartoncotton .com) publishes a small booklet with Scripture texts combined with the Collects of *The Roman Missal* as prayer texts for each mystery.

Another popular autumnal feast day falls on October 4, the Memorial of St. Francis of Assisi, the patron saint of animals and ecology. A text for the Order of Blessing Animals can be found in the *Book of Blessings.* In addition to gathering pets and their guardians, invite attendees to bring donated items for the local pet shelter (toys, food, blankets, towels, health products, and so on). Contact your local shelter for a list of items they are in most need of and publish it in the parish bulletin weeks in advance. Even parishioners without pets may be happy to participate.

October also carries the title of Respect Life Month. The United States Conference of Catholic Bishops has a wealth of online resources (www.usccb.org/respectlife). Every year a theme is announced in late summer, providing materials for parish use, including bulletin inserts, suggestions for the Universal Prayer, and other prayer services.

Regarding All Saints Day, does the parish own any relics that might be stored away? Consider displaying them on the holy day, interspersed with small votive candles. A nearby chart identifying "who's who" will be appreciated by parishioners.

A wonderful way to connect the Eucharistic table to the Thanksgiving Day table is to invite parishioners to bring a few items that will be part of the day's meal for a blessing at the Mass. Volunteers can erect long thin tables (remembering not to impede the Communion line) to be placed down the center aisle draped with a homemade full length cloth. Filling the table with items to be blessed is a wonderful sign of God's bounty. Offering the Order of Blessing of Food for Thanksgiving from the *Book of Blessings*, the presider can sprinkle the food with holy water at the end of the Mass.

Evangelization

JOSHUA told the people of the tribes of Israel at Shechem to decide whom they will serve, the Lord or the gods of their ancestors. His declared his decision: "As for me and my household, we will serve the LORD" (Joshua 24:15). As we embark on the lengthy period of Ordinary Time, the decision Joshua asks of the tribes of Israel becomes our decision. Will our families and parishes serve the Lord? How will others know we serve the Lord? How will we welcome and encourage others to decide to do the same?

Serving the Lord is a journey. Jesus' disciples discovered this after he sent them forth two by two with nothing but a walking stick, sandals, and a second tunic. Following their Teacher's example, they preached and cured. They tried to plant small seeds to grow the Kingdom of God. Sometimes they were rejected. Other times there were so many people who wanted to draw close to Jesus and perhaps follow him as disciples, they had to find respite. Yet even in rest, just like their Teacher, the work of compassionate evangelization needs to occur. Even with reduced activities in parishes and summer vacations for families, evangelization continues.

If our households choose to serve the Lord, we too, plant the Kingdom's seeds in our homes and parishes, and also in the world. People might reject the message of the Kingdom and misunderstand the food and drink that nourishes uses. We might speak prophetic words as we live in the interim before the Second Coming and experience rejection in our families and hometowns, but our supply of food and drink for the journey is eternal. Christ is our Bread of Life.

Our mission during this Ordinary Time is a mission to provide food and drink to others, to respond to their physical hunger and thirst. Our invitation to others is Wisdom's invitation to eat of her food and drink. During this period when we celebrate the Solemnities of the Most Holy Trinity and the Most Holy Body and Blood of Christ, offer to our families, parishes, and the world the beauty of the gift of communion with God and one another. For what a feast of love this is that Christ can celebrate with even the smallest amount of food—five loaves and two fish! Believing that Christ is the living bread is not easy. The disciples themselves knew this was hard to accept.

Although the journey of belief is difficult at times, our faith tells us we make the journey together—with God and one another—and with Mary, the Holy Mother of God, as a model of faith for us and John the Baptist, whose birth we celebrate on a Sunday this year, as examples of what it means to evangelize. The Good News of our communion with God and one another is the focus of the Good News we share over the coming months of Ordinary Time.

The Parish and the Home

AT home, the beginning of this season of Ordinary Time coincides with the start of summer vacation for children, longer periods of daylight, and occasional breaks in the normal routines for everyone. Carrying our faith into daily life requires commitment and some planning. Hold a family meeting at the beginning of the season. Mark a calendar with Sunday Mass, special family dates, including vacation, camps, holidays and planned activities. Talk together about how faith will be lived throughout the season. Regularly visit an elderly family member or neighbor, determine a monthly service commitment as a family, plan a walk or hike and reflect on the beauty of creation. With extra time together, children sometimes find themselves in conflict, calling them to forgive and show mercy toward others.

This season is also a perfect time to develop new habits within the family, such as making the Sign of the Cross on the foreheads of children at bedtime, reading stories of the lives of the saints, and beginning each day with a simple prayer. Set aside a few moments on Sunday to affirm one another for something done in the previous week. This helps to create a pattern in which family members look for and recognize the good in each person.

There are many feasts and solemnities upon which the family may reflect in this season. It is good to note Holydays of Obligation: August 15, the Assumption of the Blessed Virgin Mary, and November 1, All Saints Day. Children will benefit from a greater understanding of the origins of Halloween (October 31) and its connection to All Saints and All Souls' days. Parishes sometimes offer a Halloween gathering in which children dress as saints and adults reflect on the witness of the saints and the faithful departed whom they remember with reverence.

While not a day on our liturgical calendar, Thanksgiving is for many people a "holy day." Pausing to recognize the blessings in our lives, thanking God for the many gifts we are given, is a sacred call. Gratitude leads to generosity; thankfulness for the abundant blessings received leads to response by caring for and sharing with others. Parishes often tie a food or clothing drive with Thanksgiving, ending the liturgical year with an outpouring of love for the least among us as our readings call us to reflect on the end of time and Christ's reign over all.

Mass Texts

◆ TROPES FOR THE PENITENTIAL ACT, FORM C (SUMMER)

Lord Jesus, you call us to follow you in faith and in trust: Lord, have mercy.

Lord Jesus, you acknoweldge us before your heavenly Father: Christ, have mercy.

Lord Jesus, you take us to yourself, to shine like the sun in your Father's Kingdom: Lord, have mercy.

◆ TROPES FOR THE PENITENTIAL ACT, FORM C (FALL)

Lord Jesus, you are the heavenly King who summons us to the eternal wedding banquet: Lord, have mercy.

Lord Jesus, you call us to love God and to love neighbor as ourselves: Christ, have mercy.

Lord Jesus, you are the Master who opens the door to those who knock: Lord, have mercy.

◆ DISMISSAL FOR CHILDREN'S LITURGY OF THE WORD (SUMMER)

Even when school is not in session, we continue to learn from parents, friends, the books we read, and even television. It's important that we never stop learning, especially about God and his great love for us. We don't take a break from learning about God because he is more important than anything else in our lives. God speaks to us through the sun and the moon and the stars and through all his creatures. And now he will speak to you through his Word and through your teacher.

◆ DISMISSAL FOR CHILDREN'S LITURGY OF THE WORD (FALL)

Dear children, just as your lives and rhythms may be in transition as you return to school, or begin new activities, we begin to see changes in our Scriptures, and in Jesus' life. Jesus is telling us about the end times and the direction his ministry will take. We invite you now to journey with him as he travels towards Jerusalem. Go in peace.

◆ DISMISSAL for Catechumens (Summer)

As summer's temperatures fluctuate, sometimes wildly, you are committing to a relationship with Christ that won't change with the seasons nor grow tepid with time. We pray with you that the springtime of your formation will flourish under the glow of the summer sun and yield a lifetime harvest of joyful discipleship. May your sharing today deepen your commitment and hasten the day when you join us at the table of the Eucharist as fully-initiated members of our faith community.

◆ DISMISSAL FOR CATECHUMENS (FALL)

As we break open the life of Christ and the life of being a Christian, we know that it is not easy. Some weeks we will hear how difficult it was for Jesus and his disciples on the journey. As those preparing to enter into a deeper relationship with the Church, you will run into naysayers, or those who will challenge you for your faith. Be strong and courageous, taking up your cross and following Christ your Lord. Go in peace.

May 2018
Month of Our Lady

Weekdays during Ordinary Time

Except for the days of the First and Thirty-Fourth Weeks in Ordinary Time, *The Roman Missal* does not provide prayer texts for the weekdays in Ordinary Time. Instead, priest celebrants and those who prepare the liturgy may select from among the prayers provided for the Sundays in Ordinary Time.

Optional Memorials during Ordinary Time

On all Saturdays during Ordinary Time that do not have an obligatory memorial, a memorial to the Blessed Virgin Mary may be celebrated. The prayers may be selected from the Common of the Blessed Virgin Mary. Commentary below is only provided for Sundays, solemnities, feasts, and obligatory memorials. The following should be consulted for celebrating optional memorials during Ordinary Time: For the celebration of other optional memorials:

> On weekdays in Ordinary Time, there may be chosen either the Mass of the weekday, or the Mass of an Optional Memorial which happens to occur on that day, or the Mass of any Saint inscribed in the Martyrology for that day, or a Mass for Various Needs, or a Votive Mass. (GIRM, 355c)

MON 21 (#341)   green
Weekday / Seventh Week in Ordinary Time

Optional Memorial of St. Christopher Magallanes, Priest, and Companions, Martyrs / red

The Liturgy of the Word

◆ FIRST READING: This week the First Readings all come from the Letter to St. James. Today's reading opens with a question that calls us to reflect on whether or not we are wise and understanding. True Wisdom comes from above and leads to the fruits of purity, peace, gentleness, compliance, mercy, and righteousness. When we grow peace, we enact Wisdom.

◆ RESPONSORIAL PSALM 19: Our Responsorial Psalm was also the psalm for Monday of the First Week of Lent, although with a different refrain. Today's refrain speaks to the joy of the Lord's precepts. We most certainly will bear fruit following the Wisdom of the Lord's law over the demonic ways of jealousy and selfish ambition.

◆ GOSPEL: Jesus heals a boy wracked with convulsions. Faith is all Jesus requires of the boy's father. Embrace the possibility of healing from Jesus is the Lord's invitation. The disciples had been unsuccessful at exorcising the evil spirit in the boy, but Jesus triumphed over it. Jesus concluding words to the disciples remind them and us of the power of prayer.

Today's Saint

St. Christopher Magallanes was a Mexican priest whose years of ministry coincided with an extreme anticlerical era in Mexico. He was falsely accused of promoting rebellion and arrested while on his way to celebrate Mass. Christopher was killed without trial after absolving his executioners, saying, "I die innocent, and ask God that my blood may serve to unite my Mexican brethren." He and his companions died between 1915 and 1928. He was canonized by Pope John Paul II on May 21, 2000, along with twenty-one priests and three laymen, also martyred for resisting the anti-Catholic Mexican government of the 1920s.

TUE 22 (#342)   green
Weekday

Optional Memorial of St. Rita of Cascia, Religious / white

The Liturgy of the Word

◆ FIRST READING: Choose humility. Come close to God. Love God, not the world. Ask for help living in this manner, rather than raging wars and letting your passions get out of hand, James advises. When we foster our relationship with God and not the Devil, we will know God is present with us. God will exalt us.

◆ RESPONSORIAL PSALM 55 is a personal lament in which the psalmist reflects on his betrayal by close friends in light of his relationship with God. In the words of the refrain, we express our confidence that the Lord will support us and care for us. The Lord will save us from the violence and evil that surround us. Indeed, the Lord knows our desire to flee the wickedness. Would that we only flee faster to the Lord!

◆ GOSPEL: Now journeying through Galilee and arriving and Capernaum, Jesus inquires of his disciples as he did in yesterday's Gospel reading about what they are arguing. We, like the disciples, would be embarrassed to admit we were quarreling about who was the greatest, especially after Jesus just told them the Son of Man would be killed and then rise three days later. Jesus teaches the disciples and us to live as servants and to receive children in his name.

Today's Saint

St. Rita of Cascia lived in Italy from 1377 to 1457. Against her wishes, her parents arranged for her to marry a man who ended up abusing her. She had two sons with him; both followed their father's bad example. Rita's husband converted toward the end of his life, but he was murdered by an old enemy. Her sons died soon after. Rita was refused entrance to an Augustinian monastery several times because she was a widow, but eventually she was admitted and lived there until her death. She is depicted with a wound in her forehead because she asked to suffer in union with Jesus and was given a wound from a thorn in his crown.

WED 23 (#343) green
Weekday

The Liturgy of the Word

◆ FIRST READING: Are there times when we boast in our arrogance? When we do boast in our arrogance, James says, it is also sin, because we know our call is to live out the Lord's will for us, not our own desires. When we go life alone without the Lord, deciding to move from place to place solely to make a profit for ourselves, we need to be reminded to enter ourselves in the Lord and his will for our lives.

◆ RESPONSORIAL PSALM 49: The refrain for today's Responsorial Psalm comes from Matthew's version of the Beatitudes and reminds us that the poor in spirit are blessed. It is they who will receive the Kingdom of heaven. The verses align with the First Reading's focus on our call to do God's will. We cannot redeem ourselves; only God can do that.

◆ GOSPEL: John speaks for the other disciples and expresses their concern that someone who is not following Jesus is exorcising demons in his name. Jesus instructs the disciples to allow people who perform wondrous deeds in his name the freedom to do so. They are not against Jesus and his disciples.

THU 24 (#344) green
Weekday

The Liturgy of the Word

◆ FIRST READING: St. James continues to admonish those who think their ways are better than God's way. Today, James reproaches the rich who store up wealth and withhold wages from workers in order to prepare themselves for the last days. The selfishness of the rich does not serve them well. In their wanton disregard for others, they have condemned and murdered the Righteous One. His justice will prevail.

◆ RESPONSORIAL PSALM 49: Today's Responsorial Psalm comes from the latter half of the same psalm that we prayed yesterday. The refrain, like yesterday's refrain comes from Matthew 5:3. The verses instruct us that earthly wealth does not go with us when we die. Our confidence in God must replace dependence on riches on their unjust usage.

◆ GOSPEL: Jesus teaches his disciples about the effect of their actions on others. We can badly influence others, although the choice to sin is still theirs. Through the use of the physical imagery of hands, feet, and eyes, Jesus makes his point clear: sin does not lead one to enter the Kingdom of God, but should make one wary of Gehenna. Jesus short sayings about salt at the end of the Gospel reading, compel us to consider how we can remain at peace with others by keeping the flavor of salt within ourselves and not letting it turn bland.

FRI 25 (#345) green
Weekday

Optional Memorial of St. Bede the Venerable, Priest and Doctor of the Church / white; St. Gregory VII, Pope / white; St. Mary Magdalene de' Pazzi, Virgin / white

The Liturgy of the Word

◆ FIRST READING: St. James's words are straightforward today. The prophets, even Job, persevered in faith. We should, too. Complaining about our brothers and sisters does no good. We must not do so, for the Judge stands waiting. Lastly, St. James exhorts us to say what we mean. We must follow through on the oath of our yes and no, for when we say yes and no, it is matter of speaking and living our faith in the Lord.

◆ RESPONSORIAL PSALM 103: The Responsorial Psalm tempers the strict ideal of the words of the First Reading, with God's kindness and mercy. The psalm writer knows of God will have mercy on his people despite their sin. Nothing exceeds God's kindness. Our God does not hold a grudge; he will not only remove our sin, but will place it miles and miles away from us.

◆ GOSPEL: Jesus now moves into the district of Judea and across the Jordan where Pharisees question him about the legality of a husband divorcing his wife. Jesus' response holds up the ideal of the permanence of marriage in God's plan from the beginning of creation. The disciples continue the conversation with Jesus as they move inside. Inside the house, Jesus speaks of the relationship between divorce and adultery.

Today's Saints

Venerable Bede (672/73–735) was a Benedictine monk at the Abbey of Jarrow in England. He devoted his life to scholarly pursuits, including the study of Scripture, the composition of commentaries based on the ideas of Church Fathers, and extensive research and writing regarding the history of the Church in England. He is credited with educating over 600 monks and popularizing the use of AD (*anno Domini* — "in the year of our Lord") to refer to the Christian era.

St. Gregory VII (c. 1028–1085) joined the Benedictine monks, but was eventually called beyond the cloister to serve the larger Church as pope. Recognized as one of the greatest reformer popes, St. Gregory instituted what is known as the Gregorian reform. Through this reform he wanted to end rampant and widespread abuses in the Church.

St. Mary Magdalene de'Pazzi (1566–1607) was the daughter of a prominent family in Florence. She developed a love of prayer at an early age and began having mystical experiences. Her parents sent her to be educated in a convent but brought her home when they decided she should marry. Fortunately, Mary persuaded them that she had a vocation to be a Carmelite, and they allowed her to return. Her life was marked by prayer, penance, devotion to the Eucharist, and love for the poor.

S A T 26 (#346) white
Memorial of St. Philip Neri, Priest

The Liturgy of the Word

◆ FIRST READING: Prayer is powerful! With a series of questions, St. James instructs the early Christian community to pray for the suffering and the sick. The presbyters should anoint the sick, and those who good spirits should sing praise to God. The example of Elijah shows how pray truly works: he prayed that it would not rain and for three and a half years, no rain came!

◆ RESPONSORIAL PSALM 141 is also a psalm of Evening Prayer. As incense rises up to the Lord, so too, do our prayers. We raises our hands up to God knowing God will answer our the desires of our heart. We turn to God our refuge — God who protects us from harm and holds us in his love.

◆ GOSPEL: Today's Gospel reading provides us another example of where Jesus welcomes children. Recall last Tuesday, instructed his disciples that when they receive a child in his name, they receive Jesus himself. In today's passage, Jesus teaches the disciples not to hinder children from coming to him. The Kingdom of God belongs to children and those who live humbly and unencumbered like children.

The Roman Missal

The prayers for this Mass are proper and can be found in the Proper of Saints section of the Missal at May 26.

Today's Saint

St. Philip Neri (1515–1595) was an Italian priest and founder of the Congregation of the Oratory or Oratorians. Philip was known for his joyful spirit, believing that it is more Christian to be cheerful than melancholy. A well-known figure in the Eternal City, he was known as the "Apostle of Rome" during his lifetime. Philip was ahead of his time in urging more frequent reception of Holy Communion, and he introduced the Forty Hours' devotion with exposition of the Blessed Sacrament. He was apt to go into ecstasy when celebrating Eucharist, so he had to try to distract himself so he could finish the rites.

☀ 27 (#165) white
Solemnity of the Most Holy Trinity

About Today's Solemnity

"In the name of the Father, and of the Son, and of the Holy Spirit." Christians who use this phrase repeatedly could easily lose sight of the powerful mystery it expresses. Today, Trinity Sunday, the Scriptures call for reflection on this central belief of Christianity: the Trinity. One of the greatest gifts of the Christian faith is the dogma of the triune God: God is three (tri) in one (une). Christians name God as a Trinity of Father, Son, and Spirit, but only in light of Jesus Christ does such language and insight fully emerge.

The Liturgy of the Word

◆ FIRST READING: Moses addresses the people and asks them to reflect about the greatness of their experience with God. His rhetorical questions about the people hearing the voice of God in fire and God taking a rescuing the people from slavery in Egypt, lead Moses to declare there is no other God but the Lord. The Christian God — Father, Son, and Holy Spirit — is the same God who chose the people of Israel as his own. May we keep his commandments today and always so that we may know his promise of prosperity.

◆ RESPONSORIAL PSALM 33 reminds us that it was through the Lord's word that creation took place. The Lord's command brought into being all life. Christians believe that the Trinity—Father, Son, and Holy Spirit was present at creation. God the Trinity is the God we fear, the one whose kindness we pray in the psalm to be upon us for he has chosen us as his own.

◆ SECOND READING: Paul gives testimony to our familial relationship with God. Through the working of the Holy Spirit we are children of God, God's sons and daughters. Paul teaches us that because we are God's children, we are heirs, and will inherit everlasting life with Christ. We suffer earthly trials with Christ, but in the end we will share in his glory.

◆ GOSPEL: Even the eleven remaining disciples who went to the mountain with Jesus and worshipped, doubted. Matthew does not explain why they doubted, but just that they did. Perhaps they were concerned about what was to come. Perhaps they were concerned about Jesus leaving them. When Jesus came near and spoke to them, he gave them what is known as the "Great Commission." Power in heaven and earth was given to Jesus, and now he sends his disciples forth to form more disciples. They are to baptize the disciples-to-be in the "name of the Father, and of the Son, and of the Holy Spirit"—the Trinitarian formula the Church has used for centuries when the baptismal water is poured. Jesus concludes with words of reassurance to his disciples. He will be with them as they go forth in mission and will remain with them forever, until the end of time.

The Roman Missal

The texts for this solemnity are found after the texts for the Thirty-Fourth Week in Ordinary Time, toward the end of the "Ordinary Time" section of the Missal, and several pages before the "Order of Mass" section begins.

The Gloria and the Creed are sung or said today.

The Collect expresses for us the meaning of this solemnity not in terms of some dry theological doctrine but rather in terms of the active, dynamic power of the triune God: the Father sends into the world the Word of truth and the Spirit of sanctification and, in so doing, reveals to the human race his own "wondrous mystery." The prayer affirms that through the Trinity we know the very life of God himself.

The Prayer over the Offerings makes the important liturgical point that as we make the offering of our lives at this liturgy — "this oblation of our service" — its ultimate purpose is that by it we might be made "an eternal offering to you." The prayer expresses how in the liturgy we are swept up into the life of the Trinity so that our entire life might be lived with the same self-emptying, self-giving love as exists between the divine Persons.

The Preface, "The Mystery of the Most Holy Trinity," is proper for today and its text is given along with the other texts for the Mass; there is both a text with and without musical notation. The text reiterates the theological meaning of God being "one God, one Lord: / not in the unity of a single person, / but in a Trinity of one substance, equal in majesty."

The Prayer after Communion also gives voice to the basic statement about the Trinity nonetheless being "undivided Unity." Since there should be a certain emphasis given to how the life of the Christian should be a reflection of and a participation in the life of the Trinity, perhaps the formula "Go in peace, glorifying the Lord by your life" would be an appropriate choice for the dismissal today.

Other Ideas

Today is a good time to remind people of the powerful significance of making the Sign of the Cross, the gesture that professes our faith in the Triune God. Signs of the Trinity include the shamrock and the pansy, with their trefoil shape.

Recently, the holy season of Ramadan (May 15 and continue through June 15) began for our Muslim brothers and sisters. Fasting is one of the five pillars of Islam, and observant Muslims fast from dawn until dusk. Each day, the fast is broken with the *Iftar* or evening meal. This is a good time to reach out to Muslim friends and neighbors with the intent of greater interreligious understanding. Pope Francis called the Catholic community to greater dialogue with the Muslim community in *Evangelii gaudium* (see EG, 251–253). Increasing Islamophobia, as well as growing Christian-Muslim violence, are issues throughout the world. Consider making connections with an area mosque or providing learning experiences for the parish.

This is also Memorial Day weekend. Include a prayer remembering all those who have sacrificed their lives while serving in the nation's armed forces. Invite members to bring in pictures of their fallen heroes, both friends and family members to place in the gathering space. Display them with candles and the verse from John: "No one has greater love than this, to lay down one's life for one's friends" (John 15:13). The gathering space is also an appropriate place for the American flag.

M O N 28 (#347) green
Weekday / Eighth Week in Ordinary Time

The Liturgy of the Word

◆ FIRST READING: From the Letter to St. James, we shift to the First Letter of St. Peter for this week's First Readings. Today's reading opens with a short prayer of praise to God for the Resurrection of Jesus Christ. The joy of the Resurrection will buoy us up when we face life's trials and difficulties. Through these struggles, St. Peter instructs us to hold on to the precious gift of our faith. We will know salvation.

◆ RESPONSORIAL PSALM 111: The psalm writer recounts some of the many ways God has been faithful to the people of Israel. God has fed them, delivered them, and performed powerful works. All God's actions testify to his faithfulness to the covenant. The psalm refrain expresses our confidence that even in the future, we trust God will remain faithful to his covenant.

◆ GOSPEL: How many earthly possessions do you have? When the man asks Jesus what he needs to do to gain eternal life, Jesus names the commandments he must follow. The man responds that he has faithfully observed the commandments throughout his life. Yet Jesus points out to him that he lacks one thing. He must sell his possessions, give to the poor, and follow Jesus. It seems impossible to enter the Kingdom of God—or is it? The Gospel reading ends with Jesus' affirmation of the possibility of salvation in God—possible for God, but not possible for us to earn on our own.

T U E 29 (#348) green
Weekday

The Liturgy of the Word

◆ FIRST READING: St. Peter admonishes us to holiness because God in Jesus Christ is holy. Living holy lives means choosing differently. Whatever we formerly desired before we had faith in Jesus Christ, we must leave behind. We are to focus our minds on the grace he offers us. The Spirit of Christ who was active in the prophets helps us to be holy.

◆ RESPONSORIAL PSALM 98: Today's psalm acclaims the saving power of God. As Christians, we believe Christ made this salvific power visible. Salvation is not available only to one corner of the earth, but extends to the ends of the earth. We sing songs of praise as a suitable response to God's boundless gift of salvation!

◆ GOSPEL: Peter is correct that the disciples have given up everything to follow Jesus. Jesus confirms that the disciples, and anyone who has given up as much as they have for the Gospel, will receive in the present a hundred times more. Jesus reverses the world's wisdom at the end of today's Gospel when he teaches the first will be last and vice versa. Will you still follow Jesus knowing this?

W E D 30 (#349) green
Weekday

The Liturgy of the Word

◆ FIRST READING: In Christ, we have received new birth. The Word of God now alive and active in us calls us to love one another as God loves us in Christ. St. Peter quotes Isaiah 40:6–8 to show us that God's word will remain forever. It is not like flesh or grass that withers and dies.

◆ RESPONSORIAL PSALM 147: A psalm of praise, Psalm 147 describes how God revealed his Word in the midst of the people of Israel. As Christians, we believe Jesus is God's Word made flesh who calls us to love another as St. Peter instructed us in the First Reading.

◆ GOSPEL: As if Jesus' reversal of worldly wisdom in yesterday's Gospel reading was not enough for the disciples digest, today he asks the Twelve if they can drink the chalice he drinks and are willing to share in his baptism. To be great, is to be a servant, Jesus says. The Son of Man himself came to serve and to give his life for many. Will we go to Jerusalem with Jesus?

T H U 31 (#572) white
Feast of the Visitation of the Blessed Virgin Mary

About Today's Feast

When the angel brought Mary the amazing message that she would be the mother of God's Son, he also brought her some family news: her elderly cousin, Elizabeth, was going to have a baby as well. Immediately, Mary set out to visit her cousin and help her at what must have been a challenging time. When Mary arrived, something amazing happened: the child in Elizabeth's womb leapt up in recognition, and Elizabeth, too, was filled with the Holy Spirit and realized that Mary was carrying God's Son. Even before his birth, John the Baptist was pointing the way to Christ!

We echo Elizabeth's joyful exclamation every time we pray the Hail Mary: "Blessed are you among women, and blessed is the fruit of your womb!" (Luke 1:42). And we echo Mary's response to her cousin, her Magnificat, in the Office of Evening Prayer.

The Liturgy of the Word

◆ FIRST READING, OPTION 1: The prophet Zephaniah extols Zion to shout with joy for the Lord is in her midst! The Lord is here! The Savior is in our midst! The Lord visits his people. This we believe. We, too, sing joyfully on this feast of the Visitation.

◆ FIRST READING, OPTION 2: St. Paul exhorts the Christian

Church at Rome to Christ-like behaviors. Christians are to live in mutual love of one another. Our passion for the Gospel is to remain strong and our joy consistent despite the persecution we might face. Hospitality and care for the needs of others must mark our Christian life. Our joy and hope remain for God's justice triumphs.

◆ CANTICLE: The words of thanksgiving from the prophet Isaiah express Israel's gratitude for the Lord's presence among his people. For this the people of Israel, and we today, sing praise. God continues to work his mighty deeds among his people year after year.

◆ GOSPEL: Elizabeth proclaims Mary and the fruit of her womb blessed. Mary's trust that the Lord would fulfill his Word to her is an example for us all. To this day, we use the words of her Magnificat to praise the Lord for the salvation brought in Jesus Christ, the Savior. The mercy God shows to every generation and the hungry God fills reveal to us the loving kindness and justice he calls us to offer to others.

The Roman Missal

The texts for this Mass are all proper for the feast, and are located in the Proper of Saints at May 31. The Gloria is sung or said today, since it is a feast. The Collect tells of how the Blessed Virgin Mary, while carry inspired by God to visit Elizabeth, and then goes on to ask that we may be "faithful to the promptings of the Spirit." When we respond to the promptings of the Spirit, we, along with Mary who also was obedient, magnify God's greatness. (Notice how the prayer presumes the promptings are there; if we do not hear them, it's because we are ignoring them, not because the Spirit is not present to us.) The Prayer over the Offerings parallels the offering we make at this Sacrifice with the offering of char-

ity made by Mary—in the Visitation to Elizabeth—asking that God accept our offering as he was pleased to accept the Blessed Mother's offering. The Prayer after Communion notes how St. John the Baptist leapt for joy in "the hidden presence of Christ," and so, as appropriate for a Communion prayer, asks that we too rejoice as we receive in the Eucharist: "in this Sacrament the same ever-living Lord." The Preface assigned for today is Preface II of the Blessed Virgin Mary, appropriately echoing Mary's Magnificat as heard in today's Gospel reading from Luke. Also, the Solemn Blessing formula titled "The Blessed Virgin Mary" under the grouping "For the Celebration of the Saints" may be used at the end of Mass.

June 2018
Month of the Sacred Heart

F R I 1 (#351) red
Memorial of St. Justin, Martyr

The Liturgy of the Word

◆ FIRST READING: The First Reading opens with St. Peter declaring the nearness of the end times. His instructions that follow advise Christians on how to live during these last days. The instructions are as fitting for us today as they were in the early days of the Church. As baptized Christians, we are to love each other intensely, offer hospitality freely and generously, and serve one another by tending to God's grace. Those who preach are to do so only with the words of God. Everything we do is for God's glory. Even when we share in Christ's sufferings, we glorify God.

◆ RESPONSORIAL PSALM 96: Humanity, together with the entire earth and all its creatures, praises the Lord in this psalm. The refrain

acknowledge that judgment belongs to the Lord, for he rules the world with justice. At the end of time, when Christ comes again in glory, we believe that a final judgment will occur.

◆ GOSPEL: This Gospel reading is intense! With Jesus and his disciples in Bethany on their way to Jerusalem, Jesus attempts to find food to eat on a fig tree. Finding nothing to eat on the tree, with the disciples within earshot, he curses it. Once in Jerusalem, he drives out people engaged in commerce in the Temple area. Chief priests and scribes mull over how to put Jesus to death. The fig tree withers. Jesus teaches the disciples to ask in prayer and they will receive. The power of God in Jesus Christ presents itself in this Gospel reading over and over again. Jesus' identity as the Messiah, the Suffering Son of Man, continues to reveal itself to those who understand.

The Roman Missal

Full texts for today's memorial are found in the Proper of Saints at June 1. Use Preface I or II of Holy Martyrs.

Today's Saint

St. Justin, also called Justin Martyr (c. 100–165), was born in Judea and raised pagan by parents who were probably Greek or Roman. He studied philosophy, converted to Christianity, and spent his life teaching and writing. Justin is best known for his Apologies and for his Dialogue with Trypho. He fought against the heresy of Marcion, who rejected the Old Testament. Justin's life ended in Rome, where he was martyred under Marcus Aurelius. He is one of the first Christian apologists, and he was one of the first to employ philosophy as a tool toward greater understanding of revelation.

S A T 2 (#352) green
Weekday

Optional Memorial of Sts. Marcellinus and Peter, Martyrs / red; Blessed Virgin Mary / white

The Liturgy of the Word

◆ FIST READING: The First Reading comes from latter half of the one chapter letter of St. Jude. Jude's letter warns the Christian community about false teachers and exhorts Christians to witness to Christ through their actions. At the beginning of the reading, Jude exhorts Christians to build each other up, remain strong in God's love, and patiently await God's mercy in Jesus Christ. The final two verses of the reading compose the doxology that concludes Jude's letter. The doxology emphasizes God's glory and power, a theme that has reoccurred in the Lectionary readings of the past week.

◆ RESPONSORIAL PSALM 63 is a deeply personal prayer of the psalm writer. In the depths of his soul, the psalmist thirsts for God. In liturgy, he has looked toward God in the sanctuary and seen God's power and glory, a link to the conclusion of the First Reading. Praise is the psalm writer's response to God's glory. It is our response, too, as we continue to thirst for God.

◆ GOSPEL: Authority is the topic of today's Gospel reading. In the Temple area, the chief priests, scribes, and elders question Jesus about where he gets the authority to do things like overturn the tables of the moneychangers in the Temple area. Jesus responds with his own question to the religious leaders about the origin of John the Baptist's baptism. Rather than answer the question directly, the leaders choose to claim ignorance, thereby rejecting both John and Jesus.

Today's Saints

Almost nothing is known about Sts. Marcellinus and Peter, except that they gave their lives for Christ during the persecution of the Church under the emperor Diocletian.

(#168) white
3 Solemnity of the Most Holy Body and Blood of Christ / Corpus Christi

About Today's Solemnity

This Eucharistic day, observed with such solemnity throughout the world, began in a quiet Belgian convent in the thirteenth century, with the vision of a holy nun, St. Juliana. In her vision, she saw the moon, full and bright. It was glorious, except that one part of its disk was in shadow. The meaning of the vision was then revealed to her: the moon represented the liturgical year; the shadow, a missing feast in honor of the Blessed Sacrament. Juliana spoke to her confessor about what she had seen. Amazingly, within thirty-five years, Pope Urban IV had established the Feast of Corpus Christi, the Body of Christ, in the Church's universal calendar. Hundreds of years later, in 1849, Pope Pius IX added the Feast of the Precious Blood celebrated on July 1. Following the Second Vatican Council, the two liturgies became one solemnity in honor of the Most Holy Body and Blood of Christ. Of course, we already had

a day honoring the Eucharist: the Evening Mass of the Lord's Supper on Holy Thursday, which even includes a procession with the Blessed Sacrament. But the purpose and the mood of the two processions are strikingly different.

On Holy Thursday, we walk with Jesus to the Mount of Olives, to keep watch with him on the night of his betrayal. The sacrament is carried in the ciborium, covered with the humeral veil: and Christ's glory, too, is veiled as he undergoes his Passion. On Corpus Christi, we walk in the afterglow of Easter Time, in company with the Risen Lord. This time, the Blessed Sacrament is exposed in a monstrance: the Lord's glory is not hidden, but visible to all. Corpus Christi is one of the most Catholic of days, an expression of our faith in the Real Presence of Christ in the Blessed Sacrament. Yet this celebration is also outward looking, carrying the liturgy out of the church and into the streets. We come together in all our diversity and we celebrate our unity.

The Liturgy of the Word

◆ FIRST READING: Moses presents the people the words and ordinances of the Lord. The people acknowledge their acceptance of the Lord's commands saying they will follow everything the Lord tells them. The ritual of Moses writing down the Lord's words, building an altar, sanctifying the altar with the blood of young bulls, proclaiming the Lord's word to the people, and sprinkling the people with the blood of the covenant seals the covenant between the Lord and his people. On the solemnity of the Body and Blood of Christ we celebrate today, we commemorate the gifts of both Christ's Body and Blood that fulfilled the Mosaic covenant.

◆ RESPONSORIAL PSALM 116: In today's refrain, the psalmist names the Lord as the one responsible for his rescue and drinks the ceremonial cup of wine, the cup of salvation, as an acknowledgment of the life that is still his because of God's intervention. The stanzas call us to offer thanksgiving to the Lord and profess our vows to him for all that he has done for us.

◆ SECOND READING: Through his own blood, Christ the high priest mediates a new covenant. If the blood of animals can make holy those who have sinned, the author of Hebrews writes, the Blood of Christ will cleanse even more. So much more will Christ's blood erase our blemishes that sacrificing animals to the Lord is no longer necessary. Once for all, Christ came into the sanctuary. Through his sacrifice Christ made the gift of eternal redemption available to everyone. His Death delivered us from sin and holds out the grace of new life to us.

◆ SEQUENCE: This Sunday, the Church may sing one of the four sequences—ancient, poetic songs that precede the singing of the Gospel Acclamation. The sequence for the Most Holy Body and Blood of Christ, *Lauda Sion*, is ascribed to St. Thomas Aquinas. The sixth stanza of the sequence reminds us of the history of the Eucharistic feast. Today's sequence is optional. A musical arrangement by Richard Proulx and Alan J. Hommerding is available from World Library Publications. The composition is based on Tantum Ergo. A sample PDF is available here: www.wlp .jspaluch.com/download/008739. pdf. The sequence should be sung from the ambo; however, the assembly may be invited to take part. A worship aid with the music should be provided. Accomplished musicians should segue from the sequence into the Gospel Acclamation, allowing time for the cantor to move from the ambo to the cantor stand.

◆ GOSPEL: The Gospel reading comes from Mark's account of the Passion. Mark's Passion narrative was also proclaimed on Palm Sunday. Jesus takes, blesses, breaks, and shares the bread with his disciples. Then he repeats similar actions with the cup of wine. He takes, blesses (gives thanks), and shares the wine with his disciples. Each time we celebrate the memorial of the Eucharist, we remember and make present what Jesus said and did. His own sacrifice is the basis for the meal of the New Covenant. His is the Body we consume; his, the Blood we drink.

The Roman Missal

The Collect notes that in the Sacrament of the Eucharist, God has "left us a memorial of your Passion." The prayer goes on to ask that because of our revering of "the sacred mysteries of your Body and Blood," we may "always experience in ourselves / the fruits of your redemption." As this prayer speaks of the fruits of being redeemed, we must always remember that those fruits are expressed in a life of self-emptying love. Therefore, the focus is not so much on a passive contemplation of the Real Presence in the Eucharist, but, as with all liturgical celebration, how our participation in the mystery is a means of being transformed by God to live out the mystery that is being celebrated.

The Gloria and the Creed are sung or said.

The Prayer over the Offerings reinforces the idea that worship of the Eucharist must be expressed in the practical living out of our lives. This prayer reinforces that one of the chief results of Eucharistic celebration must be unity: as the one bread and one cup are prayed over at the one altar around which is gathered the one Body of Christ, we see in those signs the mystery of what we are to become — "one body, one

spirit in Christ," in the words of Eucharistic Prayer III.

The Preface that is given along with the other formularies for this Mass is Preface II of the Most Holy Eucharist; only the text with music is given, indicating a certain preference for chanting the introductory dialogue and the Preface itself. However, a rubric indicates that Preface I of the Most Holy Eucharist, which can be found along with the texts of other Prefaces further along in the Missal, may also be used.

The Prayer after Communion points to the important but often overlooked eschatological dimension of the Eucharist, as it reminds us that the reception of the Body and Blood of the Lord in the present age is a foreshadowing of sharing in God's divine life for all eternity. Noting that it is desirable for a Eucharistic procession to take place after Mass, the Missal gives instructions on how this is to be carried out. The host that will be carried in the procession should be a Host that has been consecrated at this Mass; thus it is made clear how worship of the Eucharist outside Mass is an extension of the grace of the offering of the sacrifice.

If such a procession is to take place after Mass, the host to be carried in procession is placed in the monstrance when the Communion of the faithful is over, and that monstrance is set on the altar. The Prayer after Communion is then prayed, but the Concluding Rite is omitted. Instead, the procession forms immediately after the Prayer after Communion. The Missal gives no further rubrics concerning the procession; liturgy preparers should consult the ritual, *Holy Communion and Worship of the Eucharist outside Mass* for specific instructions. The Missal does note, however, that the procession need not take place immediately after Mass, but may instead follow after a public and lengthy period of adoration coming at the end of Mass.

Consult LTP's new resource, *Guide for Celebrating® Worship of the Eucharist Outside of Mass.* As part of the *Preparing Parish Worship™* series, this resource provides detailed instructions for the procession on Corpus Christi.

Other Ideas

Many communities honor this day with special processions of the Eucharist, Eucharistic Exposition and Benediction, and other opportunities for prayer before the Blessed Sacrament (see LTP's *Guide for Celebrating® Worship of the Eucharist Outside Mass*). This is a good time to help parishioners understand that devotion to the Eucharist is connected to our participation at Sunday Mass. Time spent praying in the presence of the Blessed Sacrament should deepen our sense of connection to the Lord's table, the greater Church, and our ability to act prayerfully yet boldly as disciples of Christ.

(#353) green

M O N 4 Weekday / Ninth Week in Ordinary Time

The Liturgy of the Word

◆ FIRST READING: The next two days our First Reading comes the Second Letter of St. Peter. Today's reading includes the opening greeting of grace and peace in Jesus Christ. In his reflection on the gift of divine power and the wondrous and valuable promises given to us, Peter reminds to connect our faith with virtuous living. We are to live in knowledge, self-control, endurance, devotion, mutual affection, and love. These ideal virtues are the epitome of the Christian life as we await Christ's coming again.

◆ RESPONSORIAL PSALM 91: When difficulties come, do you seek refuge in the Lord? The psalm

writer's trust in God and the shelter God provides, is an example to us. When we hold tight to God, God will deliver us. We will know God's salvation. May today's psalm encourage our assemblies to place their trust in God.

◆ GOSPEL: The tenants kill the heir of the man who planted the vineyard and leased it to them. At the end of the parable, Jesus rhetorically asks the chief priests, scribes, and elders how the owner of the vineyard will respond? Jesus' responds to his own question by telling the religious leaders that the owner will kill the tenant and take the vineyard away and hand it over to others. Of course, the religious leaders wanted to seize Jesus for the parable indicted them. Fear of the throngs who followed Jesus prevent them from doing so.

(#354) red

T U E 5 Memorial of St. Boniface, Bishop and Martyr

The Liturgy of the Word

◆ FIRST READING: In today's reading, St. Peter exhorts Christians to live a life worthy of their calling. As we wait for the day of God to come and welcome the birth of a new heaven and earth, ours is the charge to avoid sin and mature in grace. Peter instructs us to view the Lord's patience as salvation. Glory be to our Savior, Jesus Christ, now and for all eternity!

◆ RESPONSORIAL PSALM 90 expresses the mourning of an entire community for the suffering they have endured, although the psalm writer does not specify what the suffering was. The refrain affirms the community's confidence in the Lord who has been by their side through the generations. God was, is, and always will be God of his people; God will always protect his children.

◆ GOSPEL: The Pharisees and Herodians attempt to manipulate Jesus by asking him about the legality of paying tax to Caesar. Seeing right through their question, Jesus tells them to bring him a coin so they might visibly perceive whose image is on it. Paying Caesar his due takes nothing away from what belongs to God. Everything belongs, and ultimately everything and everyone belongs to God.

The Roman Missal

The Collect is drawn from the Proper of Saints, with the remaining prayers taken from the Common of Martyrs: For One Martyr or of Pastors: For Missionaries. The Preface of Holy Martyrs or of Holy Pastors may be used.

Today's Saint

St. Boniface (c. 675–754) was an Anglo-Saxon Benedictine monk. He was first sent as a missionary to Frisia, which is in the vicinity of the Netherlands, but he failed because of wars between the local tribes and the Frankish king Charles Martel. Boniface then went to Rome and was commissioned by the pope to evangelize in Germany. He started by chopping down an oak tree dedicated to Thor, and when he was not immediately struck down, the people believed and became Christians. Boniface returned to evangelize the Frisians but was killed by them in AD 754. He is buried in the cathedral in Fulda.

(#355) green

W E D 6 Weekday

Optional Memorial of St. Norbert, Bishop / white

The Liturgy of the Word

◆ FIRST READING: We turn to the Second Letter of Paul to St. Timothy for the First Readings today and tomorrow. Paul greets Timothy with much affection and offers him a gentle, but strong reminder to "stir into flame" the gift of leadership in the Church he received through the laying on of Paul's hands. Neither cowardice nor shame has a place in the preaching of the Gospel as Paul witnesses to in his own life filled with hardship and suffering. Live in the life of grace and holiness to which God calls you in Christ Jesus, Paul tells Timothy. Let Paul's words today reminds us as well of our privilege to live a grace-filled and holy life.

◆ RESPONSORIAL PSALM 123: In this brief psalm, we lift our eyes to the Lord and join in the psalm writer's prayer to God. The end of Psalm 123, which is not included in today's Responsorial Psalm, speaks of the insults and disdain the Lord's people face. The psalm writer laments this suffering, yet still fixes his eyes on the Lord enthroned in heaven.

◆ GOSPEL: Seven brothers were married to her. All the brothers and the woman die. Yet Jesus speaks of the resurrection. The plot is similar to yesterday's Gospel in which the Pharisees and Herodians try to entrap Jesus with the question of paying taxes to Caesar. The Sadducees attempt to manipulate Jesus with their silly question about whose wife the woman would be at the resurrection. Jesus responds by referencing Scripture that the Sadducees should know, and in so doing, claims God is God of the living, not the dead.

Today's Saint

St. Norbert (1080–1134), a subdeacon and canon in the Rhineland, had a conversion experience similar to St. Paul, in which he was thrown from a horse during a violent thunderstorm. Following this event he had a change of heart. He became increasingly aware of the need to renounce the trappings of the world and to preach reform to the canons. His preaching led His preaching

led him to the valley of Premontre where he, along with thirteen disciples, laid the framework for a reform movement that became known as the Canons Regular of Premontre, the Premonstratensians, or Norbertines.

T H U 7 (#356) green
Weekday

The Liturgy of the Word

◆ FIRST READING: Paul's words to Timothy remind us of the Gospel of Jesus Christ, the Good News of his Resurrection. An early Christian hymn is found in the middle of the passage. This hymn recalls our participation in Jesus' Death and Resurrection. It gives us confidence that if we hold fast to the faith that we will reign with Christ in glory. Our charge, like Timothy's is to teach others of these truths of faith.

◆ RESPONSORIAL PSALM 25: In today's refrain, we ask the Lord to teach us his ways. We acclaim the Lord's kindness and friendship in the verses and acknowledge his justice. The Lord is the One from whom we seek guidance.

◆ GOSPEL: Today's Gospel is also the Gospel for Friday of the Third Week of Lent. Proclaimed during Ordinary Time, this Gospel challenges us to reflect on the two commandments Jesus gives in response to the scribe's inquiry about which commandment is first of all, and how we live those commandments during this lengthy period of Ordinary Time. Loving God completely and loving our neighbor as we love ourselves are not always easy to do. Yet we, like the scribe, understand our call to follow these commandments. The Kingdom of God is near to us in when we remain faithful to the love Jesus invites us to.

F R I 8 (#171) white
Solemnity of the Most Sacred Heart of Jesus

About Today's Solemnity

The Solemnity of the Sacred Heart of Jesus is celebrated on the Friday after the Most Holy Body and Blood of Christ. This devotion has a life outside of the liturgy as well: the nine Fridays and the twelve promises made by Jesus to St. Margaret Mary Alacoque are still familiar to many Catholics. Help people to understand and grow in love of this devotion by providing catechesis. Even something as simple as placing a printed prayer near your church's image of the Sacred Heart can help people understand how the devotion relates to their lives.

One of the most beloved aspects of our Catholic tradition is our devotion to the Sacred Heart of Jesus. In honoring the Sacred Heart, we are honoring the compassion and love of Christ: his human heart, moved with pity for his flock, his divine heart, pierced for the sins of his people. From the heart of Christ, pierced by the soldier's lance, blood and water poured out, "the wellspring of the Church's Sacraments" (Preface for the Sacred Heart). While saints and mystics, notably the thirteenth century Benedictine St. Gertrude, have long found the heart of Christ a rich subject matter for meditation, it was not until the seventeenth century, in France, that devotion to the Sacred Heart of Jesus began to take the form we know today. It was a time when the heresy of Jansenism was rampant. People were convinced that human sinfulness was too great to be forgiven, that salvation would only be granted to a few. In this climate of fear, the revelations of the Sacred Heart to St. Margaret Mary Alocoque, a religious of the Visitation order, in the French town of Paray-le-Monial, France, must have come as a complete and wonderful surprise. The devotion spread, and the feast of the Sacred Heart of Jesus was added to the universal calendar in 1856.

There are many devotions associated with the Sacred Heart of Jesus, especially the Litany of the Sacred Heart, and the devotion of the nine first Fridays, in which people attend Mass on the first Friday of each month, celebrating the Sacraments of Reconciliation and Eucharist, in keeping with the words of Christ to St. Margaret Mary, when he promised grace, peace, and consolation to those who would honor him in this way.

On the Solemnity of the Most Sacred Heart of Jesus, we give thanks to God for the infinite love of Christ, represented by the image of his heart on fire with love. Through our prayer, we also seek to make reparation for the ways that love has been rejected by human beings. This is why in the familiar image, Christ's heart is pierced and surrounded with thorns.

The Liturgy of the Word

◆ FIRST READING: In a vivid description of the development of the Lord's relationship with his child, Israel, the prophet Hosea depicts how the Lord taught Israel to walk, how he fed Israel, and how deeply his love was for his child. Even now, though his child sins, the Lord's heart is overwhelmed with mercy. The Lord will not let his anger rule his heart and lead him to destroy Ephraim again. The Lord is the Holy One who is present within Israel.

◆ CANTICLE: Isaiah's words confidently profess God as his Savior. With God, we draw not just any water, but water that comes from "the springs of salvation." What a joyous act this is! We sing praise to the Lord together with Israel, for God is in our midst.

◆ SECOND READING: The prayer of the author of Ephesians is that

Christ may live in our hearts by faith and that by his dwelling there, we might come to know the immensity of his love and plan for our salvation. Paul preached the mystery of salvation to the Gentiles. If God gave his grace to Paul who had persecuted followers of Christ, God, too, could strengthen us and fill us with his fullness to go forth and continue to make the divine plan known throughout the world.

◆ GOSPEL: A short segment of the Jesus' Passion according to John is the Gospel reading. This passage gives testimony to the reality of Jesus' Death. When the soldiers came to break Jesus' legs, they found he was already dead. Instead of breaking his legs, a solider put a lance in Jesus' side. Water and blood poured out. We can see a reference to Baptism and Eucharist here. Even those who pierced him, looked upon him. Perhaps they even worshipped him. His heart remains forever aligned with those who believe in him.

The Roman Missal

The orations are found in the Proper of Time. There are two options for the Collect. In the Prayer over the Offerings, we ask God to look at his Son's love for us in his heart — and to let our offering be "an expiation of our offenses." The proper Preface is subtitled "The Boundless Charity of Christ." In Christ, raised high on the Cross, pierced by the soldier's lance, we behold "the wellspring of the Church's Sacraments," a fountain of salvation open to all. Christ's Sacred Heart is an "open heart," offering love and life to every person. In the Prayer after Communion, we pray that we may also be "fervent with the fire of holy love," and be so drawn to Christ that "we may learn to see him in our neighbor." The Gloria and the Creed are sung or said.

About Today's Memorial

It was Pope John Paul II who raised this celebration to an obligatory memorial, a kind of liturgical sister to yesterday's solemnity of the Most Sacred Heart of Jesus. It always takes place on the Saturday following the Second Sunday after Pentecost (Most Holy Body and Blood of Christ/Corpus Christi). It was St. John Eudes, a priest and a contemporary of St. Margaret Mary, who helped make devotion to Mary's Immaculate Heart part of the life of the universal Church. When Mary brings the baby Jesus to the Temple, the aged Simeon tells her that her heart will be pierced by a sword (Luke 2:35). "And Mary kept all these things, reflecting on them in her heart" (Luke 2:19). Mary's heart is the treasury of the Lord's deeds and words, and it is the place of her anguish, in witnessing the sufferings of her Son. Just as the nine first Fridays are associated with the Sacred Heart of Jesus, so the five first Saturdays are associated with the Immaculate Heart of Mary. Through celebrating the Sacraments of Reconciliation and Eucharist, and taking fifteen minutes on the first Saturday of each month to ponder the mysteries of the Rosary, the devotion is focused on reparation to the Immaculate Heart of Mary.

The Liturgy of the Word

◆ FIRST READING: Our text begins and ends with reference to the future coming of the Lord as Judge. Those who are faithful to the end will receive a crown of righteousness from the Lord, which Paul believes that he will soon receive. Timothy is exhorted to be a faithful teacher and proclaimer of the Gospel. Notice how important "sound doctrine" is in today's text, as well as its opposite: the false teachings and myths propagated by the opponents of the Gospel.

◆ RESPONSORIAL PSALM 71: The theme of proclaiming God's justice and salvation pervades today's Psalm of praise. We, too, in the words of the refrain joyfully sing of God's salvation so that others will know its happiness.

◆ GOSPEL: A child wandering off from his parents is an ordinary occurrence. What is extraordinary is that when Jesus' parents finally found him after three days, he was in the Temple soaking up the knowledge of the teachers and as any good student would do, asking them questions. Apparently, Jesus answered some of their questions as well, for Luke's account describes to us how the teachers we astounded at not only his understanding, but also his answers. After herself questioning Jesus about why he had put his parents through such great anxiety, Mary placed all that she heard from him in her heart. She began to understand why he was in his Father's house. Surely, she had an immense heart for her Son and his mission.

The Roman Missal

The prayers for this memorial are found in the Proper of Saints, immediately following the prayers for the Visitation of the Blessed Virgin Mary on May 31. God made Mary's Immaculate Heart "a fit dwelling place for the Holy Spirit." We, too, are formed to be a "temple of [God's] glory" (Collect). In the Prayer over the Offerings, we pray that the prayers and offerings we make on this memorial may be pleasing to God, and bring us "help and forgiveness." Through the sacrament we share, we are "partakers of eternal redemption" (Prayer after Communion). We pray that God's grace may be increased in us.

10 (#89) green
Tenth Sunday in Ordinary Time

The Liturgy of the Word

◆ FIRST READING: Consequences always follow from sin. Embarrassment, fear, shame, and guilt follow, too. We know we should not have sinned. Adam knows this, which is why he hides from God and tries to pass the blame on to Eve for his eating the fruit of the forbidden tree. Eve, too, knows serious consequences will follow for her consumption of the fruit. Yet she passes the blame onto the serpent. God punishes the serpent, but also puts enmity between the serpent and humanity. Evil causes separation and broken relationships. The devil at work in the serpent has harmed humanity, yet God in Jesus Christ will ultimately triumph forever.

◆ RESPONSORIAL PSALM 130 is also a common psalm for the season of Lent. Having come in touch with our own sin while hearing of the sin of Adam and Eve in the First Reading, the psalm refrain calls us to express confidence in the Lord's mercy. When our hearts reside with the Lord, we will know his mercy. Even when we have to cry out to the Lord from the depths of despair, he offers redemption.

◆ SECOND READING: One of Paul's major themes in his second letter to the Corinthians is the transitory nature of our earthly life. We should look at everything we do here as a preparation for eternal life. While we might sense discouragement because even our bodies change with age, if our focus is on our internal self, we know that God in Jesus will help us continually renew our spirits. We live in hope that by virtue of our faith we will share in Jesus' Resurrection.

◆ GOSPEL: Evidently the scribes are confused for they attribute Jesus' power to exorcise demons to the devil, Beelzebul. Jesus' response to the accusations is to tell a parable. The message of the parable is that division has no place in relation to God's will. Divided homes and kingdoms continue to exist. This is why God forgives sins, even blasphemies. Yet no one is ever to speak against the Holy Spirit for that would mean a demonic spirit possesses him or her. A relative of Jesus does God's will.

The Roman Missal

The Collect praises God, the source of "all good things," and asks that with God's help we may "discern what is right," and, with God's guidance, do it. Prayer over the Offerings: We pray that we may grow in charity through the sacrifice we offer. The short and simple Prayer after Communion asks God to free us from evil, and "lead us to what is right." The Gloria and the Creed are sung or said.

Other Ideas

June is the season of graduations and weddings. Consider celebrating a Baccalaureate Sunday at which both high school and college graduates can be honored and blessed. Or include a prayer of blessing over the graduates at Mass this weekend. Invite graduates to present the gifts. You might consider adapting the Order of Blessing of Students and Teachers for this purpose (chapter 5 in the BB). Include your parish youth minister in the liturgical and post-Mass preparations.

Too often, we forget our newlyweds until they return to us requesting Baptism for a baby. Host a special gathering for couples that have been married at the parish in the past few years. Include a petition in the Universal Prayer for graduates, newly married couples, and those preparing to be married.

Eid al-Fitr, the completion of Ramadan, occurs on June 15 (it begins at sunset on June 14). Encourage community members to greet their Muslim friends and neighbors with *Eid Mubarak,* or "blessed celebration."

MON 11 (#580; Gospel #359) red
Memorial of St. Barnabas, Apostle

The Liturgy of the Word

◆ FIRST READING: The Holy Spirit filled Barnabas as he journeyed from Jerusalem to Antioch to encourage the people to remain faithful in their commitment to the Lord. Upon his arrival in Antioch, Barnabas rejoiced at how the grace of God was already active in believers there. From Antioch, he traveled to Tarsus to find Saul, and the two returned to Antioch together. By the grace of God and the call of the community at Antioch, Barnabas and Saul were chosen to extend God's mission.

◆ RESPONSORIAL PSALM 98 is used frequently during the liturgical year. The psalm's many references to God making his salvation known to the nations—indeed, to the ends of the earth—ties into the extension of the Church's mission through Barnabas and Saul as recounted in the First Reading. Through the ministry of the Apostles, people throughout the known world of the time came to know the Good News of Christ Jesus.

◆ GOSPEL: While Barnabas ministered as an Apostle before Matthew wrote his version of the Beatitudes, the Good News

Barnabas brought to the people on his travels surely held out to them the promise of the Kingdom of heaven. Undoubtedly, he the Apostles also personally tried to live a life that mirrored the teachings in the Beatitudes. Proclaiming God's mercy, espousing humility and peace, and enduring persecution for the sake of the Kingdom all had their place in the life of an Apostle; for theirs would be the Kingdom of heaven.

The Roman Missal

All the orations are proper for today and can be found in the Proper of Saints at June 11. The Collect recognizes the saint for his preaching of the Gospel to the nations, calling him "a man filled with faith and the Holy Spirit." The prayer goes on to ask that the Gospel may continue to "be faithfully proclaimed by word and by deed" even down to our own day. The Prayer over the Offerings asks that the offerings we make will transform us to do that work of spreading the Gospel in the same way St. Barnabas did, "set us on fire" with the same "flame of your love, / by which Saint Barnabas brought the light of the Gospel to the nations." Either Preface I or Preface II of the Apostles is the Preface to be used today. The Prayer after Communion points to the Kingdom that is revealed and anticipated in the celebration of the Eucharist, a Kingdom we hope to arrive at fully one day, as it asks that "what we celebrate in sacramental signs . . . we may one day behold unveiled."

Today's Saint

Even though St. Barnabas (first century) was not one of the original Twelve Apostles, he was given the title of "apostle" by St. Luke and the early Church fathers due to his apostolic endeavors on behalf of Christianity. His original name was Joseph, but the Apostles

gave him the surname Barnabas, meaning "son of encouragement." Together with St. Paul, he extended the missionary efforts of the Church beyond Jerusalem to Antioch, and after much success moved on to other places throughout Asia Minor. After parting ways with St. Paul over issues regarding circumcision and the Mosaic law, St. Barnabas embarked on further missionary journeys with John and Mark (see Acts of the Apostles 15:36–40).

TUE 12 (#360) green
Weekday

The Liturgy of the Word

◆ FIRST READING: Today we begin three weeks of First Readings that come from the historical books of 1 and 2 Kings. The widow of Zarephath's jar of flour did not go empty. She fed Elijah, and her son and herself. The jug of oil remained full. In the end, as Elijah had told the widow, there was nothing for her to fear. God provides. We will always have enough.

◆ RESPONSORIAL PSALM 4: Trust is the theme of Psalm 4 as it is one of the main themes of the First Reading. We believe the Lord will hear our prayers, and so we ask of him what we need. We trust the Lord will grace our hearts with happiness. Would that the Lord continuously shine his face upon us, as we pray in the refrain.

◆ GOSPEL: The familiar images of salt and light take center stage in Jesus' teaching to his disciples. Salt must retain its flavor, lest it become useless. Light must remain visible and not hidden, otherwise, it too, serves no purpose. As salt and light, disciples lead others to glorify the heavenly Father.

(#361) white

Memorial of St. Anthony of Padua, Priest and Doctor of the Church

WED 13

The Liturgy of the Word

◆ FIRST READING: The people of Israel were wishy-washy on which God to follow, the Lord or Baal. Elijah would have no more of it as he tells them to choose. Elijah offers a sacrifice to the Lord and cries out to him, asking him to show himself so that the people might know he truly is God. The Lord comes down in fire and consumes the burnt offering. No doubt remains. The Lord is God!

◆ RESPONSORIAL PSALM 16: The link between the Responsorial Psalm and the First Reading is clear as the psalm writer affirms the Lord is God. Those who choose to follow other gods mire themselves in sorrow. In contrast, the Lord will show life's path to those who follow him. They will reside joyfully in the Lord's presence.

◆ GOSPEL: "Abolish." "Fulfill." Jesus uses these antonyms to instruct the disciples about his purpose in relation to the Law and the prophets. He comes to fulfill, but he must complete his journey of suffering, Death, and Resurrection in order for the fulfillment of the Law to come to pass. The other sayings of Jesus in this Gospel reading are direct: follow the commandments and you will be great in heaven's Kingdom. Choose not to obey them and you will be least in the Kingdom. Notice, however, Jesus does not completely deny the Kingdom to those who have difficulty following the commandments.

The Roman Missal

The proper Collect for the day, found at June 13 in the Proper of Saints section of the Missal, recognizes St. Anthony of Padua "as an outstanding preacher / and an intercessor in their need." The prayer goes on to ask God that, with the saint's assistance, "we may know your help in every trial." (Thus, we can turn to St. Anthony not only when we have lost some item, but when we have lost strength and resolve in the face of struggle and difficulty.) The Prayer over the Offerings and the Prayer after Communion come from either the Common of Pastors: For One Pastor, or from the Common of Doctors of the Church, or from the Common of Holy Men and Women: For Religious. The same variety exists for the choice of the Preface today: Preface I or II of Saints, the Preface of Holy Pastors, or the Preface of Holy Virgins and Religious.

Today's Saint

St. Anthony of Padua (1195–1231), a member of a noble Portuguese family, joined the Canons Regular of St. Augustine at a young age, but later joined the Franciscans to engage in missionary work. Although his missionary dreams were halted due to illness, he received public acclaim for his preaching style, which led to the conversion of many from heresy, earning him the title "the Hammer of the Heretics." He had the privilege of meeting St. Francis of Assisi in person and was later elected provincial of Northern Italy. His writing is extensive, especially in the area of sermons; therefore, he was named a Doctor of the Church. People invoke his name when trying to find lost items. This comes from the story in the saint's biography when a young novice took Anthony's Psalter, but returned it in a hurry when the angry saint appeared to him in a vision!

THU 14

(#362) green
Weekday

The Liturgy of the Word

◆ FIRST READING: Would the rains come? Seven times Elijah sent his servant to climb up the mountain and look out to the sea. The seventh time the servant looked, he returned to report seeing a very small cloud, as small as a human hand. Elijah knew this meant rain so he warned Ahab to come down from the mountain. Ahab followed Elijah's directions, yet the Lord was with Elijah who went on ahead of Ahab.

◆ RESPONSORIAL PSALM 65: The refrain for today's Responsorial Psalm expresses how appropriate it is for the Lord's people to praise him in Zion. God has brought water, a direct connection to the First Reading making the land fertile. God's abundance is everywhere, then and now! For the bounty we enjoy, we praise God!

◆ GOSPEL: Today's Gospel reading is also proclaimed on Friday of the First Week of Lent. Leave your gift at the altar. Reconcile with your brother. Then approach the altar. These three steps are the steps Jesus teaches his disciples. When we enact these steps, our righteousness will indeed exceed that of the Pharisees. Ours is the hope then to enter the Kingdom of heaven.

FRI 15

(#363) green
Weekday

The Liturgy of the Word

◆ FIRST READING: Most daily Mass-goers will know this reading well. Elijah experiences the Lord neither in the wind, nor the earthquake, nor the fire, but in the whisper. When the Lord engages the prophet in dialogue, we find out Elijah feels abandoned, left alone by the people of Israel who themselves have left the covenant behind. The prophet fears for his life, yet the Lord sends him back to the desert to anoint two kings and a new prophet.

◆ RESPONSORIAL PSALM 27 echoes Elijah's desire to see the Lord. Elijah surely wants to hear the Lord and know his presence. Like the psalm writer, he does not want the Lord to abandon him, too, as others have already done. The final stanza in today's Responsorial Psalm expresses the psalmist's confidence that he will see the Lord, no matter how long he needs to wait.

◆ GOSPEL: Yesterday, Jesus focused on the commandment "you shall not kill" in relation to reconciliation. Today, he speaks to his disciples about the commandment "*you shall not commit adultery.*" He gives his practical instructions to the disciples using the metaphors of eyes and hands. Jesus warns his disciples to be aware of where there actions might lead. Would that our actions befit a follower of Jesus and lead us to the Kingdom of heaven and not Gehenna.

SAT 16 (#364) green
Weekday

Optional Memorial of the Blessed Virgin Mary / white

The Liturgy of the Word

◆ FIRST READING: Elisha is the new prophet the Lord sent Elijah to find. With the gesture of throwing his cloak over Elisha, we witness Elijah calling Elisha. Before he follows Elijah as his attendant, Elisha says good-bye to his parents and feeds his people with oxen just as prophets nourish their people with the Lord's word.

◆ RESPONSORIAL PSALM 16: Today's refrain emphasizes the Lord as our inheritance. Like the psalm writer we want for nothing but the Lord for all our days. The final stanza, verses 9–10 highlight the happiness of our heart and soul because the Lord will always be with us. The Lord will abandon neither Elijah nor Elisha, even if their people stray from the cove-

nant. We also can be assured of the Lord's faithfulness to us.

◆ GOSPEL: We continue to read from Jesus' Sermon on the Mount. Today, Jesus' teaches his disciples to not swear oaths. His instruction is such because he wants his disciples to say what they mean. If the disciples say yes, this should be the truth. If they say no, this should also be a truthful response. Those of us who follow Jesus are not to say yes, when we mean no, and no when we mean yes. This would be sin originating from the Evil One.

☀ 17 (#92) green
Eleventh Sunday in Ordinary Time

The Liturgy of the Word

◆ FIRST READING: Ezekiel offers his prophecy in the form of a poem about trees. The Lord is portrayed as the one who tends to the grove of trees. There is no interpretation of the poem, but we can make a few inferences. Christians could see in the young shoot that the Lord tears off and plants on a high mountain a reference to Jesus. This shoot eventually becomes a "majestic cedar." The prophet also communicates reverse wisdom similar to that we frequently hear from Jesus. God will level the high trees and make them low. The low trees God will raise. The shriveled trees will bloom and the blooming trees will die. Perhaps a question for us on this Sunday is what kind of tree are

we now and what kind do we want to be?

◆ RESPONSORIAL PSALM 92 compares the just ones to flourishing trees as in the First Reading. The just will praise and thank the Lord, for he is a just God. Their justice is rooted in divine justice. How wonderful it is for us to give thanks to the Lord when we sing the refrain. Would we plant our trees in the Lord's house so that by his justice we might live with him eternally?

◆ SECOND READING: Twice Paul tells the Corinthians that they are courageous. While they live in the body they long to be closer to the Lord. They walk by faith, though, not by their sight. They live confidently that one day they will be at home in the Lord. As they live in the interim before their death and before the Lord comes again, Paul encourages them to continue to please the Lord through their actions. Do good while you are in the body, for God will compensate you according to whether you choose good or evil.

◆ GOSPEL: While teaching the crowds about the Kingdom of God, Jesus uses parables so that they might understand its meaning. He offers his disciples private explanations of their meaning. The Gospel reading begins with Jesus describing how a sower scatters seed on the land and then one day discovers the land bearing fruit so the sower knows it is harvest time. Such is it with God's Kingdom, which is like a mustard seed, the smallest of seeds, which grows into a large plant. Birds will come to make their home in the large plant because of its shade. With the Kingdom of God, as with nature, we need to understand that God is at work in our midst—in us, in the people around us, in the Church, and in all of creation.

The Roman Missal

Without God, we "can do nothing." We ask for God's grace, that we may follow God's commands and be pleasing to him "by our resolve and our deeds" (Collect). The Eucharist is food for body and soul. We pray that this "sustenance . . . may not fail us in body or in spirit" (Prayer over the Offerings). Holy Communion is a foretaste of the promise of our union with God. We pray that this sacrament may "bring about unity in your Church" (Prayer after Communion). The Gloria and the Creed are sung or said.

Other Ideas

Today we honor biological fathers as well as all men who have showed someone a father's love. Take action as a community to honor Father's Day. Collect gifts or regifts of gently used clothing and provide them in gift bags to a local shelter or social service agency. Extend your pro-life ministry in some way that includes the fathers facing crisis pregnancy, perhaps making baby bottles available this month in which children and adults can save change, which can then be donated to an agency serving couples with needs. Collect professional attire for men who are being helped through transitions from unemployment, addiction or prison. Place a book of remembrance in the sanctuary, a "Spiritual Bouquet book," in which people can write the names of fathers who have passed into eternal life. Remember all fathers, living and deceased, in the Universal Prayer.

Juneteenth, also known as Freedom Day or Emancipation Day, is celebrated on June 19. This day on which the Union Army enforced the Emancipation Proclamation is day of public and community events celebrating equal rights and freedom for all people. Consider reprinting a portion of or providing a link to *Dignitatis humanae*, the *Declaration on Religious Freedom* of the *Second Vatican Council*, or an encyclical like Pope St. John Paul II's *Evangelium vitae* this week.

MON 18 (#365) green Weekday

The Liturgy of the Word

◆ FIRST READING: Today and tomorrow the First Readings recount a drama over a vineyard. Naboth the Jezreelite had a vineyard that King Ahab of Samaria desired, but Naboth refused to give away his vineyard that had been in his family for a long time. Ahab was frustrated and angry that he would not sell. But Jezebel, the king's wife, would not stand for his frustration so she wrote a manipulative, deceitful letters in the king's name to the leaders in Naboth's city disparaging his faith and calling upon people to stone him. Her letters worked and today's reading ends with the death of Naboth and Ahab making his way to the vineyard.

◆ RESPONSORIAL PSALM 5: The refrain of the Responsorial Psalm echoes King Ahab's frustration. Some in your assembly will feel they do not need to ask the Lord to listen to their groaning. We have all at one time or another in our lives been in the place where we do want the Lord to listen to us grumble. In the first two verses, the psalmist pleads to the Lord for help while identifying the Lord as king. In the latter verses, we hear of the Lord's hatred for evildoers. We can think of this as a foreshadowing for how the Lord will respond to Jezebel actions and Naboth's resultant death.

◆ GOSPEL: The wisdom Jesus imparts to his disciples negates the concept of revenge. When he instructs his disciples to turn the other cheek and go the extra mile, he is not suggesting that they allow people to walk over or take advantage of them. Rather, his teaching suggests that judgment belongs to God; retaliation and vengeance our not ours to determine.

TUE 19 (#366) green Weekday

Optional Memorial of St. Romuald, Abbot / white

The Liturgy of the Word

◆ FIRST READING: Today we learn King Ahab's fate after the death of Naboth. The Lord sends Elijah to find Ahab in the vineyard of which he has taken possession. For this evil Ahab has brought about, the Lord initially says that he will destroy Ahab and the males to come in his line. By the end of the reading, Ahab humbles himself before the Lord. The Lord, in turn, offers mercy to Ahab. Ahab's house will not face the Lord's wrath now, but during the future reign of his son.

◆ RESPONSORIAL PSALM 51 is a penitential psalm. Today, it reflects Ahab's recognition of his sin and his hope for God's mercy. The prayer of the psalm writer for mercy is the prayer on our lips when we sin. In the face of the evil we have done, we seek God's goodness and compassion.

◆ GOSPEL: Today's Gospel was also proclaimed on Saturday of the First Week of Lent. Jesus reverses the world's wisdom again as he instructs his disciples to not only love their neighbors, but also their enemies. We are to pray not only for those who love us, but also those who persecute us. When we follow Jesus' teaching on this, we draw closer to the Father and differentiate ourselves from tax collectors and pagans who only love those who love us.

Today's Saint

St. Romuald (c. 950–1027) was born in Ravenna and led a self-indulgent life as a young man, but when he saw his father kill an opponent in a duel, he fled to a monastery. Romuald yearned for a stricter life than he found there, and so he withdrew to become a hermit. Eventually, he founded the Camaldolese branch of the Benedictine family, integratingcommunity life with the solitary life. His monks live and work in individual hermitages but come together to celebrate the Eucharist and the Liturgy of the Hours.

WED 20 (#367) green Weekday

The Liturgy of the Word

◆ First Reading: Today we shift to the Second Book of Kings for our First Reading. The Lord takes Elijah up to heaven and Elisha succeeds him. Elisha's one request before Elijah leaves him is that he will receive double Elijah's spirit. The Lord fulfills the request as Elijah goes up to heaven. Elijah's mantle is now Elisha's and by the power and grace of the Lord, Elisha crosses over the water.

◆ Responsorial Psalm 31 is a lament, although the refrain and verses used for today's Responsorial Psalm express confidence in the Lord. In the refrain, we pray that those who hope in the Lord will find comfort in him. The verses remind us of the Lord's goodness and the refuge he offers to those in need. Our duty, like that of the prophets, is to love the Lord constantly and consistently, even when others might stray.

◆ Gospel: Interestingly, today's Gospel reading was also proclaimed on Ash Wednesday. In relation to today's First Reading, the emphasis falls on letting the righteous deeds we do speak for themselves. The Father knows our hearts and prayers, just as he did those of his prophets. We can trust that God in Jesus Christ sees everything that we do in his name and will lead us to the Kingdom of heaven. This is our repayment.

THU 21 (#368) white Memorial of St. Aloysius Gonzaga, Religious

The Liturgy of the Word

◆ First Reading: We take a one-day hiatus from our reading from the books of Kings and shift to the Book of Sirach to hear more of the narrative of Elijah and Elisha. After a litany of praise for Elijah which recounts the prophet's marvelous deeds, we hear that whirlwind envelopes Elijah. Elisha, who wished for a double portion of Elijah's spirit in yesterday's First Reading from 2 Kings, indeed received the double Elijah's spirit, and Elisha, too, performed many wondrous deeds.

◆ Responsorial Psalm 97 acclaims the Lord is King! The refrain gives voice to our joy in the Lord, the King for he rules with justice. Fire, as in the First Reading, signifies the Lord's presence. The Lord's people will see his glory as Elijah and Elisha did. Those who turn to others gods will experience shame, for these gods, too, lie prostrate before the King.

◆ Gospel: The Gospel leads us to ponder the role of prayer and forgiveness in our everyday lives as disciples. Jesus instructs his disciples and us that the Father knows what we need even before we ask. Surely, he knew that Elisha wanted and needed double Elijah's spirit.

The Roman Missal

The Mass prayers, all of which are proper for the day, can be found at June 21 in the Proper of Saints section of the Missal. The Collect describes St. Aloysius' life as one of penitence joined "to a wonderful innocence of life," applying that to our own journey by asking "that, though we have failed to follow him in innocence, / we may imitate him in penitence." The Prayer over the Offerings again uses the imagery of innocence associated with this saint by asking that "we may take our place at the heavenly banquet, / clothed always in our wedding garment." The banquet imagery is appropriate as we participate in the Liturgy of the Eucharist. The Prayer after Communion announces that we have been fed "with the food of Angels," and goes on to ask that we serve the Lord "in purity of life" and that "we persevere in constant thanksgiving." Although either one of the two Prefaces of Saints could be used today, perhaps the Preface of Holy Virgins and Religious would be a better choice.

Today's Saint

St. Aloysius Gonzaga (1568–1591) was born to a noble family in Italy who had him destined for the military. While recovering from an illness, he read the lives of the Sts. and spent time in prayer. As a result, Aloysius decided to dedicate himself to God as a Jesuit. Most of his family was against it, but he joined anyway, making his vows in 1587. In 1591, the plague broke out in Rome. Aloysius volunteered to care for the victims and became sick himself. He recovered, but he never became healthy, and he died within a few months. Many schools are named for him because he is the patron saint of Catholic youth.

FRI 22 (#369) green Weekday

Optional Memorial of St. Paulinus of Nola, Bishop / white; Sts. John Fisher, Bishop, and Thomas More, Martyrs / red

The Liturgy of the Word

◆ First Reading: Athaliah, the mother of Ahaziah, ruled ruthlessly for seven years after her son was killed. During this time, Ahaziah's sister, Jehosheba, took his son, Joash, away and cared for him in secret. In the seventh year, Jehoiada, the high priest summoned leaders to the Temple. They proclaimed the seven-year-old Joash king. Athaliah was put to death, and Jehoiada makes two new covenants: one between the Lord and the king and king's people, and the other between the king and the people. They destroy Baal's temple and peace reigns in the land.

◆ Responsorial Psalm 132 speaks to how the Lord has chosen Zion and how Zion's sons will remain on the throne so long as they keep the covenant with the Lord. The Lord's promise to Zion last forever; any of her enemies, he will put to shame.

◆ Gospel: Two topics concern Jesus today as he teaches the disciples. The first is the value of worldly possessions and the second, relates to light and darkness. Jesus coaches his disciples that their treasure must align with their heart. Worldly treasures do not last, but heavenly ones do. In the second part of the Gospel reading, the disciples learn that they need to keep their eye healthy, for it lights their entire body. An unhealthy eye leads to darkness throughout the body.

Today's Saints

St. Paulinus of Nola (c. 354–431) was raised in a family of wealthy politicians in Bordeaux. His interests were varied: everything from practicing law to writing poetry, from traveling to governing. After the death of a newly born son, he and his wife, Therasia, gave away the family fortune to the poor and to the Church. St. Paulinus and Therasia moved to Italy, where they began to live, along with some other friends, a life of prayer and service. They lived in a two-story building in which the first floor provided a place of rest for the wayward and the lost, and the second floor was their place of residence based on the rhythms of monasticism. Gaining a reputation for holiness, St. Paulinus

was ordained a priest and was eventually made a bishop of Nola.

St. John Fisher (1469–1535) and St. Thomas More (1478–1535) lived during a time of great upheaval and reformation. Both were friends and consultants to King Henry VIII, and both were executed because they would not declare the king's supremacy over the Church. St. John Fisher, born in Yorkshire, was an astute scholar recognized for his profound insight into the complex questions of life. He held many positions of esteem, serving as a tutor to the young Henry VIII, Chancellor of Cambridge University, and bishop of Rochester.

St. Thomas More, born in London, was a family man characterized by a deep affection for his wife and three daughters. He, too, held many powerful positions in the Church and in society; in particular, he was a Parliament lawyer, Speaker of the House of Commons, and Chancellor of England.

SAT 23 (#370) green
Weekday

Optional Memorial of the Blessed Virgin Mary / white

The Liturgy of the Word

◆ First Reading: We continue the story of King Joash today with a reading full of action from the Second Book of Chronicles. King Joash listens to princes who had come from Judah, and he and his people turn to idol worship. God raises up Zechariah, the prophet, who calls the people to repentance. Instead of returning to faithfulness, the people kill Zechariah. In the end, King Joash receives the punishment due him as his servants conspire to kill him.

◆ Responsorial Psalm 89 speaks of the Lord's constant love for his servant. God's faithfulness to the covenant will never waver

despite infidelity on behalf of his people. When God's people falter, God will punish them. But as the psalm reminds us, God will never withhold his mercy from anyone.

◆ Gospel: Worrying and anxiety just seem to come with being human. In today's Gospel reading, Jesus teaches his disciples not to worry about their daily needs. Worry and anxiety are the desires of pagans. We do not need to add worry upon worry, for life brings enough anxiety on its own. God will take care of those who believe and provide for their every need. God's abundant grace will replace anxiety about tomorrow with calm.

SUN 24 (#586/#587) white
Solemnity of the Nativity of St. John the Baptist

About Today's Solemnity

John the Baptist was the great prophet and herald of Jesus the Messiah. He prepared the way of the Lord and revealed Jesus to others as both the Messiah and the Lamb of God. St. John exemplifies the Christian life as one who proclaims the Gospel message of healing and repentance while he points out Christ to others and shows them the way to become united with God. This is an ancient solemnity, reaching back to the fourth century, though the date of the celebration varied in East and West. In the East, the birth of the forerunner was celebrated on the day after Epiphany, January 7, because of the association of that feast with the Baptism of the Lord. In the West, it was celebrated on June 24, in keeping with Luke 1:36, which notes that Elizabeth was six months pregnant at the time of the Annunciation of the Lord.

The Liturgy of the Word: Vigil Mass

◆ **FIRST READING:** The account of God calling Jeremiah to be a prophet is the First Reading. God knew Jeremiah even before he was in the womb. From the beginning of time God consecrated him as a prophet. Jeremiah spoke challenging words of repentance just as John the Baptist would do. Both prophets faced suffering and persecutions at the hands of those who did not appreciate their message. Yet, both prophets were faithful in their mission and the Lord fulfilled his promise to always be with them.

◆ **RESPONSORIAL PSALM 71:** The psalmist attests to how the Lord has been present with him since his mother's womb. From his childhood through his youth and the years after, the Lord has been his Rock, his refuge, his safety, and strength. The prophets Jeremiah and John the Baptist had a similar experience of the Lord.

◆ **SECOND READING:** The community the letter of 1 Peter addressed faced persecution. The author intended the words of this passage to encourage the people suffering because of their faith. He reminds them that the result of their faith will be their souls' salvation. This reading coincides with the Solemnity of the Nativity of John the Baptist because it mentions the prophets who, in their proclamation of the Good News, served the people not themselves. The prophets, of whom John the Baptist holds a special place, faithfully announced salvation despite the persecution they, too, endured.

◆ **GOSPEL:** Luke's story of the angel's annunciation to Zechariah of the conception of his son, John the Baptist is the Gospel reading. Zechariah and his wife, Elizabeth, were faithful before God. At the time of the annunciation, Zechariah was serving as a priest and preparing the incense offering. The Lord's angel tells him the Holy Spirit will fill the son he and his wife will have. So too, Elijah's spirit and power will lead the way for him. His will be the mission to make ready a people for the Lord. John the Baptist is the link between the Old Testament prophets and Jesus.

The Roman Missal: Vigil Mass

The Gloria and the Creed are sung or said today. The Collect uses the interesting appellation "the Precursor" to refer to St. John, a title somewhat unfamiliar to us but one which certainly defines his role in salvation history. The prayer asks that we may come safely to the One foretold by John.

The Prayer over the Offerings once again makes a connection between liturgy and life, petitioning God "that what we celebrate in mystery / we may follow with deeds of devoted service."

The Preface is proper for today, "The Mission of the Precursor," and the text, with and without musical notation, is located among the texts for the Mass during the Day, two pages over from the Vigil Mass texts. The Preface recalls the events associated with St. John the Baptist's life and echo the Scripture passages associated with him: how he was consecrated "for a singular honor / among those born of women"; how "His birth brought great rejoicing"; how he leapt for joy in the womb; how "He alone of all the prophets / pointed out the Lamb of redemption"; how "he baptized the very author of Baptism"; and how he gave witness to Christ by the shedding of his blood.

The Prayer after Communion emphasizes the Communion of Saints as it asks that "the prayer of Saint John the Baptist / accompany us who have eaten our fill / at this sacrificial feast." There is also a plea for forgiveness through the intercession of the saint: since he was the one to proclaim Jesus as the Lamb who would take away our sins, we ask that "he implore now for us your favor."

The Liturgy of the Word: Mass during the Day

◆ **FIRST READING:** The Lord called Isaiah before he was in the womb. The Lord formed Isaiah in the womb. The Lord gave him a challenging prophetic mission to offer hope to the Israelites in exile, a people who frequently needed the prophet to call them back to the Lord. God gave John the Baptist, like Isaiah, a prophetic role from the beginning. John was to proclaim the light that Jesus Christ would be to the nations and that through him salvation would reach to the ends of the earth. Isaiah's prophetic words that conclude the reading speak of this very promise.

◆ **RESPONSORIAL PSALM 139:** God is omnipotent and omniscient. Our ancestors in faith believed this and Christians have professed it for generations. The author of Psalm 139 acknowledges this truth in a personal way as he affirms God's intimate knowledge of him beginning in his mother's womb. The mention of the mother's womb connects with Isaiah's call story in the First Reading. For being "wonderfully made," we praise God together with the psalmist and the Lord's prophets.

◆ **SECOND READING:** The passage from Acts directly mentions John's role in heralding the coming of Jesus, the Savior of Davidic lineage. Luke describes how in John's ministry, especially near its end, the prophet would speak of his unworthiness to untie the Savior's sandals.

◆ Gospel: Luke's account of the Gospel is the only one that includes a narrative of the birth of John the Baptist. The Lord's angel had announced to Zechariah that Elizabeth would give birth to a son and he was to name him "John." After John's birth, the time for his circumcision came. A dispute ensued with the relatives over his name for they thought he should be named after his father. Elizabeth stayed strong and said his name is to be John even though none of their relatives had this name. Yet Zechariah still needed to affirm Elizabeth's words in writing since he could no longer speak. Yet once Zechariah wrote John's name, his speech returned. The Lord's presence was with the prophet and his family from the beginning.

The Roman Missal: Mass during the Day

Please note that since today is a solemnity, the Masses for this evening's Saturday night Mass, unless otherwise noted by your local bishop, are for the Solemnity of the Nativity of St. John the Baptist and not for the Sunday. This means you should use the prayers and readings from the Mass for St. John the Baptist and not the readings and prayer texts for Sunday, the Twelfth Sunday in Ordinary Time.

The Gloria and the Creed are sung or said today. The Collect speaks about the preparatory role of the Baptist as one who was raised up "to make ready a nation fit for Christ the Lord." This prayer prays that we may be directed "into the way of salvation and peace."

The Prayer over the Offerings expresses why it is fitting to celebrate the nativity of St. John: it is because he "both foretold the coming of the world's Savior / and pointed him out when he came."

The text for the proper Preface used today is located immediately following the Prayer over the Offerings. See the commentary above under the Vigil Mass.

The Prayer after Communion uses the imagery of the Lamb so closely associated with John the Baptist's announcement of Jesus, and in so doing the prayer gives voice to a rich Eucharistic theology with its phrase "Having feasted at the banquet of the heavenly Lamb. . ."

Other Ideas

Because St. John is considered a great bearer of light, himself, into the world (Jesus calls him "a burning and shining lamp" [John 5:35]) it is traditional to light an outdoor bonfire in his honor. If appropriate to their setting, people can light and enjoy a campfire together. Provide parishioners with a prayer they may use to bless their bonfire. (Or, if an outdoor fire is inappropriate, they might light an oil lamp, lantern, or candle.) Here is an example of a prayer:

Lord God, Almighty Father,
eternal light and creator of all lights,
bless this fire.
Grant that after the darkness
    of this world,
with pure hearts,
we may come to you, the
    never-failing Light.
Through Christ our Lord.
Amen.

Peter's Pence Sunday is always the Sunday nearest to the Solemnity of Sts. Peter and Paul. This collection allows the Holy Father to provide emergency assistance and to respond to request for aid where needed due to war, natural disasters, or oppression. This voluntary contribution by Catholics to the papal treasury has been in place since 1860. The USCCB has resources for this day, including bulletin announcements and inserts, on their website: www.usccb.org.

The Liturgy of the Word

◆ First Reading: Stubborn and obstinate were the children of Israel in their refusal to be faithful to the Lord, their God. Prophets spoke sternly to them about their infidelity, but they refused to change their ways. They broke the covenant the Lord made with their ancestors. One tribe, the tribe of Judah remains.

◆ Responsorial Psalm 60: Our Responsorial Psalm is a communal lament of the people of Israel. In the refrain, the people ask the Lord to help them despite the fact that he is angry with them for their idolatrous ways. Verses 4–5 of the psalm directly address the suffering the Lord has brought to Israel as a result of the people's sin. Still, the people cry to God to revive them. "Rally us" is our cry to as we seek to draw closer to our Lord.

◆ Gospel: How we like to judge others! Still teaching his disciples in the Sermon on the Mount, Jesus reminds them to recognize their own sin first before pointing out the sin of others. Jesus' words do not forbid his followers from mutually correcting one another. His words, though, do point to the hypocritical nature of identifying another's fault without even recognizing our own.

The Liturgy of the Word

◆ King Hezekiah of Judah prayed to the Lord to protect his people from Sennacherib, king of Assyria, and the approaching Assyrians. In a message from Isaiah, son of Amoz, Hezekiah learns that the Lord listened to his prayer. Zion will have survivors and Jerusalem shall have a remnant. The Lord will turn the Assyrians back.

◆ RESPONSORIAL PSALM 48 directly links to the First Reading because it reflects how God will save his holy city of Jerusalem for all eternity. Praise is due God for his mercy and justice toward his people and his beautiful dwelling place. As we pray this psalm, we call to mind how we believe God dwells in our midst today, upholding us in our faith and offering us his mercy when we waver.

◆ GOSPEL: Three sayings of Jesus compose today's Gospel reading. In the first, Jesus advises his disciples to be wary of how they deal with people who cause them difficulty in life. The second saying provides a clarification of the metaphorical language of dogs, pearls, and swine in the first. In his second saying, Jesus recalls the teaching of the Law and the prophets to do to others what we want them to do to us. The third saying is a mini-parable in which Jesus instructs us to enter the narrow gate and forgo the wide gate — a gate many will find easier to walk through, but which will lead to their ruin.

W E D **27** (#373) green
Weekday

Optional Memorial of St. Cyril of Alexandria, Bishop and Doctor of the Church / white

The Liturgy of the Word

◆ FIRST READING: Imagine the king, the elders of Judah and Jerusalem and Jerusalem's processing to the Temple of the Lord. Once there, imagine them listening to a reading of the book of the covenant. Our reading from 2 Kings describes these scenes. Having heard the duties of the covenant, the king made a covenant with the Lord, promising again the wholehearted faithfulness of his people. The people were

not passive, but active participants in the renewal of the covenant.

◆ RESPONSORIAL PSALM 119: The Responsorial Psalm comes from about one-fifth of the way through the longest psalm in the psalter. The refrain and first five verses are the psalm writer's request to the Lord to help him faithfully follow the Lord's statutes and decrees. The final verse express longing for the Lord's precepts, the writer has confidence in the justice and life they offer.

◆ GOSPEL: We are nearing the end of the Jesus' Sermon on the Mount. His words to the disciples are stern today. False prophets are deceptive. They appear as sheep, but really are voracious wolves. Their fruit is rancid. They will be thrown into the fire. Good fruit comes from good trees. Ours is the choice of which kind of tree to be and what kind of fruit to bear.

Today's Saint

As the patriarch of Alexandria, St. Cyril of Alexandria (376–444) was an avid defender of the faith; therefore, he was no stranger to conflict. He found himself at odds with Nestorius, the archbishop of Constantinople, who taught that the Blessed Virgin is the mother of Christ (*Christotokos*), not the Mother of God (*Theotokos*). St. Cyril presided over the First Council of Ephesus (431), which condemned this particular belief, known as Nestorianism, as heresy and proclaimed Mary as the Mother of God. The Council of Chalcedon (451) based its teachings regarding the two natures of Christ on the thought of St. Cyril. Due to the breadth of his writing on the Incarnation and the dignity of the human person, he was declared a Doctor of the Church.

(#374) red
T H U **28** Memorial of
St. Irenaeus, Bishop and Martyr

The Liturgy of the Word

◆ FIRST READING: The First Reading from 2 Kings informs us that King Jehoiachin did evil during his reign as leaders before him had done. What the reading does not tell us is if the evil he did caused the Babylonians to attack Jerusalem, but after naming Jehoiachin's evil, the passage from 2 Kings continues to describe the siege of Jerusalem by the Babylonians and the ensuing deportation of many to Babylon.

◆ RESPONSORIAL PSALM 79 is another communal lament. This psalm bemoans the desecration of the Lord's Temple and the destruction of Jerusalem. The community questions the Lord about how long he will be angry with his people. The people plead with God, as we sometimes do, to not remember our past transgressions, but to show us compassion. In the refrain, which comes from the final verse of the Responsorial Psalm (verse 9), we, together with the Lord's people of old, affirm the power of God's glory to bring salvation.

◆ GOSPEL: Today's Gospel marks the conclusion of the Sermon on the Mount. Jesus uses a short parable about the appropriate foundation on which to build a house to demonstrate the importance of his disciples both listening and acting on his words. We can teach in Jesus' name, but we must also live in his name. Jesus calls all his disciples to know him in word and in deed.

The Roman Missal

The prayers are proper for today and found in the Proper of Saints. Use the Prefaces for Holy Pastors or for Holy Martyrs.

Today's Saint

St. Irenaeus (†202), bishop of Lyons, faced one of the most pervasive heresies in Christian history — Gnosticism. Gnosticism was based on two fundamental beliefs: the flesh is evil, and saving truth is only available to a select few. Regarding the first belief, he demonstrated how the Incarnation and Resurrection point to the immeasurable worth of human flesh. Taking on the second belief, Irenaeus emphasized that God's saving knowledge is available to the many by appealing to apostolic succession. His stance toward the Gnostic heresy can be summed up in his own words, where he says that "the glory of God is the human person fully alive." Traditionally, he is venerated as a martyr, but there is little evidence to support this claim.

(#590/#591) red
FRI 29
Solemnity of Sts. Peter and Paul, Apostles

About Today's Solemnity

Today we commemorate Sts. Peter and Paul, martyred around the year AD 64 during Nero's persecution following the Great Fire of Rome. Tradition says that Peter fled Rome to avoid arrest and saw Jesus on the road. "Where are you going, Lord?" Peter asked. Jesus replied, "I am going to Rome to be crucified again." Peter turned back and was crucified upside down because he felt unworthy to meet his death the same way as Christ. Paul was arrested in Jerusalem and was sent to Rome, where he was placed under house arrest. He was slain by beheading, because as a Roman citizen he could not be subjected to the indignity of crucifixion.

The Liturgy of the Word: Vigil Mass

◆ FIRST READING: Peter honestly admits to the crippled beggar at the "Beautiful Gate" of the Temple that he has no money to give him, but he has another gift. In the name of Jesus Christ, Peter commands him to get up and walk. Peter helps him up and off the man went to the Temple to praise God. Others were amazed, too, at the miraculous healing of the man who had been placed at the Temple gate by others. The ministry of the Apostles Peter and Paul brought many to Jesus. By virtue of our Baptism, we are also proclaimers of the Good News.

◆ RESPONSORIAL PSALM 19 is frequently used as a Responsorial Psalm in the liturgical year. On the Solemnity of Sts. Peter and Paul, the refrain focuses on the message of God's salvation in Jesus Christ that they carried to people as the fledgling communities of the early Church formed. Their message is the message the heavens declare in the psalm: the glory of God alive and active in the heavens and on the earth.

◆ SECOND READING: The focus of the First Reading was on Peter's ministry to the disabled beggar at the Temple gate. The Second Reading turns our attention to Paul's call to preach the Gospel. Paul writes that his call did not have a human origin, rather it came directly from God. God chose Paul from the time he was in his mother's womb to preach the Gospel to Gentiles, despite the fact that he initially persecuted the Church of God and even attempted to destroy it. Paul wants to assure the Galatians that his ministry is authentic and the words he speaks, true.

◆ GOSPEL: Jesus and the disciples had just finished eating a breakfast of fish and bread, when Jesus inquired of Simon Peter about his love for his Teacher. In this post-Resurrection appearance narrative, Peter affirms his immense love for Jesus three times. Each time Peter responds, Jesus replies with a sacred duty revealing the significant leadership role Peter would have in the Church. Peter is to feed and tend Jesus' sheep, and feed them again. With the two words that Jesus has previously used to invite his disciples to come after him, Jesus now personally addresses Peter: "follow me."

The Roman Missal: Vigil Mass

The Gloria and the Creed are sung or said today. The Collect continues to honor Peter and Paul together as it affirms that "through them you gave your Church / the foundations of her heavenly office"; the prayer goes on to ask that through them the Church may be assisted on her way to eternal salvation. Remember that the Creed is said at this Vigil Mass.

The Prayer over the Offerings speaks of hopefulness and encouragement: it tells us that "the more we doubt our own merits, / the more we may rejoice that we are to be saved / by your loving kindness." We offer this Eucharist in union with the Apostles Peter and Paul who themselves, as the Scriptures so clearly tell us, were men who sinned and had their faults and weaknesses.

The Preface is proper for today, and it is found among the prayers for the Mass during the Day, a page turn away from the Vigil prayers. A text is given both with music and without; since it is a solemnity, strongly consider singing the introductory dialogue and the Preface. The Preface mentions in tandem the attributes that are the reasons we commemorate these two Apostles: Peter is "foremost in confessing the faith" and is the one "who established the early Church from the remnant of Israel"; Paul is the faith's "outstanding preacher . . . master and teacher of the Gentiles." Thus is the mission of the Church both within Israel and beyond her to the whole world avowed.

The Prayer after Communion entreats that as we have been "enlightened with the teaching of the

Apostles," so may we be strengthened by "this heavenly Sacrament."

The Solemn Blessing for Sts. Peter and Paul, Apostles (#16 under "Blessings at the End of Mass and Prayers over the People"), is suggested, and should be used today. It refers to Peter's "saving confession" and uses the image of the solid rock, and to "the tireless preaching of Saint Paul." It then brings the two together by highlighting "the keys of St Peter and the words of St Paul."

The Liturgy of the Word: Mass during the Day

◆ FIRST READING: Herod intended to execute Peter as he had James and in fact had Peter arrested and imprisoned. Luke describes to us, though, how the Church was at prayer for Peter. The night before he is to be put on trial, an angel of the Lord appears to Peter while he is sleeping. Peter thought he was dreaming as the angel helped him to escape from prison, but the escape was real. After Peter realizes he really was free, he first acknowledges the Lord's hand in his rescue. Then he makes his way to the home of Mary, the mother of John, where people were gathered together in prayer. The power of prayer and the grace of God are both clearly evident in the Apostle's experience.

◆ RESPONSORIAL PSALM 34: The refrain connects with Peter's experience of the angel of the Lord directing his escape from prison. Those who fear the Lord, we affirm, the angel of the Lord will rescue. Glory and praise are ever in our mouths, for the Lord delivers us and saves us suffering. We taste God salvation, and see with our own eyes how good it is!

◆ SECOND READING: Written by Paul at the time when his death was imminent, his self-reflection notes his fidelity to the faith and to his mission of proclaiming the Gospel to the Gentiles. Before the briefest of doxologies that concludes the reading, Paul expresses his confidence the Lord will rescue him from dangers he is yet to face and accompany him safely home to the heavenly Kingdom. In relation to the First Reading, we can see a connection between God's rescue of Peter and Paul's faith that the Lord also save him. The hope of the Apostles in this regard is our hope, too.

◆ GOSPEL: We do not know the individual responses of the other disciples to Jesus' question ("Who do you say that I am?") because Matthew records only Peter's statement of faith. Peter's confession of Jesus as the Christ, the Son of the God who lives is the rock upon which Jesus builds his Church. Everyone who follows after Peter and belongs to the Church professes this same faith. Peter's are the keys and the power to bind and loose on earth. Yet whatever Peter binds and looses on earth will remain so in heaven. His ministry of leadership and authority in the Church shows us that the Church helps lead people to the Kingdom of heaven.

The Roman Missal: Mass during the Day

The Gloria and the Creed are sung or said today. The Collect for this Mass during the Day reminds us that the Church's faith came through the Apostles Peter and Paul; it was through them that the Church "received / the beginnings of right religion."

The Prayer over the Offerings asks for the powerful intercession of these two Apostles, praying that their prayer may "accompany the sacrificial gift / that we present to your name for consecration." Again we are reminded that every Eucharist is celebrated in communion with all the saints who have gone before us.

The Preface is proper for today; see the commentary for it above, under the Vigil Mass.

Although the Prayer after Communion does not mention Peter and Paul by name, it does pray that we might persevere "in the breaking of the Bread / and in the teaching of the Apostles" — notice the reference to the Eucharist and to Tradition, without which the Church does not exist — and so live as Church as "one heart and one soul." The unity of the Church founded on the Apostles Peter and Paul is strengthened and nourished through sacrament and through authentic teaching.

As at the Vigil Mass, the Solemn Blessing for Sts. Peter and Paul, Apostles (number 16 under "Blessings at the End of Mass and Prayers over the People") is suggested for today, and should be used. The blessing mentions Peter's "saving confession" and the image of the solid rock, and Paul's "tireless preaching," also noting "the keys of St. Peter and the words of St. Paul."

S A T **30** (#376) green **Weekday**

Optional Memorials of the First Martyrs of the Holy Roman Church / red; Blessed Virgin Mary / white

The Liturgy of the Word

◆ FIRST READING: This poem from Lamentations describes the Lord's wrath toward Zion and her people. Many leaders and many of their people had been unfaithful. Now they face the consequences. The poem portrays hungry children and desperate people crying out to the Lord to change their fate. We can envision the people in a modern city today facing a similar challenge of hunger as we hear this passage.

◆ RESPONSORIAL PSALM 74: Today's psalm is again a communal lament. It could easily have been a psalm the people sang when the Temple was destroyed. In the refrain, the people plead with the Lord not to forget their souls. The verses describe in great detail the destruction of the Temple sanctuary. The people ask God to remember the covenant and keep his people safe.

◆ GOSPEL: We proceed down the mountain with Jesus today and out in mission and ministry as we read further on in the Gospel according to Matthew. In today's Gospel, Jesus performs two healings. Based on the faith the centurion expresses in the words that we say today in response to the priest raising the consecrated host after the Lamb of God, "Lord, I am not worthy . . . ," Jesus heals his servant. Upon entering Peter's house, Jesus observes that Peter's mother-in-law is sick. With the touch of his hand, Jesus cures her of a fever.

Today's Saint

Today we commemorate the martyrs who died between the years AD 64–68, around the same time as Sts. Peter and Paul. The emperor Nero was accused of starting the Great Fire of Rome, and to divert attention from himself and satisfy his appetite for cruelty, he turned the blame on the Christians in Rome. They were rounded up and killed by various means: by crucifixion, by being fed to wild animals, and by being burned as torches to provide light for parties. The Roman historian Tacitus provides an independent record of their torture and death.

July 2018
Month of the Most Precious Blood

(#98) green

1
Thirteenth Sunday in Ordinary Time

The Liturgy of the Word

◆ FIRST READING: Death does not come from God. The jealousy of the devil brought death into the world. There is neither anything within God's creatures nor in the way he created them that causes harm. From the beginning, God fashioned us for immortality. We were not made to perish because he made us in his own image—the divine image. Notice the echoes of the creation accounts from Genesis 1 and 2 in the reading.

◆ RESPONSORIAL PSALM 30: The psalmist's emphasis on the Lord rescuing him from his enemies and bringing him up from the netherworld relates to Wisdom's description of how God made us for everlasting life with him. Even when we turn from him, God is faithful. In God, our sadness and grief will always turn to dancing for we will never perish.

◆ SECOND READING: Paul invites the Corinthians to a "gracious act" of economic stewardship in support of the community at Jerusalem. He supports his invitation with the theological underpinning of Jesus

Christ's own example. Out of his richness, Jesus became poor, and through his poverty, he became rich. God became human in Jesus Christ so that our humanity could be taken up into divinity through his death, Resurrection, and Ascension.

◆ GOSPEL: As Jairus and Jesus were making their way to the synagogue official's home, a woman who was part of the large crowd following them, reached out and touched Jesus' cloak. She was now free from her twelve-year hemorrhages. Others then announce the death of Jairus' daughter, but Jesus pays no attention to their words. Rather, he simply asks the synagogue official to have faith. Jairus must have fulfilled Jesus' request, for Jesus took his daughter by the hand and upon his word to arise, she did. These two healing miracles testify to the power of Jesus and his word. In Jesus, is the presence of life, not death. This provides a connection to the passage from Wisdom in the First Reading. There is a longer and shorter form of today's text.

The Roman Missal

The Collect contrasts light and darkness. God has chosen us as "children of light." We pray that we may not be "wrapped in the darkness of error," but remain in the "bright light of truth." We pray that our "deeds" may be worthy of the "sacred gifts" we receive in this sacrifice (Prayer over the Offerings). We pray that the "divine sacrifice" we have received may so "fill us with life" that we may "bear fruit that lasts forever" (Prayer after Communion). The Gloria and the Creed are sung or said today.

Other Ideas

This first week in July is often the kick-off of vacation season in the United States since Independence Day (July 4) falls this week. While the bishop's guidelines, *Forming Consciences for Faithful Citizenship* tends to get more attention during presidential election cycles, this is a great time to educate people on what it means to be a responsible citizen. Likewise, the themes of Catholic Social Teaching are worthy of review as people celebrate their freedom as citizens of this country. Find excerpts appropriate to this day on the USCCB website (find the document here: www. usccb.org/issues-and-action/faithful-citizenship/). Consider having your parish march or provide a float in your local community parade, or set up an information table at the fireworks to encourage people to find out more about your faith community. It isn't appropriate to sing national hymns during the liturgy. Instead, consider any of the hymns that express the value of freedom and call to mission and discipleship that are found in Catholic hymnals, such as "This Is My Song," which is less well known but a meaningful sung prayer that all countries will know truth, peace, and freedom.

M O N 2 (#377) green
Weekday

The Liturgy of the Word

◆ FIRST READING: The prophet Amos' words were not easy for the people of Israel to hear. Neither are they pleasing to our ears for at times, we are guilty of the same sins as our ancestors. We trample the poor, take from those in need, and profane God's name by the immorality in our relationships. Yet through his prophet, the Lord reminds us that he brought his people out of Egypt and led them through the desert, just as he has always been with us.

◆ RESPONSORIAL PSALM 50: In the verses of Psalm 50 that are today's Responsorial Psalm, God directly addresses his people, chastising them for giving lip service to the covenant. The lack of consistency between the

people's words and their actions regarding God's laws has brought God's wrath upon them. In the final verses of the Responsorial Psalm, God offers hope for the people who do praise and glorify him, rather than forget him. Would that we are among the former so that God shows us salvation!

◆ GOSPEL: On face value, the command "follow me" seems easy to live out. Yet discipleship goes beyond face value. To walk side by side with Jesus, means that our worldly obligations no longer come first. But our obligations of faith do no matter where following Jesus leads us, for as Jesus tells the scribe who desires to follow him, the Son of Man has nowhere to lay down his head. Would that our journey of discipleship lead us to share in the Son of Man's glory when he comes again.

T U E 3 (#593) red
Feast of St. Thomas, Apostle

The Liturgy of the Word

◆ FIRST READING: St. Thomas is among the Apostles who provided a foundation for God's household. The Church, the household of God, with Jesus as the capstone continues to grow and develop through the working of the Spirit. In God's household, there are neither strangers nor travelers on the way. As St. Paul tells us, together with the holy ones, we all belong to this household founded on the Apostles and prophets.

◆ RESPONSORIAL PSALM 117: Jesus' commission of the Eleven at the conclusion of the Gospel according to Mark is the refrain for the Responsorial Psalm on the Feast of St. Thomas. Thomas was among those sent forth into the world to proclaim the Good News of the Gospel. We, too, embrace our mission to spread the Good News. We

call all nations to praise and glorify the Lord because of his everlasting kindness and faithfulness as the two verses from Psalm 117 state.

◆ GOSPEL: One would perhaps think when the Lord appeared a week after the other disciples had told Thomas they saw the Lord and Thomas asked to see the nailmarks in his hands and side, that the Lord might disparage Thomas for his lack of faith. Jesus entered the locked room with an offer of peace for the disciples. And, Jesus' peace extended to Thomas through an invitation to put his finger in Jesus' side and see the marks on his hands. Thomas came to believe by seeing, but he did come to believe. Many will believe by not seeing. Blessed are they, as well.

The Roman Missal

The texts for this Mass, all proper for the feast today, are located in the Proper of Saints section of the Missal at July 3.

The Gloria is sung or said today, since it is a feast. The Collect points to the Apostle Thomas' acknowledgment of the Lord as read in the Scriptures. The Prayer over the Offerings again refers to St. Thomas' confession, asking that the gifts God has given us—the gifts of faith—be kept safe. The Prayer after Communion again echoes the Gospel as the prayer asks that, in receiving the Sacrament of the Eucharist, "we may recognize him / with the Apostle Thomas by faith / as our Lord and our God." This recognition of the Lord, however, cannot be a passive gazing; rather, as a result of sacramental Communion, we must go on to "proclaim him by our deeds and by our life."

The Preface, proper for today, is one of the two Prefaces of the Apostles. Also, the Solemn Blessing formula titled "The Apostles" (#17 of the "Blessings at the End of Mass and Prayers over the People") is fittingly used as the final blessing at the end of Mass today.

Today's Saint

St. Thomas (first century), also called "Didymus" or "the Twin" (John 11:16) was one of the Twelve Apostles. He is remembered for doubting the Resurrection of Christ: "Unless I see the mark of the nails in his hands, and put my finger in the mark of the nails and my hand in his side, I will not believe." The following week, Thomas was with the Twelve when Jesus appeared and chided him for his lack of faith: "Have you believed because you have seen me? Blessed are those who have not seen and yet have come to believe" (John 20:25–29). After seeing the Risen Christ alive, Thomas exclaimed, "My Lord and my God!" (John 20:28). According to tradition, Thomas is the only Apostle who went outside the borders of the Roman Empire to evangelize. Although there is a Gospel account attributed to him, it is not accepted in the canon of Scripture, and is, in fact, of Gnostic origin. The people of Kerala in Southern India fervently believe that it was Thomas who evangelized them. He is represented in art with a spear, the instrument of his martyrdom. He is the patron saint of architects and builders, and of India, where today is a solemnity.

**W
E   4** (#379)   green
D   Weekday

Optional proper Mass for Independence Day (#882–886, #887–891) / white

The Liturgy of the Word: Seasonal Weekday

◆ First Reading: The words of today's First Reading come from the first and second woes of the prophet Amos to the people of Israel. The prophet instructs the people to look for good and avoid evil, for doing what is right and just

brings life. In the second half of the reading, the Lord admonishes the people himself. The inconsistency between the people's worship and how they live out their faith infuriates the Lord. All the Lord asks for is burnt offerings so that justice and goodness might prevail.

◆ Responsorial Psalm 50: The refrain expresses the same confidence found in the prophet's words from the First Reading. God will make his saving power known to those who act with goodness and justice. In the other verses of the psalm used today, the Lord explains directly to the people that he does not need their sacrifices, for he is God and everything in the world belongs to him. What God does require is praise and faithfulness to the covenant.

◆ Gospel: Jesus moved on to Gadarenes, a territory known to have many godless inhabitants, where two people possessed by demonic spirits met him. The demons ask Jesus that if he does exorcise them, that he send them to the herd of pigs in the area. Jesus fulfills their request such that the evil spirits now reside in the swine causing them to run down a bank into the sea and drown. Everyone in town wanted to meet the man whose power affected this dramatic event. The townspeople let Jesus know he was no longer welcome.

The Roman Missal: Independence Day

For the optional Mass for Independence Day, the Gloria is said or sung. Two complete sets of prayers are provided in the Proper of Saints. The first option for the Collect is a prayer that God's "peace may rule in our hearts" and God's "justice guide our lives." The second option gives thanks for all that has been accomplished, and calls on us to share the blessings we have received "with all the peoples of

the earth." The first option for the Prayer over the Offerings asks God to lead us to "true justice and lasting peace" through the Gospel. The second echoes the familiar motto, *E pluribus unum* (from many, one): God has "molded into one our nation, drawn from the people of many lands." Just as the "grains of wheat become one bread," and "the many grapes one cup," we pray that we may, as one, be "instruments of . . . peace."

The first option for the Preface speaks of Christ's message of peace as the beginning of "the vision of our founding fathers," a message that "lives on in our midst," both today and tomorrow. The second focuses on Christ's love for all peoples, "his witness of justice and truth." We are "reborn in the Spirit," and like the Spirit we are to be "filled with love for all people."

The first option for the Prayer after Communion is a prayer for unity, that together we may "build the city of lasting peace." The second is a prayer that as a nation we may trust in God, and do God's will. A proper Solemn Blessing is provided, which focuses on harmony, wisdom, love, and unity.

**T
H   5** (#380)   green
U   Weekday

Optional Memorial of St. Anthony Zaccaria, Priest / white; St. Elizabeth of Portugal / white

The Liturgy of the Word

◆ First Reading: Neither Bethel's priest, Amaziah, nor Israel's king, Jeroboam, are pleased with the prophet Amos and his message. Amos did not belong to the professional class of prophets. The Lord called him in the midst of his life as a shepherd and dresser of sycamores to preach a message of repentance and conversion to the people of Israel, and especially their leaders. In response to Amos' prophetic words, Amaziah rebelled and banished him from Bethel. The Lord's word of justice posed too great a challenge for him.

◆ RESPONSORIAL PSALM 19: The refrain given for today speaks of the truth and justice of the Lord's divine judgments, while the verses affirm the beauty and perfection of the divine commands. In light of the First Reading, the psalm presents us with the choice to follow the example of Amaziah and Jeroboam, or to return in faith to the Lord and abide by his precepts.

◆ GOSPEL: After exorcising demonic spirits, but being forced to leave the territory of the Gadarenes, Jesus returns to Capernaum, the place the Gospel reading refers to as "his own town." Once there, he forgives the sins of a paralyzed child. Scribes privately accuse him of blasphemy, but Jesus knows what they are thinking. He challenges them on their evil thoughts, and then proceeds to heal the child so he rises up and walks home. The scribes might not understand, but the crowds glorify God because of the authority that emanated from Jesus.

Today's Saint

St. Anthony Mary Zaccaria (1502–1539) was from Cremona, Italy. He was born into a noble family, and dedicated himself to the Lord from a young age. He studied philosophy, went to study medicine at the University of Padua, and practiced for three years before deciding to become a priest. Anthony had already done so much study that he was ordained quickly, in 1528. He founded three religious orders: the Barnabites or Clerics Regular of St. Paul — the first order named for St. Paul — the Angelic Sisters of St. Paul for nuns, and a lay community. The three groups worked together to reform society. Because of the implied criticism of abuses in the Church, Anthony was investigated for heresy twice, but was acquitted

both times. In addition to founding the Barnabites, he popularized the forty-hour devotion of exposition of the Eucharist. In 1539, he became ill with a fever, and because his health had been undermined by his penitential practices, he died at the age of 37. Anthony is the patron of his order, the Barnabites, and is represented in art wearing a cassock and with a lily, a cross, or a symbol of the Eucharist. Today the Barnabites can be found in sixteen countries, including Italy, the United States, Brazil, and Afghanistan.

St. Elizabeth of Portugal (1271–1336) was the grandniece of St. Elizabeth of Hungary and is known by the Spanish version of her name, Isabel. When very young, she was married to the King of Portugal. Elizabeth had been raised to be devout, but at her husband's court, she found much corruption and immorality. In spite of this, she managed to continue her life of prayer, penance, and devotion to the care of the sick. This caused resentment in the court, which Elizabeth bore quietly. After her husband, the king, died, she went to live in a convent of Poor Clares that she had founded, and she took the habit of a Third Order Franciscan. Throughout her life she was well known for her peacemaking skills, most importantly when she prevented a war between Portugal and Castile in 1336. The exertion weakened her health, and she died soon after and is buried at Coimbra. Elizabeth of Portugal is a patron saint of Franciscan Tertiaries.

F R I 6 (#381) green
Weekday

Optional Memorial of St. Maria Goretti, Virgin and Martyr / red

The Liturgy of the Word

◆ FIRST READING: The Lord's words to the prophet Amos indict those who crush the needy and destroy the poor. God will bring un-

welcome change upon the leader and their people: festive celebrations will no longer be occasions of joy, but grief. Sadness will come over the people as when a parent loses an only son. The Lord will even bring a famine, but there will not be a scarcity of food. This famine will bring a hunger and thirst for the Lord's word.

◆ RESPONSORIAL PSALM 119: Bread alone is not our livelihood, but the Word of God is. This is essence of the refrain from Matthew 4:4, which references Deuteronomy 8:3. In the verses, the psalm writer describes his own intense longing for the Lord's commands. May our yearning mirror the intensity of the psalm writer's words, for as verse 2 tells us, those who follow the law of the Lord are blessed.

◆ GOSPEL: "Follow me." In today's Gospel reading, Matthew, the man working at the customs post, receives the invitation in these two words from Jesus. It appears as if Matthew did not have to analyze the invitation; he just left what he was doing and went home with Jesus. In Matthew's house, the two, along with the other disciples, dined with tax collectors and sinners creating apprehension among the Pharisees. Jesus responds to them stating that he wishes for mercy, not sacrifice. He invites sinners, not those who have the hubris to think they are already redeemed to share in his mission.

Today's Saint

St. Maria Goretti (1890–1902) is one of the youngest saints to be canonized. She died of stab wounds after she resisted a rapist. Maria came from a poor Italian family. They lost their farm and a few years later, her father died of malaria. In spite of their hard existence as farm laborers, the family was close-knit and devout. By 1902, the family was sharing a building with another family of farm workers, one of whom was Alessandro Serenelli, who made it a habit to sexually harass Maria. One day, finding her alone, he threatened to kill her if she did not submit to him. Maria protested that what he asked was a mortal sin. Alessandro choked, and then stabbed her, leaving her bleeding to death. She was taken to the hospital, but she could not be saved and died forgiving her murderer. Shortly after Maria died, Alessandro was arrested, charged with her murder, and sentenced to twenty years in prison. He remained unrepentant until Maria appeared to him in a dream. Upon his release, he went to Maria's mother and asked for forgiveness. Eventually he became a Capuchin lay brother and was present at Maria's canonization in 1950, as was her mother. Maria Goretti is the patron saint of rape victims and teenaged girls and is shown in art dressed as a peasant farmer, holding lilies. Her story has prompted thought on the broader meaning of chastity, integrating sexual purity with personal integrity, and self-determination.

S A T 7 (#382) green
Weekday

Optional Memorial of the Blessed Virgin Mary / white

The Liturgy of the Word

◆ FIRST READING: Rather than hearing another stinging indictment from the prophet Amos, today we hear words of hope, a promise from the Lord to restore Israel through the leadership of a Davidic king. The people will rebuild their cities and live in them again. Food and drink will be abundant. Hope reigns in these prophetic words not only for the people of Israel, but for us today, who desire newness in the midst of the world's injustice.

◆ RESPONSORIAL PSALM 85: Today's refrain reflects the Lord's

words of peace to his people, a peace the restoration of Israel the Lord promises in the First Reading will bring. The verses describe the newness that will be evident when Israel comes out from the depths of ruin. Kindness, truth, justice, peace, and salvation will replace evil, falsehood, injustice, conflict, and division.

◆ GOSPEL: Jesus exorcised demons, healed the sick, dined with sinners and tax collectors, and today we find him responding to a question from John the Baptist's disciples about why they and the Pharisees fast but Jesus' disciples do not? As is often the case, Jesus responds to the question with his own question that is rhetorical in nature. Surely, wedding guests are not sad when the bridegroom is present. But when the bridegroom, Jesus, is no longer with them, the disciples will fast. Old clothing is not repaired with cloth before it is shrunk and new wineskins need new wine. Jesus brings newness that is not fully compatible with the ways of the old Law.

(#101) green
8 Fourteenth Sunday in Ordinary Time

The Liturgy of the Word

◆ FIRST READING: Most of us would have rejected the Lord's call to be a prophet to the Israelites after he calls them rebels, mentioned they

have "rebelled" against him, and that even their ancestors have "revolted." As if those words of the Lord would not have also had Ezekiel running, the Lord continues his depressing, but realistic depiction of the people, pointing out their stubbornness and "obstinate" hearts. Once more at the close of the reading, the Lord calls the people "rebellious." No doubt Ezekiel wondered what he was getting into, but the Lord's prophetic call is so strong, Ezekiel accepts. The Lord's spirit was within holding him upright on his feet.

◆ RESPONSORIAL PSALM 123: Only four verses make up Psalm 123 and we use all of them as our Responsorial Psalm. The psalm begins with an individual praying to the Lord in heaven and then shifts to the plural, where we focus our eyes on the Lord as well as the psalmist. In order for the prophet Ezekiel to fulfill his mission, his eyes had to be locked on the Lord, lest the rebellious house of Israel frustrate him so he resign his prophetic work. Why are our eyes focused on the Lord? We, like Israel, implore the Lord for mercy, for we have sinned.

◆ SECOND READING: Paul was worried about his ego growing too large, but he had to have a certain amount of confidence in the face of other preachers who proclaimed false gospels. He attempted to steer the Corinthians away from the false preachers, and in order to do so, had to clearly validate his own ministry and the Gospel he preached. In the Old Testament, "thorns" symbolized one's enemies, including Satan. Thus, when Paul faces weakness—including persecution—as when we do the Lord's grace is sufficient for us. It is all we need. It makes us strong.

◆ GOSPEL: Following the healings of the woman with hemorrhages and Jairus's daughter, Jesus and his disciples journeyed to his hometown. On the Sabbath, he taught in the synagogue where people question the source of his teachings and wisdom. Four questions populate this short Gospel reading. They center on Jesus' identity for the people in the synagogue who at first recognize his mighty deeds, then turn on him. Jesus' response is the familiar words that acknowledge the only place a prophet has no honor is the place where he grew up. Jesus and his disciples move on from this place whose people lacked faith. Yet it is not that they did nothing there since Mark informs us they healed a few sick people. A majority's lack of faith never silences the power of God in the face of a few who believe.

The Roman Missal

The Mass texts for today are found in the "Ordinary Time" section of the Proper of Time.

The Gloria and the Creed are sung or said today. The Collect points to God's raising up of our fallen world through "the abasement" of his Son. (It is hoped that the hearers at Mass do not mishear the phrase and think that a basement, as in a cellar, is being referred to!) The image is meant to reflect the Paschal Mystery of lowliness leading to glory, which brings "holy joy," as the prayer goes on to ask for "eternal gladness" to be bestowed upon those who have been rescued from slavery to sin (that is, through the Son's act of humble love).

The Prayer over the Offerings prays for purification of our lives to occur through the oblation being offered; it reminds us of the concrete changes we must make in our lives if we are going to truly live what we believe, as we pray that participating in this celebration might "day by day bring our conduct / closer to the life of heaven."

Any one of the eight Prefaces of the Sundays in Ordinary Time can

be used. In making a choice, note how Preface I, with its mention of Jesus accomplishing "the marvelous deed," or Preface II, with its mention of his humbling himself to be born of the Virgin, could echo the theme of "abasement" (humility) mentioned in the Collect, and the meekness and humility of Christ. Preface IV's reference to experiencing daily the effects of God's care could connect with the notion of "day by day conduct" referred to in the Prayer over the Offerings and also correlate with the notion of the burdened finding rest in the Lord as described in the Gospel.

The Prayer after Communion notes how the food of the Eucharist replenishes us so that "we may gain the prize of salvation / and never cease to praise you." That the Eucharist is nourishment for the journey to heaven must never be forgotten.

Other Ideas

This month of vacations often brings many visitors into our pews. An act of hospitality can be done at the end of Mass, or offered to families to do in their home. Consider using the Order of Blessing of Travelers (BB, chapter 9) or Pilgrims (BB, chapter 8).

This week the days commemorating St. Benedict and St. Kateri Tekakwitha will take place. Consider providing information about Benedictine spirituality, or a brief workshop on *lectio divina* or centering prayer. In a time of tremendous "noise" from cell phones and other media, helping people find silence and interiority can be a great service. St. Kateri, called the Lily of the Mohawks, is the first Native American saint, and she is patroness of the environment and ecology. Her novena can be prayed, and parish action and learning can be undertaken in support of the local indigenous communities (see blackandindianmission.org

/pdf/novena.pdf). If there is a Native American Catholic community near you, consider some of your members join them for prayer.

M O N 9 (#383) green
Weekday

Optional Memorial of St. Augustine Zhao Rong, Priest, and Companions, Martyrs / red

The Liturgy of the Word

◆ FIRST READING: Today through Friday of this week, the First Readings will come from the prophet Hosea. In today's passage, the Lord speaks through the prophet beautiful words spousal fidelity. The Lord will lead Israel into the desert and there, she shall respond once again in fidelity to him. Justice, love, and mercy will characterize the Lord's faithfulness toward Israel, his spouse. For her part, Israel will be faithful as a wife is to a husband.

◆ RESPONSORIAL PSALM 145 is a psalm of the Lord's kingship. Qualities of compassion, grace, and mercy mark the Lord's eternal reign. Many generations have praised the Lord for his marvelous works. The heart of his greatness lies in his goodness toward all.

◆ GOSPEL: On his way to heal the official's daughter, Jesus heals a woman who suffered for twelve years with hemorrhages on the basis of her courage and faith. Arriving at the official's house, the Gospel text describes musicians playing and the commotion of the crowd perhaps ritualizes what was thought to be the girl's death. Jesus commands them to leave, for the girl was not dead. Putting his hand in the girl's, Jesus led the girl up. She was alive! God's compassionate power in Jesus heals again!

Today's Saints

Between 1648 and 1930, eighty-seven Chinese Catholics and

thirty-three Western missionaries, some of whom were Dominicans, Franciscans, Salesians, Jesuits, and Vincentians, were martyred for their ministry or for refusing to renounce their Christian faith. Many of the Chinese converts were killed during the Boxer Rebellion, a xenophobic uprising during which many foreigners were slaughtered by angry peasants. Augustine Zhao Rong was a Chinese diocesan priest who was tortured and killed in 1815, after Emperor Kia-Kin issued decrees banning Catholicism. Augustine Zhao Rong and the other Chinese martyrs were canonized in 2000 by Pope John Paul II.

T U E **10** (#384) green **Weekday**

The Liturgy of the Word

◆ FIRST READING: The Word of the Lord that Hosea speaks today recounts historically how Israel strayed from the Lord. Kings and princes were made without the Lord's authority. The leaders and the people worshipped idols. They constructed altars for the forgiveness of sin, but they used the altars for idol and cultic sacrifices, so the altars became sin themselves. The dire consequence Israel will suffer is a return to Egypt.

◆ RESPONSORIAL PSALM 115: The Responsorial Psalm contrasts with the First Reading in that it expresses Israel's trust in the Lord. Yet it links directly with the passage from Hosea because it describes how people create idols; God does not create idols. God in heaven has the power to do what he wills, but idols do not.

◆ GOSPEL: Two different sections compose the Gospel reading. In the first, Jesus heals a mute man possessed by a demonic spirit. Once Jesus exorcises the evil spirit, much to the amazement of the crowds, the man speaks. They have never witnessed anything like this. On the other hand, the Pharisees quickly attribute the power of Jesus' exorcism to the prince of demons. The second section is a summary statement about Jesus proclaiming the Kingdom and healing diseases. He is the shepherd for the crowds who are without a shepherd. His disciples are workers for the Kingdom's harvest.

W E D **11** (#385) white **Memorial of St. Benedict, Abbot**

The Liturgy of the Word

◆ FIRST READING: Israel's heart is false says the prophet Hosea. Since they no longer fear the Lord, their idolatry has gotten out of hand. The Lord will destroy all the altars and sacred pillars in honor of other gods. For Israel, there is no other time but the present to turn back to the Lord so that Israel's people might know the Lord's justice.

◆ RESPONSORIAL PSALM 105 invites us to seek the Lord. Like Israel, we need to turn back to the Lord for his wondrous deeds will never end despite the times when we are unfaithful. The Lord is God forever. No matter how often or how long we stray from the Lord, he will always offer us an invitation to renew our relationship with him.

◆ GOSPEL: We hear the names of the Twelve Apostles in today' Gospel reading and their commission. Jesus sends them forth with authority—his authority that comes from the Father. The Apostles are to do as Jesus has done: exorcise unclean spirit and cure illness. Theirs is the task to proclaim the Kingdom of heaven to Israel's lost sheep.

The Roman Missal

The orations, all proper today, are found in the Proper of Saints at July 11. The Collect recognizes St. Benedict as being "an outstanding master in the school of divine service," a nod, of course, to his famous *Rule*. The Prayer over the Offerings asks that we follow Benedict's example in seeking God; the Prayer after Communion prays that, by being attentive to the teaching of St. Benedict, we may serve God's designs and "love one another with fervent charity" as a result of our receiving this sacrament as a "pledge of eternal life." The Preface may be either Preface I or II of Saints or the Preface of Holy Virgins and Religious.

Today's Saint

Saddened by the immoral state of society, St. Benedict of Nursia (480–553/7) left the city to live as a hermit at Subiaco. In time, more and more men were attracted to his charismatic personality as well as to his way of life. He eventually moved a group of monks to Monte Cassino, near Naples, where he completed the final version of his rule, now known as The Rule of St. Benedict, on the fundamentals of monastic life, including the dayto-day operation of a monastery. The rule asserts that the primary occupation of the monk is to pray the Divine Office in tandem with a vowed life of stability, obedience, and conversion. The whole of the monastic vocation can be summarized in the opening line of his rule, "Listen carefully." St. Benedict is considered the father of Western monasticism.

T H U **12** (#386) green **Weekday**

The Liturgy of the Word

◆ FIRST READING: The Lord's words on the mouth of the prophet Hosea read like a lament of a mother or father who is saddened by the choices a son or daughter makes. Yet the Lord will never stop loving Israel like a parent never stops loving a child. Even though Israel chose to sacrifice to other gods and failed to recognize the true Lord, he will not let the fire of Israel's evil ways consume her.

◆ RESPONSORIAL PSALM 80: The community of Israel laments some of their military defeats. Despite the people's struggles, in this hymn the Israelites still call upon their Shepherd to take care of them. In communion with the people of Israel, we plead in the words of the refrain to see the Lord's face and know his salvation.

◆ GOSPEL: Our Gospel reading begins with a repetition of the final verse of yesterday's Gospel. The Twelve Apostles Jesus sends out are to proclaim the nearness of the Kingdom of heaven. For their mission of curing the sick, driving out demons, and cleansing lepers, they are to take nothing — no money, no traveling bag, no extra clothes, and not even walking stick to help them traverse rough territory. Jesus counsels the Apostles to offer peace to each household they enter. He is also honest with the Apostles that they will encounter people who will not accept their message. Move on from them, Jesus advises the Apostles. Shake the dust of your feet, not giving second thought to the rejection.

FRI 13 (#387) green
Weekday

Optional Memorial of St. Henry / white

The Liturgy of the Word

◆ FIRST READING: Our final First Reading from Hosea comes from the last chapter in this prophetic book. The reading opens with a direct call to Israel to return to the Lord. Upon her return, Israel should ask for the Lord's forgiveness. How often we need to do the same! Nothing else, no one else — no other kings, no other countries, can save Israel. Only the Lord can. Even before Israel returns to the Lord still loves her and always will,

though she stumbles back toward him in humility, in recognition of her own sin.

◆ RESPONSORIAL PSALM 51 is a penitential psalm in which the people of Israel ask God's forgiveness for their sins and the consequences they have wrought. The connection to the First Reading in which Hosea calls Israel to return to the Lord and ask forgiveness from him, appears obvious. A clean heart is the desire of the individuals and communities who pray this psalm. They long to experience the joy of God's salvation as we do.

◆ GOSPEL: In previous Gospel readings this week, Jesus commissioned the Twelve Apostles and detailed the works they will perform. In today's passage, Jesus offers the Apostle a dose of reality that underscores the difficulty they will face as they carry out their mission. Sheep and wolves do not usually get along well. The Apostles will face persecution and undergo court trials, yet when they do Jesus assures them that the Spirit of their Father will speak through them. Never shall God abandon them.

Today's Saint

St. Henry II (972–1024) was a German king and Holy Roman Emperor, the only German king to be canonized. Henry had considered becoming a priest, but when his father died, he inherited his father's title of Duke of Bavaria. He became king of Germany in 1002 and married Cunegunda, who is also a St. He had a reputation for being learned and pious, and was a positive influence in Church-state relations. At that time, secular authorities appointed bishops and often selected their political allies. Henry appointed bishops who would be good pastors, and he supported them in their work. Although he waged many wars, he was not the aggressor but fought

only to protect his borders and preserve peace. Henry is a patron saint of Benedictine oblates and is invoked against infertility, for he and his wife were childless.

SAT 14 (#388) white
Memorial of St. Kateri Tekakwitha, Virgin

The Liturgy of the Word

◆ FIRST READING: Today's reading recounts the call of Isaiah to the prophetic ministry in 742 BC, the year King Uzziah died. May our humility be that of Isaiah's who recognizes his unclean lips and marvels that he still sees the Lord. May, we too, respond to the Lord's voice with the prophet's familiar words, "Here I am. . . . Send me!"

◆ RESPONSORIAL PSALM 93: This royal hymn celebrates the Lord's majesty and kingship. The Lord is the King who calls Isaiah to be a prophet. Isaiah will proclaim the Lord's decrees to the people. Isaiah's vision began as he saw the Lord sitting on the heavenly throne. How appropriate this enthronement psalm is as a reflection of God's glory evident to Isaiah and the angels who sang in the words we now sing in the Sanctus (Holy, Holy, Holy).

◆ GOSPEL: The Apostles are worth so much more than many tiny sparrows. This alone should lead the Apostles to trust that God will take care of them despite those who wish to do harm to both their body and soul. In their ministry, the Apostles will teach what they have learned from Jesus, their Teacher. Their ministry will not surpass his, but will be sufficient for the time as is the work of all disciples who imitate what they have learned from their teacher.

The Roman Missal

The Collect, the only prayer proper for today, can be found in the Proper of Saints at July 14. It specifically mentions both St. Kateri's Native American heritage and her innocence, praying for the unity of all believers gathered together "from every nation, tribe and tongue." The Prayer over the Offerings and the Prayer after Communion are taken from the Common of Virgins: For One Virgin. Either Preface I or Preface II of Saints would be the appropriate choice for today. Presiders should take note that the Missal was promulgated before Kateri was canonized. Be sure to use "saint" instead of "blessed" when praying the texts for today.

Presiders should take note that the Missal was published before Kateri was canonized. As such, the Collect prayer still uses the phrase "Blessed Kateri." Presiders should change Blessed to Saint.

Today's Saint

Kateri Tekakwitha (c. 1656–1680), daughter of a Mohawk warrior and a Catholic Algonquin woman, was born in a Mohawk fortress near Auriesville, New York. Her parents and brother died in a smallepidemic, and she was left with scars and weakened eyesight. Kateri's mother had made an impression on her, and she was baptized on Easter Sunday in 1676. Her conversion to Christianity caused her relatives to mistreat her, and so Kateri fled to a community of Native American Christians at Kahnawake (or Caughnawaga), Quebec. Kateri died at 24. She is called "Lily of the Mohawks," beatified by John Paul II in and canonized by Pope Benedict XVI in 2012 first Native American to be so honored.

15 (#104) green Fifteenth Sunday in Ordinary Time

The Liturgy of the Word

◆ FIRST READING: Amaziah, a priest of Bethel, flatly rejects Amos's words and orders him to leave town and go to the land of Judah. Amos was one of the twelve minor prophets. He proclaimed the Lord's words in the northern kingdom during a relatively successful period in Israel's history. Yet Amos's prophetic words disgruntled many affluent kings, priests, and other leaders whose greed caused them to trample the poor. While Amaziah aligns Amos with the professional class of prophets in today's reading, Amos is clear that he was working as a shepherd when the Lord called him. From within our ordinary, daily work, the Lord calls us, too.

◆ RESPONSORIAL PSALM 85 is a common psalm for use during the season of Advent, although the refrain for this day is different than the Advent refrain. In the refrain, we ask the Lord for the favor of his kindness and salvation. The first stanza reflects our hearing of the peace the Lord holds out to us, the same peace he held out to Israel. The second stanza paints a beautiful picture of kindness and truth and justice and peace coming together. In the final stanza, we express our confidence that justice goes before the Lord, leading his

steps. The prophet Amos is known for proclaiming prophetic words announcing the Lord's justice for the oppressed.

◆ SECOND READING: What gifts God gives us! Spiritual blessing from the heavens belongs to us. Adoption through Jesus Christ is ours. Redemption by the Blood of Christ and the forgiveness of sins is also ours. The knowledge of his will, he gives us. This great hymn of blessing that opens the letter to the Ephesians invites us to consider the many ways God the Father blesses us through Jesus Christ and give thanks. There is a longer and shorter form of today's reading.

◆ GOSPEL: Not alone does Jesus send the Twelve out, but with a partner. He sends them out in mission with authority over demonic spirits, the same authority he had that comes from God. What are the Twelve to take with them for the journey? Nothing. They do not have to worry about carrying the weight of possessions. Proper footwear is essential, but they will not need a second tunic. They are only to stay where people welcome them, following Jesus' example of leaving places that take offense at their preaching and miraculous deeds. The message of the Twelve is repentance, a change of heart akin to Amos' message to those who acted unjustly.

The Roman Missal

The Mass texts for today are found in the "Ordinary Time" section of the Proper of Time. The Gloria and the Creed are sung or said today. The Collect addresses the living of the Christian life, as it reminds us that God shows the light of truth "to those who go astray," praying that "they may return to the right path." However, we must always remember that we are all among those who could at any time go astray; hence, the prayer goes on to ask that all who "are accounted Christian" may be given "the grace to reject whatever is contrary to the name of Christ." Being converted to the Gospel is an ongoing journey for us all, one that is never complete. The Prayer over the Offerings speaks to the effects of participating in the sacred meal of the Eucharist, noting that the ultimate end of the offerings (of bread and wine) is that of being consumed "by those who believe." Thus, the prayer asks that those offerings "may bring ever greater holiness" to those who consume them. The Prayer after Communion directly picks up on this by its opening reference to the action that has just taken place: "Having consumed these gifts, we pray, O Lord . . ." Notice how participation in Eucharistic liturgy is highlighted here by the sacred actions of offering and of eating and drinking. It is only participating in the sacred actions that we can in any way hope that the "saving effects upon us may grow." Any one of the eight Prefaces of the Sundays in Ordinary Time could rightly be used to equal pastoral advantage today.

Other Ideas

Usually, St. Bonaventure is honored on June 15. Of course, since today is a Sunday, his memorial is omitted. However, there are still ways to honor this saint today and throughout the month of June. Bonaventure was a bishop and doctor of the Church and one of the great Franciscan saints. His devotion to the Blessed Mother is recognized through the recitation of three Hail Mary's on this day by those remembering him. Remembered for his brilliant erudition, he is also remembered for his conviction that all followers of Christ can lead a holy life. This month is a good time to regroup and do some personal "care of the soul" through retreat time, reading, prayer and reflection, practices that are often

intruded on by the busyness of parish life and leadership. Legend tells of a time St. Bonaventure made a papal delegation wait for him to finish washing the dishes. Encourage community members to honor the sacredness of ordinary, daily life some way this week.

MON 16 (#389) green
Weekday

Optional Memorial of Our Lady of Mount Carmel / white

The Liturgy of the Word

◆ FIRST READING: The words of the Isaiah from the opening chapter of his prophetic book make direct demands upon the people. The princes of Sodom are to hear the Lord's Word. The people of Gomorrah are to listen to God's commands. God's frustration with the people and their leaders not following his Word is evident. Still, God invites them to wash themselves clean, to turn away from evil and toward justice.

◆ RESPONSORIAL PSALM 50: In relation to today's First Reading, verse 21 tells us that the Lord does not shy away from bringing the sin of his people to their attention. The Lord does indeed desire the faithfulness of his people as seen in consistency between their words and actions. To the righteous—to those who act with justice—God will show his saving power.

◆ GOSPEL: The Gospel opens with Jesus telling the Apostles the exact opposite of what they would think. Jesus has not come to bring peace to the world, but the sword. Divisions, even within families, will occur because of him. The other commands in this reading, to lose one's life, to receive Jesus, to welcome a prophet and a righteous person, and to provide cold water to one who thirsts all reflect a disciple's actions that will lead to his or her reward.

Today's Optional Memorial

Mount Carmel is part of a mountain range in northern Israel, significant to Christians for its biblical association with the prophet Elijah (see 1 Kings 18). In the twelfth century, the Carmelites were founded at a site that is supposed to have been Elijah's cave and soon built a monastery there. For this reason, the Carmelites honor the Blessed Virgin Mary under the title Our Lady of Mount Carmel. The English Carmelite St. Simon Stock (feast day, May 16) is believed to have been given the brown scapular by Our Lady, and those who wear it believe they can be sure of her help at the hour of their death.

TUE 17 (#390) green
Weekday

The Liturgy of the Word

◆ FIRST READING: An attack on Jerusalem fails in today's First Reading. The Lord sends Isaiah out to meet King Ahaz and counsel him to stay calm and hold fast against the plots he faces. The Lord will not permit the destruction of his city and people if their faith remains firm. Yet Ahaz would rather trust the Assyrians than God. Later in Isaiah 7, Ahaz refuses to ask God for a sign, but the Lord will provide one anyway. The Lord's sign is the birth of a son named Immanuel, to the virgin.

◆ RESPONSORIAL PSALM 48 follows upon the First Reading's theme that the Lord stands by his holy city of Jerusalem forever. The psalm is a hymn to Zion that speaks of the city as the city of the Lord, the King. People gather in Zion because its splendor is unsurpassed.

◆ GOSPEL: Jesus thoroughly instructed the Twelve Apostles about their mission and now he has proceeded to go out and teach and preach in the towns and villages. Today, Jesus admonishes the towns that stubbornly refuse to repent. Chorazin, Bethsaida, Capernaum—places in which Jesus had performed mighty deeds—refuse to turn to Jesus and believe in him. Even the cities of Tyre and Sidon, known for their wickedness, Jesus says, will find the judgment day more tolerable because their people would have changed their ways if Jesus performed his work for them. So, too, the day of judgment will be more bearable for Sodom. Woe to us who witness Jesus' marvelous deeds, but who do not repent!

WED 18 (#391) green Weekday

Optional Memorial of St. Camillus de Lellis, Priest / white

The Liturgy of the Word

◆ FIRST READING: The passage from the prophet Isaiah reads as if the Lord sends Assyria against Israel in anger and wrath for their infidelity. Yet a remnant will return in justice. The Lord will care for his people who reside in Zion. Do not fear the Assyrians, the Lord instructs the people of Zion, later in Isaiah 10. The Lord will triumph, for Immanuel will come to rule the earth. For Christians, Jesus Christ is Emmanuel, God's Son, the Savior of the world.

◆ RESPONSORIAL PSALM 94: The Lord will remain in relationship with his people forever and ever. Today's Responsorial Psalm expresses this aspect of our faith. It links with the First Reading in which the Lord will not abandon his people in Zion. Even though the psalm writer laments the evil ones who would do him harm, still his words communicate confidence in that the Lord's judgment for the just will prevail.

◆ GOSPEL: Jesus offers words of praise to the Father in a marked shift from the stern tone of his

words of warning to unbelieving towns in yesterday's Gospel. Jesus' words speak of his unique relationship with the Father and how the reciprocity that exists is in their knowledge of one another. Would that we be among the childlike to whom Jesus and the Father reveal faith's truth!

Today's Saint

Laying aside a life of violence and gambling, St. Camillus de Lellis (1550–1614) was ordained a priest and later founded the Order of Clerks Regular Ministers to the Sick (the Camillians), a religious order dedicated to the sick, especially those afflicted with the plague. Whether they were ministering in a hospital or tending to the wounded on the battlefield, the Camillians were easily identified by their black habit with a large red cross on the breast. St. Camillus implemented many innovative approaches to hospital care, including proper ventilation, suitable diets, and isolation of people with infectious diseases. He is also credited with the establishment of military hospitals and the setup of field ambulances. Along with St. John of God, he is patron saint of hospitals, nurses, and the sick.

THU 19 (#392) green Weekday

The Liturgy of the Word

◆ FIRST READING: Taken from a song of the prophet Isaiah, this passage praises the Lord for the justice he brings. The prophet expresses his deep desire and that of the people for the Lord. He recognizes that the Lord scrutinized and chastised them for their infidelity, but his prophetic words announce the resurrection of the dead. From the dust, people will rise.

◆ RESPONSORIAL PSALM 102 is both a lament and penitential psalm.

The verses today come from the second of three sections of the psalm. In these verses, the psalm writer displays confidence in the Lord's faithfulness and the mercy he will show to Zion. From heaven, the Lord takes care of his people on earth.

◆ GOSPEL: Jesus' offers gentle words of invitation to those who labor. To the workers, he provides rest. Moreover, when those who follow Jesus take his yoke on their shoulders, they will not only learn from Jesus' humility and meekness, but they will find rest. Ours is the choice to take on Jesus' yoke, which might initially seem burdensome. Along the way, we will discover the contrary; it is truly light.

FRI 20 (#393) green Weekday

Optional Memorial of St. Apollinaris, Bishop and Martyr / red

The Liturgy of the Word

◆ FIRST READING: Isaiah informs Hezekiah, king of Judah, that he is about to die and should put his affairs in order. Instead of adhering to the prophet's advice, Hezekiah prays to the Lord asking him to remember Hezekiah's faithful service. Hezekiah's fate then changes when the Lord sends the prophet back to him with a message of healing. The Lord heard Hezekiah's prayer and saw his tears. Not only will the Lord heal Hezekiah, but he will also save his city from the king of Assyria. The Lord is merciful!

◆ CANTICLE: Having received healing from the Lord, Hezekiah sings his gratitude to God. The refrain proclaims that God saved the king's life. Divine protection from the Lord is ours as well as Hezekiah's. The Lord gives us health and instills life in our spirits. Ours is the privilege to join in Hezekiah's song of thanksgiving.

◆ GOSPEL: When they were hungry, David and his companions ate the bread offering, the bread only priests could legally consume. Priests who serve in the Temple on the Sabbath also transgress the law, but remain innocent of the transgression. Jesus responds to the Pharisees who criticize his disciples for picking grain on the Sabbath with these two example. Jesus desires mercy, not sacrifice. Practical compassion is Jesus' manner; he does not follow the way of punitive justice. Satisfying hunger is more important than worrying about what day of the week his disciples scavenge for food.

Today's Saint

Not much is known about St. Apollinaris (dates unknown) except that he was from Antioch, a Syrian, and the first bishop of Ravenna. Tradition says he was appointed bishop by St. Peter himself. Apollinaris was exiled with his people during the persecution of Emperor Vespasian. As he left the city, he was pointed out as the leader of the Christians. He was tortured and executed with a sword. St. Apollinaris is a patron St. of those suffering from epilepsy or gout and is shown in art with a sword, the instrument of his martyrdom.

S A T 21 (#394) green
Weekday

Optional Memorials of St. Lawrence of Brindisi, Priest and Doctor of the Church / white; Blessed Virgin Mary / white

The Liturgy of the Word

◆ FIRST READING: For three days, we will hear words from the minor prophet Micah who spoke the Lord's words in the southern kingdom of Judah around the same time as Isaiah. Micah is often referred to as the prophet of social justice. His words in today's passage condemning those who cheat

to get ahead in society by taking another's inheritance show why. In the assembly of the Lord's people, no one will mark divisions of land.

◆ RESPONSORIAL PSALM 10: In the Responsorial Psalm refrain we appeal to the Lord to not forget the poor. The verses speak of the evil person who seeks to harm the innocent and also of the Lord's ability to see those who suffer evil and mourn as a result of the damage done to them. The Lord's help is theirs for God's compassion and justice triumph over the harassment and godless ways of the wicked.

◆ GOSPEL: After the Pharisees questioned Jesus about the disciples picking grain on the Sabbath, Jesus heals a man with a withered hand in the synagogue on the same day. Needless to say, this act raised the ire of the Pharisees to the extent that they plotted to put Jesus to death. Jesus fully comprehended what the Pharisees were up to, and went forth from the synagogue continuing to heal many. Crowds followed him, but he counseled them not to make his identity known in order to fulfill words of the prophet Isaiah from the Servant Song in Isaiah 42:1–4, which he quotes at the conclusion of today's Gospel reading.

Today's Saint

St. Lawrence of Bridnisi (1559–1619) was born at Brindisi in what was then the Kingdom of Naples. He joined the Capuchins and was sent to be educated at University of Padua. Lawrence was known for his intelligence, and he became fluent in most Europeans and Semitic languages. It was said that he knew the entire Bible in the original languages. His known writings comprise eight volumes of sermons, two treatises on oratory, commentaries on Genesis and Ezekiel, and three volumes of religious polemics annotated in Greek and Hebrew. He was canonized by Pope Leo XIII

in 1881 and proclaimed a Doctor of the Church in 1959 by Pope John XXIII. St. Lawrence is the patron saint of the city of Brindisi and is depicted leading an army against the Turks, bearing the child Jesus, because of his role in battle against the Ottoman Empire.

22 (#107) green
Sixteenth Sunday in Ordinary Time

The Liturgy of the Word

◆ FIRST READING: Jeremiah's prophetic words in the first oracle are a warning to those who mislead the Lord's people. The shepherds who did not care for their people, the Lord will punish. No longer will they have their jobs, for the Lord will replace them with shepherds who will tend to their flocks. In the second oracle, Jeremiah communicates the Lord's promise that he will raise up a "righteous shoot" to David. The king will save both Israel and Judah through his reign of justice. As Christians, we believe Jesus Christ is the fulfillment of this oracle. He is our justice, the justice of the world.

◆ RESPONSORIAL PSALM 23 is the beautiful poem of how closely the Lord shepherds his people. It is written in the first person as an individual's account of how the Lord cares for the psalm writer even when he walks in dark valleys. The Lord's table nourishes him. The Lord's oil lavishly covers him.

The brim of his cup overflows such is the Lord's goodness. In the end, the psalmist knows he will live in the Lord's house for years and years. For what more could we ask!

◆ SECOND READING: Christ Jesus abolishes the wall that once divided Jews and Gentiles. They are now one Body in Christ existing in peace. All the legalities and detailed commands of the Mosaic law are no longer necessary. What is necessary is that we strive as a people to live the unity of the one Church in reality. We can remind each other of the peace Jesus brought so as to overcome factionalism when it does appear.

◆ GOSPEL: Last Sunday, Jesus sent the Twelve out to proclaim repentance, to exorcise demons, and to heal the sick. In this Sunday's Gospel, the Twelve return and provide Jesus with a summary report. True to his form as an evangelist of few words, Mark does not describe to us what the Twelve reported. Their mission, however, must have exhausted them because Jesus invites them to come away and rest by themselves. Crowds followed them even when they left by boat. Jesus' mercy took over as he responds to crowds who desperately need a shepherd. Perhaps the Twelve were still able to rest and Jesus' mercy extended to them as well as the crowds he taught.

The Roman Missal

The Mass texts for today are located in the "Ordinary Time" section of the Proper of Time.

The Gloria and the Creed are sung or said today. The Collect, in asking God to "mercifully increase the gifts of your grace," can be seen as setting a tone for hearing the parables in today's Gospel.

The Prayer over the Offerings reminds us that Christ's "one perfect sacrifice" completed all prior offerings of the law and asks that our sacrifice, like Abel's, will be made holy; the communal aspect of our worship is highlighted as the prayer gives the reason we ask the sacrifice to be made holy: "so that what each has offered to the honor of your majesty / may benefit the salvation of all."

The Prayer after Communion is a prayer used frequently in Easter Time; it asks that we "pass from former ways to newness of life" as a result of our having been "imbued with heavenly mysteries." The passage of the Paschal Mystery focused on so intently during Easter Time is, of course, at the heart of every celebration of the Eucharist.

Any one of the eight Prefaces of the Sundays in Ordinary Time may be selected for today. Using Eucharistic Prayer I, the Roman Canon, with its mention of "Abel the just" could provide a connection with today's Prayer over the Offerings.

Other Ideas

The fourth Sunday of July is National Parents' Day, a fairly new day of observance in the United States. Consider an event that honors parents, or a parish-based babysitting afternoon or evening that allows parents to take some time to nurture their relationship in honor of this day, or a regular "Parents' Day Out" program. There are several options for the blessing of parents in chapter 1 of the *Book of Blessings*. Natural Family Planning (NFP) Awareness Week is also this week. Consider recognizing the anniversary of the papal encyclical *Humanae vitae* (July 25) or providing information about NFP to interested couples. This week also includes the Memorial of Sts. Joachim and Anne (July 26), the parents of the Blessed Mother.

<table>
<tr><td>M
O
N</td><td>**23**</td><td>(#395)   green
Weekday</td></tr>
</table>

Optional Memorial of St. Bridget, Religious / white

The Liturgy of the Word

◆ FIRST READING: The court-like setting finds the Lord questioning his people about what he has done for them. Instead of waiting for their answer, the Lord provides his own response, declaring how he brought his people out of Egypt freeing them from slavery. The reading then shifts to the people's question about what they should bring to the Lord as an offering in response to his goodness. No offering is necessary; neither will one suffice. In the prophet's often quoted words, all that is required is acting rightly, living goodness, and walking humbly with God. This is no small task, indeed!

◆ RESPONSORIAL PSALM 50: The Responsorial Psalm restates the theme of the First Reading. Burnt offerings and sacrifice the Lord does not require. Instead, he desires discipline and right action. It is one thing to profess the Lord's commands, but it is another more righteous deed to live them. God gifts the upright who offer praise as the only suitable sacrifice with salvation.

◆ GOSPEL: The Pharisees who have plotted Jesus' death, now demand a sign from him. In response, Jesus references Jonah's three days and three nights in the belly of the whale. The Son of Man, Jesus says, will remain in the "heart of the earth" for the same amount of time. His statement foreshadows not only his death, but his Resurrection. The sayings about judgment in the Gospel remind us that those who remain unfaithful and choose to reject Jesus, will face condemnation at the final judgment.

Today's Saint

St. Bridget was the founder of the Bridgettines. She was happily married to a Swedish lord and had eight children, one of whom was St. Catherine of Sweden. The couple went on pilgrimage to Santiago de Compostela in the early 1340s, and Bridget's husband died soon after their return. Bridget had a series of visions that heavily influenced the way the Nativity is represented in art: Mary is blond-haired, and Jesus is not born naturally but arrives as a beam of light, so that Mary is able to kneel immediately with St. Joseph to adore him. St. Bridget is a patron saint of Europe and of widows, and is shown in art bearing a pilgrim's staff and bag, or wearing a crown.

TUE 24 (#396) green Weekday

Optional Memorial of St. Sharbel Makhlūf, Priest / white

The Liturgy of the Word

◆ FIRST READING: Taken from the final chapter in Micah, today's passage follows upon the prophet's words that the Lord will restore the promised land to his people. The verses are often considered a prayer from after the exiles return. God's uniqueness is upheld, for there is no one like him who shepherds his people, forgives sin, offers compassion, and does not hold a grudge.

◆ RESPONSORIAL PSALM 85 follows upon the acclamation in the First Reading that God does not remain angry with his people forever, for he is a God of mercy, offering clemency to those in need of freedom from wrongdoing. In the refrain we ask the Lord to reveal his mercy and love to us. There is never a time when we are not in need of his forgiveness and love. The psalmist also wonders whether God will always be angry with his people. Sometimes we might feel that way, but we believe that the Lord's kindness supersedes our sense that he anger will last forever.

◆ GOSPEL: The Pharisees asked for a sign in yesterday's Gospel and in response received a statement from Jesus about his own death. In today's Gospel, Jesus is still speaking with the crowds, perhaps inside, because his mother and brothers are said to be "outside." A person in the crowd alerts him to the fact that they wish to speak with him. Yet in response, Jesus' question inquire about who of us is in fact his mother and brothers. His simple gesture of extending his hand toward his disciples speaks volumes. His disciples are among his closest relatives, for they do they will of his Father.

Today's Saint

St. Sharbel Makhlūf (1828–1898) was a Maronite Catholic monk and priest in Lebanon. He joined the monastery of St. Maron at 23, and after living in community became a hermit from 1875 to his death. His reputation for holiness drew visitors who sought a word of wisdom or blessing. Sharbel observed a strict fast and had great devotion to the Eucharist. Although dedicated to his life as a hermit, he always willingly went out to perform priestly ministry in local villages when requested. Sharbel died on Christmas Eve 1898, after becoming ill while celebrating Eucharist. He was canonized in 1977.

WED 25 (#605) red Feast of St. James, Apostle

The Liturgy of the Word

◆ FIRST READING: On this Feast of the St. James the Apostle, the First Reading is Paul's reflection on his ministry, the ministry of the Gospel of Jesus Christ. Paul's words remind us of what sometimes seems the enigma of ministry. While we proclaim Christ crucified and risen, we experience suffering and despair in our service to the Gospel. We are approaching death, even as we live. As people of faith, we live in confidence that we too, will be raised.

◆ RESPONSORIAL PSALM 126: The Responsorial Psalm resounds with hope that marked the conclusion of the First Reading. Psalm 126 is a song the captives of Zion sang upon their return to the Promised Land. They sowed in tears, and now they rejoice. In the midst of their suffering, the Lord has done "great things." So, too, we pray in the final stanza of the Responsorial Psalm for the Lord to "Restore our fortunes," when we experience difficult times as his followers.

◆ GOSPEL: The request of the mother of James and John that her sons sit at Jesus' left and right in his Kingdom, follows upon Jesus' third prediction of his Passion in the Gospel according to Matthew. In reply to her request, Jesus asks her two sons if they are willing to drink of the chalice he must drink. They respond that they can. Even though James and John responded positively to Jesus' question about their willingness to share in his suffering, he points out to them that his Father is the One who assigns places in the Kingdom. This angers the other ten disciples, and leads Jesus to speak about the relationship between greatness and servanthood. The Son of Man served to the point of giving his life "as a ransom for many."

The Roman Missal

The texts for this Mass, all proper for the feast, are located in the Proper of Saints section of the Missal at July 25.

The Gloria is sung or said today, since it is a feast. The Collect acknowledges the martyrdom of St. James as it notes that God "consecrated the first fruits of your Apostles / by the blood of Saint James."

The Prayer over the Offerings continues this recognition by referring to the saint as "the first among the Apostles / to drink of Christ's chalice of suffering." As the prayer goes on to ask that "we may offer a sacrifice pleasing to you," we cannot help but be challenged to know that such sacrifice involves our willingness to participate in that same chalice of suffering.

The Prayer after Communion proclaims that we receive the holy gift of the Eucharist with joy on this feast day.

The Preface, proper for today, is one of the two Prefaces of the Apostles.

Also, the Solemn Blessing formula titled "The Apostles," number 17 of the "Blessings at the End of Mass and Prayers over the People," may be used as the final blessing at the end of Mass today.

Today's Saint

The St. James we honor today is the brother of the Apostle John, one of the "Sons of Thunder" (Mark 3:17) who were privileged witnesses of some of Jesus' greatest signs: the raising of the daughter of Jairus from the dead, the Transfiguration, and the agony in the garden. James was the first Apostle to suffer martyrdom and the only one to have his death recorded in the Acts of the Apostles. According to legend, his friends carried his remains away in a rudderless boat that drifted all the way to Spain. Many centuries later, they were discovered, and a great cathedral was built over the spot (*Santiago de Compostela*), which became one of the most popular pilgrimage destinations of the Middle Ages. To this day, hundreds of thousands of pilgrims make their way to that remote corner of Spain to venerate the relics of St. James. He is depicted in art dressed as a pilgrim with a scallop shell on his hat, the way pilgrims to Compostella dress. He is venerated as the patron saint of Spain, Nicaragua, and Guatemala.

(#398) white
THU 26 Memorial of Sts. Joachim and Anne, Parents of the Blessed Virgin Mary

The Liturgy of the Word

◆ FIRST READING: Today's First Reading comes from one of Jeremiah's earliest prophecies in which, with spousal imagery, he reminds Israel of her original devotion to the covenant. But Israel became unfaithful. Priests, shepherds, and kings turned against the Lord to worship "useless idols." Not only have God's people forsaken him, but the cisterns they have built do not even hold water.

◆ RESPONSORIAL PSALM 36: The Responsorial Psalm contrasts with the First Reading in that it consistently speaks of the life that comes from the Lord. God's mercy shows his people that he is "the fountain of life." None of the idols Israel worshipped will bring life as evidenced by their empty cisterns.

◆ GOSPEL: Jesus has taught his disciples that his family members are those who follow him as disciples. The parable of the sower immediately precedes today's Gospel, which opens with the disciples asking Jesus a question many of us would probably have liked to pose to him about why he speaks sin parables. Jesus' explanation leads us to see that only those who take time and have the courage to reflect on the meaning of the parables he tells will come to know the mysteries of the Kingdom. The righteous act responsibly on the meaning of the parables. Their eyes will not remain closed as in the words of Isaiah's prophecy Jesus cites. They, as the disciples, will be able to see God in Jesus.

The Roman Missal

All the orations are proper for today, and are to be found in the Proper of Saints at July 26. The Collect asks Sts. Joachim and Anne to pray that we may attain salvation. The Prayer over the Offerings gives an implicit acknowledgment of the two saints' role in salvation history by asking that "we may merit a share in the same blessing / which you promised to Abraham and his descendants." Either Preface I or Preface II of Saints would be the proper choice for today, with perhaps Preface I being the better choice of the two. The Prayer after Communion reminds us of the divine exchange as it notes that God's Only Begotten Son was "born from among humanity" so that "humanity might be born again from you." The prayer goes on to ask that those who have been fed with the heavenly Bread of the Eucharist might be sanctified "by the spirit of adoption." Thus, the role of Sts. Joachim and Anne as parents to the Blessed Virgin Mary continues to be a theme underlying the texts for today.

Today's Saints

The tradition of Sts. Joachim and Anne (first century) is not scriptural but comes mostly from the apocryphal Protoevangelium of James. It became popular in the thirteenth century when Jacobus de Voragine retold the story in his *Golden Legend*, which was very popular in the Middle Ages. The story of the conception of Mary echoes that of Samuel (see 1 Samuel 1:20): Joachim and Anne are a childless couple who pray to have children and promise to dedicate their child to God. Each is told by an angel that they will conceive, and afterward they meet at a gate of Jerusalem and embrace in joy. This event has been depicted in art by artists such as Dürer and Giotto.

F R I 27 (#399) green
Weekday

The Liturgy of the Word

◆ FIRST READING: Moving ahead one chapter in Jeremiah, we hear our strong Israel's renunciation of the Lord is. The Lord calls them "rebellious children." Yet the passage's first word, "Return," expresses the Lord's invitation to his children to come back to him. Jeremiah's prophetic words continue with a description of how the Lord will actually bring his people back to Zion, providing them will shepherds who root themselves in the Lord's own heart. The remnant of Israel who will come together with Judah will form a covenant with the Lord such that all nations will gather together in Jerusalem, the Lord's throne.

◆ CANTICLE: Today we hear a canticle from the book of the prophet Jeremiah. With the mention of the Lord guarding his people as a shepherd guards his flock, we find a direct connection to the shepherds mentioned in the First Reading. The stanzas of the canticle describe the joyful occasion of Israel's return from exile. Mourning becomes joy. Song and dance accompany the celebratory journey on the road home.

◆ GOSPEL: After Jesus explains to the disciples why he speaks to the crowds in parables and the blessedness of hearing *and* understanding his teaching his disciples have, he proceeds to enlighten the meaning of the parable of the sower to his disciples, although from the context in Matthew it is difficult to determine whether the crowds also hear the explanation or not. The crowds do hear a number of parables, which follow the explanation of the parable of the sower. The seed on rich soil represents the one who hears and understands God's word, and by living it bears abundant fruit. Even as disciples who have heard the parable of the sower numerous times, we need Jesus' explanation to jog our memories about the relationship between hearing, understanding, and acting on the Word!

S A T 28 (#400) green
Weekday

Optional Memorial of the Blessed Virgin Mary / white

The Liturgy of the Word

◆ FIRST READING: The prophet Jeremiah delivers his prophetic words in chapter 7–20, mainly during the reign of King Jehoiakim, a son of King Josiah who follows on his rule, but is a cruel and callous leader. In today's passage, Jeremiah receives a message from the Lord to proclaim to Judah a message of reform from the Temple gate. When the people choose to act on behalf of those whom society considers the least—the immigrants, the orphans, and the widows—and when the people choose not to worship idols, then God will choose to remain present with them. The Lord sees what is happening with his house and his people and wants to see a change.

◆ RESPONSORIAL PSALM 84 describes the longing of God's people to live in his presence. God, too, yearns for his people to reside in the joy of his presence. This is why God pleads with his people in the passage from Jeremiah to reform their lives. As the psalmist's poetry describes, even for us to spend one day in God's courts is like spending a thousand elsewhere. No matter how beautiful that other place is, God's house is a lovely dwelling place, a home for those who praise him.

◆ GOSPEL: The parable we find Jesus telling the crowds in today's Gospel reading is unique to Matthew. As you read the passage, consider why the man who had sown good seed would not allow his servants to pick the weeds his enemy had sown into his field. The Master denies their logical request to weed, stating that they will uproot the wheat with the weeds. Only at harvest will the two be separated. For now, the wheat and weeds will grow together, a realistic metaphor for our life on earth. At the harvest, only God will judge, and the wheat God will gather into his barn, while the weeds he will burn. We will need to wait a few days to hear Jesus' interpretation of this parable.

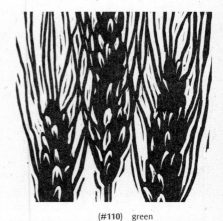

29 (#110) green
Seventeenth Sunday in Ordinary Time

The Liturgy of the Word

◆ FIRST READING: Twenty barley loaves and some fresh grain the man from Baal-Shalishah brought to Elisha to feed a hundred people. Who would believe that this would be enough food for that many people? Elisha's servant did not. But Elisha, the prophet who succeeded Elijah, refuses to rescind his instructions to the servant. Indeed, there was enough food and even some left over. The miracle story of Elisha feeding the one hundred pairs with the story of the multiplication of the loaves and fish in the Gospel reading. God's abundant care for his people is evident in both. In God, we will never go hungry.

◆ RESPONSORIAL PSALM 145: The refrain provides the obvious

connection to the First Reading as it affirms how the Lord's hand feeds us and how the Lord answers our needs. The reference in the second stanza to the Lord providing the faithful the food they need also relates to the feeding story from 2 Kings. Overall, the psalmist in Psalm 145 conveys the bounty of the Lords goodness toward his people. For the goodness of our gracious Lord, we give thanks.

◆ SECOND READING: Ephesians 4 begins a section of the letter that offers moral instructions to Christians. The verses we proclaim today provide a list of virtues that teach us what it means to live as Christians. The statement of unity that includes seven "one" statements reveals how deep the communion among Christians within the Church is. The Church makes visible the unity founded on the "one Lord, one faith, one baptism," one God, and one Spirit because the Church is the one Body of Christ.

◆ GOSPEL: From today through the end of August, the Gospel readings come from John 6 concern Jesus' identity as the Bread of Life. We begin in this chapter with the story of the multiplication of the five barley loaves and two fish. At the beginning of the story, Jesus inquires of Philip where they are going to procure enough food for the large crowd. Philip response does not provide a practical solution, but simply restates the problem in monetary terms. Andrew notes the boy with the barley loaves and fish. Foreshadowing the Eucharist, Jesus gives thanks and distributes the food. The disciples gather the leftovers. Through the miracle, Jesus provides more than enough for everyone to have their fill. Jesus rejects the earthly kingship he knows this great sign would bring, so he withdraws to the mountain again. His work is a ministry of nourishment for it is the will of his Father that he should feed people, even with his very life.

The Roman Missal

The Gloria and the Creed are sung or said today. The Collect speaks eloquently of God as the firm foundation of our lives; with that foundation, we can "use the good things that pass / in such a way as to hold fast even now / to those that ever endure." The sense of the imminent-yet-not-fully-realized Kingdom of God that underlies this Collect connects well with the Gospel parables today.

The Prayer over the Offerings continues to acknowledge the need to progress in the life of the Kingdom, which is both here and yet-to-come: we bring our offerings from the abundance of God's gifts (the already of the Kingdom), and we pray that "these most sacred mysteries may sanctify our present way of life / and lead us to eternal gladness" (growing in grace toward a future fulfillment).

Any one of the eight Prefaces of the Sundays in Ordinary Time may be selected for today. The dismissal formula "Go in peace, glorifying the Lord by your life" would reinforce the need for us to live life in a way whereby we grow in the ways of the Kingdom. The Prayer after Communion highlights the nature of every Eucharistic celebration as anamnesis — the "perpetual memorial of the Passion of your Son."

Other Ideas

Tuesday, July 31 is Memorial of St. Ignatius Loyola, founder of the Jesuit order. Consider offering the community information on Jesuit spirituality (such as the *examen* or the spiritual exercises) through the bulletin or website, or invite in a Jesuit speaker. Consider including links to the many Jesuit spirituality resources now on the Web for their use, such as the daily prayer site Sacred Space offered by the Irish Jesuits: www.sacredspace.ie. The Memorials of St. Alphonsus Liguori (August 1) and St. John Vianney (August 4) are also this week. Include prayers for priestly vocations in the Universal Prayer at Mass.

M O N 30 (#401) green
Weekday

Optional Memorial of St. Peter Chrysologus, Bishop and Doctor of the Church / white

The Liturgy of the Word

◆ FIRST READING: The prophet Jeremiah's vision of the rotted loincloth near the river Parath (the Euphrates) symbolizes the refusal of the people of Judah to obey the Lord's words. Their corruption, including that of their leaders, will result in their decay. God made his people to be close to him. At this time in history, the people fail to listen to God, though he still wants them to return. They are his cherished and beautiful people.

◆ CANTICLE: Verses from the Song of Moses in the book of Deuteronomy form the Responsorial Psalm. The refrain directly addresses God's people and reminds them of how they have forgotten God, God who gave them their very life. The people's forgetfulness of God links with the refusal of the people of Judah in the First Reading to live in obedience to God's Word. In this way, they forget God. God charges his people with a lack of loyalty in Moses' song for they have turned to idols.

◆ GOSPEL: Another nature parable makes up today's Gospel reading. The parable of the mustard seed, a parable that many in our assemblies could recite from memory, teaches us that the kingdom of heaven, like the smallest of seeds, becomes the largest of plants. An often overlooked detail of the parable is that *a person* has to take the seed and sow it in order for it to grow. As disciples, our responsibility is to sow kingdom seeds. We aid in the expansion of the Kingdom of heaven by faithfully following embracing Jesus' mission of teaching and healing, and extending to many the invitation to dwell in the Kingdom so that it gloriously expands and becomes akin to the large bush frequented by the many birds of the sky make their home on its branches.

Today's Saint

Not much is known about St. Peter, who lived from approximately 380 to 450. He was bishop of Ravenna from about the year 433. One hundred seventy-six of his homilies survive, brief and to the point, in which he explains the Incarnation, the Creed, and the major heresies of his day. He was given the name Chrysologus, or "golden-worded," for his eloquent preaching.

(#402) white

TUE 31 Memorial of St. Ignatius of Loyola, Priest

The Liturgy of the Word

◆ FIRST READING: Jeremiah has the difficult job of prophesying words of doom to the false prophets who claim to speak in the Lord's name. These prophets will face the sword and endure hunger and famine. No one will even do them the courtesy of burying them. Nevertheless, Jeremiah's words conclude with a confession. Using the plural "we," he admits to the Lord the wickedness and guilt of the people. We have sinned against the Lord. Jeremiah begs the Lord not to reject his people and remember the covenant he made with them. Only the Lord provides rain in a time of drought. The prophet recognizes the history of the Lord's faithfulness. No god among the people's idols has provided for them as the Lord has.

◆ RESPONSORIAL PSALM 79: Today's refrain expresses Israel's prayer to deliver her for the glory of the Lord's name. Israel's request mirrors the prophet's wish in the First Reading. The occasion for the composition of Psalm 79 could have been the destruction of the Jerusalem by the Babylonians in 587 BC. As was common (and reflected in the stanzas of today's Responsorial Psalm), the people link their sinfulness in a causal way with the destruction. In the final stanza, they promise again to give thanks to the Lord forever and declare his praise throughout all generations.

◆ GOSPEL: Today we hear Jesus' interpretation of the parable at the request of the disciples. Having dismissed the crowds and entered the house once again, Jesus clarifies the symbolism of the weeds, the good seed, the enemy, the Sower, the field, the harvesters, and the harvest. The end of the age does not bode well for the weeds — those who cause people to sin and those who do evil. The righteous, however, will shine brilliantly as they take their place in their Father's kingdom. We must have ears to hear, to truly understand, this message now.

The Roman Missal

All the orations, located at July 31 in the Proper of Saints, are proper for this obligatory memorial. The Collect reflects aspects often associated with Ignatian spirituality with its references to the greater glory of God's name and fighting the good fight on earth. The Prayer over the Offerings describes the sacred mysteries we are celebrating as "the fount of all holiness." In view of this, perhaps it would be good to be sure to use Eucharistic Prayer II today, with its mention of the Lord as "the fount of all holiness." Preface I or Preface II of Saints or the Preface of Holy Pastors are all appropriate choices

for today's Preface. The Prayer after Communion asks that the "sacrifice of praise" we have offered here on earth may bring us to the joys of eternity where we will "exalt your majesty without end."

Today's Saint

St. Ignatius of Loyola (1491–1556) was the founder and first Father General of the Society of Jesus, or Jesuits, and author of the *Spiritual Exercises.* Born in the Basque region of Spain, he joined the army and was severely wounded in battle. While recovering, he read a life of Christ and lives of the saints and decided to emulate them. He laid his military equipment before a statue of Mary at the Benedictine Abbey of Montserrat, and spent several months in a cave near Manresa. After making a pilgrimage to the Holy Land, he enrolled at the University of Paris, and he gathered six companions who would become the first Jesuits.

August 2018
Month of the Immaculate Heart of Mary

(#403) white

WED 1 Memorial of St. Alphonsus Liguori, Bishop and Doctor of the Church

The Liturgy of the Word

◆ FIRST READING: Jeremiah complains to the Lord for he is continuously in pain. The joy and happiness the Lord's words promised to him when he discovered them, is no longer evident. He suffers at the hands of the Lord's people who have chosen infidelity. In response to Jeremiah's complaints, the Lord issues another call to repent. If the people rebel against Jeremiah, the Lord will protect his prophet.

◆ RESPONSORIAL PSALM 59: The psalmist complains about his enemies like Jeremiah complained in the First Reading. The psalm refrain affirms the psalmist's trust that God is his refuge even when he is in distress. Would that we, too, have the strength in difficult times to still sing of God's own strength and mercy as the psalmist does in the last three stanzas of the Responsorial Psalm.

◆ GOSPEL: A treasure hidden in a field. A wholesaler looking for high-value pearls. Jesus uses these two short parables in the Gospel to teach his disciples about the Kingdom of heaven. Often the focus is on the treasure and the pearls in the parables; however, in both instances there is an actor — the person who finds and hides the treasure in the field and the merchant who searches for the valuable pearls. Are we willing to engage in the journey to the Kingdom of heaven? Are we willing, like the person who finds the treasure and the merchant who searches for fine pearls to sell everything we have when we discover the joy of the God's Kingdom?

The Roman Missal

The proper orations for this obligatory memorial are taken from August 1. The Collect points to St. Alphonsus as an example of virtue and it notes his "zeal for souls." The Prayer over the Offerings makes reference to the Holy Spirit, asking God "to enkindle our hearts / with the celestial fire your Spirit," so that we might make a holy offering of ourselves just as St. Alphonsus offered himself. Preface I or Preface II of Saints, or the Common of Holy Pastors, are the choices from which to select the Preface for today. Pointing to the stewardship and preaching of St. Alphonsus, the Prayer after Communion asks that we too, in receiving "this great mystery," may praise God without end.

Today's Saint

St. Alphonsus Mary Ligouri (1696–1787) enjoyed a successful career as a lawyer, but when he lost a legal case, he believed this to be a sign from God to change his life. So, he studied for the priesthood. At the suggestion of a bishop friend, he founded the Congregation of the Most Holy Redeemer, also known as the Redemptorists, a community of priests dedicated to preaching, hearing confessions, and administering the sacraments. One of his most important contributions to the Church is his prolific writing in the area of moral theology. Also included among his writings are many devotional works regarding Mary and the saints. He influenced the Church not only through his writings, but also through his leadership as a bishop. Due to his many accomplishments, he was declared a Doctor of the Church and is recognized as one of the greatest moral theologians in Church history.

THU 2 (#404) green Weekday

Optional Memorial of St. Eusebius of Vercelli, Bishop / white; St. Peter Julian Eymard, Priest / white

The Liturgy of the Word

◆ FIRST READING: The Lord sends Jeremiah to the potter's house for his next message. The image of the potter turning an ugly object of clay into a beautiful ceramic becomes the metaphor for how God molds his people. Israel is in God's hands, for God to treat how God chooses. Still, Israel has its own choice to make about whether to repent and return to faithfulness. The people's choice will impact God's decision to follow through on the good he promises.

◆ RESPONSORIAL PSALM 146: The God of Jacob is our help. Neither princes nor any mortals can save us as God does. Our life is in

God's hands. Having discovered this truth in his own life, the psalmist praises the Lord from the depths of his soul. God will help us like no other person or god will. Such is the truth the comparison of God to the potter in the First Reading teaches us. Yet like Israel, ours is the ongoing invitation to turn to God and repent from sin — to recognize that God is our help.

◆ GOSPEL: Again, Jesus offers us another image of the kingdom of heaven. It is like a net thrown into the sea that catches many different kinds of fish. Those who fish must not only throw the net into the open waters, but must haul it back in when fish fill it to the brim. In contrast to yesterday's parables that emphasize the actions of the person who finds a buried treasure and the merchant that searches for fine pearls, today's parable draws our attention to the fishers separating the good and bad fish. At the end of the age, angels will separate the righteous and the wicked in a similar manner. The Kingdom's joy is at stake for us. Would that we accept the cross of discipleship and live as God's righteous people now?

Today's Saints

St. Eusebius († 371) was born in Sardinia. He was made the first bishop of Vercelli, probably in the 340s, and formed his clergy into a monastic community. At the 355 Synod of Milan, he refused to condemn Athanasius for opposing the Arian heresy, which undermined belief in the full divinity of Christ. As a result, he was exiled to Syria, to Cappadocia, and later to Egypt. When he was finally allowed to return from exile, he joined Athanasius at a synod that affirmed the divinity of the Holy Spirit and urged merciful treatment of repentant bishops who had signed Arian creeds. Once he returned to Vercelli, he joined Hilary of Poitiers to defeat the Arian heresy in the

West. He died in 371 but was probably not martyred.

St. Peter Julian Eymard (1811–1868) was a French Catholic priest who founded two religious orders, the Congregation of the Blessed Sacrament and, for women, the Servants of the Blessed Sacrament. Originally rejected as a candidate for the priesthood because of poor health, he was eventually ordained for the Diocese of Grenoble and later joined the Marist Fathers. Peter Julian Eymard worked tirelessly to encourage frequent reception of Holy Communion and has been called the "apostle of the Eucharist." He was a friend of his contemporaries, St. Peter Chanel and St. John Vianney, and advised the sculptor Auguste Rodin not to give up art to become a lay brother in his Congregation.

FRI 3 (#405) green
Weekday

The Liturgy of the Word

◆ FIRST READING: Jeremiah, perhaps more than any other prophet, prefigures Jesus. Having heard Jeremiah prophesy about the people's fate for disobeying the Lord and neither following his Law nor listening to his prophets, the priests and other prophets (presumably false prophets), and the people cry for Jeremiah to be put to death. The leaders and their people do not trust that Jeremiah is actually prophesying in the Lord's name, predicting their city will become desolate and deserted should they not repent.

◆ RESPONSORIAL PSALM 69: The anguish of the psalmist reflects Jeremiah's own suffering. Even in the face of his enemies' hatred and the insults he bears from them, the psalmist prays to the Lord that God's favor will come upon him. The psalmist's profound trust in the Lord's kindness and the constancy of his help becomes tangible to us as we pray the words of this lament.

◆ GOSPEL: His disciples responded affirmatively that they understood his teachings about the Kingdom of heaven, and then Jesus moved on to Nazareth, his hometown. In the synagogue he taught people, and they were amazed at his wisdom and the marvelous deeds he performed. Ironically, after they inquire among themselves about his identity and the source of his wisdom, their amazement turns rejection. Like Jeremiah in the First Reading, the people of Jesus' native place reject him. They simply lacked faith.

SAT 4 (#406) white
Memorial of St. John Vianney, Priest

The Liturgy of the Word

◆ FIRST READING: The priests, prophets, and people called for Jeremiah's death in yesterday's First Reading. As today's passage begins, we find them presenting the charge against Jeremiah to the princes and all the people. They say, Jeremiah has prophesied against their city. In response to their charge, Jeremiah remains a faithful prophet claiming his authority to prophesy comes from the Lord. It is the Lord who desires the people to reform. Once they do, the Lord himself will repent of the evil he threatens to bring upon them. Jeremiah willingly tells the people to decide freely about his fate as they think just. His would be an innocent death. In fact, all the parties involved do decide Jeremiah does not deserve to lose his life.

◆ RESPONSORIAL PSALM 69: Today's Responsorial Psalm comes from the same psalm as we heard yesterday. The refrain is the same, as is the psalmist's affirmation of the Lord's tremendous love and his request for the Lord to answer his prayer. The stanzas come from later verses in the Psalm 69. In the opening stanza the psalmist uses metaphorical language of mire, flood-waters, and abyss as he please with the Lord to rescue him. Stanzas two and three emphasize the psalmist's confidence that the Lord will hear his plea. For the Lord's redemption, he offers a song of praise.

◆ GOSPEL: Having heard of the reputation Jesus was gaining, Herod the tetrarch confuses Jesus with John the Baptist. But John the Baptist must then have been raised from the dead for that could be the only explanation of the powers that enable Jesus to perform his mighty deeds. The rest of the Gospel continues with the account of the death of John the Baptist and Herod's fulfillment of the request of Herodias' daughter for the head of John the Baptist.

The Roman Missal

The Collect is proper and is found in the Proper of Saints for August 4. The remaining prayers may be from those for Ordinary Time or from the Common of Pastors: For One Pastor.

Today's Saint

The suppression of the Church during the French Revolution (1786–1759) resulted in an unchurched and ignorant generation. St. John Mary Vianney desired to draw these lost souls back to the Church and reeducate them in their faith. As the *curé* (parish priest) of the isolated village of Ars, he began by living a life of austerity and mortification, and brought catechesis and the sacraments, especially the Sacrament of Reconciliation, back to the people. His reputation for holiness spread throughout France—so many wished to see the *Curé d'Ars*, that one could wait over a week to see him, and it was said that if all priests were like him, everyone in France would be Catholic. St. John Vianney is the patron saint of priests, especially those who work in parishes.

(#113)   green

5 Eighteenth Sunday in Ordinary Time

The Liturgy of the Word

◆ FIRST READING: Who would not grumble if they were in the middle of a desert hungry for food? Would not we, in the midst of our despair, prefer as the Israelites did to have died in the land of their enemies where at least they had bread to eat? The Lord heard the Israelites grumble and told Moses he would send bread from heaven for them to eat. The people would have to gather their food as a test to see whether they would remain faithful to the Lord's instructions. When the Israelites saw the manna from heaven, they did not recognize it. But the Lord remained faithful to his promise to provide for his people.

◆ RESPONSORIAL PSALM 78 depicts the many ways the Lord provided for his people throughout the generations. The refrain from verse 24b specifically notes that the Lord provided bread from heaven to the Israelites as the First Reading from Exodus details. To tell the story of God's marvelous deeds to each generation is the responsibility of the faithful. In the telling, the story of salvation is not forgotten; it becomes a living story.

◆ SECOND READING: Last Sunday's Second Reading from Ephesians presented the sevenfold unity of Christians in the one Body of Christ. In the verses between last Sunday's passage and the beginning of today's reading, the author of Ephesians describes the diversity of gifts within the Church. The old selves that the Ephesians had in their previous life before Baptism, would have seen their gifts put in hierarchical order, as the Corinthians did in Paul's first letter to them. Yet their new selves in Christ live God's righteousness. Though the author of Ephesians did not face the same conflict among believers with diverse gifts, he wanted to make sure that Christians knew that in Christ all gifts are used for the same purpose, to build up the body and bring the Church to fulfillment in Christ.

◆ GOSPEL: Jesus knows the intent of the crowd who relentlessly followed him. He had fed them, and now they wanted to know more. The crowd asks him a series of three questions. In the first, they only want to know when he arrived across the sea. In the second, they want to know what their part is in accomplishing God's works. To this Jesus replies, believe in the one God sent. In the third question, the crowd asks Jesus for a sign so that they might believe in him. They reference their ancestors eating manna in the desert to substantiate their request. Jesus identifies himself as the Bread of Life. Whether the crowd understood what he was saying, John leaves unsaid.

The Roman Missal

The Collect points to how God constantly gives life to his creation: he creates, and he also restores what he creates and keeps safe what he restores. This is the reason we glory in God as our "Creator and guide." The Prayer over the Offerings highlights the theme of offering, which is central to every celebration of the Eucharist, as it petitions that we may be made an eternal offering to God. The Prayer after Communion returns to the theme of protection heard in the Collect, asking that those renewed with the heavenly gifts of the Eucharist might be worthy of eternal redemption. Of the eight Prefaces of the Sundays in Ordinary Time that could be used today, Preface III echoes the idea of God's protection and restoration as it speaks of God coming to our aid with his divinity. Preface VI speaks about the daily effects of God's care. The Gloria and the Creed are sung or said today.

Other Ideas

Tomorrow, the Church celebrates the Feast of the Transfiguration of the Lord. The Orthodox Churches observe this day in an all-night vigil beginning this evening. This is a good day to provide information about what Catholics and Orthodox Christians hold in common, and what separates the traditions — which officially refer to each other as "sister Churches." This month is a good time to attend to details related to liturgical life, such as cleaning vestments and albs, checking candle and incense supplies and ordering other provisions for the fall. Begin planning training for existing participants in liturgical ministries, and strategize with colleagues and leaders in your ministry about expanding participation. These plans can be implemented at a ministry fair or other information session this fall. In rural settings, parishes will prepare the Order of Blessing on the Occasion of Thanksgiving of the Harvest. This is traditionally celebrated on August 15, the Assumption of Mary. Be sure to include prayers in the Universal Prayer for those who grow our crops and humanely raise the animals that provide meat to local grocers.

(#614) white

MON 6 Feast of the Transfiguration of the Lord

About Today's Feast

The Feast of the Transfiguration of the Lord reminds us about the depth of mystery that surrounded Jesus Christ — mystery in the sense that we can never exhaust who he really is or categorize him in any way. Fully human, he may indeed have needed a tent or a place to camp on the mountain, like Peter asked. But just when the Apostles may have been getting really comfortable with their understanding of Jesus as friend and teacher, they catch a glimpse of his heavenly glory, challenging them to remain open to Christ communicating to them who he is as Son of God. We have moments like the Apostles each time we encounter and grapple with a new and challenging image of God in the Scriptures. Remaining humble and open to the revelatory action of God's Word and Spirit is a way to enter ever more deeply into the mystery of who God is for us in Jesus Christ.

The Liturgy of the Word

◆ FIRST READING: The brightness of the Ancient One's clothing in Daniel's vision mirrors the brilliant white of Jesus' clothes in Mark's account of the Transfiguration in the Gospel reading. Daniel's vision continued during the night and in one of them he saw "One like a Son of man coming" and going to the Ancient One. From him, the "one like a Son of man" received the authority to rule over the nations. The glory of a king was given him. His reign would be everlasting. Christians see in the vision of Daniel a foreshadowing of the coming of Jesus Christ, who receives power and glory from the Father.

◆ RESPONSORIAL PSALM 97: The references to the Lord's Kingship and throne resonate with similar images in the First Reading. In the refrain, we proclaim the Lord as King and affirm his rule over all the earth. He is above all other gods; idols no longer have power. Those who worship idols, God will judge justly. While clouds and darkness might surround the Lord as the opening stanza of the psalm describes (v. 2), the Lord still reigns from his throne. His justice prevails.

◆ SECOND READING: In this passage the author of 2 Peter wants to bolster the confidence of his audience regarding the truth of the Gospel message. To achieve this goal, he first notes how they had been eyewitnesses to the majesty of Jesus Christ and his reception of glory and honor from his Father. The author's citation of the Father's quote found in the Gospel accounts of the Transfiguration strengthens his claim about the authenticity of the Gospel of Jesus Christ.

◆ GOSPEL: *Please note that the Gospel is proper to the Sunday Lectionary cycle. Use the Gospel for Year B.*

Upon the high mountain Jesus' transfiguration occurred. His power and glory shown forth to Peter, James, and John. Elijah and Moses appeared and conversed with Jesus. Mark provides no details on what they discussed, but we do know the disciples wanted to pitch tents and remain on the mountaintop. A voice then comes from the cloud declaring Jesus' identity as "my beloved Son." The disciples and we are to listen to him. Willingly or not, we also do not know, but the disciples journeyed down the mountain with Jesus. Not until after the Resurrection, were the disciples to tell anyone of their experience on top of the mountain. In the Resurrection, Jesus' mission of life would come full circle and complete itself; we would fully witness his glory — the glory of eternal life.

The Roman Missal

The orations for this feast are all proper for the feast today, and are located in the Proper of Saints section of the Missal at August 6.

The Gloria and the Creed are sung or said today. The Collect places the meaning of the Transfiguration not as some event that took place in the past, but rather as something that serves as an invitation to explore ever more deeply the reality of who God reveals himself to be. Thus, in the Collect we are enjoined to listen to the voice of God's beloved Son, that is, now, in the present, so that "we may merit to become co-heirs with him." We must recall that all liturgical celebration is about our entrance at the present into the mystery that is being made manifest and present through the ritual actions and the anamnesis of the Church.

The Prayer over the Offerings employs imagery of the Transfiguration by referring to the "radiant splendor" of the Son. The Preface, "The Mystery of the Transfiguration," is proper for today, and is given in the pages along with the other Mass texts. Music is provided, so perhaps today would be a good day to sing the introductory dialogue and the Preface.

This Preface reminds us, as with so many of the mysteries of our faith, that the reality we celebrate about Christ is a reality we are called to also experience — we are all called to be transfigured with Christ, as his Transfiguration shows us "how in the Body of the whole Church is to be fulfilled / what so wonderfully shone forth first in its Head."

The Prayer after Communion, which also uses the imagery of radiance and splendor, picks up the theme of transformation: we pray that the "heavenly nourishment" we have received will "transform us into the likeness of your Son." We are reminded that our reception of Holy Communion is never simply a passive reception, but it is always to be an active participation in being transformed into what we receive.

TUE 7 (#408) green
Weekday

Optional Memorials of St. Sixtus II, Pope, and Companions, Martyrs / red; St. Cajetan, Priest / white

The Liturgy of the Word

◆ FIRST READING: The First Reading contains the Lord's words from an oracle to Israel and Judah that the prophet communicated. The Lord has punished his people for their infidelity, but they are not to mire themselves in guilt for their previous sins. This is the message with which the reading opens. Then a noticeable shift in tone occurs. Rather than the Lord stating the incurable nature of Israel's wound, his words offer hope for the restoration of the people. Sounds of laughter and music will once again fill the air of cities and palaces signifying the mended personal relationship between God and his people.

◆ RESPONSORIAL PSALM 102: The refrain of the Responsorial Psalm confidently expresses that the Lord will restore Zion, and when the restoration occurs, he will gloriously appear. The stanzas of this penitential psalm used today remember the Lord's promises to hear the prayers of the poor and the concerns of prisoners, and to free those captive facing death. Once more, people will praise the Lord's name in Jerusalem. Mourning turns to joy, as in the First Reading, and as happens every time have confidence the Lord will restore after we sin, for the Lord will.

◆ GOSPEL: Jesus and his disciples had just finished feeding the five thousand, when the disciples board a boat and Jesus goes up the mountain to pray alone. The boat tosses and turns and struggles in the wind. As if that in itself did not instill enough fear in the disciples, they see what they think is a ghost walking on water toward them. Jesus identifies himself, but yet Peter needs more proof. Using one word, "Come," Jesus invites Peter to walk on water. When are we like Peter, who accepts Jesus' invitation, but shortly thereafter experiences an onset of fear caused by doubt and cries out to Jesus to save him? When are we like the disciples in the boat, who from a distance acknowledge Jesus as the Son of God?

Today's Saints

St. Sixtus II was pope for less than a year, from August 30, 257, to August 6, 258. He restored relations with the African and Eastern Churches, which had been broken off over the question of heretical Baptism. Pope Sixtus, along with several deacons, was one of the first victims of the persecution begun by the emperor Valerian in 258. He is referred to by name in Eucharistic Prayer I.

St. Cajetan—not to be confused with Thomas Cardinal Cajetan— was, was born in 1480 and founded the Order of the Clerics Regular, or Theatines, which was canonically erected by Clement VII in 1524. The idea behind the Order was to combine the spirit of monasticism with active ministry. He died in 1547. He is a patron saint of workers, gamblers, and the unemployed, and is especially venerated in Argentina.

WED 8 (#409) white
Memorial of St. Dominic, Priest

The Liturgy of the Word

◆ FIRST READING: Jeremiah's words in today's passage follow the good news of the restoration of Israel and Judah we heard yesterday with more good news. God's people that have found life in the desert will relish in the fruits of the vineyards they will plant on the mountains of Samaria. The Lord will have delivered his people, the remnant of Israel. What a joyful occasion, too, when we reunite with the Lord after having wandered in the desert of our transgressions and missteps in our relationships and in life.

◆ CANTICLE: The Responsorial Psalm comes from the same chapter in Jeremiah as our First Reading. What a joyful time it will be when the people return! People of all ages will sing and dance for God brings happiness to them after enduring much sorrow. All will gather in Zion to partake of the abundance of grain, wine, and oil with which the Lord will bless them. Having scattered his people, the Lord now gathers them, and watches over them like a shepherd.

◆ GOSPEL: In today's Gospel, we find Jesus in the region of Tyre and Sidon where a Canaanite woman approaches him and asks for his mercy because a demon plagues her daughter. His disciples want Jesus to ask her to go away, but Jesus reminds them that he was sent to the lost sheep of Israel. Not giving up, the woman asks Jesus for help a second and third time. In the end, as he does many times, Jesus affirms the woman's tremendous faith and performs the exorcism.

The Roman Missal

The orations are all to be found at August 8. The Collect not surprisingly underscores Dominic's reputation as an outstanding preacher. The Prayer over the Offerings prays for protection, "through the great power of this sacrifice," for "those who champion the faith," thus reminding us that we are called to be preachers of the truth, like St. Dominic. The Prayer after Communion again highlights St. Dominic's preaching: since the Church flourished by means of his preaching, we also ask that we might be "helped through his intercession." In view of St. Dominic's life and preaching, the Preface of Holy Pastors would appear to be the most apt choice for today, although Preface I or II of Saints could also be used.

Today's Saint

St. Dominic (c. 1170–1221), a contemporary of St. Francis of Assisi, founded a mendicant order of men (those who rely on the charity of others), called the Order of Preachers or Dominicans, to preach against theological error. One of the pressing issues facing the newly established Order was the Albigensian heresy, claiming that matter, specifically the body, is evil. In order to fight against this heretical thinking, the Black Friars, as they were commonly known because of the color of the cape they wore over their white habit, went from town to town preaching the goodness of the body. In order to preach sound doctrine with clarity, St. Dominic exhorted his sons to engage in rigorous academic study. He eventually started a contemplative female branch of the Dominicans to support the apostolate of the men through prayer.

THU 9 (#410) green
Weekday

Optional Memorial of St. Teresa Benedicta of the Cross, Virgin and Martyr / red

The Liturgy of the Word

◆ FIRST READING: The Lord will write the New Covenant on the hearts of his people, not on stone tablets. The Law of the Lord will reside within us. This covenant will last for all ages. Never, even when we do evil, will we have cause to doubt that the Lord is our God and we, the Lord's people. Truly this is a noticeably different covenant than the covenant the Lord made with the ancestors of Israel and Judah.

◆ RESPONSORIAL PSALM 51: A Lenten psalm and the most well-known of the penitential psalms, Psalm 51 carries with it a simple, yet beautiful refrain today. We merely ask God to fashion us a clean heart. With the psalmist, we pray for the renewal of the spirit of faith within us. We want to rekindle the joy that comes from knowing God's salvation. All that we ask for in the Responsorial Psalm will come because we are God's people, a people of the New Covenant.

◆ GOSPEL: The last time we encountered Peter, he accepted Jesus' invitation to walk on water, but then doubt overcame him — he started sinking, and had to cry out for the Lord to save him. In today's Gospel, Jesus inquires of his disciples about who people think he is. After some of the disciples respond that people think he is either John the Baptist, Elijah, Jeremiah, or another one of the prophet, Jesus personalizes the question, asking who the disciples think he is. Matthew only records Peter's response, a confession of Jesus' identity as the Messiah. Jesus, the Messiah, is the fulfillment of the New Covenant and Peter, the one upon whom Jesus builds his Church.

Today's Saint

St. Teresa Benedicta of the Cross was born Edith Stein at Breslau in 1891 into an observant Jewish family, but by the time she reached her teens, she had become an atheist. She went on to study philosophy and received her doctorate at Freiburg under the philosopher Edmund Husserl but left her university career to teach at a girls' school when Husserl did not support her further studies. Influenced by her study of scholastic theology and spirituality, she became a Catholic in 1922. In 1932, she became a lecturer at Munster, but anti-Semitic laws passed by the Nazis forced her to resign, and she

entered the Carmel at Cologne in 1933. In an attempt to protect her from the Nazis, she was transferred to a Carmel in the Netherlands, but when the Dutch bishops condemned Nazi racism, the Nazis retaliated by arresting Jewish converts like herself. Teresa Benedicta, along with her sister Rosa, who had also become a Catholic, was deported to Auschwitz and died in the gas chamber on August 9, 1942.

FRI 10 (#618) red
Feast of St. Lawrence, Deacon and Martyr

The Liturgy of the Word

◆ FIRST READING: The context of today's reading is Paul's plea for the Corinthians' generosity in contributing to the needs of the Church in Jerusalem. This focus on the poor or those in need is particularly appropriate for St. Lawrence who is known for his great concern for the poor. Paul's words challenge us not only regarding alms, but also with respect to the manner in which we serve others and do good works. We are never diminished by our self-giving but are enriched by God because of it.

◆ RESPONSORIAL PSALM 112: The theme of concern for the poor continues. Psalm 112 acclaims the wisdom and happiness of one who heeds God's command to help those in need.

◆ GOSPEL: The blood of the martyr is the seed of the Church, wrote Tertullian (author's paraphrase), an early Church father. He was put to death because he was a Christian. His life was the grain of wheat that bore witness and gave life — new life to the Church, eternal life to himself.

The Roman Missal

The prayers for the feast are found in the Proper of Saints for August 10. The Gloria is said or sung. The simple petition in the Collect might be spoken of any saint: "grant that we may love what he loved / and put into practice what he taught." Use the Preface I or II for Holy Martyrs.

Today's Saint

St. Lawrence († 258) was one of seven deacons of ancient Rome martyred under Emperor Valerian in 258. Tradition says that he was deacon to Pope St. Sixtus II. According to St. Ambrose, Lawrence met the pope being taken to execution and is supposed to have said, "Where are you going without your deacon?" Sixtus prophesied that he would follow in three days. Lawrence is said to have been martyred by being cooked alive on a grill. He is portrayed in art holding a gridiron, the instrument of his martyrdom, and wearing a dalmatic, the vestment of a deacon. St. Lawrence is a patron saint of the city of Rome and of comedians because of the quip he is reputed to have made to his executioners: "Turn me over; I'm done on one side."

S A T 11 (#412) white
Memorial of St. Clare, Virgin

The Liturgy of the Word

◆ FIRST READING: At the time of Habakkuk's prophecy, the threat from the Babylonians was real. The question of the evil ways of the wicked destroying the just and righteous is the focus of much this short, prophetic book. Today's First Reading is an example of Habakkuk questioning God's role in permitting the wicked to trounce the just. At the conclusion of the reading, the Lord responds to his prophet, declaring the just person will live. Their faith will bring them life.

◆ RESPONSORIAL PSALM 9: The Responsorial Psalm reads like a response to Habakkuk's complaint in the First Reading. In the refrain, we assert our confidence that God will not abandon those who seek

him. In the stanzas, we declare how the Lord judges. Justice and equity are his guiding principles. We praise the Lord who is enthroned in Zion for the always remembers the poor.

◆ GOSPEL: The analogy of the mustard seed comes up again, this time in relation to the disciples' modicum of faith, which prevented them from driving out a demon from a boy. The boy's father brought him to the disciples first, yet they could not exorcise the demon. Not willing to give up, the man approached Jesus, asking him to have mercy on his son. Frequently Jesus comments on the faith of the person asking for healing either for themselves or on behalf of someone else. In today's Gospel, Jesus comments to the disciples after they approach him perplexed as to why they could not help the boy. Faith the size of a mustard seed is all they—all we— need to perform miracles and extend Jesus' compassion to others.

The Roman Missal

It is the Collect, found in the Proper of Saints at August 11, that is proper for today, and it speaks of Clare's life of poverty. Consequently, the prayer goes on to ask that we too will follow Christ "in poverty of spirit" and so merit to contemplate God in the heavenly kingdom. The texts for the Prayer over the Offerings and the Prayer after Communion are taken either from the Common of Virgins: For One Virgin, or from the Common of Holy Men and Women: For a Nun. Possible Prefaces are Preface I or II of Saints, or the Preface of Holy Virgins and Religious.

Today's Saint

St. Clare of Assisi (c. 1193–1253) was one of first followers of St. Francis of Assisi and the foundress of the Poor Clares. Her parents wanted her to marry a rich man, but she fled and Francis received her into religious life. She remained close

to Francis and cared for him in his illnesses. After Francis died, Clare fought to maintain the unique spirituality of the Poor Clares, and is the first woman known to have written a monastic rule. She is depicted holding a monstrance, ciborium, or pyx because of a tradition that she warded off invaders in 1234 by displaying the Blessed Sacrament. Her sister, Agnes of Assisi, followed her into religious life and is also a canonized saint.

(#116) green

12 Nineteenth Sunday in Ordinary Time

The Liturgy of the Word

◆ FIRST READING: The prophet Elijah has had enough, and he asks the Lord to take his life. The prophetic mission seems to have gotten the best of him. While he was sleeping underneath a broom tree, the Lord's angel wakes him and instructs him to eat. A cake and jug of water lie by his head. Eating and drinking once, though, was not enough for the journey that was ahead. Elijah fell back asleep, but the angel came by a second time with the same instructions. Elijah ate and drank. The food nourished him for a journey of forty days and forty nights to Mount Horeb, God's mountain.

◆ RESPONSORIAL PSALM 34: The next three Sunday's the Responsorial Psalm comes from

Psalm 34, a song of thanksgiving. The refrain for all three Sundays in the same, while the verses vary slightly. Psalm 34 is also a common psalm for the season of Ordinary Time. Following on the theme of eating and drinking for the journey of faith in the First Reading, the refrain invites us to "taste and see" the Lord's goodness. In the verses, we praise the Lord for the glory of his name. With the mention of the Lord's angel in the final stanza (verse 8), we also have a connection to the angel in the First Reading.

◆ SECOND READING: The author of Ephesians contrasts vices and virtues as the reading opens. As Christians, we are to forgive as God forgives us in Christ. As children of God, God calls us to imitate him. The love Christ has for us is the love in which we are to live. He loved us to the point of sacrificing himself for us. While most of us will not be asked to sacrifice our lives in death for another, still God calls us to let sacrificial love guide our life journey, our walk of faith.

◆ GOSPEL: Three questions from the Jews, or more accurately a few of their leaders, open the Gospel. The first two questions are rhetorical and question Jesus' identity as the son of Joseph and whether or not they know his father and mother. The third question asks about his authority, and how he can claim to have come down from heaven. Jesus' response develops his relationship with the Father and the role of the Father in drawing believers to Jesus. Jesus then solemnly teaches those gathered that eternal life comes to those who believe. Again, he self-identifies as the Bread of Life and the "living bread" in "I Am" statements.

The Roman Missal

The Gloria and the Creed are sung or said today. The Collect echoes St. Paul's words in Galatians 4:6:

"As proof that you are children, God sent the spirit of his Son into our hearts, crying out, 'Abba, Father!'" We are "taught by the Holy Spirit" and "dare to call [God] our Father." We ask God to bring to perfection within us this "spirit of adoption," that we may come to our promised inheritance.

We ask God to receive the offerings of his Church, the gifts he himself has given and will transform for us, for our salvation (Prayer over the Offerings).

We ask God to save us and teach us through the sacrament we have received (Prayer after Communion).

Other Ideas

Honoring the outcome of hard work is important not only for those who provide our food, but for all people who toil. This week the Church also honors St. Maximillian Kolbe, priest and martyr, who offered up his life in place of another inmate at Auschwitz. Provide learning opportunities connected to the *Shoah*, or holocaust, perhaps with the help of leaders of a local synagogue. The Solemnity of the Assumption of the Blessed Virgin Mary, a Holyday of Obligation, takes place this week.

M O N 13 (#413) green Weekday

Optional Memorial of Sts. Pontian, Pope, and Hippolytus, Priest, Martyrs / red

The Liturgy of the Word

◆ FIRST READING: For the next two weeks, the weekday First Readings come from the book of the prophet Ezekiel. As he was among the exiles by the river Chebar, the prophet had a marvelous vision of God's glory. This vision begins his book and we proclaim it today. In the vision, the prophet describes the splendor of the Lord's throne and "one who had the appearance of a man." Christians see in Ezekiel's vision of "God

appearing in human form" a prefiguring of Jesus Christ.

◆ RESPONSORIAL PSALM 148 rings out with praise of God. Heaven and earth are both full of God's glory, a declaration we also make in the Sanctus. The psalm is a fitting response to the Ezekiel's vision in the First Reading as the vision, too, affirms the connection between heaven and earth. Moreover, praise from God's faithful ones seems the only suitable response to his glory.

◆ GOSPEL: Jesus' second prediction of his Passion opens the Gospel reading. Notice, Matthew describes the disciples' reaction to the prediction. Grief overwhelms them. Yet the continue on with Jesus to Capernaum, where the Temple tax collectors inquire of Peter about whether or not Jesus pays the Temple tax to support the maintenance of the Temple. Since Jesus and his disciples belong to God's Kingdom in heaven, they are exempt from paying the tax. But not wanting to upset anyone, Jesus sends Peter to the sea. The first fish Peter catches will have a coin valued at twice the Temple tax and will serve as payment for both him and Jesus.

Today's Saints

Little is known about St. Pontian (c. † 236), save that he was pope from 198 or 199 to 236. After the schism of St. Hippolytus ended, Emperor Maximinus exiled Pontian to the Sardinian mines, where he died.

St. Hippolytus (c. 170–236) was a prolific writer and probably a disciple of Irenaeus. He wrote the *Refutation of All Heresies* and exegeses of the Song of Songs and Daniel, but he is best known as a possible author of the *Apostolic Tradition*, an invaluable source of information on customs and liturgy during the first centuries of the Church. Ironically, Hippolytus shares this day with Pope Pontian, against whom he led a schism.

(#414)   red

T U E 14 Memorial of St. Maximilian Kolbe, Priest and Martyr

The Liturgy of the Word

◆ FIRST READING: Ezekiel receives his prophetic call to the rebellious house of Israel. He feasts on the scroll of the Lord's Word and tastes how sweet the Word is. Sweet as honey it is, and its sweetness will enable the prophet to approach the rebellious people with difficult news about the destruction of Jerusalem.

◆ RESPONSORIAL PSALM 119: Taken from the longest psalm in the Psalter, the Responsorial Psalm focuses on the sweetness of the Lord's word, echoing the theme of the First Reading. Delight and joy are words that express the psalm writer's reaction to the Law. Would that we yearn and seek the Lord's commands as he does, for they are our inheritance.

◆ GOSPEL: Today's Gospel has three parts. In the first, the disciples approach Jesus with a question as they often do, for they want to learn from their Teacher. They want to know who is the greatest in the Kingdom of heaven. Jesus' response, that they must humble themselves and become like children for they are the greatest, might have surprised the disciples, but Matthew does not let on that it does. The second part is Jesus' clear instruction not to loathe even one child, while the third part is the familiar parable of the lost sheep. Jesus calls us to experience the joy of the shepherd when he finds his one lost sheep. Our heavenly Father does not want even one person to stray from his side.

The Roman Missal

The Collect, the Prayer over the Offerings, and the Prayer after Communion are all proper for today and are taken from August 14. The Collect recognizes the saint for his "zeal for souls and love of neighbor" as well as his Marian devotion. The Prayer over the Offerings asks that through the oblations we present at this celebration, "we may learn / from the example of St. Maximilian / to offer our very lives to you." Indeed, the offering of our lives is the heart of our participation in the Eucharistic celebration. One of the two Prefaces of Holy Martyrs would probably be most appropriate today, although the Preface of Holy Pastors or even one of the two Prefaces of Saints could also be considered. The Prayer after Communion reminds us of our communion with the saints in the Eucharist, as it asks that through the Eucharist "we may be inflamed with the same fire of charity / that St. Maximilian received from this holy banquet."

Today's Saint

St. Maximilian Maria Kolbe (1894–1941) was a Polish Franciscan who volunteered to die in place of a stranger in Auschwitz. From an early age, Maximilian had a strong devotion to the Virgin Mary, and in 1907, he entered the Conventual Franciscans along with his brother. He was sent to study at the Pontifical Gregorian University in Rome, and seeing anti-Catholic demonstrations, he decided to form the Militia Immaculata. He was innovative in his use of modern media, especially printing technology and radio, for catechesis, publishing first a monthly magazine, and then a daily newspaper that soon had the widest circulation in Poland. During the 1930s, he started a mission in Japan and built a monastery in Nagasaki that was one of the few buildings left undamaged by the atomic bomb dropped at the end of World War II. Because he hid Jews from the Nazis in his monastery in Poland, the Gestapo arrested Maximilian, and eventually he was transferred to Auschwitz. When three prisoners escaped, the camp commandant selected ten men to die by starvation. One of the men cried out, "My wife! My children!" and Maximilian volunteered to take his place in the bunker. He survived for two weeks, outliving the others, dying only when the guards injected him with carbolic acid. St. Maximilian Kolbe was canonized by Pope John Paul II in 1982. He is a patron saint of journalists, amateur radio operators, and of prisoners, and he is often depicted wearing the striped uniform of a death-camp inmate.

(#621/#622) white

W E D 15 Solemnity of the Assumption of the Blessed Virgin Mary

HOLYDAY OF OBLIGATION

About Today's Solemnity

The dogma of the Assumption of the Blessed Virgin Mary was proclaimed in 1950, but this observance has been celebrated on this day from the middle of the fifth century. On this solemnity, we profess our belief that Mary has gone before us, body and soul, into heaven. For her, the resurrection of the dead has taken place already. And thus the Assumption is technically an "Easter feast." God invites us to eternal life, to enjoy the glorious new creation of his Son in body, soul, and spirit. Our final hope is the resurrection of our own bodies at the end of time to exist forever in this new order of creation. The Solemnity of the Assumption is our great celebration of this final hope. Mary is a pioneer for us in faith. She was the first among us to accept Jesus Christ into her life. In her bodily assumption, she is also the first fully to enjoy eternal life at the side of her risen son in the glory of heaven. Where she has gone, we hope to follow. We rejoice in the fulfillment of God's promise in her, as we turn to her to guide us to the side of her risen son who reigns in heaven.

The Liturgy of the Word: Vigil Mass

◆ First Reading: Catholic tradition likens Mary to the Ark of the Covenant referred to in the passage from 1 Chronicles. Mary carried Jesus in her womb similar to how the people of Israel recognized the presence of God in the Ark. In the First Reading, the Levites process the Ark of the Covenant to Jerusalem according to David's instructions. Together they ritualized the placement of the Ark within the tent David pitched for it.

◆ Responsorial Psalm 132 is a processional song used when God's people carried the Ark of the Covenant to the Temple. The verses chosen for the Vigil Mass of the Assumption reflect the Ark's journey to Zion the place the Lord prefers to dwell. The middle stanza (vv. 9–10) offers a prayer for both the priests and the faithful. The psalmist requests of God that the priests wear clothes of justice and the faithful respond to God in joy. Both the justice of the priests and the joy of the faithful echo Mary's own expression of the Lord's justice in the Magnificat and her joy and that of Jesus in her womb.

◆ Second Reading: Jesus Christ accomplished victory over death in his Resurrection. Paul hints at this declaration throughout his entire letter. But now his presentation of the Gospel is complete. Humanity and divinity come together in Jesus Christ, who is the Lord of Life. Death no longer has power over him. And, the one Body of Christ that Paul told the Corinthians they are is the Risen Body of Christ! Thanks be to God for Mary who bore the Savior and whose Resurrection she participates in! She provides an example that shows us one day we, too, will share in eternal life.

◆ Gospel: Jesus was speaking to the crowds about unclean spirits returning in people and actually multiplying their wickedness, when a woman from the crowd interrupts him to affirm Mary's blessedness. Jesus' response to her is not a denial of Mary's blessedness, but rather emphasizes the holiness of those who hear and live the Word of God. Mary is an example par excellence of living what she hears.

The Roman Missal: Vigil Mass

The Prayers and Preface for the solemnity are found in the Proper of Saints. The Gloria and the Creed are said or sung today. Please note that there are two full sets of prayers. Those of the Vigil can be used on the afternoon or evening of August 14, with those of the Day reserved for August 15. The Collect echoes Mary's Magnificat. God looked "on the lowliness of the Blessed Virgin Mary, / [and] raised her to this grace." We pray that, with the help of her prayers, we, too, may be saved and "exalted . . . on high." The sacrifice we offer today is "the sacrifice of conciliation and praise." We pray that we may both know God's "pardon" and rejoice "in perpetual thanksgiving" (Prayer over the Offerings).

The Prayer after Communion is a simple prayer for protection as we honor Mary's Assumption into heaven. The Solemn Blessing of the Blessed Virgin Mary may be used.

The Liturgy of the Word: Mass during the Day

◆ First Reading: We understand the woman clothed in the brilliance of the sun and adorned with a crown to be Mary, the Mother of Jesus Christ and the Mother of the Church. Protected by God, the dragon neither harms the woman nor her child. The voice from heaven declares that salvation and power have come—the Kingdom of God is a reality. As God's Kingdom lasts throughout all time, so too, the Church will endure forever, a belief long held by the Christian community.

◆ Responsorial Psalm 45: Originally, Psalm 45 was a marriage psalm sung by the court poet at the weddings Davidic kings. The refrain speaks of the queen standing at the king's right hand adorned in gold. When we sing the refrain, the reference of the queen refers to Mary, Queen of Heaven, whose Assumption we celebrate today. She resides in the palace of the King forever. Many joyfully acclaim her as Queen as they come to live with her in heaven.

◆ Second Reading: Like the Second Reading for the Vigil Mass, this reading comes from the culminating chapter of 1 Corinthians. Its focus is Christ's Resurrection from the dead. Paul testifies that all are brought to life in a particular order. Christ had to be raised first; he is the first fruits. Then those who belong to Christ will be raised. Mary, assumed body and soul into heaven, participates before us in a unique way in Christ's Resurrection. She shows us how in Christ, God brings everything to life, and so looks forward to our own participation in the Resurrection.

◆ GOSPEL: The Gospel reading begins as a journey of one relative to visit another. When Mary arrives and greets Elizabeth, the baby jumped in her womb, and she proclaimed both Mary's blessedness and that of the child she was carrying. Elizabeth recognizes what it took for Mary to believe that she would conceive through the power of the Holy Spirit as the Lord told her she would. Mary's response to her family member is the Magnificat, her words of joy proclaiming the Lord's greatness throughout the generations now present in a new way in the child in her womb, the Savior to whom she will give birth.

The Roman Missal: Mass during the Day

Mary has gone "body and soul into heavenly glory." We pray that we may keep our eyes fixed where she has gone, "attentive to the things that are above," and come one day to share her glory (Collect).

Through Mary's intercession, we pray that our hearts may be "aflame with the fire of love" and longing for God (Prayer over the Offerings).

God would not allow decay to touch Mary's body, because from her body Christ, "the Author of all life," was born. In Mary's Assumption, we glimpse our own destiny—"the beginning and image / of your Church's coming to perfection / and a sign of sure hope and comfort to your pilgrim people" (Preface).

We ask Mary's intercession, that "we may be brought to the glory of the resurrection" (Prayer after Communion). The Solemnity of the Assumption flows from the Resurrection of Christ, in which Mary already shares, body and soul.

The Gloria and the Creed are said or sung today.

THU 16 (#416) green Weekday

Optional Memorial of St. Stephen of Hungary / white

The Liturgy of the Word

◆ FIRST READING: The Lord instructs Ezekiel to act like he is going into exile with the hope that the rebellious house of Israel will see and understand that his actions represent their own destiny. Ezekiel does as the Lord commands, and all his actions the people witness. We know the people observe him, because the text tells us the people are "looking on," watching him carefully both in the daytime as he brings out his baggage and in the evening as he goes out like one going into exile. We know the people's eyes saw Ezekiel, but we do not know if they really saw their fate in him, nor do we know if their ears actually heard it when the prophet spoke the Lord's words about the oracle.

◆ RESPONSORIAL PSALM 78 offers a historical account of the relationship of God with his chosen people throughout the generations. The refrain reminds us not to forget the Lord's works. In the psalm, parents were to recite the Lord's works to their children so each ensuing generation would remember all the Lord has done for them. On the other hand, the stanzas describe how the people rebelled against God, God rejected them, and then sent them into captivity and as such present us an obvious connection to the First Reading.

◆ GOSPEL: In this Gospel reading, Peter seems to be looking for Jesus to give him a numerical, measurable answer to his question, how often must he forgive his brother who sins

against him? We should already be alert to the fact from Jesus' previous responses to questions that he will not provide a direct answer. Numerically, Jesus response, "seven times seventy" translates to infinity. After Jesus responds, he continues with the parable of the servant whose own debt his master forgave, but who was himself unwilling to forgive the debt of a fellow servant. The heavenly Father will tolerate no such hypocrisy.

Today's Saint

St. Stephen († 1038) is thought of as the founder of the kingdom of Hungary, was its first king, and established Christianity there. According to legend, he was baptized by St. Adalbert of Prague. Hungarians believe that Pope Silvester II sent Stephen a jeweled gold crown, along with a letter recognizing him as king. This crown is venerated by the people of Hungary, although the Crown of St. Stephen that we have today probably dates from the twelfth century. St. Stephen discouraged the practice of pagan customs, brought priests in to serve as missionaries, and founded several dioceses. He had hoped to retire and lead a life of prayer and contemplation after handing the kingdom to his son, Emeric, but Emeric died young, breaking his father's heart. Stephen ruled until his death in 1038 on August 15, the celebration of the Assumption of the Blessed Virgin Mary. As he died, he asked Mary to look after the people of Hungary as their queen. Stephen was the first canonized "confessor king," a new category, and is venerated as the patron saint of Hungary. He is also the patron saint of kings, masons, and children who are dying.

FRI 17 (#417) green
Weekday

The Liturgy of the Word

◆ FIRST READING: The longer form of the First Reading recounts how Jerusalem and its people became the Lord's chosen from birth. To symbolize the Lord's intent of taking Jerusalem as his bride, he covers her nakedness with his cloak. God adorns her with the finest clothes and jewelry and feeds her with the premium foods. She was treated like a queen, but her ego took over and she turned from God to harlotry. The shorter form of the reading begins at the conclusion of the longer form and describes how God will deal fairly with her and still remember the covenant he made with her. In fact, the Lord will set up an "everlasting covenant."

◆ CANTICLE: The Responsorial Psalm is replaced with a canticle that comes from the early part of the book of the prophet Isaiah and is part of Israel's song of thanksgiving to the Lord. Even though the Lord was angry with Israel, his anger has subsided. Israel recognizes God as her strength, courage, and Savior. He is the fountain of salvation from whom Israel will draw water.

◆ GOSPEL: After teaching about forgiveness, Jesus leaves Galilee and goes across the Jordan to the district of Judea as he journeys toward Jerusalem. There, he fields a question not from his disciples, but from some Pharisees who are curious about the legality of a man divorcing his wife. Jesus returns their question with one of his own regarding God's word in Genesis. The Pharisees asks a follow-up question about Moses' command for a man to give a woman a bill of divorce. In sum, Jesus' teaching upholds the marriage ideal for the sake of Kingdom of heaven. The Gospel ends with the summary statement noting whoever can accept the teaching should.

SAT 18 (#418) green
Weekday

Optional Memorial of the Blessed Virgin Mary / white

The Liturgy of the Word

◆ FIRST READING: In Ezekiel's time, it was a common belief that sin causes death. Thus, the Lord's words the prophet Ezekiel speaks in today's passage center on virtuous living. They give no less than sixteen directives on how to be virtuous so that one's life will not result in death. The Lord will judge Israel and us according to how we have live his commands. From the start we need to trust the Lord's word at the end of the reading. The Lord God surely does not take pleasure in anyone's death for he is a God of life — the God who calls us to return!

◆ RESPONSORIAL PSALM 51: In the context of today's First Reading, the psalmist asks God for the clean heart of a virtuous person. We cooperate with God in the creation of our clean heart, for ours is the decision to live virtuously according to his commands.

◆ GOSPEL: After Jesus' instruction on marriage in response to the Pharisees' question, people bring children to him so that he might lay hands on them and pray with them. Amazingly, after Jesus had just taught the disciples that the greatest in the Kingdom of heaven has childlike humility and not to loathe even one child, they choose to rebuke those who brought the children to Jesus. Again, he reiterates the Kingdom of heaven belongs to those like the children.

☀ 19 (#119) green
Twentieth Sunday in Ordinary Time

The Liturgy of the Word

◆ FIRST READING: Wisdom built her house. She prepared a meal. She sent her maidens to invite guests from the hills overlooking the city. The invitation to attend Wisdom's banquet goes out not to the rich or wealthy, not to people who think they understand everything, and not to pretentious, the arrogant. No, Wisdom instructs her maidens to invite the simple and those who have yet to encounter Wisdom's truth. These are the people she invites with the one word "Come," the word Jesus will also use to invite his disciples to follow him and share in his Wisdom.

◆ RESPONSORIAL PSALM 34: What more fitting a response to the First Reading than the refrain which invites us to "taste and see" the Lord's goodness! We also prayed this psalm of thanksgiving as the Responsorial Psalm last Sunday. Our soul glories in the Lord who saves us from sin and delivers us from fear! May the psalm lead our hearts and minds to reflect on the bounteous feast of the Eucharist. In the Eucharistic feast we partake of Christ's Body and Blood, and share in his divine Wisdom.

◆ SECOND READING: In the Second Reading, the author of Ephesians contrasts foolish persons with wise persons and provides us here a connection the First Reading in which Wisdom desires those who participate in her banquet renounce foolishness and embrace a life of Wisdom. A life lived according to Wisdom is a life lived in the Spirit. It is a life of prayer—of singing psalms and hymns, of playing instruments. It is a life lived in thanks and praise to God for all God does for us in Jesus Christ.

◆ GOSPEL: Our Gospel from the Bread of Life discourses begins with a repetition of the verse on which last Sunday's Gospel ended, reminding us that Christ is the "living bread" from heaven. The bread he gives us is truly his flesh for the life and sake of the world. The Jews do not understand how it is possible that Jesus can give his flesh for people to eat. Christ solemnly teaches that his flesh is "true food" and his blood "true drink." Eternal life and participation in the Resurrection awaits those who feast on his food. When we participate in the Eucharist and eat Christ's Body and drink his Blood, we partake of his Wisdom and choose forsake foolishness.

The Roman Missal

The Mass texts for today are found in the "Ordinary Time" section of the Proper of Time.

The Gloria and the Creed are sung or said today. The Collect speaks to the need to keep God as the highest priority in our lives as it asks that we might love him "in all things and above all things." Ultimately, it is God alone who can fulfill us since what he promises surpasses every human desire.

The Prayer over the Offerings reminds us once again that the celebration of the Eucharist is a "glorious exchange"—we offer what God has first given to us, and, in receiving those offerings back, we receive God's very self.

The Prayer after Communion expresses how partaking of the Eucharist transforms us now as it conforms us to Christ's image on earth, and then goes on to ask that "we may merit also to be his coheirs in heaven." The transformation begun through sacramental communion reaches its fulfillment in union with Christ in heaven.

Consider using Eucharistic Prayer IV today; use of this prayer means you also must use its proper Preface, not one of the Prefaces of Sundays in Ordinary Time.

Other Ideas

Honoring the Blessed Mother continues when this week the Church celebrates the Memorial of the Queenship of the Blessed Virgin Mary. This provides an opportunity to share cultural experiences of the Virgin Mary as she has appeared to various people over the century, including Our Lady of Knock and Our Lady of La Vang (LTP's *Companion to the Calendar, Second Edition*, includes explanations of a number of these apparitions and associated devotions). Do not assume that all families know or use prayers like the Hail Mary. Offer the words of the prayer as well as information on how to pray the Rosary.

On August 22, the Muslim community will celebrate the second of two great religious feasts: *Eid al-Adha* (the other being *Eid-Al-Fitr*), which commemorates the moment that Gabriel held back the hand of Abraham (*Ibrahim*) from slaying his son Isaac. Consider hosting an experience that allows community members to learn more about the common father of Christians, Jews, and Muslims: Abraham.

This is the week of the Memorial of St. Bartholomew, patron of butchers, cobblers, leatherworkers, plasterers and more. Look through the *Book of Blessings*, and see if there are blessings that would be of interest to your members, such as offices, factories, or shops (chapter 18); the blessing of boats and fishing gear (chapter 22); or the blessing for tools and work equipment (chapter 24).

(#419) white

MON 20 Memorial of St. Bernard, Abbot and Doctor of the Church

The Liturgy of the Word

◆ FIRST READING: What the prophet Ezekiel does, the people of Jerusalem should also do when their city is destroyed. They should prepare themselves to leave, with turbans on their heads and sandals on their feet. They should not wallow in grief, nor participate in any customary mourning practices, for they will have no time to do so. If they do as Ezekiel did, the people will know the Lord is God.

◆ CANTICLE: In relation to today's First Reading, the words of Moses bemoan a lack of loyalty on the part of God's people. Ezekiel faced a rebellious people who had also forgotten God who had birthed them.

◆ GOSPEL: At the beginning of the Gospel reading, it is a young man this time who poses the question to Jesus about what good he has to do to merit eternal life. Jesus gives the logical response: keep the commandments. But the astuteness of the young man leads him to probe deeper for he has kept the commandments. His follow-up question inquires as to what he is missing. Jesus tells him he must sell all he has and give to the poor. Recall that the person who searched for the treasure in the field and the merchant who looked for the finest pearls also sell all they have for the Kingdom. The young man's grief at hearing what he needed to do to be "perfect," is reasonable in light of the life he would be leaving behind. Yet his joy in the Kingdom will surely replace his sorrow.

The Roman Missal

All three of the orations are proper for today, found in the Proper of Saints at August 20. The Collect describes St. Bernard with bright and energetic terms such as "zeal for your house," "a light shining and burning in your Church" and asks that "we may be on fire with the same spirit / and walk always as children of the light." Such phrases point to the remarkable influence St. Bernard had on the people of his time. The Prayer over the Offerings continues to extol St. Bernard as a role model as it refers to him as "a man outstanding in word and deed, who strove to bring order and concord to your Church." Such concord is appropriate in this prayer as it names the sacrament we offer at this celebration as "the Sacrament of unity and peace." We can never forget that unity, concord, and peace must be the fruits that result from Eucharistic celebration. The Prayer after Communion prays that the Eucharist we receive will truly have an effect on our life. Preface I or II of Saints or the Preface of Holy Virgins and Religious are appropriate choices today.

Today's Saint

St. Bernard (1090–1153) joined the Cistercian Abbey at Cîteaux, known for its strict and austere way of life. Within a short time he was noticed for his leadership; hence, he was appointed abbot of a new monastery at Clairvaux. His monastic vision at Clairvaux led to the foundation of several monasteries throughout France, Britain, and Ireland. In the solitude he wrote numerous theological and spiritual classics, including his treatise *On Loving God*, eighty-six sermons on the Song of Songs, and a major work *On Consideration*, a reflection on papal spirituality. St. Bernard had a special devotion to Mary, earning him the titles "Our Lady's faithful chaplain" and "Mary's harper." Due

to his abundant writing and influence upon the Church, he was declared a Doctor of the Church.

21 TUE (#420) white Memorial of St. Pius X, Pope

The Liturgy of the Word

◆ **FIRST READING:** So many problems come when a human person thinks he or she is god. The prince of Tyre faced severe consequences when his ego reached such heights that he thought he was god. Ezekiel reminded the prince of his humanity, denied his divinity, but yet still affirmed his limited practical wisdom though he was wiser than Daniel. Vicious nations desiring war would come against the prince as a result of his haughtiness. They would not spare his life. Such would be the result of confusing humanity and divinity.

◆ **CANTICLE:** Again, the Responsorial Psalm is replaced with a canticle from the Song of Moses in the book of Deuteronomy. In the context of today's First Reading, the people lacking reason mentioned in verse 28 of the second stanza alludes to Israel's enemies and other nations who champion themselves rather than the Lord, the true God who deals death and gives life (v. 39c).

◆ **GOSPEL:** God is the author of salvation. No human being can save. This is Jesus' point to the disciples after the young man with many possessions walked away from Jesus after Jesus told him to sell all he had and give to the poor to gain eternal life. Using the familiar saying about a camel finding it easier to pass through the eye of a needle than for a rich person to enter God's Kingdom, Jesus again reiterates how earthly possessions do not qualify one neither for salvation nor the Kingdom of God. Those who give up everything to follow him will inherit eternal life. Another time, perhaps this time

hoping the disciples will trust the wisdom inherit in the teaching, Jesus states the reversal of the first and last. In God's Kingdom, a new order will exist.

The Roman Missal

Texts for today can be found at August 21. The Collect acknowledges the saint's desire to "restore all things in Christ" as it recognizes his intelligence and great accomplishments. The Prayer over the Offerings reminds us of the reverence with which we must always celebrate the divine mysteries, and the Prayer after Communion asks that "the power of this heavenly table" may make us "constant in the faith." The Preface of Holy Pastors would be a good choice for today since St. Pius X was a pope. You may also use the prayers found in the Common of Pastors: For a Pope.

Today's Saint

St. Pius X (1835–1914) was born Giuseppe Sarto in Riese, Italy. He grew up poor but was able to attend seminary on a scholarship. As pope he was a reformer but at the same time conservative in matters of theology. He published the first *Code of Canon Law*, which gathered the laws of the Church into one volume. His early pastoral experience influenced him to encourage frequent reception of Communion, his lasting legacy. He reformed the liturgy, especially the breviary (Liturgy of the Hours), and encouraged the use of Gregorian chant, replacing the ornate Baroque and Classical compositions that were commonly used. Pius X lowered the "age of reason" from twelve to seven, making it possible for younger children to receive the Eucharist. It is said that the onset of World War I caused him so much distress that he died in 1914, as the war began. Pius X is a patron saint of first communicants for his role in lowering the age of first Holy Communion.

WED 22 (#421) white
Memorial of the Queenship of the Blessed Virgin Mary

About Today's Memorial

Today's Memorial of the Queenship of the Blessed Virgin Mary is a relatively new one on the Catholic calendar, established by Pope Pius XII in 1954. But its roots reach deep into our Catholic tradition. The early Church Fathers recognized that the Mother of Christ, the King, is herself a Queen. Through the centuries, artists have loved to paint the humble Virgin, crowned by the Holy Trinity amid the glories of heaven. In the Litany of Loreto, we call upon Mary as "Queen of Angels," "Queen of All Saints," "Queen Conceived without Sin," "Queen Assumed into Heaven," "Queen of the Rosary," and "Queen of Peace." Mary is our Queen, but she is also our Mother. In the words of St. Thérèse, the Little Flower, "She is more Mother than Queen."

The Liturgy of the Word

◆ FIRST READING: These words addressed to Israel's shepherds are actually addressed to her kings who had the responsibility to shepherd and care for her people as a shepherd cares for his flock. Israel's kings have failed greatly, and we have here a vivid description of bad shepherds. We also have God's promise that he will shepherd his people in their place.

◆ RESPONSORIAL PSALM 23: Today's beautiful psalm of confidence continues the theme of the last line in today's reading, and depicts God doing for Israel all that a good shepherd should do for his flock.

◆ GOSPEL: Yet another image for God is found in today's Gospel: that of a landowner. As parables are wont to do, this one completely overturns what we, like the workers, would think to be just and fair by our reckoning. The landowner *is* fair as he himself points out. God is extraordinarily generous. What is our response when we see this toward others?

The Roman Missal

All the orations for this obligatory memorial are proper for today and are located in the Proper of Saints at August 22. The Collect acknowledges the Blessed Virgin Mary as our Mother and our Queen. The Prayer over the Offerings makes explicit the connection between the offering we make and Christ's offering on the Cross, while the Prayer after Communion points to eschatological fulfillment as it asks that through this Eucharist we "may merit to be partakers at your eternal banquet." The Preface is one of the two Prefaces of the Blessed Virgin Mary; if Preface I is used, the correct phrase to use is "on the feast day."

THU 23 (#422) green
Weekday

Optional Memorial of St. Rose of Lima, Virgin / white

The Liturgy of the Word

◆ FIRST READING: Ezekiel speaks of the new heart and new spirit the Lord will give his people. The Lord's kindness and care for his people is almost overwhelming! The Lord will bring his people back to their homeland, sprinkle clean water on them to wash them of their sins; the hardened hearts of the stiff-necked people he will exchange for "natural hearts." His very own spirit he will now place within the people, marking a restored relationship.

◆ RESPONSORIAL PSALM 51: The refrain accompanying the verses from Psalm 51 is the verse from the First Reading that describes the divine action of God pouring clean water on his people to wash away their sins. In Baptism, the pouring of water symbolizes the forgiveness of original sin.

◆ GOSPEL: Will those invited to the Kingdom feast come? Will they come prepared? Will they be among the chosen? These are the questions the parable of the wedding feast addresses. Jesus tells this parable as tensions between the authorities and him continue to mount. The man who stood out to the king because he was not dressed in a wedding garment provides us a connection to the First Reading. As Christians today, we can see in the wedding garment a reference to the white baptismal garment that symbolizes our new life in Christ, having been cleansed from sin. In Baptism, God cleanses our heart and we receive the new heart he promises his people in the First Reading.

Today's Saint

During St. Rose of Lima's (1586–1617) brief life, people noticed her physical beauty, declaring her *como una rosa* ("like a rose"), but the beauty of her soul far surpassed her physical appearance. St. Rose longed to live solely for God, so she renounced the institution of Marriage by claiming Christ as her spouse. Basing her life upon St. Catherine of Siena, she lived a penitential life, setting up an infirmary in the family home to care for impoverished children and the sick. She gained popularity due to her selfless service to the needy. As the first canonized saint of the Americas, she is the patron saint of South and Central America, the Philippines, and the West Indies.

FRI 24 (#629) red
Feast of St. Bartholomew, Apostle

The Liturgy of the Word

◆ FIRST READING: In today's First Reading, John, the Christian prophet, is shown a vision of the heavenly Jerusalem. He describes the walls of this heavenly city in great detail. Fittingly, the names of the Twelve Apostles are inscribed on the foundation stones of the wall. How true it is that the Church is founded upon the witness of these Apostles, sent out by the Risen Lord to all the nations.

◆ RESPONSORIAL PSALM 145: The antiphon evokes a text from John's account of the Gospel where Jesus tells the Apostles they are his "friends" (John 15:15). In the context of the psalm, God's friends are his faithful ones who praise God and speak of his name and kingdom, a fitting description of Jesus' Apostles.

◆ GOSPEL: Tradition associates Bartholomew with Nathanael, thus the choice of this text for today's Gospel. Can you imagine Philip's excitement when he went to Nathanael? The latter is a man of caution; a Messiah from Nazareth was not his understanding of what the Scriptures prophesied. It is in the moment of personal encounter with Jesus that Nathanael comes to believe. Our faith will grow and deepen in precisely the same way.

The Roman Missal

The prayers for the feast are found in the Proper of Saints. The Gloria is said or sung today. The Preface of the Apostles is used. We pray that God may strengthen us in the faith to which the Apostle Bartholomew "clung wholeheartedly" (Collect) and that through his prayers we may know God's help (Prayer over the Offerings).

Today's Saint

Not much is known about St. Bartholomew (first century) other than the fact that he was one of the Twelve Apostles. He is also mentioned in the Acts of the Apostles as one of the disciples waiting for the descent of the Holy Spirit. According to a sec-

ond-century Alexandrian teacher Pantaenus, an early Christian community in India claims St. Bartholomew as its founder. Tradition states that he preached throughout Persia, Mesopotamia, Lycaonia, and Phrygia. It is believed that he was skinned alive and beheaded at Albanopolis, on the west coast of the Caspian Sea. He is patron saint of tanners due to the loss of his skin during his martyrdom.

S A T 25 (#424)   green
Weekday

Optional Memorial of St. Louis / white; St. Joseph Calasanz, Priest / white; Blessed Virgin Mary / white

The Liturgy of the Word

◆ FIRST READING: Our First Reading is the last in the two week series of readings from Ezekiel. The prophet's vision comes full circle from where he began. In his initial visions, he saw the destruction of Jerusalem. Now, he witnesses the restoration of the Temple and the return of the Lord's presence to its courts. The Lord sits enthroned once more in his temple. He will always abide and live with his people. Never again will they be separated.

◆ RESPONSORIAL PSALM 85: The refrain expresses the confidence of God's people that his glory will dwell in their land. Ezekiel's vision in the First Reading is about the return of the Lord's glory to the Temple and the land of his people. In the stanzas we are reminded that in God is the Giver of all benefits. Indeed, God's promises he fulfills are among the benefits he gives to us.

◆ GOSPEL: Practice what you preach is an age-old adage that is center stage in the Gospel reading. Jesus draws his disciples' attention to the fact that the Pharisees do not practice what they preach. Their hypocrisy is self-evident, and is opposite the life of a true disciple.

Disciples are not masters, only the Messiah is. The greatest serve; the humble God exalts. Jesus has been clear about this all along, and restates this teaching at the conclusion of the Gospel.

Today's Saints

Becoming King of France at the age of twelve, St. Louis (1214–1270) imbued French culture with a deep sense of divine justice. Although he enjoyed the finer things in life, including good wine and food, he never lost sight of the poor. It was not uncommon for him to feed the less fortunate from his own table, but he felt this was not enough, so he provided homes for them. Even with the many constraints upon his time, he managed to spend several hours a day in prayer.

The priest St. Joseph Calasanz (1556–1648) formed a religious order, the Clerks Regular of the Pious School, to set up free schools for the education of poor children. He believed that education would free the young from the dismal life of the slums and end the cycle of poverty when they are given the necessary skills to build a brighter future. During the plague of 1595 he ministered to the sick with St. Camillus de Lellis.

(#122) green

☀ 26 Twenty-First Sunday in Ordinary Time

The Liturgy of the Word

◆ FIRST READING: Joshua, the successor of Moses, gathers the tribes of Israel at Shechem to renew their covenant with the Lord. The choice he presents to them, is also our choice. Who will we serve? Joshua's household will serve the Lord. The people of Israel chose similarly based on the history of God's faithfulness to them. No other god can compare to God's faithfulness to us in Christ Jesus, so may this reading lead us to respond in service to the Lord as Joshua and the Israelites did.

◆ RESPONSORIAL PSALM 34: For the third Sunday in a row, the Responsorial Psalm comes from Psalm 34, although most of the verses this week are from later in the psalm. These verses emphasize the Lord's care for the just and his delivery of them from their foes. God's justice is the goodness his people taste and see. In response to God's justice, we choose to serve him.

◆ SECOND READING: The mutual love between husband and wife symbolizes the love between Christ and the Church. Such a tremendous mystery is the love between husband and wife and Christ and the Church, that even a lifetime of love with not completely unfold it. There is a longer and shorter form of the reading.

◆ GOSPEL: Last Sunday's Gospel began with the Jews argued among themselves because they did not understand how Jesus could give his flesh for people to eat. This Sunday's Gospel opens with the disciples murmuring about how hard Jesus' saying about eating his flesh and drinking his Blood to have life within them is. Some disciples would return to their previous life and others would remain followers of Jesus. Jesus' question to the Twelve about whether they also want to leave parallels Joshua's question to the tribes of Israel. Simon Peter's corresponds to Joshua's in that it is an affirmation of faith. He believes that Jesus has the words of eternal life.

The Roman Missal

The Mass texts for today are found in the "Ordinary Time" section of the Proper of Time. The Gloria and the Creed are sung or said. The Collect asks that we might love what God commands and desire what God promises. The Prayer over the Offerings reminds us that we have been gathered by God to become one people "through the one sacrifice offered once for all," and therefore we pray for "the gifts of unity and peace in your Church." The Prayer after Communion asks for completion of the works of God's mercy, thereby implying that those works have begun in our sacramental communion. Preface I of the Sundays in Ordinary Time describes how we have been summoned "to the glory of being now called / a chosen race, a royal priesthood, a holy nation, a people for your own possession, to proclaim everywhere your mighty works"; this would certainly pick up on a theme heard in the Prayer over the Offerings. Similarly, so would Preface VIII, which speaks about the people gathered and formed as one, made the Body of Christ, and now manifest as the Church. One

of those two Prefaces might be a good choice for today.

Other Ideas

St. Augustine, bishop and doctor of the Church, and his mother St. Monica are remembered this week. An excerpt from his writings (perhaps from his spiritual autobiography, *The Confession*, his book *The City of God*, or his writings on Eucharist, *Grace or Salvation*) can introduce people to this brilliant theologian. St. Monica is honored as the patron saint of mothers, due to her ongoing prayer for her then-wayward son's conversion.

(#425) white

MON 27 Memorial of St. Monica

The Liturgy of the Word

◆ FIRST READING: Paul, Silvanus, and Timothy greet the Church of the Thessalonians whom they love dearly. The Church at Thessalonica is a flourishing community marked by their love for one another. When Paul and his partners preach to other communities, they use the Thessalonians as an example of perseverance in faith. The phrase "Kingdom of God" appears in this passage, one of the few times its does in Paul's letters. Here, there reference is to the Thessalonians worthiness to reside in God's Kingdom for which they endure suffering.

◆ RESPONSORIAL PSALM 96: This psalm of praise calls us to praise God above all other gods, for indeed the Lord is the only God. His are the "marvelous works" we proclaim in the refrain; his are the salvation and glory we announce to the peoples and nations of our world.

◆ GOSPEL: Twice Jesus calls the Pharisees hypocrites. In last Saturday's Gospel, we had a clear sense of the hypocritical nature of the Pharisees for Jesus criticized them for not practicing what they preach. Today, Jesus identifies their phoniness as hypocrisy. What they preach is leading people to Gehenna, rather than to the Kingdom of heaven. Would that the Pharisees would proclaim God who sits on his throne in heaven!

The Roman Missal

The proper Collect for today, found in the Proper of Saints at August 27, des ibes St. Monica as one who wept "motherly tears . . . for the conversion of her son Augustine." The Prayer over the Offerings and the Prayer after Communion are taken from the Common of Holy Men and Women: For Holy Women, and either Preface I or Preface II of Saints is the Preface to be used for today.

Today's Saint

St. Monica (c. 33–387) knew the pain of disappointment, an unfaithful husband named Patricius who drank too much, and a promiscuous son, St. Augustine of Hippo, who lived an immoral youth. Through patience and love, her husband had a change of heart, choosing to become a Christian. St. Augustine's conversion was a much more difficult task. St. Monica prayed constantly and fasted daily, but nothing seemed to work, so she consulted St. Ambrose, bishop of Milan, for guidance. Through the intervention of God the two of them managed to lead St. Augustine to the waters of Baptism. St. Monica exemplifies that unconditional love and persistence are portals for God's saving grace.

(#426)   white

**T
U
E 28**
Memorial of
St. Augustine,
Bishop and Doctor
of the Church

The Liturgy of the Word

◆ FIRST READING: Paul offers encouraging words meant to bolster the Thessalonians in their faith as they face deception from false teachers who claim to be preaching a message that comes from Paul himself. As part of Paul's encouragement, he offers a prayer to strengthen the Thessalonians in their words and actions. The prayer recognizes the Lord Jesus Christ and God the Father as their source of love and endless encouragement.

◆ RESPONSORIAL PSALM 96: In light of the First Reading, the refrain of the Responsorial Psalm affirms that the Lord will come to judge the earth. This is the day for which the Thessalonians prepare as they struggle to remain faithful to Paul's message, not that of false teachers. The Lord's judgment will rest on justice for justice characterizes his everlasting reign. Because of this, the heavens and the earth exult!

◆ GOSPEL: More "woes" face the Pharisees. An additional two times, Jesus calls them hypocrites. They pay tithes, but forget the more importance facets of the Law: "judgment and mercy and fidelity." They follow purity laws, but their internal motivation lacks humility. Arrogance is incentive. Their blindness to Jesus and the Kingdom of heaven prevents them from looking the same inside and outside. May the woes Jesus' addresses to the Pharisees leads us to reflect on our own consistency between our external and internal selves.

The Roman Missal

The Prayer over the Offerings and the Prayer after Communion are all proper for today, located at August 28. In the Collect we pray for the same spirit as that which inspired St. Augustine to thirst for "the sole fount of true wisdom." The Prayer over the Offerings prays that this Eucharist may be for us "the sign of unity / and the bond of charity"; we can recall how that was a major theme of St. Augustine's

preaching about the Eucharist. The Prayer after Communion echoes Augustinian preaching on the Eucharist once again as it asks that "being made members of his Body, / we may become what we have received." The Preface of Holy Pastors would be a most apt choice for today, although either Preface I or II of Saints would be acceptable.

Today's Saint

St. Augustine of Hippo (354–430) is one of the four great Latin Fathers of the Church. Augustine was born in North Africa in present-day Algeria. His mother was St. Monica and his father, Patricius, a pagan. Augustine showed early promise as a scholar, but he disappointed his mother by espousing Manicheism (gnostic religion) and leading a hedonistic life (a life devoted soley to pleasure), even living with a mistress with whom he had a child. Eventually, due to Monica's prayers, he decided to become a Christian and was baptized by St. Ambrose in Milan. He became a priest, and later, the bishop of Hippo. Augustine was a prolific writer and is credited with writing one of the first autobiographies, his *Confessions*. His books, homilies, and letters are a rich source of theological insight still mined today by students of every Christian denomination or ecclesial community.

(#427; Gospel #634)   red

**W
E 29
D**
Memorial of the
Passion of St. John
the Baptist

The Liturgy of the Word

◆ FIRST READING: Paul and his companions in the mission of preaching the Gospel worked and took no food for free when they were among the Thessalonians. The false preachers among the Thessalonians do not imitate Paul and his companions, but rather choose to act not according to "the tradition" they received from them. According to Paul, one must be willing to work in order to eat. Nothing comes for free but the grace of God.

◆ RESPONSORIAL PSALM 128: Those who follow the ways of the Lord, the Lord will bless. Paul was encouraging the Thessalonians in the First Reading to continue to walk in the ways of the Lord. Psalm 128 tells us that those who do walk in the Lord's ways will feast on the fruit of his handiwork. They will know prosperity.

◆ THE Gospel for the Passion of John the Baptist is the evangelist Mark's account of the Baptist's death. Of note is that King Herod feared John because he was a "righteous and holy man." John's words confused, but intrigued Herod, yet it was Herod who imprisoned him. It was also Herod who granted the request of the daughter of Herodias, his brother Philip's wife, for the head of John the Baptist. Knowing the authenticity of the message he preached, John's disciples gave him the proper burial.

The Roman Missal

The texts for the memorial are to be found in the Proper of Saints at August 29. The Collect reminds us that St. John the Baptist was a forerunner (precursor) of the Lord not only in his birth, but also in his death. We pray in this prayer that "we, too, may fight hard / for the confession" of what God teaches. The Prayer over the Offerings employs imagery and phrases closely associated with the Baptist ("make straight your paths"; "that voice crying in the desert") in the way it asks that the offerings have an effect in our lives. The text for the Preface, "The mission of the Precursor," is given along with the other texts for this Mass, and it is the same Preface as used on the Nativity of St. John the Baptist in June (the text with music can be found there if the Preface is to be sung). The Prayer

after Communion prays that we will recognize both what the sacrament signifies and what it effects in us.

Today's Saint

"I tell you, among those born of women, no one is greater than John," Jesus told the crowds (Luke 7:28). John the Baptist, the forerunner, came to prepare the way of the Lord, and he did that from the first moments of his life. In his mother's womb, he leapt for joy at the nearness of the Lord. As an adult he preached repentance to the people, preparing them for the coming of the Kingdom, and baptizing them with water so that they might be prepared to receive baptism "with the Holy Spirit and with fire." At his death, John prepared the way for the Lord. He boldly told Herod that he was violating the Law in taking his brother's widow as his wife, and Herod had him arrested and imprisoned and then executed.

THU 30 (#428) green Weekday

The Liturgy of the Word

◆ FIRST READING: The next three and a half weeks, our the weekday First Reading come from St. Paul's First Letter to the Corinthians. We begin today with the opening verses of the letter — Paul's greeting to the Corinthians. In the greeting Paul affirms how the Corinthians have every spiritual gift they need as they live in the interim until Christ comes again in glory. How the Corinthians used and viewed their spiritual gifts caused divisions within the community that Paul would address later in his letter.

◆ RESPONSORIAL PSALM 145: Today's refrain is the opening verse of Psalm 145. Together with the psalmist declare that we will praise the Lord's name forever. We thank God as Paul did in the First Reading

for the many ways God has blesses his people.

◆ GOSPEL: The Gospel sounds like an Advent reading! "Stay awake," Jesus tells his disciples. The disciples do not know the day when the Lord will come. Neither do we. But we must be prepared for the coming of the Son of Man. Jesus calls us to be the wise and faithful servant whom the master puts in charge of his household. Regardless of when the Son of Man comes, may he find us not having lost our patience for his arrival, but rather distributing food to everyone!

FRI 31 (#429) green Weekday

The Liturgy of the Word

◆ FIRST READING: Ours is the wisdom of Christ crucified not the signs or philosophical rhetoric of others. While the Cross might seem foolish to those in the world who are passing away, Paul shows us again, that the Cross is true wisdom to those whom God saves. From the Cross comes life — the life of resurrection, although Paul does not complete his presentation of this truth until the climactic fifteenth chapter of 1 Corinthians. God's wisdom surpasses human wisdom. Those of us who preach the Gospel preach God's wisdom, offering its promise to others.

◆ RESPONSORIAL PSALM 33: The connection between the Responsorial Psalm and the First Reading lies in the contrast between God's Word and the human word found in Psalm 33. This parallels the contrast Paul makes between divine wisdom and human wisdom. The Lord's plan because it came into being through his Word, will last forever, but human plans will perish. We confidently attest to how full the earth is with the Lord's goodness as we pray the refrain.

◆ GOSPEL: The contrast between the foolish and the wise continues in the Gospel reading of the parable of the ten virgins. How foolish were the five virgins who did not bring oil for their lamps! One wonders about the wisdom of the give virgins who did have oil but sent the foolish ones to buy oil from a merchant at midnight. The bridegroom came while they were away, but would there even have been oil for purchase in the wee hours of the morning? "Stay awake" is Jesus' message for the second day in a row.

September 2018

Month of Our Lady of Sorrows

S A T 1 (#430)   green
Weekday

Optional Memorial of the Blessed Virgin Mary / white

The Liturgy of the Word

◆ FIRST READING: Paul continues to elaborate on the theme of the foolish and the wise applying it to the Corinthians' own experience. Before God chose them, they were foolish, although wise according to the standards of this world. In Christ Jesus, who is the Wisdom of God, the Corinthians boast, for they now know God's wisdom. A parallel theme Paul begins to develop in this passage in that of the weak and the strong. When the divisions in the Corinthian community occur, Paul always advises them to consider the impact their decisions will have on the weak among them.

◆ RESPONSORIAL PSALM 33: In the First Reading, Paul described how God chose both the foolish and the weak in the world as his own. In the refrain, we recognize that the ones the Lord has chosen are blessed. Psalm 33, a psalm of praise was also yesterday's Responsorial Psalm. Later verses in the psalm compose the stanzas for today. In these verses, we see the Lord's watches over those who fear him and saves them from famine and death. Our soul is the soul who waits for the Lord. As Christians, ours is the wisdom of patience as we await the return of Christ Jesus, the Wisdom of God.

◆ GOSPEL: Two of the three servants doubled the amount of money their master gave them. The third buried the money. We know the master's response when he returns. Two of the servants are good and faithful; the other is wicked and lazy. He could have at least put it in the bank to earn interest. Obviously, Jesus calls us to be good and faithful servants as we await the Master's return. How will we invest all that God has given us?

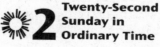
(#125)   green
2 Twenty-Second Sunday in Ordinary Time

The Liturgy of the Word

◆ FIRST READING: Moses instructs the people to listen and observe the Lord's commandments. By living the commandments, the people of Israel will show their wisdom to other nations. Because of their witness, others will know how deeply the Lord loves his people. The Lord's law is just like no other law.

◆ RESPONSORIAL PSALM 15: In the words of Psalm 15, we attest that those who do justice will live in the Lord's presence. We follow the Lord's law of truth, of kindness toward our neighbors, of honor to all who fear the Lord.

◆ SECOND READING: The Word requires both hearing and action. Caring for those whom society deems the least constitutes doing the Word. In humility, we invite the Word into our hearts for the salvation of our souls.

◆ GOSPEL: Our motivations, our thoughts, our inners workings, these taint us and cause us to do evil. Evil is not our failure to follow the external prescriptions of the law. This is the evil of which the Pharisees accused Jesus' disciples. In response to the Pharisees, Jesus points out their hypocrisy between their what is in their hearts and their strict adherence to the law.

The Roman Missal

The Mass texts for today are found in the Ordinary Time section of the Proper of Time.

The Gloria and the Creed are sung or said today. The Collect reminds us of our absolute dependence on God as we turn to him beseeching that he "nurture in us what is good" and keep safe what he has nurtured; thus are we reminded of the constant care God offers us.

The Prayer over the Offerings in effect points to the sacramental principle and the efficacy of symbols in liturgical celebration as it asks that this offering may "accomplish in power . . . what it celebrates in mystery."

The Prayer after Communion calls the Eucharist "the food of charity," thus reminding us that the Eucharist should bear fruit in us by stirring us up to serve God in our neighbor.

Other Ideas

On Monday, Labor Day is celebrated in the United States and Canada. Many Catholics do not know the rich social justice tradition defending the rights and dignity of the worker. Many encyclicals, particularly the famed *Rerum novarum*, as well as the documents of the Second Vatican Council, specifically, *Gaudium et spes*, speak to issues related to labor and laborers. The USCCB issues a statement each year on Labor Day. Consider publishing it online and in the bulletin for your community. This is a good day to highlight the great challenges faced in this country by the "working poor." Include prayers for labor-related issues in the Universal Prayer. There are multiple resources available on the USCCB website, including guidelines for the Examination of Conscience for Business Leaders (go to www.usccb.org/issues-and-action/human-life-and-dignity/labor-employment/upload/labor-day-statement-supplemental-aid.pdf).

(#431)   white

MON 3 Memorial of St. Gregory the Great, Pope and Doctor of the Church

Optional Proper Mass for Labor Day / white

The Liturgy of the Word

◆ FIRST READING: Paul speaks to his brothers and sisters in the Corinthian community about how he approached his ministry with them. His words reflect humility. He did not preach to them in sizable, multisyllable words that were difficult to comprehend. He did not preach with an arrogance that said he claimed to know everything. Rather, Paul admits he was afraid perhaps because the message he brought was so beyond human wisdom. Yet God chose him to proclaim a powerful message. The

Corinthians should base their faith on the power of God.

◆ RESPONSORIAL PSALM 119: We pray Psalm 119 frequently during the liturgical year. It is the longest psalm in the psalter. Today's verses come from approximately halfway through the psalm. They communicate in first-person language the psalmist's love for the Lord's commands and his resulting "understanding" and "discernment" that comes from the Lord's words. The wisdom the psalmist gains from the Lord's instructions corresponds to the Wisdom Paul preaches.

◆ GOSPEL: The Spirit filled Paul. On a Sabbath, in the synagogue in his hometown, Jesus reads aloud Isaiah 61:1–2. Jesus' citation of Isaiah reveals his mission to the people in the synagogue and to us. He is God's anointed one. His mission is freedom and healing. His mission is grace as communicated in his "gracious words." Yet the people in his hometown struggled with his identity and rose up against him. Jesus recognizes this and proceeds to tell them of the widow of Zarephath to whom Elijah was sent, the Naaman the Syrian, the man with leprosy, whom Elisha healed. God's power extended to these outsiders and will continue to do so through Jesus even when his "own native place" turns against him.

The Roman Missal

All the orations, proper for the day, are found in the Proper of Saints at September 3. The Collect points to the way St. Gregory was exemplary in his shepherding role in the Church as pope. The Prayer over the Offerings recalls the forgiveness that comes to us through the Eucharist, since it notes how "through its offering" God has "loosed the offenses of all the world." The Prayer after Communion uses the image of Christ the teacher to ask that

those who have been fed with the living bread may learn God's truth, and express it in works of charity." The appropriate Preface to use for today would be either the Preface of Holy Pastors or Preface I or II of the Saints.

The Mass "For the Sanctification of Human Labor" (Masses for Various Needs and Occasions, #26) may be used on this Labor Day with Preface V of the Sundays in Ordinary Time.

Today's Saint

St. Gregory the Great (540–604) was a mayor, a monk, a pope, and a writer. Unhappy with his life as mayor of Rome, St. Gregory allocated half of his fortune to the poor and the other half to the foundation of seven monasteries. After joining a monastery in pursuit of a simple life, he was elected to the papacy. As pope, he cared for the poor, implemented the reforms to improve Church governance and clerical behavior, promoted the monastic vocation, and renewed the liturgy. His name is often associated with Gregorian chant (plainsong) and Eucharistic Prayer II (along with St. Hippolytus). A prolific writer and Doctor of the Church, St. Gregory composed numerous theological texts and is cited 374 times in St. Thomas Aquinas' *Summa Theologiae*.

(#432)   green

TUE 4 Weekday

The Liturgy of the Word

◆ FIRST READING: Ours is the mind of Christ. This is the message Paul gives to us as we conclude the reading of chapter 2 in his first letter to the Corinthians. A "natural" person of this world does not follow the Spirit of God because it is foolish to do so. We who are "spiritual," however, receive the Spirit's wisdom openly. The mind of Christ allows us to see ourselves and the world in spiritual terms. The wisdom of Christ's mind helps us to know everything comes from God and God infuses his Spirit all he has created.

◆ RESPONSORIAL PSALM 145: We affirm the "Lord is just" in the refrain. Today's verses describe God's graciousness and mercy and God's kindness and compassion. The psalmist attests to God's faithfulness and holiness as well as his care for those who struggle. We ponder God's glorious and everlasting kingdom and our possibility of sharing in it.

◆ GOSPEL: From Nazareth, Jesus goes to Capernaum in Galilee where again he teaches in a synagogue on a Sabbath. A man possessed by a demonic spirit approaches Jesus who, through the power of his word, silences the evil spirit and commands him to exit the man. The power and authority of Jesus amazes the people. We recognize Jesus' power to be the power of God and the Spirit alive in him to be the Spirit of God. Jesus is fulfilling his mission he gave voice to when he read the scroll with the words of the prophet Isaiah. Of course, the Good News of Jesus would spread!

W E D 5 (#433) green
Weekday

The Liturgy of the Word

◆ FIRST READING: In these nine verses, Paul begins to lay out many of the major themes of his first letter to the Corinthians. Among them are the contrast between spirit and flesh, which the Corinthians need to place their allegiance in, and how to address the divisions within the community. At the end of the reading, Paul identifies the Corinthians are "God's coworkers," "God's field," and "God's building." All three of these images emphasize that, as people of faith,

the Corinthians belong to God in Christ and together they are the place in which the Word of God grows and develops. No longer confined to a four-walled building, God's Word lives in his people. These people, sinful and human as they are, Paul will go on to identify as the Body of Christ.

◆ RESPONSORIAL PSALM 33 continues the focus on God's chosen people we saw at the end of the First Reading. The refrain affirms the blessedness of those whom the Lord has chosen. How blessed we are to be God's coworkers, and the field and building in which God's word takes root and resounds for others to hear. We rejoice in our God and trust in his name! How grateful we are that God fashions our hearts!

◆ GOSPEL: Still in Capernaum, Jesus leaves the synagogue after exorcising the man's evil spirit and proceeds to Simon's house. While in the house, he extends his healing grace to Simon's mother-in-law who was suffering under the weight of a high fever. The mother-in-law's immediate response to the Jesus' healing words is service. As sunset comes this day, we witness the effect of Jesus exorcising the man's demon and healing the Simon's mother-in-law: two single episodes lead to exorcism of many demons and the healing of many who were sick. The demons recognize Jesus' power when they identify him as the "Son of God." Despite the crowds clinging to him, the next day Jesus' informs them his proclamation of the Kingdom of God must extend to people of other towns. No one citizenry possesses God's Kingdom. All those who believe in his Son are kingdom people.

T H U 6 (#434) green
Weekday

The Liturgy of the Word

◆ FIRST READING: Paul cites both Job 5:13 and Psalm 94:11 as he instructs the Corinthians to espouse the wisdom of God, not the wisdom of the world. To God, the world's wisdom is foolishness, and to the world, God's wisdom is folly. Paul attempts to show the Corinthians that no divisions should exist among them—no arguments about whom to pledge their loyalty—for everyone and everything belongs to Christ and Christ belongs to God.

◆ RESPONSORIAL PSALM 24: Today's refrain is verse 1 of Psalm 24 and echoes the conclusion of the First Reading by declaring the earth and all that is in it belong to the Lord. This processional psalm invites us to ascend the Lord's mountain to receive the blessing he offers to those who seek him.

◆ GOSPEL: Jesus moved on to proclaim the Good News in the synagogues of Judea. By the Lake of Gennesaret the crowd again attempted to get as close as they could to him to listen to God's word. Jesus choose to get into Simon's boat and teach the crowds from there. After instructing the crowd, Jesus instructs Simon to lower a net for a catch, despite Simon's objection on the grounds they had caught nothing all night. In Jesus is abundance. In Jesus is forgiveness. Simon found both as the net filled with fish and he asks for Jesus' mercy. James and John, along with Simon immediately followed the Lord and accepted his mission to catch people.

F R I 7 (#435) green
Weekday

The Liturgy of the Word

◆ FIRST READING: Since we belong to Christ and Christ belongs to God, we are Christ's servants and caretakers of the divine mysteries. We are to be trustworthy in our ministry. Ours is not to judge others or to even judge ourselves as we serve. Paul is clear that the Lord judges him, and ultimately the Lord judges us when he comes at the "appointed time."

◆ RESPONSORIAL PSALM 37: The Responsorial Psalm addresses the question of good and evil in the world, and our responsibility for it. In this way, it follows well upon Paul's teachings in the First Reading about our responsibility as stewards of God's mysteries. As the refrain announces, salvation for the just comes from the Lord. Those who reject evil and do good will live with the Lord forever.

◆ GOSPEL: We move ahead to end of Luke 5 where we find the scribes and Pharisees inquiring of Jesus as to why his disciples do not fast, but rather eat and drink. Jesus responds with a rhetorical question that alludes to the absurdity of wedding guests fasting while the bridegroom is present. When the bridegroom leaves, the guests will fast. Jesus then shares a parable about the relationship between the new and the old. New wine must logically be poured into new wineskins. As disciples, we are believers in the newness of Jesus.

S A T 8 (#636) white
Feast of the Nativity of the Blessed Virgin Mary

About Today's Feast

Exactly nine months after the Solemnity of the Immaculate Conception of the Blessed Virgin Mary (December 8), we come to an observance in honor of Mary's birth. This is one of only three birthdays in the Church's calendar, the other two being the birthdays of Jesus and of John the Baptist. This solemnity, like all Marian days, is less about Mary than it is about the

wondrous work of God in Mary. As St. Andrew of Crete said in a homily long ago, "The present festival, the birth of the Mother of God, is the prelude, while the final act is the foreordained union of the Word with flesh. . . . Justly then do we celebrate this mystery since it signifies for us a double grace. . . . Today this created world is raised to the dignity of a holy place for him who made all things. The creature is newly prepared to be a divine dwelling place for the Creator" (Office of Readings, Volume IV, p. 1371).

The Liturgy of the Word

◆ FIRST READING, OPTION 1: Micah's prophecy tells us that the ruler of Israel will come from Bethlehem-Ephrathah, one too small to even be among Judah's clans. Christians see in the reference to the woman who will give birth, a reference to Mary. The greatness of her Son is God's greatness. Her Son is peace.

◆ FIRST READING, OPTION 2: Paul reminds us that when we love God, all things "work for good." Mary was called according to God's purpose and will. God knew from the very beginning what her role would be, and that she would give birth to his Son. God called her, from the beginning of time to be the Mother of God. God justified and glorified her. God calls us all with a specific vocation and mission. We, too, will know God's justification and glory.

◆ RESPONSORIAL PSALM 13: The refrain comes from Isaiah 61:10 and expresses the prophet's joy at both the restoration of Jerusalem and his own salvation. It mirrors Mary's expression of joy in the Magnificat. The brief two verses from Psalm 13 communicate the psalmist's thanksgiving for the goodness and mercy of the Lord present in his life.

◆ GOSPEL: The long form of the Gospel reading includes Matthew's genealogy of Jesus who the evangelist tells us is the Christ. The short form of the Gospel begins with the birth narrative of Jesus. Matthew's account of Jesus' birth records Mary's pregnancy by the Holy Spirit and Joseph's desire to quietly divorce her so she didn't experience shame. The Lord's angel calmed Joseph's fears and he went on to take Mary as his wife and into his home. Jesus, Emmanuel, is born fulfilling Isaiah's prophecy. There is a longer and a shorter form of today's Gospel.

The Roman Missal

The prayers of the day make it clear that this feast of Mary's birth is really all about Jesus. The Collect and the Prayer over the Offerings speak not of Mary's birth, but of the birth of her son "who from her was pleased to take flesh." We remember not so much what Mary did, as what God did for her. The Gloria is sung or said today.

☀ 9 (#128) green
Twenty-Third Sunday in Ordinary Time

The Liturgy of the Word

◆ FIRST READING: The prophet's message offers hope to a frightened people. God will come to save them. What marvelous healing will take place when God comes: the blind will see, the deaf will hear, the lame will leap, and the mute will sing! Nature will reflects God's coming, too, as life-giving waters will appear in deserts and grasslands, on dry ground and within burning sands.

◆ RESPONSORIAL PSALM 146 resounds with praise for God who comes in our midst, echoing Isaiah's words that the Lord will give sight to the blind. Indeed, all the downtrodden, the Lord will raise.

◆ SECOND READING: Favoritism has no place in Christian assemblies. Our attention should go equally to the rich and the poor, for human distinctions matter not in God's community. In fact, James reminds his beloved brothers and sisters in faith, that God chose the poor to acquire the riches of faith and inherit God's Kingdom.

◆ GOSPEL: Jesus fulfills Isaiah's words and heals a deaf man with a speech impediment. In Jesus, the deaf hear and the mute speak! Jesus opens our lives to the gift of salvation he offers. Time after time, he astonishes us, like he did the crowds centuries ago. Will we proclaim him as they did?

The Roman Missal

The Mass texts for today are found in the Ordinary Time section of the Proper of Time.

The Gloria and the Creed are sung or said today. The Collect gives a description of those gathered to enact worship: they are redeemed, adopted by God, and are therefore "beloved sons and daughters." We pray that in belonging and in believing in Christ, we "may receive true freedom / and an everlasting inheritance."

The Prayer over the Offerings designates two fruits we are hoping for as a result of making the offering this day: that it might allow us to "do fitting homage" to God's "divine majesty," and that it may unite us with one another in mind and heart.

The Prayer after Communion acknowledges that the celebration of the Eucharist nourishes us with both "Word and heavenly Sacrament"; we should never forget the inherent unity of the Liturgy of the Word and the Liturgy of the Eucharist, the two parts of the Mass that are so intimately connected that they form one act of worship.

Other Ideas

This week the Church celebrates the Exaltation of the Holy Cross, commemorating the finding of wood from the "true cross" by St. Helena, mother of Constantine. Encourage parishioners to bring crosses from home to be blessed at Mass. Use the Order of Blessing of Religious Articles (chapter 44 in the BB). If your parish has multiple processional and other crosses, consider setting up a display with information somewhere people might enjoy seeing it, such as where you extend after-Mass hospitality. Educate the community about this remarkable family, perhaps including information about holy relics and their place in Catholic piety. Visit relics that are held by your local cathedral, monasteries, or religious communities. Rosh Hashanah, the Jewish New Year, begins today (and concludes on Tuesday, September 11). And the United States will observe the National Day of Mourning and Remembrance on September 11. This year is the seventeenth anniversary of this tragic event. Both of these occasions can be recognized in the Universal Prayer this Sunday.

M O N 10 (#437) green Weekday

The Liturgy of the Word

◆ FIRST READING: Immorality was a major issue in the Corinthian community, and Paul tackles it head on in today's reading. Those living immoral lives, including those participating in incestuous relation-ships, and then boasting about their corrupt choices, the community is to deliver to Satan. Their flesh Satan will destroy, but their spirit the Lord will save. Using the analogy of yeast, Paul instructs the Corinthians to root out corruption and become new—new unleavened bread. Made anew through Christ, they celebrate the Paschal Lamb with genuineness and honesty—the qualities of the new unleavened bread. In Christ, they are changed.

◆ RESPONSORIAL PSALM 5: The contrast between good and evil continues in the Responsorial Psalm. The psalmist knows that God hates evil, deceit, and arrogance. On account of this, the psalmist asks the Lord to direct him to justice. Those who act uprightly will reside in the Lord's care and protection forever.

◆ GOSPEL: Jesus has taught on the Sabbath, exorcised demons on the Sabbath, and worked with his disciples in the fields on the Sabbath. So, it should be no surprise to the watchful scribes and Pharisees how he will respond to the man with a withered right hand on a Sabbath in the synagogue. In fact, he beats the scribes and Pharisees at their game, calling the man forward and then directly inquiring of them whether it is legal to do good instead of evil on the Sabbath. Jesus does not wait for their response. He simply heals the man's hand. Jesus is Lord of the Sabbath. His mission is to "save life," to make people whole. His mission is overcoming death. How threatening this is the scribes and Pharisees!

T U E 11 (#438) green Weekday

The Liturgy of the Word

◆ FIRST READING: Paul is upset that Christians are suing members of their own faith community in pagan courts when they should be able to resolve their differences within the community of believers. Only the just will inherit the Kingdom of God, but some among the Corinthians are acting unjustly, behaving immorally. Paul provides a list of vices that will not permit people from entering God's Kingdom and then concludes with a reminder to the Corinthians of their justification in Jesus Christ through Baptism.

◆ RESPONSORIAL PSALM 149: The next to last psalm in the psalter offers us an invitation to sing praise to the Lord in the assembly of his people. The psalm is a proclamation of the Lord's love for us, and all his people. Let our voices resound in "Alleluias" to the glory of God's name for the world to hear!

◆ GOSPEL: Having restored the man's hand that once was withered, Jesus leaves the synagogue and heads to the mountain to pray. The evangelist Luke does not describe what Jesus prayed for, but simply that he prayed to God through the whole night. The next day, Jesus chose Twelve from out of his disciples as Apostles. Together, they journeyed down the mountain where they encountered more disciples and crowds who had come from near and far to witness Jesus' power, the power of the Word and the power of healing.

W E D 12 (#439) green
Weekday

Optional Memorial of the Most Holy Name of Mary / white

The Liturgy of the Word

◆ FIRST READING: Paul offers his advice, which he clearly identifies as not the Lord's commandment, about how the Corinthians should live in the present before the Parousia. The status quo ought to be the norm. Changes in relationships do not need to take place for the world is not eternal. It is passing away. Paul's recommendation to

Christians is that they live knowing that their life in the world is only temporary as they await the Lord's coming.

◆ RESPONSORIAL PSALM 45 is a song for the marriage of a Davidic king. Today's verses come from the latter half of the psalm and describe the beauty of the bride, the king's daughter who will now be queen. The wedding is a joyous occasion as weddings are today. Gladness fills the air as the bride and her attendants enter the palace. When this world has passed away, the entrance of God's people into the divine Kingdom is sure to be an occasion of unparalleled joy.

◆ GOSPEL: Jesus has called the Twelve Apostles from out of his disciples. Today begins the section in Luke known as the "Sermon on the Plain," in which Jesus instructs not only the Apostles, but all of his disciples about what it means to follow him. At times, Jesus also addresses his words to the crowds gathered. The first of his teachings is what we know as the Beatitudes, statements of blessedness. Four statements of woe follow the four Beatitudes. The theme of joy connects the Gospel reading with the First Reading and Responsorial Psalm. Our reward will be great in heaven!

Today's Optional Memorial

Three days after the Feast of the Nativity of the Blessed Virgin Mary, the Church observes an optional memorial honoring the Most Holy Name of Mary. In Hebrew, the name *Mary* is "Miryam," or "Miriam," which means "bitter sea." The name is an important one for the Jewish people: Miriam, the sister of Moses, sang in thanksgiving to God after the crossing of the Red Sea, and it was a common name for Jewish women (in the Gospel account of the Resurrection of Christ,

three women visit the tomb in the rock, and all of them are named Mary!). In the Middle Ages, the name *Mary* was often translated as "star of the sea," a title attributed to Mary.

T H U 13 (#440) white
Memorial of St. John Chrysostom, Bishop and Doctor of the Church

The Liturgy of the Word

◆ FIRST READING: Once again Paul addresses the issue of arrogance in the Corinthian community. This time arrogance occurs when those who eat meat sacrificed to idols do not recognize that they can cause harm to those in the community who are unaware that the one God of Jesus Christ is the only God. Paul wants the strong among the Corinthians to know their responsibility for the weak, for together they are one community of faith.

◆ RESPONSORIAL PSALM 139: How personally God knows us. How deeply God cares about our life's journeys. How familiar God is with our habits. And, why would he not be? As the psalmist's words remind us, God created us in our mother's womb. Our relationship with God is ongoing. As we pray the psalm, we ask God to continue to guide us and to lead us back when we go astray.

◆ GOSPEL: Jesus' instructions to his disciples seem at odds with commonsense. Love our enemies. Do good to those who hate us. Bless the ones who slander us. Pray for those who harm us. Turn the other cheek. Give another piece of our clothing. What could be the rationale behind Jesus' words? Nothing less than a disciple's mercy should mirror God's mercy. When we live God's mercy, we champion the qualities of God's Kingdom. We will know the joy of the Kingdom.

The Roman Missal

The prayers for today's memorial are proper and found in the Proper of Saints.

Today's Saint

After a short stint as a monk, St. John Chrysostom (c. 350–407), whose surname means "golden mouth," returned to Antioch, where he was ordained a priest and became a noted preacher. During his free time he wrote commentaries on the Pauline letters as well as the Gospel according to Matthew and according to John. Due to his reputation for preaching and writing, he was appointed bishop of Constantinople. As bishop he initiated a program of reform that challenged clerical abuses and the extravagant lifestyle of the upper class. His reforms were not always received well, especially on the part of Empress Eudoxia; therefore, he was exiled from the city for a period of time. St. John Chrysostom bears two distinctive titles in the Church: Father of the Church and Doctor of the Church.

F R I (#638)   red

14 Feast of the Exaltation of the Holy Cross

About Today's Feast

Today's Feast of the Exaltation of the Holy Cross began as a commemoration of a unique event: the miraculous finding of the True Cross by St. Helena, the mother of Emperor Constantine. Helena journeyed to the Holy Land to see the place of the Lord's Crucifixion. She found the spot and tore down a temple she found there honoring the Greek goddess Aphrodite, and she began to build a new basilica in honor of Christ. As they began to lay the foundations, the remains of three crosses were discovered, but they did not know which was the true Cross. The Cross of Christ was eventually revealed when a dying woman was healed after touching one of the crosses. The basilica was completed, and the Church in both East and West observes this feast in honor of the Cross on the anniversary of dedication.

The Liturgy of the Word

◆ FIRST READING: The Israelites grumble against both Moses and God, and in response God sends serpents among them. The people confess their sin to Moses and ask him to intercede to the Lord on their behalf. Moses follows the Lord instructions to mount a bronze serpent on a pole for the people to gaze upon. When they do, they shall live. Christians see in serpent on the pole a foreshadowing of Christ on the Cross. The Cross of Christ is the Cross of life, not death.

◆ RESPONSORIAL PSALM 78: Often in Israelite history, God's people lacked faithfulness to the covenant. Sometimes we forget the Lord's works. The Lord forgives our sin and extends mercy to us. May this psalm help us remember the Lord and his teaching, and those areas in our lives we need to call to mind the covenant in new ways.

◆ SECOND READING: The passage is from an early Christian hymn cited by Paul. The hymn speaks eloquently of how Christ came in "human likeness" and how he humbled himself, accepting Death on a Cross. His exaltation by God followed. This is why generations have confessed Christ as Lord and why we witness to his glory of God in Christ today.

◆ GOSPEL: The Son of Man descended from heaven to earth, becoming human like us in all things but sin. The Son of Man ascended back from earth to heaven to reside forever with his Father in the Kingdom of glory. The reference to Moses lifting up the serpent is a direct connection to the First Reading. The Son of Man is lifted up so that we who believe might receive the gift of eternal life. He saved the world.

The Roman Missal

All the texts are taken from September 14 in the Proper of Saints. The Gloria is sung or said today. The Creed is not said at this Mass, since the feast falls on a Thursday. The Preface is proper for today, "The victory of the glorious Cross," and the text, with and without musical notation, is located right there amid the other texts for the day. This Preface puts forth a very positive theology of the Cross, not focused on Christ's sufferings, but rather on the new life that flows from his sacrifice.

S A T (#442; Gospel, #639)   white

15 Memorial of Our Lady of Sorrows

About Today's Memorial

In the Gospel according to Luke, as Simeon holds the infant Christ in his arms, he tells Mary that her life will be full of suffering. Her son will be "opposed," and "a sword will pierce [Mary's] soul, too" (Luke 2:34, 35). That prophecy is fulfilled when Jesus is crucified and Mary stands at the foot of his Cross. The image of the *Mater Dolorosa*, the Sorrowful Mother, is the subject of one of the most famous works of art, Michelangelo's *Pietà*, which shows Mary with the dead Christ in her arms, her face revealing peace and acceptance, and yet profound grief. Today we ask the intercession of this sorrowful Mother for all mothers who suffer for their children, and especially those who have lost a child.

The Liturgy of the Word

◆ FIRST READING: Paul has been so concerned about the divisions in the Corinthian community caused by such issues as immorality, the strong eating meat sacrificed to idols, and people dividing their allegiance among Paul, Apollos, Cephas, and Christ. Today's reading provides us the theological reason behind Paul's concern. The meal that the Corinthians share in *is* the Body and Blood of Christ. Even though they are many, they are one just as Christ's Body is one. They must strive to overcome divisions and live the unity of the one Body.

◆ RESPONSORIAL PSALM 116: In the opening stanza, the psalmist asks how he can repay the Lord for saving him from danger. The psalmist's answer is to offer thanksgiving and take up the "cup of salvation." Psalm 116 is also the Responsorial Psalm on Holy Thursday, although with a different refrain and a few additional verses. Used today, the psalm connects to Paul's reference in the First Reading to our participation in the Blood of Christ through the cup of blessing.

◆ SEQUENCE: The sequence for today, the *Stabat Mater*, is optional. This thirteenth century text reflects on the suffering the Blessed Virgin Mary endured while watching her Son's crucifixion and death. Arrangements of the familiar hymn, "At Her Cross Her Station Keeping," may be used as the sequence.

◆ GOSPEL: Simeon's words to Mary after she and Joseph had presented Jesus in the Temple declare his destiny. Mary will witness her child's suffering and persecution. She herself will know the challenges of following the Christ, and what it means to hear God's Word and put it into action as one who believes in the Savior of the world.

The Roman Missal

All the orations are proper for today, and can be found in the Proper of Saints at September 15. The Collect draws a direct connection between yesterday's feast and today's memorial as it reminds us that when Christ was "lifted high on the Cross," his Mother was standing close by and sharing his suffering. Thus, we ask that we, with Mary, may also participate in the Passion of Christ so as to share in his Resurrection. Of course, our participation in that Paschal Mystery is effected most completely in the liturgy.

The Prayer over the Offerings describes the Blessed Virgin Mary as "a most devoted Mother" who stood by the Cross of Jesus; we can do the same by our fidelity to participation in the Eucharist.

Either Preface I or Preface II of the Blessed Virgin Mary is the Preface to be used today, but if Preface I is used, then the phrase "on the feast day" is the correct phrase to use.

The Prayer after Communion relates how our participation in "the Sacrament of eternal redemption" is a participation in the Paschal Mystery, including the suffering of Christ.

Although the Missal does not mention it, there is nothing to prevent the use of Solemn Blessing number 15, "The Blessed Virgin Mary," at the end of Mass today, particularly if your weekday Mass will see an increased attendance because of a particular devotion to the Blessed Mother under this title.

(#131) green

16 Twenty-Fourth Sunday in Ordinary Time

The Liturgy of the Word

◆ FIRST READING: This third of the four servant songs in Isaiah shows how the Servant has given himself to those who persecuted and beat him. In spite of his suffering, the Servant still professes the Lord is his help. Will anyone disprove the Lord's nearness and support of his Servant?

◆ RESPONSORIAL PSALM 116 reflects the same confidence in the Lord the servant has in the First Reading. Facing death, the psalmist calls upon the Lord who is gracious and merciful. The Lord frees his soul from death and now he walks in front of the Lord in the land of the living.

◆ SECOND READING: Faith and works are a pair. Neither exists without the other. Faith does not belong to one person and the responsibility of demonstrating faith by works to another. Our life of faith is a life of works in response to the gift of faith. Let our faith be alive in our actions!

◆ GOSPEL: The verses from chapter 8 stand as the turning point in Mark's account of the Gospel. Jesus inquires of his disciples who people say he is. His second question is personal. He wants to know who the disciples say he is. Peter's affirmation of him as the Christ leads to a warning not to let on to others about his identity, a prediction of his Passion, and an instruction to the disciples to take up their Cross and follow Jesus.

The Roman Missal

We pray that we may "serve [God] with all our heart" and so "feel the working" of his mercy in our lives (Collect).

We pray that the offering of each of us "may serve the salvation of all." We are one Body in Christ: the love and faith, the needs and hopes we each bring to our prayer touches others in ways we cannot imagine (Prayer over the Offerings).

We pray that the "heavenly gift" we have received may so work in us that God's will may prevail over our own desires (Prayer after Communion). The Gloria and the Creed are sung or said today.

Other Ideas

This week our Jewish brothers and sisters celebrate Yom Kippur, a solemn day of atonement focused on fasting and prayer. Yom Kippur is considered by many to be the most important of all the observances of the year.

This week also includes the Feast of St. Matthew, the tax collector Levi who was called by Jesus to join the Apostles and who is also one of the four evangelists. Traditions of the day include eating "silver dollar" pancakes (because Matthew was a tax collector). Encourage parishioners to spend time with the Gospel according to Matthew this week, particularly his "calling" as recounted in Matthew 9:9. Tradition holds that after the Death and Resurrection of Jesus Christ, he preached in Ethiopia, Syria, and other countries of the region. It is also held that he died a martyr. This is a good week for deepening our parishioner's understanding of what it takes to be an effective evangelist

to those who have yet to fully hear the Gospel of the Lord.

Today is Catechetical Sunday. Bless and commission the parish's catechists, particularly acknowledging those who have stepped into this important role for the first time. The Order of Blessing of Students and Teachers is found in chapter 5 of the Book of Blessings. The United States Bishops' website also provides a commissioning service that can be used (www.usccb.org/beliefs -and-teachings/how-we-teach/cate chesis/catechetical-sunday/commis sioning-service.cfm). Invite the entire community to recall their own baptismal commission to share the Good News of the Gospel. The word catechist has the Greek word "echo" or "resound" as its root. This is a good moment to remind parents that they are the primary catechists or teachers of the faith for their children. For this reason, the United States Bishops' blessing includes the option for blessing parents and guardians. Take a look at the calendar for religious education, and determine moments that would be well served with prayer resources for catechists.

M
O
N **17** (#443) green
Weekday

Optional Memorial St. Robert Bellarmine, Bishop and Doctor of the Church / white

The Liturgy of the Word

◆ FIRST READING: How human the Corinthians are! Divisions characterize their gatherings. Factions and cliques exist among them. Paul particularly concerns himself with the people who eat their own meal while others go hungry and still others become intoxicated. Paul recommends that when the Corinthians come together to eat they wait for each other. The earliest account of the institution of the Eucharist supports Paul's instructions. When the Corinthians offer the bread and

wine, they do so in remembrance of the Lord Jesus, the one Lord. They should be united as one when they participate in this meal.

◆ RESPONSORIAL PSALM 40: The refrain comes from 1 Corinthians 11:26b, a verse in the First Reading that links our participation in the Eucharist with the proclamation of the Lord's Death; a connection we also when we proclaim the mystery of faith in the Eucharistic Prayer. The psalmist recognizes that the Lord wants obedience over burnt-offerings and sin-offerings. Aligning God's will with our will is the desire of God's heart.

◆ GOSPEL: Today's Gospel reading includes the centurion's words that we now say in response to the priest's words acclaiming the consecrated host as the Lamb of God who takes away the sins of the world. As a result of the centurion's faith, Jesus heals his servant who had been at the point of death. The "good health" of the servant came from Jesus, the Savior who makes people whole.

Today's Saint

St. Robert Bellarmine (1542–1621), bishop and Doctor of the Church, was an astute scholar with a knack for diplomatically responding to the controversies of his day. As a Jesuit priest embroiled in the Protestant Reformation, he sensitively communicated through word and writing the Catholic perspective, especially regarding the relationship between Church and state. One of his most important contributions to the Church is a three-volume work, *Disputations on the Controversies of the Christian Faith*, which explained Catholic fundamentals in a nondefensive, systematic way. St. Robert, a devotee of St. Francis of Assisi, demonstrated heroic virtue by praying for his opponents, living simply, and embracing spiritual discipline.

TUE 18 (#444) green **Weekday**

The Liturgy of the Word

◆ FIRST READING: Paul identifies the Corinthians as Christ's Body. The identification of the two makes it clear why Paul desires that the Corinthians overcome their divisions and live together in unity. Living in unity does not mean negating individual differences and gifts. It means quite the opposite. Through Baptism, the one Spirit welcomes us into the one Body. The gifts God gives are many as are the roles to which God calls us. All are equally necessary and important in sustaining the living community of the one Body of Christ.

◆ RESPONSORIAL PSALM 100: The psalmist's words emphasize the close relationship of God with his people. God's enduring faithfulness leads us sing praise and thanks to him. We are the sheep of God's flock. God's flock is one, but with many sheep, just as the Body of his Son is one with many members.

◆ GOSPEL: Jesus' compassion extends toward the widow of Nain whose son has died. At the command of Jesus' words, the dead man arose. Already we see Jesus has power over death. Fear compels "all" — the disciples and the crowd — and leads them to glorify God. Jesus is not only a "great prophet," but in him God has come to his people.

WED 19 (#445) green **Weekday**

Optional Memorial of St. Januarius, Bishop and Martyr / red

The Liturgy of the Word

◆ FIRST READING: The spiritual gifts of faith, hope, and love endure. The greatest gift is love. Many of us can recite this beautiful passage and its poetic description of the importance of love. This passage from Paul is often proclaimed at the marriage liturgy. Paul proclaimed these words to the Corinthians in his continuing effort to focus them on how to build unity among themselves. When we know God face to face, we will know Love.

◆ RESPONSORIAL PSALM 33: The Lord calls us to be his people. We are blessed. Our response to God is thanks and praise for God is justice and kind. In the psalmist's words, we ask God to shower his kindness upon us. May God's kindness produce in us faith, hope, and love to build up the one Body of Christ today.

◆ GOSPEL: Jesus is speaking to the crowds about John the Baptist after his messengers had left. The illustrative sayings Jesus uses reproach those such as the scribes and Pharisees who were not baptized by John and rejected God's plan. They are also rejecting Jesus. God's wisdom active in both John and Jesus, though in different ways, will triumph.

Today's Saint

St. Januarius (c. † 305) was bishop of Benevento in Italy during the Diocletian persecutions. After suffering the fate of a martyr — being thrown to wild beasts and then beheaded — his relics were transported to Naples where it is said that a vial of his blood liquefies on three feast days related to his life: today, the day he supposedly prevented an eruption of Mount Vesuvius in 1631 (December 16), and the Saturday before the first Sunday in May, commemorating the transfer of his relics.

THU 20 (#446) red **Memorial of Sts. Andrew Kim Tae-gŏn, Priest, and Paul Chŏng Ha-sang, and Companions, Martyrs**

The Liturgy of the Word

◆ FIRST READING: Paul's words summarize the Gospel he has preached to the Corinthians. He testifies once again to the salvation that is theirs through Christ's Death and Resurrection. His presentation is that of the *kerygma*, the tradition of faith in Jesus Christ that has developed in the early Christian communities. In the end, Paul acknowledges, as he frequently does, that God's grace allows him to be the Apostle he is. God's grace compels us to proclaim the Gospel, too.

◆ RESPONSORIAL PSALM 118 is a psalm of Easter Time. This thanksgiving psalm is a fitting response to Paul's repetition of the *kerygma*. Christ is risen! For this we give thanks! Through Christ, God's mercy truly lasts forever. With the psalmist, we recognize that through the Lord's power we will not die, but live. Ours is the mission to announce the marvelous works of the Lord!

◆ GOSPEL: A Pharisee invites Jesus to eat with him in his house. A "sinful woman" seeking Jesus enters the Pharisees' house. So overcome with emotion, her tears fall on Jesus' feet and she anoints him with the oil she brought. The Pharisee, thinking Jesus cannot hear his words, mumbles about Jesus allowing the sinful woman to touch him. Jesus does hear and presents him with a parable about forgiveness. After the parable, Jesus recounts all the woman has done for him since entering the Pharisees' house, while the Pharisee has done little. Her love for Jesus is great. Her faith is the source of her salvation. The Pharisee has room for improvement in both.

The Roman Missal

All the orations for this memorial of the martyrs of Korea are proper for today, and can be found in the Proper of Saints at September 20. The Collect acknowledges the blood of these martyrs as the seed that bears fruit. The Prayer over the Offerings reminds us that in celebrating the Eucharist, we are to offer ourselves, both at the liturgy and in all of life, as it asks that through the intercession of these martyrs "we ourselves may become / a sacrifice acceptable to you / for the salvation of all the world." The Prayer after Communion labels the Eucharistic food as "the food of the valiant," thus designating it as the nourishment that strengthens us to cling faithfully to Christ and to "labor in the Church for the salvation of all." Either Preface I or Preface II of Holy Martyrs would be the appropriate choice for today.

Today's Saints

· During the eighteenth and nineteenth centuries, approximately eight thousand adherents to the Catholic faith in Korea were martyred (from 1839 to 1867); 103 of them were canonized by Pope John Paul II in 1988. The canonized martyrs were victims of a particularly heinous series of persecutions happening between 1839 and 1867. During this time, Korea was ruled by an anti-Christian dynasty that did everything possible to eliminate Catholic ideology and influence, including maliciously murdering Christian missionaries and their followers. Two of the more notable martyrs are St. Andrew Kim Taegŏn, priest and martyr; and St. Paul Chŏng Ha-sang, a layman, both of whom were dedicated to the revitalization of the Church in Korea.

(#643)   red

FRI 21 Feast of St. Matthew, Apostle and Evangelist

About Today's Feast

St. Matthew (first century), referred to as the "tax collector," is one of the Twelve Apostles and the Evangelist who authored the first of the four accounts of the Gospel. His account has a twofold purpose: one, to announce that Jesus is the eternal king of all creation; and two, to encourage faith in the face of doubt, especially regarding persecution. We have very little information about him, other than he invited Jesus to his home to dine with societal outcasts (see Matthew 9:9–13), and that he preached the Good News after the Resurrection. Tradition says he began preaching in Judea, then moved on to Ethiopia, Persia, Syria, Macedonia, and possibly Ireland. He is venerated as a martyr, even though history does not tell us how or where he died.

The Liturgy of the Word

◆ FIRST READING: The unity of Christians is Trinitarian from the earliest days. One God and Father, one Lord, and one Spirit unite all who believe. While God gifts each of us with his grace, God also calls us to different roles in the building up of the Body of Christ. God called St. Matthew as an Apostle and Evangelist and to use his gifts to uphold the sevenfold unity of the Body of Christ — one Body, one Spirit, one hope one Lord, one faith, one Baptism, one God.

◆ RESPONSORIAL PSALM 19: The heavens and the earth declare God's glory. They speak of God's wisdom evident in his Word. Their message extends throughout the whole earth. The psalmist's words connect to the words of the great commission Jesus speaks to his disciples at the of Matthew's account Gospel. They are to make disciples of *all* the

---

nations, baptizing them, and teaching them to follow the Wisdom of Jesus' commands.

◆ GOSPEL: Jesus calls Matthew as he was fulfilling his job responsibilities as a tax collector. Upon hearing Jesus two words "Follow me," Matthew follows Jesus. Ironically, Jesus led Matthew to his own home where the disciples and many other tax collectors and sinners joined them for a meal. The Pharisees, of course, cannot comprehend why Jesus eats with tax collectors and sinners and inquire of his disciples. But Jesus overhears the Pharisees and instructs them to learn about mercy.

The Roman Missal

The prayers for the feast are found in the Proper of Saints. The Gloria is said or sung today. The Preface of the Apostles is used. The Collect emphasizes the "untold mercy" of God, who chose Matthew "the tax collector" to be both Apostle and Evangelist. We pray that we may imitate him, and "hold firm in following" the Lord. The Prayer after Communion echoes the Gospel account of the call of St. Matthew: Jesus is glad to dine with this tax collector, because he "did not come to call the righteous but sinners" (Matthew 9:13). Just as Matthew rejoiced to welcome "the Savior as a guest in his home," so we rejoice to welcome Christ who has come to dwell with us through the sacrament we share. The Solemn Blessing of the Apostles may be used.

(#448)   green

SAT 22 Weekday

Optional Memorial of the Blessed Virgin Mary / white

The Liturgy of the Word

◆ FIRST READING: Some among the Corinthians denied the resurrection of the dead and some are even asking what kind of body the

---

dead will return with. Paul has built up his entire proclamation of the Gospel in his first letter up to this point. The dead are raised in Christ Jesus! When we are raised, we will share in the image of the heavenly one. Our spiritual bodies will be glorious and incorruptible. We will live forever!

◆ RESPONSORIAL PSALM 56: The psalmist faces oppression from his attackers, yet he confesses that God is with him. He exudes the confidence of faith because God has rescued him from death. The refrain paints a beautiful visual image of the psalmist walking in God's presence led by the light of all those who live in God.

◆ GOSPEL: After forgiving the sinful woman, Jesus continues his journey from town to town. The Twelve along with Mary Magdalene, Joanna, Susanna, and many others traveled with him. Surrounded by a large crowd, Jesus tells the parable of the sower. Ours is the choice where to let the seed of God's Word fall: on the path to be trampled and eaten, on rocky ground, among thorns, or on good soil. Will we hear the Word, take it into our hearts, and bear its fruit?

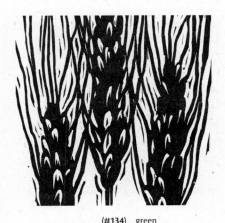

(#134)   green

23 Twenty-Fifth Sunday in Ordinary Time

The Liturgy of the Word

◆ FIRST READING: The wicked plot to persecute the just one and put him to a shameful, dishonorable death. They figure if he is the son of God, God will protect him from his enemies. Christians see in the references to the just one and the son of God, allusions to Jesus Christ.

◆ RESPONSORIAL PSALM 54: In the psalmist's words, we can hear the just one of the First Reading crying out to God for help. The wicked have risen up against him. Despite the evil they wish to bring upon him, he still acknowledges the Lord's upholds his life.

◆ SECOND READING: Human passions often cause conflict. When we covet and desire to possess wrongly, war results. Ours is the task to nurture peace. As a result, James instructs his brothers and sisters to follow "wisdom from above." God's wisdom leads to the "fruit of righteousness" sown in peace.

◆ GOSPEL: The disciples do not understand Jesus' second prediction of his Passion, Death, and Resurrection, and out of fear, they do not question him about it. The disciples argue about who's the greatest and Jesus teaches those who wish to be first will be last and will serve oth-

ers. Welcoming a child signifies welcoming Jesus and his Father.

The Roman Missal

The Mass texts for today are found in the "Ordinary Time" section of the Proper of Time. The Gloria and the Creed are sung or said today.

The Collect notes how all the commands of God's sacred Law are grounded in one foundation: the unity of love of God and love of neighbor.

The Prayer over the Offerings prays that we may truly possess what we "profess with devotion and faith"; since the context for this possession is asking God to receive our offerings, then it is the offering of ourselves in union with Christ that we are professing, and it is the offering of ourselves in union with Christ that we pray will become more and more a reality through our participation in the offering of the Eucharist.

Any one of the eight Prefaces of the Sundays in Ordinary Time are appropriate for today.

The Prayer after Communion also makes an important connection between liturgical celebration and everyday life: it asks that redemption might be ours "both in mystery [liturgical celebration] and in the manner of our life."

Other Ideas

This week is the Memorial of St. Vincent de Paul, a French priest who founded the Vincentian order and the Daughters of Charity. If your parish hosts a Vincent de Paul society, highlight current needs or promote services within the diocese that serve both the material and physical needs of those who struggle.

MON 24 (#449) green
Weekday

The Liturgy of the Word

◆ FIRST READING: Today we begin a series of First Readings from the Wisdom literature. The verses from Proverbs contain short practical sayings about how live in relationship with our neighbors and what it means to act justly and avoid evil.

◆ RESPONSORIAL PSALM 15: The focus of the Psalm 15 on living justice parallels the emphasis in the passage from Proverbs on what it means to be a just person. Like the First Reading, the Psalm 15 speaks of neither harming another person nor unjustly accusing one's neighbor. Those who live justly will reside on the Lord's holy mountain.

◆ GOSPEL: How practical and ordinary is Jesus' teaching! Of course, when we light a lamp, it gives off light! We do not light the lamp only to cover up its brightness. So, if we hear the Word of God, we must not conceal it from others. We must proclaim it! If we do not want to proclaim it, we might as well not hear it. Once again the message is: hearing and living the Word of God go together.

TUE 25 (#450) green
Weekday

The Liturgy of the Word

◆ FIRST READING: A collection of ten sayings comprises the First Reading. These various proverbs coalesce around the theme of living justly similar to yesterday's First Reading. Those who are just hear the poor's cry lest when they are in need, their cry not be heard. The Lord works in our hearts to direct us toward justice.

◆ RESPONSORIAL PSALM 119: In the refrain, we ask the Lord to guide us in following his commands. Our prayer is to know and live God's wisdom, to understand God's laws. In order to do this, we need discernment. The psalmist also prays for this gift. Knowing God accompanies us as we live his Law, we are able to remain faithful to it forever.

◆ GOSPEL: Jesus spoke the parable of the sower and explained its meaning. He offered the saying about concealing the light of a lamp. Now his mother and brothers attempts to get close to him but the size of the crowd prohibits them. Someone informs Jesus that the desire to see him. Jesus' words in response reveal to us that his mother and brothers are those who both hear and act on God's word. Listen and live the Word is our call if we desire to be close to Jesus.

WED 26 (#451) green
Weekday

Optional Memorial of Sts. Cosmas and Damian, Martyrs / red

The Liturgy of the Word

◆ FIRST READING: An unknown person referred to in Proverbs as Agur requests two things from God: that God prevent him from untruth and lying, and instead of having him live in either poverty or wealth, give him only the food he needs. His wish is never to deny the Lord or blaspheme his name because he resorts to stealing.

◆ RESPONSORIAL PSALM 119: Yesterday's Responsorial Psalm also came from Psalm 119. Today's verses come from much later in the psalm. They speak of the precious and enduring nature of God's word and the psalmist's hatred for that which is not true. The refrain reminds us Jesus' saying about the unreasonableness of hiding the light of a lamp. In the refrain, we claim the light of the Lord's word to direct our journey.

◆ GOSPEL: Jesus and his disciples sailed to Gerasenes, a terrority opposite of Galilee. While there, they faced rejection and the people asked them to leave. They returned home to Galilee, which is the setting for today's Gospel. After healing Jairus's daughter and the woman with a hemorrhage, Jesus gives the Twelve the power and authority to do the same. They will need nothing for their journey. And, when they face rejection, they are to move on as Jesus had done for the proclamation of the Kingdom of God must continue.

Today's Saints

Sts. Cosmas and Damian (c. †287) were brothers, possibly twins, who practiced medicine without accepting money for their services. They became known in the East as the *anargyroi*, meaning "moneyless ones" or "moneyless healers." As vibrant witnesses to the Christian faith, they were arrested during the Diocletian persecutions. When they refused to renounce their faith and engage in idolatrous worship, they were beheaded and cast into the sea. They are patron saints of twins, confectioners, the sightless, and many medical professions (for example, physicians, nurses, and dentists). Their names are included in Eucharistic Prayer I.

THU 27 (#452) white
Memorial of St. Vincent de Paul, Priest

The Liturgy of the Word

◆ FIRST READING: The First Reading comes from the opening chapter of Ecclesiastes, a book concerned with the meaning of human life lived in relation to the divine plan for our existence. The author declares the vanity or futility of everything. Nothing is new. Everything has existed before we existed. The passage concludes with the author stating how nothing is remembered — neither people or events of the past, present, or future. But what he does not say at this point is God knows. God remembers.

◆ RESPONSORIAL PSALM 90 is the lament of a community who has suffered hardship. The opening verse of the psalm serves as the refrain. In it, we attest to how God has been our refuge throughout the generations. In the stanzas, we pray for God's guidance throughout our days so that we might have "wisdom of heart." We cry out to God to make our work productive lest the vanity Qoheleth announces be the ultimate reality.

◆ GOSPEL: Herod concerns himself with trying to figure out Jesus' identity because he had heard about the healings and exorcisms Jesus performed, not to mention how his teaching was intriguing people. The answer to the question, "Who Jesus is?" baffled the tetrarch. Some thought Jesus to be Elijah or another ancient prophet. Still others thought John the Baptist had been raised from the dead after Herod had him beheaded. Herod desperately tried to keep seeing Jesus. His curiosity about Jesus was perhaps not for the same reasons the crowds desired to be in his company.

The Roman Missal

All the orations are found in the Proper of Saints at September 27. The Collect, not surprisingly, recognizes the saint for his "apostolic virtues" in working for the relief of the poor and, as is sometimes overlooked, for the formation of the clergy. The Prayer over the Offerings describes how St. Vincent imitated "what he celebrated in these divine mysteries"; therefore, we ask that we too may imitate them and become what we receive, that is, "be transformed into an oblation acceptable to you." The Prayer after Communion asks that in being renewed by this heavenly sacrament, we may both be prompted by the example of St. Vincent and be sustained by his prayers. Either the Preface of Holy Pastors or one of the two Prefaces of Saints would be appropriate for today.

Today's Saint

St. Vincent de Paul (1581–1660), a French priest, gradually became aware of the growing disparity between the rich and poor; therefore, he laid the framework for the Servants of the Poor, which provided for the physical needs of the poor. Recognizing the call to care for not only their physical needs, but also their spiritual needs, he established a society of priests, the Congregation of the Mission (Vincentians), dedicated to preaching to peasants, catechezing the marginalized, and performing other charitable works. In collaboration with St. Louise Montfort de Marillac, he founded the Daughters of Charity, a new community of sisters not bound by traditional vows or enclosure who are devoted to the sick, orphaned, and imprisoned. St. Vincent is the patron saint of charitable societies. Many day care centers, hospitals, thrift stores, and soup kitchens are named in his honor.

F R I **28** (#453) green
Weekday

Optional Memorials of St. Wenceslaus, Martyr / red; St. Lawrence Ruiz and Companions, Martyrs / red

The Liturgy of the Word

◆ FIRST READING: God's time is not always our time. So goes this beloved reading from Ecclesiastes. The author remarks that he has pondered the job God has given human persons. Eternity is already in our hearts. We do not need to discover all the work God has done. We need to accept the rightness of God's time in which things happen.

Our toil will work out, for God wants nothing more.

◆ RESPONSORIAL PSALM 144: The psalmist acclaims the blessed of the Lord, his Rock. This is our acclamation in the refrain as well as his. When life seems not to be working out the way we imagined, we draw strength from the Lord. We know in the words of the psalm that though we are "like a breath" and our days passing, the Lord is mindful of us.

◆ GOSPEL: At prayer, Jesus asks his disciples who the crowds of people that have been following him think he is. The disciples' responses parallel the answers Herod was receiving: John the Baptist, Elijah, or another ancient prophet. Then Jesus personalizes his question and Peter is the first to respond, testifying that he is the Christ. For now, only the disciples are to know this. Interestingly, Jesus does not require the disciples to keep his prediction of the Son of Man's suffering, death, and resurrection that follows to themselves.

Today's Saint

Most people are familiar with St. Wenceslaus (c. 907–929), due to the popular Christmas carol "Good King Wenceslaus." Although this ancient carol is not based on historical events, it illustrates the fame King Wenceslaus received because of his heroic life. As a Christian king in Bohemia, a primarily pagan country, he worked fervently to Christianize his people. His attempt to evangelize the Bohemians was not received well by some, including his brother who eventually murdered him. As he was dying, he prayed that God would forgive his brother. Shortly following his death, people proclaimed him a martyr.

St. Lawrence Ruiz (1600–1637), a married man with three children, fled to Japan from Manila to escape an unjust charge. Upon arrival, he was greeted with hostility, due to a recent edict that banned Christianity. When he and fifteen other companions would not adhere to the state religion and trample on religious images associated with the Catholic faith, they were executed. St. Lawrence and his companions join 231 other Catholics martyred in Japan between the sixteenth and seventeenth centuries.

SAT 29 (#647) white
Feast of Sts. Michael, Gabriel and Raphael, Archangels

About Today's Feast

We celebrate the feast of three Archangels, Sts. Michael, Gabriel, and Raphael, the great heralds of salvation and defenders against the power of evil. St. Michael is guardian and protector of the Church, from its roots in Israel to the Church of today and beyond. In Hebrew, his name means "who is like God?" St. Gabriel, whose name means "hero of God," announces that John the Baptist will be born to Elizabeth and Zechariah. He is entrusted with the most important task of revealing to Mary that she will bear the Son of God. Then there is St. Raphael, whose name is Hebrew for "God has healed." He is named in Tobit 12 as the one standing in the presence of God and in 1 Enoch (early Jewish writing) as the healer of the earth.

The Liturgy of the Word

◆ FIRST READING, OPTION 1: We share in Daniel's vision of God's heavenly throne. Note the attributes of the Ancient One (God)—he has snow-white clothing, his throne is flashing fire, he is surrounded by angelic hosts. This latter point no doubt influenced the choice of this reading for today. Similar imagery is found in the Book of Ezekiel and in Isaiah 6. Daniel also sees "one like a son of man" (Daniel 7:13) who receives glory in the presence of the Ancient of Days. The phrase at its most basic level signifies a human being, but in later Judaism it was used in a titular sense with reference to a specific person and his mission on behalf of Israel.

◆ FIRST READING, OPTION 2: The description of Michael and his angels engaged in battle against the dragon is part of the larger vision of the woman giving birth who would rule the nations. The dragon was going to devour the woman's son, but God took the child up to his throne. This led to the war described in today's reading. The dragon, symbolic of Satan, loses again. God prevent him from devouring the woman's child and God ensures he loses the battle. The Blood of the Lamb overcomes Satan. In Christ, salvation has come!

◆ RESPONSORIAL PSALM 138: The words of the psalm express the author's gratitude for God's rescue. In the refrain, the word "angels" links directly with today's feast. Like the psalmist, we cannot keep our praise of God to ourselves. The angels witness it. The kings and leaders of the earth join in it. Our worship acclaims the Lord's glory.

◆ GOSPEL: Jesus is in the process of calling the disciples to follow him. Philip invites Nathanael to follow him and see whether anything good can come from Nazareth. Jesus acclaims Nathanael, unlike Jacob, as one in whom no dishonesty and unfaithfulness is found. While Nathanael appears to believe in Jesus because he saw Nathanael under a fig tree, Jesus tells him he will see "greater things" in the future, including the opening of heaven and God's angels ascending and descending on the one known as the Son of Man.

The Roman Missal

The texts for this Mass, all proper for the feast day, are located in the Proper of Saints section of the Missal at September 29. The Gloria is sung or said today, since it is a feast. The text for the Preface proper for today is given right there along with the other texts for this Mass; musical notation is provided. The Preface reminds us that when we pay honor to the angels, in fact we are praising God, since their great dignity and splendor shows how great God is.

☀ 30 (#137) green
Twenty-Sixth Sunday in Ordinary Time

The Liturgy of the Word

◆ FIRST READING: The Lord's spirit extended from Moses and rested on seventy elders. Eldad and Medad, who had already left camp, also received the Spirit. Joshua, son of Nun, would hear nothing of their prophetic words and asks Moses to stop them. Moses responds to Joshua's jealousy by announcing the wonder of all the Lord's people serving as prophets!

◆ RESPONSORIAL PSALM 19: Today's refrain expresses the joy the Lord's commands bring to our heart. Psalm 19 also recognizes the power and freedom of God's Spirit. This psalm clearly extols the value of God's law. The law of God is no burden. It is a "perfect" and "trustworthy" gift that gives joy to the psalmist's heart. Yet despite the full-throated praise of God's law, the psalm recognizes that something beyond the law is required. Even with a sincere effort to follow the law, "unknown faults" (13) can occur. These failings emerge in spite of the clear and good teaching of the law.

◆ GOSPEL: James chastises the rich for their wealth has brought misery upon them. While they have stored up treasure for the end times, they have also withheld wages from their workers. Through their wanton luxury, gluttony, and greed they have condemned the righteous one and put him to death.

◆ GOSPEL: Jesus instructs his disciples not to prevent anyone performing a mighty deed in his name. Anyone not against him is for him. Anyone who provides for you because you belong to Christ will retain his or her reward. But whatever causes you to sin, cut it off so that you will not experience Gehenna, but rather the Kingdom of God.

The Roman Missal

The Mass texts for today are found in the "Ordinary Time" section of the Proper of Time. The Gloria and the Creed are sung or said today. In choosing the Preface for today, you might consider Preface II of the Sundays in Ordinary Time, with its mention of Christ responding with compassion to "the waywardness that is ours"; Preface IV, with its emphasis on Christ bringing renewal, on his canceling out our sins, and on his opening the way to eternal life; or Preface VII, as it mentions our disobedience, which has been overturned by Christ's obedience. Consider also Eucharistic Prayer for Reconciliation I, with its Preface, as another possibility; all of these would echo the theme of the return of the sinner.

Other Ideas

The first day of October (tomorrow) is the Memorial of St. Therese of the Child Jesus, also known as the "Little Flower." Place roses in the sanctuary or encourage them to be placed in the home to remember her.

October 4 is the Memorial of St. Francis, and it is traditional to bless pets and animals in his honor. Consider providing a parish experience of blessing animals in the church or in an outdoor setting that is appropriate. For many reasons, not everyone is able to bring their animals to church (some might be fearful to be other animals and it can be a stressful situation for them). In addition to the communal blessing, provide parishioners with a blessing that they can do in their own homes with their pets, or in natural settings like backyards, parks, lakes, and rivers to bless the wild animals of the land and the air such as deer and birds. These gestures remind us that all of God's works are wonderful. We should be aware that habitats are being destroyed and many animals are raised in inhumane conditions (factory farming, puppy mills, and so on). While on this day we are particularly aware of animal care and rights, Franciscan spirituality calls us to care for all creation. If you have a Franciscan community of sisters, brothers, or priests nearby, consider inviting a guest speaker on Franciscan spirituality in action. This could take place at the blessing, outside of Mass at an event on creation, or at all the Sunday Masses following the Prayer after Communion.

October 2018
Month of the Most Holy Rosary

(#455) white

M O N **1** Memorial of St. Thérèse of the Child Jesus, Virgin and Doctor of the Church

The Liturgy of the Word

◆ FIRST READING: A seeming contest between God and Satan for Job's heart comes forth from their exchange in the first half of the reading. Satan destroys all that belongs to Job. Only a few messengers are left to communicate the awful news to Job. Job himself survives, and the reading ends with his words that all that the Lord gave him, the Lord has indeed taken away. Nevertheless, Job acclaims the holiness of the Lord's name. He does not sin. How faithful is Job in the face of complete loss, at least at this point.

◆ RESPONSORIAL PSALM 17: The psalmist prays that the Lord hear his cries and bring justice. Like Job, the author of the psalm innocently suffered at the hands of his enemies and recognizes the Lord tests his heart, trying him with the heat of fire. Like Job, too, the psalmist states God will find no evil in him. All he wants is the Lord to listen to him and hear his prayer.

◆ GOSPEL: One would think the disciples might be discussing something more profound after Jesus' second prediction of his Passion than who among them is the greatest. Rather than demeaning their conversation, but yet still wanting to change their hearts' intention, Jesus merely takes a child and instructs them that hospitality toward the child in Jesus' name is hospitality toward him and the Father. Our reception of a child shows our comprehension of Jesus teaching that the least among us is the greatest.

The Roman Missal

All the orations are proper for today, as found in the Proper of Saints at October 1. The Collect explicitly mentions the "Little Way" of St. Thérèse, noting how God's Kingdom is open "to those who are humble and to little ones." The Preface of Holy Virgins and Religious would seem to be the most appropriate choice for a Preface today, although certainly Preface I or II of Saints could also be used.

Today's Saint

St. Thérèse of the Child Jesus (1873–1897), also known as the "Little Flower," was the youngest of Blessed Zélie and Blessed Louis Martin's five daughters. Zélie died of breast cancer when Thérèse was only four years old, a blow from which Thérèse took years to recover. The family moved to Lisieux, to be closer to Zélie's brother and his family. After their mother's death, Thérèse became very close to her sister, Pauline, but five years later, Pauline entered the Carmel of Lisieux. Eventually, all five sisters would become nuns, four of them at the Lisieux Carmel. Because she was so young, Thérèse had to obtain permission from the diocesan bishop to join the Carmel, and she was able to at age fifteen. As a Carmelite nun, she overcame the narrow, negative spirituality prevalent in nineteenth-century France, and focused on love—her love of God and God's love for her. She called her path of holiness the "Little Way," referring to her belief that every act, no matter how small, brings us as close to God as do heroic acts performed by spiritual giants such as St. Ignatius of Loyola or St. Teresa of Avila. She developed tuberculosis when she was only twenty-four and was unable to join a Carmel in the missionary territory of Vietnam. A year later, when only twenty-five, she died of the disease, after suffering through a period in which she doubted the existence of heaven. Thérèse left behind a memoir, *L'histoire d'une âme* (*The Story of a Soul*), which she wrote under obedience to her sister, Pauline, who had become prioress. It was published posthumously, after heavy editing by her sisters brought it into conformity with their idea of piety, but recent editions have restored the original material. Translated into over fifty languages, it has inspired faith in skeptics and strengthened the souls of believers. Because of her missionary spirit, Thérèse of Lisieux is the patron saint of the missions. Pope John Paul II declared her a Doctor of the Church in 1997, one of only three women so honored, along with Teresa of Avila and Catherine of Siena.

TUE 2 (#456; Gospel, #650) white
Memorial of the Holy Guardian Angels

The Liturgy of the Word

◆ FIRST READING: Everything Job had, he lost. That was his first test. In his second test, Satan struck Job's body from head to toe with boils. Job still did not sin against God. However, Job does curse the day. His hope wanes. He questions why laborers receive light and the resentful ones, life. He is unsure of his path forward. We can empathize with Job's growing despair for while we do not seek despair, at some point it comes our way simply as part of the ebb and flow of life.

◆ RESPONSORIAL PSALM 88: We pray in the words of the psalmist (whose death nears) for God to hear our needs. It is not difficult to imagine Job's words to God being similar to those in this psalm as he despairs. From the base of the pit, the psalmist cries from the depths of his soul for God to hear him. Without his own strength, he seeks God's to rescue him from death.

◆ GOSPEL: Jesus does not want his disciples to act in a childish manner. What he wants them to take from his example of the child he draws near, is the child's humility. Humility—not arrogance, nor greatness, nor false pride—is the mark of the greatest in the Kingdom of heaven. When we welcome a child in Jesus' name, we welcome Jesus. The children have heavenly angels who watch over them. The humble surely have angels in heaven, too. *Note:* Just yesterday we heard Luke's account in which Jesus taught the disciples the least is the greatest in the Kingdom of God, using the example of a welcoming a child.

The Roman Missal

The orations are proper again for today, and these are found at October 2. The Collect pleads that God will always have the holy angels guard and defend us. The Prayer over the Offerings also asks for the protection of our guardian angels, so that "we may be delivered from present dangers / and brought happily to life eternal." The proper Preface, "God glorified through the Angels," is given right there along with the other texts for this memorial. This Preface describes how the honor we pay to angels results in God being glorified; to venerate the angels is to praise God. The Prayer after Communion reminds us that the nourishment we receive in the Eucharist is nourishment for eternal life; we therefore ask this day that the angels guide us into that life.

Today's Memorial

While not a defined teaching of the Church, the belief that each person has a guardian angel has roots deep in antiquity among Christians and non-Christians. The ancient Babylonians and Assyrians believed in angels, and they are mentioned in the Old Testament as well, beginning in the Book of Genesis, where they deliver God's punishment on the cities of the plain and rescue Lot and his family from the destruction (see Genesis 28—29). Perhaps one of the best and most touching examples of the activity of angels is found in the Book of Tobit, where the archangel Raphael leads and advises Tobiah on his journey (see Tobit 6—12). In the New Testament, Jesus himself seems to indicate that each of us is assigned a guardian angel when he says, "Take care that you do not despise one of these little ones; for, I tell you, in heaven their angels continually see the face of my Father in heaven" (Matthew 18:10).

WED 3
(#457) green
Weekday

The Liturgy of the Word

◆ FIRST READING: Job opens his second speech to his friends with the question, "How can a man be justified before God?" Job does not answer this question directly. In much of the first part of the speech, which is today's First Reading, Job testifies to God's power and control over the heavens and the earth. Yet when God draws near to Job, he is unable to see God. Job no longer believes that God will hear his words. Has God forsaken him?

◆ RESPONSORIAL PSALM 88: Today's Responsorial Psalm continues our prayer of Psalm 88. Except for verse 9 the verses for today begin where yesterday's left off. The refrain is the same. Our misery and disappointment with God seems to grow along with that of Job and the psalmist. Perhaps we are at a similar point in our own life as they were in theirs. Or perhaps we know someone. If the latter is the case, may we join our prayers with theirs as they ask God to hear their cries and come to them in a way that they can see his loving presence.

◆ GOSPEL: Jesus has set his eyes on his journey to Jerusalem with his disciples. Along the route, an anonymous person unequivocally tells Jesus, "I will follow you wher-

ever you go." The person's statement did not require a response from Jesus. However, Jesus speaks, explaining the unqualified, absolute commitment required for following him. Even family obligations such as burying relatives cannot distract from the proclamation of God's Kingdom. Disciples always look forward to the Kingdom, not behind to their past life.

THU 4
(#458) white
**Memorial of
St. Francis of Assisi**

The Liturgy of the Word

◆ FIRST READING: Job's tone appears to have changed his tone in this his fifth reply to his friends. Today's passage comes from about halfway through this reply. Job pleads for pity from his friends for God's hand struck him, yet his friends continue to treat him as if he was divine. Job, however, sets the record straight: he knows that his Redeemer lives and he will see God! He pines for the day to come when this will be reality.

◆ RESPONSORIAL PSALM 27: The refrain mirrors Job's confidence expressing in first person the psalmist's hope that he will see the good things of the Lord. The psalmist is confident that he will make his home where the living dwell. Ours is the prayer of the psalmist for the Lord to have mercy on us and to answer us. We, too, believe God is our help.

◆ GOSPEL: Jesus previously sent the Twelve out on mission. Now, he sends seventy-two others out as disciples. Their mission is to labor is to harvest the Master's fields. Their instructions are similar to those Jesus gave to the Twelve: take nothing, heal the sick, proclaim the Kingdom of God, and exit the towns where the people reject them. The disciples are to offer peace to the homes they enter and to share meals with those who live there. Imagine

today yourself as one of these disciples, for today this is your calling by virtue of your Baptism.

The Roman Missal

Once again all the orations are proper for the day; these are found at October 4 in the Proper of Saints. The Collect, as we might expect, gives special recognition to the poverty and humility of St. Francis, praying that by walking in the footsteps of the saint we might also follow Christ. The Prayer over the Offerings observes how St. Francis "ardently embraced" the mystery of the Cross, the mystery that is celebrated in the Eucharist. The Prayer after Communion prays that the holy gifts of the Eucharist may transform us to imitate "the charity and apostolic zeal of Saint Francis" and thus speak God's love everywhere. Preface I or II of Saints would be good choices for today's Preface.

The Book of Blessings

The blessing of animals has become a popular event given St. Francis' love of animals and all of God's creation. This blessing could be celebrated on the day of the memorial, or the Sunday before, if that is more convenient for those who work. A simple prayer service might include the beautiful hymn, "All Creatures of Our God and King" or the "Canticle of the Sun." The Book of Blessings includes an order of service (chapter 25) that can be adapted to the situation. Provide refreshments for the people and the pets! If animals will be blessed individually with holy water, be careful that they don't become spooked. Encourage pet guardians to bring animals on leashes and/or in carriers to prevent squabbles and animals getting loose.

Today's Saint

The son of a wealthy merchant, St. Francis of Assisi (1182–1226) seemed destined for grand castles, exquisite clothing, and fine food. After a conversion experience, he relinquished the trappings of this world to minister to the leper and preach to the spiritually hungry. His home became the earth; his clothing, humility; and his identity, an impoverished beggar seeking God. Many young men joined St. Francis in this new way of life, leading to the foundation of the *frati minori* ("lesser brothers"), which eventually became known as the Friars Minor. He is perhaps one of the most popular saints. in Church history due to his love of creation as exemplified in his famous "Canticle of the Sun." Pope Pius XI described St. Francis as an *alter Christus*, which means "another Christ."

FRI 5 (#459) green
Weekday

Optional Memorial of Bl. Francis Xavier Seelos, Priest / white

The Liturgy of the Word

◆ FIRST READING: Job replied often to his friends and tried to justify his case before them and God. His friends refused to answer him, but in Job 32—37, Elihu expressed his anger at Job for what he thought was Job's self-righteousness. Now in Job 38, the Lord takes his turn. The Lord's words reduce Job to silence for he has never commanded the land or the sea. He has never offered people a way to the "dwelling place of light." Only the Lord has. In traditional, theological language this passage affirms God's omnipotence and omniscience.

◆ RESPONSORIAL PSALM 139: In the First Reading, Job learns of God is all-knowing. The author of Psalm 139 knows this in a very personal way. God is familiar with who he is and what he does. Nowhere can he go without the Lord. God's hand is always guiding him. God created him, "fearfully" and "wonderfully."

God created each and everyone one of us in the same manner.

◆ GOSPEL: What is our response to Jesus' healing and exorcisms, to his proclamation of the Kingdom of God? Chorazin and Bethsaida face divine judgment for they have not repented. Tyre and Sidon would have sat in sackcloth and ashes had they witnessed Jesus' wondrous acts. How will Capernaum respond? Will they listen to Jesus or reject him? Capernaum's choice is our choice.

Today's Saint

Francis Xavier Seelos was a German a member of the Congregation of the Most Holy Redeemer (Redemptorists). He came to the United States of America in 1843 to minister to German immigrants. The following year he was ordained a priest in the Church of St. James in Baltimore, Maryland. He was known to be very kind, pastoral, and concerned for the poor. Many sought his help as confessor and spiritual advisor. Although he was proposed as Bishop of Pittsburgh, he instead became a missionary throughout the United States traveling to New Jersey, New York, Ohio, Pennsylvania, Connecticut, Rhode Island, Illinois, Michigan, Missouri, Wisconsin, and Louisiana. It was in Louisiana that he became ill with yellow fever and died in 1967. He was only forty-eight years old. If you are celebrating this optional memorial, the approved texts for this Mass can be found on the USCCB website: www.usccb.org /about/divine-worship/liturgical -calendar/blessed-francis-xavier -seelos.cfm.

SAT 6 (#460) green
Weekday

Optional Memorials of St. Bruno, Priest / white; Blessed Virgin Mary / white; Bl. Marie Rose Durocher, Virgin / white

The Liturgy of the Word

◆ FIRST READING: Our last reading from Job tells the end of his story. He takes the opportunity to respond to the Lord, affirming the Lord is all-powerful and all-knowing. Job repents of his words that disparaged the Lord. For his repentance, the Lord gifts Job with prosperity and progeny. Job had a full life. His story shows us how no life is without suffering, but for a faithful person, suffering is not the end of the story.

◆ RESPONSORIAL PSALM 119: Much like Job, the psalmist acknowledges that good can come from suffering. Through suffering we can learn the Lord's ways. The justice and light of the Lord's decrees become clearer to us. We realize we do not have God's mind and need to continuously learn God's wisdom. So, we pray in the refrain for God's face to shine on us.

◆ GOSPEL: The seventy-two disciples return. Upon their return they report to Jesus how the demons were subject to them because of the power of Jesus' name. Jesus affirms their report, noting how he has seen Satan fall like bolts of lightning from the sky. Yet Jesus does not want the disciples to be overcome with arrogance at what they have accomplished. They need always to remember to rejoice not because of they accomplish, but because their names are inscribed in heaven. They are blessed because of what they see — the power of Jesus at work.

Today's Saint

St. Bruno (c. 1035–1101) longed for a deeper relationship with God, nourished by solitude and austerity; thus, he and six companions built an oratory surrounded by several small hermitages, or cells, in a remote area in the French Alps known as La Chartreuse. This marks the beginning of the Carthusian order whose motto is *Stat crux dum volvitur orbis*, Latin for "The cross is steady while the world is turning." Carthusian monks strictly follow *The Rule of St. Benedict* and live an eremitical (reclusive) life solely seeking the will of God through prayer and manual labor.

Blessed Marie-Rose Durocher (1811–1894) was raised in a large family just outside of Montreal, Quebec. From a young age, she expressed the desire to join a religious order, but her poor health stood in the way of this dream. With the approval of the bishop, she founded the Congregation of the Sisters of the Most Holy Names of Jesus and Mary dedicated to the education of the young and poor. Little did she know the ministry of the sisters would spread beyond Canada to the United States and some third-world countries.

(#140)   green

7 Twenty-Seventh Sunday in Ordinary Time

The Liturgy of the Word

◆ FIRST READING: God created human beings for companionship with all of creation and with each other. Husband and wife become one flesh. God created them as partners in their relationship.

◆ RESPONSORIAL PSALM 128: God will bless those who walk in his pathways. The household who lives in faith will prosper and will know the abundance of Jerusalem all the days of their lives.

◆ SECOND READING: We are brothers and sisters of Christ, for God made him holy just as he, in turn, consecrates us. God perfected Jesus through his suffering and death so that having shared fully in our humanity, he might be the high priest who makes us holy.

◆ GOSPEL: The Pharisees and the disciples both question Jesus about the legality of a husband divorcing his wife. What God has joined, Jesus says, human beings must not separate. The longer form of the Gospel reading includes Jesus' instruction to his disciples who were turning back the people bringing their children to him, to let the children come. There is a longer and shorter form of today's reading.

The Roman Missal

The Mass texts for today are found in the "Ordinary Time" section of the Proper of Time. The Gloria and Creed are sung or said today.

The Collect recalls that God's love and grace are super-abundant and overflowing; that is the basis for our asking God "to pardon what conscience dreads / and to give what prayer does not dare to ask." God will always surpass our expectations and fill us with life and love, despite our unworthiness.

The Prayer over the Offerings recalls that the sacrifice we celebrate today was instituted by divine command, and its purpose is to continue the sanctifying work by which we are redeemed (in the liturgy, the work of our redemption is actually being accomplished).

Any one of the eight Prefaces of the Sundays in Ordinary Time is equally appropriate today.

The Prayer after Communion speaks of the important action of transformation: we are to "be transformed into what we consume." (Shades of St. Augustine!)

Other Ideas

The first Sunday in October is Respect Life Sunday. This day emphasizes the "seamless garment of life" (a phrase coined by Eileen Egan, cofounder of the Pax Christi organization) which must be protected from conception until natural death. Help people, through the Universal Prayer, as well as written resources online and in the bulletin, to see that many issues must be championed by the faithful, including opposition to genocide, murder, euthanasia, mutilation, as well as abortion and assisted suicide. The USCCB website offers extensive resources for prayer and information (www.usccb.org/about/pro-life-activities/respect-life-program/). Columbus Day is this Monday. While this day was traditionally one of celebration by many with European roots, particularly the Italian community, many now consider the arrival of Columbus to the Americas as a tragic moment considering the ensuing genocides, oppression, and displacement. Some cities have renamed the celebration Indigenous People's Day. This tension needs to be recognized and dealt with sensitively. If your parish has a chapter of the Knights of Columbus, the good works of the millions of members of this fraternal organization can be recognized in the Universal Prayer. The needs of indigenous people in North, Central, and South America should also be recognized.

MON 8 (#461) green
Weekday

The Liturgy of the Word

◆ FIRST READING: For the next nine weekdays, the First Reading comes from Paul's letter to the Galatians. Usually Paul's letters begin with an extended greeting and thanksgiving, but not his letter to the Galatians. Paul faces the need to be forthright with the Galatians because they are forsaking the Gospel of Christ for other perverted gospels. The Gospel of Christ is the one, true Gospel because it does not come from a human being, but from a "revelation of Jesus Christ." As quickly as some of the Galatians turned from the true Gospel, they should return to it.

◆ RESPONSORIAL PSALM 111 details the manifold ways in which God was present to his people, Israel, throughout the generations. The refrain provides us the opportunity to voice our confidence that the Lord will continue to remember his covenant as he did with Israel. As Christians, we confess God sent deliverance to us through Jesus Christ and forever sealed a new covenant in him.

◆ GOSPEL: Picture a legal scholar questioning Jesus about what must be done to inherit eternal life. This is how today's Gospel begins. Jesus replies to the scholar asking what the law says and how the scholar interprets it. As expected, the scholar cites the law correctly. But the task of the legal scholar is to *live* the love of God, neighbor as self as the law requires. It is one thing to believe and have knowledge of the truth. It is another to live it. The Good Samaritan lived mercy toward his neighbor. We are to do the same.

TUE 9 (#462) green
Weekday

Optional Memorial of St. Denis, Bishop, and Companions, Martyrs / red; St. John Leonardi, Priest / white

The Liturgy of the Word

◆ FIRST READING: In an autobiographical passage, Paul recalls his former way of life when, as a Jew, he persecuted the Church of God. Despite his persecution of the Church, he believes that through grace, God called him from within his mother's womb to proclaim the Gospel of Christ to the Gentiles. Churches in many regions to which Paul traveled accepted the Gospel, and as Paul attests, probably more factually than arrogantly, gave glory to God because of him and their knowledge of his conversion.

◆ RESPONSORIAL PSALM 139: The refrain reflects the psalmist's desire for the Lord to guide him along the path that leads to eternal life, "the everlasting way." We believe with Paul that the Gospel of Christ is this way.

◆ GOSPEL: Sometimes in life we simply need to sit and take in the wisdom of another. Mary chose to listen attentively to the Lord while Martha served him. Martha was none too pleased with Mary's decision, and since Martha had "much serving" to do, one might surmise

there were many others in the house with the Lord and the two sisters. Rather than keep her feelings to herself, Martha asks the Lord whether or not he cares that she has to do the working of serving by herself. Of course the Lord cares, but he cares about Martha's anxiety and worry. The Lord's words only serve to help Martha see she needs to draw closer to him and take in the Wisdom of his Word.

Today's Saints

St. Denis of Paris († 258) was the bishop of Paris during the third century, martyred during the persecution by the emperor Decius. It's possible that Denis came from Italy to convert Gaul, settling in Paris on the Île de la Cité in the River Seine. According to Gregory of Tours, he was beheaded with a sword on Montmartre, the highest hill in Paris, which may have been a druidic holy place, and local tradition holds that the martyrdom of St. Denis gave the hill its name. After his death, his body and those of his companions, Sts. Eleutherius and Rusticus, were recovered by the Christian community and buried. Later, St. Geneviève started the construction of a basilica on the spot. St. Denis of Paris is often confused with Dionysus the Areopagite, who was converted by St. Paul in Athens (Acts of the Apostles 17:34), and with Pseudo-Dionysius the Areopagite, a sixth-century theologian who's best known for describing the ranks of angels in the *Celestial Hierarchy*. Because he was martyred by beheading, St. Denis is portrayed decapitated, dressed in bishop's vestments, and holding his own head. He is a patron saint of France, the city of Paris, and is one of the Fourteen Holy Helpers, invoked against headaches, rabies, and demonic possession.

St. John Leonardi (c. 1541–1609) was an Italian priest who founded the Confraternity of Christian

Doctrine. Born in Diecimo, his father sent him to pharmacy school when he was seventeen, and John plied this trade for ten years before realizing that he had a vocation to the priesthood. He was ordained in 1572 and developed an apostolate among young peoplewith the Confraternity of Christian Doctrine. In 1574, he founded a community of priests, the Order of Clerks Regular of the Mother of God. After Paul V approved his new order, John moved to Rome, where he cofounded the seminary of the Propagation of the Faith. He died during an influenza epidemic, after caring for his stricken brothers. St. John is the patron saint of pharmacists.

W E D **10** (#463) green
Weekday

The Liturgy of the Word

◆ FIRST READING: The truth of the Gospel Paul preached is that its Good News is for all — for Jew and Gentile — circumcised and uncircumcised — alike. When Paul went to Jerusalem with Barnabas and Titus, they shared the right hand of partnership with James, Cephas, and John. God's grace was active in all those who preached the Gospel, though they struggled with the Jewish laws the Gentiles would need to follow in order to participate fully in the fledgling Christian communities. Paul's question to Cephas at the end of the reading is apt: how could they require Gentiles to live as Jews? What is truly necessary to live the Gospel?

◆ RESPONSORIAL PSALM 117: The mission the Risen Christ gave the eleven remaining disciples is our mission. It is the mission Paul and his partners in ministry embraced. It is the mission we announce each time we utter the refrain for today's Responsorial Psalm that comes from Mark 16:15. We are to go out into the world — its neighborhoods and its places of work — and speak the Gospel. The two short stanzas come from Psalm 117. They call the nations and all their peoples to praise the Lord for the Lord is ever faithful in his kindness toward his people.

◆ GOSPEL: How appropriate that after the Gospel passage of Martha and Mary, we find Jesus praying, and after he completes his prayer, one of his disciples, who Luke does not name, asks him to teach them how to pray. Apparently John the Baptist had instructed his disciples about prayer. Jesus does not give his disciples a lecture on prayer. He simply offers them a model prayer, what we know as the "Our Father." It is a prayer in which we ask for bread and forgiveness and commit ourselves to the practice of forgiveness. It is a prayer of the Father's kingdom.

T H U **11** (#464) green
Weekday

Optional Memorial of St. John XXIII, Pope / white

The Liturgy of the Word

◆ FIRST READING: Paul spares no words as he chastises the Galatians. He refers to them as "stupid" to open the passage. Surely they were foolish and senseless because some of them were listening to the false and perverted interpretations of the Gospel others were preaching. These interpretations required the Galatians to perform "works of the law," such as circumcision for their justification. The only requirement of the Gospel Paul preaches is faith. For the Galatians to not believe correctly about the Gospel, Paul believes, puts their salvation at risk.

◆ CANTICLE: The Canticle of Zechariah from the Gospel according to Luke includes Zechariah's prophetic words declaring how God raised up a Savior from the house of David. Through the words of the refrain, we acclaim the blessedness of Israel's God who has visited his people. In Christ, salvation is available to all.

◆ GOSPEL: Jesus continues to teach his disciples about prayer. Three things we are to do in prayer: ask, seek and find. When we do these, we will receive, we will find, and we will be able to walk through an open door. Through prayer, we will receive the Holy Spirit from the Father in heaven. We, too, will learn how to share our bread with a neighbor in need in the middle of the night, if only because of his or her persistence.

Today's Saint

Known for his modesty and pastoral concern, "Good Pope John" dedicated his ministry to placing the needs of the world at the service of the Church. As supreme pontiff, John XXIII refused to be a prisoner of the Vatican, and instead modeled the Good Shepherd, visiting the prisons of Rome, reaching out to the sick, and welcoming visitors of every faith and nation. He surprised the world by announcing the Second Vatican Council on January 25, 1959. His hope was that the Council would signal a "new" style for the Church and its authority.

F R I **12** (#465) green
Weekday

The Liturgy of the Word

◆ FIRST READING: According to Paul, not only are those who depend on the works of the law foolish, they are also cursed. God does not justify via the law, but through faith. Abraham had faith and we today who have faith, share in his blessing. We are God's children by faith. By faith, we receive the Spirit's promise.

◆ RESPONSORIAL PSALM 111: The psalmist praises the Lord in the assembly of the Lord's people. Why? Because the Lord's works are wondrous! Through the Lord's works the people of Israel experienced his faithfulness to the covenant. We communicate our confidence that the Lord will forever remain faithful to the covenant in the psalm refrain.

◆ GOSPEL: After Jesus taught his disciples about prayer, he drove out a demon from a mute person, and the person began to speak. The crowd gathered thought Jesus' power came from Beelzebul. Those that thought otherwise asked Jesus to perform a sign from heaven. Instead of acquiescing to their request, Jesus taught them how divided kingdoms will not stand. Since Jesus' power has come from "the finger of God," the Kingdom of God is a present reality in the midst of the people.

SAT 13 (#466) green
Weekday

Optional Memorial of the Blessed Virgin Mary / white

The Liturgy of the Word

◆ FIRST READING: Faith makes us children of God. Paul's teaching in this regard takes the pressure off of us to earn our justification. There is nothing we can do that will merit our status as God's children. Only faith brings us into this relationship. In Baptism, we have put on Christ. We are Abraham's descendants. God's promise is ours. We share our identity in Christ with all who are baptized, and all who, by faith, believe in Jesus Christ. God's promise of salvation is theirs, too.

◆ RESPONSORIAL PSALM 105: The refrain today from Psalm 105 is similar to yesterday's refrain from Psalm 111. In yesterday's refrain we declared our future confidence that the Lord will remember his covenant. Today, we acknowledge in the present tense that the Lord indeed does remember his covenant, and not just now, but for ever. In verses 6 at the beginning of the final

stanza, we find the connection with the First Reading. We are descendants of Abraham and sons of Jacob. Their God is our God! We are God's children, God's chosen ones.

◆ GOSPEL: A woman interrupts Jesus as he was teaching the crowd about how unclean spirits attempt to find their home again in the people from which they were exorcised. The woman announces the blessedness of Mary carrying Jesus in her womb and nursing him. Jesus' response to her expands the notions of blessedness to include all who hear and act on the Word of God.

14 (#143) green
Twenty-Eighth Sunday in Ordinary Time

The Liturgy of the Word

◆ FIRST READING: The author prefers prudence and the spirit of wisdom to riches. Wisdom's value surpasses that of health. With wisdom comes a different kind of goodness and incomparable riches unequaled by monetary or material gains.

◆ RESPONSORIAL PSALM 90: In the words of the community's lament, we sing to God to provide us with "wisdom of heart." We ask God to fill us with his love and help the work of hands to flourish so that we might once again sing for joy.

◆ SECOND READING: The Word of God gets into the marrow of our bones and finds its way in between our soul and spirit. So alive is God's Word that it knows our self-reflections and musings of our heart. We might try, but we can hide nothing from the Word.

◆ GOSPEL: Living God's commandments puts us on the path to eternal life. However, as the man with many possessions finds out, he also must sell everything he has, give to the poor, and then follow Jesus. Surely, the man thought this a lot to ask. But in his sadness, what he does not yet recognize is salvation is impossible for human beings, but not for God. There is a longer and shorter form of today's reading.

The Roman Missal

We ask that God's grace may be with us always, going before and following after us, and that we may be "determined / to carry out good works" (Collect). It is the perfect formula for a holy life! We ask God to accept our prayers together with the "sacrificial offerings" we present, that we may "pass over to the glory of heaven" (Prayer over the Offerings). The Gloria and the Creed are sung or said today.

Other Ideas

In these weeks before Advent, check supplies and if you have not already done so, and order the resources for prayer that you would like to distribute to parishioners, and the annual resources you will need for next year's liturgical preparations. Check any supplies used in the liturgical environment to see if they need freshening. Make sure that you have an attractive book in which members can inscribe the names of the dead during the month of November.

The Memorial of St. Teresa of Jesus, also known as Teresa of Avila, happens this week (October 15). One of the first women to be made a doctor of the Church, she is known for her reforms of the Carmelite order. A great contemplative, Teresa was also a great spiritual thinker and an energetic, lively person. She was a friend and mentor to collaborator the great mystic St. John of the Cross. This week, offer the community the Prayer of St. Theresa of Avila:

> Let nothing disturb you, Let nothing frighten you, All things are passing away: God never changes. Patience obtains all things Whoever has God lacks nothing; God alone suffices.

The Taizé piece, *Nada te turbe*, is based on her prayer. Consider using it at Mass today either as a prelude, during the Preparation of the Gifts, or as the Communion song. The Feast of St. Luke is also this week (October 18). Encourage reading of his Gospel.

(#467) white
MON 15 Memorial of St. Teresa of Jesus, Virgin and Doctor of the Church

The Liturgy of the Word

◆ FIRST READING: Paul makes the contrast between slavery and freedom by using an allegory based on the Abraham's two sons, Isaac and Ishmael, and their birth mothers, Sarah (Abraham's wife) and Hagar (the slave). It is important to note the limitations of this allegory and to see in Paul's writing his main point that in Christ we are free. Our lives are meant to be free, and to represent a newfound freedom to the world that God in Christ offers to everyone.

◆ RESPONSORIAL PSALM 113 invites the Lord's servants to praise his name, not just in one moment of the day but continuously, from the rising of the sun to its setting. The rhetorical question in verses 5a–6 asks for someone who is like the Lord watching over the heavens and the earth. Of course, no one

compares to the Lord who raises up the poor and lowly.

◆ GOSPEL: Today's Gospel reading is also proclaimed on Wednesday of the First Week of Lent. In last Friday's Gospel, people in the crowd had asked Jesus for sign because they wondered from where his power to exorcise the demon from the mute person came. In today's Gospel, Jesus begins by noting the need of this generation for a sign. Jonah's prophetic mes sage of repentance is the sign as it was for the Ninevites. The Son of Man also preaches repentance, for the Kingdom of God is at hand. The difference between the two: something greater than Jonah is at work in Jesus. Will this generation repent?

The Roman Missal

All the orations are proper for this obligatory memorial, and they can be found in the Proper of Saints at October 15. It would seem that the Preface of Holy Virgins and Religious would be the most logical choice for the Preface today.

Today's Saint

St. Teresa of Jesus (1515–1582), more commonly known as St. Teresa of Avila, joined the Carmelite Convent of the Incarnation at the age of 21. Disheartened by the laxness of its observance of the Carmelite Rule, in particular its opulent nature and overly social atmosphere, she began a reform movement laying the framework for the Discalced Carmelites. This new branch of Carmelites modeled themselves on the poor and crucified Christ, adopting a life of poverty and abstinence. In collaboration with St. John of the Cross, she helped bring this new way of life to the male Carmelite communities. Although their reforms were met with great resistance, they moved forward with faith and persistence. Among her many writings, she is well known for two classics: *The*

Way of Perfection and *The Interior Castle*.

TUE 16 (#468) green
Weekday

Optional Memorials of St. Hedwig, Religious / white; St. Margaret Mary Alacoque, Virgin / white

The Liturgy of the Word

◆ FIRST READING: Freedom. Paul's tells us this is why Christ set us free. This is so important that today's reading begins with the same verse yesterday's reading ended on. Paul wants to make sure the Galatians understand that the Gospel of Christ teaches us that the law does not justify. Outward signs such as circumcision or uncircumcision do not matter. Our faith that is evident in our actions of love matters.

◆ RESPONSORIAL PSALM 119: An obvious connection to Paul's discussion of freedom in the First Reading is found in the fourth stanza (verse 45). The psalmist recognizes he will walk freely because he pursues the Lord's commands. In Christ Jesus, the greatest of the commandments is the law of love: love of God with all your heart, mind, and soul, and love of neighbor as ourselves. In this love others see our faith, and we are free. Often, though, we are in need of the Lord's mercy for we do not love as we should. In the refrain, we ask for divine mercy to come upon us.

◆ GOSPEL: A Pharisee invites Jesus to share a meal at his home. Luke remarks that the Pharisee observed, but did not say anything about Jesus not following the purity laws for washing before eating. Perhaps the Pharisee rolled his eyes or made another gesture to alert Jesus to his displeasure, because next we know Jesus forthrightly criticizes the Pharisees as a whole for their hypocrisy. Our insides must match our outsides for God created both.

Today's Saint

St. Hedwig of Silesia (1174–1243) was Duchess of Silesia and of Poland and an aunt of St. Elizabeth of Hungary. When only twelve, she was married to Henry I of Silesia. They lived a devout life, performed penitential practices, and together supported the founding of many religious communities in Silesia. When Henry died in 1238, Hedwig went to live in the Cistercian convent her husband had founded at her request. Hedwig was canonized in 1267 and is a patron saint of orphaned children.

St. Margaret Mary Alacoque (1647–1690) was a French Visitation nun and mystic, whose visions of Jesus led her to promote devotion to the Most Sacred Heart as we know it today. Margaret was a pious child and practiced prayer and penance. She entered the Visitation convent in Paray-le-Monial in 1671. Unfortunately, the nuns there were suspicious of her, and Margaret Mary found her vocation tried, especially by the delay of her profession. The following year, she began having the visions that revealed the devotion to the Sacred Heart and its practices such as communion on First Fridays, and the holy hour of Eucharistic adoration on Thursdays. She was discouraged from spreading this devotion until the convent's Jesuit confessor, St. Claude la Colombière, declared that her visions were genuine. St. Margaret Mary died in 1690, but after her death, the Jesuits spread the devotion to the Sacred Heart. She is a patron saint of polio sufferers, orphans, and those devoted to the Sacred Heart.

(#469) red

W E D 17
Memorial of St. Ignatius of Antioch, Bishop and Martyr

The Liturgy of the Word

◆ FIRST READING: The fruit of the Spirit stands in contrast with the works of the flesh. Only we who allow the Spirit to lead us will inherit the Kingdom of God. To be bound by the flesh, according to Paul, is to be bound by the law and immorality. To live by the Spirit is to be free in Christ. The fruits of the Spirit blossom a hundredfold in those who belong to Christ Jesus.

◆ RESPONSORIAL PSALM 1: Similar to Paul's contrast between those who live by the Spirit and those who live by the flesh, the opening psalm in the Psalter compares the blessed person and the wicked. The blessed follow the way of the Lord and are like trees that bear fruit in their time. The wicked are chaff blown away by the wind. The psalm refrain comes from the second half of John 8:12. In the first half of the verse Jesus identifies himself as the Light of the World. Those who follow him will receive the light of life as their inheritance now and forever.

◆ GOSPEL: Jesus denounces the Pharisees again. Their hypocrisy overtly shows itself in three ways. They pay tithes, but neither give heed to God's judgment nor love God. They take delight in sitting in places of honor. And, they lead others to break the law despite their own hang up with the law. A legal scholar also claims to be insulted by Jesus' words. Perhaps he should not have spoken, for Jesus responds by rebuking the scribes. They place burdens on people, but they do not see fit to help. Neither the Pharisees nor the scribes exhibit behaviors worthy of the Kingdom of God. Do we?

The Roman Missal

All the orations, found at October 17, are proper for today. The Collect highlights the "glorious passion of St. Ignatius of Antioch." The Prayer over the Offerings includes a wonderful reference to the saint's proclamation before his martyrdom that he was the wheat of Christ, to be ground by the teeth of beasts (a statement that is used as today's Communion Antiphon); the prayer asks that just as St. Ignatius was accepted as the wheat of Christ, so may our oblation be pleasing to God. In other words, may we too be wheat and bread, transformed into an offering acceptable to God as this gift of bread will be transformed. The Prayer after Communion connects with this thought in asking that the heavenly bread we receive this day renew us "and make us Christians in name and in deed"—the deed perhaps including martyrdom, following the example of St. Ignatius. Given the emphasis on martyrdom in the orations, the most likely choice for the Preface would be one of the Prefaces of Holy Martyrs, although the Preface of Holy Pastors or even one of the two Prefaces of Saints could not be excluded as possibilities.

Today's Saint

St. Ignatius of Antioch (c. 37–107), an apostolic father and possible disciple of John the Evangelist, served the community of Antioch as bishop. Living during the anti-Christian reign of the Roman emperor Trajan, he was sentenced to be fed to animals in the Roman Colosseum because he would not engage in idol worship. His journey to Rome was marked by extensive writing in which he composed seven letters. These letters, directed to various churches, emphasized the humanity and divinity of Christ, the centrality of Eucharist, and the importance of Church unity.

THU 18 (#661) red Feast of St. Luke, Evangelist

About Today's Feast

St. Luke the Evangelist (first century) is traditionally known as the author of the Gospel that bears his name as well as of the Acts of the Apostles. He is also identified with the "beloved physician" referred to by St. Paul (Colossians 4:14). Luke was a Gentile from Antioch in Syria, and his roots show both in his writing style and in his sympathetic treatment of Gentiles in the Gospel that bears his name. According to Acts of the Apostles, he accompanied St. Paul on some of his evangelizing journeys, and he stays with Paul when he is imprisoned in Rome. Some sources claim he was martyred, but it is thought that he died an old man of natural causes. A tradition states that he was the first icon painter, and the Black Madonna of Częstochowa is attributed to him. His symbol is an ox or bull because the Lucan Gospel begins with Zechariah, the father of John the Baptist, offering a sacrifice in the Temple. St. Luke is patron saint of artists and physicians.

The Liturgy of the Word

◆ First Reading: Paul describes some difficult trials he faced in his ministry. A number of his ministerial colleagues deserted him, but Luke stayed the course. Alexander was an enemy of the Gospel Paul preached. When Paul needed the support of witnesses, no one stood by him. Despite this, Paul asks that the Lord judge them mercifully. Through it all, Paul retains his faith and acknowledges the constancy of the Lord's companionship. The preaching of the Gospel to the Gentiles must continue.

◆ Responsorial Psalm 145: God's Kingdom is glorious! We who are friends of God reveal this truth to others. God's companionship comes to those who call upon him. There is nothing quite like God's justice and holiness and the enduring nature of God's Kingdom.

◆ Gospel: The focus of today's reading appears on the seventy-two disciples who were sent out, not alone, but in pairs to companion one another in their proclamation of the Kingdom of God. Luke remained a faithful companion to other disciples. His account of the Gospel endures as written testament to the announcement of the Kingdom.

The Roman Missal

The texts for this Mass, all proper for the feast today, are located in the Proper of Saints section of the Missal at October 18. The Gloria is sung or said today, since it is a feast. The Collect employs themes typically associated with St. Luke's Gospel account: God's love for the poor, and the universality of the Gospel as it goes out to all nations. The Prayer over the Offerings prays that the food of this Eucharist may bring us freedom of heart to serve God, in addition to healing and glory. The Prayer after Communion asks for strength from the Eucharist so that we might continue to be strong "in the faith of the Gospel which Saint Luke proclaimed." The proper Preface designated for today is Preface II of the Apostles.

FRI 19 (#471) red Memorial of Sts. John de Brébeuf and Isaac Jogues, Priests, and Companions, Martyrs

The Liturgy of the Word

◆ First Reading: God chose us in Christ to be sealed with the Holy Spirit. In Paul's words, this is the "first installment of our inheritance." We are on the way to the fullness of salvation. Twice Paul reminds us that our response to our destiny in Christ is praise of God. We are to direct all we say and do to the praise of God.

◆ Responsorial Psalm 33 is frequently used to Ordinary Time. It is a fitting as a Responsorial Psalm today because its theme of praise connects with Paul's teaching that we exist for the praise of God. The other connection between this psalm and the First Reading is seen in the refrain that attests to the blessedness of the people the Lord calls as his own.

◆ Gospel: Having criticized the Pharisees for their hypocrisy, Jesus now cautions the disciples about it. Even if the Pharisees think no one notices their hypocrisy, God does. What we speak in the dark, God hears in the light. Our whispers, God shouts from the rooftops. God cares for even the smallest of birds, the sparrow. There is nothing to fear on the journey of discipleship. Ours is the mission to faithfully live the words we proclaim. Ours is the task to not imitate the hypocrisy of the Pharisees, but to imitate the love of Jesus.

The Roman Missal

The Collect for the memorial is found in the Proper of Saints, with the remaining prayers drawn from the Common of Martyrs: For Missionary Martyrs.

Today's Saints

On this day the Church honors the saints who gave their lives to spread the Catholic faith in North America: two Jesuit priests, St. Isaac Jogues (1607–1646) and St. John de Brébeuf (1593–1649), and their companions. St. Isaac was captured and tortured for his preaching of the Gospel. He escaped and returned to Europe, but only to seek permission to offer Mass with his scarred and mutilated hands. The pope granted his wish, and St. Isaac returned to the New World where he was put to death in 1646. Jean de Brébeuf dedicated himself to preaching the Gospel among the Huron peoples in what is now up-state New York and Canada. He translated the Catechism into the Huron language and wrote a series of "Instructions for Missionaries" that mingled divine and practical counsels: "Love the Hurons as brothers," he urged, "and bear with their shortcomings. Never keep them waiting, and learn to get into a canoe without carrying sand or water with you. Eat first thing in the morning, because that's what the Indians do. Work as they do, and serve them in whatever way you can." Jean de Brébeuf knew that only by understanding the Indians could missionaries hope to help them understand the Gospel. North American martyrs, pray for us.

S A T 20 (#472) green
Weekday

Optional Memorials of St. Paul of the Cross, Priest / white; Blessed Virgin Mary / white

The Liturgy of the Word

◆ FIRST READING: Two-thirds of the First Reading is a prayer. Paul offers thanks to God for the Ephesians and prays that God may gift them with a spirit of wisdom and revelation that leads to a deeper knowledge of God. Paul prays for enlightened hearts for the people to the hope of God's call. The passage culminates with the identification of the Church with Christ's Body.

◆ RESPONSORIAL PSALM 8 reflects on God's grandeur seen throughout the heavens and the earth. The psalmist describes the smallness of human persons in relation to God through a rhetorical question that wonders why God would even bother to care for them. What a gracious act of God to create humankind, and then to appoint us stewards over creation.

◆ GOSPEL: Jesus instructs the disciples that their choice and ours is clear: either we acknowledge him or we deny him. If we choose the former, he presents us before God's angels, but if we decide for the latter, he will deny us before those same angels. While this seems black and white, Jesus goes onto extend God's forgiveness to those who speak against the Son of Man. Should disciples face persecution and be put on trial, they need not worry about having the right words to say, the Holy Spirit will guide them.

Today's Saint

After having a vision of himself clothed in a black habit, St. Paul of the Cross (1694–1775) established the Congregation of the Passion (the Passionists, or Congregation of the Discalced Clerks of the Most Holy Cross and Passion of Our Lord Jesus Christ). The Passionists, a community of priests, were to live a strict monastic life while fostering an intense devotion to the Passion of Christ through preaching and missions. Along with the traditional vows of other religious communities, they took a fourth vow to spread the memory of Christ's Passion. Unique to their habit is a large badge in the shape of a heart bearing a cross and the words *Jesu XPI Passio* (Passion of Jesus Christ). As they grew in numbers, they engaged in ministry to the sick and dying. Toward the end of his life, St. Paul founded a community of Passionist nuns.

(#146) green
21 Twenty-Ninth Sunday in Ordinary Time

The Liturgy of the Word

◆ FIRST READING: The two verses from the fourth and final servant song in Isaiah describe how the sinless servant of the Lord justifies many through his own suffering. He gives his life as a sin offering. The Lord accomplishes his will through his servant.

◆ RESPONSORIAL PSALM 33 becomes our prayer for God's mercy. We place our trust in the Lord and hope that he will deliver us from death and preserve us from suffering.

◆ SECOND READING: Despite being without sin, Jesus, our high priest, can sympathize with our weaknesses for he shares in the fullness of humanity. With confidence, we approach the throne of our high priest to receive his gifts of mercy and grace. We confess Jesus, the Son of God, risen and reigning forever with the Father in heaven.

◆ GOSPEL: To be great is to serve. To be first is to serve. The Son of Man provides the example par excellence of this teaching for he came to "give his life as a ransom for many." The longer form of the Gospel reading includes Jesus' response to James and John share in the cup he drinks and be baptized with his baptism. With good reason, the other ten Apostles became irate with the sons of Zebedee. There is a longer and shorter form of today's reading.

The Roman Missal

The Mass texts for today are found in the "Ordinary Time" section of the Proper of Time. The Gloria and the Creed are sung or said today.

The Collect prays that we might always conform our will to God's will, and serve him in sincerity of heart. This petition might in some way be seen as connecting with the Gospel for today, in that discernment of God's will is important in figuring out how we are to live as both citizens of heaven and citizens of the civil society in which we find ourselves. That kind of discernment demands that we constantly seek to purify our actions and our motives, to be focused on the values of the kingdom, and so the Prayer over the Offerings appropriately prays for that purification through our participation in this celebration: that "we may be cleansed by the very mysteries we serve." We need to look at everything through the lens of the Paschal Mystery, celebrated in the Eucharist, in order to properly discern. The Prayer after Communion also assists us in this discernment as it describes how, from our participation in heavenly things (that is, this Eucharist), "we may be helped by what you give in this present age and prepared for the gifts that are eternal."

In choosing a Preface for today, consider how Preface I of the Sundays in Ordinary Time describes for us how we are to live in the world, namely, as a chosen race, a holy nation, and a people belonging to God who proclaim everywhere his mighty works. Also consider using Eucharistic Prayer IV this week, with its own proper Preface; the sweeping résumé of salvation history it gives sets our notions of civil society in its proper perspective before God's majesty.

Other Ideas

World Mission Sunday is celebrated each year in every parish in the world. Collections gathered this day support a wide range of international pontifical mission societies. The efforts of this day, organized by the society for the propagation of the faith, is "an important date in the life of the Church, because it teaches how to give: as an offering made to God, *in* the Eucharistic celebration and *for* all the missions of the world" (*Redemptoris missio*, 81). This week, highlight the mission activities of your parish and diocese. Members of the community who have experienced the value of missions can contribute short articles for use in the bulletin and on the parish website or social media page. If there is a guest homilist or speaker (those who are not ordained may provide reflections following the Prayer after Communion), provide hospitality so parishioners can speak to this person after Mass. The last full week in October is also Pastoral Care Week. Consider providing tables of information about the many services the parish provides as well as information about how to get involved with pastoral ministries, such as bringing the Eucharist to those who are ill or homebound, supporting the bereaved, and visiting the sick.

MON 22 (#473) green Weekday

Optional Memorial of St. John Paul II, Pope / white

The Liturgy of the Word

◆ FIRST READING: Ours is the mercy of God through Christ. Twice Paul tells us in this eloquently written, kerygmatic passage that we have been saved by grace. Our salvation is a gift. We do not earn salvation by our works. Our sins surely caused our death, but God raised us up with Christ. Life is ours in him!

◆ RESPONSORIAL PSALM 100: Our security rests in the God who made us. We belong to God and will never have to worry that God will abandon us. Our response to being God's chosen people is praise and blessing and thanksgiving.

◆ GOSPEL: Material possessions have limited value. We do not find richness in them. Greed is overrated. We do not find happiness in greed. Jesus tells the parable about the rich man whose land produced such an abundant harvest that lacking space to store the harvest, he decided to build larger barns. The meaning of the parable: disciples find richness in what concerns God not in amassing material wealth.

Today's Saint

In the early years, Catholics and non-Catholics alike were attracted to the athletic man who sneaked out of his villa to ski and reached out to the young at World Youth Days. People of many faiths prayed for him when he was shot in St. Peter's Square and were awed with the mercy he granted his assailant. None escaped the poignancy of a feeble John Paul II praying at the Western Wall in Israel, leaving a prayer inside the wall. Even a scant follower of the pope knew that the man who forgave his assailant, traveled the world to evangelize, and sought healing in relations with the Jewish people looked to the Blessed Virgin as a model of faith. For Mass, use the texts from the Common of Pastors: For a Pope.

TUE 23 (#474) green Weekday

Optional Memorial of St. John of Capistrano, Priest / white

The Liturgy of the Word

◆ FIRST READING: Christ's Blood has drawn us near to God offering peace—a peace that overcomes divisions and hatred, a peace that reconciles in his one Body. Through Christ Jesus we are share citizenry with the holy ones in God's household. Christ is the cornerstone of the entire building. He is building God's people together in unity in the Holy Spirit.

◆ RESPONSORIAL PSALM 85: In today's refrain, acknowledge the peace the Lord speaks to his people. The verses poetically portray the meeting of kindness and truth, and peace and justice. As Christians, we affirm their ultimate meeting in Christ Jesus. In him, Truth has once for all sprung out of the earth.

◆ GOSPEL: With a month left in the liturgical year, we hear in the weekday readings an increasing sense of urgency about the Master's return. Will he find us vigilant? Will we be ready to open the door immediately when he knocks? Will he bless us and share a meal with us upon his return because we have lived faithful lives?

Today's Saint

St. John of Capistrano (1386–1456) was an Italian Franciscan priest. He was born in the Kingdom of Naples and studied law at Perugia, got married, and became a magistrate. During a war, he was sent as a peace ambassador but was thrown in prison, and during this time realized that he was called to be a priest. He and his wife had never consummated their marriage, so they separated, and John entered the Franciscans. He applied himself to a life of extreme asceticism and developed a reputation as a powerful preacher, in Italy as well as in countries such as Germany and Poland. So great were the crowds who came to hear him that no church could hold them, and he had to preach outdoors. In addition to preaching, John fought heresy through his writing and led an army against an invasion of Turks. He survived the battle but died of bubonic plague in 1456. St. John of Capistrano is a patron saint of those in the legal profession. The famous Mission San Juan Capistrano in southern California is named for him.

W E D **24** (#475) green **Weekday**

Optional Memorial of St. Anthony Mary Claret, Bishop / white

The Liturgy of the Word

◆ FIRST READING: This self-reflective passage might draw out in us a need to reflect on our own ministry and service to the Gospel. Paul considers his own ministry to the Gentiles who are "coheirs" and "copartners" with the Jews. The two are members of the same Body, the Body of Christ, the Church. Paul did not become a minister on his own accord, but God's grace. So, too, it is with us.

◆ CANTICLE: Israel's word could easily be Paul's words as well as ours. In the thanksgiving, Israel expresses gratitude to the Lord. Once angry with Israel because of her infidelity, the Lord turned away from anger and saved Israel.

◆ GOSPEL: Be vigilant. Be prepared. The Son of Man will not announce the hour when he will come. He will come unexpectedly just as thief does not announce his or her arrival. Peter questions who the Lord intends to hear the parable. Rather than answer Peter's question directly, Jesus offers another parable. The faithful and wise servant is the prepared servant.

Today's Saint

As a successful weaver and skilled printer in Spain, St. Anthony Mary Claret (1807–1870) felt called to be ordained a priest and preach parish missions. He eventually gathered young men together in community to preach missions, which led to the foundation of a new religious congregation called the Claretians. Later in life he was appointed archbishop of Santiago, Cuba, a huge diocese with many problems, including racism, slavery, and anti-Christian persecution. His Christian response to the posing problems (for example, establishing credit unions to loan money to the poor) resulted in fifteen assassination attempts upon his life. Following his tenure as bishop, he served as confessor to Queen Isabella II and was able to exert his influence in the court to implement new projects, such as starting a natural history museum and schools of music and languages.

T H U **25** (#476) green **Weekday**

The Liturgy of the Word

◆ FIRST READING: Paul offers beautiful prayer for the Ephesians. He prays to the Father to strengthen their inner selves through the Spirit. He prays that Christ may dwell in their hearts. He prays that they may know the immeasurable dimensions of Christ's love. A doxology acknowledging God's power already at work in Paul and the Ephesians concludes his prayer. Imagine praying this prayer for your faith community.

◆ RESPONSORIAL PSALM 33: The Responsorial Psalm frequently comes from Psalm 33. Most recently the Psalm 33 and its verses appointed for today were used Friday, October 19, 2018. An additional two verses, verses 18–19 are included as the final stanza for today. In them, the psalmist affirms God's help and care for those who hope in him.

◆ GOSPEL: Jesus ratchets up his rhetoric in today's Gospel reading. He has come to set the earth on fire. Peace he does not bring, but division he does—division even among family members. His Passion and Death will be his baptism. Only the disciples hear these words of Jesus. Luke does not record their reaction to them, but one might think they do not completely understand their meaning. If they have heard in Jesus' words a call to whole-hearted commitment to him and his message of the Kingdom, they have grasped enough.

FRI 26 (#477) green
Weekday

The Liturgy of the Word

◆ FIRST READING: Humility, gentleness patience, and love are the virtues of a life that reflects God's call. In everything we do as Christians, we try to maintain the unity that is God's gift to us through the one Spirit and the one Body. May we open ourselves to hearing anew the seven unity phrases in this passage so that we might ponder how we orient our lives to preserving and enacting the oneness of which Paul speaks.

◆ RESPONSORIAL PSALM 24: The psalm's emphasis on the Lord's glorious kingship aligns with the First Reading's focus on the declaration of the one God whose presence permeates everyone and everything.

◆ GOSPEL: Apparently the people in the crowd can interpret the signs of nature, but not what they see before them in Jesus in the present time. How could they have missed his healings and exorcisms or misunderstood his teaching about the Kingdom of God? Choosing to reconcile with one's adversary surely reveals one as a disciple of Jesus. Not to mention it prevents one from facing the undesirable consequences of imprisonment and monetary payment.

SAT 27 (#478) green
Weekday

Optional Memorial of the Blessed Virgin Mary / white

The Liturgy of the Word

◆ FIRST READING: Christ descended to earth and ascended back to heaven. As the descending and ascending One, he is the head of the whole Body, the Church. He directs the functions of the Body and has appointed people to have different roles in the building up of the Body. As members of the Body, we build up the Body in love, the love of Christ.

◆ RESPONSORIAL PSALM 122 is also the Responsorial Psalm for Wednesday of the Fifth Week of Easter. This psalm is a processional psalm pilgrims sang on their way to Jerusalem. In the context of the First Reading, the Lord's house to which we go rejoicing is community of the faithful who form the Church, Christ's Body. What joy we have to be part of this household of faith whose head is Christ.

◆ GOSPEL: How enduring is God's tolerance for us! God's patience for our repentance seems endless. The first half of the Gospel reading recounts the death of the Galileans on Pilate's watch and the loss of life of those on whom the tower of Siloam fell. Jesus links their fate with people's ongoing need for repentance. Despite the urgency in Jesus' tone, the second half of the Gospel reading is a parable of the gardener giving a fig tree one more chance to bear fruit. The gardener's patience symbolizes God's patience with us.

☀ 28 (#149) green
Thirtieth Sunday in Ordinary Time

The Liturgy of the Word

◆ FIRST READING: Joy marks the return of a remnant—a large throng—from exile in the desert. The Lord has delivered his people. Their tears of departure contrast with the happiness upon their return. One point could not be clearer: the Lord has always been and will always be the Father of Israel.

◆ RESPONSORIAL PSALM 126: We rejoice with the people the Lord brings back and proclaim the great things he has done for us and the joy that now fills us. Psalm 126 mirrors the movement of the people's emotions from sorrow to joy found in the passage from Jeremiah.

◆ SECOND READING: Jesus Christ is the Son of the Father from whom his high priesthood comes. The Father glorifies Christ and makes him a priest forever in the order of Melchizedek. Christ deals patiently with our sins because he shares in the fullness of our humanity. He offers himself for our sins because he also shares in the fullness of divinity.

◆ GOSPEL: Despite the rebuke of many, the blind beggar, Bartimaeus, would not stop calling out to Jesus for pity. Jesus does not ignore his cries, but rather calls him near and asks him what he desires. Bartimaeus simply wants to see. Jesus heals the blind man, noting that his faith saved him. Bartimaeus responds to his newly-gained sight by following Jesus.

The Roman Missal

The Mass texts for today are found in the "Ordinary Time" section of the Proper of Time. The Gloria and the Creed are sung or said today. Of the eight Prefaces of the Sundays in Ordinary Time that can possibly be used today, perhaps. The prayers for today ask God to "increase our faith, hope, and charity," so that we may do as he commanded—to "love."

Other Ideas

Halloween, with all of its secular fanfare, tends to dwarf All Saints Day, a Holyday of Obligation, which occurs this Thursday. This day honors all the saints who are not otherwise honored throughout the liturgical year. On the Solemnity of All Saints, enshrine in an accessible location the book you have chosen for parishioners to use in inscribing the names of those who have departed earthly life. Keep this book available through the entire month of November. In the evening, encourage parishioners to light a candle and pray the Rosary in remembrance of their beloved dead in preparation for All Souls' Day, It was widely held in folklore throughout the world that the souls of the dead return to earth on All Souls' Day. In many countries, it is customary to visit the graves of loved ones, and to even have a festive meal in the graveyard. In Mexico, this day–*Día de Muertos*–is particularly festive. Parishioners can also remember those that have passed by setting out photos along with candles in their homes.

MON 29 (#479) green
Weekday

The Liturgy of the Word

◆ FIRST READING: Kindness, compassion, forgiveness, and gratitude are virtues of God's children. They contrast with the vices of immorality, impurity, greed, and obscenity. The latter mark those who worship other gods, not the one Lord. Those who live in sin will not inherit the Kingdom that belongs to Christ and to God. God calls us to live as children of light. Darkness is for those who do not belong to God.

◆ RESPONSORIAL PSALM 1: The refrain is Ephesians 5:1, a verse from the First Reading that challenges us to live in a manner befitting our identity as God's beloved children. Today, the verses of the psalter's opening psalm, call to mind the blessedness of those who reject evil and choose to walk in the Lord's way. They help us respond to the First Reading emphasis on the living the Christian virtues.

◆ GOSPEL: It has been a while, but Jesus returns to teach in a synagogue on a Sabbath. In the synagogue he encounter a woman beset by a spirit that made her unable to stand up straight. She does not even need to ask Jesus for healing. Upon seeing her, Jesus heals her. The synagogue's leader is none too happy, but instead of rebuking Jesus, he addresses the crowds attempting to incite them against Jesus. Jesus turns the tables naming the leader's hypocrisy in a declaration that he presumably also aimed at some in the crowd. A person's freedom is what is a stake for Jesus, and what better day to heal than on a Sabbath!

TUE 30 (#480 or First Reading, #122) green
Weekday

The Liturgy of the Word

◆ FIRST READING: The reading from Ephesians continues Paul's discussion of Christian love in the context of the relationship between a husband and wife. Love is what defines the spousal relationship just as love defines the relationship between Christ and the Church. It is not just any love, but a love the supports and treasures the other. It is a love that befits members of Christ's Body.

◆ RESPONSORIAL PSALM 128: The psalmist contemplates God's blessing for the person who fears the Lord and walks in the Lord's ways. The second stanza (verse 3) specifically describes how the Lord will bless the husband's wife and children and thus specifically connects with the First Reading.

◆ GOSPEL: After many teachings on the Kingdom of God and performing actions of healing and exorcism that reveal the presence of God's Kingdom in the midst of the people, Jesus himself now asks the question about what the Kingdom of God is like and to what he can compare it. His own questions he answers with two brief parables, the first about the mustard seed that becomes a large bush and home for many birds and the second about yeast mixed with flour to form leavened bread. We can think of the Kingdom of God as the home that can be ours. In the Kingdom, present now, but fully yet to come, we will feast forever on the Bread of Life. The Kingdom will expand and expand. It is a large home with food a plenty.

**W
E 31** (#481) green
D **Weekday**

The Liturgy of the Word

◆ FIRST READING: Yesterday the First Reading spoke of the centrality of love in the relationship between husband and wife. Today, the passage from Ephesians discusses the important relationship between children and their parents. The Lord calls children to obey and honor their parents. The reading specifically mentions fathers not upsetting their children so as to make this angry. This reasonably seems to apply also to mothers. At the time of the writing of Ephesians, Paul also needed to address the relationship between the slaves and their masters in the context of faithful living. His point about the Master in heaven showing no partiality applies well today to any relationships, including that between a supervisor and his or her employee. As people of faith, we serve the Lord in all our relationships

◆ RESPONSORIAL PSALM 145: Often when the Responsorial Psalm comes from Psalm 145, the focus is on the Lord's glorious kingship in the refrain. Today's underscores the Lord's faithfulness in his words. For the Lord's faithfulness in his words and the holiness in his works, we give thanks. To our responsibility to live out our gratitude to the Lord in all our relationships, we say yes; we too accept our call to faithfulness.

◆ GOSPEL: To the yes or no question regarding whether only a few people will be saved, Jesus offers a lengthy response. Many will try to get through the narrow gate, but will not succeed, he says. The Master of the house will lock the door and not recognize where you are from. He will cast many out, but many others from all directions will have a seat at the Kingdom's table. They were last, but now are first. They are people of faith. They have believed. Their lives and relationships have testified to Jesus and witnessed to the Kingdom. Jesus recognizes them.

November 2018
Month of All Souls

☀ **1** (#667) white
**Solemnity of
All Saints**

HOLYDAY OF OBLIGATION

About Today's Solemnity

On this day, the Church honors all the saints, those who have finished the race and now rejoice in God's presence. We honor the towering figures like Sts. Peter, Paul, Augustine, Francis, and Thérèse of the Child Jesus, and we honor the humble saints as well, those whose names are known to few or to none: the grandparents and ancestors, the friends and teachers who lived their faith to the full and inspired faith in others. This is a day to celebrate them all.

An observance in honor of all the saints has been celebrated on November 1 since at least the seventh century, and it originated even earlier, with a feast in honor of all martyrs in the year 359. "Why should our praise and glorification, or even the celebration of this feastday mean anything to the saints?" asked Saint Bernard of Clairvaux in a homily on All Saints' Day. "Clearly, if we venerate their memory, it serves us, not them. But I tell you, when I think of them, I feel myself inflamed with a tremendous yearning. Calling the saints to mind inspires, or rather arouses in us, above all else, a longing to enjoy their company. . . . We long to share in the citizenship of heaven to dwell with the spirits of the blessed. . . . In short, we long to be united in happiness with all the saints" (Office of Readings, Volume IV, p. 1526). All holy men and women, saints of God, pray for us.

The Liturgy of the Word

◆ FIRST READING: The angel marks 144,000 people representing every tribe of Israel with "the seal of the living God." A great and diverse multitude of people from throughout the world wear white robes, hold palm branches, and stand before the throne of the Lamb announcing salvation comes from God and the Lamb. Others prostrate themselves in worship, acclaiming the glory and power of God. Like many of the saints who are also martyrs, the ones wearing white have survived persecution and trial. The Lamb's blood saved them.

◆ RESPONSORIAL PSALM 24 originally served as a processional psalm as people carried the Ark of the Covenant to its place in the Temple. On the solemnity of All Saints, we can see in the psalm visions of the saints ascending the Lord's mountain. They now reside will God forever and have met him face to face. We, too, desire to see the Lord's face and receive blessing from him.

◆ SECOND READING: We do not need to wait to be God's children. This is our identity *now*. Our future remains undetermined, yet we wait in hope for one thing we are sure of is that we will be like God. We will see God just as God is for in this life, we have sought God's face. Therein lies a connection between the Second Reading and the Responsorial Psalm.

◆ GOSPEL: Once Jesus saw the crowds he went up the mountain and sat down. His disciples followed him up the mountain. Their lesson this day would be about blessedness. The saints lived this lesson of the Beatitudes in many and varied ways. Ours is the call to live the Beatitudes and through our lives to teach others about blessedness as Jesus taught his disciples on the mountain. Great will be our reward in heaven. In our knowledge of this, we rejoice and sing with the saints!

The Roman Missal

The Gloria and the Creed are sung or said today. The Collect reminds us of the great cloud of witnesses by which we are surrounded as it tells of how in this one celebration we venerate the merits of all the saints. Thus, we can take comfort in asking for the reconciliation with God "for which we earnestly long" because we can count on the intercession of so many saints.

The Prayer over the Offerings reiterates that we live our lives, and offer this Eucharist, in the Communion of Saints, and therefore they celebrate with us. We can experience their solidarity with and concern for us because they are assured of immortality in the Lord.

The Preface, titled "The glory of Jerusalem, our mother," is given, with and without musical notation, right there among the pages for all the other texts for this Mass. The Preface points to Jerusalem as our mother and the heavenly city where our brothers and sisters who have gone before us give God eternal praise. The key point to be emphasized is that we as pilgrims seek to advance to the heavenly Jerusalem as well, and our hope of arriving there is not unfounded since we

have the strength and good example of the saints to assist us. This reminds us that the liturgical celebration of All Saints is not only about those faithful upon whom the Church has designated the title of sanctity, but it is also about our call to that same sanctity.

Eucharistic Prayer I, the Roman Canon, with its two listing of saints' names, might be considered an appropriate choice for use at this solemnity.

The Prayer after Communion reminds us that the holiness of the saints is only possible because it is rooted in God's holiness, God who alone is holy. In addition, although not explicitly so, the image of the heavenly Jerusalem — the eschatological aspect inherent in every Eucharist — is once again invoked as the prayer asks that "we may pass from this pilgrim table to the banquet of our heavenly homeland."

The Solemn Blessing formula for All Saints, found in the section of the Missal "Blessings at the End of Mass and Prayers over the People," is suggested for today, and would be well used. Also, in light of the call to sanctity that is given to us all as we strive to imitate and be in communion with the saints, perhaps the dismissal formula "Go in peace, glorifying the Lord by your life" would be the most appropriate form of dismissal for today.

(#668, #1011-1016) white or violet or black

F R I 2 The Commemoration of All the Faithful Departed (All Souls' Day)

About Today's Commemoration

On the day after All Saints comes All Souls' Day, the Commemoration of the Faithful Departed, in which the Church prays for all who have died. As Catholics, we believe in Purgatory. Not everyone necessarily has to pass through purgatory. Today, we pray for them, trusting that God will hear and an-

swer our prayers that they know eternal light, happiness, and peace.

As we remember and pray for our loved ones who have died, the reality that we ourselves must one day die is also brought home to us as a gentle, insistent reminder. In Mexico, the Day of the Dead (*Día de Muertos*) is a way of praying for our ancestors, remembering and celebrating them, and making friends with death. As St. Ambrose wrote, "Death is then no cause for mourning, for it is the cause of mankind's salvation. Death is not something to be avoided, for the Son of God did not think it beneath his dignity, nor did he seek to escape it" (Office of Readings, Volume IV, p. 1539). May the souls of all the faithful departed through the mercy of God rest in peace.

The Liturgy of the Word

There are numerous options for today's readings. This year the author has chosen to reflect on these options from Lectionary #668: Isaiah 25:6, 7–9 (option 3 of 3); Psalm 25 (option 2 of 3); Romans 6:3–9 (option 3 of 13); and Luke 23:44–46, 50, 52–53; 24:1–6a (option 5 of 12).

◆ FIRST READING: Isaiah's prophetic words remind us this day of God's triumph over death. The mountain of Zion symbolizes the heavenly Jerusalem, the home in which we are confident our loved ones and all the faithful departed now dwell. There and here, God gently wipes away our tears and consoles us in our grief. God has saved them! God will provide for them forever!

◆ RESPONSORIAL PSALM 25: The Lectionary provides two options for the refrain. In the first, we name the act of lifting our souls to God. In the second, we express confidence that the Lord will receive those who wait for him, and not put them to shame. Both refrains come from Psalm 25, a lament of an individual writer. The psalmist's words give voice to our prayer that the Lord remembers his compassion and kindness toward our loved ones and toward us.

◆ SECOND READING: Paul's words are a bold proclamation to the Romans that in Christ's Resurrection is the final and lasting victory over death. Christ has put death's power to death. In Baptism, we participated both in Christ's Death and Resurrection. Ours is new life in him. We hope, together with all the faithful departed, to share in his Resurrection on the last day.

◆ GOSPEL: The opportunity to sit at the bedside of a dying person is a privilege. The sense of their spirit returning to God is palpable. For this reason, the Gospel passage from Luke when Jesus commended his spirit to the Father befits the liturgy for All Souls' Day. But the reading does not end with Jesus' Death, it continues by describing how Joseph and others took care of Jesus' body and performed the prescribed burial rituals. On the first day of the week, they found Jesus' tombstone rolled away. They sought the living among the dead. Jesus had been raised!

The Roman Missal

Because this Commemoration replaces the Sunday in Ordinary Time, all the texts are taken from November 2 in the Proper of Saints. Any one of the three sets of formularies may be chosen, at the discretion of the priest celebrant or, as appropriate, the parish's liturgy preparation/worship team. All the texts proclaim the centrality of the Paschal Mystery in understanding the meaning of Christian

death: because of Jesus' Death and Resurrection, death leads to new life for all those united to Christ. Therefore, because of our faith in the Risen Christ, we can find hope in death. Some of the Mass prayers (the Prayer over the Offerings in formulary set 2; the Prayer after Communion in formulary set 3) explicitly mention Baptism; thus, calling to mind the baptismal symbols used in the funeral Mass (sprinkling with holy water, Paschal candle, white garment). Any one of the five Prefaces for the Dead may be used today, again at the discretion of the priest celebrant or according to the preparations made by a parish committee. Also, the Solemn Blessing formula "In Celebration for the Dead" (number 20 under "Blessings at the End of Mass and Prayers over the People") is suggested and should be used for all Masses today. The Gloria is not sung or said on All Souls' Day.

S A T 3 (#484) green Weekday

Optional Memorial of St. Martin de Porres, Religious / white; Blessed Virgin Mary / white

The Liturgy of the Word

◆ FIRST READING: For the next week, the First Readings come from Paul's letter to the Philippians. Paul's extols the Philippians to proclaim Christ. Doing so has been Paul's own life after his conversion. As we draw closer to the end of the liturgical year, we see in this passage Paul's reflection on how he strongly desires to no longer live in the flesh, but to live with Christ. We hope for to live our lives in Christ now, so that we will live forever with him in the future.

◆ RESPONSORIAL PSALM 42: The psalmist's thirst for the "living God" parallels Paul's yearning to be with Christ. Just as a deer craves running water, our souls long for God. We deeply desire to see God's face. We can describe our lives as a journey to God's house, akin to the psalmist's depiction of leading the people to temple.

◆ GOSPEL: Again, we find Jesus dining with a Pharisee. During the meal, Jesus tells a parable, much like we tell stories when sharing a meal with friends and relatives. But Jesus' story means to instruct the Pharisees and to motivate them to change their ways. The Pharisees seek places of honor around the dining table, but the guests at the wedding banquet should take the lowest place. God will raise up the humble, and those who raise themselves up, God will humble.

Today's Saint

St. Martin de Porres (1579–1639) had a special love for the marginalized in society; he knew what it was like to feel unaccepted. As the son of an unwed couple, a Spanish knight and a freed slave from Panama, he hardly fit the norm. His father essentially disowned him because he inherited his mother's features, primarily her skin color. Instead of wallowing in his own pain, he chose to become a Dominican brother, focusing on ministry to the "forgotten" in society. St. Martin, called the "father of charity," cared for sick people in the monastery, fed the needy with food from the monastery, and began a home for abandoned children. He had a close friendship with St. Rose of Lima and is considered patron saint of racial justice.

4 (#152) green
Thirty-First Sunday in Ordinary Time

The Liturgy of the Word

◆ FIRST READING: Moses instructs the people of Israel to keep the Lord's commandments. Land, prosperity, and progeny will be theirs. Only the Lord is God. The Lord is the God of Israel whom the people shall love with their heart, soul, and strength. Moses' words call us to take the Lord's statutes into our hearts this day.

◆ RESPONSORIAL PSALM 18: We sing our thanks to the Lord for the rescuing us from our enemies and express our love of the Lord, for God is our strength and our rock. As Christians, we believe ours is the victory the Lord gave us in Christ Jesus.

◆ SECOND READING: Jesus the high priest is unlike the Levitical priests who needed to offer repeated sacrifice for their sins and the sins of their people, and whose priesthood ceases at death. Jesus' Death on the Cross is a "once for all" sacrifice, which he never needs to repeat. His priesthood is eternal and the salvation he offers to people, constantly available.

◆ GOSPEL: Jesus' words in response to the scribe who inquires about the most important commandment echo the Moses' words in the First Reading. To the commandment of honor the Lord God alone with love of one's heart, mind, and strength, Jesus adds the second commandment to love your neighbor as yourself. Understanding these commandments brings one near to the Kingdom of God.

The Roman Missal

Even to praise God is God's gift. We pray that "we may hasten without stumbling" to the promises of God (Collect). We pray that our "sacrificial offerings" to God may be pure and bring us "a holy outpouring" of God's mercy (Prayer over the Offerings). We pray that God's power might be at work in us, so that the gift we receive in the Eucharist may prepare us to receive what it promises: eternal life (Prayer after Communion). The Gloria and the Creed are sung or said today.

Other Ideas

The Feast of the Dedication of the Lateran Basilica in Rome occurs this week. It is the highest ranking of the four major Basilica's in Rome, and also the oldest basilica in the Christian community. Given to the pope by Emperor Constantine the Great after the latter's conversion experience, it was consecrated by Pope Sylvester in the year 324. Invite parishioners to experience the online virtual tour of this historic church (www.vatican.va /various/basiliche/san_giovanni /vr_tour/index-en.html). Encourage trips this week to your local cathedral or basilica, and consider partnering in some aspect of their ministries. Since this is the Holy Father's Church, this is also a good time to pray for the pope and his ministries in the Universal Prayer.

This week is the week-long celebration of vocations in National Vocation Awareness Week. Prayers for an increase in the number of people embracing the priesthood, diaconate, and consecrated life may be included in the Universal Prayer.

The Hindu community worldwide will celebrate *Diwali*, the festival of lights, on November 7. This festival celebrates all forms of light overcoming darkness, such as knowledge overcoming ignorance, goodness triumphing over evil, and more. Pray for those of all faiths in the Universal Prayer.

MON 5 (#485) green
Weekday

The Liturgy of the Word

◆ FIRST READING: Paul's words to the Philippians introduce the Christ hymn that is tomorrow's First Reading. The Apostle encourages the Philippians to be of the "same mind," the mind of Christ. Christ's mind marked itself with generosity and humility, not selfishness and vanity. As Christ looked out for others, so they ought to take care of others. Love as Christ loved.

◆ RESPONSORIAL PSALM 131: The psalmist has found peace in the Lord. Paul sought this same peace. He had encouraged the Philippians to be of the same mind as Christ for their doing so would bring Paul joy. The psalmist reflects on how he has neither a proud heart nor selfish eyes; he is like a child resting on his mother's lap. Living in humility, may we find also find peace in God who cares for us as a mother cares for her child.

◆ GOSPEL: We find Jesus still at table in the home of a leading Pharisee. Having instructed the Pharisee and the other guests about the relationship between humility and exaltation, Jesus continues the lesson, but this time he only speaks to the Pharisee who hosts the gathering. Jesus teaches the Pharisee specifically whom to invite so he does not end up feeling obligated to accept a return invitation. How shocked the Pharisee must have been when he heard he should invite the least in society — the poor and those who suffer from ailments. Perhaps Jesus appeased his shock when he told him the righteous will be repaid at the Resurrection.

TUE 6 (#486) green
Weekday

The Liturgy of the Word

◆ FIRST READING: The first half of the reading speaks of Christ Jesus' actions. Though he was God, he became human. He humbled himself obediently accepting his Death on the Cross. The second half defines what God did because of Jesus' actions. God exalted him and made it such that everyone should confess his name and Lordship. For the Philippians and us to be of the same mind as Christ Jesus is to follow his example of humility. God made us to worship Jesus Christ the Lord.

◆ RESPONSORIAL PSALM 22 is a suitable response to the First Reading because even though the psalmist laments his suffering, he still praises the Lord. He praises the Lord, not alone, but in the midst of God's people. The words of the psalm assist us in making the psalmist's worship our worship, our praise of God. For we, too, know, in God our souls will live.

◆ GOSPEL: Jesus still remains at table in the Pharisees' home. Today's Gospel begins with one of the Pharisees' guests stating the truth: the ones who feast in God's Kingdom are blessed. Jesus tells another parable in response to the guest. The guests the master in the parable invited to dinner, all were unable to come. As a result, the master instructs his servant to go out into the streets and invite those Jesus told the Pharisee in the previous Gospel reading to welcome to his banquet. So much room will there be in the Kingdom, that the Master wanted the servant to invite more people. God wants the joy of a full house in his Kingdom.

WED 7 (#487) green
Weekday

The Liturgy of the Word

◆ FIRST READING: Paul exhorts the Philippians to live in obedience as they have faithfully done so far. When we, like the Philippians, labor, it is God who works in us leading us to do what is right. While we do the best we can, sometime we grumble, although Paul advises the Philippians neither to complain nor question, but to shine as the children of God to the world. Even though Paul suffers, he rejoices and asks the Philippians to share his joy. Let us find joy in our work as God's children.

◆ RESPONSORIAL PSALM 27: The refrain picks up the First Reading's image of light as we affirm the Lord as our light and salvation. We are children of the light, because God is Light. The psalmist's words remind us that we have nothing to fear. We wait patiently to dwell in the Lord's house.

◆ GOSPEL: Hate our relatives? Renounce all our possessions? Jesus seems a bit unreasonable in his instructions to the huge crowds who were traveling with him. Exaggeration does sometimes help to make a point. Jesus' point could not be more obvious: we have a choice to follow him, carry our cross, and be a disciple, or not. Our decision impacts our place in God's Kingdom.

THU 8 (#488) green
Weekday

The Liturgy of the Word

◆ FIRST READING: True confessions of Paul fill this reading. Paul was circumcised according to the law, but he ended up persecuting the Church until his conversion. Whatever he experienced as positive in his former way of life, pales in comparison to the truth he finds in Christ Jesus as his Lord. His words to the Philippians intend to show them how they, too, are God's people. They preach Christ and not the flesh. They worship through the Spirit.

◆ RESPONSORIAL PSALM 105: Today's refrain encourages people who look for the Lord to rejoice in their hearts. The author of the psalm invited Israel to praise the Lord for his wondrous deeds. In the final stanza (verse 6), we recognize ourselves as among Abraham's descendants. The Lord is our God.

◆ GOSPEL: Like the joy of a shepherd finding one lost sheep and a woman recovering one lost coin, God will celebrate the repentance of a single sinful person. Surely the tax collectors and sinners who gathered around Jesus to hear him teach, felt a joy they had never felt before upon hearing this. The Pharisees and scribes, who were complaining about Jesus welcoming sinners and eating with them, even before even he told the parable, most certainly will raise the intensity of their grumbling after hearing Jesus' words.

FRI 9 (#671) white
Feast of the Dedication of the Lateran Basilica

About Today's Feast

Today the Church throughout the world celebrates a feast in honor of a church in Rome: the Basilica of St. John Lateran. St. John Lateran is not just any church: it is the cathedral of the Bishop of Rome, who is, of course, the pope.

"Lateran" was the name of a Roman family whose lands were seized by Emperor Constantine in the fourth century. He proceeded to build a great basilica dedicated in honor of St. John the Baptist, but the name of the family that had once owned the land remained associated with it, and the church is called *San Giovanni in Laterano*, or "St. John in the Lateran." For centuries, the old Lateran palace was the residence of the popes. It was only when the popes returned to Rome following the Avignon exile in the fourteenth century that they moved their residence to the Vatican Hill, which they considered to be a healthier part of the city. St. John Lateran continues to serve as the pope's cathedral and is as a sign of our unity as a Church under the leadership of the Holy Father. As we recall the dedication of this important church, the "mother church" of all the churches of the world, we should look inward as well.

The Liturgy of the Word

◆ FIRST READING: Water flows from the Temple overcoming dryness. In every direction it flows. Trees along the riverbanks bear fruit, and the fruit of the trees will feed people. Tree leaves will heal others. We receive life in God in the waters of Baptism. Baptism leads us to the Eucharist, where we find a lifetime of nourishment at God's table.

◆ RESPONSORIAL PSALM 46: The psalm refrain attests to the life-giving waters in God's city. We cannot exist as human without water. As God's people, a people of faith, the joy that comes from the abundant waters God created, provide us with life and protection. They symbolize God's presence among us and his overflowing care for us.

◆ SECOND READING: Paul identifies the Corinthians as God's building. The foundation of their building is Jesus Christ. It will take time for the Corinthians to grasp the meaning of their identity, but Paul moves on to also tell them they are God's temple. The Holy Spirit lives in them. They are holy. They are to come together as one, overcoming the divisions that exist among them. For if someone destroys one person, they destroy God's Temple, and will face the

consequence of their own destruction. All are holy.

◆ GOSPEL: Jesus drives out those doing business in the Temple area. He overturns the tables of the money-changers. Jesus' point: commercial enterprise is not the purpose of his Father's house. In a perplexing answer to the Jews requesting a sign for supporting his actions, Jesus foreshadows his own Death and Resurrection. His Body is the living Temple.

The Roman Missal

The texts for this Mass are all found in the Proper of Saints section of the Missal, at November 9.

The Gloria is sung or said today, since it is a feast. Since today is Thursday, the Creed is not sung or said today.

There is a choice between two options for the Collect today. The first option uses the imagery of living stones to refer to the dwelling place of God, and thus asks for an increase of the spirit of grace in the Church. When the prayer goes on to ask that God's faithful people build up the heavenly Jerusalem by "new growth," it is presumably by a growth in holiness and grace, although certainly growth by the incorporation of new living stones (new members) could also be understood as well. The second option for the Collect uses the imagery of the Church as the Bride of Christ and has a little more of an eschatological focus as it specifically asks that the people of God may be led to attain God's promises in heaven.

The Prayer over the Offerings, in asking God to accept the offering being made, also asks that those who make that offering may receive "in this place / the power of the Sacraments / and the answer to their prayers." We can note an emphasis intended by inclusion of the phrase "in this place," thus, highlighting the Church both as the living stones and as a people who

gather in a sacred space to enact the Divine Liturgy.

The text for today's proper Preface is given right along with the other texts for this Mass, and it is given both with and without musical notation. The Preface, titled "The mystery of the Church, the Bride of Christ and the Temple of the Spirit," reiterates the imagery of the people as the temple of the Spirit who make the Church resplendent through their living lives acceptable to God. The visible buildings that make up the Church are foreshadows of her heavenly glory.

The Prayer after Communion continues this eschatological theme of foreshadowing by addressing God as the one "who chose to foreshadow for us / the heavenly Jerusalem / through the sign of your Church on earth." Thus, the prayer goes on to ask that by our partaking of the Eucharist, "we may be made the temple of your grace / and may enter the dwelling place of your glory." Indeed, we can be reminded that it is only by celebrating the Eucharist that the Church can be Church; without Eucharist, the Church does not exist.

(#490) white

S A T **10** **Memorial of St. Leo the Great, Pope and Doctor of the Church**

The Liturgy of the Word

◆ FIRST READING: As individuals, we like to be self-sufficient. Paul was no different. He prided himself on taking care of his own material needs. He knew how to live humbly. Yet sometimes we just need the assistance of others. In this passage, Paul expresses his gratitude to the Philippians for the monetary gift they sent him. They were the only Church to share their resources with him. Paul assures the Philippians that God will provide for them in return through the bounty of Christ Jesus.

◆ Responsorial Psalm 112: The Lectionary gives two options for the refrain. The first affirms the blessedness of the one who fears the Lord. The second is a single "Alleluia." The verses speak of the blessings of posterity and exaltation that the Lord grants the one who fears him. Generosity of spirit characterizes the person in the psalm as it did the Philippians.

◆ Gospel: Jesus had just finished telling the parable of the dishonest steward and in today's Gospel passage he applies the parable to the life of his disciples. He instructs the disciples to be trustworthy even with wealth that another has entrusted to them, even if it is dishonest wealth. Disciples only serve God, not money. Certainly, the Pharisees who cherished money were not pleased when the overheard Jesus' teaching. God knows our hearts, too.

The Roman Missal

All the orations are proper for today, as found in the Proper of Saints at November 10. The Collect communicates to us the place of greatness among the successors to the Apostles that Pope St. Leo holds in the life of the Church as the prayer asks the intercession of St. Leo to stand firm in the truth and to "know the protection of lasting peace." Such firmness and protection is assured because God is addressed as the one who never allows the gates of hell to prevail against the Church, founded firmly as it is on apostolic rock. The Prayer over the Offerings prays particularly for those who shepherd the Church, asking that they may be pleasing to God, and also prays that the flock everywhere may prosper. The Prayer after Communion also speaks of governance, noting that it is God who governs the Church he nourishes with the Eucharist; the prayer also asks that under God's direction, "she may enjoy ever greater freedom / and persevere in integrity of religion." Although the Prayer over the Offerings and the Prayer after Communion do not specifically mention Pope St. Leo by name, they certainly reflect the virtues that he lived as pope, and the concerns he faced and addressed in his ministry. Certainly the Preface of Holy Pastors would be perhaps the most appropriate choice for today, although Preface I or II of Saints could also be used.

Today's Saint

As pope and Doctor of the Church, St. Leo the Great († 461) strongly supported the teachings of the Council of Chalcedon, especially on the humanity and divinity of Christ. He advocated papal authority by moving from the traditional approach that the pope is a successor to St. Peter's chair to the pope as St. Peter's heir. Under his leadership, uniformity of pastoral practice was encouraged, liturgical and clerical abuses were corrected, and priests were sent on a mission to extinguish Priscillianism, a heresy that claimed the human body was evil. St. Leo is recognized as a "protector of the people" because he persuaded Atilla the Hun to not invade the city of Rome and later prevented the Vandals (Germanic invaders) from torching the city of Rome and massacring its people.

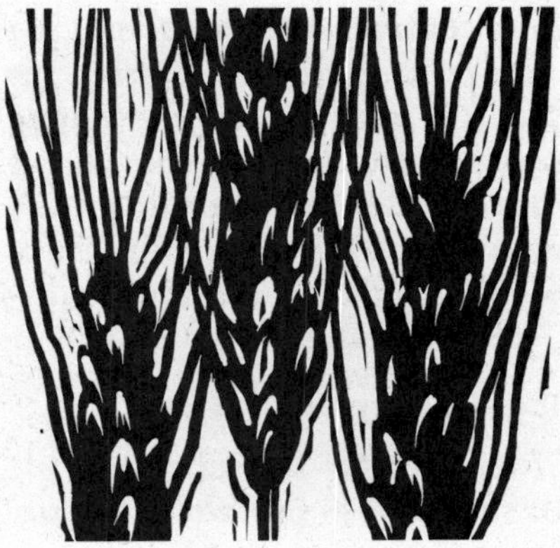

(#155) green

11 Thirty-Second Sunday in Ordinary Time

The Liturgy of the Word

◆ First Reading: Will God provide enough? While the widow of Zarephath worries she does not have enough to provide for herself, her son, and Elijah, the prophet announces to her that her jar of flour and jug of oil will not go empty. Her trust in the Lord's words from Elijah bore fruit as all could eat for a year.

◆ Responsorial Psalm 146: The Lectionary provides two options for the psalm refrain. In the first, we offer a short exclamation of our praise of God. In the second, a single "Alleluia" declares our praise of God. The verses of the Psalm 146 evidence God's providential care for his people.

◆ Second Reading: The author of Hebrews reiterates Christ's "once for all" sacrifice that we proclaimed last Sunday. The reading concludes with a statement of our belief that Christ will come a second time in order to bring salvation to those who wait for him. Christ resides in heaven, appearing before God for us, until he comes again.

◆ Gospel: The shorter form of the Gospel reading includes Jesus' condemnation of the scribes for their lavish and arrogant lifestyle and their destruction of the homes and lives of widows. The longer form continues with Jesus offering a concrete example to illustrate his point. A poor widow gives to the treasury from the little she has, but the rich people give from their surplus. Which is truly giving? There is a longer and shorter form of today's reading.

The Roman Missal

We ask God to "keep from us all adversity," not so that we may carry out our own plans, but so that "we may pursue in freedom of heart / the things that are" God's (Collect). In the Mass, we celebrate "in mystery" the Passion of Christ. We pray that we may always honor this great mystery with "loving devotion" (Prayer over the Offerings). We ask "the grace of integrity" for all those who have received God's "heavenly power" through sharing in the "sacred gift" of the Eucharist (Prayer after Communion). The Gloria and the Creed are sung or said today.

Other Ideas

Tomorrow, the United States celebrates Veterans' Day, remembering all those who have served in the armed forces in service to their country. Many parishes offer a special Mass for veterans. Invite members to create an information page about any loved ones who are currently serving in the Army, Navy, Marines, Air Force, National Guard, or Coast Guard and display them, inviting prayers. Building awareness of posttraumatic stress disorder, high suicide rates, reentry challenges as well as addictions and other hardships faced by veterans can be valuable this week. Make sure petitions in the Universal Prayer are gender inclusive, recognizing that both men and women have served their county. If you have homebound veterans, be sure to send ministers of care to give them Communion on this day. Resist having veterans stand to be acknowledged at Mass; some

experienced great hardship in their reentry and do not want to be recognized in this way. Consider profiling the soldiers at Jesus' baptism and Crucifixion, as well Cornelius and Julius from Acts of the Apostles in your bulletin this week. Invite members to bring in pictures of their veterans and display them with the American flag in the vestibule or gathering space.

MON 12 (#491) red
Memorial of St. Josaphat, Bishop and Martyr

The Liturgy of the Word

◆ FIRST READING: For the next three days the First Reading comes from the pastoral letter to Titus. Today's reading contains Paul's opening greeting and his instruction to Titus to appoint presbyters in every town in Crete. Paul lists the qualities a presbyter and bishop must have in order to preach "sound doctrine" and refute opponents of the Gospel message.

◆ RESPONSORIAL PSALM 24: As the conclusion of the liturgical year rapidly approaches, we express our longing as a people to see God's face and to ascend his mountain as our reward for faithfully serving him.

◆ GOSPEL: Jesus appears realistic at the beginning of the Gospel reading when he acknowledges that sin will happen. He goes on to teach the disciples how to address the person who commits sin. They must tell the person who sinned and if the person repents of his or her sin, the disciples should offer forgiveness. Even if the sin occurs often, God still asks the disciple to forgive the sinner. The Gospel transitions to the disciples asking the Lord to increase their faith. Perhaps after hearing how often they would have to forgive, the disciples felt the need to ask the Lord for greater faith. Yet even having mustard-seed-size faith is enough.

The Roman Missal

All the orations are proper today, and are taken from November 12. Given the emphasis in the orations today, one of the two Prefaces of Holy Martyrs would seem to be the most logical choice for a Preface; the Preface of Holy Pastors or one of the two Prefaces of Saints could also be considered.

Today's Saint

As a young man St. Josaphat (c. 1580–1623) was excited about the possibility of the Orthodox metropolitan city of Kiev, comprising Belarussians and Ukrainians, reuniting with the Church of Rome. When he was elected archbishop of Polotsk, Lithuania, he worked tirelessly to continue the efforts to bring the Orthodox communities of Kiev in full communion with the Catholic Church. Many people were strongly opposed to this reunion; therefore, they established a rival hierarchy and set up groups to defame his name. While preaching in a particularly hostile city, he was murdered. His commitment to ecumenical relations was eventually realized in the Byzantine Rite of Catholicism. St. Josaphat, the martyr, is the first Eastern saint to be formally canonized.

TUE 13 (#492) white
Memorial of St. Frances Xavier Cabrini, Virgin

The Liturgy of the Word

◆ FIRST READING: The First Reading includes advice for aging men and women, and young men. Self-control and moral behavior lies at the heart of the advice. By his grace, God has saved us. As a faithful response to our salvation, we are to live moderately, justly, and sincerely in Jesus Christ. How we live in the interim as we await the blessed hope of Christ coming again in glory reflects our faith.

◆ RESPONSORIAL PSALM 37: The words of Psalm 37, like the First Reading, call us to "do good" and rejoice in the Lord. For the good we do, the Lord will grant us life forever and a dwelling place in his land. The Lord will feed us his security. We will be safe. Our salvation comes from him.

◆ GOSPEL: Jesus continues to teach the Apostles in response to their desire to grow their faith. In Jesus' parable, we hear about the master who would, even after a hard day's work in the field, demand his servant prepare a meal for him and serve him. We do not know whether or not the master expresses gratitude to the servant for his work. What we do know is that God freely gives his grace to us. Ours is the mere duty to act responsibly in light of all God gives us without regard for desiring more of God.

The Roman Missal

The Collect is the only proper for today, and it is found at November 13. The prayer describes how the saint was called from Italy to serve the immigrants of America, and then goes on to ask that we might be taught to have the same concern for the stranger and all those in need. The Prayer over the Offerings and the Prayer after Communion are taken from either the Common of Virgins: For One Virgin, or from the Common of Holy Men and Women: For Those Who Practiced Works of Mercy. An appropriate Preface for this celebration would be either the Preface of Holy Virgins and Religious or Preface I or II of Saints.

Today's Saint

St. Frances Xavier Cabrini (1850 –1917), also known as Mother Cabrini, was an Italian immigrant to the United States. She was the first American citizen to be canonized. As a girl, Frances dreamed of sailing to China as a missionary. In 1880, she founded the Missionary Sisters of the Sacred Heart of Jesus, and her community's work drew the attention of Pope Leo XIII. She hoped that he would send her to China, but he instead sent her to New York City in 1889 to minister to Italian immigrants, saying "Not to the East, but to the West." She founded sixty-seven institutions throughout the United States, Europe, and South America. After her death, her sisters fulfilled her dream of working in China. St. Frances Cabrini is the patron saint of immigrants.

WED 14 (#493) green
Weekday

The Liturgy of the Word

◆ FIRST READING: God saved us through Jesus Christ by the Holy Spirit to be heirs of eternal life. What possibly could be an adequate response to this gift of mercy, love, and hope? While still on the earth, we must live Christian virtues such as those named in the passage from Titus. Among them are living in peace ad consideration for others, and acting graciously to all. The way of life in faith differs considerably from our prior life of foolishness and hate.

◆ RESPONSORIAL PSALM 23: Used today this beloved psalm, which often serves as the Responsorial Psalm for the Mass of Christian Burial, focuses us on how the Lord guides and shepherds us, leading us to dwell eternally in his house. Nothing shall we want for in this life and the life to come. The Lord will guide us away from evil and give us the courage to do live virtuously.

◆ GOSPEL: All ten lepers had asked Jesus for mercy. And, without questioning them further, Jesus responded. He cleansed all ten as they traveled to see the priests. Only one leper, the Samaritan, returned to give thanks to God. His faith had saved him. What is our response to God saving us by faith in Jesus? How do our lives express our worship of the One who saves us?

THU 15 (#494) green
Weekday

Optional Memorial of St. Albert the Great, Bishop and Doctor of the Church / white

The Liturgy of the Word

◆ FIRST READING: Paul sends Onesimus, a runaway slave, back to his master. The master is to welcome Onesimus back as a partner in the Gospel now that he has converted to Christ. No difference should exist between the way the master would treat Paul and how he will treat Onesimus upon his return. Paul's instructions provide us guidance for how we are to live in relationship with one another as Christians. We are all partners in the proclamation of the Gospel.

◆ RESPONSORIAL PSALM 146: The Lectionary provides two options for the psalm refrain. The first affirms the blessedness of the one whose help comes from the God of Jacob. The second is a single "Alleluia." The verses from Psalm 146 describe the Lord's care for the oppressed, the hungry, for captives, the blind, strangers, the fatherless, and the widow. All these will know wholeness in the Lord.

◆ GOSPEL: The Pharisees request a date for the arrival of the Kingdom of God. Jesus responds to them by saying no one will tell them exactly when and where the Kingdom is. Jesus simply tells them the Kingdom of God is already present among them. Perhaps the Pharisees just need to look more closely. Jesus then speaks personally to his disciples in descriptive language about his Death and Resurrection.

Today's Saint

To the great disappointment of his father, St. Albert the Great (1206–1280), known as "the universal doctor," entered the Dominican order, where he was recognized for his acumen. Ahead of his time, he believed that learning did not take place in a vacuum; one must be an interdisciplinary learner. He loved the world of academia, anywhere from studying the natural sciences to unearthing the connection between reason and experience to learning the geography of the earth. As a prestigious teacher, he had the privilege of instructing and mentoring St. Thomas Aquinas, author of the *Summa Theologiae*. Toward the end of his life he began to experience memory loss and dementia, which led to his gradual demise. He was declared a Doctor of the Church by Pope Pius XI.

FRI 16 (#495) green Weekday

Optional Memorials of St. Margaret of Scotland / white; St. Gertrude, Virgin / white

The Liturgy of the Word

◆ FIRST READING: The presbyter who serves as the author of 2 John writes to the "Chosen Lady" and to her children as representative of a Christian community that struggles with deceivers who do not acknowledge the fullness of Jesus' humanity. The author reminds the Lady of the original commandment to "love one another." Following this commandment helps people to remain within the parameters of Christ's teaching.

◆ RESPONSORIAL PSALM 119: Today's refrain is the opening verse of the psalm and emphasizes that our blessedness comes from following the Lord's Law. Just as the author of the First Reading stressed the importance of the following the commandment of love, so too, the psalm encourages us to observe the Lord's laws with our whole heart and to see their beauty with our eyes.

◆ GOSPEL: The day the Son of Man comes will resemble the time of the flood in the days of Noah and the fire and brimstone on the day Lot left Sodom. The Son of Man's will come suddenly and unexpectedly. As we live in preparation for his coming, we must not hang onto our life too tightly, but rather lose it to God to gain salvation.

Today's Saint

St. Margaret of Scotland (c. 1045–1093), the wife of King Malcolm III of Scotland, managed to raise eight children while promoting Church reform, especially in the area of liturgical practice. As a woman of great faith, she founded and restored monasteries, provided hospitality to pilgrims, spoke out on behalf of the falsely accused, and fed the poor from her own dining table. All of her charitable activity was grounded in a strong prayer life.

St. Gertrude the Great (1256–1302) was a nun at the Benedictine monastery of Helfta, the abbey where two other great female spiritual writers lived: Mechtilde of Magdeburg and St. Mechtilde (Matilda von Hackeborn-Wippra). Through prayer she was graced with many mystical and ecstatic experiences, which are recorded in a five volume work titled *Legatus divinae pietatis*, commonly called *The Life and Revelations of St. Gertrude the Great*. Her spirituality focused on the humanity of Christ and was characterized by a strong devotion to the Sacred Heart of Jesus. According to many scholars, St. Gertrude's writings should be on the same shelf with other influential mystics, such as St. Teresa of Avila.

SAT 17 (#496) white Memorial of St. Elizabeth of Hungary, Religious

The Liturgy of the Word

◆ FIRST READING: The presbyter/author of 3 John commends Gaius for the hospitality he has shown to the visiting missionaries, and asks him to continue supporting them. The missionaries are partners with the presbyter and Gaius, and all who proclaim the truth of the Church's faith.

◆ RESPONSORIAL PSALM 112: The behaviors described in today's First Reading—and in the stanzas of the psalm as well—are evidence of a fear and reverence for the Lord, especially when we receive others in the name of the Lord. Those who do so will be abundantly blessed.

◆ GOSPEL: In the midst of Jesus' intense teaching to the disciples about preparing themselves and being vigilant for the Son of Man, he appears to switch topics in today's Gospel reading. "Pray always," he instructs his disciples. Pray and do not grow tired. In his example parable, we find a dishonest judge who did weary of the persistent widow's demand for justice. The end of the reading reveals that Jesus did not switch topics. Unlike the dishonest judge, God will respond quickly and with justice for his people. The question is, when the Son of Man comes, will he find faith in us?

The Roman Missal

The Collect, found at November 17 in the Proper of Saints, is the prayer that is proper for today. The Collect recognizes St. Elizabeth's ministry to the poor and therefore asks "that we may serve with unfailing charity / the needy and those afflicted." Ministry to the poor is not something that is optional in the Christian life; it is part-and-parcel of what it means to follow Christ.

The Prayer over the Offerings and the Prayer after Communion come from the Common of Holy Men and Women: For Those Who Practiced Works of Mercy. For the Preface, use either Preface I of Saints or Preface II of Saints.

Today's Saint

St. Elizabeth of Hungary (1207–1231), the Queen of Hungary and mother of four children, had a special love for the downtrodden. She built a hospital in the basement of her castle, nursed the sick, fed the hungry, and provided life-giving work for the poor. After the death of her husband, she took the habit of a Franciscan tertiary (Third Order Franciscan), devoting herself to a life of simplicity and almsgiving. Along with her selfless service to those in need, she actively pursued God through prayer and spiritual discipline. St. Elizabeth is the patron saint of Franciscan tertiaries, bakers, beggars, brides, the homeless, and charities (among others).

(#158)   green

18 Thirty-Third Sunday in Ordinary Time

The Liturgy of the Word

◆ First Reading: Daniel's apocalyptic vision portends a time of distress when some will live forever and others will know eternal shame and horror. Those who are wise will emit a bright glow in the sky. Those who lead others to justice will be like eternal stars. Would that our light shine forever in the Lord!

◆ Responsorial Psalm 16: In the words of Psalm 16, we affirm the Lord is our inheritance. The Lord shows us the path of life, a path opposite the road that leads to the netherworld — a path of joy.

◆ Second Reading: No other offering is necessary for our sins. Christ the high priest offered his one sacrifice for sins. Now he sits at God's right hand. His one offering did more for us than the daily offerings of every other priest. Through Christ's offering, he has made us perfect forever. He consecrates us and makes us holy.

◆ Gospel: How ominous, yet hopeful Jesus' words to his disciples are! Darkness will follow the tribulation. The Son of Man will come with power and glory to gather his chosen ones from all directions. Both heaven and earth will pass away, but Jesus' words will not. Our hope is in the word for it tells of our salvation in Jesus. When all this will take place, we do not know. We must be vigilant each day.

The Roman Missal

The Gloria and the Creed are sung or said today. The Collect identifies for us where the source of "constant gladness" and "full and lasting happiness" is to be found: it is to be found in serving "with constancy / the author of all that is good." This Collect asks that we make sure we are using all our gifts and resources to serve God well; it is only by doing so that we can hope to share in the fullness of the joy of the kingdom. We must also stay alert and sober so we can serve with constancy. The Prayer over the Offerings has an eschatological focus, appropriate for this penultimate Sunday of the liturgical year, as it asks that what we offer at this Eucharist may "gain us the prize of everlasting happiness." The Prayer after Communion, however, is focused more on the present as it implores that, having partaken of "the gifts of this sacred mystery," we may be given "a growth in charity." Any one of the eight Prefaces of the Sundays in Ordinary Time are appropriate options for today, but perhaps Preface V might be considered the best choice with its emphasis on God setting humanity "over the whole world in all its wonder"; the text could serve to reinforce the theme of taking responsibility for using the gifts God has given us and building the Kingdom of God.

Other Ideas

In these last two weeks of Ordinary Time before Advent, provide clear information about the parish's observance of the holy season about to commence. Thanksgiving, the national day of gratitude that is observed by Americans of almost all beliefs, happens this week. Provide a blessing of the food on Wednesday evening and a special Mass on Thursday. The Order for the Blessing of Food for Thanksgiving Day is found in chapter 58 of the *Book of Blessings*. Consider an ecumenical or interfaith prayer service that honors all people of goodwill that are expressing gratitude this week.

This is a day to honor human rights, particularly religious freedom, and to recall the centrally important task of evangelization for all disciples. Today, the Sunday before Thanksgiving, a special collection is gathered in support of the Catholic Campaign for Human Development, which provides a range of grants to important causes related to social change and Catholic social teaching. In particular, it supports programs designed to break the cycle of poverty.

MON 19 (#497) green
Weekday

The Liturgy of the Word

◆ FIRST READING: From today until the end of the liturgical year, the weekday First Readings take us on a journey through the book of Revelation. We begin with the opening greeting that announces that the contents of the book are the revelation of Jesus Christ given by angel to John to seven Churches in Asia. The number seven is the biblical number symbolizing completeness. Thus, the seven Churches represent the whole Church. The second half of the reading part of a letter to the angel of the Church at Ephesus calling the people to repent and love the way they originally did.

◆ RESPONSORIAL PSALM 1: Today's refrain comes from John 8:12 and affirms those who follow the Lord will know the "light of life." The refrain links with the John's statement in the First Reading that unless the people of the Church in Ephesus repent, they will lose their lampstand. No longer will they have light.

◆ GOSPEL: Upon the blind man's inquiry, the crowd lets him know Jesus is walking by. The blind man calls out for pity, much to the dismay of the people in front of him. Their rebuke does not deter him, and he again calls out for Jesus' mercy. Once Jesus stops, the blind man asks Jesus for his sight. Jesus gifts him with sight because of his faith. The blind man's faith leads to the conversion of the people who rebuked him. Our faith can lead others to faith.

TUE 20 (#498) green
Weekday

The Liturgy of the Word

◆ FIRST READING: At the Lord's direction, John writes his fifth letter to the Church in Sardis and his seventh to the Church in Laodicea. Repentance is the call to both Churches. The people will not know when the Lord will come, for the Lord will come like a thief. When he comes, the blameless ones, wearing white garments, will approach the Father on his throne. Let the image of the white garments lead us to ponder how faithful we have recently been to our baptismal commitments as another liturgical year rapidly comes to a close.

◆ RESPONSORIAL PSALM 15: Today's refrain is from Revelation 3:21, a verse from the First Reading in which the Lord declares he will seat the victor beside him on the throne. The verses describe the just and kind behavior of the blameless ones who will eternally share life with God.

◆ GOSPEL: Check the time in the liturgical year. With all the readings about repentance and forgiveness it seems as though we are in Lent. As Jesus approached Jericho, he healed the blind beggar who asked for mercy. Now in the town, he witnesses Zacchaeus, the chief tax collector, in a tree. With a sense of urgency in his voice, Jesus commands Zacchaeus to come down and tells him he is staying at the tax collector's home. The rest of the story is this: Zacchaeus repents and Jesus offers salvation, *today*.

WED 21 (#499) white
Memorial of the Presentation of the Blessed Virgin Mary

About Today's Memorial

The Gospel accounts tell of the Presentation of the Lord Jesus in the Temple but do not speak of the Presentation of Mary. Nevertheless, Christians in the East and the West have observed a day in honor of Mary's Presentation for centuries. Many artists have depicted the scene: a tiny girl (Mary is said to have been three or four years old when she was presented in the Temple), climbing the steps to go into the Temple to offer herself to God. This memorial speaks of Mary's total openness to God. God kept her free from sin from the moment of her conception, so that she, whose presentation in the Temple we commemorate today, would become a Temple of the Holy Spirit.

The Liturgy of the Word

◆ FIRST READING: Glorious details about the throne's appearance, the elders who surround it, the spirits of God, and the entire environment around the throne fill John's vision. His vision builds like a doxology. Living creatures continuously praise the Lord seated on the throne with the familiar words of the opening line of the *Holy*. Their praise resounds in declaration of his glory, honor, and power. They acclaim the Lord for he was Lord in the past, is Lord now, and will come again as Lord.

◆ RESPONSORIAL PSALM 150 acclaima the holiness of our "mighty God." The verses form a grand hymn of praise. Instruments of every kind praise the Lord. People in the sanctuary sing to praise of his name. You are the people offering praise today! Let your voices resound!

◆ GOSPEL: Todya's parable presents a nobleman who gives ten servants ten gold coins each. Upon his return, we find out what three servants did. The first made 100 percent on top of the original coins, the second 50 percent more, and the third, only returned the original coin. The nobleman is demanding. The faithful servants made money. The other servant he condemned. Jesus left the people with this parable and proceeded on to Jerusalem. No doubt he led the people to consider their willingness to follow him faithfully, accepting the demands of the cross.

The Roman Missal

The proper Collect is found at November 21 in the Proper of Saints. The prayer asks for the intercession of the Blessed Virgin Mary as we venerate her on this day. The Prayer over the Offerings and the Prayer after Communion are to be taken from the Common of the Blessed Virgin Mary, with the Preface being either Preface I or Preface II of the Blessed Virgin Mary; use "on the feast day" as the choice of phrasing in Preface I.

THU 22 (#500) red
Memorial of St. Cecilia, Virgin and Martyr

Optional Proper Mass for Thanksgiving Day (#943–947) / white

The Liturgy of the Word

◆ FIRST READING: Christ is the Paschal Lamb. With his Blood, he saved us. He has won the victory. Together with the elders, we glorify Christ who broken open the seals on the scrolls, welcomed us into God's Kingdom and made priests for God who will lead the Church. At Baptism, we were anointed to share in the priestly, prophetic, and kingly ministry.

◆ RESPONSORIAL PSALM 149: The refrain comes from Revelation 5:10, the concluding verse of the First Reading. Every time we pray the refrain, we acknowledge we are a kingdom of priests serving God because of Christ, the Paschal Lamb's sacrifice. In the verses, the psalm writer calls Israel to rejoice in their Maker and praise his name in song and dance. The Church, the "new Israel," we join our voices in one grand chorus of praise to God in Jesus Christ.

◆ GOSPEL: Jerusalem was destroyed in AD 70, and since Luke wrote his account of the Gospel

after that date, he could have in mind the city's destruction in this passage. In the Gospel reading, Jesus mourns for Jerusalem for it does not know that belief in him would make for peace. Peace is in their midst, if they would recognize Jesus. Since they do not acknowledge that his peace and their salvation that comes from him, their devastation will befall their city.

The Roman Missal

The Collect for the memorial, the only prayer proper for today, is found at November 22. The Collect asks that we might imitate the example of the saint, one of the most famous and revered of the early Roman martyrs. The Prayer over the Offerings and the Prayer after Communion come from either the Common of Martyrs: For a Virgin Martyr, or from the Common of Virgins: For One Virgin. One of the Prefaces of Holy Martyrs would be an apt choice for today, and consider using Eucharistic Prayer I, the Roman Canon, since St. Cecilia's name is mentioned in it.

Today's Saint

According to legend, St. Cecilia (c. third century) was beheaded because she would not forsake her vow of virginity and would not make sacrifices to the gods.

FRI 23 (#501) green
Weekday

Optional Memorials of St. Clement I, Pope and Martyr / red; St. Columban, Abbot / white; Bl. Miguel Agustín Pro, Priest and Martyr / red

The Liturgy of the Word

◆ FIRST READING: God's people will suffer and also taste victory. When John takes the scroll from the angel and consumes it, he tastes sour and sweet, which represent the suffering the people will face and

their ultimate triumph through Christ, the Son of Man and the Son of God.

◆ RESPONSORIAL PSALM 119: Verse 103a from the psalm is the refrain. This verse mirrors the sweetness of the scroll in the First Reading. God's promise to his people is truly sweet — "sweeter than honey." The other verses of today's Responsorial Psalm describe the joy and delight of the Lord's decrees. We want to breathe in God's word so strongly and immediately, that we gasp with the psalm writer in the final stanza as we long for God's commands.

◆ GOSPEL: Jesus has entered Jerusalem and the Temple area. As his first act in the holy city, he purifies the Temple, driving out the commercial entrepreneurs and laying claim to the Temple as his house. Jesus then merges words from Isaiah and Jeremiah to declare his house as a "house of prayer," not "a den of thieves," that the entrepreneurs have made it. People yearned for every word of Jesus, but those who had struggled with his teaching all along — the chief priest, scribes, and others in authority — wanted to kill him.

Today's Saints

St. Clement I (c. † 100) was pope during a rather tumultuous time, when the early Christian communities were experiencing growing pains. He is most remembered for a letter referred to as 1 Clement, which was written to the Christian community at Corinth. His letter addressed division within the community, urging its members to live in charity and unity. An unverified tradition, but one accepted by the early Church historian Tertullian and St. Jerome, claims that St. Clement was consecrated by St. Peter as his immediate successor. He is venerated as a martyr but the manner of his death is unknown.

St. Columban (Columbanus) (c. 543–615) was an Irish monk and missionary who established many religious houses in France and Italy. Through word and example, he urged the Church (and especially the clergy) to ever greater holiness.

Bl. Miguel Agustín Pro (1891–1927), a Jesuit priest and martyr, lived under an anticlerical and anti-Christian political regime in Mexico. He was executed by a firing squad because he would not abandon his clerical call to care for the oppressed.

(#502) red
S A T 24 Memorial of St. Andrew Dũng-Lạc, Priest, and Companions, Martyrs

The Liturgy of the Word

◆ FIRST READING: Two prophets become martyrs. At their death, those who do not believe in God rejoice. Arrogance is their attitude. For three and a half days they have a chance to think they have won the victory. But God brings life to the prophets with his breath—the breath of life. The prophet-martyrs God takes up to heaven to live forever. The victory of life belongs to God!

◆ RESPONSORIAL PSALM 144: In this psalm, a leader, perhaps a king, extols God as his rock, refuge, and fortress. The leader attributes victory to God, who brings David safely home from his enemies. To God be praise and glory for he shields his people from evil.

◆ GOSPEL: As we draw close to the end of the liturgical year, the readings focus more on the Resurrection. The Sadducees, who themselves do not believe in the resurrection of the dead, attempt to get Jesus wrapped up in their scenario about the seven brothers who upon each of their deaths, each marry the deceased brother's wife. She eventually dies childless. The Sadducees want Jesus to tell them

whose wife she will be at the resurrection. Their question is irrelevant —if not laughable. God is God not of the dead, but of the living!

The Roman Missal

All the orations are proper for today, and are found in the Proper of Saints at November 24. It would seem that one of the two Prefaces of Holy Martyrs would be the most appropriate choice of Preface for today, although certainly Preface I or II of Saints could also be chosen.

Today's Saint

St. Andrew Dũng-Lạc (1795–1839), a Vietnamese priest canonized in 1988, was one of 117 martyrs who died trying to establish and spread the Catholic religion in Vietnam. This effort, which began in 1533 and continued well into the nineteenth century, was fraught with periods of persecution. Although St. Andrew was born into a Buddhist family, he was raised Catholic. His priestly ministry involved evangelization, parish catechesis, and service to the persecuted. Living under a particularly oppressive edict, St. Andrew was killed because he would not renounce his Christian apostolate and succumb to idolatrous ritual.

(#161) white
☀ 25 Solemnity of Our Lord Jesus Christ, King of the Universe

About Today's Solemnity

On the Solemnity of Our Lord Jesus Christ, King of the Universe, we honor the unique kingship of Christ. His kingdom is not here: his kingdom is with his Father, and yet it is being mysteriously built in our very midst. His is "an eternal and universal kingdom, / a kingdom of truth and life, / a kingdom of holiness and grace, / a kingdom of justice, love and peace" (Preface of Christ, King of the Universe).

The Liturgy of the Word

◆ FIRST READING: "One like a Son of man" comes. He is king! Glory and dominion belong to him! They are everlasting. No one can destroy his reign. Everyone serves him. On this solemnity we acclaim Christ as the King of the Universe and see identify him as the One who comes in our midst.

◆ RESPONSORIAL PSALM 93: We sing of the majesty of the Lord, the King, and declare his everlasting reign. The Lord's decrees deserve our trust, the trust of his holy people.

◆ SECOND READING: The passage from Revelation also includes a reference to Jesus Christ coming in the clouds. He is the past, present, and future. The "ruler of the kings" has made us priests for God, his Father. We are a kingdom people who give glory, honor, and praise to Christ forever.

◆ GOSPEL: Jesus does not identify himself as a king in response to Pilate's question, but Jesus does admit to having a kingdom. His Kingdom, though, does not belong to the world. He only came to testify to the truth of his Kingdom, a kingdom in which the last will be first, and the first will be the servant of all. Do we belong to the truth? Have we listened to his voice throughout this year?

The Roman Missal

The Gloria and the Creed are sung or said today. In the Collect, we call on all of creation to serve and to praise God. In the Prayer over the Offerings, we pray that Christ may grant to all the nations his unity and peace. And in the Prayer after Communion we pray that all who follow Christ, the King of the Universe, may come to eternal life in the kingdom of heaven. The beautiful Preface, which is proper, praises God, who anointed Christ as eternal Priest and King, to save us and lead us to a new kind of kingdom: "a kingdom of truth and life, / a kingdom of holiness and grace, / a kingdom of justice, love, and peace." It is found with the other prayers in the Proper of Time.

Other Ideas

Will this Sunday look different from the Fourteenth Sunday in Ordinary Time? This is a great solemnity and the end of our liturgical year. Are there banners in the procession? Will incense be used? Will there be a sprinkling rite? Will there be more flowers? This is the Last or Thirty-fourth Sunday in Ordinary Time. Next Sunday a new liturgical year begins. Announce the schedule for Advent this week. Encourage parishioners to make (or purchase) an Advent wreath for their homes. Or schedule a wreath-making workshop for households this afternoon. Invite them to bring the necessary materials and provide them with the blessing and prayers for their use at home.

26 MON (#503) green
Weekday / Thirty-Fourth or Last Week in Ordinary Time

The Liturgy of the Word

◆ FIRST READING: Mount Zion represents the heavenly Jerusalem. On the mount, the faithful gather to acclaim the Lamb. The great number—one hundred forty-four thousand—will follow the Lamb wherever he journeys. We see in the pure, faithful ones, a foreshadowing of our own resurrection and our eternal life with the Lamb of God.

◆ RESPONSORIAL PSALM 24: Today's refrain emphasizes our longing to see the Lord's face. People sang this processional psalm as the Ark of the Covenant made its way into the Temple. Our lives are a journey of faithfulness to God. On the last day, we hope to process into the heavenly Jerusalem where we will know everlasting life with the Lamb.

◆ GOSPEL: What is our entire livelihood? For the poor widow, the two coins worth a small amount that she placed in the treasury were her means of support. We do not know the amount of the offerings the wealthy people gave, but Jesus' commendation of the widow leads us to believe what they did contribute came only from their surplus and had little impact on their lives. Where does their true attachment lie—to material possessions or to God?

27 TUE (#504) green
Weekday

The Liturgy of the Word

◆ FIRST READING: Christians see in John's vision of the one who resembled a son of man a reference to Jesus Christ crowned in glory. Now is the time for the final judgment. The harvest is ripe. The time for self-evaluation and action has long since ended. Now is the time for the harvest.

◆ RESPONSORIAL PSALM 96 underscore the Lord's Kingship and divine judgment. The Lord rules the earth he created with justice. The Lord faithfully governs his people. There should be no question of the Lord's fairness when he comes to judge the earth.

◆ GOSPEL: Admirers in the Temple commented on the beauty of its expensive stones and votive offerings in place. Jesus' words predicting the Temple's destruction unnerved them so much that they asked for the date and a sign when it would occur. Do not follow false preachers who claim to come in Jesus' name. Lay fear aside when wars and uprisings come. Natural disasters will signify the coming Day of Judgment. Follow Jesus by living faithfully now and you will have no concern.

28 WED (#505) green
Weekday

The Liturgy of the Word

◆ FIRST READING: John sees two signs. In the first, he perceives seven angels with the seven final plagues through which God's wrath will leave a lasting impression. In the second, the victorious people stand on a glassy sea and playing God's harp for their accompaniment, sing the canticle of Moses, which the author of Revelation also identifies as the song of the Lamb. Both Exodus 15 and the words of Moses' song as cited in today's First Reading express declare the triumph of God's saving power.

◆ **RESPONSORIAL PSALM 98:** Today's refrain is a verse from the song of Moses in the First Reading declaring the wonder of the Lord's works. The verses announce the Lord's salvation and describe the voices of creation that resound in praise of the mighty God.

◆ **GOSPEL:** Jesus' words describing the coming persecution of his followers must have seemed even more worrisome. Just as the Lord's Word has triumphed over evil spirits and death so far, its wisdom will defend his followers against their adversaries. The perseverance of Jesus' followers will lead to salvation.

THU 29 (#506) green
Weekday

The Liturgy of the Word

◆ **FIRST READING:** Babylon (Rome) will fall because of infidelity. Salvation belongs to God who judges justly and calls the blessed to the "wedding feast of the Lamb." Their reward in heaven is great. Their faithfulness returned in kind.

◆ **RESPONSORIAL PSALM 100:** We sing our thanks to God who calls us to the feast of the Lamb. We enter his courts with thanksgiving knowing that we belong to God.

◆ **GOSPEL:** Predictions of destruction and persecution turn to portentous warnings about the events leading up to the coming of the Son of Man. Disciples must not shrink in terror, but rather stand tall for their redemption comes.

FRI 30 (#684) red
Feast of St. Andrew, Apostle

The Liturgy of the Word

◆ **FIRST READING:** Believe with your heart and confess with your mouth. God in Jesus Christ who is Lord of all, whether Jew or Greek, will justify and save you.

◆ **RESPONSORIAL PSALM 19:** We sing Psalm 19's beautiful words about the sweet and precious law of the Lord, which brings life to all.

◆ **GOSPEL:** Jesus calls Peter and Andrew in the midst of their ordinary workday as fishermen. He also invites the brothers James and John to follow him. The immediacy of the fours acceptance of Jesus' call offers us food for thought about the time we spend scrutinizing his invitation to come after him before we say yes.

The Roman Missal

Today we turn to the Proper of Saints for the prayer texts for St. Andrew. All of the texts are proper. The Gloria is sung or said today. There is no Creed. Use one of the Prefaces of the Apostles.

Today's Saint

St. Andrew (first century) was the first of the Twelve to meet Jesus. Tradition says that he may have preached in parts of Asia Minor and Greece before being crucified on an X-shaped cross.

December 2018
Month of the Divine Infancy

SAT 1 (#508) green
Weekday

Optional Memorial of the Blessed Virgin Mary / white

The Liturgy of the Word

◆ **FIRST READING:** The water of life flows from the throne of God and of the Lamb. Darkness is overcome and the only light necessary is the light that comes from the Lord. Our eternal participation in God's reign will be wondrous and filled with the abundance of divine life.

◆ **RESPONSORIAL PSALM 95:** The refrain from 1 Corinthians 16:22b (Revelation 22:20c) leads us into Advent as we pray "Maranatha!" and ask the Lord Jesus to come. Psalm 95 sings of the Lord's greatness and our worship of him.

◆ **GOSPEL:** A disciple lives his or her life with vigilance—always attentive for the coming of the Son of Man. We notice the lackadaisical patterns of our daily life and strive to change them, lest they trap us. Our prayer is for strength to flee the coming trials that will herald the final judgment.